Governance and Ownership

Critical Governance in the New Global Economy

Series Editors: Kevin Keasey
Leeds Permanent Building Society Professor of Financial Services and Director of the International Institute of Banking and Financial Services, Leeds University Business School, UK
Steve Thompson
Professor of Strategic Management, Nottingham University Business School, UK
Mike Wright
Professor of Financial Studies and Director of the Centre for Management Buy-out Research, Nottingham University Business School, UK

Wherever possible, the articles in these volumes have been reproduced as originally published using facsimile reproduction, inclusive of footnotes and pagination to facilitate ease of reference.

For a list of all Edward Elgar published titles visit our site on the World Wide Web at www.e-elgar.com

Governance and Ownership

Edited by

Robert Watson

Professor of Financial Management
University of Durham, UK

CORPORATE GOVERNANCE IN THE NEW GLOBAL ECONOMY

An Elgar Reference Collection
Cheltenham, UK • Northampton, MA, USA

584595564

Published by
Edward Elgar Publishing Limited
Glensanda House
Montpellier Parade
Cheltenham
Glos GL50 1UA
UK

Edward Elgar Publishing, Inc.
136 West Street
Suite 202
Northampton
Massachusetts 01060
USA

A catalogue record for this book is available from the British Library

ISBN   1 84376 831 3

Printed and bound in Great Britain by MPG Books Ltd, Bodmin, Cornwall

Contents

Acknowledgements

The editor and publishers wish to thank the authors and the following publishers who have kindly given permission for the use of copyright material.

Academy of Management via Copyright Clearance Center, Inc. for articles: Peter Wright, Stephen P. Ferris, Atulya Sarin and Vidya Awasthi (1996), 'Impact of Corporate Insider, Blockholder, and Institutional Equity Ownership on Firm Risk Taking', *Academy of Management Journal*, **39** (2), April, 441–63; Parthiban David, Rahul Kochhar and Edward Levitas (1998), 'The Effect of Institutional Investors on the Level and Mix of CEO Compensation', *Academy of Management Journal*, **41** (2), April, 200–208.

Administrative Science Quarterly for article: Randolph P. Beatty and Edward J. Zajac (1994), 'Managerial Incentives, Monitoring, and Risk Bearing: A Study of Executive Compensation, Ownership, and Board Structure in Initial Public Offerings', *Administrative Science Quarterly*, **39** (2), June, 313–35.

Blackwell Publishing Ltd for articles: Ken Robbie and Mike Wright (1995), 'Managerial and Ownership Succession and Corporate Restructuring: The Case of Management Buy-ins', *Journal of Management Studies*, **32** (4), July, 527–49; Rafael La Porta, Florencio Lopez-de-Silanes and Andrei Shleifer (1999), 'Corporate Ownership Around the World', *Journal of Finance*, **LIV** (2), April, 471–517.

Elsevier for articles: Hamid Mehran (1995), 'Executive Compensation Structure, Ownership, and Firm Performance', *Journal of Financial Economics*, **38**, 163–84; Bernard S. Black and Ronald J. Gilson (1998), 'Venture Capital and the Structure of Capital Markets: Banks versus Stock Markets', *Journal of Financial Economics*, **47** (3), March, 243–77; Helen Short and Kevin Keasey (1999), 'Managerial Ownership and the Performance of Firms: Evidence from the UK', *Journal of Corporate Finance*, **5**, 79–101; Rakesh Duggal and James A. Millar (1999), 'Institutional Ownership and Firm Performance: The Case of Bidder Returns', *Journal of Corporate Finance*, **5**, 103–17; Robert F. Bruner (1999), 'An Analysis of Value Destruction and Recovery in the Alliance and Proposed Merger of Volvo and Renault', *Journal of Financial Economics*, **51**, 125–66; David J. Denis and Atulya Sarin (1999), 'Ownership and Board Structures in Publicly Traded Corporations', *Journal of Financial Economics*, **52**, 187–223; Brian F. Smith and Ben Amoako-Adu (1999), 'Management Succession and Financial Performance of Family Controlled Firms', *Journal of Corporate Finance*, **5**, 341–68; Charles P. Himmelberg, R. Glenn Hubbard and Darius Palia (1999), 'Understanding the Determinants of Managerial Ownership and the Link between Ownership and Performance', *Journal of Financial Economics*, **53**, 353–84; Robert C. Hanson and Moon H. Song (2000), 'Managerial Ownership, Board Structure, and the Division of Gains in Divestitures', *Journal of Corporate*

Finance, **6**, 55–70; Mara Faccio and M. Ameziane Lasfer (2000), 'Do Occupational Pension Funds Monitor Companies in Which They Hold Large Stakes?', *Journal of Corporate Finance*, **6**, 71–110; Marc Goergen and Luc Renneboog (2001), 'Investment Policy, Internal Financing and Ownership Concentration in the UK', *Journal of Corporate Finance*, **7**, 257–84.

Emerald Publications Ltd for article: John Holland (1998), 'Influence and Intervention by Financial Institutions in their Investee Companies', *Corporate Governance*, **6** (4), October, 249–64.

Institute for Operations Research and the Management Sciences (INFORMS) for article: William S. Schulze, Michael H. Lubatkin, Richard N. Dino and Ann K. Buchholtz (2001), 'Agency Relationships in Family Firms: Theory and Evidence', *Organization Science*, **12** (2), March–April, 99–116.

Journal of Financial and Quantitative Analysis for article: Sunil Wahal (1996), 'Pension Fund Activism and Firm Performance', *Journal of Financial and Quantitative Analysis*, **31** (1), March, 1–23.

Oxford University Press for article: Julian Franks and Colin Mayer (2001), 'Ownership and Control of German Corporations', *Review of Financial Studies*, **14** (4), Winter, 943–77.

Every effort has been made to trace all the copyright holders but if any have been inadvertently overlooked the publishers will be pleased to make the necessary arrangement at the first opportunity.

In addition the publishers wish to thank the Library of Indiana University at Bloomington, USA for their assistance in obtaining these articles.

Introduction

Robert Watson

The papers in this collection address a variety of corporate governance issues associated with different forms of corporate ownership. The issues investigated include:

- the international and within-country diversity in both corporate and ownership forms and their corporate control implications
- the effectiveness of different owners in monitoring and materially influencing the incentives of executives to enhance corporate value
- the role of owners in appointing and removing poorly performing executives
- the decision processes and value consequences of ownership and control changes arising from corporate restructuring and merger activities
- the motivations of different classes of owners and their ability and willingness to influence major corporate investment and financing decisions.

All of the above issues have been the subject of much academic research and public policy interest in recent years. For the editor of a collection of studies on those topics, the wide variety of good quality published research now available is both a blessing and a curse. The choice set is huge and, therefore, it is a relatively easy task to find 20 or more papers that will inform and interest researchers and practitioners in the field. The major difficulty of course is deciding on which 20 papers to include from the many high quality contributions available.

The decision criteria adopted necessarily reflect to some extent the editor's specific interests and biases. Given the broad sweep of topics, research methods and policy issues that the subject covers, it is highly likely that there will not be a close correspondence between the interests and biases of the editor and a significant proportion of the intended readership. Hence, some discussion (framing) of the heuristics and choice criteria used is clearly required. This is the main purpose of the following section, 'Ownership and Corporate Governance: Themes and Issues'. This section is not intended to be a conventional literature review since each of the papers in the collection contains its own review of the most relevant aspects of the literature.[1] A section follows which summarises how the collection is organised into subsections each dealing with one of the broad themes listed above. This section also provides a brief discussion of each of the papers in terms of their specific focus, research method, contribution and findings. The final section provides a brief discussion of how the research to date has enhanced our understanding of the relationships between ownership and corporate governance and concludes with some suggestions for future research.

Ownership and Corporate Governance: Themes and Issues

Broadly defined, corporate governance refers to the array of external and internal control mechanisms that motivate senior corporate executives to make decisions that are expected to enhance the value of the firm and/or the wealth of its major stakeholders. This definition is broad enough to encompass the huge diversity in both international and within-country corporate governance systems that currently exists. For example, the legal and institutional infrastructure and corporate governance mechanisms of many highly developed market economies, such as the US and UK, are largely oriented towards restricting the notion of 'stakeholders' to the firms' equity owners (shareholders). In other, equally complex and developed market economies – the examples of Germany and Japan are most frequently mentioned in this context – legal rights and other institutional mechanisms require managerial decisions to take some account of the interests of other stakeholder groups, such as employees, their creditors and/or their corporate network.

The international differences in corporate governance are matched by a similarly wide variety of corporate governance practices operating within any individual economy. Within national economies, corporate variety in terms of differences in firm size, legal and regulatory status, exposure to product market competition, financial requirements and perceived risks, clearly influence the relative effectiveness and usage by individual firms of particular governance mechanisms. Indeed, several of the papers in this collection address these inter-relationships and the implications of corporate heterogeneity upon the efficiency of the market for corporate control, insider shareholdings, equity-based compensation initiatives and the incentives of different types of external blockholders.

The efficiency of corporate governance mechanisms are important to shareholders because their wealth depends on the actions of corporate executives over whom they necessarily have limited control. Limited control is inevitable since, in order to fulfil their duties, executives require a large degree of discretion over the day-to-day use of the firm's assets and in regard to the formulation and implementation of corporate strategies. That is to say, executive employment contracts are necessarily 'incomplete' because 'complete contracting', i.e., fully specifying ex ante the precise actions the executives should take in all possible circumstances, is an impossibility due to bounded rationality,[2] asymmetric information and the costs associated with becoming informed (Hart, 1995).

In the case of firms characterised by a significant degree of separation of ownership from control, there is an ever-present danger that executives may develop priorities and/or preferences that differ from those of shareholders. For example, due to their high firm-specific risk exposure, executives may be more risk averse than diversified shareholders with respect to firm investment decisions. Hence, executives may prefer not to undertake risky but positive NPV projects, the so-called 'under-investment' hazard. Alternatively, executives may use corporate free cash flows to invest in negative NPV projects (the 'over-investment' problem). However, a typical diversified individual investor will generally own only a small proportion of the firms' equity and therefore, is unlikely to have sufficient incentive or skills to adequately monitor and control executive discretion. Thus, incomplete contracts, monitoring and information costs in relation to evaluating performance and effectively disciplining poorly performing executives and conflicts of interest expose executives to moral hazards and shareholders to agency costs. In this context, the role of corporate governance mechanisms is to minimise these dangers by motivating executives to use their managerial discretion to enhance shareholder value (Hart, 1995).

The potential problems arising from the separation of ownership from control has been a dominant theme (i.e., 'frame') in corporate governance studies since Berle and Means (1932) first drew attention to the issue, which they saw as a major distinguishing characteristic of the modern corporation. These concerns were later developed by Jensen and Meckling (1976) into what has subsequently become known as 'agency theory'. Following Berle and Means, Jensen and Meckling focused on the separation of ownership from control in widely held firms and how to minimise the agency costs associated with executive discretion. Berle and Means (1932) were clearly correct in drawing attention to the new widely held ownership structures and potential control problems that could arise when no individual shareholder actually held a significant equity stake in the business. Nevertheless, the widely held firm has survived and, indeed, this ownership structure often characterises the largest firms in several developed economies such as the US and the UK. This suggests that, whatever the supposed agency problems between its shareholders and its management, the widely held firm has other advantages and/or its agency costs are mitigated by other external or internal control mechanisms such as the market for corporate control or the adoption of independent board members.

Even so, it is not obvious why the agency problems of the widely held firm should have become the central issue of corporate governance research. The widely held ownership structure was not particularly common even amongst the largest US firms when Berle and Means first published their work (see, for example, Holderness et al., 1999). This remains the case in the US today and international comparisons suggest also that it is in fact a comparatively rare organisational form even amongst the largest businesses of many developed economies (see La Porta et al., 1999). Though it is true that the vast majority of individual shareholders are neither involved in the management of the business nor hold a controlling stake, most firms do in fact have one or more significant blockholders. Frequently these blockholders consist of a controlling family, the State, executives and other board members or other corporate entities and financial institutions.

The existence of one or more blockholders with a controlling interest in the firm has also cast doubt upon Jensen and Meckling's original idea that the most important agency relationship was necessarily between executives with no ownership stake and widely held shareholders. To be applicable to the majority of firms, the Jensen and Meckling agency ideas have had to be extended to include the possibility of conflicts of interests between different classes of shareholder. In some recent theoretical models (e.g., Shleifer and Vishny, 1986), the owners of large equity blocks are assumed to have sufficient incentive to monitor executives since by definition they have a large non-diversified financial interest in ensuring that executives pursue only value increasing opportunities. As the benefits associated with this monitoring are also shared with other shareholders (the so-called 'shared benefits of control'), the existence of such a blockholder can be viewed as being in all shareholders' interests. However, blockholders are not all identical and some types of controlling blockholders may be primarily motivated by the prospect of obtaining benefits not shared with other shareholders (the 'private benefits of control'). Moreover, as argued by Short (1994), institutional shareholders often suffer from their own agency problems and conflicts of interests between maximising corporate pension fund business and seeking to control the actions of executives on behalf of their other investors. Thus, it may be plausible to argue that an external blockholder, such as a pension fund that does not depend on the firm for any significant level of business, may have an interest in monitoring managerial actions. It is, however, probably unrealistic to expect internal blockholders (such as management or another corporate entity or family that controls the board of directors) to be so motivated.

This considerable diversity in terms of corporate characteristics, the existence of other institutional control mechanisms and the variety of possible blockholder motivations and objective functions are precisely what makes ownership and governance an interesting and dynamic field of research. However, these inter-related factors also help explain why neither the conclusions of theoretical models nor the findings of empirical studies usually have much of an impact on corporate governance practitioners and policy makers. It is clear that poor corporate performance will frequently be the result of factors that have nothing to do with inadequacies in corporate governance. In addition, research design and econometric problems regarding the direction of causation and adequately controlling for the endogeneity of ownership characteristics also create immense difficulties in empirically evaluating whether, for example, blockholders have an impact upon corporate outcomes, whether the private benefits of control is what motivates blockholders and/or whether private benefits significantly reduce the wealth of other shareholders. Clinical studies that include data and analyses from a variety of viewpoints and sources, e.g., detailed case studies, rather than relying solely on large-scale empirical analyses of highly heterogeneous firms, may perhaps be more likely to shed light on some of these complex inter-relationships.

The Papers in this Collection

The 20 papers in this collection on ownership and corporate governance research are intended to provide the reader with an appreciation of the wide variety of issues currently being addressed by researchers in this field. As discussed above, bounded rationality, incomplete contracts, judgmental inadequacies (of owners, managers and corporate governance policy makers) and conflicts of interests are why corporate governance is of economic importance. The diversity in international and national corporate governance and ownership characteristics, and the conceptual and data requirements involved in adequately modelling and empirically testing corporate governance hypotheses also makes bounded rationality a central issue for researchers in the field. Thus, the papers in this collection reflect both the variety of research methods used in corporate governance studies and the diversity with respect to the types of firms, ownership and corporate governance systems that currently exist. To help guide the reader through this work, I have chosen to split the collection into the following four main parts:

Part I   Forms of Ownership and Corporate Diversity
Part II   Insider Ownership, Monitoring by Blockholders and Corporate Performance
Part III   Ownership, Managerial Succession and Corporate Restructuring
Part IV   Ownership, Executive Compensation and Corporate Decision Making

Of course, given the interconnected nature of many of the issues examined by individual papers, this division is somewhat arbitrary because several papers could have appeared in more than one of the four sections. A brief discussion of each of the sections and papers in the collection is undertaken below.

Part I. Forms of Ownership and Corporate Diversity

The international diversity in ownership structures is empirically examined by Chapter 1, La Porta et al. (1999). These authors examine the ownership structures and the identity of the ultimate controlling shareholders of the 20 largest corporations in 27 wealthy economies. With their comparative database the authors are able to empirically evaluate the following four broad questions related to the Berle and Means (1932) thesis:

> First, how common are widely held firms in different countries, as opposed to firms that have owners with significant voting rights? Second, to the extent that firms have significant owners, who are they?... Third, how do these owners maintain their power and, fourth, what explains differences between countries in their ownership patterns? (pp. 472–3)

The main findings of the study are that, except in economies with very good shareholder protection, the Berle and Means image of the widely held ownership structure of large corporations is relatively uncommon – as, indeed, is the so-called 'German' model whereby banks acquire controlling equity stakes (see Jenkinson and Ljungqvist, 2001). Rather, for most countries, the controlling shareholders of large corporations consist of either 'the State' or 'families' and, moreover, through the use of pyramid structures and their participation in the management of the corporation, these controlling shareholders typically have control rights significantly in excess of their cash flow rights. The authors conclude that these findings suggest that the most relevant corporate governance perspective for most countries is one that focuses upon the incentives and opportunities of controlling shareholders to both benefit and expropriate the minority shareholders.

An interesting finding of the La Porta et al. study is that, though their relative importance varies significantly between countries, family-based controlling stakes in large corporations are ubiquitous. Indeed, La Porta et al. show that family control is generally far more common than either widely held ownership structures or firms in which the State or a financial institution has a controlling interest. On average, using a definition of control as an equity stake of 10 per cent or more, families appear to control some 35 per cent of the largest firms in the richest economies, compared to only 24 per cent and 20 per cent that are respectively widely held or controlled by the State. Moreover, as family control is the dominant ownership form found in unlisted and small and medium sized enterprises, the above statistics based upon the largest public corporations in each country clearly provide a gross underestimate of the actual importance of family ownership to the governance of firms around the world. Even so, despite the prevalence of family control, there is a relative lack of academic research into the theory and practice of family ownership and control. One of the possible reasons for this relative neglect is theoretical. Typically it has been assumed that agency costs are generally low and formal governance mechanisms unnecessary in relation to family firms because of their limited separation of ownership from control and the advantages families have in 'monitoring and disciplining related decision agents' (Jensen and Meckling, 1976; Fama and Jensen, 1983). Another, more practical, reason for the relative lack of empirical research into the governance of family firms concerns the difficulties in obtaining reliable and consistent information on family ownership and practices.

Chapter 2, Schulze et al. (2001), 'Agency Relationships in Family Firms: Theory and Evidence', is a rare attempt to examine the theory and evidence relating to the governance of family firms. Drawing on the behavioural insights of, amongst others, Becker (1981), Stulz (1988) and Thaler and Shefrin (1981), these authors argue that private ownership and family management actually expose such firms to a number of unique agency hazards that prevent them from minimising the agency costs of ownership. Using data from a 1995 survey of American family businesses, the authors field test six hypotheses of the relationship between family firm governance characteristics and performance (sales growth). Though the empirical results offer some support for several of the hypotheses, they may lack credibility with some researchers due to the inherent limitations of the available survey data and the relatively unsophisticated empirical methods that had to be employed. Nevertheless, as unlisted owner-manager and family firms are not required to disclose much in the way of financial and other information to outsiders, survey methods are likely to remain one of the few ways that quantitative analyses can be undertaken in respect of this important sector of the corporate landscape.

Chapter 3, by Black and Gilson (1998), entitled 'Venture Capital and the Structure of Capital Markets: Banks versus Stock Markets', examines another relatively neglected area of corporate governance, the governance roles of venture capital and its relationship with the stock market and the market for corporate control. These authors develop a model that explains why venture capital is so much more prevalent in economies such as the US and UK that have both a stock market-centred system and an active market for corporate control than the more bank-centred financial systems characteristic of Germany and Japan. Their basic argument is that in a stock market-centred system, venture capital provides entrepreneurs and venture capitalists with the

> opportunity to enter into an implicit contract over control, which gives a successful entrepreneur the option to reacquire control from the venture capitalist by using an initial public offering as the means by which the venture capitalist exits from a portfolio investment. (p. 243)

As these features are not easily duplicable in a bank-centred capital market, the authors suggest rather optimistically

> that the best strategy for overcoming path dependent barriers to a venture capital market in bank-centred systems is to piggyback on the institutional infrastructure of stock-market-centred systems. (p. 274)

Chapter 4, by Franks and Mayer (2001), 'Ownership and Control of German Corporations', provides an interesting analysis of the distinctive ownership structures of German corporations. They provide evidence that suggests that the more bank-centred, or 'insider' system in Germany is more similar to the US and UK than has often been acknowledged. They also argue that, in Germany, how control changes take place and the motivations and benefits to the blockholders involved are different from what is generally the case in the US. These authors show that despite the obvious differences in ownership characteristics compared with both the US and UK, there is a similar strong relationship between executive turnover and firm performance and limited evidence that ownership concentrations are associated with managerial disciplining or that pyramid structures are actually used for control purposes. Nevertheless, they also find that in terms of changes in ownership, the German system operates very differently from the market-centred systems of the US and UK. In Germany changes in control occur via an active market in share blocks that primarily benefit the blockholders rather than the minority shareholders. However, the benefits of control changes appear, overall, to be relatively small and the authors suggest that the benefits accruing to the blockholders demonstrate the exploitation of the private benefits of control.

Part II. Insider Ownership, Monitoring by Blockholders and Corporate Performance

The Franks and Mayer (2001) paper demonstrated that, despite the differences in ownership, the German corporate governance system operated in ways that were in many important respects very similar to the supposedly very different US and UK systems. Chapter 5, by Short and Keasey (1999), entitled 'Managerial Ownership and the Performance of Firms: Evidence from the UK', provides evidence of significant differences between the two supposedly very similar US and UK corporate governance systems in terms of both insider (management) and outside blockholder characteristics and in the relationship between insider ownership and corporate performance. Short and Keasey extend the predominantly US empirical literature that has focused on whether managerial equity ownership succeeds in aligning managerial and shareholder interests or whether beyond some level of ownership managers become 'entrenched'. They argue that in the UK, with institutional differences such as the limited availability of anti-takeover defences and the greater prevalence of institutional investors, a higher level of equity ownership than in the US will be required in order for managerial entrenchment to occur. Their empirical results, using both accounting and stock market valuation measures confirm the US findings of a non-linear relationship between managerial ownership and firm performance but, as expected, managerial entrenchment in the UK appears to occur at a significantly higher level of equity ownership than was apparent from the US studies.

The results of Short and Keasey (1999) and the extensive US literature on the relationship between managerial ownership and firm performance appear to suggest that many firms operate with suboptimal compensation and incentive alignment systems. In contrast, Chapter 6, Himmelberg et al. (1999), 'Understanding the Determinants of Managerial Ownership and the Link between Ownership and Performance', builds upon the work of Demsetz and Lehn (1985) to propose an equilibrium interpretation of observed differences in corporate ownership structures. These authors argue that observed differences in managerial ownership are endogenously determined by both observable and non-observable heterogeneity in the contracting environment facing firms. So, for example, for firms with low exposure to moral hazard and/or where monitoring by shareholders is relatively easy to accomplish, a very low level of managerial ownership may be optimal. Using a panel dataset of large US firms, the authors test the extent to which managerial ownership is endogenously determined by including in their estimating equations fixed effects (to control for unobserved firm heterogeneity) and variables such as stock price variability, firm size, capital intensity, Research and Development (R&D) intensity, advertising intensity, cash flow and investment rate, to proxy for differences in the firm's exposure to moral hazard. The main findings are first, the proxies for firms' contracting environment strongly predict the structure of managerial ownership and that these results are robust to the inclusion of firm-level fixed effects; second, the coefficient on managerial ownership was not robust to the inclusion of fixed effects which indicates that both managerial ownership and firm performance are determined by common (observed and unobserved) characteristics; and third, via the use of instrumental variables, there was some tentative evidence to support a causal link from ownership to performance.[3]

Chapters 7, Wahal (1996), 'Pension Fund Activism and Firm Performance', and 8, Faccio and Lasfer (2000), 'Do Occupational Pension Funds Monitor Companies in Which They Hold Large Stakes?', both focus on the monitoring role of pension funds and conduct empirical analyses to evaluate whether pension fund activism or pension fund equity stakes have a significant impact on firm performance. The Wahal (1996) paper examines pension fund activism in the US and shows that for the firms targeted there is no evidence of long term performance improvements. Wahal concludes that these results cast considerable doubt on the effectiveness of pension fund activism as a substitute for an active market for corporate control. Using a UK sample of large firms, the Faccio and Lasfer paper focuses on firms with large pension fund stakes and shows that these firms do not outperform their industry counterparts and, in a similar fashion to Wahal (1996) conclude that the evidence suggests that pension funds are not effective monitors.

Chapter 9, by Holland (1998), 'Influence and Intervention by Financial Institutions in their Investee Companies', details the (often private) corporate governance role of financial institutions in their portfolio companies. Holland employs a research method based primarily upon detailed case studies and interviews with senior directors and fund managers of UK financial institutions to explore the ways in which they attempt to exert what he calls 'implicit influence' (or 'voice') on their investee companies. What becomes clear from this analysis is that institutional voice is typically highly constrained by financial institutions' relative powerlessness and general unwillingness to interfere during periods of good corporate performance. The quasi insider knowledge gained by financial institutions was typically held 'in reserve' until such time as they felt that they had greater influence, i.e., during periods of poor performance. Holland's findings have obvious relevance to the findings of the previous two chapters. Namely, that the private information gathering of financial institutions and the building of relationships with their portfolio companies certainly generate costs but, due to their unwillingness to confront management and/or perceived lack of influence, institutional investors neither act on this information during good times nor do they share their private information with other investors. Given these behavioural constraints it is clear that expecting financial institutions to intervene prior to a crisis or expecting any sort of superior performance from firms that have a large institutional shareholder base may be unrealistic. Holland's findings do, however, suggest that UK financial institutional shareholdings may be associated with speedier replacement of incompetent executives or more efficient restructuring once a financial crisis has surfaced.

Part III. Ownership, Managerial Succession and Corporate Restructuring

Chapters 10 to 15 all examine different aspects of the relationships between ownership structures and dynamics and the ability and willingness of owners to intervene in managerial succession decisions and/or corporate restructuring of one sort or another. Chapter 10, by Denis and Sarin

(1999), entitled 'Ownership and Board Structures in Publicly Traded Corporations', focuses on the dynamics of ownership (and board) structures and whether these may be caused by fundamental changes in the firms' business environment. The study utilises both a large sample of US firms and a number of detailed case studies to evaluate the empirical evidence on the evolution and changes in both ownership and board structures and how such changes are related to managerial succession and asset restructuring decisions. The main findings are that ownership and board structures are considerably less stable than has generally been believed and appear to be responses to fundamental changes in the firms' operating environment. Ownership and board changes are also strongly related to top management changes, corporate control threats, asset restructuring and prior share price performance.

Chapter 11, Smith and Amoako-Adu (1999), 'Management Succession and Financial Performance of Family Controlled Firms', examines both the immediate and long-term share price effects of family and non-family managerial successions for a sample of family controlled Canadian public corporations. The authors show that around 62 per cent of these family controlled firms make use of dual class capitalisations to maintain family control. Even so, filling managerial positions with family members is not without its costs. Family successions tend to be associated with significantly negative abnormal returns around the announcement date, whilst for non-family successors, who are generally only appointed after a period of poor firm performance, no such negative reaction is found. The authors indicate, however, that for the family successors, most of the negative reaction appears to be due to their relative youth and lack of experience vis-à-vis the non-family appointments.

Chapter 12, Robbie and Wright (1995), 'Managerial and Ownership Succession and Corporate Restructuring: The Case of Management Buy-ins', provides a review and case study evidence relating to management buy-ins, a particularly interesting form of corporate restructuring since a buy-in involves simultaneously changing both management and ownership structures. Typically, due to information asymmetries between the vendors and the new management and ownership teams, particular problems arise in respect of incentivising management, matching entrepreneurs to the firms and business context, monitoring and control by financiers (principally, venture capitalists) and the implementation of corporate strategies. The common behavioural bias of 'overconfidence' in the face of uncertainty certainly appears to inflict buy-in teams. Indeed, the authors conclude

> that managers in a buy-in may be well-incentivised and that there may be systematic and responsive monitoring in place, but that the efficacy of these mechanisms may be swamped by problems which arise when the business context ex post was not what it appeared to be ex ante ... As a result, although they may already have a track record as effective managers and be highly incentivised, they are in a comparatively weak position to take appropriate restructuring action. (pp. 545–6)

Chapter 13, Hanson and Song (2000), 'Managerial Ownership, Board Structure and the Division of Gains in Divestitures', provides an empirical analysis of 326 corporate divestment decisions and whether the shareholder wealth effects of such decisions are related to internal control characteristics, i.e., managerial ownership and board structure. The study shows that on average the 326 divestitures appeared to be in shareholder's interests since small, but positive excess returns around the announcement date were observed for both buyers and sellers. The average divestiture transaction created a 'synergy gain' (the total Dollar excess returns) of approximately US$20 million (in constant 1981 dollars), with US$8.7 million and US$11.3 million respectively accruing to the sellers and buyers of the assets. Hanson and Song's regression results indicate that when the divestiture produces positive synergy gains, the seller's shareholders receive gains that are significantly related to both managerial ownership and the proportion of outside directors on the firm's board. The authors interpret the managerial ownership results as evidence consistent with the alignment of interests hypothesis since high managerial ownership appears to provide an incentive to both sell assets that create negative synergies and to negotiate the best price for shareholders. The authors are similarly optimistic regarding the interpretation of their board composition results. The relationships between seller gains, total synergy gains and the proportion of outside directors are interpreted as supporting notions that outside directors fulfil two important, though perhaps contradictory, corporate governance roles, namely independent monitors of management and effective advisors and members of the firm's top management team.

Chapter 14, Duggal and Millar (1999), 'Institutional Ownership and Firm Performance: The Case of Bidder Returns', focuses on outside (institutional) ownership and its relationship to takeover decisions and corporate performance. Though their Ordinary Least Squares (OLS) regression estimates indicate a positive relationship between bidder returns and institutional ownership, these authors show that institutional ownership is itself significantly determined by firm size, Standard and Poor's (S&P) 500 membership and insider ownership. Using a 2-stage recursive regression estimation procedure, in which the bidder returns were regressed on the predicted values of institutional ownership, the positive relationship between bidder gains and institutional ownership estimated by the OLS regression disappears. As these authors also report that active institutional investors, such as the California Public Employees' Retirement System (CalPERS), as a group do not appear to enhance the efficiency of corporate control, they suggest that their findings cast doubt on the supposed superior selection and monitoring abilities of institutional investors.

Chapter 15, Bruner (1999), 'An Analysis of Value Destruction and Recovery in the Alliance and Proposed Merger of Volvo and Renault', provides a very contrasting view of the potential roles and wealth effects of institutional activism in this area. The paper presents a detailed case study of the attempted merger between Volvo and Renault. The attempted merger temporarily destroyed over US$1billion of Volvo's value. What is particularly interesting about this study is that Bruner analyses these wealth-destroying actions as arising from managerial entrenchment (due to a complex structure of cross-shareholdings, joint committees and a poison pill) and the consequent lack of checks on their behavioural biases generated unconstrained hubris and the escalation of commitment. The merger was, however, abandoned only after a rebellion by a small group of Swedish financial institutions who, though collectively holding a minority of the firm's shares, were able to force through changes in management, strategy and governance – actions that were accompanied by positive abnormal returns. Thus, the case illustrates both the potential causes of sub-optimal managerial decision making and the potential efficacy of institutional shareholder activism in remedying the situation.

Part IV. Ownership, Executive Compensation and Corporate Decision Making

Chapters 16 to 18 each examine different aspects of the relationships between executive compensation decisions, the role of insider and/or outsider ownership, firm performance, the level and mix of Chief Executive Officer (CEO) compensation or initial public offering decisions. Chapter 16, Mehran (1995), 'Executive Compensation Structure, Ownership, and Firm Performance', provides evidence that the form and not merely the level of compensation matters since firm performance is positively related to the percentage of managerial equity and to the percentage of their total compensation that is equity-based. Moreover, firms with more outside directors appear to make more extensive use of equity-based compensation whilst other firms with more insider and outsider block ownership tend to rely upon equity-based compensation to a much lesser extent. Mehran suggests that his results indicate that compensation decisions are, as expected, much more focused on incentive alignment concerns in the absence of high managerial ownership and/or direct monitoring by external blockholders.

Chapter 17, David et al. (1998), 'The Effect of Institutional Investors on the Level and Mix of CEO Compensation', conceptualises CEO compensation decisions as the outcome of a political power struggle between CEOs and owners. CEOs attempt to extract the most favourable pay packet whilst owners try to limit the level of compensation and to increase the proportion of long-term incentives. Thus, the relative power between CEOs and owners largely determines pay outcomes. David et al. categorise institutional investors into three groups depending upon their ability and incentives to resist managerial pressure. Their main findings, based upon 125 US firms, suggest that institutional owners that have only an investment relationship with the firm ('pressure resistant' institutions) are able to influence CEO compensation in a manner consistent with shareholder preferences. In contrast, 'pressure sensitive' institutions, i.e., those that depend on a firm for business, appear to be unable to influence CEO compensation levels or the proportion of long-term incentives in total pay.

Chapter 18, Beatty and Zajac (1994), 'Managerial Incentives, Monitoring and Risk Bearing: A Study of Executive Compensation, Ownership and Board Structure in Initial Public Offerings', adopts a contingency framework to examine the complex trade-offs between incentive alignment, monitoring and managerial risk-bearing that owners and board compensation committees have to consider in order to decide upon an appropriate level and structure of executive pay. Beatty and Zajac empirically evaluate a number of trade-off hypotheses relating to incentives and risk bearing and monitoring and incentives using a sample of US Initial Public Offerings (IPOs). Their main findings are as follows. First, there is an inverse relationship between levels of firm risk and the use of incentive pay for top managers and, second, firms that face the most severe managerial incentive problems are more likely to have governance structures that provide a higher level of monitoring of managerial behaviour.

Chapter 19, Wright et al. (1996), 'Impact of Corporate Insider, Blockholder and Institutional Equity Ownership on Firm Risk Taking' also examines the influence of equity ownership structures upon corporate growth-oriented risk taking. Their empirical findings suggest that the wealth portfolios of managers influence the level of risk taking and that at high levels of equity ownership, i.e., entrenchment, managers appear to take decisions inconsistent with growth-oriented risk taking. Although the role of non-institutional blockholders appeared negligible, institutional owners exerted a positive and statistically significant influence on corporate risk taking.

The differing incentives of individual (inside and outside) blockholders and their ability to form coalitions in order to exercise a greater degree of control over important corporate decisions is also the focus of Chapter 20, Goergen and Renneboog (2001), 'Investment Policy, Internal Financing and Ownership Concentration in the UK'. Goergen and Renneboog address the relationships between free cash flow, capital structure and suboptimal corporate investment decisions. Their empirical analysis utilises a six-year panel of 240 UK firms listed on the London Stock Exchange and, to avoid the well-known measurement problems associated with Tobin's q, the authors estimate a Euler-equation model which allows for a direct test of the first-order condition of an intertemporal maximisation problem. Of especial interest, however, is their analysis of the differing corporate under- and over-investment outcomes associated with particular categories, concentrations and/or coalitions of blockholders. Their main findings suggest that large shareholdings by industrial companies, particularly when their voting power is combined with the equity stakes of families, are associated with increased over-investment. The presence of large institutional shareholdings, however, reduces the positive relationship between investment spending and cash flows which suggests that institutional ownership tends to mitigate the over-investment problem. Moreover, low levels of managerial ownership appear not to be associated with either under- or over-investment problems. Interestingly though, a high concentration of executive director control, far from reducing corporate risk-taking, appears to render under-investment less likely.

Concluding Remarks

The papers in this collection reflect the diversity of research currently being undertaken in this field. What should be apparent from the brief summaries given above is that there is an equally wide diversity in the types of ownership structures, individual blockholder incentives to take actions that either increase or decrease the value of the firm and the mechanisms used by owners to control managerial discretion. Such diversity in subject matter and methods naturally makes it difficult to summarise the contribution of this research to our understanding of the relationships between ownership forms and corporate governance. Nevertheless, an excellent recent review article, Holderness (2003), successfully summarised the findings of the (largely, US-based) empirical research as follows:

> surprisingly few major corporate decisions have been shown to be different in the presence of a blockholder. One exception is that external blockholders appear to monitor the form and level of managerial compensation. Conversely, there is little evidence that blockholders affect leverage. Ownership concentration appears to have little impact on firm value. If one wants a single 'take-away' point from the rapidly growing literature on ownership concentration, it is that small shareholders and regulators have little reason to fear large percentage shareholders in general, especially when a large shareholder is active in firm management. (p. 60)

Though the above is a fair reflection of the findings 'in general' of the large-scale econometric studies, the limitations of the data used in terms of its level of detail, the typically restricted sample coverage (predominantly only large surviving firms) leave room for considerable doubts. Moreover, it is no consolation to an investor of a failed firm to be told that 'in general' this is (or has been in the past) a relatively unusual occurrence. Indeed, Holderness's 'take-away' point is probably unwisely complacent given the evidence of detailed case studies that owners can often make a significant (positive or negative) impact on corporate decisions, and the behavioural studies that suggest that most corporate governance failures result from a combination of complacent investors and over-confident executives. Future research in this area should perhaps concentrate on integrating more realistic institutional and behavioural assumptions into their hypotheses and empirical analyses regarding the motivations of different groups of owners to monitor and control executive discretion.

Notes

1. Several excellent published reviews are available elsewhere (see, for example, Daily et al. (2003), Denis (2001), Holderness (2003) and Short (1994)).
2. The concept of bounded rationality was first coined by Herbert Simon (1955) and its decision making implications are of central importance to corporate governance research. Bounded rationality stems from the limitations of human cognitive powers and, in many instances, leads to a *satisficing* (i.e., a satisfactory) rather than an 'optimal' solution. This is because, in order to cope with the complex information and decisions they face, human beings rely upon simplified cognitive processes and decision criteria, called *heuristics*. These cognitive processes result in judgmental biases and decisions based on inappropriate anchoring, stereotypes, frame dependencies, overconfidence and the escalation of commitment (see the original contributions to this literature in Kahneman et al. (1982)). Recent reviews of the research into the judgmental biases of agents in economics, investment and managerial decision making can be found respectively in Conlisk (1996), Shefrin (2000) and Bazerman (2002).
3. See also the empirical analyses and similar results provided by Demsetz and Villalonga (2001).

References

Bazerman, M. (2002), *Judgement in Managerial Decision Making* (5th edn), New York/Chichester: John Wiley Publishers.

Becker, G.S. (1981), *A Treatise on the Family*, Cambridge, MA: Harvard University Press.

Berle, A. and G.C. Means (1932), *The Modern Corporation and Private Property*, New York, Macmillan Publishers.

Conlisk, J. (1996), 'Why Bounded Rationality?', *Journal of Economic Literature*, **34**, 669–700.

Daily, C.M., D.R. Dalton and N. Rajagopalan (2003), 'Governance Through Ownership: Centuries of Practice, Decades of Research', *Academy of Management Journal*, **46**, 151–8.

Demsetz, H. and K. Lehn (1985), 'The Structure of Corporate Ownership: Causes and Consequences', *Journal of Political Economy*, **93**, 1155–77.

Demsetz, H. and B. Villalonga (2001), 'Ownership Structure and Corporate Performance', *Journal of Corporate Finance*, **7**, 209–33.

Denis, D.K. (2001), 'Twenty-five Years of Corporate Governance Research ... and Counting', *Review of Financial Economics*, **10**, 191–212.

Fama, E. and M.C. Jensen (1983), 'Agency Problems and Residual Claims', *Journal of Law and Economics*, **26**, 325–44.

Hart, O. (1995), 'Corporate Governance: Some Theory and Implications', *Economic Journal*, **105**, 678–89.

Holderness, C.G. (2003), 'A Survey of Blockholders and Corporate Control', *Economic Policy Review*, Federal Reserve Bank of New York, 51–64, April.

Holderness, C.G., R.S. Kroszner and D.P. Sheehan (1999), 'Were the Good Old Days that Good? Changes in Managerial Stock Ownership since the Great Depression', *Journal of Finance*, **54**, 435-69.

Jenkinson, T. and A. Ljungqvist (2001), 'The Role of Hostile Stakes in German Corporate Governance', *Journal of Corporate Finance*, **7**, 397–446.

Jensen, M.C. and W.H. Meckling (1976), 'Theory of the Firm: Managerial Behaviour, Agency Costs and Ownership Structure', *Journal of Financial Economics*, **3**, 305–60.

Kahneman, D., P. Slovic and A. Tversky (eds) (1982), *Judgement under Uncertainty: Heuristics and Biases*, Cambridge: Cambridge University Press.

Shefrin, H. (2000), *Beyond Greed and Fear*, Boston, MA: Harvard University Business School Press.

Shleifer, A. and R.W. Vishny (1986), 'Large Shareholders and Corporate Control', *Journal of Political Economy*, **94**, 461–88.

Short, H. (1994), 'Ownership, Control, Financial Structure and the Performance of Firms', *Journal of Economic Surveys*, **8** (3), 203–49.

Simon, H.A. (1955), 'A Behavioural Model of Rational Choice', *Quarterly Journal of Economics*, **69**, 99–118.

Stulz, R.M. (1988), 'On Takeover Resistance, Managerial Discretion, and Shareholder Wealth', *Journal of Financial Economics*, **20**, 25–54.

Thaler, R.H. and H. Shefrin (1981), 'An Economic Theory of Self-Control', *Journal of Political Economy*, **89**, 392–406.

Part I
Forms of Ownership and Corporate Diversity

[1]

THE JOURNAL OF FINANCE • VOL. LIV, NO. 2 • APRIL 1999

Corporate Ownership Around the World

RAFAEL LA PORTA, FLORENCIO LOPEZ-DE-SILANES,
and ANDREI SHLEIFER*

ABSTRACT

We use data on ownership structures of large corporations in 27 wealthy economies to identify the ultimate controlling shareholders of these firms. We find that, except in economies with very good shareholder protection, relatively few of these firms are widely held, in contrast to Berle and Means's image of ownership of the modern corporation. Rather, these firms are typically controlled by families or the State. Equity control by financial institutions is far less common. The controlling shareholders typically have power over firms significantly in excess of their cash flow rights, primarily through the use of pyramids and participation in management.

IN THEIR 1932 CLASSIC, *The Modern Corporation and Private Property*, Adolph Berle and Gardiner Means call attention to the prevalence of widely held corporations in the United States, in which ownership of capital is dispersed among small shareholders, yet control is concentrated in the hands of managers. For at least two generations, their book has fixed the image of the modern corporation as one run by professional managers unaccountable to shareholders. The book stimulated an enormous "managerialist" literature on the objectives of such managers, including the important work of Baumol (1959), Marris (1964), Penrose (1959), and Williamson (1964), as well as Galbraith's (1967) popular and influential account. More recently, the modern field of corporate finance has developed around the same image of a widely held corporation, as can be seen in the central contributions of Jensen and Meckling (1976) or Grossman and Hart (1980). The Berle and Means image has clearly stuck.

In recent years, several studies have begun to question the empirical validity of this image. Eisenberg (1976), Demsetz (1983), Demsetz and Lehn (1985), Shleifer and Vishny (1986), and Morck, Shleifer and Vishny (1988) show that, even among the largest American firms, there is a modest concentration of ownership. Holderness and Sheehan (1988) have found in the United States several hundred publicly traded firms with majority (greater

*Harvard University. We are grateful to Alexander Aganin, Carlos Berdejo-Izquierdo, David Grossman, Bernardo Lopez-Morton, Tatiana Nenova, Ekaterina Trizlova, and David Witkin for help with assembling the data, to Lucian Bebchuk, Marco Becht, Mihir Desai, Oliver Hart, Louis Kaplow, Mark Roe, Roberta Romano, René Stulz, Robert Vishny, Luigi Zingales, and two anonymous referees for advice, and to the NSF for financial support.

than 51 percent) shareholders. Holderness, Kroszner and Sheehan (1999) have found, moreover, that management ownership in the United States today is higher than it was when Berle and Means wrote their study.

Studies of other rich countries reveal more significant concentration of ownership in Germany (Edwards and Fischer (1994), Franks and Mayer (1994), and Gorton and Schmid (1996)), Japan (Prowse (1992), Berglof and Perotti (1994)), Italy (Barca (1995)), and seven OECD countries (European Corporate Governance Network (1997)). In developing economies, ownership is also heavily concentrated (La Porta et al. (1998)). This research suggests that in many countries large corporations have large shareholders and, further, that these shareholders are active in corporate governance (e.g., Kang and Shivdasani (1995), Yafeh and Yosha (1996)), in contrast to the Berle and Means idea that managers are unaccountable.[1]

As a result of this research, the Berle and Means image of the modern corporation has begun to show some wear. Still, we have relatively little systematic evidence about the ownership patterns of large publicly traded firms in different countries, and we lack a comparative perspective on the relevance of the Berle and Means description of the firm. This paper attempts to provide some such evidence. Specifically, we look at the ownership structures of the 20 largest publicly traded firms in each of the 27 generally richest economies, as well as of some smaller firms so that we can keep size constant across countries. We focus on the largest firms in the richest economies precisely because, for these firms, the likelihood of widely dispersed ownership is the greatest—and we find that this is indeed the case. Our principal contribution is to find wherever possible the identities of the *ultimate* owners of capital and of voting rights in firms, so when shares in a firm are owned by another company, we examine the ownership of that company, and so on.[2] For most countries, this is the only way to understand the relationship between ownership and control. These data enable us to address, in a comparative perspective, four broad questions related to the Berle and Means thesis.

First, how common are widely held firms in different countries, as opposed to firms that have owners with significant voting rights? Second, to the extent that firms have significant owners, who are they? Are they families, the government, financial institutions, or other, possibly widely held, firms? How often do banks control companies—a big issue in corporate finance in light of the extensive discussion of the German corporate governance model? Third, how do these owners maintain their power? Do they use shares with superior voting rights that enable them to exercise control with

---

[1] There is a parallel theoretical literature on the role of large shareholders, including Shleifer and Vishny (1986), Stulz (1988), Grossman and Hart (1988), Harris and Raviv (1988), Bebchuk (1994), and Burkart, Gromb, Panunzi (1997, 1998).

[2] La Porta et al. (1998) examine first level ownership of the 10 largest publicly traded firms in 49 countries, but do not look for the ultimate owners. This paper attempts to establish the identities of the ultimate owners.

only limited ownership of capital? Alternatively, do they create complicated cross-ownership patterns to reduce the threat to their control? Or do they build pyramids, whereby they control firms through a chain of companies—another form of separating ownership of capital and control? By answering these questions empirically, we hope to provide a comprehensive description of ownership patterns of large firms in rich countries.

The fourth question we address is: What explains the differences between countries in their ownership patterns? Why, for example, is the Berle and Means image of a widely held firm so much more descriptive of the United States than of Mexico or Italy? Our earlier work (La Porta et al. (1997, 1998)) suggests that the Berle and Means widely held corporation should be more common in countries with good legal protection of minority shareholders (which are often the rich common law countries). In these countries, controlling shareholders have less fear of being expropriated themselves in the event that they ever lose control through a takeover or a market accumulation of shares by a raider, and so might be willing to cut their ownership of voting rights by selling shares to raise funds or to diversify. In contrast, in countries with poor protection of minority shareholders, losing control involuntarily and thus becoming a minority shareholder may be such a costly proposition in terms of surrendering the private benefits of control that the controlling shareholders would do everything to keep control. They would hold more voting rights themselves and would have less interest is selling shares in the market.[3] In view of this analysis, we assess the relationship between ownership concentration and minority shareholder protection in terms of the voting rights of the principal shareholders rather than their cash flow rights.[4]

Relatedly, we evaluate the relationship between shareholder protection and the incidence of various control arrangements, including cross-shareholdings, differential voting rights, and pyramids. The theory in this area is not completely developed, but some articles do help us think about the data. Grossman and Hart (1988) and Harris and Raviv (1988) suggest that deviations from one-share one-vote should be larger when private benefits of control are higher, which must be the case in countries with poorer shareholder protection. Wolfenzon (1998) argues that pyramids should also be more common in countries with poor shareholder protection, because it is easier for controlling shareholders there to make minority shareholders in existing firms pay for starting up new firms as partial subsidiaries without fully sharing with these minorities the benefits of a new venture. Pyramids and multiple classes of stock are of course two different ways of separating cash flow and control rights in firms.

---

[3] Bebchuk (1998) establishes in a formal model that dispersed ownership is unstable when private benefits of control are large because raiders would gain control of companies with dispersed ownership at low prices and extract these benefits of control.

[4] The distinction between control and cash flow rights is due to Grossman and Hart (1986). For the various ways in which the controlling shareholders can divert resources to themselves, and thereby obtain the "private benefits of control," see Shleifer and Vishny (1997).

The controlling shareholders face strong incentives to monitor managers and maximize profits when they retain substantial cash flow rights in addition to control. These incentives, emphasized by Jensen and Meckling (1976) and Shleifer and Vishny (1986), also restrain the diversion of corporate resources by the controlling shareholders, and enhance the value of minority shares.

In our empirical work, we find that the Berle and Means corporation is far from universal, and is quite rare for some definitions of control. Similarly, the so-called German model of bank control through equity is uncommon. Instead, controlling shareholders—usually the State or families—are present in most large companies. These shareholders have control rights in firms in excess of their cash flow rights, largely through the use of pyramids, but they also participate in management. The power of these controlling shareholders is evidently not checked by other large shareholders. The results suggest that the theory of corporate finance relevant for most countries should focus on the incentives and opportunities of controlling shareholders to both benefit and expropriate the minority shareholders.

The next section of the paper describes our data, and presents a number of examples of ownership patterns in particular companies. Section II presents the basic results on the incidence of various ownership structures around the world. Section III concludes.

I. Data

A. Construction of the Database

This paper is based on a new database of ownership structures of companies from 27 countries. As we detail below, the data on corporate ownership are often difficult to assemble, and this limitation determines many of the choices we make. We generally use the richest countries based on 1993 per capita income, but exclude a number of them that do not have significant stock markets (e.g., Kuwait, United Arab Emirates, Saudi Arabia).[5] For each country, we collect two samples of firms. The first sample consists of the top 20 firms ranked by market capitalization of common equity at the end of 1995 (with some exceptions detailed below). This sample runs into the objection that the largest companies in some countries are much larger than the largest companies in other countries. This is a particularly serious issue for a study of ownership because larger companies presumably have less concentrated ownership, and hence we should be careful that our measures of block ownership do not simply proxy for size. Accordingly, the second sample collects, whenever possible, the smallest 10 firms in each country with market capitalization of common equity of at least $500 million at the end of 1995. We call the first sample "large firms" and the second sample "medium firms." For countries with small stock markets, the two samples intersect.

---

[5] If we include the poorer countries, the incidence of family and State control would only be higher, and the prevalence of widely held firms significantly lower.

Moreover, for six countries (Argentina, Austria, Ireland, New Zealand, Greece, and Portugal) we do not have 10 publicly traded firms with capitalizations above $500 million. Overall, we have 540 large firms in the large firm sample, and a total of 691 different firms (out of a possible maximum of 810).[6]

There are a few additional restrictions on these samples of companies. First, for both samples, we exclude all affiliates of foreign firms. A firm is defined as an affiliate of a foreign company if at least 50 percent of its votes are directly controlled by a single foreign corporate owner. Further, we exclude banks and utilities from the sample of medium firms, to prevent the domination of this sample by these two industries. Finally, by construction, neither sample includes companies that are owned either wholly privately or wholly by the government, and therefore are not listed. This restriction biases our results toward finding fewer firms with significant government and family ownership than actually exist.

As a rule, our companies come from the WorldScope database. In four countries for which WorldScope coverage is limited (Argentina, Israel, Mexico, and the Netherlands), we use other sources (see the Appendix for data sources). We generally rely on annual reports, 20-F filings for companies with American Depositary Receipts (ADRs), proxy statements, and, for several countries, country-specific books that detail ownership structures of their companies. We also found the Internet to be very useful because many individual companies (e.g., in Scandinavia), as well as institutions (e.g., the Paris Bourse and *The Financial Times*) have Web sites that contain information on ownership structures. Virtually all of our data are for 1995 and 1996, though for a few observations the data do come from the earlier years, and for a few from 1997. Since ownership patterns tend to be relatively stable, the fact that the ownership data do not all come from the same year is not a big problem.

For several countries, our standard procedures do not work because disclosure is so limited. For Greece and Mexico, we cannot work with the 20 largest firms because we do not have enough ownership data. For Greece, we take the 20 largest corporations for which we could find ownership data (mostly in *Bloomberg Financial Systems*). For Mexico, we take the 20 largest firms that have ADRs. For Israel, we rely almost entirely on Lexis/Nexis and Internet sources. For Korea, different sources offer conflicting information on corporate ownership structures of business groups (chaebols). We were advised by Korean scholars that the best source for chaebols contains information as of 1984, so we use the more stale but reliable data.

To describe control of companies, we generally look for all shareholders who control more than 10 percent of the votes. The cutoff of 10 percent is used because (1) it provides a significant threshold of votes; and (2) most

---

[6] Note that medium firms are, on average, larger in countries with smaller stock markets than in countries with larger stock markets because the latter countries have more firms with capitalizations just above $500 million. In the medium firm sample, therefore, the size bias is toward finding less ownership concentration in countries with poor shareholder protection.

countries mandate disclosure of 10 percent, and usually even lower, owner-ship stakes. For most countries and companies, we have some information on smaller shareholdings, but focus only on shareholders who control more than 10 percent of the votes. In many cases, the principal shareholders in our firms are themselves corporate entities and financial institutions. We then try to find the major shareholders in these entities, then the major share-holders in the major shareholders, and so on, until we find the ultimate controllers of the votes. In some cases, the ultimate controller is the State, a widely held financial institution, or a widely held corporation. In other cases, it is an individual or a family. We do not attempt to get inside families, and assume that every family owns and votes its shares collectively.

B. Definitions of Variables

We ask whether firms have substantial owners. We do not try to measure ownership concentration, because a theoretically appropriate measure re-quires a model of the interactions between large shareholders, which we do not have. Rather, we try to define owners in a variety of ways, summarized in Table I and discussed in this subsection. In the following subsection, we illustrate these definitions using several companies from our sample.

Our definitions of ownership rely on voting rights rather than cash flow rights. Recall that Berle and Means want to know who controls the modern corporation: shareholders or managers. We too want to know whether cor-porations have shareholders with substantial voting rights, either directly or through a chain of holdings. This idea motivates our definitions.

We divide firms into those that are *widely held* and those with *ultimate owners*. We allow for five types of ultimate owners: (1) a family or an indi-vidual, (2) the State, (3) a widely held financial institution such as a bank or an insurance company, (4) a widely held corporation, or (5) miscellaneous, such as a cooperative, a voting trust, or a group with *no single controlling investor*. State control is a separate category because it is a form of concen-trated ownership in which the State uses firms to pursue political objectives, while the public pays for the losses (Shleifer and Vishny (1994)). We also give widely held corporations and widely held financial institutions separate categories as owners because it is unclear whether the firms they control should be thought of as widely held or as having an ultimate owner. A firm controlled by a widely held corporation or financial institution can be thought of either as widely held since the management of the controlling entity is not itself accountable to an ultimate owner, or as controlled by that manage-ment. For these reasons (and because bank ownership is of independent interest), we keep these categories separate.

As a first cut, we say that a corporation has a controlling shareholder (ultimate owner) if this shareholder's direct and indirect voting rights in the firm exceed 20 percent. A shareholder has x percent indirect control over firm A if (1) it directly controls firm B, which in turn directly controls x percent of the votes in firm A; or (2) it directly controls firm C, which in turn controls firm B (or a sequence of firms leading to firm B, each of which has control over the next one, i.e., they form a control chain), which directly controls x percent of the votes in firm A. Table I provides a more precise definition. The idea behind using 20 percent of the votes is that this is usually enough to have effective control of a firm. Indeed, below we present evidence that, in the majority of cases, our ultimate owners are also part of the management of the firm.

In the simplest case, each sample firm would have an ultimate owner of the above five types. There may, alternatively, be a legal entity that has more than 20 percent voting rights in our sample firm, which itself has a shareholder with more than 20 percent of the votes, and so on. We classify all firms that do not have such a 20 percent chain of voting rights as widely held, and firms with such a chain as having owners. On this definition, if company B has 23 percent of the votes in company A, and individual C has 19 percent of the votes in B, we still classify A as controlled by a widely held corporation (unless C has additional indirect control in A; see the discussion of Korea below). In addition to the definition of ultimate owners using this 20 percent of votes rule, we consider a second definition that relies on a chain of more than 10 percent of voting rights.

The preceding definitions give us a reasonably conservative way to answer the question: Does the firm have shareholders with a substantial amount of control, or does it have *ultimate owners*? But this is not the only interesting aspect of ownership. To evaluate the potential for agency problems between ultimate owners and minority shareholders, we also want to know whether the cash flow ownership rights of the controlling shareholders are substantially different from their voting rights. One way in which the ultimate owners can reduce their ownership below their control rights is by using shares with superior voting rights; another way is to organize the ownership structure of the firm in a pyramid. Finally, the ultimate owners might wish to solidify their control through cross-shareholdings—having the firm own shares in its shareholdings.

We describe the role of multiple classes of shares in the simplest possible way. For each firm in the sample, we ask: What is the minimum percentage of its capital at par value that the immediate shareholder (who might be different from the ultimate owner) needs to own to have 20 percent of the voting rights under the existing structure of share types of that firm (as opposed to what might be allowed by law)? For example, if a firm has 50 percent of its capital in the form of shares that have 100 percent of voting rights, and 50 percent in the form of nonvoting shares, we would say that a shareholder must own at least 10 percent of capital (in the form of the first kind of shares) to have 20 percent of the votes. Note that we are only computing this measure for the firms in the sample; we do not capture a deviation from one-share one-vote if a publicly held corporate shareholder in our sample firm itself has multiple classes of stock.

We say that a firm's ownership structure is a pyramid (on the 20 percent definition) if: (1) it has an ultimate owner, and (2) there is at least one publicly traded company between it and the ultimate owner in the chain of 20 percent voting rights. Thus, if a publicly traded firm B has 43 percent of

478   *The Journal of Finance*

Table I
Definition of the Variables

Variable	Description
Antidirector Index	An index aggregating shareholder rights which we label as "antidirector rights." The index is formed by adding one when: (1) the country allows shareholders to mail their proxy vote to the firm; (2) shareholders are not required to deposit their shares prior to a General Shareholders Meeting; (3) cumulative voting or proportional representation of minorities in the board of directors is allowed; (4) an oppressed minorities mechanism is in place; (5) the minimum percentage of share capital that entitles a shareholder to call an Extraordinary Shareholders Meeting is less than or equal to 10 percent; or (6) shareholders have preemptive rights that can only be waived by a shareholders vote. The index ranges from 0 to 6. Source: La Porta et al. (1998).
Widely Held	Equals one if the there is no controlling shareholder. To measure control we combine a shareholder's *direct* (i.e., through shares registered in her name) and *indirect* (i.e., through shares held by entities that, in turn, she controls) *voting* rights in the firm. A shareholder has an *x percent indirect control* over firm A if: (1) it controls directly firm B which, in turn, directly controls x percent of the votes in firm A; or (2) it controls directly firm C which in turn controls firm B (or a sequence of firms leading to firm B each of which has control over the next one; i.e., they form a control chain), which, in turn, directly controls x percent of the votes in firm A. A group of n companies form a *chain of control* if each firm 1 through $n - 1$ controls the consecutive firm. Therefore, a firm in our sample has a controlling shareholder if the sum of a shareholder's direct and indirect voting rights exceeds an arbitrary cutoff value, which, alternatively, is 20 percent or 10 percent. When two or more shareholders meet our criteria for control, we assign control to the shareholder with the largest (direct plus indirect) voting stake.
Family	Equals one if a person is the controlling shareholder, and zero otherwise.
State	Equals one if the (domestic or foreign) State is the controlling shareholder, and zero otherwise.
Widely Held Financial	Equals one if a widely held financial company is the controlling shareholder, and zero otherwise.
Widely Held Corporation	Equals one if a widely held nonfinancial company is the controlling shareholder, and zero otherwise.
Miscellaneous	Equals one if Widely Held, Family, State, Widely Held Financial, and Widely Held Corporation are all equal to zero, and zero otherwise. When it equals one, it includes control by pension funds, mutual funds, voting trusts, management trusts, groups, subsidiaries (firms that, in turn, are at least 50 percent owned by the firm in the sample), nonprofit organizations, and employees.
Cap = 20% V	Minimum percent of the book value of common equity required to control 20 percent of the votes. Source: *Moodys International*.
Cross-Shhs	Equals one if the firm both has a controlling shareholder (i.e., it is not widely held) and owns shares in its controlling shareholder or in a firm that belongs to her chain of control, and zero otherwise.
Pyramid	Equals one if the controlling shareholder exercises control through at least one publicly traded company, and zero otherwise.
%Mkt Fam	Aggregate market value of common equity of firms controlled by families divided by the aggregate market value of common equity of the 20 largest firms in a given country.

Corporate Ownership Around the World   479

Table I—*Continued*

Variable	Description
Firms/Avg Fam	Number of firms among the top 20 controlled by an average family in a given country.
Management	Equals one if a member of the controlling family is also the CEO, Honorary Chairman, Chairman, or Vice-Chairman of the Board, and zero if they do not hold any of the mentioned positions.
%Mkt WHF	Aggregate market value of common equity of firms controlled by widely held financial firms divided by the aggregate market value of common equity of the 20 largest firms in a given country.
Firms/Avg WHF	Number of firms among the top 20 controlled by an average widely held financial firm in a given country.
Independent Financials	Equals one when a (widely held) financial institution controls at least 10 percent of the votes and its control chain is separate from that of the controlling owner, and zero otherwise. More precisely, the variable takes the value of one when the following three conditions are met: (1) it controls at least 10 percent of the votes of the firm; (2) it is not the controlling owner; and (3) its control chain does not overlap with that of the controlling owner.
Associated Financials	Equals one when a (widely held) financial institution controls at least 10 percent of the votes and its control chain overlaps with that of the controlling owner, and zero otherwise. More precisely, equals one when a financial institution meets the following three conditions: (1) it controls at least 10 percent of the votes of the firm; (2) it is not the controlling owner; and (3) its control chain overlaps with that of the controlling owner.
Controlling Shareholder is Alone	Equals one if the firm has a 20 percent controlling owner and no other shareholder has control of at least 10 percent of the votes through a control chain that does not overlap with that of the controlling shareholder. Equals zero if the firm has a shareholder other than the controlling one with at least 10 percent of the votes through a control chain that does not overlap with that of the controlling shareholder. The variable is otherwise set to missing.
Common Law Origin	Equals one if the origin of the commercial law of a country is English Common Law, and zero otherwise. Source: Reynolds and Flores (1989).
Civil Law Origin	Equals one if the origin of the commercial law is the French Commercial Code, the German Commercial Code, or if the commercial law belongs to the Scandinavian commercial-law tradition, the Scandinavian Commercial Code, and zero otherwise. Source: Reynolds and Flores (1989).
Strong Banks	Equals one if commercial banks are allowed to own majority stakes in industrial firms and to invest at least 60 percent of their capital in a portfolio of industrial firms, and zero otherwise. Source: Institute of International Bankers (1997).
Private Claims/ GDP	Ratio of the claims of the banking sector on the private sector to gross domestic product in 1995. Source: International Monetary Fund (1998).
Corporate Dividends are Taxed	Equals one if corporate taxes are levied on dividends received from an investment representing at least 20 percent of the share capital of the dividend-paying corporation, and zero otherwise. Source: Price Waterhouse (1995) and Ernst & Young (1994).
Consolidation for Tax Purposes	Equals one if the tax authorities permit the use of consolidated accounting for tax purposes; that is, they allow corporations to offset the profits of one subsidiary against the losses of another. Source: Price Waterhouse (1995) and Ernst & Young (1994).

Table I—*Continued*

Variable	Description
Restrictions on Cross-Ownership	Equals one if the commercial law places restrictions on cross-ownership or reciprocal ownership, and zero otherwise. Source: Tomsett and Betten (1997).
GDP per Capita	Gross domestic product per capita in dollars in 1995. Source: World Bank (1997).
Corruption Index	Transparency International's corruption perception index for 1996. Average of up to 10 independent surveys on businessmen's perception of the degree of corruption in a given country. Scale from 1 to 10, with lower scores for higher levels of corruption. Source: Transparency International (1996).

the votes in a sample firm A, and an individual C has 27 percent of the votes in firm B, we would say that C controls A, and that the ownership structure is a pyramid. But if B is 100 percent owned by C, we would still call C the ultimate owner, but would not call the ownership structure a pyramid. Pyramids require publicly traded intermediate companies. We also use a parallel definition of pyramids with 10 rather than 20 percent of voting rights.

We say that there is cross-shareholding by sample firm A in its control chain if A owns any shares in its controlling shareholder or in the companies along that chain of control. So, if firm B has 20 percent of the votes in A, a publicly held firm C owns 20 percent of the votes in B, and A owns two percent of the votes in C, we would say that C is the ultimate owner of A, that A is owned through a pyramid, and that there is a cross-shareholding by A. On the other hand, if, instead of A owning 2 percent in C, it were the case that B owned two percent in C, we would not call this a cross-shareholding by A because B is not a firm in our sample. We do not look for cross-shareholdings by firm A in firms outside its control chain because of data limitations.

We use some further measures of ownership which are summarized in Table I, but introduce them later as we present our findings in Section II. First, we present some examples.

C. Examples of Ownership Structures

To describe the database and to illustrate our variables, we present several cases of ownership structures of individual companies, in roughly increasing order of complexity.

Begin with the United States. The three most valuable firms in the United States at the end of 1995, General Electric, AT&T, and Exxon, are all widely held. The fourth most valuable, Microsoft, has three large shareholders (Figure 1): the cofounders Bill Gates (with 23.7 percent of the votes as well as shares) and Paul Allen (with nine percent), and Steven Ballmer (with five percent). We say that Microsoft has an ultimate owner on the 20 percent (as

Corporate Ownership Around the World 481

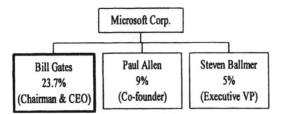

Figure 1. Microsoft Corporation (USA). The principal shareholders of Microsoft (the fourth largest company in the United States) are shown. All shares carry one vote. Under the 20 percent rule, we assign control to Bill Gates and represent his control chain with a thick bordered box.

well as on the 10 percent) definition, namely Bill Gates, and is a family-owned firm. It is obviously not a pyramid, does not have cross-shareholdings, and it takes 20 percent of the capital to amass 20 percent of the votes.

The fourth most valuable company in Canada is Barrick Gold, and it has a more complex ownership structure (Figure 2). Its founder, Chairman, and CEO is Peter Munk, who is also Chairman and CEO of a holding company called Horsham, that owns 16.3 percent of votes and capital in Barrick Gold. Munk controls the publicly traded Horsham with 79.7 percent of its votes, but only 7.3 percent of capital. Even though Munk evidently controls Barrick, we say that Barrick Gold is widely held on the 20 percent definition of control because Horsham only has 16.3 percent of the votes. On the 10 percent definition, Barrick Gold has an ultimate owner, a family. Since Horsham is publicly traded, we call Barrick's ownership structure a pyramid on the 10 percent but not the 20 percent definition. Finally, even though Horsham has multiple classes of stock, it takes 20 percent of Barrick's capital to have 20 percent of the votes, and so the company has a one-share/one-vote structure.[7]

The next example is Hutchison Whampoa, the third most valuable company in Hong Kong (Figure 3). It is 43.9 percent controlled by Cheung Kong Holdings, which happens to be the fifth largest publicly traded company in Hong Kong and is therefore also in our sample. In turn, the Li Ka-Shing family owns 35 percent of Cheung Kong. Hutchison Whampoa and Cheung Kong are thus both family controlled companies, except the former is owned through a pyramid but the latter is not. Note that the Li Ka-Shing family controls three of the 20 largest companies in Hong Kong (also the eleventh-largest Hong Kong Electric Holdings), a number that we keep track of.

---

[7] Tufano (1996) shows that, among gold-mining firms in North America, those with higher management ownership do more hedging of gold prices. This result is consistent with the dominance of the controlling shareholders' motives rather than minority shareholders' motives in the hedging decisions because costly hedging is more attractive to the undiversified controlling shareholders than to the diversified minority shareholders.

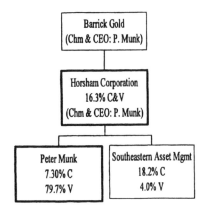

Figure 2. Barrick Gold (Canada). The principal shareholders of Barrick Gold (the fourth largest company in Canada) are shown. All shares in Barrick Gold, but not in Horsham Corporation, carry one vote. Ownership stakes are denoted with "C" and voting stakes with "V." We classify the firm as widely held at the 20 percent level. Under the 10 percent rule, we assign ultimate control to Peter Munk and represent his control chain with thick-bordered boxes.

After the State-controlled NT&T, Toyota Motor is the most valuable company in Japan (Figure 4). Toyota has several nontrivial shareholders, but none of them is very large. Four of these shareholders (Sakura Bank, Mitsui Fire and Marine, Mitsui T&B, and Mitsui Life) are part of the Mitsui Group and together control 12.1 percent of both capital and votes in Toyota. This is a common situation in Japan, and we say that Toyota is widely held on the 20 percent definition, but "miscellaneous" on the 10 percent definition, because that is where we put business groups as well as voting trusts. There are no pyramids or deviations from one-share one-vote here, but Toyota has cross-shareholdings in firms in the Mitsui Group.[8]

Ownership in Japanese companies is straightforward relative to that in Korean ones, as the example of Korea's second largest firm, Samsung Electronics (Figure 5), illustrates. Lee Kun-Hee, the son of Samsung's founder, controls 8.3 percent of Samsung Electronics directly. But he also controls 15 percent of Samsung Life, which controls 8.7 percent of Samsung Electronics, as well as 14.1 percent of Cheil Jedang, which controls 3.2 percent of Samsung Electronics directly and 11.5 percent of Samsung Life. Lee Kun-Hee has additional indirect stakes in Samsung Electronics as well. Because there are no 20 percent ownership chains, we call Samsung Electronics widely held on the 20 percent definition. But we classify it as a family-controlled firm on the 10 percent definition because the total of Lee Kun-Hee's direct

---

[8] Because Toyota does not have a controlling shareholder, and because we only report cross-shareholdings by the sample firms in the firms in their control chains, Toyota and similar Japanese firms would not appear in Table IV as having cross-shareholdings.

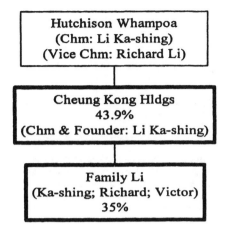

Figure 3. Hutchison Whampoa Ltd. (Hong Kong). The principal shareholders are shown for Hutchison Whampoa Ltd. (the third largest company in Hong Kong). All shares in Hutchison Whampoa and Cheung Kong Holdings carry one vote. Under the 20 percent rule, we assign ultimate control to the Li family and represent their control chain with thick-bordered boxes.

holdings and his holdings in Samsung Life is more than 10 percent of the votes in Samsung Electronics. It is also controlled through a pyramid on that definition because, for example, Samsung Life is publicly traded.

Finally, to illustrate the really complicated cases, we consider the ownership structure of five companies from Continental Europe. We begin with Germany, where the most valuable company is Allianz Insurance (Figure 6). Allianz is a one-share one-vote company with several large shareholders, of whom the largest, with a 25 percent stake, is Munich Reinsurance, the third most valuable company in Germany. However, Allianz has cross-shareholdings in most of its large shareholders, including a 25 percent stake in Munich Reinsurance (Allianz also has a 22.5 percent stake in Dresdner Bank, which has a 10 percent stake in Munich Reinsurance). Allianz presents a difficult case: One could argue that it is widely held because it controls its controlling shareholder, that it is controlled by a widely held financial institution, or that it belongs in the "miscellaneous" category. We allocate it to the first category, while (happily) recognizing that there are only four such controversial cases in the sample, including Munich Reinsurance itself.

The fourth largest company in Germany is Daimler Benz (Figure 7). It is 24.4 percent owned by Deutsche Bank, so its ultimate owner is a widely held financial institution (the largest shareholder in Deutsche Bank is Allianz, with five percent). Other shareholders of Daimler Benz form an enormous pyramid, but we do not call its ownership structure a pyramid because it does not involve publicly traded firms in the control chain and does not lead to the ultimate owner. Although there are other greater than 10 percent

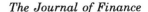

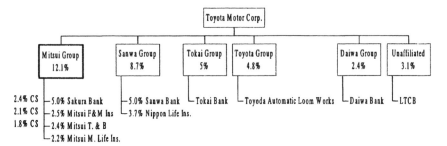

Figure 4. Toyota Motor (Japan). The principal shareholders are shown for Toyota Motor (the second largest company in Japan). All shares carry one vote. Members of the Mitsui group (Sakura Bank, Mitsui F&M, Mitsui T&B, and Mitsui M. Life Ins.) hold 12.1 percent of Toyota's shares. Therefore, under the 10 percent rule, we assign ultimate control to the Mitsui Group and represent its control chain with a thick bordered box. In turn, Toyota Motors owns shares in members of the Mitsui Group (i.e., there are cross-shareholdings). For example, Toyota Motor owns 2.4 percent of the shares of Sakura Bank. Cross-shareholdings are denoted with "CS".

shareholders and chains of shareholders in Daimler Benz, for the purposes of most of our analysis we look only at the largest shareholder, namely Deutsche Bank. Also, by looking only at the banks' own equity ownership, we ignore the voting arrangements that enable Deutsche Bank and other German banks to vote the shares they hold in custody for their brokerage clients, thereby biasing our results in favor of Berle and Means.

The fourth most valuable company in Sweden is ABB (Figure 8). Like five of the top 10 most valuable companies in Sweden, ABB is controlled by the Wallenberg family, characteristically through a pyramid of companies that have shares with differential cash flow and voting rights. Incentive, the 17th most valuable company in Sweden, owns 24.3 percent of capital and has 32.8 percent of the votes in ABB. The Wallenberg Group owns 32.8 percent of the capital, but has 43.1 percent of the votes in Incentive. The Wallenberg Group is a voting arrangement controlled by Investor (which has 35.7 percent of the Group's total of 43 percent of the votes in Incentive). Investor is the fifth most valuable company in Sweden, controlled by the Wallenberg Group with 41.2 percent of the votes. Here we have family control, pyramids, and deviations from one-share one-vote.

ABB is a good company to illustrate how we measure the extent of deviations from one-share one-vote. The company has 24,345,619 shares with 0.1 votes per share and a par value of 50 SEK, as well as 66,819,757 shares with one vote per share and a par value of 5 SEK. Here the cheapest way to buy a 20 percent voting stake is to acquire the second kind of shares only. The number of required votes is $13{,}850{,}865 = 0.2 * (24{,}345{,}619 * 0.1 + 66{,}819{,}757)$, and each of these votes costs 5 SEK at par value. The par value of the firm is SEK 1,551 billion. Therefore, the cost of buying the required votes as a percentage of the total book value of the firm's capital is

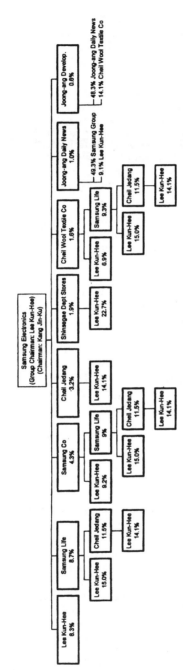

Figure 5. Samsung Electronics (South Korea). The principal shareholders in Samsung Electronics (the second largest company in South Korea) are shown. There are no deviations from the one-share one-vote rule on the graph. We classify the firm as widely held at the 20 percent level. Under the 10 percent rule, we assign ultimate control to Lee Kun-Hee and represent his control chain with thick-bordered boxes.

Figure 6. Allianz Holding (Germany). Principal shareholders of Allianz Holdings (the largest company in Germany) are shown. There are no deviations from the one-share one-vote rule on the graph. Allianz and Munchener Ruckversicherung own 25 percent of the shares of each other. Allianz also owns 22.5 percent of Dresdner Bank, which in turn owns 9.99 percent in Munchener Ruckversicherung. We classify Allianz as widely held since it, arguably, controls its largest shareholder.

(SEK 5 * 13,850,864)/(SEK 1,551 billion) = 4.46 percent. To acquire 20 percent of the votes in ABB, one can buy only 4.46 percent of the capital, a sharp deviation from one-share one-vote.

The third most valuable company in Italy is Fiat (Figure 9). Many of its shares are controlled by a voting trust, of which the most important member is Ifi, with 14.8 percent of the capital and 22.3 percent of the votes. Another large shareholder is Ifil, with 6.1 percent of the capital and 9.2 percent of the votes. Ifi is controlled by Giovanni Agnelli and his family, who have 41.2 plus 8.75, or 49.95, percent of the capital and 100 percent of the votes. Ifi also controls Ifil with 26.5 percent of the capital and 52.25 percent of the votes. Here we have family control through pyramids and voting trusts, though no evident cross-shareholdings by Fiat. The majority of Fiat's shares are ordinary, but there are a few savings shares with no voting rights. As a consequence, one can control 20 percent of Fiat's votes with 15.47 percent of its capital.

The last, and possibly most complicated, example we present is Electrabel, the largest listed company in Belgium (Figure 10). Fortunately, voting and cash flow rights are the same here. One can see that 26.34 percent of Electrabel is controlled by Powerfin, the eleventh largest company in Belgium. In turn, 60 percent of Powerfin is owned by Tractebel, which is the third largest company in Belgium, and which also controls 16.2 percent of Electrabel directly. But who owns Tractebel? The Belgian bank, Générale de Belgique, owns 27.5 percent of the company directly, and also controls 8.02 percent of the votes held by Genfina. Générale de Belgique does not itself enter the Belgian sample because it is 49.4 percent owned by a French bank, Compagnie de Suez, and hence is defined to be a foreign affiliate. Thus, through this pyramid, Electrabel is controlled by a widely held financial institution. Tractebel, however, has an additional significant set of owners. Actually, 20 percent of its shares are owned by Electrafina, the twelfth largest company in Belgium. Electrafina, in turn, is controlled with a 46.6 percent stake by Groupe Bruxelle Lambert, a holding company that is the ninth largest in Belgium. Groupe Bruxelle Lambert is in turn controlled with

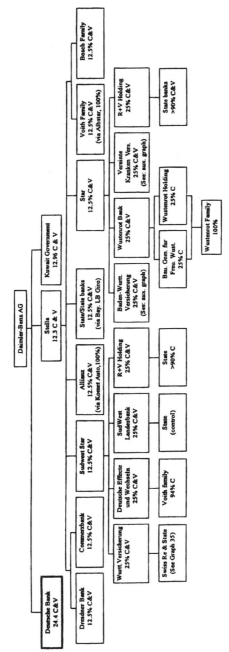

Figure 7. Daimler Benz (Germany). The principal shareholders are shown for Daimler Benz (the fourth largest company in Germany). Ownership stakes are denoted with "C" and voting stakes with "V." Under the 20 percent rule, we assign ultimate control to Deutsche Bank and represent its control chain with a thick-bordered box.

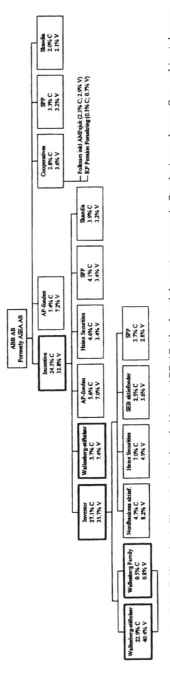

Figure 8. ABB AB (Sweden). The principal shareholders in ABB AB (the fourth largest company in Sweden) are shown. Ownership stakes are denoted with "C" and voting stakes with "V." Under the 20 percent rule, we assign ultimate control to the Wallenberg family and indicate its control chain with thick-bordered boxes.

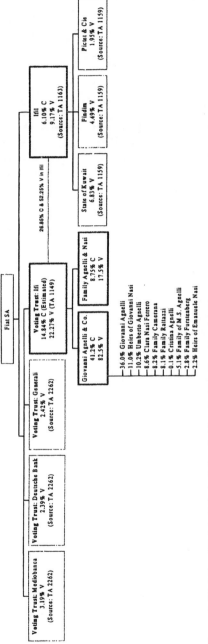

Figure 9. Fiat Spa (Italy). Principal shareholders in Fiat Spa (the third largest company in Italy) are shown. Ownership stakes are denoted with "C" and voting stakes with "V." A voting trust formed by Mediobanca, Deutsche Bank, Generali, Ifi, and Ifil controls 39.44 percent of the votes in Fiat. Members of the Agnelli family control 100 percent of the votes in Ifi, Fiat's largest shareholder. In addition, Ifi controls 52.25 percent of the votes in Ifil, Fiat's second largest shareholder. Therefore, we assign ultimate control (under the 20 percent rule) to the Agnelli family and indicate its control chain with thick-bordered boxes.

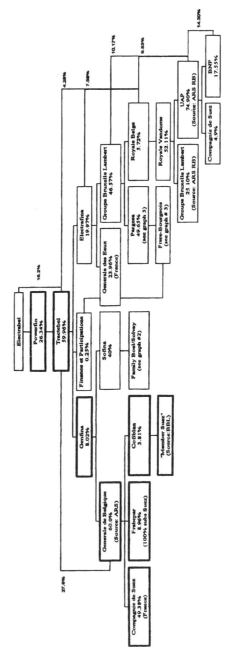

Figure 10. Electrabel SA (Belgium). Principal shareholders are shown for Electrabel SA (the largest company in Belgium). There are no deviations from the one-share one-vote rule on the graph. Under the 20 percent rule, we assign ultimate control to Compagnie de Suez because it is the largest shareholder in Tractebel. In turn, Tractebel owns directly 16.2 percent of Electrabel and controls Powerfin's 26.34 percent stake by virtue of its 59.96 percent investment in Powerfin. We represent Suez's control chain with thick-bordered boxes.

49.7 percent by Pargesa, a Swiss-listed holding controlled by the Belgian Frere family. Thus the Freres can also be viewed as the owners of Electrabel, except that we count only the largest ultimate owner, and hence Electrabel goes to Compagnie de Suez. There are many other relationships between the various companies in these pyramids, which are presented in Figure 10. Electrabel offers a good reason to look only at the largest shareholders rather than measure ownership concentration.

The preceding examples are not intended to prejudge the reader's opinion as to the relative frequency of widely held versus owner-controlled firms, but rather to show how complicated ownership structures can be, and to illustrate our biases toward classifying firms as widely held. In the next section, we abstract from the many subtleties of ownership and present the simple statistics on the relative frequency of different arrangements.

II. Results

A. Who Owns Firms?

Tables II and III present the basic information from our sample on who the ultimate owners of firms are in different countries. We divide the 27 countries in the sample into 12 with better than median shareholder protection using the scores from La Porta et al. (1998) (four and five), and 15 with median and worse than median protection (zero, one, two, and three). These scores aggregate a number of legal shareholder protections used in different countries (Table I). The good protection subsample is dominated by common law countries, and the bad protection subsample by civil law countries. We describe average ownership patterns for each country, and then compare average patterns for the world (meaning the 27 rich countries), the good protection countries, and the bad protection countries. We have two tables because we do each calculation for the large and the medium firm samples.

Within each country, for a given sample and a given definition of control, we classify every firm following the rules described in the previous section as one of six types: widely held, family-controlled, State-controlled, controlled by a widely held financial institution, controlled by a widely held corporation, or miscellaneous. We then compute and report the frequency of each type of firm in each country, and take appropriate averages. The *t*-tests comparing groups of countries treat each country's average as one observation.

Table II, Panel A, shows that, for the sample of large firms, and using the 20 percent definition of control, 36 percent of the firms in the world are widely held, 30 percent are family-controlled, 18 percent are State-controlled, and the remaining 15 percent are divided between the residual categories. To us, the fact that only slightly more than one-third of the firms in the richest countries, selected for their large size and using the stiff 20 percent chain definition of control, are widely held suggests that the image of the Berle and Means corporation as the dominant ownership structure in the world is misleading. It is true that, on this definition, all 20 firms in the United

492   *The Journal of Finance*

Table II

Control of Large Publicly Traded Firms around the World

This table classifies countries according to their ranking in antidirector rights. We form two groups of countries: (1) high antidirectors; and (2) low antidirectors, based on whether the country's antidirector index is above the median or not. Panel A (B) presents means for each variable using 20 (10) percent as the criterion for control for a sample of the 20 largest firms (by stock market capitalization of equity at the end of 1995) in 27 countries. (Definitions for each of the variables are given in Table I.) This table also reports tests of means for countries above and below the median antidirector rights.

Panel A: 20% Cutoff					
Country	Widely Held	Family	State	Widely Held Financial	Widely Held Corporation	Miscellaneous
Argentina	0.00	0.65	0.15	0.05	0.15	0.00
Australia	0.65	0.05	0.05	0.00	0.25	0.00
Canada	0.60	0.25	0.00	0.00	0.15	0.00
Hong Kong	0.10	0.70	0.05	0.05	0.00	0.10
Ireland	0.65	0.10	0.00	0.00	0.10	0.15
Japan	0.90	0.05	0.05	0.00	0.00	0.00
New Zealand	0.30	0.25	0.25	0.00	0.20	0.00
Norway	0.25	0.25	0.35	0.05	0.00	0.10
Singapore	0.15	0.30	0.45	0.05	0.05	0.00
Spain	0.35	0.15	0.30	0.10	0.10	0.00
U.K.	1.00	0.00	0.00	0.00	0.00	0.00
United States	0.80	0.20	0.00	0.00	0.00	0.00
High antidirector avg.	0.4792	0.2458	0.1375	0.0250	0.0833	0.0292
Austria	0.05	0.15	0.70	0.00	0.00	0.10
Belgium	0.05	0.50	0.05	0.30	0.00	0.10
Denmark	0.40	0.35	0.15	0.00	0.00	0.10
Finland	0.35	0.10	0.35	0.05	0.05	0.10
France	0.60	0.20	0.15	0.05	0.00	0.00
Germany	0.50	0.10	0.25	0.15	0.00	0.00
Greece	0.10	0.50	0.30	0.10	0.00	0.00
Israel	0.05	0.50	0.40	0.00	0.05	0.00
Italy	0.20	0.15	0.40	0.05	0.10	0.10
South Korea	0.55	0.20	0.15	0.00	0.05	0.05
Mexico	0.00	1.00	0.00	0.00	0.00	0.00
Netherlands	0.30	0.20	0.05	0.00	0.10	0.35
Portugal	0.10	0.45	0.25	0.15	0.00	0.05
Sweden	0.25	0.45	0.10	0.15	0.00	0.05
Switzerland	0.60	0.30	0.00	0.05	0.00	0.05
Low antidirector avg.	0.2733	0.3433	0.2200	0.0700	0.0233	0.0700
Sample average	0.3648	0.3000	0.1833	0.0500	0.0500	0.0519
Test of Means (*t*-statistic)					
Low vs. high antidirector	−1.95	1.09	1.20	1.70	−2.38	1.40

Table II—*Continued*

	Panel B: 10% Cutoff					
Country	Widely Held	Family	State	Widely Held Financial	Widely Held Corporation	Miscellaneous
Argentina	0.00	0.65	0.20	0.10	0.05	0.00
Australia	0.55	0.10	0.05	0.05	0.25	0.00
Canada	0.50	0.30	0.00	0.00	0.15	0.05
Hong Kong	0.10	0.70	0.05	0.05	0.00	0.10
Ireland	0.45	0.15	0.00	0.05	0.05	0.30
Japan	0.50	0.10	0.05	0.00	0.00	0.35
New Zealand	0.05	0.45	0.25	0.05	0.20	0.00
Norway	0.05	0.25	0.40	0.10	0.00	0.20
Singapore	0.05	0.45	0.45	0.00	0.00	0.05
Spain	0.15	0.25	0.45	0.15	0.00	0.00
U.K.	0.90	0.05	0.00	0.05	0.00	0.00
United States	0.80	0.20	0.00	0.00	0.00	0.00
High antidirect. avg.	0.3417	0.3042	0.1583	0.0500	0.0583	0.0875
Austria	0.05	0.15	0.70	0.00	0.00	0.10
Belgium	0.00	0.50	0.05	0.35	0.00	0.10
Denmark	0.10	0.35	0.20	0.05	0.00	0.30
Finland	0.15	0.10	0.35	0.25	0.00	0.15
France	0.30	0.20	0.20	0.20	0.10	0.00
Germany	0.35	0.10	0.30	0.25	0.00	0.00
Greece	0.05	0.65	0.30	0.00	0.00	0.00
Israel	0.05	0.50	0.40	0.00	0.05	0.00
Italy	0.15	0.20	0.50	0.00	0.00	0.15
South Korea	0.40	0.35	0.15	0.00	0.05	0.05
Mexico	0.00	1.00	0.00	0.00	0.00	0.00
Netherlands	0.30	0.20	0.05	0.00	0.10	0.35
Portugal	0.00	0.50	0.25	0.20	0.00	0.05
Sweden	0.00	0.55	0.10	0.30	0.00	0.05
Switzerland	0.50	0.40	0.00	0.05	0.00	0.05
Low antidirector avg.	0.1600	0.3833	0.2367	0.1100	0.0200	0.0900
Sample average	0.2407	0.3481	0.2019	0.0833	0.0370	0.0889
	Test of Means (*t*-statistic)					
Low vs. high antidirector	−1.92	0.88	1.05	1.50	−1.50	0.06

Kingdom, 18 out of 20 in Japan, and 16 out of 20 in the United States fit the widely held description. Still, in Argentina, Greece, Austria, Hong Kong, Portugal, Israel, or Belgium, there are hardly any widely held firms in this

Table III

Control of Medium-Sized Publicly Traded Firms around the World

This table classifies countries according to their ranking in antidirector rights. We form two groups of countries: (1) high antidirectors; and (2) low antidirectors, based on whether the country's antidirector index is above the median or not. Panel A (B) presents means for each variable using 20 (10) percent as the criterion for control for a sample of 10 firms with stock market capitalization of common equity at the end of December of 1995 of at least $500 million or higher in 27 countries. (Definitions for each of the variables are given in Table I.) This table also reports tests of means for countries above and below the median antidirector rights.

				Panel A: 20% Cutoff		
Country	Widely Held	Family	State	Widely Held Financial	Widely Held Corporation	Miscellaneous
Argentina	0.00	0.80	0.20	0.00	0.00	0.00
Australia	0.30	0.50	0.00	0.00	0.20	0.00
Canada	0.60	0.30	0.10	0.00	0.00	0.00
Hong Kong	0.00	0.90	0.00	0.00	0.00	0.10
Ireland	0.63	0.13	0.00	0.00	0.13	0.13
Japan	0.30	0.10	0.00	0.00	0.00	0.60
New Zealand	0.57	0.29	0.14	0.00	0.00	0.00
Norway	0.20	0.40	0.20	0.10	0.00	0.10
Singapore	0.40	0.40	0.20	0.00	0.00	0.00
Spain	0.00	0.30	0.20	0.40	0.10	0.00
U.K.	0.60	0.40	0.00	0.00	0.00	0.00
United States	0.90	0.10	0.00	0.00	0.00	0.00
High antidirector avg.	0.3750	0.3850	0.0867	0.0417	0.0358	0.0775
Austria	0.00	0.17	0.83	0.00	0.00	0.00
Belgium	0.20	0.40	0.30	0.10	0.00	0.00
Denmark	0.30	0.40	0.20	0.00	0.00	0.10
Finland	0.20	0.20	0.20	0.10	0.10	0.20
France	0.00	0.50	0.20	0.20	0.00	0.10
Germany	0.10	0.40	0.20	0.20	0.10	0.00
Greece	0.00	1.00	0.00	0.00	0.00	0.00
Israel	0.10	0.60	0.30	0.00	0.00	0.00
Italy	0.00	0.60	0.00	0.00	0.10	0.30
South Korea	0.30	0.50	0.00	0.00	0.20	0.00
Mexico	0.00	1.00	0.00	0.00	0.00	0.00
Netherlands	0.10	0.20	0.10	0.00	0.10	0.50
Portugal	0.00	0.50	0.50	0.00	0.00	0.00
Sweden	0.10	0.60	0.20	0.00	0.00	0.10
Switzerland	0.50	0.50	0.00	0.00	0.00	0.00
Low antidirector avg.	0.1267	0.5047	0.2020	0.0400	0.0400	0.0867
Sample average	0.2370	0.4515	0.1507	0.0407	0.0381	0.0826
			Test of Means (*t*-statistic)			
Low vs. high antidirector	−2.86	1.24	1.64	−0.45	0.18	0.16

Table III—*Continued*

| | | | | Widely Held | Widely Held | |
Country	Widely Held	Family	State	Financial	Corporation	Miscellaneous
Argentina	0.00	0.80	0.20	0.00	0.00	0.00
Australia	0.10	0.50	0.00	0.10	0.20	0.10
Canada	0.40	0.50	0.10	0.00	0.00	0.00
Hong Kong	0.00	0.90	0.00	0.00	0.00	0.10
Ireland	0.50	0.25	0.00	0.00	0.00	0.25
Japan	0.20	0.10	0.00	0.00	0.00	0.70
New Zealand	0.00	0.86	0.14	0.00	0.00	0.00
Norway	0.10	0.40	0.20	0.10	0.00	0.20
Singapore	0.10	0.60	0.30	0.00	0.00	0.00
Spain	0.00	0.30	0.30	0.40	0.00	0.00
U.K.	0.10	0.60	0.00	0.10	0.00	0.20
United States	0.50	0.30	0.00	0.00	0.00	0.20
High antidirector avg.	0.1667	0.5092	0.1033	0.0583	0.0167	0.1458
Austria	0.00	0.17	0.83	0.00	0.00	0.00
Belgium	0.10	0.40	0.30	0.20	0.00	0.00
Denmark	0.00	0.40	0.20	0.00	0.00	0.40
Finland	0.00	0.20	0.20	0.20	0.10	0.30
France	0.00	0.50	0.20	0.20	0.00	0.10
Germany	0.10	0.40	0.20	0.30	0.00	0.00
Greece	0.00	1.00	0.00	0.00	0.00	0.00
Israel	0.10	0.60	0.30	0.00	0.00	0.00
Italy	0.00	0.80	0.10	0.00	0.00	0.10
South Korea	0.00	0.80	0.00	0.00	0.20	0.00
Mexico	0.00	1.00	0.00	0.00	0.00	0.00
Netherlands	0.10	0.20	0.10	0.00	0.10	0.50
Portugal	0.00	0.50	0.50	0.00	0.00	0.00
Sweden	0.10	0.60	0.20	0.10	0.00	0.00
Switzerland	0.40	0.50	0.00	0.00	0.00	0.10
Low antidirector avg.	0.0600	0.5380	0.2087	0.0667	0.0267	0.1000
Sample average	0.1074	0.5252	0.1619	0.0630	0.0222	0.1204

Panel B: 10% Cutoff

Test of Means (*t*-statistic)

Low vs. high antidirector	−1.83	0.28	1.47	0.20	0.44	−0.65

sample and on this definition. A critic might remark that most of the value of the world stock market is in the United States, United Kingdom, Japan, and other countries with Berle and Means firms, so who cares about Argentina or Austria? We care because to understand corporate governance in most countries in the world, to appreciate what is essential about the countries where Berle and Means corporations are common, and consequently to see how corporate governance *is changing or can be changed*, it is important to recognize how much of an exception widely held corporations really are.

Among corporations with owners, the principal owner types are the families and the State. The high percentage of companies with State control in this sample is not surprising given that we are sampling the largest firms, and privatization is not finished in most countries. Still, the fact that 70 percent of the largest traded firms in Austria, 45 percent in Singapore, and 40 percent in Israel and Italy are State-controlled is a reminder of massive post-war State ownership around the world. Indeed, the magnitude of State ownership among the largest companies would be even higher if we included firms that are entirely State owned, and hence do not trade publicly. It is perhaps more surprising that by far the dominant form of controlling ownership in the world is not that by banks and other corporations, but rather by families.

A comparison of countries with good and poor shareholder protection shows that widely held firms are more common in countries with good protection: 48 percent versus 27 percent. This difference is statistically significant ($t = -1.95$). Countries with poor shareholder protection have more of most other types of firms, including family-controlled: 34 versus 25 percent ($t = 1.09$), and State-controlled: 22 versus 14 percent ($t = 1.20$). Interestingly, firms in countries with good protection are more commonly controlled by a widely held corporation: eight percent versus two percent ($t = -2.38$). These results suggest that dispersion of ownership goes together with good shareholder protection, which enables controlling shareholders to divest at attractive prices.

Table II, Panel B, presents the results for the sample of large firms using the 10 percent chain definition of control. Under this definition, only 24 percent of the large companies in rich countries are widely held, compared to 35 percent that are family-controlled, 20 percent are State-controlled, and 21 percent are in the three residual categories. We stress that using the 10 percent control chain to define control is not incredibly tough on the Berle and Means thesis; many people would consider 10 percent ownership of a U.S. firm to be sufficient for control. Indeed, 90 percent of the large U.K. firms, 80 percent of the large U.S. firms, and 50 percent of the large Japanese firms remain widely held.[9] Still, in the rich world as a whole, dispersed ownership is rare on this definition.

One finding shown in Panel B is that many Japanese firms shift into the miscellaneous category because, like Toyota, they are controlled by groups with no dominant members. Individual members of these groups hold very

---

[9] Some seminar participants have argued that the larger the firm, the smaller the percentage of equity needed to control it. If that were the case, many of the firms in the United States, Japan, and the United Kingdom that we designate as widely held would also have controlling shareholders, further diminishing the Berle and Means category. Our sample of medium firms, which holds size roughly constant across countries, addresses this point as well.

small equity stakes in sample companies, and even groups as a whole often have stakes of 10 to 20 percent. In this respect, the Japanese model of ownership seems to be closer to that in other countries with good shareholder protection, like the United States or the United Kingdom, than it is to the continental European model. Specifically, most shares in Japanese firms are owned by small individual shareholders and relatively small corporate shareholders (French and Poterba (1991)), there are few controlling shareholders per se, and even the groups have a relatively small share of the total votes. Of course, the groups may have control in excess of their voting rights because of lending and supply arrangements.

A comparison of countries with good and poor shareholder protection shows that widely held firms remain more common in the former: 34 percent versus only 16 percent in countries with poor shareholder protection ($t = -1.92$). The latter countries have relatively more firms with ultimate owners in almost all categories: family, the State, and financial institutions, though the differences are not statistically significant. The bottom line is that the largest firms typically have ultimate owners, particularly in countries with poor shareholder protection.

What about the medium-sized firms, defined here as those with market valuations above, but near, $500 million? Recall that we focus on these firms in part to address the criticism that firms in countries with good shareholder protection are larger, and hence have more dispersed ownership. Table III presents the results for these firms using the 20 percent chain definition of control. Among the medium firms, the world average incidence of dispersed ownership is 24 percent, compared to 36 percent for the large firms. So going down in size has the same effect as relaxing the strictness of the definition of control: it makes widely held firms more scarce. Note, however, that in the United States and the U.K., though not in Japan, the medium firms remain mostly widely held—a testimony to the attractiveness of selling out in the United States and the U.K.. For medium firms, the percentage of firms controlled by families rises to a world average of 45 percent, making it the dominant ownership pattern.

The comparison of countries with good and poor shareholder protection reinforces this picture. Only 13 percent of the medium firms in poor protection countries are widely held, compared to 38 percent in good protection countries ($t = -2.86$). Families control 39 percent of medium firms in the good shareholder protection countries, and 50 percent in the poor investor protection countries (this difference is not statistically significant). State control is more common in bad protection countries: 20 percent versus nine percent ($t = 1.64$, significant at the 10 percent level). Using even the tough definition of control, we see that medium-sized firms generally have owners, especially in countries with poor shareholder protection.

Table III, Panel B, shows that, if we soften the definition of control by using the 10 percent control chain, only 11 percent of the medium-sized firms in the world are widely held (50 percent in the United States and Ireland.) By contrast, 53 percent of firms are family controlled, 16 percent are State controlled, and the remaining 20 percent are in other categories. Using this perfectly reasonable definition of control for medium firms makes dispersed ownership truly an exception.

Not surprisingly, dispersed ownership is even more of an exception in countries with poor shareholder protection, where only six percent of the firms are widely held, compared to 17 percent in countries with good investor protection ($t = -1.83$). In both groups, the predominant ownership pattern is family control. The conclusion from this evidence is inescapable: If we look at the largest firms in the world and use a very tough definition of control, dispersed ownership is about as common as family control. But if we move from there to medium-sized firms, to a more lenient definition of control, and to countries with poor investor protection, widely held firms become an exception. Berle and Means have created an accurate image of ownership of large American corporations, but it is far from a universal image.

B. How are Firms Owned?

In this subsection, we describe some of the mechanisms through which controlling shareholders exercise their power in the large firm sample. We address several related questions. First, how commonly are voting rights separated from cash flow rights through multiple classes of stock, cross-shareholdings, and pyramids? Second, how do families that control firms do so, and in particular is management separate from ownership in these firms? Third, do financial institutions play a bigger role in the control of firms than our earlier discussion has indicated? And finally, who, if anyone, monitors the controlling shareholders? By answering these questions, we hope to provide a more detailed picture of ownership of very large firms, as well as suggest what might be some of the problems in the governance of such firms.

Table IV begins by showing, for each country, the average fraction of book capital needed to control 20 percent of the votes, the incidence of cross-shareholdings by the sample firms, and the frequency of pyramids in firms with controlling owners at the 20 percent control level.

For the large firms, the *magnitude* of deviations from one-share one-vote through shares with differential voting rights tends to be small. In our sample, it takes on average about 18.6 percent of capital to control 20 percent of the votes, assuming that the only mechanism at the disposal of a controlling shareholder is shares with differential voting rights *in the sample firm*.[10] Companies obviously do not use anything like the opportunities for high and low voting shares allowed by national laws (La Porta et al. (1998)).[11] Indeed, even in countries with poor shareholder protection, it takes on average 17.7 percent of capital to buy 20 percent of the votes, compared to 19.7 percent for

---

[10] We do not, in this calculation, take account of the voting caps and other possible restrictions on voting in different countries.

[11] De Angelo and De Angelo (1985) and Zingales (1994) report similar findings for the United States and Italy, respectively.

Table IV

One-Share One-Vote, Cross-Shareholdings, and Pyramids

This table classifies countries according to their ranking in antidirector rights. We form two groups of countries: (1) high antidirectors; and (2) low antidirectors, based on whether the country's antidirector index is above the median or not. This table presents means for each variable using 20 percent as the criterion for control for a sample of the 20 largest firms (by stock market capitalization of equity at the end of 1995) in 27 countries. (Definitions for each of the variables are given in Table I.) This table also reports tests of means for countries above and below the median antidirector rights.

Country	Cap = 20% V	Pyramid and Not Widely Held	Cross-Shhs
Argentina	19.6013	0.05	0.00
Australia	20.0000	0.14	0.10
Canada	19.3618	0.13	0.00
Hong Kong	19.5107	0.39	0.05
Ireland	20.0000	0.00	0.00
Japan	20.0000	0.00	0.00
New Zealand	20.0000	0.36	0.00
Norway	18.1548	0.13	0.00
Singapore	20.0000	0.41	0.10
Spain	20.0000	0.38	0.00
U.K.	20.0000	.	0.00
United States	19.1927	0.00	0.00
High antidirector avg.	19.6518	0.1808	0.0208
Austria	19.8933	0.47	0.15
Belgium	20.0000	0.79	0.05
Denmark	14.8661	0.08	0.00
Finland	15.7533	0.00	0.00
France	19.9957	0.38	0.00
Germany	18.6137	0.40	0.20
Greece	20.0000	0.11	0.00
Israel	20.0000	0.53	0.00
Italy	18.0399	0.25	0.00
South Korea	20.0000	0.33	0.05
Mexico	16.4490	0.25	0.00
Netherlands	15.0000	0.14	0.00
Portugal	20.0000	0.44	0.05
Sweden	12.6283	0.53	0.10
Switzerland	14.1783	0.00	0.00
Low antidirector avg.	17.6945	0.3137	0.0400
Sample average	18.5644	0.2575	0.0315
Test of Means (*t*-statistic)			
Low vs. high antidirector	−2.53	1.64	0.91

good shareholder protection countries ($t = -2.53$). Some countries, particularly in Scandinavia, have much more significant deviations, but the average deviation from one-share one-vote is small. The results suggest that multiple classes of shares are not a central mechanism of separating ownership and control. They are also consistent with the notion that the controlling shareholders may need to hold on to significant cash flow rights as a commitment to limit the expropriation of minority shareholders.

At the same time, fully 26 percent of firms that have ultimate owners are controlled through pyramids. That fraction is 18 percent in countries with good shareholder protection, and 31 percent in countries with poor protection. Relative to shares with differential voting rights, pyramidal ownership appears to be a more important mechanism used by controlling shareholders to separate their cash flow ownership in sample firms from their control rights. These results are consistent with Wolfenzon's (1998) theory on pyramids, which suggests that they can be used by controlling shareholders to make existing shareholders pay the costs, but not share in all the benefits of new ventures, particularly in countries with poor shareholder protection. Through pyramids, more so than through high voting rights shares, controlling shareholders acquire power disproportionate to their cash flow rights.

Finally, with the exception of a few countries, such as Sweden and Germany, cross-shareholdings by sample firms in the firms that control them or in the controlling chain are rare. This is particularly interesting because cross-shareholdings are restricted by law in only six of our sample countries (Belgium, France, Germany, Italy, Korea, and Spain), and, if anything, appear to be *more* common in the countries where they are restricted.[12]

Table V examines the firms that are controlled by families more specifically.[13] The second column shows that in an average country, the *ultimate family owners* control, on average, 25 percent of the value of the top 20 firms. Following up on the predominance of the Wallenbergs in Sweden, we also ask how many of the largest firms a controlling family controls, on average. Our sample average answer is 1.33, though in countries such as Israel and Sweden, an average *ultimate family owner* controls 2.5 of the top 20 firms. Again, this is evidence of very significant control of productive resources by the largest shareholding families.

The next-to-last column of Table V speaks to the crucial issue concerning family control, namely the separation of ownership and management. We ask how often a member of the controlling family is the CEO, the Chairman, the Honorary Chairman, or the Vice-Chairman of the firm that the family controls. We do not catch all the family members by this procedure because a CEO who is married into the family but does not have the same last name would not be recorded as a family member. For the universe as a whole, the answer is that (at least) 69 percent of the time, families that control firms also participate in management. In countries with good shareholder protection, this fraction is 75 percent, whereas in countries with poor protection, it

---

[12] The Japanese Commercial Code prohibits cross-shareholdings by subsidiaries in their parents, and places restrictions on voting by companies with large cross-shareholdings (Kita (1996)). However, modest cross-shareholdings are not restricted and are widely used.

[13] On preliminary calculations, about one-third of the family-controlled firms are run by their founders, and the rest by the descendants of founders or families that came to own them later.

Table V
Family Control in a Sample of Large Publicly Traded Firms around the World

This table classifies countries according to their ranking in antidirector rights. We form two groups of countries: (1) high antidirectors; and (2) low antidirectors, based on whether the country's antidirector index is above the median or not. This table presents means for each variable using 20 percent as the criterion for control for a sample of the largest 20 firms (by stock market capitalization of equity at the end of 1995) in 27 countries. (Definitions for each of the variables are given in Table I.) This table also reports tests of means for countries above and below the median antidirector rights.

Country	Family	%Mkt Fam	Firms/Avg Fam	Management	Pyramids
Argentina	0.65	0.5258	1.18	0.62	0.00
Australia	0.05	0.1218	1.00	1.00	0.00
Canada	0.25	0.2770	1.25	1.00	0.20
Hong Kong	0.70	0.6342	1.56	0.86	0.50
Ireland	0.10	0.0417	2.00	1.00	0.00
Japan	0.05	0.0287	1.00	1.00	0.00
New Zealand	0.25	0.1511	1.00	0.60	0.40
Norway	0.25	0.1327	1.00	0.80	0.00
Singapore	0.30	0.1514	1.20	0.67	0.67
Spain	0.15	0.1697	1.50	0.67	0.33
U.K.	0.00	0.0000	.	.	.
United States	0.20	0.1827	1.00	0.75	0.00
High antidirector avg.	0.2458	0.2014	1.2441	0.7475	0.1909
Austria	0.15	0.0620	1.50	0.33	0.67
Belgium	0.50	0.4124	1.67	0.50	0.80
Denmark	0.35	0.3167	1.17	0.57	0.14
Finland	0.10	0.0613	1.00	0.50	0.00
France	0.20	0.2569	1.00	0.75	0.25
Germany	0.10	0.0751	1.00	0.50	0.00
Greece	0.50	0.4746	1.00	0.60	0.00
Israel	0.50	0.3099	2.50	0.60	0.60
Italy	0.15	0.1424	1.50	1.00	0.33
South Korea	0.20	0.2160	1.33	0.75	0.50
Mexico	1.00	1.0000	1.05	0.95	0.25
Netherlands	0.20	0.0610	1.00	0.50	0.25
Portugal	0.45	0.3798	1.80	0.44	0.44
Sweden	0.45	0.3545	2.50	0.56	0.78
Switzerland	0.30	0.2874	1.00	1.00	0.00
Low antidirector avg.	0.3433	0.2940	1.4010	0.6367	0.3343
Sample average	0.3000	0.2528	1.3347	0.6859	0.2736
Test of Means (t-statistic)					
Low vs. high antidirector	1.09	1.06	0.94	−2.33	1.34

is 64 percent ($t = -2.33$). This result shows that the standard problem of separation of ownership and management is not important for most of these firms, which is not to say that controlling shareholders act in the interest of minorities.

Relative to the power of the families, significant ownership of equity by banks is rare, as Table VI illustrates. The first column repeats the results from Table II, Panel A that only five percent of our large firms are controlled by financial institutions (mostly banks, but also insurance companies), and that this number is much higher in countries with poor than with good shareholder protection (seven percent versus two percent). But even in the former countries, bank ownership of equity is surprisingly small outside of Belgium (where it comes from French banks) and Germany. We also note that where banks are controlling shareholders they often control several of the largest firms, as is the case in Belgium, Portugal, and Sweden.

One reason for the scarcity of financial institutions as controlling shareholders in the largest firms may be that such institutions control small, though influential, ownership stakes. We look for financial institutions *outside* the 20 percent control chains in two ways. First, we look for financials that have more than 10 percent of votes, but are not part of the 10 percent control chain (independent financials). As the fourth column of Table VI shows, only six percent of the firms in the sample have such financials as shareholders. Second, we look for financial institutions that are themselves a link in a 10 percent control chain (associated financials). Only three percent of the firms in the sample have such institutions. Thus, even on looser definitions of significant ownership, financial institutions do not play a huge role as *significant shareholders* in governance outside a few countries, most notably Germany (Franks and Mayer (1994)).

These results leave us with a very different picture of separation of ownership and control than that suggested by Berle and Means. Widely held firms appear to be relatively uncommon, unless we look at specific countries, or focus on very restrictive measures of control and very large firms. In contrast, family control is very common. Families often have control rights over firms significantly in excess of their cash flow rights, particularly through pyramids, and typically manage the firms they control. They are, indeed, the ultimate owners with control in the Berle and Means sense. Moreover, financial institutions do not typically appear as controlling shareholders, although they may exercise influence through board representation and lending. The question this evidence raises is: Who keeps the controlling families from expropriating the minority shareholders, especially in countries with weak legal protection of these shareholders, where family control is even more common? *Who monitors the families?*

One possibility is that there are other large shareholders, and that the large shareholders monitor each other, preventing each other from taking too much (see Pagano and Roell (1998)). The second possibility is that no one monitors the families. We can try to distinguish between these possibilities by asking whether family (or other) controlling shareholders have other large shareholders in their firms.

Table VII addresses this question. We say that the 20 percent controlling shareholder has a potential monitor if there is another shareholder that has a nonoverlapping 10 percent chain of control. Thus, we suppose that moni-

Table VI

Control by Financial Institutions in a Sample of Large Firms in Twenty-Seven Countries

This table classifies countries according to their ranking in antidirector rights. We form two groups of countries: (1) high antidirectors; and (2) low antidirectors, based on whether the country's antidirector index is above the median or not. This table presents means for each variable using 20 percent as the criterion for control for a sample of the 20 largest firms (by stock market capitalization of equity at the end of 1995) in 27 countries. (Definitions for each of the variables are given in Table I.) This table also reports tests of means for countries above and below the median antidirector rights.

Country	Widely Held Financial	%Mkt WHF	Firms/ Avg WHF	Financ. Inst. Not Dominant		Pyramid
				Independent	Associated	
Argentina	0.05	0.0241	1.00	0.05	0.05	0.00
Australia	0.00	0.0000	.	0.00	0.00	.
Canada	0.00	0.0000	.	0.00	0.00	.
Hong Kong	0.05	0.0838	1.00	0.05	0.00	0.00
Ireland	0.00	0.0000	.	0.15	0.00	.
Japan	0.00	0.0000	.	0.00	0.00	.
New Zealand	0.00	0.0000	.	0.00	0.00	.
Norway	0.05	0.0177	1.00	0.20	0.00	1.00
Singapore	0.05	0.0169	1.00	0.00	0.00	0.00
Spain	0.10	0.0386	1.00	0.05	0.05	0.00
U.K.	0.00	0.0000	.	0.00	0.00	.
United States	0.00	0.0000	.	0.00	0.00	.
High antidirector avg.	0.0250	0.0151	1.0000	0.0417	0.0083	0.2000
Austria	0.00	0.0000	.	0.00	0.10	.
Belgium	0.30	0.4258	3.00	0.25	0.30	1.00
Denmark	0.00	0.0000	.	0.05	0.00	.
Finland	0.05	0.0156	1.00	0.15	0.00	0.00
France	0.05	0.0507	1.00	0.10	0.05	1.00
Germany	0.15	0.1304	1.50	0.10	0.15	0.67
Greece	0.10	0.0317	2.00	0.00	0.00	0.00
Israel	0.00	0.0000	.	0.05	0.00	.
Italy	0.05	0.0442	1.00	0.00	0.00	0.00
Korea (South)	0.00	0.0000	.	0.05	0.00	.
Mexico	0.00	0.0000	.	0.00	0.00	.
Netherlands	0.00	0.0000	.	0.10	0.00	.
Portugal	0.15	0.1021	3.00	0.05	0.00	0.67
Sweden	0.15	0.2074	3.00	0.10	0.05	0.33
Switzerland	0.05	0.0077	1.00	0.00	0.00	0.00
Low antidirector avg.	0.0700	0.0677	1.8333	0.0667	0.0433	0.4074
Sample average	0.0500	0.0443	1.5357	0.0556	0.0278	0.3333
Test of Means (t-statistic)						
Low vs. high antidirector	1.70	1.53	5.88	0.94	1.40	0.85

504 *The Journal of Finance*

Table VII

Probability That the Controlling Shareholder Is Alone

This table classifies countries according to their ranking in antidirector rights. We form two groups of countries: (1) high antidirectors; and (2) low antidirectors, based on whether the country's antidirector index is above the median or not. This table presents means for each variable using 20 percent as the criterion for control for a sample of the 20 largest firms (by stock market capitalization of equity at the end of 1995) in 27 countries. The last column presents the country mean across all observations reported in the table. (Definitions for all other variables are given in Table I.) This table also reports tests of means for countries above and below the median antidirector index and against the sample mean of firms with controlling shareholders.

Country	Family	State	Widely Held Financial	Widely Held Corporation	All
Argentina	0.85	0.33	1.00	0.67	0.75
Australia	1.00	1.00	.	0.80	0.86
Canada	1.00	.	.	1.00	1.00
Hong Kong	0.86	0.00	1.00	.	0.81
Ireland	0.00	.	.	0.50	0.25
Japan	1.00	1.00	.	.	1.00
New Zealand	0.80	0.60	.	0.00	0.50
Norway	0.40	0.71	1.00	.	0.62
Singapore	0.83	1.00	0.00	0.00	0.82
Spain	1.00	1.00	1.00	0.50	0.92
U.K.	.	.	.	.	.
United States	1.00	.	.	.	1.00
High antidirector avg.	0.7939	0.7050	1.0000	0.4957	0.7756
Austria	0.67	0.79	.	.	0.76
Belgium	0.50	1.00	1.00	.	0.71
Denmark	0.43	1.00	.	.	0.60
Finland	0.00	1.00	0.00	1.00	0.73
France	0.75	0.67	0.00	.	0.63
Germany	0.50	0.80	0.33	.	0.60
Greece	0.70	1.00	1.00	.	0.83
Israel	0.70	0.63	.	0.00	0.63
Italy	1.00	1.00	1.00	1.00	1.00
South Korea	0.75	1.00	.	1.00	0.88
Mexico	0.80	.	.	.	0.80
Netherlands	1.00	1.00	.	1.00	1.00
Portugal	0.56	0.80	0.67	.	0.65
Sweden	0.50	1.00	0.00	.	0.43
Switzerland	0.83	.	1.00	.	0.86
Low antidirector avg.	0.6457	0.8990	0.5552	0.8000	0.7396
Sample average	0.7084	0.8251	0.6921	0.6225	0.7548
Test of Means (t-statistic)					
Versus sample mean	−0.44	1.11	−0.75	−0.93	0.00
Low vs. high antidirector	−1.31	1.27	−2.82	1.27	−0.46

toring the controlling shareholder does not require one to be as large. In the example of Electrabel from Section I.C, the Frere family would be classified as a potential monitor of Suez. Using this definition, we find that large shareholders of all kinds, including family, are typically alone. Overall, the controlling shareholder does not have another large shareholder in the same firm in 75 percent of the cases, and this number is 71 percent for family controlling shareholders. These results are inconsistent with the hypothesis that controlling shareholders are usually monitored by other large shareholders.

In sum, this subsection has demonstrated that (1) controlling shareholders often have control rights in excess of their cash flow rights, (2) this is true of families, who are often the controlling shareholders, (3) controlling families participate in the management of the firms they own, (4) banks do not often exercise much control over firms as shareholders, and (5) other large shareholders are usually not there to monitor the controlling shareholders. Family control of firms appears to be common, significant, and typically unchallenged by other equity holders.

C. Alternative Hypotheses

One of our main findings is the higher incidence of widely held Berle and Means firms in countries with good legal protection of minority shareholders. In this subsection, we address a number of questions about the robustness, and possible alternative explanations, of this finding.

All the results we discuss are presented in Table VIII, which shows mean percentages of companies that are widely held in variously classified groups of countries, for our two samples (large and medium) and for the two definitions of widely held firms (20 percent and 10 percent criteria for control).

First, the classification of countries based on the legal rules for protecting minority shareholders may be endogenous. In particular, countries with economically and politically powerful controlling shareholders may enact laws that entrench such shareholders and reduce minority rights. One way to address this concern, suggested by La Porta et al. (1998), is to classify countries based on the origin of their commercial laws rather than on the actual legal rules, because the legal origin is both historically predetermined and highly correlated with shareholder protection. Specifically, common law countries tend to have better protection of minority shareholders than civil law countries do. Accordingly, Panel A of Table VIII divides countries into those with civil and common law origins of commercial laws. The results in Panel A show that, using both samples and both definitions of control, common law countries have a significantly higher fraction of widely held firms than civil law countries do. (In one instance, the difference, while substantively large, is statistically not quite significant; in the other three instances, the difference is both large and statistically significant.) Thus, our results do not appear to be a consequence of the endogeneity of legal rules.

Table VIII
Robustness of the Results

The table reports means and *t*-statistics for the fraction of widely held firms based on the 20 percent and the 10 percent criteria of control for both the sample of the 20 largest firms (by stock market capitalization of equity at the end of 1995) and the sample of medium firms (i.e., the 10 smallest firms with market capitalization of common stock exceeding U.S. $500 million in 1995). We report means for countries grouped according to the following eight independent criteria: (1) legal origin of commercial code or company law, (2) bank regulation, (3) the size of the banking sector, (4) the existence of taxes on dividends received by a corporation, (5) rules regarding the consolidation of profits of subsidiaries, (6) restrictions on cross-ownership, (7) GDP per capita, and (8) the level of corruption. (Definitions for all criteria are given in Table I.)

Country	N	Sample of Large Firms		Sample of Medium Firms	
		20% Definition of Control	10% Definition of Control	20% Definition of Control	10% Definition of Control
Panel A: Legal Origin					
Common Law Origin = 1	9	0.4778	0.3833	0.4552	0.2000
Civil Law Origin = 1	18	0.3083	0.1694	0.1278	0.0611
t-statistic common vs. civil law origin		1.4779	2.1900	3.9725	2.3526
Panel B: Bank Regulation					
Strong Banks = 1	13	0.4154	0.2846	0.2382	0.1000
Strong Banks = 0	14	0.3179	0.2000	0.2357	0.1143
t-statistic strong vs. weak banks		0.8779	0.8533	0.0249	−0.2323
Panel C: Size of Banking Sector					
Private Claims/GDP ≥ median	14	0.4536	0.3321	0.2765	0.1214
Private Claims/GDP < median	13	0.2692	0.1423	0.1942	0.0923
t-statistic large vs. small banks		1.7292	2.0379	0.8404	0.4752

	N				
Panel D: Taxes on Corporate Dividends					
Corp. Dividends are Taxed = 1	9	0.4333	0.2556	0.2444	0.1111
Corp. Dividends are Taxed = 0	18	0.3306	0.2333	0.2331	0.1056
t-statistic tax vs. no tax on corp. div.		0.8726	0.2086	0.1075	0.0852
Panel E: Consolidation of Subsidiaries for Tax Purposes					
Consolidation for Tax Purposes = 1	16	0.3969	0.2656	0.2498	0.1000
Consolidation for Tax Purposes = 0	11	0.3182	0.2045	0.2182	0.1182
t-statistic consolidation vs. no-consolidation		0.6926	0.6014	0.3135	-0.2910
Panel F: Restrictions on Cross-Ownership					
Restrictions on Cross-Ownership = 1	6	0.3750	0.2250	0.1000	0.0333
Restrictions on Cross-Ownership = 0	21	0.3619	0.2452	0.2760	0.1286
t-statistic restricted vs. unrestricted cross-own.		0.0966	-0.1675	-1.5435	-1.3322
Panel G: GDP per Capita					
GDP per Capita ≥ median	14	0.3786	0.2321	0.2357	0.1214
GDP per Capita < median	13	0.3500	0.2500	0.2382	0.0923
t-statistic high vs. low GDP per capita		0.2536	-0.1763	-0.0249	0.4750
Panel H: Corruption Index					
Corruption Index ≥ median (low corruption)	14	0.4321	0.2857	0.3354	0.1500
Corruption Index < median (high corruption)	13	0.2923	0.1923	0.1308	0.0616
t-statistic high vs. low corruption index		1.2797	0.9450	2.2624	1.5000

A second concern is that our results might be a spurious consequence of an association between minority shareholder protection and the more general structure of financial systems. Thus firms in "bank-centered" financial systems might rely on debt finance, making it unnecessary for controlling shareholders to sell their equity to raise funds, but also making legal rules protecting minority shareholders less essential. In contrast, firms in "market-centered" financial systems rely on equity finance, forcing founders to give up control to raise capital, as well as making the protection of minority shareholders necessary. Our finding of greater ownership concentration in countries with poor investor protection might then simply reflect greater reliance on debt rather than equity finance in such countries.[14]

As a preliminary comment, we note that, in general, the distinction between "bank-centered" and "market-centered" financial systems is tenuous. As a legal matter, banks are allowed to underwrite and trade securities in some archetypal market-centered systems, such as the United Kingdom, and are severely restricted in these activities in some archetypal bank-centered systems, such as Japan (Institute of International Bankers (1997)). As an empirical matter, market-centered systems often have better-developed debt markets than bank-centered systems (La Porta et al. (1997)). Despite our skepticism about the usefulness of the distinction, we try to address the concern that our findings are related to it.

To do so, we divide up countries in two distinct ways. First, we look at legal restrictions on bank investment in industrial firms (Institute of International Bankers (1997)). Some countries restrict such investment by prohibiting ownership of controlling stakes; others restrict the amount of capital that banks can invest in the equity of industrial firms. We define the "strong bank" group as consisting of the 13 countries in the sample where banks are allowed to both own majority stakes in industrial firms and invest more than 60 percent of their capital portfolio in such firms (Institute of International Bankers (1997)). The strong bank countries include Austria, Finland, France, Germany, Greece, Ireland, Israel, Korea, Netherlands, New Zealand, Spain, Switzerland, and the United Kingdom. The remaining 14 countries have "weak banks," and they include Argentina, Australia, Belgium, Canada, Denmark, Hong Kong, Italy, Japan, Mexico, Norway, Portugal, Singapore, Sweden, and the United States. Our definition of strong banks gets at the heart of one aspect of bank-centered corporate governance, but there are of course other elements, such as banks' power through lending, as well as less formal mechanisms of restricting banks' power as shareholders. To supplement this legal view of bank-centeredness, we also divide the countries according to whether the ratio of claims of the banking sector on the private sector to GDP in 1995 is above or below the median. This outcome-based measure associates "bank-centered" financial systems with the greater

---

[14] Rajan and Zingales (1995), however, do not find systematically higher leverage in bank-centered corporate governance systems in seven OECD countries.

reliance on bank finance. Note that, like Rajan and Zingales (1998), we cannot separate the claims of the banking sector on corporations from those on individuals.

Panel B of Table VIII shows that, for all of our samples, there are no significant differences between strong and weak bank countries in the incidence of widely held firms. If anything, there is statistically insignificant evidence that countries with strong banks have more widely held firms. Panel C of Table VIII shows that countries with more bank finance have a greater incidence of widely held firms, in direct contrast to the "bank-centered" financial system hypothesis. This result, however, is consistent with the finding of La Porta et al. (1997) that countries with successful equity markets also have successful debt markets. In short, to the extent we have measured "bank-centeredness" successfully, our results do not appear to be driven by a difference between "bank-centered" and "market-centered" corporate governance.

A third concern is that our results are driven by differences in the tax rules. We have little doubt that tax rules in different countries influence ownership structures. We have more difficulty understanding why tax rules are correlated with the rules protecting minority shareholders, unless the tax rules themselves are endogenous (e.g., concentrated owners may lobby for tax rules that discourage ownership dispersion). Nonetheless, we consider two types of tax rules that might influence the incidence of widely held firms. First, if intercorporate dividends are taxed, as they are in some countries, it may be advantageous for firms to separate completely or to consolidate completely rather than to own equity in each other. This may have the effect of increasing the incidence of widely held firms. Second, if tax rules permit the use of consolidated accounting for tax purposes, it may be more advantageous for firms to own partial equity stakes in other firms, since they would then be able to use the losses in one firm to offset the profits in another. We would thus expect to see more widely held firms in countries where consolidated accounting is prohibited. Panels D and E present the results from dividing countries according to these two aspects of the tax law. We find no evidence that these particular rules influence the incidence of widely held firms.

A fourth concern is that the differences we find in the incidence of widely held firms are a consequence of some other specific aspect of the corporate governance system, and not the protection of minority shareholders. One such aspect is cross-ownership. According to Morck and Nakamura (1998), in Japan, cross-ownership of shares has developed (despite a legal prohibition) as an antitakeover device. According to Bolton and von Thadden (1998), takeovers and concentrated ownership are substitute mechanisms of corporate control because lower ownership concentration makes stock markets more liquid and thus facilitates takeovers. Putting these ideas together, countries that restrict cross-ownership of shares should have more widely held firms, as well as more liquid markets. Panel F shows that, for the large firms, there is no difference in the incidence of widely held firms according to whether

510   *The Journal of Finance*

cross-ownership is restricted. For the medium firms, countries that do not restrict cross-ownership have in fact a higher incidence of widely held firms. The data thus do not validate this particular concern.

A more straightforward version of the stock market liquidity argument is that large shareholders in the less liquid markets may be stuck with their equity stakes, whereas in the more liquid markets they can get rid of them more easily (Bhide (1993), Maug (1998)). Perhaps the greater concentration of ownership in poor investor protection countries is a consequence of their lower market liquidity. Market liquidity is itself endogenous, and is likely to be at least in part determined by the legal rules. Since we do not have direct measures of market liquidity, one way to address this concern is to observe that the level of economic development may be a partial proxy for market liquidity, and to verify whether the level of development is related to ownership concentration. This test might also be useful because, in more developed countries, the largest firms tend to be older, and hence if their controlling shareholders were interested in selling out, they have sometimes had a few decades to do so, perhaps long enough to sell at the ask. Panel G presents the results. It reveals no relationship between per capita GDP, our proxy for the level of development, and the incidence of widely held firms in our samples.

A final concern, has to do with the enforcement of legal rules and corruption. One version of this concern, discussed by La Porta et al. (1998), states that the protection of minority shareholders is determined not just by the legal rules but also by the quality of their enforcement. If corruption is a sign of poor enforcement of minority protection, and if it is moreover correlated with poor legal protection, then our results may be picking up the effects of poor law enforcement rather than that of legal rules on ownership concentration. Another version of this concern, suggested by Luigi Zingales, deals with corruption more directly. In most countries, the largest firms operate in a complicated political environment, and need to deal with a large number of laws and regulations that restrict (or subsidize) their activities. In many countries, to avoid the restrictions, or to get the subsidies, firms need to bribe politicians and regulators. Family control may facilitate corruption because it gives the controlling shareholders enormous autonomy in decision making, keeps the potential whistle-blowers out of major corporate decisions, and thus reduces the risk of getting caught. According to this theory, family control is especially important in the most corrupt countries. If these countries also happen to protect minority shareholders poorly, the relationship we have identified might be spurious. In fact, some evidence indicates that French civil law countries, which tend to have particularly poor minority protection, are also relatively more corrupt (see La Porta et al. (1999)). *Prima facie*, then, both versions of the concern about corruption potentially have merit.

The last panel of Table VIII divides countries into those with high and low corruption scores according to an international ranking (Transparency International (1996)). The data show that low corruption countries have a higher incidence of widely held firms, although the results are generally statistically insignificant. At the same time, if we run a cross-sectional regression with 27 country observations of the percentage of firms that are widely held on the shareholder rights score (or legal origin) and the corruption score, the former is important and significant, but the latter is not.[15] It is likely, therefore, that corruption shows up in Table VIII as weakly related to ownership concentration because it is itself related to legal origin and to minority protection.

In summary, the results suggest that the quality of investor protection, as measured either by the shareholder rights score or by legal origin, is a robust determinant of the incidence of widely held firms. In particular, this measure seems to be a better predictor of ownership concentration than plausible proxies for "bank-centered" corporate governance systems.

III. Conclusion

Our results present a different picture of the ownership structure of a modern corporation than that suggested by Berle and Means and widely accepted in the finance literature. The Berle and Means widely held corporation is only a common organizational form for large firms in the richest common law countries, one of which, the United States, Berle and Means actually had in mind. As we look outside the United States, particularly at countries with poor shareholder protection, even the largest firms tend to have controlling shareholders. Sometimes that shareholder is the State; but more often it is a family, usually the founder of the firm or his descendants.

The controlling shareholders typically have control over firms considerably in excess of their cash flow rights. This is so, in part, because they often control large firms through pyramidal structures, and in part because they manage the firms they control. As a consequence, large firms have a problem of separation of ownership and control, but not the one described by Berle and Means. These firms are run not by professional managers without equity ownership who are unaccountable to shareholders, but by controlling shareholders. These controlling shareholders are ideally placed to monitor the management, and in fact the top management is usually part of the controlling family, but at the same time they have the power to expropriate the minority shareholders as well as the interest in so doing. Cash flow ownership by the controlling shareholder mitigates this incentive for expropriation, but does not eliminate it. As a consequence, equity markets are both broader and more valuable in countries with good legal protection of minority shareholders (La Porta et al. (1997)).

The result that ownership concentration is a consequence of poor legal protection of minority shareholders casts doubt on the theory of Roe (1994), who attributes ownership dispersion in the United States to U.S.-specific policies that discourage ownership concentration undertaken under political

---

[15] La Porta et al. (1998) also present such a regression using their ownership data.

pressure from the professional corporate managers. The trouble is that the United States shares relatively high ownership dispersion with other countries with good shareholder protection, particularly the other rich common law countries. Roe's U.S.-specific theory of ownership dispersion is unlikely to be the whole story unless U.S.-style antiblockholder policies are common to all the countries with good protection of minority shareholders.

Our analysis raises the obvious question of how the agency conflict between the controlling and the minority shareholders can be reduced. One obvious strategy is to improve the legal environment so as to make expropriation of minority shareholders more difficult. The European Corporate Governance Network (1997) stresses improved disclosure as the crucial element of such a strategy. This is surely an important element of reform, but it does not directly address the problem of poor shareholder protection.[16] The Cadbury Committee (Charkham (1994)) proposes changes in the structure of the boards of directors in European companies. Still other proposals suggest the mandatory requirement of one-share one-vote in European countries. As our evidence indicates, this requirement will not make much difference as long as pyramids remain the principal strategy of separating ownership and control by the controlling shareholders. Indeed, legal reforms may need to be considerably more radical in nature, and give shareholders explicit rights to either prevent expropriation or seek remedy when it occurs, such as the opportunity to sue directors (perhaps through derivative or class action suits) for oppressive conduct (see also Berglof (1997)).

An alternative view is that corporations seeking external capital will opt into legal regimes that are more protective of minorities without explicit legal reforms. The issuance of ADRs in New York by many Mexican and Israeli companies, with the attendant increases in corporate disclosure though not minority shareholder rights, exemplifies this phenomenon. Unfortunately, a New York listing is prohibitively expensive for many companies. Alternatively, companies in countries with good shareholder protection, which have easier access to external funds, may acquire the less valuable companies in countries with poor investor protection, thereby bringing the assets of the latter into a more protective legal regime.[17] Lastly, companies may simply try to change their charters to attract portfolio investors.

Despite these ongoing market adjustments, it seems more likely that the existing ownership structures are primarily an equilibrium response to the domestic legal environments that companies operate in. Moreover, the controlling shareholders generally do not appear to support legal reform that would enhance minority rights; in fact, they typically lobby against it. This may seem puzzling because the value of dividend rights that controlling shareholders retain would increase significantly if minority protections are

---

[16] In a personal communication, Marco Becht of the European Corporate Governance Network notes that even this reform has proved controversial at the European Commission.

[17] A related phenomenon is for multinational firms to raise funds in countries with good investor protection to finance projects in countries with poor investor protection (Desai (1998)).

improved. The puzzle disappears once it is recognized that, as the potential to expropriate the minority shareholders diminishes, so would the value of control, which may be a significantly larger part of the controlling shareholders' total wealth. Improvement of minority protections are thus, in the first instance, a transfer from the controlling to the minority shareholders. Another potential agent of lobbying for corporate governance reform is the entrepreneurs who are interested in issuing equity in the future, but they do not usually have nearly as persuasive a political voice as the established corporate families. This reasoning makes us skeptical about the imminence of convergence of corporate ownership patterns, and of governance systems more generally, to the Berle and Means model.

Appendix

Panel A classifies the sources of ownership data for each country and gives the year of the ownership data.

Panel B gives a list of books and Internet resources for each country.

					Panel A: Sources of Ownership Data					
	Data Sources					Year of Data			
Country	Primary Source	Book	Lexis/ Nexis	Internet	Other	Yr < 95	Yr = 95	Yr = 96	Yr = 97
Argentina	8	7	1	0	4[a]	1	7	7	5
Australia	30	0	0	0	0	0	1	28	1
Canada	3	27	0	0	0	0	28	2	0
Hong Kong	27	1	0	1	1[b]	0	9	20	1
Ireland	8	4	0	7	1[c]	0	2	13	5
Japan	0	30	0	0	0	0	21	0	9
New Zealand	9	10	0	0	1[b]	1	3	16	0
Norway	18	0	0	2	0	0	4	16	0
Singapore	28	1	0	1	0	0	8	22	0
Spain	25	0	0	2	1[d]	0	13	13	2
UK	0	30	0	0	0	0	0	30	0
US	30	0	0	0	0	0	0	3	27
High antidirector total	186	110	1	13	4	2	96	170	50
Austria	0	20	0	0	0	0	20	0	0
Belgium	0	30	0	0	0	0	0	30	0
Denmark	6	0	8	5	1[b]	4	5	5	6
Finland	12	0	2	8	0	1	2	17	2
France	20	0	0	10	0	3	17	7	3
Germany	3	0	27	0	0	0	24	5	1
Greece	0	3	1	0	16[e]	1	2	14	3
Israel	14	0	2	0	4[f]	1	6	12	1
Italy	2	26	2	0	0	0	0	30	0
South Korea	0	28	1	0	1[b]	4	1	23	2
Mexico	20	0	0	0	0	0	5	12	3
Netherlands	6	22	1	0	1[g]	0	4	26	0
Portugal	1	0	4	10	5[b]	1	8	9	2
Sweden	0	30	0	0	0	0	0	30	0
Switzerland	1	29	0	0	0	0	0	30	0
Low antidirector total	85	188	48	33	28	15	94	250	23
Sample total	271	298	49	46	32	17	190	420	73

Panel B: Resources	
Country	Book/Internet Resource
Argentina	*Argentina Company Handbook 95/96* (The Reference Press, Austin, Texas).
Australia	*ASX All Ordinary Index. Companies Handbook*, 1997 (Australian Stock Exchange, Sydney, N.S.W.).
Austria	*Hoppenstedt Companies and Executives in Austria* (Lexis/Nexis).
Belgium	*Actionnariat des Sociétés Beleges cotées á Bruxelles, 1996* (Banque Bruxelles Lambert, Department Etudes et Stratégie).
Canada	*Survey of Industrials 1996* (The Financial Post Datagroup, Toronto, Ontario).
	Survey of Mines 1996 (The Financial Post Datagroup, Toronto, Ontario).
Denmark	http://www.huginonline.com/
Finland	http://www.shh.fi/ffn/
	http://www.huginonline.com/
France	*French Company Handbook 1997* (The Herald Tribune, SFB-Paris Bourse).
	http://www.bourse-de-paris.fr/bourse/sbf/emett/acemet.fcgi?GB
Germany	*Hoppenstedt Aktienführer 1997 (Hoppenstedt, Darmstadt, Germany).*
Hong Kong	http://www.ft.com/
Ireland	*The Price Waterhouse Corporate Register, 1997* (Hemmington Scott Publishing, London).
	http://www.hemscott.co.uk/equities/
Italy	*Taccuino Dell'Azionista 1997* (Il Sole 24 Ore Radiocor, Milan, Italy).
Japan	*Industrial Groupings in Japan, The Anatomy of the "Keiretsu,"* 1996–1997 (Dodwell Marketing Consultants, Tokyo).
	Japan Company Handbook, Spring 1997 (Toyo Keizai Inc., Japan).
Korea (South)	Korea Investors Service, Inc., 1990, Seoul, Korea.
	Zaebols in Korea, 1989, Bankers Trust Securities Research, Seoul, Korea.
Netherlands	*Handboek Nederlandse Beursfondsen, 1996/97*, 1997 (Het Financieele Dagblad/HFD Informatie).
New Zealand	*The New Zealand Company Register*, 1996 (Mercantile Gazette Marketing, Christchurch).
	http://www.nzse.co.nz/companies/
Norway	http://www.huginonline.com/
Portugal	http://www.ft.com/
Singapore	*Stock Exchange of Singapore Ltd., Company Handbook*, 1996 (Stock Exchange of Singapore, Research and Publications Department, Singapore).
Spain	*The Maxwell Espinosa Shareholder Directory*, 1994 (S.P.A. Unión Editorial, Madrid).
Sweden	*Ägarna Och Makten I Sveriges Börsföretag*, 1996 (Dagens Nyheter, Stockholm).
	http://www.huginonline.com/
	http://www2.fti.se/foretag/#i
Switzerland	*Swiss Stock Guide*, 1996 (Union Bank of Switzerland, Zurich).
United Kingdom	*The Price Waterhouse Corporate Register*, 1997 (Hemmington Scott Publishing, London).
	http://www.hemscott.co.uk/equities/
United States	http://www.sec.gov/

Superscript letters correspond to the following sources: [a] shareholder meeting records; [b] WorldScope; [c] *Irish Times*; [d] *Forbes Magazine*; [e] *Bloomberg* in twelve cases, *Euromoney* and *World Scope* in two cases each; [f] *WorldScope* in three cases, *Moodys International* in one case; [g] *Moodys International*.

Corporate Ownership Around the World   515

REFERENCES

Barca, Fabrizio, 1995, On corporate governance in Italy: Issues, facts, and agency, Unpublished manuscript, Bank of Italy, Rome.

Baumol, William, 1959, *Business Behavior, Value and Growth* (MacMillan, New York, N.Y.).

Bebchuk, Lucian, 1994, Efficient and inefficient sales of corporate control, *Quarterly Journal of Economics* 109, 957–994.

Bebchuk, Lucian, 1998, A theory of the choice between concentrated and dispersed ownership of corporate shares, Unpublished manuscript, Harvard University.

Berglof, Eric, 1997, Reforming corporate governance: Redirecting the European agenda, *Economic Policy* 1997, 93–123.

Berglof, Eric, and Enrico Perotti, 1994, The governance structure of the Japanese financial keiretsu, *Journal of Financial Economics* 36, 259–284.

Berle, Adolf, and Gardiner Means, 1932, *The Modern Corporation and Private Property* (MacMillan, New York, N.Y.).

Bhide, Amar, 1993, The hidden cost of stock market liquidity, *Journal of Financial Economics* 34, 31–51.

Bolton, Patrick, and Ernst-Ludwig von Thadden, 1998, Blocks, liquidity, and corporate control, *Journal of Finance* 53, 1–26.

Burkart, Mike, Denis Gromb, and Fausto Panunzi, 1997, Large shareholders, monitoring, and fiduciary duty, *Quarterly Journal of Economics* 112, 693–728.

Burkart, Mike, Denis Gromb, and Fausto Panunzi, 1998, Why higher takeover premia protect minority shareholders, *Journal of Political Economy* 106, 172–204.

Charkham, Jonathan, 1994, *Keeping Good Company: A Study of Corporate Governance in Five Countries* (Clarendon Press, Oxford, U.K.).

DeAngelo, Harry, and Linda DeAngelo, 1985, Managerial ownership of voting rights, *Journal of Financial Economics* 14, 33–69.

Demsetz, Harold, 1983, The structure of ownership and the theory of the firm, *Journal of Law and Economics* 26, 375–390.

Demsetz, Harold, and Kenneth Lehn, 1985, The structure of corporate ownership: Causes and consequences, *Journal of Political Economy* 93, 1155–1177.

Desai, Mihir, 1998, A multinational perspective on capital structure choice and internal capital markets, Unpublished manuscript, Harvard University.

Edwards, Jeremy, and Klaus Fischer, 1994, *Banks, Finance and Investment in West Germany since 1970* (Cambridge University Press, Cambridge, U.K.).

Eisenberg, Melvin, 1976, *The Structure of the Corporation: A Legal Analysis* (Little, Brown and Co., Boston, Mass.).

Ernst & Young, 1994, *Worldwide Corporate Tax Guide and Directory* (Ernst & Young International, New York, N.Y.).

European Corporate Governance Network, 1997, *The Separation of Ownership and Control: A Survey of 7 European Countries Preliminary Report to the European Commission*. Volumes 1–4 (European Corporate Governance Network, Brussels).

Franks, Julian, and Colin Mayer, 1994, The ownership and control of German corporations, Unpublished manuscript, London Business School.

French, Kenneth, and James Poterba, 1991, Were Japanese stock prices too high?, *Journal of Financial Economics* 29, 337–364.

Galbraith, John Kenneth, 1967, *The New Industrial State* (Houghton-Mifflin, Boston, Mass.).

Gorton, Gary, and Frank Schmid, 1996, Universal banking and the performance of German firms, Working paper 5453, National Bureau of Economic Research, Cambridge, Mass.

Grossman, Sanford, and Oliver Hart, 1980, Takeover bids, the free-rider problem, and the theory of the corporation, *Bell Journal of Economics* 11, 42–64.

Grossman, Sanford, and Oliver Hart, 1986, The costs and benefits of ownership: A theory of vertical and lateral integration, *Journal of Political Economy* 94, 691–719.

Grossman, Sanford, and Oliver Hart, 1988, One share-one vote and the market for corporate control, *Journal of Financial Economics* 20, 175–202.

Harris, Milton, and Artur Raviv, 1988, Corporate governance: Voting rights and majority rules, *Journal of Financial Economics* 20, 203–235.

Holderness, Clifford, Randall Kroszner, and Dennis Sheehan, 1999, Were the good old days that good? Changes in managerial stock ownership since the Great Depression, *Journal of Finance* 54, 435–469.

Holderness, Clifford, and Dennis Sheehan, 1988, The role of majority shareholders in publicly held corporations: An exploratory analysis, *Journal of Financial Economics* 20, 317–346.

International Monetary Fund, 1998, *International Financial Statistics* (International Monetary Fund, Washington, D.C.).

Institute of International Bankers, 1997, Global survey 1997, mimeo, New York, N.Y.

Jensen, Michael, and William Meckling, 1976, Theory of the firm: Managerial behavior, agency costs, and ownership structure, *Journal of Financial Economics* 3, 305–360.

Kang, Jun-Koo, and Anil Shivdasani, 1995, Firm performance, corporate governance, and top executive turnover in Japan, *Journal of Financial Economics* 38, 29–58.

Kita, Ryoyu, 1996, *A Compendium of Japanese Commercial Law* (Kindaibungeisha, Tokyo).

La Porta, Rafael, Florencio Lopez-de-Silanes, Andrei Shleifer, and Robert Vishny, 1997, Legal determinants of external finance, *Journal of Finance* 52, 1131–1150.

La Porta, Rafael, Florencio Lopez-de-Silanes, Andrei Shleifer, and Robert Vishny, 1998, Law and finance, *Journal of Political Economy* 106, 1113–1155.

La Porta, Rafael, Florencio Lopez-de-Silanes, Andrei Shleifer, and Robert Vishny, 1999, The quality of government, *Journal of Law, Economics, and Organization*, forthcoming.

Marris, Robin, 1964, *The Economic Theory of Managerial Capitalism* (Free Press, Glencoe, Ill.).

Maug, Ernst, 1998, Large shareholders as monitors: Is there a tradeoff between liquidity and control?, *Journal of Finance* 53, 65–98.

Morck, Randall, and Masao Nakamura, 1999, Banks and corporate control in Japan, *Journal of Finance*, 54, 319–339.

Morck, Randall, Andrei Shleifer, and Robert Vishny, 1988, Management ownership and market valuation: An empirical analysis, *Journal of Financial Economics* 20, 293–315.

Pagano, Marco, and Ailsa Roell, 1998, The choice of stock ownership structure: Agency costs, monitoring, and the decision to go public, *Quarterly Journal of Economics* 113, 187–226.

Penrose, Edith, 1959, *The Theory of the Growth of the Firm* (Basil Blackwell, Oxford, U.K.).

Price Waterhouse, 1995, *Corporate Taxes: A Worldwide Summary* (Price Waterhouse Center for International Taxation, New York).

Prowse, Stephen, 1992, The structure of corporate ownership in Japan, *Journal of Finance* 47, 1121–1140.

Rajan, Raghuram, and Luigi Zingales, 1995, What do we know about capital structure? Some evidence from the international data, *Journal of Finance* 50, 1421–1460.

Rajan, Raghuram, and Luigi Zingales, 1998, Financial dependence and growth, *American Economic Review* 88, 559–586.

Reynolds, Thomas, and Arturo Flores, 1989, *Foreign Law: Current Sources of Basic Legislation in Jurisdictions of the World* (Rothman and Co., Littleton, Col.).

Roe, Mark, 1994, *Strong Managers Weak Owners: The Political Roots of American Corporate Finance* (Princeton University Press, Princeton, N.J.).

Shleifer, Andrei, and Robert Vishny, 1986, Large shareholders and corporate control, *Journal of Political Economy* 94, 461–488.

Shleifer, Andrei, and Robert Vishny, 1994, Politicians and firms, *Quarterly Journal of Economics* 109, 955–1025.

Shleifer, Andrei, and Robert Vishny, 1997, A survey of corporate governance, *Journal of Finance* 52, 737–783.

Stulz, René, 1988, Managerial control of voting rights: Financing policies and the market for corporate control, *Journal of Financial Economics* 20, 25–54.

Tomsett, Erik, and Rijkele Betten, 1997, *The International Guide to Mergers and Acquisitions* (IBFD Publications BV, Amsterdam).

Transparency International, 1996, www.transparency.de.

Tufano, Peter, 1996, Who manages risk? An empirical investigation of risk management practices in the gold mining industry, *Journal of Finance* 51, 1097–1138.

Williamson, Oliver, 1964, *The Economics of Discretionary Behavior: Managerial Objectives in a Theory of the Firm* (Prentice Hall, Englewood Cliffs, N.J.).

Wolfenzon, Daniel, 1998, A theory of pyramidal ownership, mimeo, Harvard University.

World Bank, 1997, *World Development Report: The State in a Changing World* (Oxford University Press, New York, N.Y.).

Yafeh, Yishay, and Oved Yosha, 1996, Large shareholders and banks: Who monitors and how? Unpublished manuscript, Hebrew University, Jerusalem.

Zingales, Luigi, 1994, The value of the voting right: A study of the Milan stock exchange experience, *The Review of Financial Studies* 7, 125–148.

[2]

Agency Relationships in Family Firms: Theory and Evidence

William S. Schulze • Michael H. Lubatkin • Richard N. Dino • Ann K. Buchholtz

Case Western Reserve University, Weatherhead School of Management, 10900 Euclid Avenue, Cleveland, Ohio 44106-7235
University of Connecticut, Box U-41 Mgmt., 368 Fairfield Road, Storrs, Connecticut 06269
University of Connecticut, 368 Fairfield Road—U-41FB, Storrs, Connecticut 06269-2041
The University of Georgia, Terry College of Business, Department of Management, Athens, Georgia 30602-6275
schulze@po.cwru.edu • mike@ba.uconn.edu • rdino@sbu.uconn.edu • abuchholtz@terry.uga.edu

---

The authors have conducted the kind of research here that we all reach for but too often fail to grasp. That is, this study of the governance of family firms is theoretically rich and practically relevant. Our colleagues have pressed the limits of agency theory to explore the control of owners' opportunistic behavior, behavior that interestingly just might be rooted in an altruistic impulse. They have done this by empirically examining privately-held, family-managed firms. While such firms embody the dominant form of organization in the world today, they are very underrepresented in our study of organization and management. This research simultaneously advances our understanding of agency theory and draws much needed attention to these kinds of firms. Spend some time with this paper. I think you will be glad that you did.

James Walsh

Abstract

Does owner management necessarily eliminate the agency costs of ownership? Drawing on agency literature and on the economic theory of the household, we argue that private ownership and owner management expose privately held, owner-managed firms to agency threats ignored by Jensen's and Meckling's (1976) agency model. Private ownership and owner management not only reduce the effectiveness of external control mechanisms, they also expose firms to a "self-control" problem created by incentives that cause owners to take actions which "harm themselves as well as those around them" (Jensen 1994, p. 43). Thus, shareholders have incentive to invest resources in curbing both managerial *and* owner opportunism. We extend this thesis to the domain of the family firm. After developing hypotheses which describe how family dynamics and, specifically, altruism, exacerbate agency problems experienced by these privately held, owner-managed firms, we use data obtained from a large-scale survey of family businesses to field test our hypotheses and find evidence which suggests support for our proposed theory. Finally, we discuss the implications of our theory for research on family and other types of privately held, owner-managed firms.

(*Agency Theory; Altruism; Privately-Owned Firms; Family Business*)

Must privately held, family-managed firms (henceforth, family firms) offer pay incentives and use other formal governance mechanisms to mitigate agency threats to their performance? There are no clear empirical or theoretical answers to this question, largely because family firms have been virtually overlooked in the mainstream economic and management journals.[1] What makes this oversight remarkable is that family firms are far more common than widely held public firms; have at least as much economic impact and, as we will soon argue, represent a theoretically distinct form of governance.[2]

Nevertheless, we can infer three reasons from Jensen's and Meckling's (1976) model[3] three reasons why family firms, at least those that are privately held and family-managed, need not incur significant agency costs. First, owner management should reduce agency costs because it naturally aligns the owner-managers' interests about growth opportunities and risk. This alignment reduces their incentive to be opportunistic, sparing firms the need to maintain "costly mechanisms for separating the management and control of decisions" (Fama and Jensen 1983a, p. 332). Second, private ownership should reduce

1047-7039/01/1202/0099/$05.00
1526-5455 electronic ISSN

ORGANIZATION SCIENCE, © 2001 INFORMS
Vol. 12, No. 2, March–April 2001, pp. 99–116

W. S. SCHULZE, M. H. LUBATKIN, R. N. DINO, AND A. K. BUCHHOLTZ   *Agency Relationships in Family Firms*

agency costs because property rights are largely restricted to "internal decision agents" whose personal involvement assures that managers will not expropriate shareholder wealth through the consumption of perquisites and the misallocation of resources (Fama and Jensen 1983a, p. 332). Finally, family management should further reduce agency costs because shares tend to be held by ". . . agents whose special relations with other decision agents allow agency problems to be controlled without separation of the management and control decisions. For example, family members . . . therefore have advantages in monitoring and disciplining related decision agents" (Fama and Jensen 1983b, p. 306).

It may not be surprising, therefore, that some have speculated that family firms represent one of the least costly (most efficient) forms of organizational governance (e.g., Daily and Dollinger 1992, Kang 2000). Indeed, Jensen and Meckling (hereafter J/M) imply that formal governance mechanisms at family firms are not necessary and that their expense may even detract from firm performance. We disagree. Drawing from theory developed by Becker (1981), Stulz (1988), Thaler and Shefrin (1981) and others, we argue that private ownership and family management expose firms to agency hazards. For example, private ownership frees firms from the discipline imposed by the market for corporate control (Jensen 1993) and increases the agency threat posed by self-control—a problem that arises when owner-managers have incentive to take actions that can "harm themselves as well as those around them" (Jensen 1998, p. 48). Firms also face an increased threat of adverse selection due to the effect of private ownership on the efficiency of their labor markets. Finally, altruism alters the incentive structure of family-managed firms such that many of the agency benefits gained (e.g., commitment) are offset by self-control and moral hazard problems. Because these agency problems can prevent the alignment of ownership interests, we conclude that owner management does not minimize the agency costs of ownership within privately held, family-managed firms.

We believe that a positive relationship exists between agency costs incurred by family firms and performance. In this paper we develop theory and field-test six hypotheses concerning agency costs in privately held, family-managed firms. We conclude with a discussion of the implications of our theory for research on family firms, as well as for agency theory in general.

Agency in Privately Held and Owner-Managed Firms

Agency relationships arise when one self-interested individual (the principal) delegates some decision-making authority to another (the agent). This delegation of authority exposes agents to risks for which they are not fully compensated, giving them incentive to seek additional compensation through noncompensatory means such as free-riding or shirking (Jensen and Meckling 1976). It also creates information asymmetries that make it possible for agents to engage in activities that, if left unchecked, would threaten firm performance and may ultimately harm the welfare of owners and agents alike. Information asymmetries and incentives therefore combine and pose a moral hazard to agents, which owners can reduce by monitoring agent conduct, gaining access to their firm's internal information flows, and providing incentives that encourage agents to act in the owners' best interests. Accordingly, Jensen and Meckling conclude that the cost of reducing information asymmetries and the accompanying moral hazard is lowest when owners directly participate in the management of the firm. Owner-managed firms thus have little need to guard against this agency threat.

This claim is predicated on two assumptions: That owner management is an efficient substitute for the costly control mechanisms that non-owner-managed firms use to limit the agency costs of managerial discretion, and that the separation of ownership and control is the source of agency costs in firms (Alchian and Woodward 1988).[4] We challenge both assumptions.

The Agency Cost of Private Ownership. We begin our challenge by noting that the J/M model recognizes a variety of external governance mechanisms that reduce agency costs in publicly held firms. For example, efficient capital markets reduce monitoring costs by tracking firm performance and making this information available in the form of share price. They also reduce the detrimental effects of overinvestment by providing the firm's decision makers with liquidity and distributing the firm's risk among a large number of shareholders (Fama and Jensen 1983b, Reagan and Stulz 1986). Product market competition and the market for corporate control also place a variety of limits on managerial discretion (Jensen 1993). Finally, competitive labor markets make it less costly for firms to recruit qualified applicants and reduce the threat of precontractual opportunism or *adverse selection* which arises when applicants are able to hide information about themselves that prospective employers need to properly evaluate an applicant's quality and worth (Fama 1980, Hansmann 1996).

Private ownership, however, compromises the efficiency of the firm's factor markets and the external governance that these markets provide. For example, economists recognize that a self-selection or *sorting* process

100

occurs in labor markets whenever the terms of the employment contract systematically influence the characteristics of the individuals whom firms can hire. Higher paying jobs, for example, attract more able workers, while pay-for-performance contracts attract risk takers (Besanko et al. 1996). Private firms, however, cannot offer prospective employees the same terms of employment as public firms. For example, while public firms may offer stock options to prospective employees, privately held firms cannot, due to limited liquidity and the fact that majority shareholders are generally not willing to dilute their control of the firm (Lew and Kolodzeij 1993, Morck 1996). Public firms can also promise talented employees promotional opportunities; typically, because important management positions are "chosen on the basis of wealth and willingness to bear risk as well as for decision skills" (Fama and Jensen 1983a, p. 332), such positions in private firms tend to be held by shareholders (La Porta et al. 1999).

These inefficiancies have five important implications for the cost of governing private firms and, by extension, for the relative efficiency of owner management. First, the risk that these firms will inadvertently hire lower-quality agents is increased because sorting reduces the size, character, and quality of the labor pool which serves them.[5] Second, firms face increased risks of hiring inferior and/or opportunistic employees because reduced competition and accompanying market inefficiencies make it more costly for firms to guard against adverse selection (Mohlo 1997). Third, reluctance to dilute ownership hampers these firms' ability to post the bonds that public firms offer talented applicants to assure them that the firm will not take advantage of them (Rajan and Zingales 1998).[6] Private ownership thus weakens the institutional safeguards that help to protect public firms from adverse selection and prospective agents from a form of owner opportunism known as hold-up (Williamson 1985). Fourth, private ownership increases monitoring costs, because inferior compensation and limited promotion opportunities reduce these agents' incentive to monitor each other's conduct (Fama and Jensen 1983b, p. 310) and to compete with one another for advancement (Besanko et al. 1996). Finally, private ownership increases the cost of monitoring firm performance because share price is not determined by the market. By shielding the firm from the disciplinary pressure of the market for corporate control (Stulz 1988), "it [can be] extremely difficult for adjustment to take place until long after the problems have become severe, and in some cases even unsolvable" (Jensen 1993, p. 847). Private ownership therefore increases monitoring costs while exposing the firm to precontractual agency threats rooted in "hidden information" and to postcontractual agency threats associated with "hidden actions." Hence, owner management is not an efficient substitute for the costly control mechanisms that non-owner-managed firms use to limit the agency costs of managerial discretion.

The Agency Cost of Owner Management. The J/M model assumes that separation of ownership from control is the principal source of agency costs in firms, and that these costs are eliminated when the firm is managed by a single owner (Fama and Jensen 1983a). The model also presumes that while conflicts of interest may arise when ownership is shared, these conflicts do not generally engender agency costs because they are resolved efficiently.[7]

Three mechanisms make this possible. First, J/M assume that voting minimizes the economic cost of settling more divisive issues because votes are assumed to reflect the proportionate distribution of economic risks and rewards among the owners. Second, liquid markets limit the agency costs of owner conflict by making it possible for conflicting parties to cut their losses simply by selling their shares (Alchian and Woodward 1988; Jensen and Smith 1985). This assures economic efficiency because it prevents any owner or group of owners from transferring a portion of their ownership costs onto others. Finally, owners are assumed to be rational and principally motivated by economic incentives: Ownership, it follows, substantially aligns their interests and gives them incentive to develop rules and policies aimed at minimizing conflict and limiting the cost of settling disputes. In this light, the J/M model presumes that owner management minimizes, but does not eliminate, the agency cost of conflict among owners.

However, the model recognizes that significant agency costs arise when these assumptions are violated. Jensen (1993), for example, notes that failures in the market for corporate control allow inside owners to advance their personal interests at the expense of outside owners. Private ownership exacerbates this problem because the absence of a liquid market for the firms' shares increases the threat of hold-up, which arises whenever owners use their voting rights or their control over a firm-specific resource to take the ownership interests of other owners "hostage." As long as the loss the hostaged owners might suffer from giving in to the hostage-taker is less than the cost they would incur from not giving in and/or selling their stake in the firm, the hostage-taker has incentive to force the firm to take actions that favor his or her interest. It follows that the ability to transfer ownership at low cost guards owners from this important agency threat (Williamson 1985).

Finally, the notion that the agency cost of conflict among owners is negligible rests on the assumptions about the economically rational behavior of owners. However, the assumption that all preferences can be expressed in economic terms is problematic because individuals have preferences or tastes for noneconomic as well as economically motivated behaviors, and people are naturally driven to maximize the utility they gain from each[8] (Arrow 1963; Buchanan 1975; Becker 1974, 1981; Thaler and Shefrin 1981).

The presence of noneconomic preferences creates two problems: First, while owners may be expected to share common economic interests, there is little reason to presume that they have common noneconomically motivated preferences. Further, because the value of noneconomically motivated preferences cannot be fully expressed or calibrated in terms of a commodity like money (Bergstrom 1989), the J/M model cannot assume that ownership necessarily reduces agency costs because money (i.e., equity ownership and monetary incentives) cannot guarantee the alignment of owners' attitudes towards growth opportunities and risk.

Second, conflicts of interests may arise because some noneconomically motivated preferences can cause owners to take actions that threaten their own welfare as well as those around them. These "agency problems with oneself" (Jensen 1998, p. 48) persist because the utility individuals gain from indulging personal tastes (e.g., a taste for drug consumption or the exercise of power) is functionally indistinguishable from that gained from rationally motivated pursuits (Becker and Murphy 1988, Thaler and Shefrin 1981). Attempts to maximize one's welfare can therefore cause individuals to take actions that do not advance the common (economic) good. For example, a powerful owner might veto a new venture because it threatens the status quo, entails too much effort, or is not in their personal financial interest (Jensen and Meckling 1976, Wright et al. 1996). And, because power is not symmetrically distributed in a firm, an owner can engage in exploitive behavior with subordinates, in what Perrow (1986, p. 227) refers to as "owner opportunism." Although Jensen admits that he "failed for more than a decade to see the generality and importance of this self-control issue" (1994, p. 45), his subsequent publications, including the versions of Fama and Jensen (1983a, 1983b) that appear in his 1998 book, make no mention of this agency problem when discussing owner management.

In sum, we posit that private ownership not only fails to minimize the agency costs of ownership, but can actually engender agency costs in these firms for reasons

which are entirely overlooked in the J/M model.[9] Moreover, private ownership reduces external governance and exacerbates the self-control problems that arise whenever firms are led by a powerful owner-manager, a threat which is particularly troublesome when privately held firms are owned and managed by family.

Agency Threats and Costs in the Family Firm

While Fama and Jensen (1983a, p. 332) contend that family management is especially efficient, we propose instead that family relations tend to make agency problems associated with private ownership and owner management *more* difficult to resolve due to self-control and other problems engendered by altruism.

Economists model altruism as a trait that positively links the welfare of an individual to the welfare of others (Becker 1981, Bergstrom 1995). As such, altruism is self-reinforcing and motivated by self-interest because it allows the individual to simultaneously satisfy both altruistic (other-regarding) preferences and egotistic (self-regarding) preferences (Lunati 1997).[10] Parents, it follows, are not only generous to their children because they love them, but also because they would harm their own (the altruist's) welfare if they acted otherwise (Becker 1981). Simon (1993) and Eshel et al. (1998), for example, note that altruism compels parents to care for their children, encourages family members to be considerate of one another, and makes family membership valuable in ways that both promote and sustain the family bond. These bonds, in turn, lend family firms a history, language, and identity that make it special. Communication and some types of decision making are facilitated by the intimate knowledge about others that family members bring into the firm (Gersick et al. 1997). Altruism also fosters loyalty, as well as a commitment among its leadership to the firm's long-run prosperity (Ward 1987). Kang (2000), for example, concludes that family-managed firms are patient investors, capable of sticking with strategies through circumstances and over periods of time that nonfamily-managed firms cannot.

Buchanan (1975) notes, however, that altruism can cause parents to threaten their children with moral hazard. Because altruism partly stems from a parents' desire to enhance their own welfare, parents have incentive to be generous even though that increased generosity may cause their children to free-ride (e.g., leave an assigned household chore for a parent to complete, or squander their parent's money). This agency threat is likely to be pronounced in family firms, because control over the firm's resources makes it possible for owner-managers to be unusually generous to their children and relatives. The typical family firm, for example, provides family members with secure employment, as well as perquisites and privileges that they would not otherwise receive (Gersick et al. 1997, Ward 1987). Kets De Vries (1996) reports that family-firm founders have a tendency to lavish their children with gifts, perhaps to make up for their absence from the household when their children were young. Altruism therefore adds a theoretically distinct set of self-control problems to the set of agency problems identified earlier.

Consequently, the agency problems associated with private ownership and owner management, as well as those engendered by altruism, threaten the performance of privately held, family-managed firms. In the next section, six hypotheses (two dealing with the costs of monitoring agents, two with the costs of monitoring and settling disputes among owner-managers, and two with configurations of governance mechanisms) describe how family dynamics influence governance practices in these firms.

Hypotheses

The Agency Costs of Monitoring Agents. We argued previously that failures in external labor markets increase the need for privately held, owner-managed firms to monitor agent conduct, while internal labor market failures increase the cost of monitoring. Owner supervision, if possible, minimizes monitoring costs; if not, owner-managers can discourage agents from pursuing their own interests by making a portion of their pay contingent on achieving a performance objective (Eisenhardt 1989). Given limits to owner supervision and the fact that owner-managers are unable or at least highly reluctant to use equity to compensate or bond agents (Berk et al. 1988), it should not come as a surprise that between 73% and 85% of these firms offer agents pay incentives in the form of cash bonuses (Fraser 1990, Greco 1997, *INC* 1996, Small Business Reports 1993).

While theory leads us to expect a positive relationship between family-firm performance and incentive compensation paid to nonfamily agents, the same may not be true for family agents (i.e., family members employed by family firms), who, as de facto owners,[11] already have their personal wealth tied to the value of the firm. It follows from the J/M model that incentive compensation should not affect family agent performance because their interests are already aligned with those of the owners.

On the other hand, we infer from the economic literature on altruism that family agents have incentive to free-ride and that parent owner-managers will have difficulty monitoring and disciplining their conduct. Because altruism biases parental perceptions (*My kids are such hard workers!*) it becomes difficult for family agents to take actions that might harm another family member's welfare. One solution to this conundrum is to tie a portion of the family agent's wage to outcomes that can be effectively monitored and objectively assessed, like firm performance (Andersen 1985). In this light, family agent pay incentives are akin to parents making a portion of their children's allowance contingent upon completing certain chores. This mitigates the self-control problem by allowing parent owner-managers to satisfy their need to be altruistic while reducing the risk of spoiling (and thereby harming) their children (Becker 1981, Bergstrom 1989). Also, pay incentives should improve firm performance by controlling the family agents' tendency to free-ride (Chami 1997). As such, and contrary to the J/M model, we posit that privately held, family-managed firms should offer pay incentives to both family and nonfamily agents to mitigate agency threats to their performance.

HYPOTHESIS 1A (H1A). *Pay incentives to nonfamily agents are positively related to the performance of privately held, family-managed firms.*

HYPOTHESIS 1B (H1B). *Pay incentives to family agents are positively related to the performance of privately-held, family-managed firms*

Jensen and Meckling (1995) note that monitoring costs are not only associated with observing, measuring, and rewarding various agent behaviors, but also entail costs associated with the host of administrative practices that firms use to control agent behavior. Managerial hierarchies, for example, enhance accountability by separating decision authority from operating responsibility. Budgets help direct agent activity while their accompanying rules and regulations limit agent discretion. Finally, strategic plans have both manifest (intended) and latent (unintended but nevertheless consequential) effects (Merton 1968) that enhance organizational control and limit agency costs. Jensen and Meckling (1995), for example, note that strategic plans reduce information asymmetries within the firm, and hence the threat of moral hazard, by encouraging agents to gather and share information that does not ordinarily flow through the firm's communication channels. Strategic planning also requires agents to systematically assess firm performance relative to internal and external benchmarks. It promotes the alignment of attitudes toward growth opportunities and risk by forcing agents to define the firm's mission and values, promotes consensus by requiring that agents from different levels

W. S. SCHULZE, M. H. LUBATKIN, R. N. DINO, AND A. K. BUCHHOLTZ   *Agency Relationships in Family Firms*

in the hierarchy agree on goals and strategies, and imposes discipline by insisting that these objectives guide day-to-day activities. Thus, strategic planning can be a valuable tool for achieving good agency, especially when firms lack the discipline imposed by capital markets and are less able to assess performance objectively due to the absence of a market-determined share price.

Paradoxically, family-managed firms are less likely to use formal monitoring and control mechanisms than other firms (Daily and Dollinger 1993, Geeraerts 1984). Our analysis suggests an agency explanation: We believe that conflict between the self- and the other-regarding interests of the owner-managers can discourage or even prevent them from engaging in activities that they have economic incentive to undertake. Ward (1988), for example, observes that family owner-managers tend to view strategic planning and similar administrative processes as laborious and time-consuming, taking them away from running the business while providing them with little in the way of new strategic insights or other benefits. They may also be reluctant to commit to jointly determined courses of action that limit their discretion. Finally, family members may avoid strategic planning if it requires them to deal with emotionally charged issues like disciplining family agents, or to make decisions that have ramifications for familial relations both inside and outside the firm (Meyer and Zucker 1989, Ward 1987). Thus, in contrast to research which attributes variance in the use of strategic planning to exogenous factors like the competitiveness of the markets in which privately held firms compete (e.g., Powell 1992), we attribute this variance to agency problems associated with self-control and the potential for conflict among owner-managers. Hence:

HYPOTHESIS 2 (H2). *There is a positive relationship between the use of strategic planning and the performance of privately held, family-managed firms.*

The Agency Cost of Monitoring Owners. As argued earlier, agency problems can arise in privately held, owner-managed firms because noneconomically motivated preferences give owners incentive to take actions that threaten their personal welfare as well as the welfare of those around them (e.g., deciding against a new venture because it threatens the status quo or refusing to take actions which compromise their individual welfare). External governance cannot curb these forms of owner opportunism (e.g., hold-up) because such firms face a failed capital market and, with it, a failed market for corporate control. Consequently, all shareholders, especially those with a significant portion of their wealth invested in the firm, have economic incentives to adopt and enforce gover-

nance practices which prevent these self-control problems from undermining the viability of the firm. Therefore, privately held, owner-managed firms need vigilant boards whose ability to monitor and discipline top management is not compromised by the CEO's power and authority and/or his or her hegemony over the board (Lin 1996).

Widely held firms reduce executive or board turnover (entrenchment) and increase board autonomy and vigilance with rules regarding CEO and board tenure, the appointment of outside directors, and other measures (Finkelstein and Hambrick 1996, Lin 1996). Privately held, family-managed firms, however, are less likely to implement such policies because ownership rights and the formal authority of office combine with family status to reduce turnover (and hence increase entrenchment) in the board and executive ranks (Finkelstein and D'Aveni 1994, Ford 1988). For example, family-firm CEOs can use the promise of familial succession and/or future ownership to lock in continued support from board members. The absence of a liquid market for their shares, as well as the opportunity to exercise their ownership rights in a manner that enhances personal welfare, prolongs tenure. Not surprisingly, the CEOs of most family firms are firmly entrenched, with an average tenure of 24 years (Beckhard and Dyer 1983), twice what Hambrick and Fukutomi (1991, p. 736) observed at widely held firms.

Family dynamics and self-control problems also combine and undermine the effectiveness of outside directors. The advantages of outside directors in widely held firms are clear: They are better able to monitor firm performance; discipline or even dismiss managers since they are not beholden to the firm and/or the powerful CEO for their livelihood (Finkelstein and D'Aveni 1994, Lin 1996, Walsh and Seward 1990); and bring needed expertise and perspective to boards which might otherwise lack diversity (Finkelstein and Hambrick 1996). In spite of the advantages of outside directors, however, family firms are less likely to use them. First, they exact an agency cost on family owners in terms of a perceived loss of control and discretion. Second, because outsiders almost never attain the status of large-block ownership that they sometimes do in widely held firms, they are likely to be less motivated than family directors (Alderfer 1988). Third, while their "impartial" status can enhance their ability to offer advice on some decisions, they have little influence on decisions involving family members or other family matters (Nelsen and Frishkoff 1991). Finally, the tendency of family-firm CEOs to appoint outside directors to their boards who are close friends and/or happen to have a fiduciary relationship with the firm (e.g., their attorneys or accountants) further compromises director

104

autonomy (Ward and Handy 1988).[12] Thus, "hand-picking" outside directors for reasons other than strong board oversight can undermine their effectiveness (Ford 1988, Rubenson and Gupta 1996). Consequently, we anticipate that problems associated with family dynamics, self-control, and owner control make family-firm boards prone to entrenchment. Hence:

HYPOTHESIS 3 (H3). *The greater the board entrenchment, the lower the performance of privately held, family-managed firms.*

The Agency Costs of Settling Disputes Among Owners. Shares in privately held firms have limited transferability, making it necessary for owners to "specify rights in net cash flows and procedures for transferring residual claims to new agents" (Fama and Jensen 1983b, p. 308). While a seemingly straightforward process, conflicts between self- and other-regarding interests may cause family-firm CEOs to keep the specific conditions of their share transfer intentions private. They may fear that they will cause a jealous rift among the other family agents if they disclose their share transfer and estate plans. The involvement of extended family members complicates planning and virtually assures that some family agents will feel slighted, and perhaps even disenfranchised, once the plan is revealed (Barnes and Hershon 1976). Some CEOs might be reluctant to disclose their intentions because they feel that their chosen successor still lacks the skills and experience needed to lead the firm (Handler 1990). Disclosure is also risky because creditors and other stakeholders may attempt to protect their interests by tying contract renewal dates to the execution date of the announced plan (Gersick et al. 1997). Still other CEOs may wish to put off the share transfer or delay retirement until they have secured their "nest egg" (Rubenson and Gupta 1996). The result is that these plans are kept confidential. As Ellen Gordon, principal owner and president of Tootsie Roll Industries put it, "We have a succession plan, but we don't have to announce what it is." (*Forbes* 2000, p. 131)

Unfortunately, uncertainty regarding share transfer plans increases agency problems because the ambiguous promise of ownership and/or leadership serves to "lock" the hopeful heirs into a dependent relationship with the firm (Nelton 1995). CEOs can reduce information asymmetries, and hence the threat of hold-up and other agency problems, by naming a successor and/or announcing how ownership and voting rights will be distributed (Barnes and Hershon 1976, Fama and Jensen 1983a; Gersick et al. 1997, Handler 1990). Incentive pay, for example, will be more effective because it gives family agents the information they need to more accurately calculate both the

short- and long-term value of their efforts (Bergstrom 1989). Information asymmetries and rivalries among family agents should also decline because they have little reason to continue lobbying the CEO for favor once his or her share transfer intentions have been declared. Thus, although principal shareholders have incentive to keep information about their share transfer plans private, this secrecy increases agency costs within family firms.

HYPOTHESIS 4 (H4). *Disclosure of the major shareholder's estate and share transfer intentions is positively associated with the performance of privately held, family-managed firms.*

Configurations and a System of Agency Threats. To this point, we have dealt with each agency threat and its corresponding governance mechanism as if their effects were independent and additive. The reality, however, is that agency threats tend to become causally and sequentially entwined in a manner that makes their effects difficult, if not impossible, to tease apart. Using our earlier example, failed labor markets may engender the threat of adverse selection, which in turn exacerbates the threat of moral hazard to privately held, family-managed firms. While these entwined effects make it nearly impossible to reliably trace a specific agency cost to a specific agency threat, they also make it possible that a given control mechanism, such as pay incentives or strategic planning, can simultaneously mitigate theoretically distinct agency threats. Bonds, for example, reduce the threat posed by adverse selection and moral hazard (McAfee and McMillan 1987). Governance mechanisms might also operate as a group, such that one governance mechanism can complement and/or substitute for another (Johnson et al. 1993, Rediker and Seth 1995).

Firms may therefore end up adopting a set of control mechanisms whose effects on agency costs are complementary and possibly synergistic. Over time, firms may bundle some or all of the governance mechanisms highlighted in our first four hypotheses into an internally consistent set or configuration of governance practices that addresses the agency problems which typically arise in privately held, family-managed firms (Ketchen et al. 1993). If successful, relationships among these governance mechanisms should be self-reinforcing, promoting enhanced control of agency costs and, presumably, firm performance.

Of course, not all family-managed firms have the same goals. Some parent owner-managers may make decisions based more on what is best for themselves than for their families, or on what is best for their families as opposed to what is best for the firm as a going concern. As a result, self-control problems can cause some owner-managers to refrain from commitments that limit their discretion, block the introduction of governance practices which limit their ability to use the firm's resources as they see fit, and take other actions, perhaps unintentionally, that undermine the effectiveness of current governance practices. The path to the control of agency costs in family firms might therefore be like a slippery slope, with one side leading to the adoption of a complimentary set of good governance practices, and the other side leading away from adoption of those practices. Our speculation about the complementary and self-reinforcing character of the relationships between agency costs and governance practice ground H5 and H6.

HYPOTHESIS 5 (H5). *Some privately held family-managed firms are characterized by a configuration of good governance practices, while others are not.*

HYPOTHESIS 6 (H6). *Privately held, family-managed firms characterized by a configuration of good governance practices will outperform firms that are not.*

Sample and Methods

Data. Reliable information on family firms is extremely difficult to obtain (Wortman 1994). Public information is unreliable because the majority of family firms are privately held and have no legal obligation to disclose information. Government documents and Dunn and Bradstreet are also of little use because family-managed firms are not listed as a separate category of business organization. Finally, it is difficult for researchers to collect primary data and/or target selected groups of family-managed firms for study because there is no reliable way to identify family firms a priori (Daily and Dollinger 1993). Consequently, researchers are forced to rely on self-reported data, sample from a broad population, and identify family-managed firms ex post (Daily and Dollinger 1992, 1993; Handler 1989).

We field-tested our hypotheses using data from a 1995 survey of American family businesses. The survey had been designed and administered by The Arthur Andersen Center for Family Business. One of the largest and most comprehensive surveys ever conducted on family firms (Gersick et al. 1997), it covers the range of agency issues that we address. Because all of the firms in the sample are privately held and the data are confidential and proprietary, we were unable to independently establish the data's reliability. Andersen's statisticians assure us, however, that they are reliable and representative of the sample.

While the use of secondary data can limit generalizability, Ilgen (1986) and Sackett and Larsen (1990, p. 435) point out that representativeness is less of a concern when the sample is prototypical of the relevant population and the research question concerns whether hypothesized effects can occur as opposed to determining the frequency or relative strength of the observed effects. The Arthur Andersen data are well suited to this task because the surveys were designed to obtain "reliable benchmarks" about American family businesses (Arthur Andersen & Co. 1995, p. 3).

Before mailing the survey to chief executives of 37,304 privately held U.S. family businesses, items in this survey were reviewed by a focus group of family-business owners and pilot-tested on a holdout sample. A single mailing yielded 3,860 responses within one month, or a response rate of 10.3% that is comparable to "the 10–12 percent rate typical for studies which target executives in upper echelons" (Geletkanycz 1998, Hambrick et al. 1993, Koch and McGrath 1996), and chief executives in small to mid-sized firms (MacDougall and Robinson 1990).

Because of the a priori selection problems, Andersen survey respondents range from "mom and pop" proprietorships to large family-managed corporations. We therefore applied a number of ex post screening criteria to the data. First, we deleted 334 partnerships and proprietorships because different laws and tax policies influence their share transfer and compensation practices. Second, we dropped 1,650 cases due to missing data about firm ownership and/or board composition, and another 297 due to some missing information about the other (15) variables included in the regression. (We tested and found no difference in performance or the mean values of our model's independent variables between cases that include data about ownership or board composition and those that do not). Finally, by deleting 203 firms that had $5 million or less in sales, we excluded "lifestyle firms,"—i.e., small firms that might be operated mainly for the purpose of income substitution—(Allen and Panian 1982), as well as others for whom growth may not be a strategic objective (Carland et al. 1984, Rubenson and Gupta 1996). Larger firms are less likely to be operated in this manner because the demands of managing them mitigate the family/CEO's primary motive for suppressing growth, to more easily maintain managerial and ownership control (Daily and Dollinger 1992, Whisler 1988). The final sample thus consists of 1,376 firms. Our average firm has annual sales of $36 million, has 195 employees, and has been in business for 49 years.

Dependent Variable. Consistent with Jensen's and Meckling's (1976) assertion that agency relationships

106

within the firm have a strong bearing on its growth rate, family-firm performance is defined in terms of sales growth. This is considered to be a more reliable measure of family-firm performance than income-based measures because privately held firms have incentive to minimize reported taxable income and no incentive to minimize reported sales (Daily and Dollinger 1992, Dess and Robinson 1984). Indeed, "The goal of a good family business should be to break even each year at a record high level of sales" (Dreux 1997). Finally, this measure is recommended by ecologists whenever private ownership or other factors make it difficult to obtain other organization-specific indicators of firm performance (Baum 1990, 1996; Baum and Singh 1996; Haveman 1993).

Like Cavusgil and Zou (1994), the Andersen survey measured *Sales Growth* as a five-year average, using a six-point, nominal scale ranging from Decreased, No Change, Increased 1–5%, Increased 6–10%, Increased 11–20%, to Increased 21% or more. The scale is appropriate because the construct is expected to be both right-censored (few firms experience sustained double-digit growth) and left-censored (few firms survive a sustained decline in sales). Although performance is self-reported, such measures have been shown to be reliable (Nayyar 1992, Tan and Litschert 1994), particularly when reported by executives on anonymous surveys (Dillman 1978, Nunnelly 1978). The impact of common-method bias, which arises when a common method (survey) is used to gather data about both independent and dependent variables, should be less here than it might be for other types of studies. Crampton and Wagner (1994) found that the percept-percept bias that results from common-method variance does not have the broad comprehensive effects that many have expected (though it does have a modest influence on bivariate relationships). Of good news to us is the finding that social desirability and other sources of bias are diminished when one or both of the variables are demographic, descriptive, and/or nonaffective, as are most of our variables. Spector (1987, p. 442) is more bold, stating that, "Method variance is a frequent criticism of research using affective and perceptual variables. The data and research summarized here suggest the problem may in fact be mythical."

Independent Variables. We use two items to proxy for incentive pay, *Family Pay Incentives* and *Nonfamily Pay Incentives*. Both are dummy variables (1/0) from the survey which identify firms that offer pay incentives as annual and/or long-term cash bonuses to family members or to nonfamily employees. Family firms "rely heavily on cash incentives" (Fraser 1990, p. 58) due to both a concern for maintaining control of the firm (Morck 1996),

and the fact that cash holds a greater incentive than stock for employees when the firm's equity is not publicly traded (Berk et al. 1988).[13] In total, 75% of the firms in our sample indicated that they offer pay incentives to family members, while 72% offered the same to nonfamily agents, figures fully consistent with the range reported in the four previously cited surveys. To assure that the use of these incentives is not influenced by variance with respect to the family's involvement in the firm, we include both the reported percentage of *Family Ownership* and the *Number of Family Members* employed by the firm as covariates in the regression. To assure that cash bonuses paid to family agents are indeed contingent portions of salary and not simply dividend payments that are distributed as salary bonuses to reduce the tax burden on family members, we identify firms that pay *Dividends* with a dummy variable, and include it as one of the eleven covariates described in the Appendix.

Strategic Planning (H2) is measured by asking if the firm has a strategic plan and how well these plans are known within the organization. We code the construct as a three-level categorical variable: "No Strategic Plan," "Strategic Plan Exists but is Not Well Known to Company Management," and "Strategic Plan is Well Known by Company Management."

We use three variables to proxy for board entrenchment (H3). *CEO Tenure* is measured with a 5-level scale, ranging from "11 or more years until retirement" to "Semi-retired," which conforms with other indirect measures of tenure available from the survey. For example, the bivariate correlation between CEO tenure and CEO age is high ($r = 0.62$, $p < 0.001$), particularly because scaling differences naturally deflate the correlation between the two variables. Also, the mean age of the CEO (54 years) and the mean age of the heir apparent at the time of this designation (38 years) differ, as expected, by about one generation. Like Finkelstein and Hambrick (1990), we measured *Average Board Tenure* as the average number of years each member has served on the board. Lastly, we measure *Outside Board Member* using a continuous variable to identify the number of outside directors (i.e., individuals who are neither family members nor employees, as a percentage of the total number of board directors). Our final variable, *Transfer Intentions* (H4), is measured with a dummy variable (1/0) that indicates whether significant shareholders of the business know each others' estate and share transfer intentions. Our notion that CEOs and major shareholders have incentive to keep this information confidential is supported by the fact that share and estate transfer plans are not known in approximately one-third of the firms.

W. S. SCHULZE, M. H. LUBATKIN, R. N. DINO, AND A. K. BUCHHOLTZ   *Agency Relationships in Family Firms*

Control Variables. We included eleven covariates to reduce variance that is extraneous to the research question or may confound interpretation: *Family Ownership, Number of Employed Family Members,* and *Dividends, Firm Size, Firm Age, Technological Intensity, Export Sales, Capital Intensity, Industry Growth Rate, Multiple Family Ownership,* and *Ownership Goal.* A complete description of each is provided in the Appendix.

Results

Table 1 contains descriptive statistics (unstandardized) and Pearson correlations while regression results are reported in Table 2. The F-statistic associated with the covariate set is 5.40 ($p \leq 0.00$), and the F-statistic associated with the set of seven hypothesized variables, after hierarchically adjusting for the set of eleven covariates, is 5.66 ($p \leq 0.00$).

Consistent with the notion that agency conditions in family-managed firms engender a variety of agency costs, the data indicate support for H1A but not H1B: A positive relationship is found for *Nonfamily Pay Incentives* ($p \leq 0.03$), but not for *Family Pay Incentives* ($p \leq 0.23$). The data also indicate support for H2 (*Strategic Planning* ($p \leq 0.04$) was positively related to firm performance) and for H3: *CEO Tenure* is negatively associated with firm performance ($p < 0.05$), *Average Board Tenure* ($p \leq 0.01$) and *Outside Directors* ($p \leq 0.00$). Finally, H4: *Transfer Intentions* is positively associated with firm performance ($p \leq 0.09$).

Using the seven independent variables used to test the first four hypotheses, we performed a complete linkage cluster analysis and identified two sets of internally consistent configurations of governance mechanisms posited by H5. Complete linkage is preferred because it requires potential cluster members to bear similarity to all members of the cluster (Norusis 1993). Following generally accepted procedures (Ketchen et al. 1993), we visually inspected dendograms to identify the number of clusters, and then confirmed cluster membership using K-means iterative partitioning. Table 3 shows the results of the cluster analysis along with a test of pairwise differences. Consistent with H5, two distinct profiles emerged, the one that shows generally high values for our seven governance variables and the other showing generally low values. Further, univariate F-statistics show that all but mean CEO tenure differ between groups as predicted. Finally, ANCOVA results (Table 4) confirm that the two profiles differ as predicted (H6) with respect to firm performance ($F = 5.11, p \leq 0.02$). This finding is consistent with the logic used in H5 to define "good" family governance practices.

Discussion

We attempt to explain why private ownership, owner management, and family do not eliminate the agency costs of ownership. Drawing on various economic theories, we describe problems that accompany private ownership and owner management, noting that each exposes the firm to agency problems that are overlooked by the J/M model. Next, we inferred that agency problems may be more pronounced in family-managed firms due to self-control and other agency threats engendered by altruism. Conflict of interests, both within and among family-firm owners, combine with the effects of external market failures to threaten performance in this type of privately held, owner-managed firm. Contrary to conventional wisdom, we conclude it is essential that family-managed firms incur agency costs (i.e., invest in the kinds of internal control mechanisms that are deemed necessary for widely held firms). Secondary data from 1,376 family firms yielded evidence that is consistent with our thesis. Thus, owner management in general, and family ownership in particular, may not be the kind of governance panacea that agency theory assumes it to be.

Ironically, the tenets of the J/M model may have prevented this governance theory from being explicitly extended to privately held, family-managed firms, a domain "plagued by conflict" and governance failures (Levinson 1971, p. 90; Meyer and Zucker 1989). We try to suggest such an extension, and point the way toward a fruitful research agenda. In addition to further research on privately held, family-managed firms, the influence of family management on public corporations merits investigation. There is a need to develop more fully specified agency models for different types of owner-managed or privately held firms (e.g., new ventures). Finally, our theory underscores the importance of incorporating both altruism and the agency problem of self-control into existing agency literature.

Our agency model of the family firm and our empirical results also extend understanding of the owner management/firm performance relationship that was theorized by Stulz (1988) and empirically examined by Demsetz and Lehn (1985), McConnell and Servaes (1990), and Morck et al. (1988). Specifically, these studies found that the impact of the market for corporate control on owner conduct is positive up to the point that insider ownership is about 40 and 50 percent, after which the relationship begins to slope downward. Due to theoretical and sampling restrictions,[14] however, these studies are silent about the nature of the slope at higher levels of inside ownership. Our study, the first to theorize and examine this relationship in privately held family-managed firms (see Endnote

W. S. SCHULZE, M. H. LUBATKIN, R. N. DINO, AND A. K. BUCHHOLTZ   *Agency Relationships in Family Firms*

Table 1   Descriptive Statistics[1]

Variable	Mean	S.D.	1	2	3	4	5	6	7	8	9	10	11	12	13	14	15	16	17	18
1. Sales Growth	3.96	1.38	—																	
2. Sales Revenues	36.21	83.79	0.08	—																
3. Company Age	49.47	27.44	-0.12	0.05	—															
4. Family Ownership (%)	73.40	38.60	0.03	-0.12	-0.02	—														
5. Industry Growth	0.56	0.49	0.07	0.03	-0.01	-0.08	—													
6. Capital Intensity	0.70	0.45	0.05	0.06	-0.01	-0.03	0.51	—												
7. Multiple Family Ownership	1.16	0.53	0.02	0.02	-0.02	-0.07	0.02	-0.01	—											
8. No. Family Employees	3.47	2.06	0.05	0.08	0.02	-0.06	0.03	-0.02	-0.06	—										
9. Export Sales	1.51	0.81	0.08	0.08	0.03	-0.06	0.27	0.19	-0.03	-0.03	—									
10. Ownership Goal	1.61	0.92	0.05	-0.03	-0.04	0.03	0.10	0.07	-0.02	-0.13	-0.06	—								
11. IT Intensity	3.08	0.91	0.15	0.16	-0.01	0.07	-0.01	0.04	0.03	-0.03	-0.03	0.10	—							
12. Dividends	0.17	0.37	-0.02	0.08	0.08	-0.05	0.02	0.03	0.03	0.07	0.04	0.03	0.01	—						
13. Nonfamily Pay Incentives	0.72	0.45	0.15	0.15	-0.06	0.03	-0.04	-0.08	-0.06	-0.05	0.06	0.06	-0.02	0.09	—					
14. Family Pay Incentives	0.75	0.43	0.17	0.09	-0.01	0.06	-0.05	-0.07	0.02	-0.04	0.06	0.02	0.01	0.04	0.03	—				
15. Strategic Planning	1.41	1.36	0.08	0.13	0.04	0.02	0.02	0.03	0.03	-0.05	0.09	0.09	-0.01	0.03	0.08	0.61	—			
16. Outside Board Member	0.06	0.18	-0.06	0.16	0.05	-0.10	0.09	0.04	-0.01	-0.11	0.11	0.11	0.04	0.18	-0.01	0.04	0.04	—		
17. CEO Tenure	2.42	1.12	-0.07	-0.11	-0.09	0.01	0.02	-0.01	-0.01	0.11	-0.04	-0.04	-0.11	0.05	0.14	0.06	0.01	0.08	—	
18. Average Board Tenure	17.34	7.61	-0.05	0.02	0.05	0.06	0.03	-0.02	0.02	0.10	-0.11	-0.11	-0.02	-0.06	-0.02	-0.03	-0.03	-0.02	-0.03	—
19. Transfer Intentions	0.67	0.46	0.02	-0.07	-0.01	-0.01	-0.12	0.04	-0.04	-0.05	-0.07	-0.08	0.04	0.08	0.01	-0.05	0.15	-0.06	0.01	0.04

Note. [1]$N = 1,376$; Correlations larger than 0.06 are significant at $p \leq 0.05$

W. S. SCHULZE, M. H. LUBATKIN, R. N. DINO, AND A. K. BUCHHOLTZ   *Agency Relationships in Family Firms*

Table 2   Moderated Hierarchical Regressions

Variables	Sales Growth
1. Sales Revenue	0.07**
2. Company Age	−0.11***
3. Family Ownership (%)	0.01
4. Industry Growth	0.08**
5. Capital Intensity	−0.00
6. Multiple Family Ownership	0.01
7. No. Family Employees	0.04
8. Export Sales	0.03
9. Ownership Goal	0.04
10. IT Intensity	0.08**
11. Dividends	0.00
12. Nonfamily Pay Incentives	0.07*
13. Family Pay Incentives	0.04
14. Strategic Planning	0.06*
15. Outside Board Member	−0.08**
16. CEO Tenure	−0.05*
17. Average Board Tenure	0.07**
18. Transfer Intentions	0.05†

$F_{covariate}$	5.40***
$F_{regression}$	5.66***
R^2	0.07
Adj R^2	0.06
N	1,376

Note. $p \leq 10$†; $p \leq 0.05$*; $p \leq 0.01$**; $p \leq 0.001$***

Table 3   Results of Analysis of Variance: Governance Profiles

Variable	Profile One Mean/sd	Profile Two Mean/sd	Univariate F
1. Nonfamily Pay Incentives	0.70 (0.45)	0.75 (0.43)	4.05*
2. Family Pay Incentives	0.73 (0.44)	0.79 (0.41)	6.05*
3. Strategic Planning	0.04 (0.20)	2.66 (0.47)	206.10***
4. Outside Board Member	0.05 (0.13)	0.09 (0.20)	20.34***
5. CEO Tenure	2.42 (1.16)	2.43 (1.12)	0.00
6. Average Board Tenure	17.78 (7.68)	16.97 (7.55)	4.48*
7. Transfer Intentions	0.61 (0.49)	0.75 (0.43)	37.36***
N	771	882	

Note. $p \leq 10$†; $p \leq 0.05$*; $p \leq 0.01$**; $p \leq 0.001$***

Table 4   Results of ANCOVA Test of Performance Difference Between Governance Profiles

Variable	F
Model	6.78***
1. Sales Revenue	6.80**
2. Company Age	31.94***
3. Family Ownership (%)	0.89
4. Industry Growth	4.37*
5. Capital Intensity	0.87
6. Multiple Family Ownership	0.38
7. No. Family Employees	3.13†
8. Export Sales	0.49
9. Ownership Goal	1.75
10. IT Intensity	13.88***
11. Dividends	0.49
12. Governance Profile	5.10**
R^2	0.07
N	1376

Note. $p \leq 10$†; $p \leq 0.05$*; $p \leq 0.01$**; $p \leq 0.001$***

1), shows that ownership structure engenders various agency threats to firm performance, threats that originate with altruism, market failures, and self-control.

The importance of altruism in the family firm should not be understated. Litz (1995) and others have struggled with the question of whether family firms represent a form of governance that is theoretically distinct from other closely held forms. In our view, altruism makes agency relationships in these owner-managed firms different from those found in other organizational forms, a notion consistent with Litz and others who suggest that family firms are distinguished by both the active involvement of family in firm management and the intent that future ownership will remain in the hands of family members. Our theoretical approach allows us to specify, in relatively precise terms, how altruism alters agency relationships and hence owner-manager conduct, and to show how many of the assumed benefits of family owner management are offset by agency costs as well as other costs of ownership (see Endnote 4). In this light, altruism helps explain why family firms can ask for and receive the types of employee self-sacrifice and commitment required to found and grow firms, and yet have so much difficulty managing conflict. A better understanding of these dynamics may explain why family-controlled and family-managed firms are, in fact, more common than ostensibly superior widely held firms (La Porta et al. 1999).

Why do a large percentage of the firms in our sample

Governance and Ownership

offer pay incentives to family agents, even though these incentives do not appear to be positively associated with firm performance? The justice literature suggests that if pay incentives are offered to nonfamily agents to motivate them and signal professionalism, then fairness concerns may obligate the family-firm CEO to do the same for family agents. We would then expect a null performance effect, because the principal purpose of the family agent pay incentive is to avoid the harm that the perceived inequities might cause, rather than to enhance firm performance. Altruism, on the other hand, can make parent owner-managers unable or unwilling to properly administer incentive programs. The altruist's ability to enforce agreements is often compromised by the ramifications that such actions might have on familial relationships, both within and among the extended family. Both phenomenons, if carried into the family firm, make it difficult for owner-managers to discipline family agents and enforce agreements. The Small Business Administration, for example, reports that family business owners find it extremely difficult to fire relatives (Levinson 1989), and a well-intentioned family-firm CEO recently told us that he felt obligated to give a car to every family member employed by the firm after giving a company car to the child responsible for outside sales!

Another possibility is that well-governed firms show higher levels of firm performance and are more apt to offer pay incentives to family agents than those that are not, suggesting that family agent pay incentives may contribute to superior performance when coupled with other complementary governance mechanisms, and yet have a negligible independent effect on firm performance. More research and different research designs are needed to sort out which explanation is responsible for our results.

Why does outsider representation on family-firm boards show a significant negative independent effect on firm performance? While Ford (1988) found the same, our findings are nevertheless at odds with the conventional understanding of the role of outsider directors. First, consistent with the logic of H3, outside directors may be ineffective because they lack the independence they enjoy when serving on the boards of widely held firms. Second, the observed relationship might be spurious if the relatively few firms that placed outsiders on the board (only 19% percent of our sample) have done so because they were *already* experiencing performance problems.[15] Third, the independent performance effect of outsiders may not tell the whole story, because well-governed family firms show higher overall levels of outsider representation than do firms in the poorly governed configuration. As with pay incentives, outsiders may impart a positive effect only when coupled with complementary governance mechanisms.

Finally, this anomaly could be the product of ineffective governance, and not evidence that outside directors, when properly used, threaten the performance of family firms. For example, few firms in the sample have outside directors, the average board size is four members, and board directors, as a rule, are not compensated for the one to two meetings that the average firm in this sample held each year. In contrast, family firm experts recommend that these boards have 30 to 40 percent outside representation, consist of five to nine member boards, and compensate directors for meeting frequently (Nash 1988). Lin (1996) agrees, citing the need to expand the board to include more outside directors, hold frequent meetings, delegate certain tasks to outside directors, offer director compensation, and limit director tenure.

The findings for pay incentives and board representation from the cluster analysis are intriguing because they highlight the complementary and self-reinforcing nature of governance mechanisms. Furthermore, they may explain why some family firms, prosper while others fail. Simply put, and as our fifth and sixth hypotheses suggest, there may be two types of family firms, one that recognizes the need to adopt the kind of internal governance mechanisms used by successful widely held firms to compensate for the agency problems that they face, and another that does not.

The slippery slope leading to poor governance and an increased risk of firm failure is not the product of malevolent leadership. To the contrary, altruism adds a distinctive set of self-control problems to those that arise from being privately held and owner-managed, making it very difficult for family-business owners to make decisions that represent their own best interests, much less those of the firm or other family members. For example, altruism can make a well-intentioned family CEO a "bad agent" in the sense that the CEO's generosity increases the threat of moral hazard within the firm. Similarly, a heartfelt concern for the firm's prosperity may cause some CEOs to remain in office long after they have ceased to be effective, harming firm performance and increasing the agency costs of hold-up. Interestingly, while neither act is selfish in the conventional sense—both require that CEOs sacrifice their own welfare for the ostensible benefit of others—altruism explains why these behaviors are common and yet so difficult to circumscribe. We attribute the persistence of these and other family-firm behaviors to the firm's incentive structure, the context in which governance decision are made, and the trade-offs these decisions involve, as opposed to family conflict or the host of other situationally dependent variables often cited in the family-business literature (Gersick et al. 1997, Wortman 1994).

W. S. SCHULZE, M. H. LUBATKIN, R. N. DINO, AND A. K. BUCHHOLTZ   *Agency Relationships in Family Firms*

This study suggests a theoretical grounding for this economically important yet underresearched domain of firms. The purpose of this empirical study was to lend credibility to our concepts, not to confirm their validity. Indeed, we cannot claim that our tests were confirmatory because we used cross-sectional data and relied upon survey data gathered for other purposes. However, we think these tests lend credibility to our theory because the firms represented by the Andersen survey are prototypical of a population of firms that is rarely studied and whose data are difficult (and quite expensive) to obtain (Gersick et al. 1997, p. 25 Sackett and Larsen 1990). The size of the sample also gives us sufficient power to detect small effects and yet conclude with a high degree of confidence that these results are not the product of chance. Although some of the measures are coarser than we would have liked (i.e., the use of categorical instead of continuous measures), that coarseness also lends a conservative bias to the analysis, because categorical measures deflate the amount of variance explained by the regression equation, as well as the likelihood of obtaining significant results (Hunter and Schmidt 1990). We are also encouraged that these coarse indicators produced results consistent with those of other studies (e.g., the influence of outside directors on firm performance and these firms' use of incentive compensation), and that, despite the quality of the measures and the use of eleven covariates, the general pattern of positive and negative results is consistent with theory. This consistency lends convergent validity to our measures and results.

Family business research to date has been hampered by the absence of well-developed theory, as well as by a paucity of data about this important segment of the economy (Wortman 1994). Our extension of agency theory to this domain, coupled with the Arthur Andersen data, helps to illuminate the insidious character of agency problems in family firms while paving the way to future avenues for research.

Acknowledgments

The authors would like to thank Jack Veiga, Steve Floyd, Deborah Kidder, Peter Lane, and the anonymous reviewers at *Organization Science* for their encouragement and critique of earlier versions of the paper. Survey data were provided courtesy of the Arthur Andersen Center for Family Business. The support of the Family Business Program at the University of Connecticut is also acknowledged.

Appendix

Description of the Eleven Covariates Employed in the Study

Eleven covariates were included to reduce variance that is extraneous to the research question or may confound interpretation. We controlled for *Firm Size* using the log transformation of total firm sales to correct for its skewed distribution. We controlled for *Firm Age* by using a continuous measure calibrated in years. Age may be linked to performance due to a self-selection bias; older firms might be present simply because they are successful. Differences in rates of sales growth associated with *Export Sales* are controlled using a five-level indicator ranging from 0 through >50%. Variance in performance and agency due to *Technological Intensity* is controlled using an item which asked: *How important are investments in information technology for the accomplishment of your future goals?* This item is measured with a four-level scale, ranging from *Not Important* to *Very Important*. The potential influence of *Multiple Family Ownership* on the CEO's ability to determine compensation and other management practices is controlled with a dummy variable that identifies firms in which two or more families own at least 15% of the firm. We controlled for the *Number of Employed Family Members*, because family compensation practices should have more impact in firms that employ a larger number of family members. We use *Family Ownership* to control for the effect of ownership concentration on governance practices, measuring this variable as the reported percentage of the firm's shares held by the eight largest family shareholders. It is not necessary to use an independent control for the percentage of firm ownership represented on the board because it is empirically indistinguishable from the reported percentage of the firm owned by family members. (The correlation between the two is 0.96). Finally, an item which asked the respondent to rate the likelihood that the family will retain control of the firm in the foreseeable future, *Ownership Goal*, controls for variance in the strategic direction of the family firm.

We also control for *Capital Intensity*, because the agency effects of debt (Fama 1980) are likely to have greater salience in capital-intensive, as opposed to non-capital-intensive industries. Because the industry categories identified in the Andersen survey do not correspond directly to SIC-based industry descriptions, *Capital Intensity* was coded 1 if the mean on the reported debt/equity ratio for the industry category was greater than the median debt/equity ratio for all industry categories, and 0 if below the median. The resulting dummy variable thus identifies industries which rely more heavily on debt relative to other industries. Another dummy variable, *Industry Growth*, controls for variation in sales growth across the industries represented in the sample and is coded in the same manner. While coarse-grained, the resulting measures distinguish capital-intensive industries (e.g., manufacturing, real estate, and transportation), from those that are not (e.g., retail and other service-based industries), as well as industries that enjoyed high levels of sales growth during this period (e.g., manufacturing and telecommunications), from those that did not. Further, we were unable to employ financial statistics derived from SIC-based data for control purposes because such data includes information from large, widely held businesses whose capital structure differs markedly from that of family firms.

Endnotes

[1] We identified only one study that examined these firms in the *Academy of Management Journal* (Trostel and Nichols 1982) and only three such studies in *Administrative Science Quarterly* (Trow 1961, Davis 1968, Geeraerts 1984). The bulk of existing research has been published by a fairly recently founded journal, *The Family Business Review*. We updated Chrisman et al. (1996) to find the number of articles published by major journals since 1956. They are: *Harvard Business Review* (17), *Entrepreneurship, Theory and Practice* (8), *Organization Dynamics*

(5), *Journal of Small Business Management* (7), *Administrative Science Quarterly* (3), *Human Relations* (3), *Sloan Management Review* (2), *Academy of Management Journal* (1), *Academy of Management Review* (1), *Journal of Management* (1), *Journal of Management Studies* (1), *Organization Studies* (1), and *Journal of Business Venturing* (2).

[2]The Internal Revenue Service (1996) reports that about 215,000 U.S. firms had $5 million or more in annual revenues. Of these, only 15,000 were widely-held corporations (i.e., listed by the NASDAQ, NYSE, or other exchange). While we do not know the precise figure (neither the government nor Dun and Bradstreet track this data), experts estimate that sixty to eighty percent are likely to be family managed (Gersick et al. 1997, *The Economist* 1996). These estimates are consistent with the results of the 1993 National Survey of Small Business Finance, conducted by the Federal Reserve, which found that a single family controlled at least 50% of the ownership in approximately 65% of the firms that had more than $5 million in revenue.

Family ownership of public corporations is also important. In their authoritative study of corporate ownership around the world, La Porta, Lopez-de-Salanes, and Shleifer (1999) found that family members participate in the management of at least 69% of the firms they control. (Control is defined as 10% ownership). Moreover, families on average control 35% of the largest firms in the richest countries in the world, compared to the 24% that are widely held and the 20% that are controlled by the state. Family control becomes more prevalent as firm size falls, with families controlling approximately 53% of the world's medium-sized firms ($500 million in revenues), compared to the 20% that are state-controlled and 11% that are widely held. (The remaining percentage of firms in these samples are owned by financial institutions or by cooperatives, trusts, or other groups that lack a single controlling investor).

Of course, the importance of family management varies greatly around the world. In the United States and Canada, families control about 30% of the largest public firms and directly participate in the management in about a third of them (*Forbes* 2000, Kang 2000). And while families control only 10% of the largest firms in Australia, Japan, Finland, and Germany, they control 50% of the largest firms in Belgium and Israel, 55% in Sweden, 65% in Argentina and Greece, 70% in Hong Kong, and 100% in Mexico (La Porta et al. 1999). As these statistics indicate, the influence of the family on firm governance is an important but astonishingly neglected topic in management research.

[3]While we focus on the 1976 J/M model due to its clarity and widespread acceptance, our discussion of that model is informed by more recent research, including Fama (1980), Fama and Jensen (1983a, 1983b, 1985), Jensen (1993, 1994, 1998), Jensen and Meckling (1995) and Jensen and Murphy (1990). Important exceptions and/or modifications to the 1976 J/M model by these or other researchers are noted.

[4]More formally, Fama and Jensen (1985, p. 118) state that the "restriction of residual claims (to decision agents) avoids the costs of controlling agency problems between decision agents and residual claimants, but at the cost of inefficiency in risk-bearing and a tendency toward under-investment." The effect is that the choice of organizational form (i.e., public vs. private) involves a trade-off between agency costs and other costs that accompany private ownership. These other costs arise because "The residual claimant-decision agents (of closed corporations) tend to choose lower levels of investment in plant, equipment, etc. that reduce future production costs, and they choose different

technology than when residual claims allow unrestricted risk-bearing arrangements. These organizations survive in the face of such inefficiency when the agency costs that are avoided by restricting residual claims to decision agents exceed the higher costs induced by forgone investments and inefficiency in residual riskbearing" (Fama and Jensen 1985, p. 119). Of course, the conclusion that private ownership and family management reduce the efficiency (and hence value) of the firm is somewhat at odds with La Porta et al., (1999: 28) who conclude that "by far the dominant form of controlling ownership in the world is not that by banks or corporations but by families."

[5]Akerloff (1972) observed that inefficient markets lower the average quality and price of goods traded. Ironically, poor-quality goods occasionally get a premium price and attract more poor-quality goods, further suppressing average product quality. The lemon effect, in this manner, sorts markets by the quality of the goods and services offered. Besanko et al. (1996) describe the effect of sorting in labor markets on managerial talent in their text.

[6]The threat of hold-up explains, at least in part, why firms grant some executives and other potentially valuable employees stock options as terms of employment. This "bond" protects the prospective agent from employer (owner) opportunism (Reagan and Stulz 1986).

[7]The model recognizes that conflicts of interest arise with fractional ownership of the firm because every owners' ability and/or willingness to bear risk varies with the relative size of their stake in the firm and their personal preference for risk (Fama and Jensen 1983a, 1983b; Reagan and Stulz 1986; Wiseman and Gomez-Mejia 1998). For example, owners who have a large portion of their wealth invested in the firm may prefer less risk than more diversified investors, and older owners are likely to be more risk averse than younger owners.

[8]While single-preference utility functions are the norm in neoclassical economics, dual-preference utility functions are found in a variety of literatures (Lunati 1997, p. 28), including the economic theory of the household (Becker 1974), public choice (Buchanan 1975), cooperation (Arthur 1991, Margolis 1982), and sociobiology (Krebs 1987, Nowak and May 1992).

[9]Jensen (1994: 45) states "Constrained at the time (1976) by our economists' view of rationality, Meckling and I discussed only one source of agency costs, that which emanate from the conflicts of interests between people. There is clearly a second major source of agency costs, the costs incurred as a result of self control problems . . ."

[10]While this definition of altruism is "impure" in the sense that it views altruism as being driven, at least in part, by exchange, it is common, and "for many (economists) the only acceptable" approach to altruism (Lunati 1997, p. 22). She and Piliavan and Charng (1990) explore the implications of this definition at length.

[11]Family members are de facto owners of the firm in the sense that each acts in the belief that they have a residual claim on the family's wealth, and/or the right to have a say in determining its use (Holtz-Eakin et al. 1993, Stark and Falk 1998). This belief is not only enhanced by the extent to which altruistic CEOs grant family members perquisites and privileges, but also in the common law which, in the absence of a will, distributes the family estate in equal shares among the surviving members.

[12]Family-firm CEOs most frequently identify attorneys and accountants as their closest and most trusted advisors (Arthur Andersen & Co. 1995, Ward and Handy 1988). Gersick et al. (1997) lament their tendency to name them to their boards.

[13]While some suggest the control problem is ostensibly solved by using phantom or shadow stock plans—classes of stock which are not publicly traded, but accrue value according to an established formula—a variety of factors limit their use (Berk et al. 1998, Lew and Kolodzeij 1993). Statistics bear this out. A 1990 *INC* survey (Fraser 1990) found that fewer than 5% of the INC 500 firms used phantom or shadow stock as incentives. In our sample, only 4% have shadow stock plans and/or use them as part of their compensation packages.

[14]Stulz (1988) attributes the nonlinear relationship between owner management and firm performance to the failure in the market for corporate control. The domain of Stulz's theory is limited, however, because market failures should have no influence on owner conduct once inside ownership exceeds 50%. Our theory is not subject to this limitation because external market failure is but one of the multiple sources of agency costs.

[15]We were unable to identify any statistical difference between the performance of firms with outside directors and those without.

References

Akerloff, G. A. 1972. The market for "lemons": Quality, uncertainty, and the market mechanism. *Quart. J. Econom.* **84** 488–500.

Alchian, A. A., Woodward, S. 1988. The firm is dead: Long live the firm. A review of Oliver E. Williamson's, *The economic institutions of capitalism. J. Econom. Literature* **26** 65–79.

Alderfer, C. P. 1988. Understanding and consulting to family business boards. *Family Bus. Rev.* **1**(3) 249–261.

Allen, M. P., S. K. Panian. 1982. Power, performance, and succession in the large corporation. *Admin. Sci Quart.* **27** 538–547.

Andersen, E. 1985. The salesperson as outside agent or employee: A transaction cost analysis. *Marketing Sci.* **4**(3) 234–254.

Arrow, K. J. 1963. *Social Choice and Individual Values.* Wiley, New York.

Arthur Andersen & Co. 1995. 1995 *American Family Business Survey.* Arthur Andersen Center for Family Business, St. Charles, IL.

Arthur, W. B. 1991. Designing economic agents that act like human agents: A behavioral approach to bounded rationality. *Amer. Econom. Rev.* **81**(2) 353–359.

Barnes, L. B., S. A. Hershon. 1976. Transferring power in the family business. *Harvard Bus. Rev.* **54**(4) 105–114.

Baum, J. A. C. 1990. Inertial and adaptive patterns in the dynamics of organizational change. J. L. Wall, L. R. Jauch, eds. *Acad. Management Pro.* San Francisco, CA, 165–169.

——. 1996. Organization ecology. S. R. Clegg, C. A. Haroy, W. R. Nord, eds. *Handbook of Organization Studies.* Sage, London, U.K. 77–114.

——, J. V. Singh. 1996. Dynamics of organizational responses to competition. *Social Forces,* **74**(4), 1237–62.

Becker, G. S. 1974. A theory of social interaction. *J. Political Economy* **82** 1063–1093.

——. 1981. *A Treatise on the Family.* Harvard University Press, Cambridge, MA.

——, K. M. Murphy. 1988. A theory of rational addiction. *J. Political Economy* **96**(4) 675–700.

Beckhard, R., W. G. Dyer Jr. 1983. Managing continuity in the family owned business. *Organ. Dynam.* (Summer) 5–12.

Bergstrom, T. C. 1989. A fresh look at the rotten kid theorem and other household mysteries. *J. Political Economy* **97** 1138–1159.

——. 1995. On the evolution of altruistic rules for siblings. *Amer. Econom. Rev.* **85**(5) 58–81.

Berk, K. H., J. A. Hechtman, K. A. Goldstein. 1998. The competitive edge: Creating attractive incentive plans for privately-held entities. *J. Corporate Taxation* **25**(2) 133–148.

Besanko, D., D. Dranove, M. Shanley. 1996. *Economics of Strategy.* John Wiley & Sons, New York.

Buchanan, J. M. 1975. The Samaritan's dilemma. E. S. Phelps, ed. *Altruism, Morality and Economic Theory.* Russell Sage Foundation, New York.

Carland, J. W., F. Hoy, W. Boulton, J. A. C. Carland. 1984. Differentiating entrepreneurs from small business owners: A conceptualization. *Acad. Management Rev.* **9** 354–359.

Cavusgil, S. T., S. Zou. 1994. Marketing-strategy performance relationship: An investigation of the empirical link in export market ventures. *J. Marketing* **58** 1–21.

Chami, R. 1997. What's different about family business? Working paper series, file no. 98061505, Social Science Research Network: Organizations and Markets Abstracts, Internet.

Chrisman, J. J., J. Chua, P. Sharma. 1996. *A Review and Annotated Bibliography of Family Business Studies.* Kluwer Academic Publishers, Boston, MA.

Cohen, J., P. Cohen. 1983. *Applied Multiple Regression/Correlation Analysis for the Behavioral Sciences.* Lawrence Erlbaum Associates, Hillsdale, NJ.

Crampton, S. M., J. A. Wagner. 1994. Percept-percept inflation in microorganizational research: An investigation of prevalence and effect *J. Applied Psych.* **79**(1) 67–76.

Daily, C. M., M. J. Dollinger. 1992. An empirical examination of ownership structure in family and professionally-managed firms. *Family Bus. Rev.* **5**(2) 117–136.

——, ——. 1993. Alternative methods for identifying family vs. nonfamily managed small businesses. *J. Small Bus. Management* **31**(2) 79–90.

Davis, S. M. 1968. Entrepreneurial succession. *Admin. Sci. Quart.* **13** 402–416.

Demsetz, H., K. Lehn. 1985. The structure of corporate ownership: Causes and consequences. *J. Law and Econom.* **26** 375–390.

Dess, G. D., R. B. Robinson. 1984. Measuring organizational performance in the absence of objective measures: The case of the privately held firm and conglomerate business unit. *Strategic Management J.* **5** 265–273.

Dillman, D. A. 1978, *Mail and Telephone Surveys: The Total Design Method.* John Wiley, New York.

Dreux, D. R. IV. 1997. Invited research symposia. 1997 International Family Business Program Association, Northhampton, MA.

Economist. 1996. In praise of the family firm (editorial). **46** (March 9).

Eisenhardt, K. M. 1989. Agency theory: An assessment and review. *Acad. Management Rev.* **1** 57–74.

Eshel, I., L. Samuelson, A. Shaked. 1998. Altruists, egoists, and holligans in a local interaction model. *Amer. Econom. Rev.* **88**(1) 157–179.

Fama, E. 1980. Agency problems and the theory of the firm. *J. Political Economy* **88** 288–307.

Fama, E., M. C. Jensen. 1983a. Agency problems and residual claims. *J. Law and Econom.* **26** 325–344.

——, ——. 1983b. Separation of ownership and control. *J. Law and Econom.* **26** 301–325.

——, ——. 1985. Organizational forms and investment decisions. *J. of Financial Econom.* **14** 101–119.

Federal Reserve Board of Governors. 1994. *National Survey of Small Business Finances.*⟨www.federalreserv.gov⟩.

Finkelstein, S., R. A. D'Aveni. 1994. CEO duality as a double-edged sword: How boards of directors balance entrenchment avoidance and unity of command. *Acad. Management J.* **37**(5) 1079–1108.

——, D. C. Hambrick. 1990. Top management team tenure and organizational outcomes: The moderating role of managerial discretion. *Admin. Sci. Quart.* **35** 484–503.

——, ——. 1996. *Strategic Leadership: Top Executives and their Effects on Organizations.* West, St Paul, MN.

Forbes. 2000. Are dynasties dying? **165**(6) 126–131.

Ford, R. H. 1988. Outside directors and privately-held firms: Are they necessary? *Entrepreneurship Theory and Practice* **13**(1) 49–57.

Fraser, J. A. 1990. Executive compensation survey: Missed opportunities. *INC Magazine* **12**(11).

Geeraerts, G. 1984. The effect of ownership on the organization structure in small firms. *Admin. Sci. Quart.* **29** 232–237.

Geletkanycz, M. A. 1998. The salience of 'Culture's Consequences:' The effect of cultural values on top executive commitment to the status quo. *Strategic Management J.* **18**(8) 615–634.

Gersick, K. E., J. A. Davis, M. M. Hampton, I. Lansberg. 1997. *Generation to Generation: Life Cycles of the Family Business.* Harvard Business School Press, Cambridge, MA.

Greco, S. 1997. Employee package deal. *INC Magazine* **19**(15) 30.

Hambrick, D. C., G. D. S. Fukutomi. 1991. The seasons of a CEO's tenure. *Acad. Management Rev.,* **16**(4) 719–742.

——, M. A. Geletkanycz, J. A. Fredrickson. 1993 Top executive commitment to the status quo: Some tests of its determinants. *Strategic Management J.* **14**(6) 401–418.

Handler, W. C. 1989. Methodological issues and considerations in studying family business. *Family Bus. Rev.* **1**(4) 257–276.

——. 1990. Succession in owner-managed and family firms. A mutual role adjustment between the entrepreneur and the next generation. *Entrepreneurship Theory and Practice* **15**(19) 37–51.

Hansmann, H. 1996. *The Ownership of Enterprise.* Harvard University Press, Cambridge, MA.

Haveman, H. A. 1993. Follow the leader: Mimetic isomorphism and entry into new markets. *Admin. Sci. Quart.* **38** 593–627.

Hirschhorn, L., T. Gilmore. 1980. The application of family therapy concepts to influencing organization behavior. *Admin. Sci. Quart.* **25** 18–37.

Holtz-Eakin, D., D. Joulfian, H. S. Rosen. 1993. The Carnagie conjecture: Some empirical evidence. *Quart. J. Econom.* **108** 413–435.

Hunter, J. E., F. L. Schmidt. 1990. *Methods of Meta-analysis: Connecting Error and Bias in Research Findings.* Sage, Newbury Park, CA.

Ilgen, D. R. 1986. Laboratory research: A question of when, not if. E. A. Locke, ed. *Generalizing from Laboratory to Field Settings.* Heath, Lexington, MA. 257–267.

INC Magazine. 1996. INC 500 Almanac, 1997. **17**(15) 23–26.

Internal Revenue Service. 1996 returns of active corporations: Selected balance sheet, income statement, and tax items by industrial division and size of business receipts.

Jensen, M. C. 1993. The modern industrial revolution, exit, and the failure of internal control systems. *J. Finance* **48**(3) 831–880.

——. 1994. Self-interest, altruism, incentives, and agency. J. Appl. Corporate Finance. **7**(2).

——. 1998. Self-interest, altruism, incentives, and agency. *Foundations of Organizational Strategy.* Harvard University Press, Cambridge, MA.

——, W. H. Meckling. 1976. Theory of the firm: Managerial behavior, agency costs, and ownership structure. *J. Financial Econom.* **3** 305–360.

——, ——. 1995. Specific and general knowledge and organization structure. *J. Applied Corporate Finance,* **8**(2) 4–18.

——, K. Murphy. 1990. Performance pay and top management incentives. *J. Political Economy* **98** 225–263.

——, C. L. Smith. 1985. Stockholder, manager and creditor interests: Applications of agency theory. E. I. Altman, M. G. Subrahmanyam, eds. *Recent Advances in Corporate Finance.* Irwin, Homewood, IL. 95–131.

Johnson, R. A., R. E. Hoskisson, M. A. Hitt. 1993. Board of director involvement in restructuring: The effects of board versus managerial controls and characteristics. *Strategic Management J.* **14**(Summer) 33–50.

Kang, D. 2000. The impact of family ownership on performance in public organizations: A study of the U.S. Fortune 500, 1982–1994. 2000 Academy of Management Meetings, Toronto, Canada.

Ketchen, D. J. Jr., J. B. Thomas, C. C. Snow. 1993. Organizational configurations and performance: A comparison of theoretical approaches. *Acad. Management J.* **36**(6) 1279–1314.

Kets De Vries, M. 1996. *Family Business: Human Dilemmas in the Family Firm.* Thomson Business Press, London, U.K.

Koch, M. J., R. G. McGrath. 1996. Improving labor productivity: Human resource management policies do matter. *Strategic Management J.* **17**(5) 335–354.

Krebs, D. 1987. The challenge of altruism in biology and psychology. C. Crawford, M. Smith, D. Krebs, eds. *Sociobiology and Psychology.* Erlbaum, Hillsdale, N.J.

La Porta, R., F. Lopez-de-Salanes, A. Shleifer. 1999. Corporate ownership around the world. *J. Finance* **54**(2) 471–517.

Levinson, H. 1971. Conflicts that plague family business. *Harvard Bus. Rev.* (March–April) **49** 90–98.

Levinson, R. E. 1989. Problems in managing a family owned business. Business Development Publication MP3, Small Business Administration, ⟨www.sba.gov⟩.

Lew, M. I., E. A. Kolodzeii. 1993. Compensation in a family-owned business. *Human Resources Professional* **5**(3) 55–57.

Lin, L. 1996. The effectiveness of outside directors as corporate governance mechanism: Theories and evidence. *Northwestern University Law Rev.* **90** 898–951.

Litz, R. A. 1995. The family business: Toward definitional clarity. *Proc. Acad. Management* 100–114.

Lunati, M. T. 1997. *Ethical Issues in Economics: From Altruism to Cooperation to Equity.* MacMillan Press, London, U.K.

Margolis, H. 1982. *Selfishness, Altruism and Rationality.* Cambridge University Press, Cambridge, U.K.

MacDougall, P., R. B. Robinson. 1990. New venture strategies: An empirical identification of eight 'archetypes' of competitive strategies for entry. *Strategic Management J.* **11**(6) 447–468.

McAfee, R. P., J. McMillan. 1987. Competition for agency contracts. *Rand J. of Econom.* **18**(2) 296–307.

McConnell, J. J., H. Servaes. 1990. Additional evidence on equity ownership and corporate value. *J. Financial Econom.* **27** 595–612.

Merton, R. K. 1968. *Social Theory and Social Structure.* The Free Press, New York.

Meyer, M., L. G. Zucker. 1989. *Permanently Failing Organizations.* Sage, Newbury Park, CA.

Mohlo, I. 1997. *The Economics of Information: Lying and Cheating in Markets and Organizations.* Blackwell, Oxford, U.K.

Morck, R. 1996. On the economics of concentrated ownership. *Canadian Bus. Law J.* **26** 63–85.

——, A. Shleifer, R. W. Vishney. 1988. Management ownership and market valuation: An empirical analysis. *J. Financial Econom.* **20** 293–315.

Nash, J. M. 1988. Boards of privately-held companies: Their responsibility and structure. *Family Bus. Rev.* **1**(3) 263–369.

Nayyar, P. R. 1992. On the measurement of service diversification strategy: Evidence from large U.S. service firms. *Strategic Management J.* **13**(3) 219–235.

Nelsen, J. F., P. A. Frishkoff. 1991. Boards of directors in family-owned business. *Akron Bus. and Econom. Rev.* **23**(8) 88–96.

Nelton, S. 1995. The agony of quitting the family firm. *Nation's Bus.* **83**(10) 62.

Nowak, M. A., R. M. May. 1992. Evolutionary games and spatial chaos. *Nature* **359** 826–829.

Norusis, M. J. 1993. *SPSS for Windows Base System User's Guide.* SPSS, Inc., Chicago, IL.

Nunnelly, J. C. 1978. *Psychometric Theory.* McGraw-Hill, New York.

Perrow, C. 1986. *Complex Organizations.* Random House, New York.

Piliavan, J. A., H. Charng. 1990. Altruism: A review of recent theory and research. *Ann. Rev. Soc.* **16** 27–65.

Powell, T. C. 1992. Strategic planning as competitive advantage. *Strategic Management J.* **13** 551–558.

Rajan, R. G., L. Zingales. 1998. Power in a theory of the firm. Social Science Research Network (www.ssrn.com).

Reagan, P. B., R. M. Stulz. 1986. Risk bearing, labor contracts, and capital markets. *Res. Finance* **6** 217–232.

Rediker, K. J., A. Seth. 1995. Boards of directors and substitution effects of alternative governance mechanisms. *Strategic Management J.* **16**(2) 85–99.

Rubenson, G. C., A. K. Gupta. 1996. The initial succession: A contingency model of founder tenure. *Entrepreneurship Theory and Practice* **21**(2) 21–35.

Sackett, P. R., J. R. Larsen Jr. 1990. Research strategies and tactics in industrial organization psychology. M. D. Dunnette, L. M.

Hough, eds. *Handbook of Industrial and Organization Psychology.* Consulting Psychologists Press, Inc., Palo Alto, CA.

Simon, H. A. 1993. Altruism and economics. *Amer. Econom. Rev.* **83** 156–161.

Small Business Reports. 1993. New pay ethics. **18**(5) 42.

Sonnenfeld, J. 1988. *The Hero's Farewell.* Oxford Press, New York.

Spector, P. E. 1987. Method variance as an artifact in self-reported affect and perceptions at work: Myth or significant problem. *J. Appl. Psych.* **72**(3) 438–443.

Stark, O. 1989. Altruism and the quality of life. *Amer. Econom. Rev.* (AEA Papers and Proceedings) **79**(2) 86–90.

——, I. Falk. 1998. Transfers, empathy formation, and reverse transfers. *Amer. Econom. Rev.*, **88**(2) 271–276.

Stulz, R. M. 1988. On takeover resistance, managerial discretion, and shareholder wealth. *J. Financial Econom.* **20** 25–54.

Tan, J. J., R. J. Litschert. 1994. Environment-strategy relationship and its performance implications: An empirical study of the Chinese electronics industry. *Strategic Management J.* **15**(1) 1–20.

Thaler, R. H., H. M. Shefrin. 1981. An economic theory of self-control. *J. Political Economy* **89**(2) 392–406.

Trostel, A. O., M. L. Nichols. 1982. Privately held companies and publicly held companies: A comparison of strategic choices and management processes. *Acad. Management J.* **25**(1) 47–62.

Trow, D. B. 1961. Executive succession in small companies. *Admin. Sci. Quart.* **6** 228–239.

Walsh, J. P., J. K. Seward. 1990. On the efficiency of internal and external control mechanisms. *Acad. Management Rev.* **15**(3) 421–458.

Ward, J. L. 1987. *Keeping the Family Business Healthy: How to Plan for Continuous Growth, Profitability, and Family Leadership.* Jossey-Bass, San Francisco, CA.

——. 1988. The special role of strategic planning for family businesses. *Family Bus. Rev.* **1**(2) 105–117.

Ward, J. L., J. L. Handy. 1988. A survey of board practices. *Family Bus. Rev.* **1**(3) 298–308.

Whisler, T. L. 1988. The role of the board in threshold firms. *Family Bus. Rev.* **1**(3) 309–321.

Williamson, O. 1985. *The Economic Institutions of Capitalism.* The Free Press, Boston, MA.

Wiseman, R. M., L. R. Gomez-Mejia. 1998. A behavioral agency model of managerial risk taking. *Acad. Management Rev.* **23**(1) 133–153.

Wortman, M. S. Jr. 1994. Theoretical foundations for family-owned business: A conceptual and research-based paradigm. *Family Bus. Rev.* **7**(1) 3–27.

Wright, P., S. P. Ferris, A. Sarin, V. Awasthi. 1996. Impact of corporate insider, blockholder, and institutional equity ownership on firm risk taking. *Acad. Management J.* **39**(2) 441–465.

Accepted by James Walsh; received July 12, 2000.

[3]

ELSEVIER   Journal of Financial Economics 47 (1998) 243–277

Venture capital and the structure of capital markets: banks versus stock markets[1]

Bernard S. Black[a],*, Ronald J. Gilson[a,b]

[a] *Columbia University School of Law, New York, NY 10027, USA*
[b] *Stanford University School of Law, Stanford, California 94305, USA*

Received 18 July 1996; accepted 29 August 1997

Abstract

The United States has many banks that are small relative to large corporations and play a limited role in corporate governance, and a well developed stock market with an associated market for corporate control. In contrast, Japanese and German banks are fewer in number but larger in relative size and are said to play a central governance role. Neither country has an active market for corporate control. We extend the debate on the relative efficiency of bank- and stock market-centered capital markets by developing a further systematic difference between the two systems: the greater vitality of venture capital in stock market-centered systems. Understanding the link between the stock market and the venture capital market requires understanding the contractual arrangements between entrepreneurs and venture capital providers; especially, the importance of the opportunity to enter into an implicit contract over control, which gives a successful entrepreneur the option to reacquire control from the venture capitalist by using an initial public offering as the means by which the venture capitalist exits from a portfolio investment. We also extend the literature on venture capital contracting by offering an explanation for two central characteristics of the U.S. venture capital market: relatively rapid exit by venture capital providers from investments in portfolio companies; and the

* Corresponding author. Tel.: 212/854-8079; fax:212/854-7946; e-mail: bblack@law.columbia.edu.

[1] The authors are grateful for helpful suggestions from the editor and an anonymous referee, and from Anant Admati, Erik Berglof, Stephen Choi, Kevin Davis, Uri Geiger, Victor Goldberg, Paul Gompers, Joseph Grundfest, Ehud Kamar, Michael Klausner, Joshua Lerner, Ronald Mann, Paul Pfleiderer, Mark Ramsayer, Charles Sabel, Allen Schwartz, and Omri Yadlin, and from participants in workshops at Columbia Law School, Harvard Law School, Stanford Law School, the Max Planck Institute (Hamburg, Germany), and the American Law and Economics Association. Research support was provided by Columbia Law School and the Roberts Program in Law and Business, Stanford Law School. We thank Laura Menninger, Nishani Naidoo, Annette Schuller, and Ram Vasudevan for research assistance.

244   *B.S. Black, R.J. Gilson/Journal of Financial Economics 47 (1998) 243–277*

JEL classification: G23; G32

Keywords: Venture Capital; Exit Strategy; IPO; Comparative corporate governance

1. Introduction

Contrasting capital markets in the United States with those of Japan and Germany has become a commonplace activity. The United States has a large number of comparatively small banks that play a limited role in the governance of large corporations, and a well developed stock market with an associated market for corporate control that figures prominently in corporate governance. In contrast, Japanese main banks and German universal banks are few in number but larger in size, relative to Japanese and German firms, and are said to play a central corporate governance role in monitoring management (e.g., Aoki, 1994; Roe, 1994). Neither country has an active market for corporate control.

Advocates of bank-centered capital markets claim that this structure fosters patient capital markets and long-term planning, while a stock market-centered capital market is said to encourage short-term expectations by investors and responsive short-term strategies by managers (e.g., Edwards and Fischer, 1994; Porter, 1992). Advocates of stock market-centered systems (e.g., Gilson, 1996) stress the adaptive features of a market for corporate control which are lacking in bank-centered systems, and the lack of empirical evidence of short-termism.

Paralleling the assessment of the comparative merits of stock market and bank-centered capital markets, scholars have also sought to explain how the United States, Germany, and Japan developed such different capital markets. Recent work has stressed that the characteristics of the three capital markets do not reflect simply the efficient outcome of competition between institutions, in which the most efficient institutions survive. The nature of the American capital market – a strong stock market, weak financial intermediaries, and the absence of the close links between banks and nonfinancial firms said to characterize the Japanese and German capital markets – reflects, at least in part, politics, history and path-dependent evolution, rather than economic inevitability (e.g., Black, 1990; Gilson, 1996; Roe, 1994). Much the same seems to be true of Germany and Japan (Hoshi, 1993; Roe, 1994). To be sure, competitively driven evolution hones efficiency, but institutions that emerge are shaped at critical stages by the random hand of events and the instrumental hand of politics.

In this article, we seek to contribute to two literatures. First, we extend the debate about the relative efficiency of bank- and stock market-centered capital markets by documenting and explaining a second systematic difference between

B.S. Black, R.J. Gilson/Journal of Financial Economics 47 (1998) 243–277   245

the two systems: the existence of a much stronger venture capital industry in stock market-centered systems.

We define 'venture capital', consistent with American understanding, as investment by specialized venture capital organizations (which we call 'venture capital funds') in high-growth, high-risk, often high-technology firms that need capital to finance product development or growth and must, by the nature of their business, obtain this capital largely in the form of equity rather than debt. We exclude 'buyout' financing that enables a mature firm's managers to acquire the firm from its current owners, even though in Europe, so-called 'venture capital' firms often provide such financing – more often, in many cases, than the financing that we call venture capital.

Other countries have openly envied the U.S. venture capital market and have actively, but unsuccessfully, sought to replicate it. We offer an explanation for this failure: We argue that a well developed stock market that permits venture capitalists to exit through an initial public offering (IPO) is critical to the existence of a vibrant venture capital market.

Understanding this critical link between the stock market and the venture capital market requires that we understand the implicit and explicit contractual arrangements between venture capital funds and their investors, and between venture capital funds and entrepreneurs. This brings us to our second contribution: We extend the literature on venture capital contracting by offering an explanation for two characteristics of the United States venture capital market. First, we explain the importance of exit – why venture capital providers seek to liquidate their portfolio company investments in the near to moderate term, rather than investing for the long-term like Japanese or German banks. Second, we explain the importance of the form of exit: why the potential for the venture capital provider to exit from a successful start-up *through an IPO*, available only through a stock market, allows venture capital providers to enter into implicit contracts with entrepreneurs concerning future control of startup firms, in a way not available in a bank-centered capital market. Thus, we make explicit a functional link between private and public equity markets: The implicit contract over future control that is permitted by the availability of exit through an IPO helps to explain the greater success of venture capital as an organizational form in stock market-centered systems.

Section 2 of this article motivates the theoretical analysis by contrasting the venture capital markets in the United States and Germany. Section 3 develops the importance of exit from venture capital investments to the viability and structure of the venture capital industry. Exit serves two key functions. First, venture capital investors specialize in providing portfolio companies with a combination of financial capital, monitoring and advisory services, and reputational capital. The combination of financial and nonfinancial services loses its efficiency advantages as the portfolio company matures. Thus, recycling venture capital investors' capital through exit and reinvestment is jointly efficient for the provider and the portfolio company. Second, exit facilitates contracting between venture capital managers (persons with expertise in identifying and developing promising new businesses) and providers of capital to venture capital managers. The exit price gives capital providers a reliable measure of the venture capital manager's skill. The exit and reinvestment cycle also lets capital providers withdraw capital from less skilled venture capital managers or managers whose industry-specific expertise no longer matches the nature of promising start-up firms. It supports an implicit contract under which capital providers reinvest in the future limited partnerships of successful venture capital managers.

Section 4 focuses on the implicit contract over control between the entrepreneur and the venture capital fund. The potential to exit through an IPO allows the entrepreneur and the venture capital fund to enter into a self-enforcing implicit contract over control, in which the venture capital fund agrees to return control to a successful entrepreneur by exiting through an IPO. This implicit contract cannot readily be duplicated in a bank-centered capital market. Section 5 compares the predictions from our informal model to evidence about the success of venture capital in other countries, including Canada, Great Britain, Israel, and Japan. Section 6 considers alternative explanations for the observed international patterns of venture capital development, especially differences in legal rules. Some of these reasons may have predictive power, but none has enough power to displace our theory as an explanation for a substantial portion of the observed intercountry variation. Section 7 considers the implications of the symbiosis between stock markets and venture capital markets for efforts by other countries to expand their venture capital markets. Section 8 concludes.

2. The venture capital industry in the United States and Germany

In this section, we compare the venture capital industries in the United States and Germany in order to motivate the theory developed in Sections 3 and 4, in which a stock market-centered capital market (present in the United States but absent in Germany) is a precondition to a substantial venture capital industry.

The United States has a much more fully developed venture capital market than Germany. The differences are of both size and substance. The United States has a larger number of funds and the funds themselves are larger relative to each country's economy. Substantively, United States funds are more heavily invested in early-stage ventures and high-technology industries, while German venture capital provides primarily later-stage financing in lower-technology industries.

The United States venture capital market is quite large. As of the end of 1994, 591 U.S. venture capital funds had total investments (from which the fund had not yet exited or written off) of around $34 billion (Venture Capital Yearbook, 1995). New investment in venture capital funds in 1996 was $6.5 billion (Fig. 1). In recent years, venture capital-backed firms have raised several billion dollars

B.S. Black, R.J. Gilson/Journal of Financial Economics 47 (1998) 243–277   247

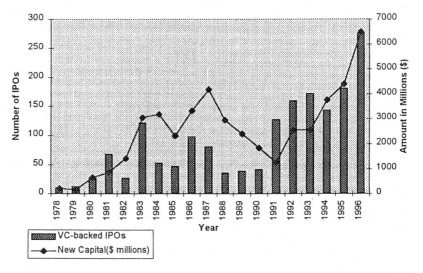

Fig. 1. Venture capital-backed IPOs and new venture capital commitments. Number of initial public offerings of venture-capital-backed companies (left-hand scale), and amount of new capital commitments to venture capital funds (right-hand scale), between 1978 and 1996. Source: Venture Capital Journal and Venture Capital Yearbook (various dates); Economist, Mar. 29, 1997 (survey of Silicon Valley)

annually through IPOs, including a 1996 total of $12 billion; they form a significant portion of the total IPO market (Venture Capital Yearbook, various years through 1997; Brav and Gompers, 1997).[2] Between 1991 and 1996, there were 1059 venture capital-backed IPOs, an average of over 175 per year (see Table 1), as well as 466 exits through acquisition of the venture-capital-backed firm.

Fig. 1 shows the annual variation in the number of venture-capital-backed IPOs, as well as the amount of new capital committed to venture capital funds. Inspection of Fig. 1 suggests a correlation between the availability of exit through IPO (proxied by the number of venture-capital-backed IPOs) and investor willingness to invest in venture capital funds (measured by new capital commitments), with perhaps a one-year lag between a change in the number of IPOs and a resulting change in the amount of capital committed. This correlation is consistent with the theory developed below on the link between the stock market and the venture capital market.

---

[2] An alternate way to measure the importance of venture-capital-backed IPOs is to measure the firms' market capitalization rather than the amount of funds raised in the IPO. The 276 venture-capital-backed firms taken public in 1996 had a mean market capitalization of $209 million and total market capitalization of $58 billion (Venture Capital Journal, April, 1997).

Table 1
VC-backed IPOs, public acquisitions, and private acquisitions

Number of initial public offerings of venture-capital-backed companies and number of sales of venture-capital-backed companies, between 1984 and 1996.

Year	VC-backed IPOs	Exits via acquisitions		
		Of private companies	Of already public companies	Total
1984	53	59	27	86
1985	47	83	18	101
1986	98	90	30	120
1987	81	113	27	140
1988	36	106	29	135
1989	39	101	45	146
1990	42	76	33	109
1991	127	65	19	84
1992	160	90	4	94
1993	172	78	14	92
1994	143	99	no data	no data
1995	183	98	no data	no data
1996	276	94	no data	no data

Source: Venture Capital Journal (various dates) (data for acquisitions of already public companies was available only through 1993)

The visual impression of a correlation between venture-capital-backed IPOs and new capital commitments to venture capital funds is confirmed by a simple regression of capital contributions in year $X + 1$ (as a dependent variable) against number of venture-capital-backed IPOs in year X (Table 2). Regression 1 below shows that the number of IPOs in year X correlates strongly with new capital contributions in year $X + 1$. Regression 2 adds year as an additional possible explanatory variable. The correlation between number of IPOs in year X and new capital commitments in the following year remains statistically significant as a predictor of new capital commitments in the following year. These regressions are not intended to fully capture the factors that affect capital commitments to venture capital funds, but do confirm the visual correlation evident from Fig. 1.

United States venture capital funds obtain capital from a range of sources, but pension funds are the largest contributor. Pension funds have provided roughly 40% of the capital raised by venture capital funds over the last 10 years or so (Table 3). In Germany, on the other hand, banks supply the majority of venture capital commitments.

Seed, startup and other early stage investments that take a company through development of a prototype and initial product shipments to customers

B.S. Black, R.J. Gilson/Journal of Financial Economics 47 (1998) 243–277   249

Table 2
Correlation between venture capital backed IPOs and new capital commitments to venture capital
funds

Least-squares regression of capital contributed to venture capital funds ($ millions) in year $X + 1$
against number of initial public offerings of venture-capital backed companies in year X. Based on
data from 1978–1996 as shown in Fig. 1. t-statistics in parentheses. *** (**) (*) = significant at 0.001
(0.01) (0.05) level.

Dependent variable	Independent variable(s)			R^2	Number of observations
	Intercept	VC-backed IPOs in year X	Year		
1 Capital contribution in year $X + 1$	1015 ($t = 2.35$)*	20.2 ($t = 4.54$)***		0.56	18
2 Capital contribution in year $X + 1$	− 137846 ($t = - 0.93$)	15.1 ($t = 2.17$)*	70.1 ($t = 0.94$)	0.59	18

Table 3
United States and Germany capital raised by venture capital funds by type of investor

Percentage of capital raised by venture capital funds in the United States and Germany, by type of
investor, for 1992–1995.

	1992	1993	1994	1995
United States				
Corporations	3%	8%	9%	2%
Private individuals & families	11	8	9	17
Government agencies	—	—	—	—
Pension funds	42	59	46	38
Banks and insurance companies	15	11	9	18
Endowments and foundations	18	11	21	22
Other	11	4	2	3
Total	100%	100%	100%	100%
Germany				
Corporations	7%	9%	8%	10%
Private individuals & families	6	7	8	5
Government agencies	4	6	7	8
Pension funds	—	—	—	9
Banks	53	52	55	59
Insurance companies	10	12	12	6
Endowments and foundations	—	—	—	—
Other	17	14	10	2
Total	100%	100%	100%	100%

Sources: European Venture Capital Association Yearbook (1995); Bundesverband Deutsche
Kapitalbeteiligungsgesellschaften Jahrbuch [German Venture Capital Association Yearbook] (various years through 1996); Venture Capital Yearbook (various years through 1997).

Table 4
United States and Germany venture capital disbursements by stage of financing

Percentage of capital disbursed by venture capital funds in the United States and Germany, by nature of investment, for 1992–1995.

	1992	1993	1994	1995
United States				
Seed	3%	7%	4%	
Startup	8	7	15	
Other early stage	13	10	18	
Expansion	55	54	45	
LBO/Acquisition	7	6	6	
Other	14	16	12	
Total	100%	100%	100%	
Germany				
Seed	1%	1%	2%	2%
Startup	6	7	8	6
Expansion	45	66	54	65
LBO/Acquisition	24	25	36	18
Other	25	—	—	8
Total	100%	100%	100%	100%

Sources: European Venture Capital Association Yearbook (1995); Bundesverband Deutsche Kapitalbeteiligungsgesellschaften (BVK) Jahrbuch [German Venture Capital Association Yearbook] (various years through 1996); Venture Capital Yearbook (various years through 1997).

accounted for about 37% of new capital invested by venture capital funds in 1994 (Table 4). Later-stage expansion financing represented another 45% of 1994 investments. Because venture capitalists usually stage their investments (Sahlman, 1990; Gompers, 1995), most expansion financing goes to companies that received early-stage financing. Thus, the bulk of venture capital investments go to firms that receive venture capital financing very early in their life. Moreover, most investments go to technology-based companies; in 1994, 68% of new investments went to these companies (Venture Economics, 1995).

Lest venture capital be dismissed as trivial in amount, and therefore not an important factor in comparing corporate governance systems, we note that mature firms which began with venture capital backing assume macroeconomic significance in the U.S. economy. They play a major, often dominant role in several important and rapidly growing sectors where the United States is recognized as a world leader, including biotechnology (for example, Genentech and Biogen); personal computers and workstations (for example, Apple, Compaq, and Sun Microsystems); many personal computer components and related devices such as hard drives and routers (for example, Seagate Technologies, Connor Peripherals, and Cisco Systems); personal computer software (for example, Lotus Development and Harvard Graphics); and semiconductors (for example, Intel and Advanced Micro Devices).

B.S. Black, R.J. Gilson/Journal of Financial Economics 47 (1998) 243–277   251

The German venture capital industry is a fraction of the size of the United States industry. Only 85 venture capital organizations existed at the end of 1994, with DM 8.3 billion ($5.5 billion) in cumulative capital commitments (European Venture Capital Yearbook, 1995) and annual investments of under $400 million. Venture capital investments were 0.01% of German GDP in 1994; only one-sixth of the U.S. level. This comparison understates the difference in venture capital activity between the two countries because the European definition of venture capital is broader than the American definition. These organizations received the majority of their capital from banks (55%) and insurance companies (12%). Pension funds are not a factor in the German market because German corporate and government pension obligations are largely unfunded.

The German venture capital industry also differs from the United States in its aversion both to early-stage investment (Table 4) and to investment in high-technology industries (Harrison, 1990). In 1994, only 8% of the venture capital invested went to startup companies, and only 2% to seed financing. Technology-related investments comprised only 11% of all new investments.

In Germany, as in the United States, exit by the venture capital fund is the norm, but the form of exit differs. Exit through the stock market is largely unavailable, although a handful of German venture capital-backed firms have gone public on Britain's AIM (Alternative Investment Market). The venture capital fund's exit therefore comes principally through the company's repurchase of the venture fund's stake (a strategy not available to the rapidly growing firms that are the predominant recipients of venture capital financing in the United States), or through selling the company. Table 5 shows the exit strategies employed by German venture capital funds for 1995. Of the 12 exits through IPO, only one was in Germany; the rest were on foreign markets.

This section has only sketched the United States and German venture capital markets. But it demonstrates the pattern we seek to explain: the existence in the

Table 5
Exits by German venture capital funds, 1995

Type of exit from portfolio companies by German venture capital funds for 1995.

Exit type	Number of firms
Buyback by portfolio company	166
Sale of portfolio company	74
Block sale of venture capital fund's stake	8
Initial Public Offering	12
(IPOs on foreign stock markets)	(11)
Other	4
Total	264

Source: Bundesverband Deutsche Kapitalbeteiligungsgesellschaften Jahrbuch [German Venture Capital Association Yearbook] (1996)

252   B.S. Black, R.J. Gilson/Journal of Financial Economics 47 (1998) 243–277

United States of a dynamic venture capital industry centered on early stage investments in high-technology companies and the absence of a comparable industry in Germany.

3. The importance of exit by the venture capital fund

The first step in understanding the link between the stock market and the venture capital market involves the importance of exit by the venture capital fund from its investments. We develop below an informal theory for why exit by venture capital providers from their successful investments is critical to the operation of the venture capital market, both for the relationship between a venture capital fund and its portfolio companies, and for the relationship between the fund and its capital providers. Florida and Kenney (1990) argue that U.S. venture investors' refusal to act as long-term investors in portfolio companies weakens United States competitiveness. Our analysis provides an efficiency justification for exit.

The need for an exit strategy does not itself explain the distinctive properties of exit through an IPO and, therefore, the special role of an active IPO market. We develop that relationship in Section 4.

3.1. Exit from the venture capital fund – portfolio company relationship

Venture capitalists provide more than just money to their portfolio companies. Three additional contributions loom large (Bygrave and Timmons, 1992; Barry, 1994; Lerner, 1995; Gorman and Sahlman, 1989): management assistance to the portfolio company, analogous to that provided by a management consulting firm; intensive monitoring of performance, reflecting the incentives to monitor arising from equity ownership and the power to act using the venture capitalist's levers of control; and reputational capital, that is, the venture capitalist's ability to give the portfolio company credibility with third parties, similar to the role played by other reputational intermediaries such as investment bankers.

3.1.1. Management assistance

The typical venture capital fund is a limited partnership run by general partners who are experienced at moving companies up the development path from the startup stage and market knowledge based on other investments in the portfolio company's industry and related industries (Sahlman, 1990; Gompers and Lerner, 1996). With this experience, the venture capitalist can assist a management-thin early-stage company in locating and recruiting the management and technical personnel it needs as its business grows, and can help the company through the predictable problems that high-technology firms face in moving

B.S. Black, R.J. Gilson/Journal of Financial Economics 47 (1998) 243–277   253

from prototype development to production, marketing, and distribution. The venture capital fund's industry knowledge and experience with prior startup firms helps it locate managers for new startups (Carvalho, 1996).

3.1.2. Intensive monitoring and control

Venture capital funds have both strong incentives to monitor entrepreneurs' performance, deriving from equity ownership. They also receive strong control levers, disproportionate to the size of their equity investment. One control lever results from the staged timing of venture capital investment. The initial investment is typically insufficient to allow the portfolio company to carry out its business plan (Gompers, 1995; Sahlman, 1990). The venture capitalist will decide later whether to provide the additional funding that the portfolio company needs. The company's need for additional funds gives its management a performance incentive in the form of a hard constraint, analogous to the use of debt in leveraged buyouts.[3]

The typical contractual arrangements between a venture capital fund and a portfolio company provide other control levers. The venture capitalist typically receives convertible debt or convertible preferred stock that carries the same voting rights as if it had already been converted into common stock (Benton and Gunderson, 1993; Gompers, 1997).[4] The venture capital fund commonly receives greater board representation – often an absolute majority of the board – than it could elect if board representation were proportional to overall voting power. Board control lets the venture capital provider replace the entrepreneur as chief executive officer if performance lags.[5] Even where the venture capitalist lacks board control, the investor rights agreement gives the venture capital provider veto power over significant operating decisions by the portfolio company.

---

[3] Gompers (1995) explains the extra control rights given to the venture capital fund as a response to adverse selection problems in early-stage financing, where information asymmetries between the entrepreneur and the venture capital fund are greatest.

[4] The standard contractual package for an early-stage venture capital investment consists of a convertible preferred stock purchase agreement; the portfolio company's certificate of incorporation; and an investor rights agreement. The purchase agreement, through detailed representations and warranties, documents the portfolio company's condition at the time of the venture capital investment. The certificate of incorporation sets out the voting and other rights of the venture capital fund's convertible debt or preferred stock. The investor rights agreement contains the portfolio company's ongoing obligations to the venture capital fund, including detailed negative covenants and such things as registration rights.

[5] Hellman (1995a) explains why an entrepreneur would give the venture capitalist this right: to reduce the cost of capital, thereby increasing the share of the equity the entrepreneur retains. We discuss the reputation market necessary to prevent the venture capitalist from misusing this power in Section 4.

3.1.3. Reputational capital

Much like an investment bank underwriting an initial public offering (Gilson and Kraakman, 1984; Booth and Smith, 1986), the venture capital fund acts as a reputational intermediary. Venture capital financing enhances the portfolio company's credibility with third parties whose contributions will be crucial to the company's success. Talented managers are more likely to invest their human capital in a company financed by a respected venture capital fund, because the venture capitalist's participation provides a credible signal about the company's likelihood of success. Suppliers will be more willing to risk committing capacity and extending trade credit to a company with respected venture capital backers. Customers will take more seriously the company's promise of future product delivery if a venture capitalist both vouches for and monitors its management and technical progress. Moukheiber (1996) provides an account of the reputational power of Kleiner, Perkins, Caufield and Byers, a leading venture capital fund. Later on, the venture capitalist's reputation helps to attract a high quality underwriter for an initial public offering of the portfolio company's stock (Lerner, 1994a; Megginson and Weiss, 1991).

The venture capital fund's proffer of its reputation to third parties who have dealings with a portfolio company is credible because the fund is a repeat player, and has put its money where its mouth is by investing in the portfolio company. The fund's reputation is crucial for its own dealings with investors in its existing and future limited partnerships, with other venture capitalists in syndicating investments in portfolio companies and in negotiating with entrepreneurs concerning new portfolio investments (Sahlman, 1990; Lerner, 1994b). Consistent with a reputational analysis, Brav and Gompers (1997) report that venture-capital-backed IPOs do not suffer the long-run underperformance reported for IPOs in general.

Like a venture capitalist's provision of financial capital, its non-financial contributions are also staged, albeit informally. A venture capitalist can choose not to make or return telephone calls to or from a portfolio company or its suppliers, customers, or prospective employees. The fund's power to withhold its management assistance and reputational capital reinforces its incentive and power to monitor.

The management assistance, monitoring, and service as a reputational intermediary that a venture capitalist provides share a significant economy of scope with its provision of capital. This scope economy arises from a number of sources. The portfolio company must evaluate the quality of the venture capital fund's proffered management assistance and monitoring. Similarly, potential employees, suppliers, and customers must evaluate the credibility of the fund's explicit and implicit representations concerning the portfolio company's future. Combining financial and nonfinancial contributions both enhances the credibility of the information that the venture capitalist provides to third parties and bonds the venture capitalist's promise to the portfolio company to provide

B.S. Black, R.J. Gilson/Journal of Financial Economics 47 (1998) 243–277   255

nonfinancial assistance. The venture capitalist will suffer financial loss if it reneges on its promise of nonfinancial support. Combining financial and non-financial contributions also lets investors in venture capital funds evaluate a fund's nonfinancial contributions by measuring its return on investment. Lin and Smith (1995) also link the venture capitalist's financial and nonfinancial investments. Finally, there is the customary role of monitoring in ensuring that the portfolio company's managers do not divert to themselves some of the company's income stream.

The non-capital inputs supplied by venture capital providers have special value to early-stage companies. As the portfolio company's management gains its own experience, proves its skill, and establishes its own reputation, the relative value of the venture capital provider's management experience, monitoring, and service as a reputational intermediary declines.[6] Thus, by the time the portfolio company succeeds, the venture capital provider's nonfinancial contributions can be more profitably invested in a new round of early-stage companies. But because the economies of scope discussed above link financial and nonfinancial contributions, recycling the venture capitalist's nonfinancial contributions also requires the venture capitalist to exit – to recycle its financial contribution from successful companies to early-stage companies.

3.2. The exit and reinvestment cycle for venture capital funds and capital providers

The efficiency of exit for the venture capitalist-portfolio company relationship complements a similar efficiency arising from the relationship between the venture capitalist and the investors in its limited partnerships. The cycle of financial commitment to early-stage firms, followed by exit from these invest-ments, responds to three contracting problems in the venture capitalist – capital provider relationship. First, capital providers need a way to evaluate venture capitalists' skill, in order to decide to which managers to commit new funds. Second, capital providers need to evaluate the risks and returns on venture capital investments relative to other investments, in order to decide whether to invest in venture capital, and how much to invest. Third, capital providers need to be able to withdraw funds from less successful managers, or from managers whose industry-specific expertise no longer matches current investment oppor-tunities. Yet the very specialization that explains why capital providers hire venture capitalists rather than invest directly ensures that capital providers

---

[6] Compare Rajan's (1992) analysis of the trade-off between a bank-like lender who has the ability to monitor the borrower's on-going performance and public investors who cannot monitor. As the borrower's quality improves, the returns to monitoring decrease, and the most efficient capital provider shifts from a monitoring bank-like lender to a non-monitoring investor. Diamond (1991) discusses a similar generational theory in which optimal investor type depends on a firm's stage in its life-cycle.

256   *B.S. Black, R.J. Gilson/Journal of Financial Economics 47 (1998) 243–277*

cannot easily assess whether a venture capital fund's ongoing investments are or are likely to become successful, or how successful they are likely to be.

Exit by the venture capital manager from specific portfolio investments provides a benchmark that lets capital providers evaluate both the relative skill of venture capital managers and the profitability of venture capital relative to other investments (Gompers, 1996). At the same time, payment of the exit proceeds to capital providers lets the capital providers recycle funds from less successful to more successful venture capital managers.

Conventional limited partnership agreements between venture capital funds and capital providers reflect the efficiency of exit for this relationship. The limited partnership agreement typically sets a maximum term for the partnership of 7–10 years, after which the partnership must be liquidated and the proceeds distributed to the limited partners (Sahlman, 1990). During the term of the limited partnership agreement, the proceeds from investments in particular firms are distributed to limited partners as realized. Moreover, venture capital funds have strong incentives to exit from their investments, when feasible, well before the end of the partnership period. A fund's performance record, based on completed investments, is the fund's principal tool for soliciting capital providers to invest additional funds in new limited partnerships.

The explicit contract between capital providers and the venture capitalist, requiring liquidation of each limited partnership, is complemented by an implicit contract in which capital providers are expected to reinvest in future limited partnerships sponsored by successful venture capital funds. The expectation of reinvestment makes it feasible for venture capital funds to invest in developing infrastructure and expertise that will outlive the term of any one limited partnership, and could not be justified by the returns on the modest amount of capital that a venture capitalist without a track record can expect to raise. Fig. 2

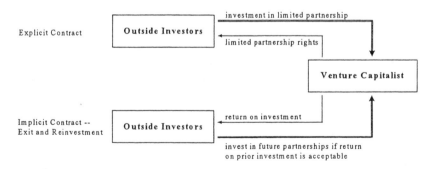

Fig. 2. Implicit and explicit contracts between venture capitalists and outside investors.

B.S. Black, R.J. Gilson/Journal of Financial Economics 47 (1998) 243–277   257

illustrates the explicit and implicit contracts between venture capitalists and their investors.

In sum, exit is central to the venture capital manager's accountability to capital providers. The efficiency of exit for the venture capital fund – capital provider relationship complements its efficiency properties for the portfolio firm – venture capital fund relationship. Taken together, they provide a strong rationale for exit from individual portfolio investments as a critical component of a viable venture capital industry.

4. The availability of exit by IPO: Implicit contracting over future control

The analysis in part 3 establishes the importance of an exit strategy to the venture capital market. But it does not differentiate between stock market-centered and bank-centered capital markets. A stock market makes available one special type of exit – an initial public offering. But another exit strategy is available to venture capital funds in both bank-centered and stock-market centered capital markets: the fund can cause the portfolio company to be sold to a larger company. Indeed, even in the United States, venture capitalists frequently exit through sale of the portfolio company rather than through an IPO (Table 1). A third exit option – leveraging the portfolio company so it can repurchase the venture capitalist's stake – is generally not feasible for the fast-growing, capital-consuming companies that are the typical focus for venture capital investing in the U.S.

Exit through sale of the portfolio company is likely to be the most efficient form of exit in some cases. For example, innovation may be better accomplished in small firms while production and marketing may be better accomplished in large firms. In this circumstance, selling a startup company to another firm with manufacturing or marketing expertise can produce synergy gains. These gains can be partly captured by the startup firm through a higher exit price (Bygrave and Timmons, 1992).

In other cases, an IPO may be the most efficient form of exit. The potential for an IPO to provide a higher-valued exit than sale of the company must be considered plausible, given the frequency with which this exit option is used in the United States. Viewed ex ante, venture capital financing of firms for which exit through IPO will (or might turn out to) maximize exit price could be a positive net present investment in a stock-market-centered capital market, but not in a bank-centered capital market. But this difference should affect investment decisions only at the margin. Thus, it cannot easily explain the dramatic differences between the venture capital industries in the United States and Germany, both in size and in type of investment.

Thus, we are only part of the way towards a theory that explains the observed link between venture capital markets and stock markets. We have shown why venture capital providers need an exit strategy. What remains to be shown is that the potential for exit through IPO, *even if exit often occurs through the portfolio company's sale*, is critical to the development of an active venture capital market. This part shows that the potential for exit through IPO allows the venture capital provider and the entrepreneur to enter into an implicit contract over future control of the portfolio company in a manner that is not readily duplicable in a bank-centered system.

4.1. The contracting framework

In a contracting framework, the relevant time to assess the influence of an IPO's availability (and therefore the importance of a stock market) on the operation of the venture capital market is when the entrepreneur and venture capital provider contract over the initial investment, not when exit actually occurs. A number of authors have modeled aspects of this contract, including the staging of the venture capitalist's funding, which vests in the venture capital provider the decision whether to continue the portfolio company's projects (Admati and Pfleiderer, 1994; Gompers, 1995), and the venture capital fund's purchase of a convertible security both to mitigate distributional conflicts between the entrepreneur and the venture capitalist associated with a future sale of the firm (Bergloff, 1994), and to solve an adverse selection problem among prospective entrepreneurs (Marx, 1994; Gompers, 1997). Our informal model seeks to explain three additional characteristics of venture capital contracting: (1) the parties' ex ante joint preference that the venture capital fund exit through an IPO; (2) how the entrepreneur's preference that the fund use this exit strategy if it becomes available ex post is expressed through a self-enforcing implicit contract over future control; and (3) how this implicit contract provides the entrepreneur with incentives that are not easily duplicated if sale of the portfolio company is the only exit option. Because the incentive properties of this contract go to the heart of the entrepreneurial process, its availability in a stock-market-centered capital market links the venture capital market and the stock market and can explain the absence of vigorous venture capital in countries with bank-centered capital markets.

Our IPO exit model requires three noncontroversial assumptions: (i) the entrepreneur places substantial private value on control over the company she starts; (ii) it is not feasible for an untested entrepreneur to retain control at the time of the initial venture capital financing; and (iii) it is feasible for a successful entrepreneur to reacquire control from the venture capitalist when the venture capitalist exits. We discuss each assumption below.

A private value for control is a standard feature in venture capital models and, more generally, in models that seek to explain the incentive properties of capital structure (Holmstrom and Tirole, 1989; Grossman and Hart, 1988; Harris and Raviv, 1988). Moreover, for entrepreneurs, the assumption appears to be

B.S. Black, R.J. Gilson/Journal of Financial Economics 47 (1998) 243–277   259

descriptively accurate. The failure rate for startup companies is high enough[7] so that, without a large private value for control, many potential entrepreneurs would decide not to leave a secure job to start a new company. It is also apparent that ceding to the venture capital provider the power, frequently exercised, to remove the entrepreneur from management is a significant cost to the entrepreneur (Hellman, 1995a).

Even if entrepreneurs value control highly, they cannot demand its retention at the time that they are seeking venture financing. The typical entrepreneur has not previously run a startup company. Venture capitalists rationally insist on retaining control to protect themselves against the risk that the entrepreneur would not run the firm successfully or will extract private benefits from the firm instead of maximizing its value to all investors.

The situation changes once a startup firm has succeeded. The entrepreneur has proved her management skill and provided some evidence that she can be trusted with other peoples' money. Returning control to the entrepreneur could now maximize firm value. Even if not, the value lost may be less than the entrepreneur's private value of control. The opportunity to regain control also provides an incentive, beyond mere wealth, for the entrepreneur to devote the effort needed for success. This possibility squarely raises the contracting problem that we address below: How can the venture capitalist commit, ex ante, to transfer control back to the entrepreneur, contingent on a concept as nebulous as 'success'?

4.2. The entrepreneur's incentive contract

When the entrepreneur sells an interest in her company to a venture capital fund, the venture capitalist receives both a residual interest in the firm's value, typically in the form of convertible preferred stock or debt and significant control rights, both explicit (for example, the right to remove the chief executive officer) and implicit (for example, the right to decide whether the firm can continue in business through staged funding). In return, the company and the entrepreneur get three things. The portfolio company receives capital plus nonfinancial contributions including information, monitoring, and enhanced credibility with third parties. This explicit contract is illustrated in Fig. 3. In addition, the entrepreneur receives an implicit incentive contract denominated in control. The structure of this incentive contract depends on the availability of an IPO exit strategy.

---

[7] See Gompers (1995) (16% of portfolio companies are liquidated or go bankrupt), Barry (1994) (one-third of venture capital investments result in losses), Sahlman (1990) (one-third of venture capital investments result in losses). Additionally, a significant percentage of would be entrepreneurs never secure venture funding at all.

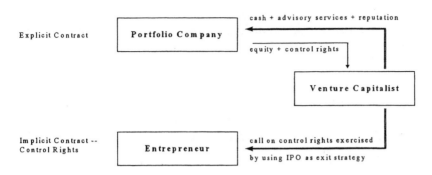

Fig. 3. Implicit and explicit contracts between venture capitalist and entrepreneur.

To begin with, an IPO is available to the portfolio company only when the company is successful. Indeed, the frequency with which a venture capital fund's portfolio companies go public is a central measure of the venture capitalist's success in the eyes of investors in venture capital funds (Gompers, 1996). When an IPO occurs, the entrepreneur receives two things. Like the venture capital provider, the entrepreneur gets cash to the extent that she sells some of her shares in the offering, plus increased value and liquidity for unsold shares. In addition, the entrepreneur reassumes much of the control originally ceded to the venture capitalist. The venture capitalist's percentage stake is reduced by its direct sale of shares,[8] by the venture capitalist's in-kind distribution of shares to its investors (Gompers and Lerner, 1997), and by the company's sale of new shares in the IPO to dispersed shareholders. The now-public firm also no longer depends on the venture capitalist for continuation decisions through staged funding; the public equity market is available. The greater liquidity of the venture capitalist's remaining investment after the IPO also reduces the venture capitalists' incentive to monitor (Coffee, 1991 discusses the tradeoff between monitoring and liquidity).[9] The venture capitalist's need to monitor the port-folio company intensively is further reduced because some of the monitoring task will now be undertaken by stock market analysts. On average, venture

[8] Over the years 1979–1990, lead venture capitalists sold shares in some 27% of IPOs of venture capital backed companies. The incidence of venture capitalist sales increased to 37% in the last three years of that period. (Lin and Smith, 1995).

[9] The increased liquidity and the venture capitalist's ability to sell off its investment gradually after the initial public offering is critical because the underwriter will typically limit the amount that the venture capitalist can sell in the IPO and over the following six months lest the market draw an unfavorable inference about the portfolio company's future value from the venture capitalist's sales (Benton and Gunderson 1993).

B.S. Black, R.J. Gilson/Journal of Financial Economics 47 (1998) 243–277   261

capital funds reduce their holdings of a portfolio company's shares by 28% within one year after an IPO (Barry et al., 1990). Three years after the IPO, only 12% of lead venture capitalists retain 5% or more of the portfolio company's shares (Lin and Smith, 1995).

Finally, and most significantly, the explicit contract between the venture capital fund and the portfolio company ensures that important control rights that were initially given to the fund, including guaranteed board membership and veto power over business decisions, disappear on an initial public offering whether or not the fund sells any shares at all in the IPO. Typically, the terms of the convertible securities held by the venture capital fund require conversion into common stock at the time of the IPO (Gompers, 1997); the negative covenants contained in the investor rights agreement also terminate on an IPO (Benton and Gunderson, 1993). In short, the venture capital fund's special control rights end at the time of an IPO, leaving the fund with only the weaker control rights attendant to substantial stock ownership. Even this control will diminish over time as the venture capital fund reduces its remaining stock position. Control becomes vested in the entrepreneur, who often retains a controlling stock interest and, even if not, retains the usual broad discretion enjoyed by chief executives of companies without a controlling shareholder.

The opportunity to acquire control through an IPO exit if the company is successful gives the entrepreneur a powerful incentive beyond the purely financial gains from the increased value of her shares in the firm. In effect, the prospect of an IPO exit gives the entrepreneur something of a call option on control, contingent on the firm's success.

Contrast this outcome with what the entrepreneur receives when the venture capital provider exits through sale of the portfolio company to an established company. As in an IPO, the entrepreneur receives cash or the more liquid securities of a publicly traded acquirer. Control, however, passes to the acquirer, even if the entrepreneur remains in charge of day-to-day management. Thus, if an IPO exit is not available, the entrepreneur cannot be given the incentive of a call option on control exercisable in the event of success. Exit through an IPO is possible only in the presence of a stock market; its role in the contract between the venture capitalist and the entrepreneur links the venture capital market and the stock market.

4.3. Feasibility of the implicit contract over control

It remains to demonstrate the feasibility of the implicit incentive contract over control and its superiority to an explicit contract. We undertake these tasks in this and the next subsection. The difficulty of defining success and the potential advantages of an implicit contract are suggested by the parties' use of an implicit contract involving staged funding to handle the pre-IPO decision as to whether and on what terms the venture capitalist will provide additional financing.

The feasibility problem is to specify a self-enforcing implicit contract: (i) whose terms are clear; (ii) whose satisfaction by the entrepreneur is observable; and (iii) whose breach by the venture capital provider would be observable and punished by the market. Consider the following stylized implicit contract: The entrepreneur will be deemed sufficiently successful to exercise her call option on control and the venture capital provider will exit through an IPO, so long as a reputable investment banker will underwrite a firm commitment offering. The need to clearly specify the conditions under which the entrepreneur can exercise the call option on control is met, not by defining numerical performance standards that the portfolio company must meet, but by delegating the performance assessment to a third party. Investment bankers have an incentive to seek out (or respond to inquiries from) portfolio companies whose performance has been strong enough to allow a successful public offering. A central feature of the investment banker's role in a public offering is as an information intermediary who proffers its reputation on behalf of the portfolio company much as the venture capitalist provides credibility to the portfolio company at an earlier stage in its development. The investment banker's internal standards for companies it is willing to take public, made credible by its willingness to commit its own capital and reputation to the offering, provide a self-enforcing statement of the conditions for exercise of the entrepreneur's call option.

The second requirement, that the entrepreneur's satisfaction of the exercise conditions be observable, is met in the same way. The investment banker's offer to take the portfolio company public is directly observable by the venture capital provider and the entrepreneur and is credible because the investment banker has the right incentives to honestly evaluate a portfolio company's performance.

The final requirement, that the venture capitalist's breach of the implicit contract be observable and punishable by the market, is also met. Observability results from the character of the venture capital market. The universe of portfolio companies sufficiently successful to merit a public offering is limited, as is the number of venture capital providers. Both sides of the market are relatively concentrated, with a significant number of portfolio companies geographically concentrated and the offices of a significant percentage of U.S. venture capital providers found along a short strip of Sand Hill Road in Silicon Valley (Saxanian, 1994). Moreover, venture capital funds typically specialize in portfolio companies geographically proximate to the fund's office.[10] While

---

[10] Lerner (1994a) reports that venture capital providers located within five miles of a portfolio company are twice as likely to have a board representative than providers located more than 500 miles distant. The fact that in 1996, 40% of total venture capital disbursements were to portfolio companies in California (Venture Capital Yearbook, 1997) provides further evidence of venture capital provider concentration sufficient to support a reputation market.

proximity facilitates monitoring, it also facilitates the emergence and maintenance of a reputation market. A claim by an entrepreneur that a venture capital provider declined to allow a portfolio company to go public when a reputable investment banker was available would quickly circulate through the community. Finally, venture capital providers are repeat players, who typically seek at regular intervals to raise funds for new limited partnerships, which must then invest in new portfolio companies, before prior limited partnerships are completed (Sahlman, 1990). In the competition to be lead venture investor in the most attractive companies, a reputation for breaching the implicit contract for control is hardly an advantage.

The viability of reputation market constraints on venture capitalist behavior is confirmed by another aspect of the overall venture capitalist-entrepreneur relationship. The venture capitalist's staged capital commitment gives the venture capitalist the option to abandon short of providing the portfolio company sufficient funds to complete its business plan. This gives the entrepreneur incentive to perform, gives the venture capitalist incentives to monitor, and reduces agency costs by shifting the continuation decision from the entrepreneur to the venture capitalist. However, this pattern, coupled with the right of first refusal with respect to future financing typically given to the venture capitalist (Sahlman, 1990), also permits the venture capitalist to act opportunistically. What can the entrepreneur do if the venture capitalist opportunistically offers to provide the second-stage financing necessary for the entrepreneur to continue at an unfair price? The entrepreneur could seek financing from other sources, but the original venture capitalist's right of first refusal presents a serious barrier: who would incur the costs of making a bid when potential bidders know that a bid will succeed only when a better informed party – the original investor – believes the price is too high? A reputation market can police this potential for opportunism.[11]

4.4. Superiority of the implicit contract over control

An explicit contract that specifies the operating performance necessary to entitle the entrepreneur to reacquire control is a difficult undertaking. Creating a state-contingent contract that specifies the control consequences of the full range of possible states of the world over the four- to ten-year average term of a venture investment, without creating perverse incentives, is a severe challenge both to the parties' predictive powers and their drafting capabilities. It is in precisely these circumstances that an implicit contract is likely to have a comparative advantage over an explicit contract.

---

[11] Admati and Pfleiderer (1994), who model the shift of the continuation decision to the venture capitalist, do not address this problem.

264   *B.S. Black, R.J. Gilson/Journal of Financial Economics 47 (1998) 243–277*

Moreover, the venture capitalist will be willing to cede control only at the time of exit, not before. Yet a mechanical formula cannot ensure that a reputable underwriter will be willing to take the portfolio company public. In addition, the venture capitalist must actively cooperate for an IPO to succeed. At the same time, the venture capitalist cannot unduly 'puff' the portfolio company's prospects, because the capital markets will punish this behavior through reduced marketability of IPOs of other portfolio companies. Thus, a supposedly explicit contract, defining when the entrepreneur and the venture capital fund have the right to take the portfolio company public, cannot easily be enforced. Such a contract would be substantially implicit in fact, even if explicit in form. Thus, it is not surprising that entrepreneurs and venture capitalists, for the most part, do not seek to contract explicitly over control.

Finally, the implicit/explicit dichotomy presented above oversimplifies the real world. In fact, some elements of the contract over control are explicit, while others are left implicit. For example, cessation of the venture capital fund's special control rights at the time of an IPO is explicitly required, while the timing of the triggering event – the IPO – is left implicit. Conversion of the venture capitalist's convertible securities into common stock special rights is sometimes explicitly required if the portfolio company achieves defined financial milestones, even without an IPO (Benton and Gunderson, 1993; Gompers, 1997). Also, consistent with the greater importance of control earlier in a firm's life, the venture capitalist's explicit control rights are generally stronger, the earlier the stage of the investment (Gompers, 1997).

4.5. Consistency with empirical evidence

In our model, successful entrepreneurs often prefer exit by IPO, and have the implicit contractual right to demand this form of exit not only when it maximizes firm value compared to the alternative of sale of the firm, but also when the entrepreneur's private value of control outweighs the entrepreneur's loss in share value. Our model predicts that the venture capitalist's successful exits will take place disproportionately through IPO. If so, IPO exits will be more profitable than exits through sale of the portfolio company, by more than can plausibly be explained by the different values available through these different forms of exit.

This prediction is confirmed. Gompers (1995) reports that venture capital funds earn an average 60% annual return on investment in IPO exits, compared to 15% in acquisition exits; see also Petty et al. (1994); Sagari and Guidotti (1993). MacIntosh (1996) reports that IPO exits are more profitable in Canada as well. It is not plausible that these large differences could arise if the venture capitalist chose in each case the exit that maximized return on investment.

B.S. Black, R.J. Gilson/Journal of Financial Economics 47 (1998) 243–277   265

5. Evidence from other countries

We have developed an informal theory in which the success of early stage
venture capital financing of high-growth, often high-technology firms, is linked
to the availability of exit through an initial public offering. The weak form of the
theory is that IPO exit is preferred by entrepreneurs. This preference leads to an
implicit contract over control between the entrepreneur and the venture capitalist, in which the entrepreneur's success is rewarded by giving the entrepreneur
the option to reacquire control through an IPO exit. This theory is consistent
with the evidence discussed in part 2 of a correlation between frequency of IPO
exit and amount of new capital contributed to venture capital funds, and the
evidence in Section 4.5 that successful exits occur disproportionately through
IPO.

The strong form of our theory is that the entrepreneur's preference for control
is strong enough to significantly impair the development of a venture capital
market in countries where exit by acquisition is the only viable option. This
section offers an informal test of the strong form of our theory: Does the theory
predict the observed success of venture capital in different countries with
different types of capital markets? We provide data on Germany and the United
States in part 2; we survey several other countries below.

5.1. Japan

We have only limited quantitative data on the size of the venture capital
industry in Japan. However, the quantitative and qualitative data that we have
(primarily from Milhaupt, 1997) is consistent with our theory: Japan, with its
bank-centered capital market, has relatively little venture capital. In 1995, there
were only 121 venture capital funds, of which more than half were affiliated with
banks and run by the parent bank's employees. The employees of bank-affiliated
funds commonly rotate through jobs in the bank's venture capital affiliate and
then return to the parent bank. Thus, they are unlikely to develop the special
skills needed to evaluate high-technology investments. Another 25 Japanese
venture capital funds were run by securities firms or insurance companies.

Unlike American venture capital funds, which primarily provide equity
financing, Japanese funds, perhaps reflecting their parentage, provide funds
mostly through loans. Where American venture capital funds concentrate on
high-tech businesses, and are the principal capital source for many startup
high-tech firms, Japanese venture capital firms rarely invest in high-technology
firms. Instead, they concentrate on manufacturing and services, including such
mundane investments as small shops and restaurants. As of 1995, Japanese
venture capital funds owned more than 10% of the stock of only one biotechnology company, two new materials firms, and 12 electronics firms.

266   B.S. Black, R.J. Gilson/Journal of Financial Economics 47 (1998) 243–277

5.2. Great Britain and Other European Countries

The similarity between Germany and Japan in the weakness of their venture capital industries strengthens the empirical support for the claim that bank-centered capital markets do not develop a strong venture capital industry. The converse claim is that stock-market centered capital markets can develop a strong venture capital industry. In particular, our theory predicts that Great Britain, with its active stock market, should have comparatively strong venture capital industries. This prediction is also supported by the evidence. British GDP is only about two-thirds of Germany's, yet its venture capital industry is almost five times larger, measured by cumulative capital committed (Economist, 1996); new capital commitments are comparable to the United States as a percentage of GDP. Ireland, with its easy access to the London stock market, also has relatively high venture capital as a percentage of GDP. Britain and Ireland are the clear European leaders in venture capital, with everyone else far behind.

Table 6 shows new funds raised by venture capital funds in 1993 and 1994 as a percentage of GDP. Great Britain's lead over everyone else would be greater still if the data were classified by the venture capital fund's home country,

Table 6
New capital committed to venture capital funds, 1993–1994 (percent of GDP)

New capital commitments to venture capital funds, as percent of national GNP, for various countries between 1993 and 1994.

Country	Year		Average: 1993–1994
	1993	1994	
United States	0.03%	0.06%	0.05%
Great Britain	0.09	0.27	0.18
France	0.06	0.07	0.06
Italy	0.02	0.02	0.02
Germany	0.01	0.01	0.01
Netherlands	0.04	0.07	0.05
Spain	0.03	0.01	0.02
Sweden	0.06	0.06	0.06
Ireland	0.04	0.25	0.15
Portugal	0.06	0.07	0.06
Belgium	0.04	0.03	0.04
Denmark	0.01	0.08	0.04
Switzerland	0.03	0.02	0.03
Norway	0.05	0.03	0.04
Finland	0.01	0.04	0.02
Iceland	0.06	0	0.03
Austria	0	0	0

Source: European Venture Capital Association, 1995.

B.S. Black, R.J. Gilson/Journal of Financial Economics 47 (1998) 243–277   267

because British-based venture capital funds invest substantial amounts through affiliates in other European countries.

These data understate the relative size of the U.S. venture capital industry. European venture capital firms are less specialized than their American counterparts and are often affiliated with commercial banks. The European Venture Capital Association defines 'venture capital' to include leveraged buyouts and buyins, and replacement of a firm's existing financing. In contrast, leveraged buyout firms in the United States are a distinct industry from venture capital firms; venture capital is also distinct from non-venture private equity financing. Non-venture uses of funds by European 'venture capital' firms are substantial. For example, in Great Britain, 47% of capital commitments in 1994 went to buyins and buyouts, and only 8% to early stage financing. In France, 40% of venture capital comes from banks, and in 1994, 51% of funds committed went to buyouts, buyins, and replacement financing, while only 9% went to early stage financing.

5.3. Canada

Our evidence on Canada is drawn primarily from the recent survey by MacIntosh (1996). Canada has a relatively open IPO market – both domestic IPOs and access to the U.S. IPO market. Thus, our theory predicts that Canada should have a relatively active venture capital industry. The Canadian data are difficult to interpret because of heavy government intervention in the venture capital industry. Labor Sponsored Venture Capital Corporations (LSVCCs), which must be formed by a labor union, receive substantial tax benefits. As a result, they dominate the Canadian venture capital industry. These funds tend to invest more conservatively than other venture capital funds. The largest single LSVCC fund, the Solidarite fund, is owned by the government of Quebec.

Still, there is substantial evidence that Canadian venture capital funds, especially private funds, play a large role in early-stage financing of high-technology Canadian firms. In 1994, private independent funds had C\$1.8 billion under management, and all Canadian venture capital firms had C\$4.5 billion under management. The latter figure is comparable to the United States after adjusting for the size of the economy. Moreover, 25% of new capital went to early-stage financing – a figure similar to that for the United States, and much higher than for European and Japanese venture capital firms. The percentage of early-stage investments is likely higher than this for non-LSVCC funds. In Canada, as in the United States, IPO exit is common and the highest-return exits are through IPOs.

5.4. Israel

Israel offers an interesting case study of how an existing venture capital industry can adapt when the option of a domestic IPO is taken away through regulation. The Israeli economy has grown rapidly during the 1990s, partly in response to deregulation of a formerly heavily government-controlled economy. High-technology startups, often financed by venture capital funds, have been an important element in this growth (Gourlay, 1996). Multiple elements have contributed to the Israeli high-technology and venture capital industries, including government guarantees against large losses by publicly traded venture capital funds in the form of a put option on the fund's shares, government creation of incubator facilities for startup firms, and a substantial influx in the early 1990s of immigrant scientists from Russia.

In the early 1990s, Israeli high-technology firms often went public on the Tel Aviv Stock Exchange at a very early stage. After a stock price crash in early 1994, the Tel Aviv Stock Exchange adopted listing rules that limited IPOs by early-stage companies. Israeli venture capital funds have nonetheless continued to flourish by shifting their IPOs from the Tel Aviv Stock Exchange to the NASDAQ market. Giza Group (1996) reports the results of 16 IPOs of venture capital-backed Israeli companies from 1993 through early 1996, of which 14 were on NASDAQ, one on the British 'AIM' small-firm market, and one on the Tel Aviv Stock Exchange. As of March 31, 1997, 62 Israeli companies had listed securities on NASDAQ, including 22 in 1996 alone; most were high-tech companies. The cumulative total exceeds any other country's except Canada's, and far exceeds any other country's relative to GDP.

6. Alternative explanations for intercountry variations in venture capital

We have developed in this paper an informal theory, based on the stock market's role in providing contracting options not available in a bank-centered capital market, that may partially explain cross-country variations in venture capital. In this section, we evaluate briefly several alternative explanations for the different levels of venture capital financing in stock market-centered and bank-centered capital markets. We first consider a claim of functional irrelevance: institutional differences between stock market-centered and bank-centered systems do not affect economic outcomes because bank-centered systems have developed functionally equivalent means for financing early-stage entrepreneurial activities. We then turn to explanations that acknowledge differences between countries in their ability to provide financing for high-technology ventures, but assign causation differently than we do.

While our analysis here is only suggestive, differential performance between the United States and Germany in industries where venture capital plays a significant role in the U.S. suggests that Germany has not yet developed a functional substitute for venture capital. Alternative explanations may account for some of this functional difference, but none appears able to fully displace the account of cross-national differences offered here.

6.1. Institutional but not functional differences

Different methods of organizing capital markets do not necessarily dictate corresponding functional or performance differences. For example, empirical research by Kaplan (1994a,b) and Kaplan and Minton (1994) suggests that Japanese and German companies change top management in response to poor earnings and stock price performance about as often and as quickly as United States companies, despite the three countries' quite different corporate governance institutions. The similar outcomes could reflect the impact of selection on path-dependent corporate governance systems. That three leading industrial economies change senior management under roughly the same circumstances may reflect a selection bias. By limiting the sample to these successful systems, we observe only systems that, within the constraints established by their particular institutions, have solved reasonably well the central corporate governance problem of replacing poorly performing managers (Gilson, 1996; Kaplan and Ramseyer, 1996).

The same functional equivalence argument can be made with respect to differences in how successful economies finance entrepreneurial activities. If other financing methods, such as bank financing of startup companies or internalization of the entrepreneurial process by large companies, yields the same performance as the United States' venture capital market, then the institutional differences are historically interesting but not functionally significant.

The empirical evidence needed to assess the functional equivalence argument for venture-capital financed industries is not available, but anecdotal evidence makes us skeptical about functional equivalence. The United States has become a world leader in precisely those industries, notably biotechnology and computer-related high technology, in which the venture capital market figures centrally (Powell, 1996). Moreover, in both Europe and the United States, large pharmaceutical companies are responding to biotechnology entrepreneurship not by funding the entrepreneurs directly, but instead by providing later-stage financing and partnering arrangements to entrepreneurial companies, mostly U.S.-based and originally financed through U.S. venture capital (Powell, 1996; Hellman, 1995b; Lerner and Merges, 1997). The result is not functional equivalence but specialization: Different activities are allocated to different countries on the basis of differences in their venture capital markets.

6.2. The role of pension fund financing of venture capital

In both Japan and Germany, pension funds do not invest in venture capital. In Germany, corporate pension obligations are typically unfunded, so large private pension plans do not exist. Japan has moderate sized corporate pension plans, but these plans are barred by law from investing in venture capital (Milhaupt, 1997). In the United States, in contrast, the Department of Labor in

1979 explicitly sanctioned pension fund investment in venture capital. As shown in Table 3, pension plans now provide over 40% of total investment in U.S. venture capital funds.

Differences in pension fund size and regulation can explain part, but in our judgment only part, of the cross-national differences in the size of the venture capital industry. Funded pension obligations, as in the United States, as opposed to unfunded pension obligations in Germany, dictate only who makes employee pension investments, not the investments themselves. A company with an unfunded pension plan, in effect, incurs an unsecured debt – its promise to pay pensions when workers retire. The company can invest the funds thus made available in any way it chooses, including in venture capital. German firms could also voluntarily fund their pension obligations, as many American firms did even before ERISA established minimum funding requirements in 1973. The pension plan could then invest in venture capital, if it so chose.

In the U.S., the unclear legality of pension fund investments in venture capital between 1973 and 1979 sterilized this pool of investable funds. Not surprisingly, the 1979 regulatory change resulted in a flow of funds into the previously restricted area. German firms have never been subject to an investment restriction similar to 1973–1979 U.S. regulation.

More generally, money is the ultimate fungible commodity, and venture capital commitments are a tiny fraction of total business investment – in the U.S., around $5 billion annually compared to gross investment of over $1 trillion. If there were attractive profits to be made from venture capital investing, it seems likely that funds would be available from other sources, even if not from pension plans. After all, the Germans and the Japanese save more than Americans as a percentage of GDP, merely in different forms.

6.3. Differences in labor market regulation

Germany and a number of other Western European countries impose substantial restrictions on layoffs, especially severance payment obligations. These rules impose costs on startup businesses and thus could discourage their formation. Variations in labor market restrictions correlate with observed national variations in venture capital. Germany has strong layoff protections and little venture capital. Japan has few formal restrictions on layoffs, but the common practice by large companies of hiring only recent college graduates and promising them lifetime employment reduces labor market mobility (Gilson and Roe, 1997). In contrast, the United States and Britain have more flexible labor markets and more active venture capital markets.

Labor market regulation and practices could well affect the vitality of venture capital. For example, Gilson (1997) argues that weak enforcement of covenants not to compete is a factor in the strength of venture capital in California; Hyde (1997) argues that the concentration of venture-capital-backed firms in Silicon

B.S. Black, R.J. Gilson/Journal of Financial Economics 47 (1998) 243–277   271

Valley both supports and depends on what he calls 'high velocity' labor markets. But labor market regulation, as a partial explanation for the vitality of venture capital markets, seems unlikely to fully displace our explanation, based on differences in capital markets.

Consider Germany as an example. Severance obligations build over time; they are much less burdensome for a startup firm that fails after a few years of operation than for a mature firm that closes a plant that has operated for decades. Moreover, unpaid severance obligations are of little significance if a firm goes bankrupt – they merely expand the pool of unsecured claims on the firm's assets.

Moreover, labor market restrictions do not map perfectly onto national patterns in venture capital activity. Canada has moderately strong labor market restrictions; Ireland and Israel have strong restrictions comparable to West Germany's. Yet these countries also have strong venture capital. This pattern is consistent with their access to stock markets: the London market for Ireland; the U.S. market for Israel; and U.S. and domestic stock markets for Canada.

6.4. Cultural differences in entrepreneurship

A final explanation is cultural. Germans and Japanese could be less entrepreneurial and less willing to risk failure than Americans, leading to lesser demand for venture capital services (Milhaupt, 1997, discusses Japanese culture). Cultural explanations for different patterns of economic activity are hard to evaluate. They can be partly tautological. In economically successful countries like Germany and Japan, the forces of economic selection will cause culture and economic institutions to become mutually supportive. Because both are endogenously determined, observing that cultural institutions support existing economic patterns tells us nothing about causation. For present purposes, the more interesting issue is not a static inquiry into the current equilibrium of culture and economic institutions, but a dynamic one: how can culture and institutions change in response to exogenous changes in the economic environment (North, 1990, 1994). We briefly consider this issue from an instrumental perspective in Section 7.

However, there is some reason for skepticism about claims of large cultural differences in willingness to take risks. People in all countries found large numbers of businesses, most of which fail. The empirical regularity to be explained is *not* why the Germans and Japanese do not start risky new businesses, but why they do not start many *high-technology* businesses, with few tangible assets on which a bank can rely for partial return of its investment. The success of immigrant entrepreneurs in countries with strong venture capital (for example, Russian immigrants in Israel and Asian immigrants in the United States) suggests that entrepreneurs will emerge if the institutional infrastructure needed to support them is available. After all, Russia and India are also not

272 *B.S. Black, R.J. Gilson/Journal of Financial Economics 47 (1998) 243–277*

known for their cultural support of entrepreneurship. Moreover, efforts to find large cross-cultural differences in entrepreneurship between the U.S. and Russia at the close of the Communist period have failed, even though these two countries ought to exhibit much larger differences than the United States, Germany, and Japan (Shiller et al., 1991, 1992).

7. Implications for venture capital in bank-centered capital markets

Exploring the implications of the link between venture capital markets and stock markets is more complicated than the simple admonition that bank-centered capital markets should create a stock market. That straightforward approach has been tried before and failed. For example, France and Germany created special stock exchange segments for newer, smaller companies during the 1980s that, by the mid-1990s, had been shuttered or marginalized (Rasch, 1994). Nonetheless, the financial press still stresses the absence of a venture capital market as being at the root of the European high technology sector's poor performance, particularly with respect to Germany (e.g., Fisher, 1996a,b), and three efforts are underway to try again to create stock markets that cater to small high-technology companies. The Alternative Investment Market of the London Stock Exchange began trading in June 1995 and now lists over 200 firms (Price, 1996). Euro NM, a consortium of the French Le Nouveau Marche', which began trading in February, 1996, the German Neur Market, and the Belgian New Market, is scheduled to begin full operation in 1997. Finally, EASDAQ, an exchange explicitly patterned after the U.S. NASDAQ and of which the NASD is a part owner, opened on September 30, 1996 (Pickles, 1996). This flurry of stock market creation, taken with the explicit goal of enhancing the European venture capital market, suggests that there may be value in exploring the normative implications of the stock market-venture capital market link.

We begin our analysis of this link by stressing the path dependency of national capital markets. It is not merely a stock market that is missing in bank-centered systems. The secondary institutions that have developed in bank-centered systems, including the banks' conservative approach to lending and investing, and social and financial incentives that less richly reward entrepreneurial zeal and more severely penalize failure (See Harrison, 1990 (Germany); Milhaupt, 1997 (Japan)), are less conducive to entrepreneurial activity than the secondary institutions of stock market-centered capital markets. More critically, experienced venture capitalists, able to assess the prospects of new venture and to provide the nonfinancial contributions that venture capitalists supply in the United States are absent, as are investment bankers experienced in taking early-stage companies public. Neither institution will develop quickly. A strong venture capital market thus reflects an equilibrium of a

B.S. Black, R.J. Gilson/Journal of Financial Economics 47 (1998) 243–277   273

number of interdependent factors, only one of which is the presence of a stock market.

For example, Germany today faces a chicken and egg problem: a venture capital market requires a stock market, but a stock market requires a supply of entrepreneurs and deals which, in turn, require a venture capital market. In addition, German entrepreneurs who care about future control of their company must trust venture capitalists to return control to them some years hence and must further trust that the stock market window will be open when they are ready to go public. The institutional design issue is how to simultaneously create both a set of mutually dependent institutions and the trust that these institutions will work as expected when called upon.

In such a path-dependent equilibrium, the cost of change is the guard rail that keeps us on the path. We remain in an equilibrium less efficient than would be possible without the transaction costs of creating the institutions needed to support alternatives (Kohn, 1995). While we do not aspire to offer a solution here, our analysis suggests an approach to creating the conditions conducive to a vigorous venture capital market: avoid the problem of creating multiple new institutions by piggybacking on another country's institutions. If this is successful, a profit opportunity and corresponding potential for the development of local institutions will be created.

Most obviously, in the increasingly global capital market, the German venture capital market could follow Israel's lead in relying on the United States stock market and its supporting infrastructure. A German company that maintains accounting records in a fashion consistent with U.S. standards – arguably much less of a burden when done from the beginning than if implemented by a conversion, as when Daimler-Benz listed its shares on the New York Stock Exchange – confronts no regulatory barrier to listing on NASDAQ, the exchange most suitable to venture-capital-backed IPOs. At present, over 100 European companies, including one German company, list their shares on NASDAQ. Many of these listings represent the initial public offering of the company's stock. With NASDAQ comes its institutional infrastructure. For example, both Hambrecht and Quist and Robertson, Stephens and Co., leading investment bankers for venture-capital-backed IPOs in the United States, are opening European offices and holding conferences to introduce American venture capital funds to European entrepreneurs (Lavin, 1996). Silicon Valley law firms are also actively recruiting European IPO candidates.

The availability of this institutional infrastructure, without the costs of establishing it from scratch, can shorten the shadow of the past and, in the medium term, induce the development of competing local institutions. For example, in the near term, foreign venture capitalists will likely find it profitable to hire and train locals to help them find profitable investment opportunities. In the medium term, some of these people, once trained, will form their own firms and compete with their former employers.

8. Conclusion

In this paper. we have examined one of the path-dependent consequences of the difference between stock market-centered and bank-centered capital markets: the link between an active stock market and a strong venture capital market. We have shown that economies of scope among financial and nonfinancial contributions by venture capital providers, plus venture capital investors' need for a quantitative measure of venture capital funds' skill, can explain the importance of an exit strategy. Moreover, the potential for exit through an IPO, possible in a stock-market-centered capital market, allows the venture capitalist and the entrepreneur to contract implicitly over control, in a manner that is not easily duplicable in a bank-centered capital market. Finally, we have suggested that the best strategy for overcoming path dependent barriers to a venture capital market in bank-centered systems is to piggyback on the institutional infrastructure of stock-market-centered systems.

Our model seeks to explain the importance of a possible IPO exit for a high-growth firm financed by a venture capital fund, for which exit by the fund is desirable at a stage in the firm's life when it is still consuming rather than generating capital. For a mature, cash-generating firm, another exit strategy that preserves the entrepreneur's control is possible: the firm itself can buy back the venture capital fund's stake, perhaps by borrowing the needed funds. This strategy permits a somewhat different implicit contract over control between the fund and an entrepreneur: if the firm is successful enough to buy out the fund, the fund will acquiesce in this strategy even if this form of exit does not maximize the fund's return on an individual investment. In the United States, this form of exit is associated not with venture capital funds but with 'leveraged buyout' funds. In Europe, which has a less clear distinction between venture capital and leveraged buyouts, this form of exit is common when venture capital funds invest in management buyouts of mature firms. We plan to explore in future work the possible extension of our model to the leveraged buyout industry.

References

Admati, A., Pfleiderer, P., 1994. Robust financial contracting and the role of venture capitalists. Journal of Finance 49, 371–402.

Aoki, M., 1994. Monitoring characteristics of the main bank system: an analytical and developmental view. In: Aoki, M., Patrick, H. (Eds.), The Japanese Main Bank System: Its Relevance for Developing and Transforming Economies. Oxford University Press, Oxford.

Barry, C., 1994. New directions in venture capital research. Journal of Financial Management 23, 3–15.

Barry, C., Muscarella, C., Peavy J., III, Vetsuypens, M., 1990. The role of venture capitalists in the creation of a public company. Journal of Financial Economics 27, 447–471.

Benton, L., Gunderson, R.,Jr., 1993. Portfolio company investments: hi-tech corporation, venture capital and public offering negotiation. In: Halloran, M., Benton, L., Gunderson, R., Jr., Kearney, K., del Calvo, J. (Eds.), Law and Business, Inc. Harcourt Brace Jovanovich, New York.

Bergloff, E., 1994. A control theory of venture capital finance. Journal of Law, Economics and Organization 10, 247–267.

Black, B., 1990. Shareholder passivity reexamined. Michigan Law Review 89, 520–608.

Booth, J., Smith, R., 1986. Capital raising, underwriting and the certification hypothesis. Journal of Financial Economics 15, 261–281.

Brav, A., Gompers, P., 1997. Myth or reality? The long-run underperformance of initial public offerings: evidence from venture and nonventure capital-backed companies. Journal of Finance, forthcoming.

Bundesverband Deutsche Kapitalbeteiligungsgesellschaften (BVK) Jahrbuch [German Venture Capital Association Yearbook], various years through 1996 (BVK, Berlin, Germany).

Bygrave, W., Timmons, J., 1992. Venture capital at the crossroads. Harvard Business School Press, Cambridge, MA.

Carvalho, A., 1996. Venture capital as a network for human resources allocation. Unpublished working paper. University of Illinois.

Coffee, J., 1991. Liquidity versus control: The institutional investor as corporate monitor. Columbia Law Review 91, 1277–1368.

Diamond, D., 1991. Monitoring and reputation: the choice between bank loans and directly placed debt. Journal of Political Economy 99, 689–721.

Economist, 1996. Going for the golden egg. Sept. 28, 1996, at 89.

Edwards, J., Fischer, K., 1994. Banks, finance and investment in Germany. Cambridge University Press, Cambridge.

European Venture Capital Association, 1995. EVCA Yearbook 1995. Ernst and Young, London, England.

Fisher, A., 1996a. A venture across the pond. Financial Times, July 24, 1996, 12.

Fisher, A., 1996b. Germans urged to take a risk for jobs. Financial Times, July 16, 1996, 2.

Florida, R., Martin, K., 1990. The Breakthrough Illusion: Corporate America's Failure to Move from Innovation to Mass Production. BasicBooks, New York.

Gilson, R., Kraakman, R., 1984. The mechanisms of market efficiency. Virginia Law Review 70, 549–644.

Gilson, R., Roe, M., 1997. Lifetime employment: Labor peace and the evolution of Japanese corporate governance. Unpublished working paper. Columbia Law School.

Gilson, R., 1996. Corporate governance and economic efficiency. Washington University Law Quarterly 74, 327–345.

Gilson, R., 1997. The legal infrastructure of high-technology industrial districts: Silicon Valley and covenants not to compete. Unpublished working paper. Stanford Law School.

Giza Group, 1996. Survey of venture capital and investment funds in Israel: August 1996 Update. Giza Group, Tel Aviv, Israel.

Gompers, P., 1997. An examination of convertible securities in venture capital. Journal of Law and Economics, forthcoming.

Gompers, P., 1996. Grandstanding in the venture capital industry. Journal of Financial Economics 42, 133–156.

Gompers, P., 1995. Optimal investment, monitoring, and the staging of venture capital. Journal of Financial Economics 50, 1461–1489.

Gompers, P., Lerner, J., 1996. The use of covenants: an empirical analysis of venture partnership agreements. Journal of Law and Economics 39, 463–498.

Gompers, P., Lerner, J., 1997. Venture capital distributions: short-run and long-run reactions. Unpublished working paper. Harvard Business School.

276   *B.S. Black, R.J. Gilson/Journal of Financial Economics 47 (1998) 243–277*

Gorman, M., Sahlman, W., 1989. What do venture capitalists do? Journal of Business Venturing 4, 231–248.

Gourlay, R., 1996. The development of a venture capital industry lies behind the economic success of a new breed of high-tech Israeli company. Financial Times, April 30, 1996, 14.

Grossman, S., Hart, O., 1988. One share-one vote and the market for corporate control. Journal of Financial Economics 20, 175–202.

Harris, M., Raviv, A., 1988. Corporate governance: voting rights and majority rules. Journal of Financial Economics 20, 203–235.

Harrison, E., 1990. The West German venture capital market. Peter Lang, Frankfurt am Main, Frankfurt, Germany.

Hellman, T., 1995a. The allocation of control rights in venture capital contracts. Research Paper No. 1362. Stanford Business School, Stanford.

Hellman, T., 1995b. Competition and cooperation between entrepreneurial an established companies: the viability of corporate venture investments. Unpublished working paper. Stanford Business School, Stanford.

Hyde, A., 1997. High-velocity labor markets. Unpublished working paper. Rutgers Law School.

Hoshi, T., 1993. Evolution of the main bank system in Japan. Unpublished working paper. University of California at San Diego.

Kaplan, S., 1994a. Top executive rewards and firm performance: a comparison of Japan and the United States. Journal of Political Economy 102, 510–546.

Kaplan, S., 1994b. Top executives, turnover, and firm performance in Germany. Journal of Law, Economics and Organization 10, 142–159.

Kaplan, S., Minton, B., 1994. Appointments of outsiders to Japanese boards: determinants and implications for managers. Journal of Financial Economics 36, 225–258.

Kaplan, S., Ramseyer, J., 1996. Those Japanese firms with their disdain for shareholders: another fable for the academy. Washington University Law Quarterly 74, 403–418.

Kohn, M., 1995. Economics as a theory of exchange. Unpublished working paper. Dartmouth College Department of Economics, Dartmouth, NH.

Lavin, D., 1996. The sky's the limit. Convergence 2, 8.

Lerner, J., 1995. Venture capitalists and the oversight of private firms. Journal of Finance 50, 301–318.

Lerner, J., 1994a. The syndication of venture capital investments. Financial Management 23, 16–27.

Lerner, J., 1994b. Venture capitalists and the decision to go public. Journal of Financial Economics 35, 293–316.

Lerner, J., Merges, R., 1997. The control of strategic alliance: an empirical analysis of biotechnology collaborations. Working paper No. 6014. National Bureau of Economic Research.

Lin, T., Smith, R., 1995. Insider reputation and selling decisions: the unwinding of venture capital investments during equity IPOs. Unpublished working paper. Claremont Graduate School.

MacIntosh, J., 1996. Venture capital exits in Canada and the U.S. Unpublished working paper. University of Toronto Faculty of Law.

Marx, L., 1994. Negotiation of venture capital contracts. Unpublished working paper. University of Rochester.

Megginson, W., Weiss, K., 1991. Venture capital certification in initial public offerings. Journal of Finance 46, 879–903.

Milhaupt, C., 1997. The market for innovation in the United States and Japan: Venture capital and the comparative corporate governance debate. Northwestern University Law Review 91, 865–898.

Moukheiber, Z., March 25, 1996, Kleiner's web. Forbes, 40–42.

North, D., 1994. Economic performance through time. American Economic Review 84, 359–368.

North, D., 1990. Institutions, institutional change, and economic performance. Cambridge University Press, Cambridge, England.

Petty, W., Bygrave, W. Shulman, J., 1994. Harvesting the entrepreneurial venture: a time for creating value. Journal of Applied Corporate Finance. Spring, 48–58.

Pickles, C., 1996. One answer to Europe's capital needs. Wall Street Journal, Europe, October 23, 1996.

Porter, M., 1992. Capital disadvantages: America's failing investment system. Harvard Business Review, Sept.–Oct, 65–82.

Powell, W., 1996. Inter-organizational collaboration in the biotechnology industry. Journal of Institutional and Theoretical Economics 152, 197–215.

Price, C., 1996. EASDAQ pins hopes on NASDAQ. Financial Times, Sept. 30, 1996, 23.

Rajan, R., 1992. Insiders and outsiders: the choice between informed and arm's length debt. Journal of Finance 47, 1367–1400.

Rasch, S., 1994. Special stock market segments for small company shares in Europe – what went wrong? Discussion Paper No. 93-13. Center for European Economic Research.

Roe, M., 1994. Strong managers, weak owners: the political roots of American corporate finance. Princeton University Press, Princeton.

Sahlman, W., 1990. The structure and governance of venture capital organizations. Journal of Financial Economics 27, 473–522.

Sagari, S., Guidotti, G., 1993. Venture capital: the lessons from the developing world for the developing world. Financial Markets. Instruments and Investments 1, 31–42.

Saxanian, A., 1994. Regional Advantage: Culture and Competition in Silicon Valley and Route 128. Harvard University Press, Cambridge, MA.

Shiller, R., Boycko, M., Korobov, V., 1991. Popular attitudes toward free markets: the Soviet Union and the United States compared. American Economic Review 81, 385–400.

Shiller, R., Boycko, M., Korobov, V., 1992. Hunting for homo sovieticus: situational versus attitudinal factors in economic behavior. Brookings Papers on Economic Activity, 127–181.

Venture Capital Yearbook, various years through 1997. Venture Economics Publishing, New York.

[4]

Ownership and Control of German Corporations

Julian Franks
London Business School

Colin Mayer
University of Oxford

In a study of the ownership of German corporations, we find a strong relation between board turnover and corporate performance, little association of concentrations of ownership with managerial disciplining, and only limited evidence that pyramid structures can be used for control purposes. The static relationship of ownership to control in Germany is therefore similar to the United Kingdom and the United States. However, there are marked differences in dynamic relations involving transfers of ownership. There is an active market in share blocks giving rise to changes in control, but the gains are limited and accrue solely to the holders of large blocks, not to minority investors. We provide evidence of low overall benefits to control changes and the exploitation of private benefits of control.

The United Kingdom and United States have "outsider systems" of corporate control with large equity markets, dispersed ownership, and active markets in corporate control. In contrast, a majority of Continental European capital markets have "insider systems" with small numbers of quoted

This article is part of an ESRC funded project on "Capital Markets, Corporate Governance and the Market for Corporate Control," no. W102251103. We are also grateful for financial support from the European Union's Training and Mobility of Researchers Network, contract no. FRMX-CT960054. This article has benefited from interviews with numerous individuals in Germany and the United Kingdom. We are particularly grateful to Gerhard Hablizer of Commerzbank, Ellen Schneider-Lenne and Ulrich Weiss of Deutsche Bank, Charles Lowe of Deutsche Bank UK, Dr. Klaus Christian Hubner and Berndt Jonas of Fried. Krupp AG, Dr. Peter Krailic of McKinsey, Peter von Elten and Andreas Buddenbrock of JP Morgan, Greg Morgan of Munger, Tolles & Olson, Malcolm Thwaites of Morgan Grenfell, Dr Kiran Bhojani and Dr Wilhelm Heilmann of Veba AG, Michael Treichl of Warburg, Nicholas Weickart of Weickart, Simon, & Westpfahl, Hans Peter Peters and Andrew Neumann of WestLB. The article has been presented at the conference on Relational Investing organized by Columbia University, at the ESF Network in Financial Markets Workshop on Corporate Finance at Lisbon, the annual meetings of the Western Finance Association in Santa Fe in 1994, and at the annual meetings of the American Finance Association in San Francisco in 1996. It has been presented at seminars at Cardiff University, Center for Financial Studies, Frankfurt, City University, London, HEC, Lausanne, Liege, London Business School, Oxford, Penn State, Southern California, Virginia, Arizona, Vienna, and Warwick. We wish to thank the following for many useful comments and suggestions: Harold Baums, Erik Berglöf, Arnoud Boot, Wolfgang Buehler, Bill Carleton, Wendy Carlin, Jeremy Edwards, Klaus Fischer, Rajna Gibson, Bob Harris, Martin Hellwig, David Hirshleifer, Kose John, Steve Kaplan, John Moore, Mark Roe, and Luigi Zingales. We are grateful to an anonymous referee and Gary Gorton (editor) for their many suggestions. We are grateful to Marc Goergen, Luis Correia da Silva, and Myriam Soria for research assistance on this project. This article records the views of the authors alone and not those of any person interviewed or their associated institutions. Any remaining errors are the sole responsibility of the authors. Address correspondence to Julian Franks, London Business School, Regent's Park, London NW1 4SA, United Kingdom.

The Review of Financial Studies Winter 2001 Vol. 14, No. 4, pp. 943–977
© 2001 The Society for Financial Studies

The Review of Financial Studies / v 14 n 4 2001

companies, concentrated share ownership, and comparatively low levels of takeover activity. Germany is a good example of an insider system. It has fewer than 800 quoted companies, compared with nearly 3,000 in the United Kingdom, and 85% of the largest quoted companies have a single shareholder owning more than 25% of voting shares. Corporate ownership is characterized by a strikingly high concentration of ownership, primarily in the hands of families and other companies. Corporate holdings frequently take the form of complex webs of holdings and pyramids of intercorporate holdings. Bank influence and control are extensive where shareholdings are widely dispersed.

How does this pattern of ownership affect corporate control? According to Shleifer and Vishny (1986), concentrated share ownership overcomes free-rider problems of corporate control that affect stock markets, such as in the United Kingdom and United States, with dispersed ownership. It should therefore be associated with more active corporate governance. On the other hand, according to Bebchuk (1999), insider systems are afflicted by private benefits to the detriment of corporate efficiency and La Porta, Lopes-de-Silanes, and Shleifer (1999) argue that the German civil code provides weak protection for minorities at the expense of the operation of its capital markets. Ownership concentrations may therefore be associated with weak rather than strong corporate governance.

We evaluate these conflicting views by investigating the relationship between board turnover and corporate performance for firms with different ownership patterns. Kaplan (1994b) has examined this issue and concluded that while management board turnover in Germany is related to performance, neither the size nor nature of ownership has much of an influence. We extend his work by using more elaborate measures of pyramids and a new database on proxy votes. We record how these control vehicles significantly influence the relationship between cash flow and voting rights and relate these new measures of ownership and control to board turnover and performance. We find, first, that board turnover in German firms is similar to that of U.K. and U.S. firms. Second, there is a close relationship between board turnover and poor performance in Germany, as has been documented in the United Kingdom and United States. Third, while large blocks of shares held by families are often owned indirectly through other companies, that is, through pyramids, they are only used for control purposes in about one-third of cases. Fourth, the relation between managerial disciplining and performance is no worse in widely held firms, where banks exercise significant control, than in companies with large concentrated ownership.

Thus far, both this article and Kaplan's take a static view of the relationship between ownership and control. However, it has recently been suggested that there may be significant differences in transfers of ownership—the dynamics of control. While there has been virtually no Anglo-American market for corporate control in Germany in the post–World War II period, there is a substantial market in sales of large share stakes. Burkhart, Gromb, and

Panunzi (1998) point to the advantages of markets in partial share stakes in overcoming free-rider problems, but Bebchuk (1999) emphasizes the private benefit problems that they may create. We find that the characteristics of this market are quite different from its Anglo-American equivalent. Block premia are much lower than target bid premia in takeovers in the United Kingdom and United States, and while sellers of large blocks of shares obtain benefits, minorities do not share at all in the bid premia. Differences between bid premia paid to sellers of large blocks and to minorities provide estimates of the private benefits enjoyed by block holders in Germany, and we find these to be significant.

One explanation for low bid premia is that gains to takeover are small as a consequence of significant impediments to managerial control by new block holders. We document these impediments in several case studies of German takeovers. We examine the extent to which share block sales are associated with managerial disciplining by relating presale performance to subsequent board turnover. We find that board turnover in share block sales is appreciably lower than in takeovers in the United Kingdom and United States and that there is little relation between board turnover and corporate performance. These observations are consistent with comparatively low gains to ownership changes.

In sum, while static aspects of ownership patterns in Germany do not translate into distinctive forms of control, the dynamics—transfers of ownership—operate quite differently. They reveal a smaller scale of merger benefits, the importance of private benefits in the German capital market, and limitations on the control that acquiring shareholders can exercise.

Section 1 describes the structure of ownership and control of German corporations and the hypotheses tested. Section 2 analyzes the static features of German ownership and control: Section 2.1 evaluates the significance of concentration of ownership, Section 2.2 pyramid ownership, and Section 2.3 the type of owner, including banks and their proxy holdings. Section 2.4 brings these variables together in regressions of board turnover on the ownership variables.

Section 3 turns from the statics to the dynamics of ownership. Section 3.1 reports bid premiums paid to block holders and minority shareholders in sales of blocks. These are used to estimate private benefits of control to block holders. Case studies of takeovers illustrate the influences on merger benefits. Section 3.2 evaluates the relationship between board turnover, performance, and sales of share blocks. Section 4 summarizes the results.

1. The Structure of German Ownership and Control and the Hypotheses Tested

In Section 1.1 we describe the datasets used and the structure of ownership and control of German corporations. In Section 1.2 we describe the hypotheses tested in the article.

The Review of Financial Studies / v 14 n 4 2001

1.1 The structure of ownership and control

Two main datasets were collected for this study. The larger set comprises 171 quoted industrial and commercial companies collected from Hoppenstedt Stockguide in 1990.[1] The companies in Hoppenstedt are a subset of the population of 477 quoted industrial and commercial companies in Germany in 1990. More detailed information on financial performance and board turnover was collected from company accounts on a second sample of 75 firms, derived from the larger sample of 171, for which data were available for the period 1989–1994. These 75 companies formed the basis of much of the analysis reported in Sections 2 and 3. Information on the remaining 96 companies was unavailable due to incomplete library records.[2]

We also examined case studies of the accumulation and role of large share stakes in three hostile takeovers that took place in Germany: the bid by the Flick brothers and then Veba AG for Feldmühle Nobel AG in 1988 and 1989, respectively; the bid for Continental AG by Pirelli in 1990 and 1991; and the bid for Hoesch AG by Krupp AG in 1991 and 1992. These were supplemented by interviews with block holders who had recently acquired control.[3]

1.1.1 Ownership.   Ownership of share stakes was classified by banks, families, industrial companiess, and different types of institutional investors. Data were collected on the size of ownership stakes greater than 25%; the type of owner, including bank, family, and corporation; and changes in ownership through sales of share stakes.[4] Disclosure of stakes smaller than 25% was not compulsory and they were included where available.

The size of holdings has been classified by those starting at 25%, 50%, and 75%; these constitute important thresholds that determine the control rights of shareholders. A minority stake greater than 25% provides a blocking minority which may be used, for example, to prevent issues of new shares or the dismissal of members of the supervisory board, and, when the company's constitution requires it, the removal of a voting restriction. A majority stake of less than 75% allows wide control over the management of the firm, but is subject to a blocking minority. For example, a simple majority is

---

[1] Twenty-nine banks and insurance companies were omitted to allow the analysis to focus on the nonfinancial sector.

[2] The first set of firms (the "171") includes the largest German quoted firms: the average size, based on market values of equity and preference shares, is 2.34 billion DM. Almost 50% fall in the highest quintile of all quoted industrial and commercial companies. The second set of 75 companies were mainly the largest companies in our sample of 171, with an average market capitalization of 4.29 billion DM; 73% were in the highest quintile of all industrial and commercial companies.

[3] Interviews were arranged with Commerzbank, Deutsche Bank, Deutsche Bank UK, Krupp AG, McKinsey, JP Morgan, Morgan Grenfell, Munger, Tolles & Olson, Warburg, Weickart, Simon, & Westpfahl, WestLB, and Veba AG.

[4] Ownership data were collected from Hoppenstedt Stockguide, supplemented by Saling Aktienfuhrer and Commerzbank's *wer gehoert zu wem*, a guide on shareholdings produced triennially.

Ownership and Control of German Corporations

Table 1
Proportion of companies with a single shareholding in excess of 25%, 50%, and 75% for the sample of 171 large industrial quoted companies in 1990

	Proportion of companies with a share stake in excess of		
	25%	50%	75%
A. Companies with a large shareholder the largest shareholder being ...	85.4%	57.3%	22.2%
1. Another German company	27.5%	21.1%	9.9%
2. An insurance company	1.8%	0.0%	0.0%
3. A trust/an institutional investor	12.9%	6.4%	1.8%
4. A family group	20.5%	16.4%	5.3%
5. A foreign company[a]	9.9%	8.8%	5.3%
6. A bank	5.8%	0.0%	0.0%
7. The German State	1.2%	1.2%	0.0%
8. Other German authorities	3.5%	2.9%	0.0%
9. Unknown	2.3%	0.6%	0.0%
B. Companies without a large shareholding greater than 25, 50, or 75%, respectively.	14.6%	42.7%	77.8%
Total[b]	100.0	100.0	100.0

The table reports the proportion of companies with a large shareholder. Companies are partitioned into those that have one shareholder owning at least 25%, 50%, and 75% of the voting equity, respectively. The table partitions large shareholders into various categories including other German companies, insurance companies, trust and institutional investors, families, foreign companies, banks, German state and other German authorities.
Sources: Hoppenstedt and own calculations.
[a] Including foreign holding companies.
[b] Discrepancies in the total may be due to rounding errors.

required to appoint members of supervisory boards when existing contracts expire, but may not be sufficient for dismissal during their contract period. In the hostile takeover bid of the German tire manufacturer Continental by Pirelli, Continental management sought protection by putting a motion to its shareholders increasing the majority required to dismiss members of the supervisory board from 50% to 75%. A stake of 75% is not subject to a blocking minority.

Table 1 describes the number and owners of share stakes larger than 25%, 50%, and 75% of voting equity in our sample of 171 quoted industrial and commercial companies in 1990. The most striking feature of the sample is that for 85% of the companies there is at least one large shareholder owning more than 25% of voting shares; for 57% of companies there is a majority shareholder and for 22% the holding is sufficiently large to prevent a blocking minority. In a similar sample of the largest 173 quoted companies in the United Kingdom in 1992, we found that only 13% of companies had one shareholder owning more than 25% of issued equity, and 6% had a shareholder with more than 50% of shares.

A second feature of the table is that other German industrial companies account for 27.5% of dominant shareholdings, and families for a further 20.5% in companies with a single shareholder owning more than 25%. German institutional investors, including trusts and insurance companies, account for only 14.7%. Their role is a relatively minor one compared with

The Review of Financial Studies / v 14 n 4 2001

that played by institutional investors in the United Kingdom and United States, in part because pension funds are usually unfunded and are financed on an ongoing basis out of firm's own earnings. Equally striking is the modest size of bank holdings that account for less than 6% of share holdings in excess of 25%. Edwards and Fischer (1994) suggest that it is banks' control over proxy votes rather than their own shareholdings that confer control upon them.

Table 1 records only the immediate ownership of the sample of 171 companies. A substantial number of stakes are held by other companies, which are in turn held by other shareholders. This raises questions as to who is the ultimate shareholder, where ultimate control lies, and the motivation for the complex pattern of ownership. We distinguish between two categories of pyramids, those motivated by control, as measured by the ratio of large voting rights to cash flow rights, and those that are simply holding companies.

When large shareholdings were held directly by companies, ownership was traced back through the various layers to the ultimate investors, who were families, the state, banks and foreign companies. Where the number of layers is greater than one, we refer to that complex shareholding as a pyramid. We recorded the number of layers in the pyramid and the shareholdings at each level. Thus we were able to determine the number of stakes at different levels in the pyramid. We classified a pyramid as being a controlling pyramid where there were significant violations of one share one vote using various benchmarks.

We find that families and banks are more prominent at the top of the complex shareholding than at the first level. Family holdings account for 33.0% of ultimate shareholdings as against the 20.5% at the first tier reported in Table 1. Banks account for 12.0% of ultimate holdings as against the 5.8% recorded at the first tier in Table 1.[5]

Figure 1 illustrates one such pyramid structure, Daimler Benz, at the beginning of the 1990s, although it has now significantly altered. There were two blocking minorities in Daimler Benz at level 1 held by Deutsche Bank and Mercedes Automobil Holdings. There were also two blocking minorities in Mercedes Automobil Holdings at level 2 held by Stern and Stella, and they in turn had four blocking minority holdings at level 3.

This case illustrates the potential for acquiring control at low cost—what Bebchuk, Kraakman, and Triantis (1999) describe as a controlling minority structure. For example, Robert Bosch GmbH at level 3 has a 25% holding in Stern Automobil that in turn at level 2 has a stake of 25% in Mercedes which owns a stake of 25% at level 1 in Daimler-Benz. As a result, Bosch's cash flow rights in Daimler Benz are 1.56%, where cash flow rights are defined as the product of the shareholdings at the different levels of the pyramid,

---

[5] Gorton and Schmid (1999) report that bank holdings of corporate equity in Germany averaged 6% in 1986; their estimate is therefore similar to our first tier number, but below our ultimate holdings.

Ownership and Control of German Corporations

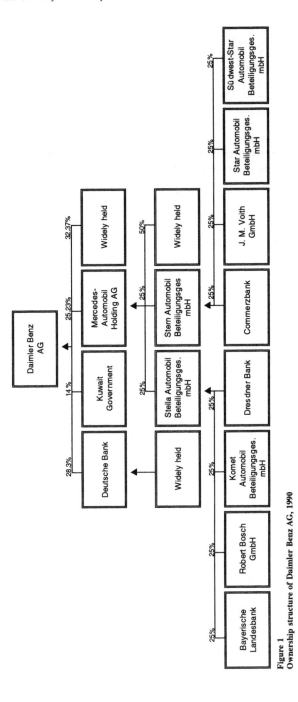

Figure 1
Ownership structure of Daimler Benz AG, 1990

949

The Review of Financial Studies / v 14 n 4 2001

whereas its voting rights are 25%. The ratio of voting to cash flow rights is therefore 16. Such shareholding structures violate the principle of one share one vote [see DeAngelo and De Angelo (1985), Grossman and Hart (1988), and Harris and Raviv (1988)].

To provide more systematic evidence on complex shareholdings, we examined the data available for 38 of the 75 firms. The data include the number of tiers of shareholdings, the size and number of stakes in excess of 25%, 50%, and 75%, and the total of disclosed stakes between 10% and 25%. Using these data we ascertained the number of cases where pyramids were control vehicles, defined as involving a significant violation of one share one vote. For there to be a violation, the ratio of voting rights to cash flow rights has to be greater than unity, and the cash flow rights and voting rights have to straddle a critical control level of 25%, 50%, or 75%. For example, a voting right of 60% and a cash flow right of 49% allow the holder to cross the critical control threshold of 50%. We found 33 pyramids, where a pyramid is defined as a company in which there is at least one large shareholder holding more than 10% of shares indirectly through another company (see Table 2). The mean number of tiers through which the pyramids are held is 2.2, where 0 describes a direct holding. Thirteen of the 33 companies had two tiers of indirect shareholdings, 10 had three tiers, 5 had four tiers, and another 5 had more than four tiers. Eleven companies had family shareholdings greater than 75%, and in 12 companies Allianz appeared as a stakeholder, reflecting its significance in German corporate holdings. The average size of all stakes in excess of 10% accumulated to 47% at level 1.

In 23 companies the ratio of voting rights to cash flow rights was greater than one. Table 2 shows that the average ratio of voting to cash flow rights was 1.6 in these companies; in five cases it exceeded 2. In 10 of the companies, voting rights and cash flow rights crossed one of the critical control levels of 25%, 50%, or 75%. Therefore, using this measure of violation of one share one vote, 10 of the 33 pyramids can be described as a controlling pyramid.

Although in 23 of the 33 pyramids no one shareholder used intermediary companies to span a control threshold, coalitions might do so. The three large shareholders in Holzmann—Deutsche Bank (25.9%), Commerzbank (10%), and Hochtief (24.9%)—have total holdings of 60.8%, with the remaining 39.2% widely held. Commerzbank and Hochtief together can form a blocking minority. In Table 2, coalitions in 30 companies could in principle vote more than 25% of shares, in 19 they could vote more than 50%, and in 4 more than 75% of shares. In 13 companies, the coalitions crossed a critical control threshold of 25%, in 11 of 50%, and in 4 of 75%.

Another form of coalition is cross-shareholdings. Examining a sample of major German banks and insurance companies which exert an important influence in widely held companies, Adams (1994) found that they protect themselves from hostile takeovers and other forms of outside control via a

Ownership and Control of German Corporations

Table 2
Incidence of controlling pyramids

Size of sample	No. of companies with multiple layers of shareholdings, i.e. pyramids	Average ratio of voting rights to cash flow rights (sample size = 23)	No. of controlling pyramids crossing thresholds of 25%, 50%, or 75%	No. with coalitions of investors exceeding thresholds of			No. of coalitions with controlling pyramids crossing thresholds of		
				25%	50%	75%	25%	50%	75%
38	33	1.6	10	30	19	4	13	11	4

The table provides an analysis of the sample of 38 German firms with multiple layers of shareholdings. Pyramids are defined as companies that are owned by at least one intermediary shareholder, i.e., there are at least two (vertical) shareholdings where the intermediary holds at least a 10% stake. The average ratio of voting to cash flow rights is calculated as voting rights of 25%, 50%, or 75% associated with block holdings divided by the product of the shareholdings at different levels of the pyramid. A controlling pyramid is one where the ratio of voting to cash flow rights is greater than one, and the pyramid enables a shareholder to cross a critical control threshold of 25%, 50%, or 75%. Coalitions are calculated as the sum of holdings at the first tier in the pyramid.

The Review of Financial Studies / v 14 n 4 2001

complex system of cross-shareholdings. Our examination of corporate ownership failed to uncover significant cross-shareholdings in industrial and commercial companies. However, since companies have traditionally only been
obliged to disclose holdings in excess of 25%, some cross-shareholdings may
have been disguised. For example, in a court case it was disclosed that Allianz
had a 25% sharcholding in Bayerische Hypotheken- Und Wechsel-Bank and
the latter had about a 5% holding in Allianz. Similarly, Allianz held a 23%
stake in Dresdner Bank, while Dresdner held a 10% stake in Allianz.[6] Such
cross-holdings may promote managerial versus ultimate shareholder control.

1.1.2 Board structure.   German companies are governed by a two-tiered
board structure [see Baums (1994) and Edwards and Fischer (1994) for a
detailed description]. The first tier is a supervisory board composed of shareholder and employee representatives and other stakeholders. The supervisory
board appoints the management board, equivalent to the executive directors
of a U.K. or U.S. board, approves the annual accounts and the firm's long-
term strategy, and can intervene when there is a serious deterioration in the
company's fortunes. The chairman of the management board is not a member of the supervisory board and does not normally attend its meetings. The
proportion of employee representatives is related to the size of the company
and the industry. For our sample it is either one-third or one-half of the total
membership depending upon the legal thresholds, which are a function of the
size of the company.

   Board data were collected from Hoppenstedt and Wer ist Wer (the Who's
Who of German companies). The data included the composition of supervisory boards and the shareholder or shareholder group responsible for appointing the member of the board, and cases of resignation due to retirement or
death. In addition to the name of the individual, the affiliation of board
members is provided in the annual reports. Data were also collected on the
members of management boards.

   Annual average turnover of members of the management and supervisory
board, including the chairmen, was calculated for the six financial years from
1989 to 1994 for the sample of 75 companies. Board turnover was defined
as the number leaving the board during the year, other than for reasons of
death or retirement, divided by the total number of board members at the
beginning of the year. Supervisory board turnover in this article refers only
to shareholder representatives and excludes employee representatives whose
turnover is expected to be unrelated to corporate performance. In addition,
the same data were collected for the sample of companies that were involved
in block sales for the three-year period straddling the year of sale.

   Table 3 reports representation on the supervisory board of the companies in
the sample of 171 in which the dominant shareholder was "another company"

---

[6] These shareholdings come from Adams (1994) and were collected by Professor E. Wenger in 1993.

Ownership and Control of German Corporations

Table 3
Categories of shareholders appointing chairman and members of supervisory boards in companies where the major shareholder is "another German company" and "families"

Investor or appointing body	Companies where major shareholder is another company		Companies where the major shareholder is a family	
	Proportion of chairmen appointed by large shareholder	Proportion of supervisory board appointed by large shareholder*a*	Proportion of chairmen appointed by large shareholder	Proportion of supervisory board appointed by large shareholder*a*
Another German company	77.8%	27.4%	5.7%	7.2%
An insurance company	2.2%	1.2%	2.9%	1.3%
A family group	2.2%	1.2%	37.1%	16.0%
A foreign company	2.2%	1.6%	0.0%	1.6%
A bank	4.4%	5.5%	5.7%	4.7%
The German state	0.0%	0.0%	2.9%	0.0%
Other German authorities	2.2%	1.4%	0.0%	0.0%
Employees	0.0%	40.3%	0.0%	37.1%
Independent members	2.2%	5.9%	20.0%	6.9%
Unknown	0.0%	15.3%	25.7%	25.1%
Total	100.0%	100.0%	100.0%	100.0%

The table reports the proportion of chairmen and members of the supervisory board appointed by different classes of investors or other appointing bodies. The table also includes the proportion of independent members who are usually, but not exclusively, nominated by the major shareholder.
Source: Own calculations based on Hoppenstedt's Handbuch der Grossunternehmen, Wer ist wer, and company accounts.
a Excluding the chairman.

or a family. The table shows that representation goes hand in hand with ownership. Where the major shareholder is another company, the shareholder appoints the chairman of the board in more than three-quarters of the sample; in addition, about one-quarter of all remaining members of the board are appointed by the largest shareholder. Where the shareholder is a family, the proportions are lower, but are still very substantial, with appointments by the family exceeding one-third of the chairmen and 16.0% of remaining board members; the latter is equivalent to 25.4% of all nonemployee members of the board. Moreover, one fifth of chairmen of supervisory boards are independent members who, despite their description, are typically associated with the controlling family.

1.1.3 Proxy votes and board representation by German banks. German banks derive their influence not only from their direct holdings of equities, but also from their holdings of proxy votes. They offer a variety of services including advice and voting on behalf of shareholders in company resolutions. The permission to use shareholders' proxies is obtained annually by the banks, although they must inform shareholders of any impending resolution and their voting intention so as to provide them with the opportunity to vote otherwise. An important advantage of this service is that it can mitigate the free-rider problems associated with dispersed ownership. On the other hand, it might exacerbate conflicts between bank and shareholder interests.

The Review of Financial Studies / v 14 n 4 2001

We have used a dataset on proxy votes collected by Nibler (1998) and data from Gottschalk (1988) and Baums and Fraune (1995).[7] Nibler (1998) provided proxy data for 49 companies in our sample. Using original data sources from commercial registers (Handelsregister) in cities where firms were registered, Nibler collected copies of the protocol of their general meetings. These contain a list of all those attending shareholder meetings, the number of votes cast by each person, and whether these were own shares or proxies. He found that three banks—Deutsche, Dresdner, and Commerzbank—held proxies in nearly all of the 93 publicly traded AGs in his sample and voted on average 14.4% of companies' voting equity. In addition, these three banks owned 6.8% of the equity in their own right. In total, the average size of bank proxies in our sample of 49 firms was 17.6%.

The three cases of hostile takeovers illustrate the importance and limitations of bank control in the form of proxy votes and the chairmanship of the supervisory board. In the bid for Feldmühle Nobel by the Flick brothers, Deutsche Bank was able to defeat a hostile change of control by casting proxy votes in favor of a resolution supporting a 5% voting right restriction. It cast 55% of the shares voted, although its direct holdings totalled only 8%. The effect was to subject the 38.5% held by the Flick brothers to the voting restriction and thereby prevent a hostile tender offer. In the case of Continental and the bid by Pirelli, the banks used their proxy votes in favor of motions favoring management entrenchment, for example, the retention of the 5% voting restriction.

However, the influence of proxies should not be overstated. Purchases of shares in the open market by predators led to the withdrawal of proxy votes held by banks. In the bid by Pirelli for Continental, Pirelli was able to withdraw proxy votes from banks by acquiring shares in the market. Similarly, when Krupp acquired 24.9% of the shares in Hoesch from open market purchases, bank influence was much reduced by the withdrawal of proxies.

We would expect proxy votes to be reflected in a high level of board representation by banks and an examination of supervisory boardroom representation of different shareholders in widely held companies confirmed this. We found banks held almost 11.0% of seats and 26.3% of the positions of chairman. Former chairmen of the management boards fill another sixth of the positions; therefore "insiders"—managers and banks—control nearly one-half of widely dispersed companies.[8]

The three case studies illustrate the potential importance of the supervisory board and bank chairmen. In the case of Continental, the chairman of the supervisory board, Dr. Weiss, a director of Deutsche Bank, wished to promote merger talks with Pirelli against the wishes of the head of the management

---

[7] Using data from Gottschalk (1988) and Baums and Fraune (1995) we find that the size of the proxy votes did not change appreciably over a six-year period between 1986 and 1992.

[8] Gorton and Schmid (1999) report that bank holdings influence their supervisory board representation.

board, H. Urban, resulting in Urban's resignation, although there was no evidence of poor corporate performance. In the case of the takeover bid for Hoesch, the chairman of the supervisory board, a director of Deutsche Bank, did not support the head of the management board and instead supported the bid by Krupp, resulting in the head of the management board's replacement. Dr. Blaschke, the chairman of the supervisory board, who was a Deutsche Bank representative, initiated the voting by Deutsche Bank for the 5% voting restriction introduced by Feldmühle Nobel.

These three cases suggest a more active role for the supervisory board than that implied by Edwards and Fischer (1994), although not necessarily successful. For example, although the bank was able to limit the voting power of the Flick brothers, the company finally succumbed to a takeover and was broken up as the Flick brothers wished. Similarly, it is doubtful if Deutsche Bank could have stopped the takeover by Krupp, and therefore their support might have reflected an acceptance of the inevitability of the outcome rather than their judgment as to what was best for the target company.

1.1.4 Sales of share stakes. The paucity of hostile takeovers in Germany and the much lower levels of merger activity than in the United Kingdom and United States suggest that until recently there has been little or no active market for corporate control. However, sales of large share stakes may provide a substitute for the traditional market for corporate control observed in the United Kingdom and United States. From the sample of 171 companies between the years 1988 and 1991 we found data on sales of share stakes for 134 companies using information published by Commerzbank's *wer gehoert zu wem*. We classify sales of share stakes by changes in major shareholders, emergence of large share stakes from widely dispersed companies, and the dispersal of large share stakes. We also report the number of cases where the size of the share block changes but does not give rise to a change in the major shareholder.

We found a substantial level of turnover of share stakes over the three years 1988 to 1991. In 21.6% of companies a new major shareholder emerged: in 13.4% of these, the major shareholder sold its entire stake as a block, and in 8.2% the company went from being widely held in 1988 to having a large stakeholder by 1991. In a further 3.7% of cases a company with concentrated ownership became widely held. Finally, in 7.4% of cases there were changes in large holdings without a change in the major shareholder.

In aggregate, the turnover of large share stakes was more than 8% per year (i.e., 32.7% over the four years) and compares with the level of takeover activity in the United Kingdom of about 4% of the capital stock of the corporate sector, at the peak of takeover activity. It is commensurate with the

The Review of Financial Studies / v 14 n 4 2001

combined level of takeover activity and share block sales reported for the United Kingdom by Franks, Mayer, and Renneboog (1999).[9]

The above describes the ownership and control of German corporations. In the next section we derive three testable hypotheses based on these features and the literature on ownership and control.

1.2 Hypotheses

1.2.1 Ownership concentration.
There is extensive literature on how performance is related to concentration of ownership. Shleifer and Vishny (1986) provide a theoretical demonstration that concentrated shareholdings can mitigate free-rider problems of corporate control associated with dispersed ownership. But as Shleifer and Vishny (1997) observe, there are significant disadvantages as well as advantages to concentrated ownership: "large investors represent their own interests, which need not coincide with the interests of other investors in the firm, or with the interests of employees or managers. In the process of using his control rights to maximize welfare, the large investor can therefore redistribute wealth—in both efficient and inefficient ways—from others" (p. 758). Bebchuk (1999) suggests that in countries where companies tend to have controlling shareholders, private benefits are large. He argues that separation of cash flow and voting rights allows owners to maintain control even where it is inefficient for them to do so.

It is therefore an empirical matter whether free-rider benefits outweigh private benefits of control. Edwards and Weichenrieder (1999) examine this proposition by evaluating how Tobin's Q is related to cash flow and voting rights of the largest and second-largest shareholders in a sample of 102 listed German companies. They find that "the largest shareholder in listed companies does obtain private benefits at the expense of minority shareholders" (p. 33).[10]

This article takes an alternative approach to analyzing whether corporate control in Germany is characterized by private benefits and examines the relation between board turnover, performance, and ownership. If concentrated ownership overcomes free-rider problems of control then we would expect to observe a closer relation between board turnover and performance in concentrated than in widely held firms. If concentrated ownership is afflicted by private benefits, then the reverse will hold. In the following hypothesis, we take the agency rather than the private benefits problem as our null. We

---

[9] In case studies of share block transactions in Germany, Jenkinson and Ljungqvist (2001) report that they are frequently opposed by target management and banks play an important role in helping predators accumulate and avoid the disclosure of large stakes.

[10] In the United States, Morck, Shleifer, and Vishny (1988), McConnell and Servaes (1990), and Wruck (1989) find that corporate performance, as measured by Tobin's Q, initially rises with low levels of concentration. For example, in Morck, Shleifer, and Vishny's study it rises with insider ownership of up to 5%, then declines up to 25%, and then rises.

also distinguish between management board and supervisory board turnover because the two, we argue, are influenced by different factors.

Hypothesis 1. *High management board turnover is associated with poor performance in companies with concentrated but not dispersed shareholdings. Supervisory board turnover is unaffected by performance unless it is the result of a failure to monitor the management board.*

1.2.2 Nature of ownership.   The nature of ownership as well as its scale may be important in the exercise of corporate control. Concentrated ownership may be more effective when it is in the hands of principals, for example, families, than when it is with agents such as banks or other companies. However, the distinction between corporate control in widely held and concentrated firms may be affected by bank intermediation. Banks may overcome free-rider problems of corporate control in widely held firms by, for example, exercising proxy votes on behalf of individual investors, as described in the previous section. Alternatively, they may create their own agency problems, with the interests of banks diverging from those of the investors they represent.[11]

Edwards and Fischer (1994) find little evidence of German banks playing a direct role in the rescue of German firms. They report that "the evidence on German bank behaviour when firms are in financial distress does not support the view that banks are able to reduce the costs of financial distress and bankruptcy by close monitoring and control ..." (p. 175). However, Gorton and Schmid (1999) find that bank control via share blocks improves the performance of companies, as measured by the market-to-book ratio or return on equity. They do not find a relationship with bank proxy holdings and performance in the absence of share blocks.

As described above, pyramid holdings are widespread in Germany. Burkart, Gromb, and Panunzi (1997) explain these in terms of the desire of controlling shareholders to minimize their stake and maximize the dilution of outside shareholdings. Pyramids achieve this through a reduction in the ratio of voting to cash flow rights and therefore the costs of control. Bebchuk, Kraakman, and Triantis (1999) argue that pyramids are control devices for separating ownership and control rights resulting in inefficient retention of control. In contrast, Emmons and Schmid (1998) suggest that pyramids are

---

[11] According to Diamond (1984), banks overcome free-rider problems of information gathering which afflict lending by a large number of dispersed investors. Similarly, Dow and Gorton (1997) argue that bank-based economies can be just as efficient as stock market economies. Hoshi, Kashyap, and Scharfstein (1990, 1991) find evidence of a role for banks in Japan in organizing and financing the rescue of failing companies. Kaplan and Minton (1994) report that Japanese bank directors manage firms in financial distress and that these appointments are associated with the disciplining of management. However, Kang and Stulz (1997) find that bank-dependent firms suffered significantly larger wealth losses and invested less than other firms during 1990–1993 when the Japanese stock market dropped appreciably. Weinstein and Yafeh (1998) record that close bank-firm ties increased the availability of capital to Japanese firms but did not lead to higher profitability or growth because of banks' market power.

The Review of Financial Studies / v 14 n 4 2001

used less as control devices and more to deal with other governance issues such as relationship-specific investments and joint ventures. Furthermore, the intermediary layers of a pyramid may diminish the ability of ultimate shareholders to exercise control. In the following hypothesis we test the view that principal controlling shareholders discipline poorly performing management and that pyramids do not dilute that control.

Hypothesis 2. *Principals with large share stakes, such as families, have greater incentives to discipline poorly performing management than agents, such as banks or insurance companies. Pyramids are control vehicles that allow ultimate shareholders to discipline management without a dilution of control.*

1.2.3 Market for corporate control. As recorded above, while there are few hostile tender offers in Germany, there is a flourishing market in large share stakes. Burkhart, Gromb, and Panunzi (1998) argue that markets in partial share stakes mitigate free riding by dispersed shareholders in takeovers, making it desirable for shareholders to acquire as few shares as possible to gain control. They predict a high incidence of auctions for controlling share stakes and lower bid premia compared with full tender offers. Gains to acquirors of large blocks of shares may therefore be large, provided that dominant shareholders can exert unimpeded control by replacing members of the boards of acquired companies. If, on the other hand, control is impeded by the continuing presence of other block holders and minorities or because of restrictions on board turnover, then gains to block holders may be modest. In the following hypothesis, we assume that block holders can exercise unimpeded control after acquisition.

By observing price differentials between sellers of blocks and other shareholders, it is possible to measure private benefits of control. Bebchuk (1999) has argued that they are extensive. This points to a distinction between the gains to holders of blocks of shares and minorities. In the United Kingdom, takeover rules require that, once 30% of the shares in a target firm have been acquired, other shareholders receive at least an equal if not higher price for their shares. In the United States, the courts actively enforce fair price rules. In Germany, there has not historically been an equal price rule and, as a consequence, gains to minorities, as measured by bid premia, can be expected to be small.[12]

Hypothesis 3. *Weak regulation of takeovers is reflected in low bid premia paid to minority shareholders and high premia to large block holders. Differences in premia paid to minority and large shareholders are a reflection of private benefits of control. Share block purchases are associated with high levels of board turnover in poorly performing companies.*

---

[12] The U.K.'s equal price rule requires that once 30% of a target's shares have been acquired, all remaining shareholders must be offered the highest price paid for shares of the target during the previous 12 months.

2. Analysis of the Relationship Between Board Turnover, Performance, and Ownership

This section analyzes how board turnover, of both management and supervisory boards, is related to performance and different patterns of ownership. Section 2.1 discusses concentration of ownership, Section 2.2 pyramiding, and Section 2.3 the type of owner, including families, banks, and corporations. In Section 2.4 we describe results of running regressions of board turnover on performance and the ownership variables.

2.1 Concentration of ownership

We begin by examining hypothesis 1, which predicts a relationship between board turnover in poorly performing companies and concentration of ownership. We compiled data on three measures of performance for the 75 companies; these were dividends per share, net after-tax income, and abnormal share price returns. The sources of data included annual reports for individual companies from Datastream and Hoppenstedt. Share price returns were measured relative to the DAX. Poor performance was indicated by earnings losses (after all provisions), dividend cuts or omissions, and abnormal returns worse than -20% in a single year.

Of the sample of 75 firms, the number of firms that had earnings losses in a particular year ranged from 3 to 16. Twenty-nine firms showed losses in at least one year. Up to 27 firms cut or omitted their dividend in a single year. There is considerable variation in earnings losses across time, with 1991–1993 being the worst performing years. In 1993 more firms cut or omitted their dividend than reported earnings losses. Most of the subsequent tables use earnings losses as the measure of poor performance.[13]

In our sample of 75 firms, average management board turnover was 11.2% and average supervisory board turnover was 12.6% for the period 1989–1994. Partitioning the sample between loss makers and non-loss makers, board turnover for non-loss makers was calculated as an annual average over the six years, 1989–1994, and for loss makers the average of the year of the loss and all subsequent years. Management board turnover for loss-making firms was 13.5% compared with 9.8% for non-loss makers, and the difference is statistically significant at greater than the 5% level.[14] Turnover of the supervisory board is similar for loss makers and for non-loss makers, 13.1% compared with 12.3%.

---

[13] Ball, Kothari, and Robin (1997) show that German managers have significant discretion over the reporting of earnings and tend to use hidden reserves to smooth earnings. In an analysis of the dividend behavior of German firms, Correia Da Silva (1996) found that German firms are far more likely to reduce their dividends in the face of temporary declines in earnings than British or American firms. As a result, dividend cuts may not be as good a measure of demonstrably poor performance as earnings losses.

[14] If board dismissal occurs rapidly after the loss, then including turnover for subsequent years may understate the level of disciplining.

The Review of Financial Studies / v 14 n 4 2001

If we compare average annual management board turnover before and after the year of the loss, we find that board turnover rises from an average of 6.6% in the two years prior to the loss to an average of 13.5% in the year of the loss and subsequent years. Average supervisory board turnover is almost identical before and after the loss. The similarity of supervisory board turnover suggests that poor performance is not perceived as a failure of monitoring or strategy. Our results for Germany are consistent with those found in other countries. Kaplan (1994a) records a significant relationship between executive board turnover and earnings losses in Japan, and Franks, Mayer, and Renneboog (1999) and Weisbach (1988) record similar relationships for the United Kingdom and United States respectively. The similarity of German results to those found in other countries suggests that very different legal rules and governance systems may still produce similar governance results [see La Porta et al. (1998)].

Table 4 reports the results of partitioning the sample of 75 into closely held and widely held companies, where the latter are defined as not having a shareholder with a stake greater than 25%. There is higher management board turnover in loss-making firms compared with non-loss-making firms for those that are both widely and closely held; even though the differences are economically large, they are only statistically significant for the closely held sample. However, there is only a small difference in turnover, less than 1%,

Table 4
Supervisory and management board turnover among loss-making and non-loss-making firms partitioned by closely and widely held companies

Panel A: Average board turnover

	Closely held firms		Widely held firms	
	Loss makers	Non-loss makers	Loss makers	Non-loss makers
Supervisory board	13.3%	12.6%	12.3%	11.3%
Management board	13.6%	10.2%	12.8%	8.5%
No. of firms	25	36	4	10
No. of firm years	141	208	24	60

Panel B: *t*-Statistics of differences in board turnover

	Loss making firms		Non-loss-making firms	
	Supervisory board	Management board	Supervisory board	Management board
Closely held minus widely held	0.38	0.24	0.55	0.97

	Closely held firms		Widely held firms	
	Supervisory board	Management board	Supervisory board	Management board
Loss makers minus non-loss makers	0.37	1.96	0.35	1.45

The table records the annual average turnover of management and supervisory board in companies with and without earnings losses. A company is classified as loss making if it makes losses in any year between 1989 and 1994 inclusive. Board turnover is measured for the year of the loss and all subsequent years to 1994 for the loss makers and all years between 1989 and 1994 for non-loss makers. The table records the annual average board turnover partitioned by whether companies are closely or widely held. Closely held companies are those with a single shareholding in excess of 25% in 1989.

Table 5
Supervisory and management board turnover among loss making and non-loss-making firms partitioned by whether there are pyramids of ownership

Panel A: Average board turnover

	Firms with pyramids		Firms without pyramids	
	Loss makers	Non-loss makers	Loss makers	Non-loss makers
Supervisory board	12.0%	11.3%	13.6%	12.7%
Management board	11.9%	8.6%	14.0%	10.4%
No. of firms	9	14	20	32
No. of firm years	46	80	119	188

Panel B: t-Statistics of differences in board turnover

	Loss-making firms		Non-loss-making firms	
	Supervisory board	Management board	Supervisory board	Management board
Pyramid minus no pyramid	−0.53	−0.75	−0.65	−1.00

	Firms with pyramids		Firms without pyramids	
	Supervisory board	Management board	Supervisory board	Management board
Loss makers minus non-loss makers	0.20	1.24	0.45	1.91

The table records the annual average board turnover reported in Table 4 partitioned by whether or not there are pyramids of share ownership in 1989. Firms with pyramids have more than one tier of ownership.

between loss makers in closely held and widely held companies, suggesting that large share ownership is not important in explaining differences in disciplining. There is therefore no support for hypothesis 1 of a difference in managerial board turnover between companies with concentrated and dispersed ownership.

2.2 Complex shareholdings and pyramiding

Table 5 reports the board turnover of companies partitioned by pyramiding and the incidence of loss makers. Management board turnover is higher for loss makers than for non-loss makers within both samples; the differences in board turnover between loss and non-loss makers are very similar, 3.3% for firms with pyramids and 3.6% for those without. Only the latter is statistically significant, but the pyramid sample is small. It is also the case that the difference in board turnover for loss-making companies that are part of a pyramid structure is not significantly different from those that are not. The comparison suggests that pyramids make little difference to the level of control exerted by ultimate shareholders. As a result, there is little support for hypothesis 2, that pyramids are control vehicles.[15]

---

[15] Pyramiding ownership schemes were widely practiced in the utility industry in the United States as a means of reducing the costs of control and extracting private benefits. They were made illegal in the Public Utility

The Review of Financial Studies / v 14 n 4 2001

Table 6
Supervisory and management board turnover among loss-making and non-loss-making firms partitioned by type of ultimate large shareholder

Panel A: Average board turnover

	Family-owned firms		Bank-owned firms	
	Loss makers	Non-loss makers	Loss makers	Non-loss makers
Supervisory board	11.7%	12.5%	9.0%	13.1%
Management board	12.1%	9.9%	13.5%	7.3%
No. of firms	12	11	7	10
No. of firm years	51	59	27	53

Panel B: *t*-Statistics of differences in board turnover

	Loss-making firms		Non-loss-making firms	
	Supervisory board	Management board	Supervisory board	Management board
Family minus bank ownership	0.69	−0.35	−0.18	1.02

	Family-owned firms		Bank-owned firms	
	Supervisory board	Management board	Supervisory board	Management board
Loss makers minus non-loss makers	−0.20	0.67	−1.18	1.87

The table records the annual average board turnover for firms with a single shareholder in excess of 25% partitioned by whether the large shareholder is a family or a bank. Where there are pyramids ownership is traced back to the ultimate owner.

2.3 Type of owner

The previous section recorded that the two owner groups most frequently found at the top of pyramids are families and banks. Hypothesis 2 suggests that families exert direct control over management. The question we examine in this section is whether there are differences in disciplining associated with family as against bank ownership. Such differences might be expected on the grounds that one owner is an agent and the other is a principal.

Using data on the disciplining of management by the supervisory board when corporate performance was poor, we compared board turnover of companies with large shareholders, represented by banks, families, and other corporations. When we measured ownership at the first level, we found that turnover of the management board was 8.9% for bank controlled companies compared with 11.3% for family controlled and 9.3% for other corporate shareholders. The differences were not significantly different. In Table 6 the other corporate holdings are traced back to their ultimate shareholders. We find very similar management board turnover in loss-making companies with bank owners as with family ownership, 13.5% compared with 12.1%. However, there is some evidence of significantly higher board turnover in loss

Holding Act of 1935, as were pyramids for registered investment funds under the Investment Companies Act of 1940. They are not illegal for other companies, but minority protection rules make them less valuable than in Germany.

makers than non-loss makers in companies where banks are large shareholders. This provides some support for banks exerting a disciplinary function, and is consistent with the conclusion of Gorton and Schmid (1999).

Given that many widely held companies are bank controlled, Table 4 provides some additional evidence on the relative disciplining of banks as intermediaries versus other corporate intermediaries. We found little evidence of a lower rate of disciplining in widely held companies compared with those with a large shareholder. This would suggest that if banks do control widely held companies, they do not discipline any less (or more) than those that are closely held.

In general, the implication is that, contrary to Hypothesis 2, there is little evidence that disciplining is related to the pattern of ownership, in particular whether the large shareholder is a principal or agent. This might be explained by the fact that banks exert effective control on behalf of dispersed shareholders in widely held companies. Alternatively, agency problems may be so pervasive as to make different patterns of ownership irrelevant to the correction of managerial failure.[16] The similar rate of board turnover in Germany compared with the United Kingdom provides some support for the former rather than the latter hypothesis.

2.4 Regression results

We performed more formal tests of Hypotheses 1 and 2 by regressing board turnover on performance and ownership for individual companies in individual years.

2.4.1 Methodology.   We performed three sets of panel data regressions of board turnover on performance and ownership. First, we ran pooled OLS regressions over the entire sample of 75 companies for six years of data. Second, we allowed for individual firm ("within") effects using firm-specific intercepts. Third, we ran a cross-sectional ("between") regression with individual-year intercepts. Interaction terms between performance and ownership variables were included.

The inclusion of a lagged dependent variable was tested using a first difference instrumental variable estimator [see Arellano and Bond (1991)]. The coefficient on the lagged dependent variable was positive but statistically insignificant, suggesting the use of a static panel data model rather than a dynamic one. Heteroscedastic consistent t-statistics are reported using a White (1980) procedure. We focus mainly on the within-firm regressions, which complement the cross-section results in Sections 2.1–2.3, but we also describe the results of alternative specifications where the results differ from those of the within-firm regressions.

---

[16] For example, the Krupp family (Alfred Krupp von Bohlen and Halbach-Stiftung), through the Krupp Foundation, has a controlling interest, but the company is managed by professional managers.

The Review of Financial Studies / v 14 n 4 2001

Several specification tests of the results were performed. These included (i) corrections for serial correlation of residuals, (ii) control for size of firms as measured by their turnover, and (iii) dummy variables for industries. We examined potential collinearity between the ownership and performance measures by excluding the earnings variables from some of the regressions and directly regressing performance on the ownership variables.

The board turnover regressions were performed on both management and supervisory board turnover, where the latter excluded employee representatives. Ownership variables were measured at both the first and the ultimate level.

2.4.2 Regression results

Hypothesis 1. Table 7 reports the results of fixed effect (within) regressions of annual management board turnover and supervisory board turnover on earnings losses and an interactive variable of concentration of ownership with earnings losses. The value of ownership is measured both at the first tier in column 1 and at the ultimate level at the top of the pyramid in column 2. Earnings loss is a zero-one dummy that takes the value of one in any year in which a company records a loss. The ownership concentration varies from year to year, reflecting sales and purchases of shares reported in Section 3.

Table 7 records that earnings losses are associated with an approximately 10% increase in management board turnover in the year of the loss and 7% in the subsequent year. The current earnings loss variable is significant at

Table 7
Regressions of management and supervisory board turnover on performance and concentration of ownership

Management board turnover	Ownership measured at the first tier	Ownership measured at the top of a pyramid
Constant	0.0973 (11.10)	0.0820 (4.57)
Earnings loss	0.105 (3.99)	0.113 (4.24)
Earnings loss (-1)	0.0703 (1.87)	0.0847 (2.41)
Concentration of ownership	—	0.0643 (0.96)
Interactive term of earnings loss and concentration of ownership (-1)	-0.0877 (1.08)	-0.166 (1.81)
R^2	0.062	0.067

Supervisory board turnover	Ownership measured at the first tier	Ownership measured at the first tier
Constant	0.118 (11.71)	0.0862 (2.73)
Earnings loss	0.0127 (0.48)	0.0150 (0.60)
Earnings loss (-1)	0.0203 (0.56)	0.0414 (1.22)
Concentration of ownership	—	0.136 (1.01)
Interactive term of earnings loss and concentration of ownership (-1)	0.0610 (0.72)	0.000172 (0.00)
R^2	0.0061	0.013

The table records within (firm effect) regressions of management and supervisory board turnover of 75 German firms between 1990 and 1994 on performance as measured by whether there are earnings losses (a zero-one dummy variable, with 1 for a loss), concentration of ownership as a continuous variable and an interactive term between concentration of ownership and performance. One year lags on variables are described as (-1). Standard errors are heteroscedastic corrected. t-statistics are shown in parentheses.

the 1% level and the lagged term at the 10% level. The first column reports results using concentration of ownership measured at the first tier and the second column reports the ultimate concentration of ownership. The first part of Hypothesis 1 predicts that board turnover will be higher in poorly performing firms (earnings loss = 1) in the presence of a high concentration of ownership, that is, a positive effect of the interactive term. When concentration of ownership is only included as part of an interactive term (earnings loss and concentration) in column 1, contrary to the prediction of Hypothesis 1, the sign is negative but not statistically significant. In column 2, when ownership is measured at the ultimate level there is some evidence of a negative interrelation effect with performance, suggesting that lower levels of concentration of ownership are weakly associated with higher board turnover in loss makers.

Several variants of the above regression were performed. First, different performance measures were used: abnormal returns, accounting earnings, dividends per share (all continuous variables), and a dummy variable for persistent losses, as reflected in losses in more than one consecutive year. Negative relations with abnormal returns were observed, but stronger relations were associated with accounting earnings, earnings losses, and persistent losses, all accounting measures. This points to the importance of accounting earnings in identifying poor performance in German firms, consistent with the prediction of Ball, Kothari, and Robin (1997). Little or no relation was observed between board turnover and either concentration of ownership on its own or the interaction of concentration with performance.

Second, OLS panel regressions were performed in place of the fixed effects, with dummy variables signifying the firm's main industry and with firm size, as measured by turnover. The earnings loss variables remained significant and the concentration of ownership effect remained insignificantly negative. Third, regressions were performed with only a concentration of ownership variable (i.e., no interactive term) to avoid potential biases from a correlation of ownership with performance. The concentration of ownership was again insignificantly negative. Fourth, time dummy variables were included to establish whether there was a cross-sectional relation between board turnover and ownership concentration. Again there was no evidence of this.

In the case of supervisory board turnover, there is little evidence of a relationship with either performance or ownership concentration. The one exception is persistent earnings losses: where there are persistent earnings losses then supervisory board turnover is significantly higher (table not shown). Thus, consistent with the second part of Hypothesis 1, there is evidence that supervisory board members are replaced when they fail to correct poor performance. However, this is not related to ownership concentration, and the results were not affected by the level at which ownership is measured or by the inclusion of size and industry dummies.

The Review of Financial Studies / v 14 n 4 2001

Table 8
Regressions of management and supervisory board turnover on ownership concentration of different types of investor and a measure of pyramiding

Management board turnover	Ownership measured at the first tier	Ownership measured at the top of a pyramid
Constant	0.0874 (4.87)	0.111 (6.32)
Earnings loss	0.110 (4.21)	0.107 (4.09)
Earnings loss (−1)	0.0488 (1.49)	0.0459 (1.40)
Bank ownership concentration (−1)	−0.0163 (0.19)	−0.196 (1.99)
Corporate ownership concentration (−1)	0.0642 (0.86)	—
Family ownership concentration (−1)	0.0437 (0.53)	0.00732 (0.10)
R^2	0.059	0.061

Supervisory board turnover	Ownership measured at the first tier	Ownership measured at the first tier
Constant	0.0800 (3.16)	0.0881 (3.73)
Earnings loss	0.0208 (0.89)	0.0147 (0.59)
Earnings loss (−1)	0.0433 (1.65)	0.0411 (1.59)
Bank ownership concentration (−1)	0.214 (1.23)	0.0998 (0.80)
Corporate ownership concentration (−1)	0.0443 (0.27)	—
Family ownership concentration (−1)	0.233 (2.14)	0.142 (1.18)
R^2	0.032	0.013

The table records within (firm effect) regressions of management and supervisory board turnover of 75 German firms between 1990 and 1994 on performance as measured by whether there are earnings losses (a zero-one dummy variable, with 1 for a loss), concentration of ownership (as a continuous variable) by different types of investor and a dummy variable taking the value of one when there was a pyramid structure. Where variables are lagged 1 year they are described as (−1). Standard errors are heteroscedastic corrected. *t*-statistics are shown in parentheses.

In sum, contrary to the first part of Hypothesis 1, the results suggest little influence of ownership concentration on board turnover as reported in Section 2.1. There is some evidence in support of the second part of Hypothesis 2, that supervisory board turnover only occurs after persistently bad performance.

Hypothesis 2: We disaggregated the ownership concentration data by type of owner (bank, corporation, or family) at the first level of the pyramid and at the ultimate level (bank or family) and included these in regressions on board turnover with performance. Table 8 shows the results using earnings loss as the performance measure. To provide further tests on the role of pyramids we also examined the effect of including a dummy variable for whether there was a pyramid in the ownership structure.

Earnings loss remains highly significant in the management board turnover regressions. However, there is no evidence that any of the ownership concentration variables are significant when ownership is measured at the first level. There is some evidence of a negative influence of bank ownership on management board turnover where ownership is measured at the ultimate level, but the result was not robust to alternative specifications reported below.

We carried out several variants of the above regressions. First, we used the different performance variables described above; little influence of different classes of ownership was observed. Second, we examined the effect of omitting the performance measures—even then ownership variables remained insignificant. Third, in addition to the ownership concentration variables, we included interactive terms of ownership with performance; again no influence of ownership concentration was observed.

We then examined the influence of pyramids in greater depth. We constructed two variables using measures provided in Table 2, recording the degree of control exercised by members of a pyramid. The first variable was the ratio of voting to cash flow rights for each company (the average value of which is shown in column 3 of Table 2). The second was a dummy variable indicating whether a coalition of shareholders could cross one of the key thresholds of voting power, namely 50% (column 5 of Table 2). Neither of these variables was significant.

We performed several tests of the influence of banks' shareholdings, including proxy votes on management and supervisory board turnover. First, using the data from Gottschalk (1988) and Baums and Fraune (1995), we included a dummy variable that took the value of unity if banks controlled more than 50% of votes and there were no other large shareholders (including banks themselves) controlling more than 25% of voting shares. Second, we replaced the dummy variable in this regression with the size of the proxy vote. Third, we aggregated banks' direct and proxy votes and included a dummy variable equal to unity when these amounted to more than 25% of voting shares. Finally, we excluded all other ownership variables and ran a regression including only performance and the proxy variable. In no case was there a significant influence of proxies on board turnover. We then used the more extensive dataset on bank proxies and banks' own shareholdings from Nibler (1998). We repeated the regressions on management turnover using this new dataset. There was some evidence of a negative influence (significant at the 10% level) of banks' proxies on management turnover, but not on supervisory board turnover. Overall, contrary to Hypothesis 2, but consistent with the evidence from Sections 2.2 and 2.3, there is little or no relation between different types of owner, pyramiding structure, and board turnover.[17]

The regression results support our earlier cross-section results:

(i)   Consistent with Section 2.1 there is a relation between management board turnover and performance but no relationship for the supervisory board except in the presence of persistently bad performance.

(ii) There is no relationship between concentration of ownership and management board turnover (Section 2.1).

(iii) There is support for interpretation of the results in Section 2.2 that pyramids do not affect the exercise of control or are not control vehicles.

---

[17] We included all of the variables in regressions that examined the influence of performance, ownership concentrations broken down by different categories of owner, pyramiding, and interactive terms with performance, turnover of firms, and industry dummies. Overall the equations provide little explanatory power of supervisory board turnover but strong explanatory power of management board turnover. Performance is a significant determinant of management but not supervisory board turnover. There is some evidence of a negative influence of bank ownership and pyramiding on management board turnover and of share changes on supervisory board turnover.

The Review of Financial Studies / v 14 n 4 2001

(iv)   As reported in Section 2.3, there is little or no relationship between the type of owner and management or supervisory board turnover and no relationship between proxy votes and board turnover.

Kaplan (1994b) also finds a relationship between management board turnover and performance. He reports some relation with supervisory board turnover, but finds that it is sensitive to the specification of the performance variable. Kaplan (1994b) provides some initial evidence on the influence of ownership on the relationship between board turnover and performance. He reports that the relationship was not significantly affected by the presence of large share blocks held by families, banks, and other investors, or by substantial bank proxy votes. This article reports that this conclusion remains valid on more detailed investigation, once account is taken of pyramid holdings and new data on proxy votes. Gorton and Schmid (1999) examine the influence of bank ownership on market-to-book ratios and rates of return on equity of AGs in 1975 and 1986. They find a positive influence of banks' own equity holdings but not of proxy votes in both years. The influence of banks' holdings exceeds that of other block holders.

3. Sales of Share Stakes

We now turn to an analysis of the dynamic effects of sales of share blocks. We collected a sample of 57 block purchases in 38 German companies for the period 1988–1997 for which data on prices of block trades were available. We compared the prices paid to sellers of blocks with bid premia to minority shareholders and we contrasted the costs of changing control in the German market with bid premia in Anglo-American markets.

   Section 3.1 reports the size of premia paid to selling block holders and other, generally minority, shareholders. In Section 3.2 we measure the extent to which sales of blocks are related to poor performance and the disciplining of management. This provides a test of whether the market in share blocks operates like an American market for corporate control.

3.1 Bid premia paid to selling block holders

There are three parties to a block sale transaction: the seller of the share block, the acquiring company, and shareholders of the acquired company which are not party to the block sale. Using the announced price for the block, we measure the control premium paid to the vendor. We also estimate the gains to other shareholders by calculating abnormal returns over the window surrounding the announcement of the sale of the block. Since controlling block holders will only be willing to sell if they receive an amount equal to the sum of their private benefits of control and the public benefits to all shareholders, then the private benefits cannot exceed the difference between the control premium and the gains to other shareholders. In relation to an

Table 9
Block premia to vendors and abnormal returns to non-selling shareholders in 57 share blocks over the period 1988–1997

	Average size of share stake	1 week	1 month	3 months
Panel A: Block premia for the whole sample				
Mean	36.32%[22]	13.85%	16.21%	9.43%
Median	33.20%	8.83%	10.51%	5.87%
Standard errors		3.21%	3.89%	4.28%
t-statistics		4.31	4.17	2.20
Panel B: Abnormal returns to nonselling shareholders				
Mean		2.34%	3.01%	0.03%
Median		−0.69%	1.45%	0.73%
Standard errors		1.18%	1.64%	2.59%
t-statistics		1.99	1.84	0.01

This table reports block premia paid to sellers of large share blocks in 57 share block transactions involving 38 target companies. Panel A of the table reports the block premia measured relative to the DAX over 1 week, 1 month, and 3 months prior to and including the announcement date. Panel B reports abnormal returns to nonselling shareholders relative to the DAX over the same periods.

equal price regulatory rule, this can also be interpreted as a measure of the exploitation of minority shareholders.

We estimated bid premia in block sales using a sample from an international database, AMDATA, over the period 1988–1997. AMDATA provided the names of acquiring and target companies, the size of the stake, the selling price of the block, and the date the purchase was reported to the German stock exchange. In addition, data on board turnover and performance were collected.

We found 85 block purchases. After excluding blocks where data were unavailable, there were 57 cases involving 38 target companies, each block purchase being considered a separate transaction. We checked all our data with original sources, including Reuters Business Briefing and Dow Jones data, and collected the price of the shares at the time of and prior to the block purchase.

In panel A of Table 9 we report the bid premium paid to the seller of the block, which is calculated as the difference between the announced purchase price of the block and the share price. The premium is calculated separately for three time windows: 1 week, 1 month, and 3 months prior to and including the announcement date. The bid premium is measured relative to market movements as measured by the DAX. Panel A of Table 9 records that the average size of block purchases was 36.32% (median 33.20%). Median abnormal returns were 8.83% for 1 week, 10.51% for 1 month, and 5.87% for 3 months prior to the announcement. All estimates of the bid premium are statistically significant at better than the 1% level.[18]

---

[18] There is little relation between the calculated bid premium and the size of stake over a one-week window.

The Review of Financial Studies / v 14 n 4 2001

The premia in share block transactions in Germany are small in relation to those in tender offers in the United Kingdom and United States. For example, Franks and Harris (1989) report premia to targets in tender offers of 24.0% in the United Kingdom and 23.3% in the United States. Barclay and Holderness (1991) report abnormal returns of up to 28.6% to shareholders of companies where there was a block trade of at least 5%, and where the company was subsequently acquired. Much lower abnormal returns accrued to targets of block trades that remained independent in the year following the block sale, possibly due to the lower probability of a control change.

In panel B of Table 9 we report abnormal returns to other (nonselling) shareholders. These are obtained by calculating the return for the period beginning 1 day after the announcement of the block sale and 1 week, 1 month, and 3 months prior to the announcement, adjusting for market movements. The median abnormal returns to these other shareholders for the three windows are small, between −0.69% and 1.45%.[19]

There are three important conclusions from the table. First, as already reported, bid premia paid to selling shareholders are small compared with the United States and United Kingdom. Even in the largest transactions, bid premia are around half those in the United States and United Kingdom. Second, other shareholders incur significant discrimination and obtain a virtually zero abnormal return. The absence of an effective equal price rule acts to the serious disadvantage of minority shareholders. Third, there is evidence of significant private benefits of control. However, the size of the private benefits is modest by the scale of total acquisition benefits in the United Kingdom and United States, as measured by bid premia.[20]

These results provide support for Burkhart, Gromb, and Panunzi's (1998) prediction that costs of changing control are lower in share block purchases than full tender offers, possibly reflecting the limited protection of minority shareholders in share block transactions in Germany. An example of this is the undisclosed accumulation of the 24.9% share stake by Krupp prior to the bid for Hoesch. This would have violated the 1989 U.K. Companies Act, requiring disclosure of stakes in excess of 3%, and the U.K. Takeover Code which requires that the price paid to shareholders should equal the highest price paid in the previous 12 months. Likewise, the takeover of Feldmühle Nobel by the Swedish company Stora would have violated the U.K. Takeover Code when Stora launched a discriminatory two-tiered offer of DM567 per share to large shareholders and DM540 to small shareholders.

---

[19] This is consistent with the share price performance of two takeover bids, Continental and Hoesch, which had negative abnormal returns for other shareholders around the announcement date. Only in the third case, Feldmühle Nobel, was there a bid premium, 12.0% before the announcement of the first bid and 12.6% prior to the second bid.

[20] The estimates of private benefits in this section are an upper bound. To the extent that the supply of blocks is imperfectly competitive, then vendors will be able to command premia in excess of their private benefits.

There are two possible explanations for the smallness of the bid premia. The first is the absence of minority rules making discriminatory pricing possible and reducing costs of changing control. While this explains the low abnormal returns to other shareholders, it does not account for the low bid premia paid to selling block holders. A second explanation is that the gains to control are limited, possibly as a consequence of the continuing presence of other block holders and minority shareholders and, as Gorton and Schmid (1998) note, codetermination agreements protecting employment contracts.

The three cases of hostile takeovers provide clear evidence of impediments to the exercise of control by acquirors in German takeovers. In Feldmühle Nobel, Veba was unable to exercise control in the face of opposition from the Flick brothers despite having acquired a shareholding of 61% by early 1990. By early 1992, Krupp had a shareholding of 62% in Hoesch. However, the merger could not be completed before December 1992 because of opposition in the courts by three small shareholders. In Continental, a proposition to remove the voting right restriction, which was supported by 66% of shareholders led by Pirelli, could not be implemented because of opposition from minority shareholders. Even the supervisory board of Continental, which decided to enter into merger negotiations, had considerable difficulty in forcing the management board to pursue negotiations with Pirelli and eventually had to dismiss the chairman of the management board, Horst Urban, to bring this about.

To gain a better understanding of the impediments to the exercise of control in German acquisitions we undertook a series of interviews with the owner of a large share block of a German company. The owner purchased a block of 65% from a German bank that had amassed a stake from several previous owners. The stake of 65% was gradually increased to 94%. Even with a 94% block, the owner felt constrained in its ability to restructure, for example, the management board would not implement the blockholders' wishes to terminate a long-standing contract. The company cited three impediments to their ability to exercise control:

- *Presence of minorities.* Minorities can require that transactions with investors holding more than 75% of shares of the firm be undertaken at arms length, that is, at market prices.
- *Inability to take out minorities.* Removal of the 5% minority through a squeeze-out rule is made difficult by the holding of shares in bearer form by banks, which are, as a consequence, in a privileged position regarding the identity of many owners of a company. Also, although a company with more than 95% of shares can compulsorily acquire the minority, a shareholder can seek redress in the courts for what they perceive to be a purchase of shares at unfair prices.[21]

---

[21] This is included in company legislation, Aktiengesetz 1965.

The Review of Financial Studies / v 14 n 4 2001

- *Opposition of boards.* Since members of the supervisory board are appointed for fixed periods, it can take a considerable period of time for block holders to gain control of the supervisory board through new appointments. The block holder cited above made it a condition of its initial block purchase that a certain number of supervisory board members resign. Notwithstanding this, the block holder claims that full control of the management board did not immediately and automatically follow. Management refused to implement policies they felt were not in the company's interest.

3.2 Management turnover, performance, and sales of stakes

The last part of Hypothesis 3 suggests that sales of share stakes are associated with the disciplining of the management board or a failure of monitoring by the supervisory board. In the United Kingdom, Franks and Mayer (1996) report a very high level of board turnover in the two years after takeovers, 90% in hostile takeovers and 50% in agreed bids. However, they do not find a relationship between incidence of hostile takeovers and performance of target firms. In contrast, in the United States, Martin and McConnell (1991) do find a relationship between disciplinary takeovers as measured by CEO turnover and poor performance of targets.

Table 10 shows the relationship between sales of share stakes and board turnover, using the sample of 75 firms, in the year of the sale and in subsequent years. Supervisory board turnover of loss makers and non-loss makers is significantly higher where there is sale of a stake compared with no sale: 18.1% compared with only 11.1%. However, the higher turnover is independent of performance; for example, where sales occurred, board turnover is slightly higher among non-loss makers than loss makers, 18.6% versus 16.7%.

The level of management board turnover provides a similar picture. Board turnover for loss makers is higher than for non-loss makers for both samples. However, the difference is only statistically significant for the sample with stable holdings. Also, the level of board turnover is higher for loss makers with stable share holdings than for those with sales: 20.9% and 14.0%, respectively. These results suggest that unlike results reported for the United States, block sales are not disciplinary in nature and do not act as a substitute for a market in corporate control.

These results are confirmed in a regression of management and supervisory board turnover on performance and changes in share ownership using the sample of 75 companies. Table 11 reports the results using earnings loss as the performance measure. There was no significant relation of either

---

[22] Where several stakes are announced contemporaneously or in close proximity, the amalgamation of these stakes raises the average size to a mean of 43.10% and median of 45.55%.

Table 10
Supervisory and management board turnover among loss-making and non-loss-making firms partitioned by sales of shareholders

Panel A: Average board turnover

	Sales of shares		No sales of shares	
	Loss makers	Non-loss makers	Loss makers	Non-loss makers
Supervisory board	16.7%	18.6%	13.1%	10.8%
Management board	14.0%	10.0%	20.9%	9.5%
No. of firms	11	11	18	35
No. of firm years	27	66	91	175

Panel B: t-Statistics of differences in board turnover

	Loss-making firms		Non-loss-making firms	
	Supervisory board	Management board	Supervisory board	Management board
Share sales minus no sales	0.88	−1.32	2.85	0.28

	Sales of shares		No sales of shares	
	Supervisory board	Management board	Supervisory board	Management board
Loss makers minus non-loss makers	−0.45	0.84	0.89	4.19

The table records the annual average board turnover reported in Table 3 partitioned by whether there are sales of share stakes in any year between 1989 and 1991 inclusive. Where sales of shares occur, board turnover is calculated from the year of the sale onwards.

management or supervisory board turnover with share block changes or with the interaction of share changes with earnings losses. There is therefore no support for the assertion in Hypothesis 3 that there is high board turnover in poorly performing companies that involve sales of share blocks.

Table 11
Regressions of management and supervisory board turnover on sales of shares

Management board turnover

Constant	0.0974 (11.20)
Earnings loss	0.110 (4.19)
Earnings loss (−1)	0.0477 (1.40)
Sales of share stakes (−1)	−0.0121 (0.33)
Interactive term of earnings loss and sales of share stakes (−1)	−0.042 (0.97)
R^2	0.058

Supervisory board turnover

Constant	0.120 (11.34)
Earnings loss	0.0124 (0.48)
Earnings loss (−1)	0.0252 (0.90)
Sales of share stakes (−1)	−0.0238 (0.59)
Interactive term of earnings loss and sales of share stakes (−1)	0.0902 (1.13)
R^2	0.0078

The table records within (firm effect) regressions of management and supervisory board turnover of 75 German firms between 1990 and 1994 on performance as measured by whether there are earnings losses (a zero-one dummy variable, with 1 for a loss) and sales of share stakes. Where a variable is lagged by 1 year it is described as (−1). Standard errors are heteroscedastic corrected. t-statistics are shown in parentheses.

The Review of Financial Studies / v 14 n 4 2001

In summary, we have found a significant level of price discrimination in German share block transactions and low overall gains to target shareholders. These low gains are associated with a weak disciplinary function of share block sales and significant impediments to the exercise of control by the new block holder. The impediments may also explain why we found little relation between ownership concentration and corporate control in Section 2.

4. Conclusion

In this article we report very high levels of concentration of ownership in German firms, particularly associated with holdings by other companies and families, and complex patterns of ownership involving pyramids. Bank ownership is of limited significance in the large proportion of highly concentrated firms, but is of importance through proxy votes, voting rights restrictions, and board representation in the minority of widely held companies with no single shareholder in excess of 25%.

The question that this article addresses is whether these distinctive ownership characteristics are associated with effective corporate governance or exploitation of private benefits. In some respects the article is consistent with a growing body of evidence [Kaplan (1994b) and Edwards and Nibler (1999)] that concludes that, while patterns of ownership of German companies are markedly different from those of U.K. and U.S. firms, corporate control is similar. Furthermore, we find little relation between concentration of ownership and the disciplining of management of poorly performing firms, and between the type of concentrated owner and board turnover.

There are therefore few distinctive features of the static aspects of corporate control in Germany, but there are marked differences in its dynamics. Although there is no hostile takeover market, there is a substantial market in share stakes that superficially bears close resemblance to an Anglo-American market for corporate control. But it differs in two crucial respects. First, it permits price discrimination between sellers of share blocks and other investors and, second, the overall gains to merger as reflected in bid premia are low in relation to those in the United Kingdom and United States. We have used price discrimination to provide evidence on the existence of private benefits of control in German capital markets. The modest gains to changes in ownership are mirrored in board turnover that is low in comparison to takeovers in the United Kingdom and United States, suggesting that control benefits for ownership changes in Germany are small in comparison to those elsewhere.

The implication of this article is that the primary distinction between financial markets does not concern the static relationship of ownership concentrations to corporate control, as suggested by much of the literature, but the dynamic aspects relating to the evolution of ownership and control. Even if flexibility in altering ownership through share block sales in Germany is similar to that in the United Kingdom and United States through tender offers, flexibility in corporate restructuring is lower and is associated with the existence of significant private benefits of control.

References

Adams, M., 1994, "Die Usurpation von Aktionaersbefugnissen mittels Ringverflechtung in der Deutschland AG," *Die Aktiengesellschaft*, 39, 148–158.

Arellano, M., and S. Bond, 1991, "Some Tests of Specifications for Panel Data: Monte Carlo Evidence and an Application to Employment Equations," *Review of Economics Studies*, 53, 205–225.

Ball, R., S. Kothari, and A. Robin, 1997, "The Effect of Institutional Factors on Properties of Accounting Earnings: International Evidence," mimeo, University of Rochester.

Barclay, N., and C. Holderness, 1991, "Negotiated Block Trades and Corporate Control," *Journal of Finance*, 46, 861–878.

Baums, T., 1994, "Corporate Governance in Germany—System and Recent Developments," working paper, Universitat Osnabruck, Germany.

Baums, T., and C. Fraune, 1995, "Institutionelle Anleger und Publikumsgesellschaft: Eine empirische Untersuchung," *Die Aktiengesellschaft*, 40, 97–112.

Bebchuk, L., 1999, "A Rent-Protection Theory of Corporate Ownership and Control," Working Paper no. 260, Harvard University.

Bebchuk, L., R. Kraakman, and G. Triantis, 1999, "Stock Pyramids, Cross-Ownership, and Dual Class Equity: The Creation and Agency Costs of Separating Control from Cash Flow Rights," Working Paper no. 6951, NBER.

Burkart, M., D. Gromb, and F. Panunzi, 1997, "Large Shareholders Monitoring, and the Value of the Firm," *Quarterly Journal of Economics*, 112, 693–728.

Burkart, M., D. Gromb, and F. Panunzi, 1998, "Why Higher Takeover Premia Protect Minority Shareholders," *Journal of Political Economy*, 196, 176–204.

Correia Da Silva, L., 1996, "Corporate Control and Financial Policy: An Investigation of the Dividend Policy of German Firms," PhD dissertation, University of Oxford.

De Angelo, H., and L. De Angelo, 1985, "Managerial Ownership of Voting Rights—A Study of Public Corporations with Dual Classes of Common Stock," *Journal of Financial Economics*, 14, 33–69.

Diamond, D., 1984, "Financial Intermediation and Delegated Monitoring," *Review of Economic Studies*, 51, 393–414.

Dow, J., and G. Gorton, 1997, "Stock Market Efficiency and Economic Efficiency: Is There a Connection?" *Journal of Finance*, 52, 1087–1130.

Edwards, J., and K. Fischer, 1994, "Banks, Finance and Investment in West Germany Since 1970," Cambridge University Press, Cambridge.

Edwards, J., and M. Nibler, 1999, "Corporate Governance in Germany: The Influence of Banks and Large Equity Holders," unpublished working paper, University of Cambridge.

Edwards, J., and Weichenrieder, 1999, "Ownership, Concentration and Share Valuation: Evidence from Germany," working paper 193, CESifo.

Emmons, W., and F. Schmid, 1998, "Universal Banking, Control Rights, and Corporate Finance in Germany," Federal Reserve Bank of St. Louis Review, July/August.

Franks, J., and R. Harris, 1989, "Shareholder Wealth Effects of Corporate Takeovers: The UK Experience, 1955 to 1985," *Journal of Financial Economics*, 23, 225–249.

The Review of Financial Studies / v 14 n 4 2001

Franks, J., and C. Mayer, 1996, "Hostile Takeovers and the Correction of Managerial Failure," *Journal of Financial Economics*, 40, 163–181.

Franks, J., C. Mayer, and L. Renneboog, 1999, "Who Disciplines Management in Poorly Performing Companies," mimeo, London Business School.

Gorton, G., and F. Schmid, 1998, "Corporate Finance, Control Rights and Firm Performance: A Study of German Co-Determination," working paper, University of Pennsylvania.

Gorton, G., and F. Schmid, 1999, "Universal Banking and the Performance of German Firms," *Journal of Financial Economics*, 43,

Gottschalk, A., 1988, "Der Stimmrechtseinfluss der Banken in den Aktionaersversammlungen der Grossunternehmen," 5 WSI-Mitteilungen, 294–298.

Grossman, S., and O. Hart, 1988, "One Share-One Vote and the Market for Corporate Control," *Journal of Financial Economics*, 20, 175–202.

Harris, M., and A. Raviv, 1988, "Corporate Governance: Voting Rights and Majority Rules," *Journal of Financial Economics*, 20, 203–235.

Hoshi, T., A. Kashyap, and D. Scharfstein, 1990, "The Role of Banks in Reducing the Costs of Financial Distress in Japan," *Journal of Financial Economics*, 27, 67–88.

Hoshi, T., A. Kashyap, and D. Scharfstein, 1991, "Corporate Structure, Liquidity and Investment: Evidence from Japanese Industrial Groups," *Quarterly Journal of Economics*, 106, 33–60.

Jenkinson, T., and A. Ljungqvist, 2001, "The Role of Hostile Stakes in German Corporate Governance," forthcoming in *Journal of Corporate Finance*.

Kang, J.-K., and R. Stulz, 1997, "Is Bank-Centred Corporate Governance Worth It? A Cross-Sectional Analysis of the Performance of Japanese Firms During the Asset Price Deflation," mimeo.

Kaplan, S., 1994a, "Top Executive Rewards and Firm Performance: A Comparison of Japan and the United States," *Journal of Political Economy*, 102, 510–546.

Kaplan, S., 1994b, "Top Executives, Turnover, and Firm Performance in Germany," *Journal of Law and Economics*, 10, 142–159.

Kaplan, S., and B. Minton, 1994, "Appointments of Outsiders to Japanese Boards: Determinants and Implications for Managers," *Journal of Financial Economics*, 36, 225–258.

La Porta, R., F. Lopes-de-Silanes, and A. Shleifer, 1999, "Corporate Ownership Around the World," *Journal of Finance*, 54, 471–517.

La Porta, R., F. Lopes-de-Silanes, A. Shleifer, and R. Vishny, 1998, "Law and Finance," *Journal of Political Economy*, 106, 1113–1155.

Martin, K., and J. McConnell, 1991, "Corporate Performance, Corporate Takeovers and Management Turnover," *Journal of Finance*, 46, 671–687.

McConnell, J., and H. Servaes, 1990, "Additional Evidence on Equity Ownership and Corporate Value," *Journal of Financial Economics*, 27, 595–612.

Morck, R., A. Shleifer, and R. Vishny, 1988, "Management Ownership and Market Valuation: An Empirical Analysis," *Journal of Financial Economics*, 20, 293–315.

Nibler, M., 1998, "Bank Control and Corporate Performance in Germany: The Evidence," PhD dissertation, Cambridge University.

Schmidt, H., J. Drukarczyk, D. Honold, S. Prigge, A. Schuler, and G. Tetens, 1996, *Corporate Governance in Germany*, Nomos Verlagsgesellschaft, Baden-Baden.

Shleifer, A., and R. Vishny, 1986, "Large Shareholders and Corporate Control," *Journal of Political Economy*, 94, 461–488.

Ownership and Control of German Corporations

Shleifer, A., and R. Vishny, 1997, "A Survey of Corporate Governance," *Journal of Finance*, 52, 737–783.

Weisbach, M., 1988, "Outside Directors and CEO Turnover," *Journal of Financial Economics*, 20, 431–460.

Weinstein, D., and Y. Yafeh, 1998, "On the Costs of a Bank Centred Financial System: Evidence from the Changing Main Bank Relations in Japan," *Journal of Finance*, 53, 635–672.

White, H., 1980, "A Heteroscedasticity-Consistent Covariance Matrix Estimator and a Direct Test for Heteroscedasticity," *Econometrica*, 48, 817–838.

Wruck, K. 1989, "Equity Ownership, Concentration and Firm Value: Evidence from Private Equity Financing," *Journal of Financial Economics*, 23, 3–28.

Part II
Insider Ownership, Monitoring by Blockholders and Corporate Performance

[5]

ELSEVIER   Journal of Corporate Finance 5 (1999) 79–101

Journal of
CORPORATE
FINANCE

Managerial ownership and the performance of firms: Evidence from the UK

Helen Short, Kevin Keasey [*]

University of Leeds, Blenheim Terrace, Leeds LS2 9JT, UK

Received 1 March 1996; accepted 1 June 1998

Abstract

Given the governance issues arising from the separation of ownership from control, the ability to align managerial and shareholder interests via the managerial ownership of equity is an important topic of inquiry. The findings of the primarily US based literature suggest that management is aligned at low and possibly high levels of ownership but is entrenched (pursuing self interests) at intermediate ownership levels. This paper extends the US based literature in a number of important ways. First, the analysis is extended to the UK where there are important differences, as compared to the US, in the governance system. A comparative analysis of key differences between the US and UK governance systems suggest that management should become entrenched at higher levels of ownership in the UK. Some of the reasons for this suggestion are that in the UK management do not have the same freedom as their US counterparts to mount takeover defenses and institutional investors in the UK are more able to co-ordinate their monitoring activities. The empirical results of the paper confirm that UK management become entrenched at higher levels of ownership than their US counterparts. Second, the results from extending the analysis to consider different measures of firm performance and a more generalized form of the relationship confirm the general finding of the US literature of a non-linear relationship between firm performance and managerial ownership. © 1999 Elsevier Science B.V. All rights reserved.

JEL classification: G32

Keywords: Managerial ownership; UK; US

---

[*] Corresponding author. Tel.: +44-113-2332618; Fax: +44-113-2332640; E-mail: kk@lubs.leeds.ac.uk

80   *H. Short, K. Keasey / Journal of Corporate Finance 5 (1999) 79–101*

1. Introduction

Given the governance issues arising from the separation of ownership and control, it is not surprising that the form of the relation between the performance of firms and managerial ownership has been the subject of empirical investigation (for example, see Morck et al., 1988; McConnell and Servaes, 1990, 1995; Kole, 1995). To date the analysis has been primarily US based and the purpose of this paper is to extend the analysis in a number of important ways. First, the analysis of the relationship between the performance of firms and managerial ownership is extended to the UK where there are important differences, as compared to the US, in the governance system. In addition, the distribution of managerial ownership in the UK is different to that of the US and it has certain properties which are a positive benefit given the nature of the present analysis. Second, the analysis is conducted with a more generalized form of the relationship between management ownership and firm performance and with different measures of the performance of firms.

The paper is structured as follows. Section 2 outlines briefly the extant literature concerning the relation between the performance of firms and managerial ownership. As a means to guiding the methodology of the present paper, Section 3 discusses how institutional differences between the US and UK might lead to differences in governance mechanisms. Section 4 details hypotheses and empirical methods. Section 5 describes the sample and data, while the empirical findings are presented in Section 6. Section 7 presents conclusions and summarizes the findings of the paper.

2. The relationship between the performance of firms and managerial ownership–evidence from the US

The early analysis of the relation between the performance of firms and ownership was linear in form (see, for example, Demsetz and Lehn, 1985), while the later analysis of managerial ownership has considered non-linear forms (see Morck et al., 1988; McConnell and Servaes, 1990, 1995; Kole, 1995). The non-linear analysis follows from two possible effects which influence the relation between a firm's performance and managerial ownership: alignment and entrenchment. The notion that shareholdings by managers help to align the interests of shareholders and managers is well documented in the agency literature (Jensen and Meckling, 1976). Jensen and Meckling's 'convergence of interest' hypothesis contends that, as managerial ownership in a firm increases, a firm's performance increases uniformly, as managers are less inclined to divert resources away from value maximization. In contrast, Demsetz (1983) and Fama and Jensen (1983) contend that market discipline will force managers to adhere to value maximization at very low levels of ownership. At certain levels of equity ownership, however, managers' consumption of perquisites (for example, an attractive salary)

H. Short, K. Keasey / Journal of Corporate Finance 5 (1999) 79–101   81

may outweigh the loss they suffer from a reduced value of the firm. Morck et al. (1988) argue that high levels of managerial ownership could lead to 'entrenchment', as external shareholders find it difficult to control the actions of such managers. That is, at certain levels of ownership, managers find it worthwhile to consume perquisites which reduces the firm's value and, moreover, they have sufficient control to follow their own objectives without fear of discipline from other ownership interests. The combination of the convergence of interest and entrenchment effects point towards a non-linear relation between the performance of firms and managerial ownership.

Using Tobin's Q [1] as a measure of performance and the percentage of shares owned by the board directors as a measure of ownership, Morck et al. employ piecewise linear regression techniques (allowing the coefficients on the ownership variable to change at the 5% and 25% ownership levels) to estimate the relation between these variables. Their results suggest a positive relation between managerial ownership and Tobin's Q in the 0% to 5% ownership range and beyond the 25% ownership level; although the magnitude of the response of performance to given changes in managerial ownership is substantially less beyond the 25% level. They also note a negative relationship in the 5% to 25% range. Morck et al. contend these results are consistent with the view that the convergence of interest effects are dominant within the 0% to 5% range and above the 25% level, with the entrenchment effect being dominant within the 5% to 25% ownership range.

Alternatively, McConnell and Servaes regress Tobin's Q against managerial ownership and managerial ownership squared, and find the coefficient on managerial ownership to be statistically significant and positive while the coefficient on managerial ownership squared is statistically significant and negative. The results suggest that the relationship between managerial ownership and the value of the firm is curvilinear, as the value of the firm first increases and then decreases as ownership becomes concentrated in the hands of managers. Specifically, a positive relation between the performance of firms and managerial ownership exists for managerial ownership positions between 0% and approximately 40–50%, which is consistent with incentive alignment occurring between these ownership levels. These findings, therefore, differ from those of Morck et al., who found entrenchment to occur in the 5% to 25% ownership range. Moreover, McConnell and Servaes were unable to replicate Morck et al.'s specific empirical findings using piecewise regression techniques. In addition, McConnell and Servaes (1995) replicate their earlier study over a later time period and report similar results.

A recent paper by Kole (1995) suggests that the different findings of Morck et al. and McConnell and Servaes are attributable to differences in the size of the firms analyzed. Specifically, Morck et al.'s sample contains only large firms (371 firms from the Fortune 500), while McConnell and Servaes' sample consists of 1173 firms in 1976 and 1093 firms in 1986. Similarly, McConnell and Servaes

---

[1] Defined as the ratio of a firm's market value to the replacement cost of its physical assets.

82 *H. Short, K. Keasey / Journal of Corporate Finance 5 (1999) 79–101*

(1995) extend their earlier work by adding a sample of 1943 firms for 1988. Hence, the samples of McConnell and Servaes' obviously contain firms which are smaller than those contained in the Morck et al. sample. Kole argues that,

> on average, the positive relationship between Tobin's Q and managerial ownership is sustained at higher levels of ownership for small firms than it is for large firms (p. 426).

Thus, in summary, using Tobin's Q as the main measure of the performance of firms, the US studies have found the relationship between the performance of firms and managerial ownership to be, generally, non-linear–with a movement from alignment to entrenchment and then, possibly, to alignment as management ownership increases. The precise functional form of the relationship is, however, open to debate.

3. US and UK governance mechanisms: A comparison of institutions

Given the above results for the US, the obvious question to ask is does the movement from alignment to entrenchment (and possibly back to alignment) as management ownership increases hold for a different system of corporate governance; namely, the UK? Moreover, given noted differences between the systems of governance for the UK and US, do the relationships between firm performance and management ownership differ in a predictable manner? Thus, the purpose of this section is to consider how differences in the corporate governance mechanisms of the UK, as compared to the US, may impact on the relationship between the performance of firms and managerial ownership. In particular, this section focuses on the nature of equity ownership, the role of regulation and the nature of board structure.

While companies in both the US and UK are often described as having widely dispersed shareholdings, Table 1 illustrates that the patterns of share ownership are quite different for the two countries. In particular, the institutional ownership of US companies is two-thirds the level of that in the UK. Insurance companies hold a significantly smaller proportion of equity in the US than in the UK, largely as a result of US legislation which restricts the amount of equity in which insurance companies can invest [a maximum of 2% of assets can be invested in a single company, while a maximum of 20% of assets can be invested in equity (Roe, 1990)]. US pension funds also hold smaller domestic equity positions than their UK counterparts. [2] Furthermore, the US has the largest percentage of shareholders in the form of households.

---

[2] US pension funds equity holdings (both domestic and international) amounted to 52% of their total assets at the end of 1993, compared to 81% for UK pension funds (source: Pension Fund Indicators 1995, PDFM). US pension funds invest a far greater proportion of their funds in domestic bonds (33%) than do UK pension funds (7%).

Table 1
Ownership structure of publicly listed corporations in the UK and US 1990–1991 (percentage holdings)

	UK (%)	US (%)
Financial sectors		
Pension funds[a]	30.4	24.8
Insurance companies	18.4	5.2
Banks[b]	0.9	0.3
Investment companies and others	11.1	9.5
Total financial sector	60.8	39.8
Non-financial sectors		
Non-financial businesses	3.6	–
Households	21.3	53.5
Government	2.0	–
Foreign	12.3	6.7
Total	100.0	100.0

[a] Public and private.
[b] All types, including bank holding companies.
Source: Adapted from Kester (1992, Table 4, p. 33).

Although the structure of stock ownership differs between the US and the UK, the corporate governance debate in both countries has, in recent years, focused on the potential for institutions to take a more active role in the governance of corporations. In general, UK institutions are thought to be more active than their US counterparts (Black and Coffee, 1994). Black (1990) and Roe (1991) argue that financial institutions in the US face excess regulation which raises the cost of participation in corporate governance. In contrast to UK institutions, US institutions are subject to various legal restrictions (see Roe (1990) for a discussion) on stock ownership, which prevents them from building significant stakes in individual corporations. As a consequence, the concentration of institutional stock ownership in the UK is higher than in the US. In addition, much of the monitoring of companies by UK institutions takes place in a private 'behind the scenes' fashion, which allows institutions to take joint action to curb managerial excesses without drawing public attention to the fact. [3] Furthermore, the nature of the City of London means that institutional shareholders are in physical close proximity to each other, which aids the formulation of informal coalitions. In contrast, institutions in the US are deterred from such practices by the requirements to make a Schedule 13D filing when a shareholder group (formal or informal) owning 5% or

---

[3] For a discussion of the problems associated with such private intervention by UK institutions, see Short and Keasey (1997).

84   *H. Short, K. Keasey / Journal of Corporate Finance 5 (1999) 79–101*

more stock is formed. The filing must contain disclosure of the group's plans with respect to the company. As Roe (1991) and Jensen (1993) argue, such requirements discourage institutional shareholders from exercising effective corporate control. In contrast, UK institutions are under no obligation to disclose the fact that they have formed informal coalitions to monitor management. Given the higher concentration of institutional stock ownership in the UK and the ability of UK institutions to form monitoring coalitions, it is to be expected that UK managers will need to have higher levels of ownership than their US counterparts before they become entrenched.

Although UK institutions face fewer restrictions with respect to their ownership and monitoring actions than US institutions, US pension funds governed by the ERISA legislation and the large public funds (such as CalPERS and the State of Wisconsin Investment Board) are typically more active than their UK counterparts. In contrast to the UK pension funds, US pension funds covered by ERISA are legally obliged to exercise their voting rights, both in the case of stock holdings in domestic and non-US companies. UK institutions, preferring to exercise any power via private meetings with company management, have typically failed to exercise their right to vote at company general meetings. [4] However, the increase in the number of US institutions holding shares in UK companies is presently causing concern among UK institutions and forcing them to review their voting policy. [5]

Both the UK and US have highly active markets in corporate control, which is seen as the dominant disciplining mechanism and the primary means of removing under performing managers. Both the US and UK have strict rules to prevent raiders from accumulating large stakes without disclosing their holdings to the target company. In the UK, stock holdings of 5% or more (3% or more from 1990) and increases in holdings above 5% of 1% or more of stock in a public company must be disclosed within 5 days (2 days from 1990) of the holding being acquired.[6] This is slightly stricter than the position in the US, which demands disclosure within 10 days of the acquisition of a 5% holding, with changes of 1% or more thereafter being promptly disclosed. Furthermore, UK quoted companies are subject to a mandatory bid threshold of 30% of equity; any shareholder breaching the 30% threshold is required to make an offer to all shareholders

---

[4] A survey by the UK National Association of Pension Funds (National Association of Pension Funds, 1994) reported that only 28% of UK pension funds exercised their right to vote whenever practicable.

[5] One of their main concerns is that US institutions will be in a position to determine the outcome of proposals put to the vote at the corporate general meeting, simply because UK institutions do not bother to vote.

[6] In addition, a person is prevented from acquiring 10% or more of the voting shares (other than from a single shareholder) within any period of 7 days if the acquisition would give the buyer more than 15% of the voting rights in the company unless a tender offer for all other shares immediately follows.

holding voting shares at the highest price paid by the offerer in the preceding twelve months. Although the slightly tighter takeover disclosure rules in the UK suggest that UK management may be less threatened by such a governance mechanism and hence may become entrenched at lower levels of ownership, the differences between the two systems in this regard can only be considered as marginal.

A potentially more important difference is the use of takeover defenses in the two systems. The adoption of poison pills and other anti takeover measures by US companies, coupled with various antitakeover legislation has meant that US corporate management is afforded much greater protection against hostile bidders than is UK management. Although there are few legal restrictions on the adoption of takeover defenses prior to a hostile bid, in practice, the adoption of such defenses is not widespread in the UK. As Black and Coffee (1994) note, the relative lack of takeover defenses is due to opposition on the part of institutional shareholders.

Finally, there are differences between the US and the UK in terms of the constitution and operation of corporate boards. Boards of directors are theoretically appointed to represent the interests of shareholders and bridge the gap between external shareholders and managers internal to the company. The effectiveness of the board of directors in the UK as an internal control mechanism, however, is likely to be diminished as a result of its structure; in that the majority of the boards of UK companies are dominated by executive directors, hence blurring the distinction between directors and management. This contrasts with the structure of the boards of US large companies, which are typically dominated by outside directors (known as 'non-executive' directors in the UK). Nonetheless, the structure of the board of UK companies has changed significantly in recent years towards the US model. A Bank of England (1983) survey examining the year 1982 reported that the average UK quoted company board comprised of 67% executive directors and 33% non-executive directors. In contrast, Conyon (1994) found that for the year 1993, the average UK quoted company board comprised of 57% executive directors and 43% non-executive directors. Furthermore, the UK Cadbury Committee on standards of corporate governance recommended that quoted company boards should incorporate at least three non-executive directors, two of whom should be independent, in that they have no financial or other ties with management (Cadbury, 1992). Although the boards of US companies are dominated by outside directors, it is by no means clear that such a structure acts as an effective internal control mechanism. As Jensen (1993) notes, the US board is typically controlled by the CEO who is usually also the chairman of the board. In the UK, the majority of quoted companies have a separate CEO and chairman. Nevertheless, the debate continues as to effectiveness of the various board structures and it is difficult to conclude a-priori as to how the different board structures in the two countries might impact upon the relationship between firm performance and managerial ownership.

In summary, there are significant differences between the US and UK with respect to corporate governance characteristics. In particular, the ability of external shareholders (particularly institutions) in the US to coordinate effective corporate governance action is severely restricted by legal and regulatory restrictions. Far fewer restrictions are placed on shareholders in the UK. While institutions in both countries are frequently criticized for their lack of public intervention in corporate governance issues, the preference by UK institutions for private 'behind the scenes' forms of intervention means that, in reality, the degree of intervention by UK institutions is greater than that publicly reported. Furthermore, the ability of US boards to adopt takeover defense mechanisms, coupled with the relative lack of power on the part of external shareholders means that US corporate management is protected from external corporate control mechanisms to a far greater extent than are their UK counterparts. While the predominance of outside directors on the board of US companies may suggest that the internal control mechanisms are stronger in the US than in the UK, the ability of the CEO to select and reward the other members of the board is likely to mean that the ability of the outside directors to act as a disciplining device is questionable. Taking all of the above arguments together, however, suggests that management in the US is more likely to become entrenched at lower levels of ownership than is the case for UK management.

4. Hypotheses and empirical method

The general hypothesis examined here is that the performance of firms is non-linearly related to the percentage of equity shares held by management. Given the nature of the results produced by Morck et al. (1988), McConnell and Servaes (1990, 1995) and Kole (1995), we test for a cubic form of the relationship between the performance of firms and managerial ownership. Specifically, the model to be tested is as follows:

$$\text{Performance} = a + \beta_1 \text{DIR} + \beta_2 \text{DIR}^2 + \beta_3 \text{DIR}^3 + \gamma \text{Control Variables}.$$

Hence, three variables are included in the model to describe managerial ownership; DIR (the percentage of shares owned by managers), DIR^2 and DIR^3 (the square and cube, respectively, of the percentage of shares owned by managers). This is a general extension of the Morck et al. piecewise model, allowing the coefficients on the managerial ownership variables to determine their own turning points. A problem with the empirical application of the Morck et al. piecewise regression model is that it only allows the coefficients on the managerial ownership variables to change at pre-determined levels of ownership (specifically at 5% and 25% of managers' ownership, in the case of Morck et al.). As Morck et al. themselves note, however, there is no theoretical guidance for the choice of turning points on the piecewise regression, hence the form of the relationship is essentially an empirical issue. [7] So as not to pre-determine the turning points in the relationship between the performance of firms and managerial ownership, a cubic form of managerial ownership is examined which allows the turning points to be determined endogenously.

If the form of the relationship is similar to that suggested by Morck et al., the coefficient on the variables DIR and DIR^3 are expected to be positive (indicating the convergence of interest with its positive effect on the performance of firms at lower and higher levels of ownership), while that on the variable DIR^2 is expected to be negative (indicating entrenchment with negative effects on the performance of firms at medium levels of ownership). However, while Morck et al. find that the entrenchment effect is dominant within the 5% to 25% ownership range, the differences between the US and UK with respect to corporate governance mechanisms, outlined in Section 3, suggest that dominance of the entrenchment effect may be felt at different (higher) levels of ownership for UK firms as compared to US firms. As previously argued, US corporate management is protected from external corporate control mechanisms to a far greater extent than are their UK counterparts. The ability of US managers to adopt antitakeover measures and the legal and regulatory restrictions placed on US institutions in terms of stock ownership and the coordination of effective corporate governance action suggests that US managers may become entrenched at lower levels of ownership than is the case for UK managers. Hence, a priori, it is hypothesized that for the present sample of UK companies, the relationship between firm performance and management ownership will be positive at levels above 5% ownership.

All of the above analysis has concerned itself with considering whether US and UK management will become entrenched at different levels of ownership. There has been no consideration given to whether the range of ownership over which entrenchment occurs might differ between the two countries. This is because there is little in the theoretical and empirical literatures to inform such a discussion. From this position, we draw the default conclusion that there is no reason to expect the ownership ranges over which entrenchment is the dominant force to differ between the US and the UK and, therefore, the negative effects of entrenchment are expected to be dominant at higher levels of ownership in the UK than is the case for the US.

---

[7] Morck et al. (1988) arrived at turning points of 5% and 25% as a result of examining a variety of piecewise formulations. Their regression including the turning points of 5% and 25% provided the 'best' regression model as it had the lowest sum of squared errors. However, they do note that the choice of 5% is motivated by the fact that this is the mandatory disclosure level of ownership interest (mandated by the SEC for their US sample) and also Herman (1981) focuses on 5% ownership as representing a non-negligible stake. The choice of a 25% turning point is motivated by the suggestion of Weston (1979) that directors' ownership of 20%–30% prohibits a successful hostile takeover bid.

88 *H. Short, K. Keasey / Journal of Corporate Finance 5 (1999) 79–101*

5. Sample and variables

5.1. Sample

The sample was chosen from all UK firms quoted on the Official List of the London Stock Exchange for the period 1988 to 1992. Although the performance data are retrieved from the on-line Datastream facility, [8] the ownership data had to be collected manually from annual company reports which conditions the size and time frame of the overall sample. To be included in the sample, the firms had to be quoted on the Official List for at least a year before the date of their accounting year end for 1988. This condition was imposed to ensure that the performance of firms, capital structure and ownership were not affected as a result of a new listing. The basis of selection was random, subject to the following exclusions.

(a) Firms in the financial and oil and gas sectors are excluded due to the different income measuring rules governing such companies, as compared to those in the manufacturing and service sectors.

(b) Privatized firms (such as Water, Electricity, Telecommunications, Steel and Gas) are excluded as their operating conditions, in terms of regulation and monopoly markets, are usually atypical.

(c) Firms in the broadcasting sector are excluded due to the regulatory nature of the sector and the changes in regulation which occurred during the period (for example, tendering for operating licenses and changes in ownership rules which are largely government controlled).

(d) Firms with ownership structures which do not confirm to the typical one vote for each ordinary share are also excluded. As this paper specifically examines the effects of ownership structure, it is important that the ownership structure and the associated voting structure of the equity shares of a particular firm can be determined. As a result, firms whose share structures included non-ordinary voting shares (such as voting A shares, management shares, founders' shares) were excluded. [9]

Having excluded firms on the above basis, a final random sample of 225 firms is derived.

5.2. Variables

The key variables of interest are measures of the performance of firms, managerial ownership and other ownership interests. Furthermore, a small number

---

[8] Datastream is an on-line international database containing data on accounting, stock market and economic variables.

[9] Non-ordinary voting shares often carried more votes per share than ordinary shares and would considerably complicate the determination of the ownership structure of individual firms. As the trend is towards share structures including only ordinary voting shares and, in addition, in many cases, firms which such atypical share structures often changed the nature of the shares in the period under consideration, exclusion of such firms should not materially affect the results.

of additional variables are used to control for effects on the performance of firms not captured by the ownership variables. The variables are summarized in Table 2. To smooth fluctuations on an annual basis, the firm performance and control variables are measured as averages over the period 1989 to 1992. The ownership variables are defined, however, as at the beginning of the period under consideration, that is at the beginning of the firms' 1989 accounting year ends (and, hence, taken from the 1988 annual reports). The implicit assumption of the current analysis is that causality runs from ownership to the performance of firms. However, any relationship between ownership and performance could reflect 'reverse' causality; that is, management may increase their stakes in higher performing firms. Ownership variables are measured at the beginning of the period under consideration in an attempt to reduce potential problems of 'reverse' causality arising between the performance of firms and ownership, but the possibility of reverse causality clearly remains.

5.2.1. Firm performance variables

This paper utilizes commonly used accounting and market measures of the performance of firms. The accounting based measure of the performance of firms is the return on shareholders' equity (RSE). The return on shareholders equity is calculated as profits attributable to shareholders, divided by shareholders' equity and reserves. The market measure used is a valuation ratio (VAL). The valuation ratio VAL is used by Leech and Leahy (1991) and is calculated as the market value of the firm at its accounting year end, divided by the book value of equity at the accounting year end. The book value of equity is calculated excluding intangible assets to eliminate differences caused by diverse accounting treatments

Table 2
Description of variables

Variables	Description
Dependent variables	
VAL	Market value of equity at the accounting year end, divided by the book value of equity at the accounting year end.
RSE	Return on shareholders' equity equal to profits attributable to shareholders divided by shareholders' equity and reserves.
Ownership variables	
DIR	Percentage of shares held by directors.
INST	Percentage of shares owned by institutions owning 5% or more.
EXTERNAL	Percentage of shares held by other external ownership interests.
Control variables	
SIZE	Log of the firm's sales.
GROWTH	Average annual growth in sales.
DEBT	Total debt divided by book value of total assets.
RDTA	Research and development expenditure divided by total assets.

90   *H. Short, K. Keasey / Journal of Corporate Finance 5 (1999) 79–101*

of brand names, patents and capitalized research and development. Due to skewness in the distribution of VAL, the log form of the variable is used throughout the analysis. In very basic terms, the market value of the firm measures the discounted present value of its expected future income stream, while the book value of equity measures the investment by shareholders in the assets utilized to generate that income stream. VAL, therefore, provides a measure of management's ability to generate a certain income stream from an asset base and is, hence, an indication of management performance. From this perspective, the VAL variable can be seen as a UK approximation to Tobin's Q.

5.2.2. Managerial ownership variables

As noted above, all ownership data have been manually extracted from the annual reports of the sample companies from the years 1988 to 1992. The available data on ownership interests contained in the annual report is determined by the Companies Act 1985 Part VI. Briefly, prior to 1990, the legislation required the details of external interests (that is, excluding directors' interests) which amounted to 5% or more of the issued share capital to be disclosed. Post June 1990, details of external interests which amounted to 3% or more of issued share capital were required to be disclosed. In contrast to the case of external shareholders, members of the board of directors must disclose the total holdings of their shares, regardless of the size of their shareholdings. Hence in the case of directors' shareholdings, there is no cut-off ownership level at which ownership is reported; that is, every ownership stake is disclosed.

Managerial ownership is measured as the percentage of equity shares owned by directors' and their immediate families at the accounting year end. This measure includes directors' ownership via corporate vehicles, for example, where directors' are majority shareholders in other firms which have direct ownership stakes in the particular firm under consideration. This definition of managerial ownership is consistent with that of Morck et al. (1988) who define managerial ownership as ownership by members of the board of directors. It does, however, differ from McConnell and Servaes who define management (or 'insider') ownership as equity owned by corporate officers and members of the board of directors. Note that ownership data in the UK are only available for individuals who legally hold the position of director of the firm, and not for other officers/managers of the firm.

Data relating to the managerial ownership of equity for the sample years is shown in Table 3. [10] As Table 3 illustrates, the percentage of equity owned by managers has decreased slightly over the period. In 1988, the mean (median)

---

[10] Although in the initial part of the analysis, managerial ownership is defined at the end of 1988, Table 2 reports ownership at the end of the years 1988 to 1992. Managerial ownership for the other years is used when examining the robustness of the results.

H. Short, K. Keasey / Journal of Corporate Finance 5 (1999) 79–101   91

Table 3
Managerial ownership

	1988	1989	1990	1991	1992
Managers' ownership (DIR)%					
Mean	13.344	13.449	12.905	11.731	11.473
Median	5.260	6.745	6.270	5.590	4.110
Standard deviation	16.279	16.093	15.394	14.657	15.495
Minimum	0.000	0.000	0.000	0.000	0.000
Maximum	62.860	62.030	57.540	57.580	75.250

ownership was 13.34% (5.26%) which compares to a mean (median) of 11.47% (4.11%) in 1992.

Comparisons can be made with the levels of managerial ownership reported in previous US research. Morck et al. (1988), using a 1980 sample, report mean ownership to be 10.6% with a median of 3.4%. Their figures are, therefore, slighter lower than for the present UK sample. However, it should be noted that Morck et al.'s figures for managerial ownership are taken from the Corporate Data Exchange which lists ownership stakes by directors who hold at least 0.2% of equity, whereas the present managerial ownership data is not subject to any minimum cut-off level of ownership. Furthermore, differences in the distribution of managerial ownership between the Morck et al. US sample and the present UK sample are apparent. In the present sample 48% of companies have managerial ownership of 5% or less of equity, whereas, the comparative figure for the Morck et al. sample is 58%. In addition, managerial ownership exceeds 25% of equity for 21% of the present sample, compared with 14% of companies in the Morck et al. sample. McConnell and Servaes (1990) find mean managerial ownership for 1986 to be 11.84% with a median of 5%. They use data collected from the Value Line Investment Survey and define management (or insider) ownership as ownership by corporate officers and members of the board of managers. Overall, given the differences in the nature of the definition of managerial ownership, there are similarities between managerial ownership in the US and UK. Nonetheless, comparisons with the Morck et al. sample suggest that the distribution of managerial ownership in UK firms is more dispersed than in US firms and this has clear benefits, given that the purpose of the analysis is to assess the nature of the relationship between firm performance and managerial ownership across the whole range of managerial ownership.

5.2.3. Other ownership variables

In addition to including managerial ownership, other ownership variables are included in the analysis. In line with McConnell and Servaes (1990), variables denoting ownership by institutions (INST) and ownership by other external shareholders (EXTERNAL) are incorporated. Due to the restrictions on the level of external ownership reported in the Annual Report, INST measures the percentage of equity ownership by institutions owning 5% or more of equity at the beginning of 1989. Similarly, EXTERNAL measures the percentage of equity ownership by other external shareholders (corporations, charities and individuals) owning 5% or more of equity at the beginning of 1989.

5.2.4. Control variables

A number of additional variables are included in the performance regression models to control for other potential influences on the performance of firms. The variables included are firm size, firm growth, debt, and research and development expenditure. [11]

The potential impact of firm size on the performance of firms is allowed for by the inclusion of the logarithm of total sales (SIZE). A firm's size potentially affects performance through at least two different avenues. First, there is a potential financing effect, in that larger firms may find it easier to generate funds internally and to access funds from external sources. A reduced financing constraint allows the firm to make greater use of profitable projects. Second, the economies of scale which accompany size enables the firm to create entry barriers with the associated beneficial effects on the performance of firms.

Following the comments of Morck et al. (1988) and McConnell and Servaes (1995), we include a variable to capture firm growth (GROWTH, measured as the percentage annual change in sales, averaged over the sample period) to control for the impact of growth on the firm's performance and for potential linkages between the firm's performance, financing structure and growth.

The variable DEBT (defined as the book value of total debt divided by total assets) is included to control for a number of factors. First, it controls for the possibility that debt holders exert significant influence over the behavior and operation of the firm and its management. Stiglitz (1985) argues that control over management actions is effectively exercised, not by shareholders, but by lenders, particularly banks. Second, as suggested by Grossman and Hart (1982) and Jensen (1986), debt may be used by management to signal that they have bonded themselves to achieving the levels of cash flow necessary to meet the debt repayments. Debt may, therefore, be used to resolve conflicts between managers and shareholders as it reduces management discretion to consume excessive perquisites and, hence, should increase the value of the firm's equity (Jensen and Meckling, 1976; Grossman and Hart, 1982).

Finally, in line with Morck et al. (1988) and McConnell and Servaes (1990), we include research and development expenditure as a control variable. This variable, RDSALES, is defined as average research and development expenditure over the period, divided by average total assets over the period.

---

[11] Both Morck et al. (1988) and McConnell and Servaes (1990) use advertising expenditures as a control variable. However, data on advertising expenditure is not publicly available in the UK.

H. Short, K. Keasey / Journal of Corporate Finance 5 (1999) 79–101   93

6. Empirical results

6.1. Multivariate results

The empirical analysis consists of a series of OLS regressions utilizing the correction technique for unknown heteroskedasticity of White (1980). Summary univariate statistics for the dependent and explanatory variables are provided in Appendix A.

Table 4 presents the results of the hypothesis that the relationship between the performance of firms and managerial ownership is cubic in form. For both the RSE and VAL regressions, the coefficients on the variables DIR, DIR^2 and DIR^3

Table 4
Regression estimates using 1988 ownership data

Variable	Dependent variables	
	RSE	VAL
	Coefficient t-statistic	Coefficient t-statistic
DIR	0.009446	0.030447
	3.816278 * *	2.418527 * *
DIR^2	−0.000416	−0.001534
	−3.730197 * *	−2.615695 * *
DIR^3	4.83E − 06	1.86E − 05
	3.548624 * *	2.659960 * *
INST	0.001111	0.001797
	1.332224	0.495025
EXTERNAL	0.000194	0.004565
	0.410438	1.563765
SALE	0.026488	0.088504
	4.642483 * *	3.441729 * *
GROWTH	0.083050	0.581489
	3.516016 * *	7.210637 * *
RDTA	0.824677	8.565263
	3.184826 * *	5.250013 * *
DEBT	−0.031094	0.244179
	−0.631782	1.070520
INTERCEPT	−0.215935	−0.806672
	−2.799769 * *	−2.379558 * *
Adjusted R^2	0.227935	0.286801
F-statistic	8.347893 * *	11.00865 * *
Inflection points	15.58%	12.99%
	41.84%	41.99%

Performance $= a + \beta_1 DIR + \beta_2 DIR^2 + \beta_3 DIR^3 + \gamma$ Control Variables.
* Significant at 10% confidence level using two-tailed test.
* * Significant at 5% confidence level using two-tailed test.

are all statistically significant at the 5% level of confidence and are of the expected sign; that is, the coefficients on the variables DIR and DIR^3 are positive, while that on the variable DIR^2 is negative. Hence, the results provide support for the general functional form of the relationship between the performance of firms and managerial ownership as suggested by Morck et al. (1988); that is, management move from alignment, to entrenchment, to alignment as their ownership stakes in the firm increase.

In terms of the other ownership variables included in the regression analysis, there is little support for the hypothesis that large shareholders (institutions and other large external shareholders) have an independent effect on the performance of firms In both regressions, the coefficients on the variables INST and EXTER-NAL are positive but statistically insignificant. The finding that institutions have no effect on the performance of firms contrasts with that of McConnell and Servaes (1990), who report a statistically significant and positive relationship between the performance of firms and institutional ownership. However, the lack of statistical significance of the coefficient on the other external ownership variable is consistent with McConnell and Servaes. The SIZE, GROWTH and RDSALES control variables are, however, statistically significant in both regressions, and DEBT is statistically significant in the VAL regression. In general, the estimated regressions explain 20 to 30% of the variation in the dependent variables.

The interesting question, however, is do the results confirm the hypothesis that UK managers will become entrenched at higher levels of ownership than their US counterparts? Calculations carried out on the coefficients of the variables DIR, DIR^2 and DIR^3 reveal that, for the RSE model, the turning points on the cubic function of managers' ownership are approximately 15.58% (a maximum point) and 41.84% (a minimum point). [12] In terms of the sample, 51 companies lie between the two turning points and 23 companies lie above the maximum point. [13] The results suggest, therefore, that the performance of firms (as measured by RSE) is positively related to managers' ownership in the 0% to 15.58% range, negatively related in the 15.58% to 41.84% range and positively related when managers' ownership exceeds 41.84%. Similarly, using VAL as the measure of the performance of firms, the turning points are 12.99% and 41.99%, respectively. Given the differences between the measures of the performance of firms RSE and

---

[12] The turning points of a cubic function are calculated as follows: Assuming all other variables are constant and denoting DIR by x: $RSE = 0.009446\,x - 0.000416\,x^2 + 4.83e^{-06}x^3$. The turning points are found by differentiating y (RSE) with respect to x, letting $\frac{\partial y}{\partial x} = 0$ and solving for x. To determine whether x is a maximum or minimum turning point, calculate the value of $\partial^2 y / \partial x^2$. If $\partial^2 y / \partial x^2 > 0$, the turning point is a maxima, if $\partial^2 y / \partial x^2 < 0$, the turning point is a minima.

[13] To gain further insight into the distribution of the managerial ownership variable (DIR), the 25th percentile of the ownership distribution has a value of 0.49%, while the 75th percentile has a value of 22.50%.

H. Short, K. Keasey / Journal of Corporate Finance 5 (1999) 79–101   95

VAL, the similarity of the turning points of managerial ownership indicates the robustness of the general relationship.

Therefore, given that Morck et al. find a negative relationship to exist between performance and managerial ownership in the 5% to 25% ownership range, the present results provide support for the hypothesis that UK managers become entrenched at higher levels (12%) of ownership than US managers. Furthermore, as managers in the present sample remain entrenched up to an ownership level of 41%, the results suggest that entrenchment effects dominate the relationship between firm performance and managerial ownership at generally higher levels of managerial ownership than is the case for the US.

Finally, the cubic relationship between performance and managerial ownership is found to exist for both market and accounting measures of performance. Morck et al. utilized an accounting measure of performance (profit rate) in addition to Tobin's Q, but found a statistically significant relationship to exist only for the positive slope in the 0% to 5% ownership range. Moreover, the coefficient on the variable denoting ownership of 25% or more, whilst being insignificant, was negative, suggesting that accounting performance did not increase as ownership rises above 25%. Hence, the present results provide additional evidence of the non-linear relationship between performance and managerial ownership affecting both market and accounting measures of performance. In addition to testing for the cubic form of the relationship between the performance of firms and managerial ownership, we also explicitly examine Morck et al.'s piecewise model using the exogenously determined turning points of 5% and 25%. As would be expected, given the results of the cubic model, the coefficients on the managerial ownership variables using such piecewise specifications are generally statistically insignificant. Finally, we also tested McConnell and Servaes' finding of a curvilinear relationship between the performance of firms and managerial ownership (including the variables DIR and DIR^2 in the regression). For both the RSE and VAL regressions, while the coefficient on the variable DIR is positive and that on the variables DIR^2 is negative (consistent with the form of the relationship found by McConnell and Servaes) all coefficients are statistically insignificant.

6.2. Robustness of results

We now conduct further analysis to determine the robustness of our results. Following Demsetz and Lehn (1985) and McConnell and Servaes (1995), it is possible that the relationship between the performance of firms and managerial ownership is spurious because the relationship between these variables is industry-specific and no control has been included in the regressions for this possibility. To investigate whether our regression results reflect industry effects, we repeated all of the above regressions after incorporating industry dummy variables, based on the firm's stock exchange industry classification. The results shown in Table 4 were not altered materially, with the cubic relationship between the performance of firms and managerial ownership still being present. For both regressions, the results for the other ownership and control variables still held. These results provide evidence against the argument that our findings are due to an industry effect.

The robustness of the reported cubic relationship between the performance of firms and managerial ownership is further examined by investigating the relationship using different sample structures. For the results reported in the previous section, the ownership variables have been measured at the beginning of the sample period (that is, ownership at the beginning of 1989). To test whether the observed cubic relationship is dependent on ownership being defined at the beginning of the period, the ownership variables are redefined to measure owner-

Table 5
Regression estimates using 1990 ownership data

Variable	Dependent variables	
	RSE	VAL
	Coefficient t-statistic	Coefficient t-statistic
DIR	0.006849 2.560419 * *	0.034546 2.243886 * *
DIR^2	− 0.000373 − 2.675031 * *	− 0.001993 − 2.474952 * *
DIR^3	$5.07E-06$ 2.664466 * *	$2.63E-05$ 2.430597 * *
INST	0.000905 1.454904	0.001107 0.427731
EXTERNAL	0.000293 0.588473	0.005848 2.098585 * *
SIZE	0.023012 3.919539 * *	0.084183 2.878986 * *
GROWTH	0.076809 3.071418 * *	0.576369 7.383331 * *
RDTA	0.771579 2.938332 * *	8.182848 5.109526 * *
DEBT	− 0.037714 − 0.764245	0.214404 0.962761
INTERCEPT	− 0.170140 − 2.035993 * *	− 0.751792 − 1.824259 *
Adjusted R^2	0.203137	0.296238
F-statistic	7.344681 * *	11.47663 * *
Inflection points	12.23% 36.82%	11.11% 39.41%

* Significant at 10% confidence level using two-tailed test.
* * Significant at 5% confidence level using two-tailed test.

ship in the middle of the sample period (that is ownership at the end of the accounting year 1990/beginning of accounting year 1991). Hence, the variables measuring managerial ownership (DIR), institutional ownership (INST) and other external shareholders (EXTERNAL) are taken at the end of the accounting year 1990.

The results of the regression analysis utilizing these redefined ownership variables are shown in Table 5. As Table 5 demonstrates, the coefficients on the

Table 6
Regression estimates using panel data

Variable	Dependent variables	
	RSE	VAL
	Coefficient t-statistic	Coefficient t-statistic
DIR	0.004960 3.166658**	0.025788 3.174584**
DIR^2	−0.000248 −3.178974**	−0.001528 −3.931388**
DIR^3	3.25E−06 3.177612**	2.05E−05 4.205575**
INST	0.000772 1.821566*	0.002453 1.253225
EXTERNAL	8.74E-05 0.319504	0.003705 2.539946**
SIZE	0.023067 6.711220**	0.108373 6.218357**
GROWTH	0.086458 2.976499**	0.594319 4.769446**
RDTA	0.864373 5.746909**	8.614726 9.217929**
DEBT	0.000677 0.016339	−0.116416 −0.890955
YEAR DUMMY 89	0.068439 6.577777**	0.258164 4.411254**
YEAR DUMMY 90	0.050749 5.173511**	0.020471 0.365123
YEAR DUMMY 91	0.012933 1.269248	0.065870 1.132622
INTERCEPT	−0.209946 −4.534504**	−1.089493 −4.541960**
Adjusted R^2	0.198000	0.240497
F-statistic	19.39276**	24.45848**
Inflection points	13.68% 37.19%	10.77% 38.92%

* Significant at 10% confidence level using two-tailed test.
** Significant at 5% confidence level using two-tailed test.

variables DIR, DIR^2 and DIR^3 are all statistically significant and of the expected sign. Hence, this suggests that the cubic relationship between the performance of firms and managerial ownership is not dependent on ownership being defined at the beginning of the period under inspection. Similarly, the statistical significance of the other variables, the adjusted R^2 and the turning points of the relationship are in line with those reported in Table 4.

As an additional test, the regressions are re-estimated using the sample data in a panel form covering the years 1989, 1990, 1991 and 1992. For each panel year, the ownership variables are defined as of the start of the year. The results of the regression analysis utilizing the panel dataset are shown in Table 6. Once again, the coefficients on the variables DIR, DIR^2 and DIR^3 are all statistically significant and of the expected sign. The rest of the regression is essentially similar to the one reported in Table 4, with some very minor variations. For example, the other ownership interests are statistically significant in one or other of the regressions and debt shows statistical significance in the RSE regression rather than the VAL regression. Nonetheless, these additional tests indicate the general robustness of the noted relationship between the performance of firms and managerial ownership.

7. Summary and conclusions

This paper has extended the US based literature on the relationship between firm performance and managerial ownership in a number of ways. First, the analysis has been extended to the UK where there are important differences, as compared to the US, in the governance system. A comparative analysis of the US and UK governance systems suggested that greater institutional monitoring and a lesser ability to mount takeover defenses within the UK should lead to management becoming entrenched at higher levels of ownership in the UK. The empirical results of the paper confirm that UK management become entrenched at higher levels of ownership than their US counterparts. Second, the results from extending the analysis to consider different measures of firm performance and a more generalized form of the relationship confirm the general finding of the US literature of a non-linear relationship between firm performance and managerial ownership. Therefore, the results suggest that the noted non-linear relationship (of alignment, entrenchment, alignment) between the performance of firms and managerial ownership is sufficiently robust to be present across samples from the UK and US, different measures of the performance of firms and an additional method of estimation.

In addition to the differences between the levels of ownership at which management appear to become entrenched, there are other notable differences between the results of the present analysis as compared to Morck et al. The present results indicate that the non-linear relationship between exists between performance and managerial ownership for both accounting and market measures of

H. Short, K. Keasey / Journal of Corporate Finance 5 (1999) 79–101   99

performance. In contrast, Morck et al. found a significant positive–negative–positive relationship to exist only for performance as measured by Tobin's Q and not for performance as measured by an accounting profit rate. In addition, the present results indicate a consistently significant and positive relationship between performance and managerial ownership at high levels of managerial ownership, consistent with the hypothesis that the convergence of interest effect dominates the entrenchment effect at high levels of ownership. While Morck et al. report a positive association between performance (Tobin's Q) and high management ownership (specifically ownership at 25% or above), the statistical significance of their variable is weak and varies according to the model specification. Hence, the present results provide somewhat stronger evidence of a positive relationship between performance and managerial ownership at high levels of ownership. This is consistent with the Jensen and Meckling (1976) model, which suggests that high levels of managerial ownership help to align the interests of shareholders and managers.

Before drawing implications for the modeling and practice of corporate governance, however, a number of caveats must be noted. The implicit assumption of the current analysis is that causality runs from managerial ownership to the performance of firms. While the present analysis has used data that attempts to protect the integrity of such an assumption, there is no escaping the fact that 'reverse' causality could underpin the estimated results. For example, the positive alignment between performance and management could simply reflect more successful firms awarding directors equity shares; here the causality runs from performance to ownership rather than vice versa. Such an argument would, however, have trouble explaining the noted negative relation between performance and managerial ownership in the 12% to 40% managerial ownership range. A further caveat is that all the analysis to date, for good reasons, has assumed that managerial ownership is homogenous in terms of its ability to influence the performance of the firm. The history and dynamics of any corporate board would tell us that such an assumption is a simplification of practice. Nonetheless, until data on the history of boards are publicly available, the present assumption is the only practicable means of quantitative analysis.

Bearing the above in mind, the results of this and previous papers offer the conclusion that aligning the interests of management and shareholders is simply not a case of providing management with larger amounts of equity. Corporate governance is concerned with complex multi-dimensional entities and the modeling/practice of governance needs to reflect this.

Acknowledgements

We are grateful to Kenneth Lehn (the editor) and the anonymous referees for valuable comments and suggestions.

100   H. Short, K. Keasey / Journal of Corporate Finance 5 (1999) 79–101

Appendix A. Summary statistics for variables

	Mean	Median	Standard deviation	Minimum	Maximum
Performance variables[a]					
Market value/equity (VAL)[c]	1.86	1.60	1.26	0.44	10.67
Return on shareholders' equity (RSE)	0.13	0.13	0.10	−0.21	0.38
Ownership variables[b]					
Managers' ownership (DIR)	13.34	5.26	16.28	0.00	62.86
Institutional ownership (INST)	7.73	5.47	9.38	0.00	45.47
External ownership (EXTERNAL)	6.87	0.00	14.94	0.00	93.90
Control variables[a]					
Sales (SIZE)[c]	408,870.40	98,817.42	821,350.90	10,429.81	4,847,875.62
Growth (GROWTH)	−0.03	−0.07	0.39	−0.94	2.04
R&D/Sales (RDSALES)	0.01	0.00	0.02	0.00	0.14
Debt (DEBT)	0.48	0.39	0.51	0.00	5.54

[a] Performance and control variables are calculated as averages over the period 1989–1992.
[b] Ownership variables are measured at the beginning of 1989.
[c] Statistics for the variables VAL and SIZE are shown in their unlogged form.

References

Bank of England, 1983. The composition of company boards in 1982. Bank of England Quarterly Bulletin, March, pp. 66–68.

Black, B.S., 1990. Shareholder passivity reexamined. Michigan Law Review 89, 520–608.

Black, B.S., Coffee, J.C., 1994. Hail Britannia?: Institutional investor behavior under limited regulation. Michigan Law Review 92 (7), 1997–2087.

Cadbury, A., 1992. Report of the Committee on the Financial Aspects of Corporate Governance. Gee Publishing, London.

Conyon, M.J., 1994. Corporate governance changes in UK companies between 1988 and 1993. Corporate Governance 2 (2), 97–109.

Demsetz, H., 1983. The structure of ownership and the theory of the firm. Journal of Law and Economics 26, 375–390.

Demsetz, H., Lehn, K., 1985. The structure of corporate ownership: Causes and consequences. Journal of Political Economy 93, 1155–1177.

Fama, E.F., Jensen, M.C., 1983. Separation of ownership and control. Journal of Law and Economics 26, 301–325.

Grossman, S., Hart, O., 1982. Corporate financial structure and managerial incentives. In: McCall, J. (Ed.), The Economics of Information and Uncertainty, University of Chicago Press, Chicago, IL, pp. 107–137.

Herman, E.S., 1981. Corporate Control, Corporate Power. Cambridge University Press, Cambridge.

Jensen, M.C., 1986. Agency costs of free cash flow, corporate finance and takeovers. American Economic Review 76, 323–329.

Jensen, M.C., 1993. The modern industrial revolution, exit, and the failure of internal control systems. Journal of Finance 48, 831–880.

Jensen, M.C., Meckling, W.H., 1976. Theory of the firm: Managerial behavior, agency costs and ownership structure. Journal of Financial Economics 4, 305–360.

Kester, W.C., 1992. Industrial groups as systems of contractual governance. Oxford Review of Economic Policy 8, 24–44.

Kole, S.R., 1995. Measuring managerial equity ownership: A comparison of sources of ownership data. Journal of Corporate Finance 1, 413–435.

Leech, D., Leahy, J., 1991. Ownership structure, control type classifications and the performance of large British companies. Economic Journal 101, 1418–1437.

McConnell, J.J., Servaes, H., 1990. Additional evidence on equity ownership and corporate value. Journal of Financial Economics 27, 595–612.

McConnell, J.J., Servaes, H., 1995. Equity ownership and the two faces of debt. Journal of Financial Economics 39, 131–157.

Morck, R., Shleifer, A., Vishny, R.W., 1988. Managerial ownership and market valuation: An empirical analysis. Journal of Financial Economics 20, 292–315.

National Association of Pension Funds, 1994. Annual Survey of Occupational Pension Schemes, National Association of Pension Funds, London.

Roe, M.J., 1990. Political and legal restraints on ownership and control of public companies. Journal of Financial Economics 27, 7–42.

Roe, M.J., 1991. A political theory of American corporate finance. Columbia Law Review 91, 10–67.

Short, H., Keasey, K., 1997. Institutional shareholders and corporate governance in the UK. In: Keasey, K., Thompson, S., Wright, M. (Eds.), Corporate Governance: Economic and Financial Issues, Oxford University Press, Oxford, pp. 18–53.

Stiglitz, J.E., 1985. Credit markets and the control of capital. Journal of Money, Credit, and Banking 17 (2), 133–152.

Weston, J.F., 1979. The tender takeover. Mergers and Acquisitions, pp. 74–82.

White, H., 1980. A heteroskedasticity-consistent covariance matrix and a direct test for heteroskedasticity. Econometrica 48, 817–838.

[6]

ELSEVIER   Journal of Financial Economics 53 (1999) 353–384

www.elsevier.com/locate/econbase

Understanding the determinants of managerial ownership and the link between ownership and performance [☆]

Charles P. Himmelberg[a], R. Glenn Hubbard[a,b,*], Darius Palia[a,c]

[a]*Graduate School of Business, Columbia University, Uris Hall, 3022 Broadway, New York, NY 10027 USA*
[b]*The National Bureau of Economic Research, USA*
[c]*1050 Massachusetts Avenue, Cambridge, MA 02138, USA*

Received 9 March 1998; received in revised form 19 October 1998; accepted 2 March 1999

Abstract

Both managerial ownership and performance are endogenously determined by exogenous (and only partly observed) changes in the firm's contracting environment. We extend the cross-sectional results of Demsetz and Lehn (1985) (Journal of Political Economy, 93, 1155–1177) and use panel data to show that managerial ownership is explained by key variables in the contracting environment in ways consistent with the predictions of principal-agent models. A large fraction of the cross-sectional variation in managerial ownership is explained by unobserved firm heterogeneity. Moreover, after

* Corresponding author. Tel.: + 1-212-854-3493; fax: + 1-212-864-6184.

E-mail addresses: cph15@columbia.edu (C.P. Himmelberg), rgh1@columbia.edu (R.G. Hubbard), dnp1@columbia.edu (D. Palia)

[☆]We are grateful for helpful comments and suggestions from two anonymous referees and from Anup Agrawal, George Baker, Sudipto Bhattacharya, Steve Bond, Charles Calomiris, Harold Demsetz, Rob Hansen, Laurie Hodrick, Randy Kroszner, Mark Mitchell, Andrew Samwick, Bill Schwert (the editor), Scott Stern, Rob Vishny, and Karen Wruck, as well as participants in seminars at Boston College, Columbia University, University of Florida, Harvard University, London School of Economics, Massachusetts Institute of Technology, Virginia Tech, the 1998 Western Finance Association meetings, and the National Bureau of Economic Research.

354   *C.P. Himmelberg et al. / Journal of Financial Economics 53 (1999) 353–384*

controlling both for observed firm characteristics and firm fixed effects, we cannot conclude (econometrically) that changes in managerial ownership affect firm performance.

JEL classification: G14; G32; D23; L14; L22

Keywords: Managerial ownership; Corporate governance

1. Introduction

Since Berle and Means (1932), the conflict between managers and shareholders has been studied extensively by researchers seeking to understand the nature of the firm. When shareholders are too diffuse to monitor managers, corporate assets can be used for the benefit of managers rather than for maximizing shareholder wealth. It is well known that a solution to this problem is to give managers an equity stake in the firm. Doing so helps to resolve the moral hazard problem by aligning managerial interests with shareholders' interests. Therefore, Jensen and Meckling (1976) suggest that managers with small levels of ownership fail to maximize shareholder wealth because they have an incentive to consume perquisites. In a similar fashion, some commentators have decried low levels of managerial ownership in U.S. corporations, and the theme has even appeared in discussions by compensation specialists and boards of directors.

In this paper, we propose an equilibrium interpretation of the observed differences in ownership structures across firms. Rather than interpret low ownership levels as per se evidence of suboptimal compensation design, we argue that the compensation contracts observed in the data are endogenously determined by the contracting environment, which differs across firms in both observable and unobservable ways. In particular, low levels of managerial ownership might well be the optimal incentive arrangement for the firm if the scope for perquisite consumption (or more generally, the severity of the moral hazard problem for managers) happens to be low for that firm. We do not deny the importance of agency problems between stockholders and managers, but rather emphasize the importance of *unobserved heterogeneity* in the contracting environment across firms.

We begin by examining the observable determinants of managerial ownership. This investigation builds upon Demsetz and Lehn (1985), who use cross-sectional data to show that the level of managerial ownership is determined by the riskiness of the firm, measured by the volatility of the stock price. They argue that the scope for moral hazard is greater for managers of riskier firms, which therefore means that those managers must have greater ownership stakes to align incentives. They also point out that riskiness makes it costlier for managers

C.P. Himmelberg et al. | Journal of Financial Economics 53 (1999) 353–384   355

to hold nondiversified portfolios (assuming that equity holdings in the firm are not easily hedged), so the relation between managerial ownership and nondiversifiable stock price risk is not necessarily monotonic.

To document the extent to which managerial ownership is endogenously determined by the contracting environment, we extend the empirical specification used by Demsetz and Lehn by including a number of additional explanatory variables other than stock price variability (see also Kole, 1996). Most importantly, we include variables (such as firm size, capital intensity, R&D intensity, advertising intensity, cash flow, and investment rate) designed to control for the scope for moral hazard. To the extent that our additional explanatory variables proxy for moral hazard, our specification clarifies the role of stock price variance as an explanatory variable for managerial ownership. We also use panel data that allow us to estimate the importance of unobserved (time-invariant) firm effects. These results show that a large fraction of the cross-sectional variation in managerial ownership is 'explained' by unobserved firm heterogeneity. In our subsequent analysis of the determinants of firm value, we argue that this unobserved heterogeneity generates a spurious correlation between ownership and performance.

The second goal of this paper is to reexamine theoretical explanations of the empirical link between managerial ownership and firm performance. Mørck et al. (1988) estimate a piecewise-linear relation between board ownership and Tobin's Q and find that Tobin's Q increases and then decreases with managerial ownership. McConnell and Servaes (1990) examine a larger data set than the Fortune 500 firms examined by Mørck et al. and find an inverted U-shaped relation between Q and managerial ownership, with an inflection point between 40% and 50% ownership. Hermalin and Weisbach (1991) analyze 142 NYSE firms and find that Q rises with ownership up to a stake of 1%; the relation is negative in the ownership range of 1–5%, becomes positive again in the ownership range of 5–20%, and turns negative for ownership levels exceeding 20%. The pattern identified by Mørck et al. has been corroborated for a cross-section of U.S. firms from 1935 by Holderness et al. (1999). Kole (1995) examines the differences in data sources used in several recent studies and concludes that differences in firm size can account for the reported differences between those studies. These studies generally interpret the positive relation at low levels of managerial ownership as evidence of incentive alignment, and the negative relation at high levels of managerial ownership as evidence that managers become 'entrenched' and can indulge in non-value-maximizing activities without being disciplined by shareholders. However, these studies do not address the endogeneity problem that confronts the use of managerial ownership as an explanatory variable, a problem noted early by Jensen and Warner (1988, p. 13).

We investigate the degree to which this heterogeneity makes managerial ownership an endogenous variable in models of firm performance. Following in the tradition of Demsetz and Lehn, we describe the contracting problem faced by the firm and develop a simple empirical model to illustrate the econometric issues that are encountered when estimating the relation among managerial ownership, its determinants, and its effect on firm performance. Distinct from Demsetz and Lehn, and in contrast to previous papers that attempt to measure the impact of managerial ownership on firm performance, we use panel data to test for the endogeneity of managerial ownership in models linking ownership to performance (measured by Tobin's Q). In particular, we use panel data to investigate the hypothesis that managerial ownership is related to observable and unobservable (to the econometrician) firm characteristics influencing contracts. If the unobserved sources of firm heterogeneity are relatively constant over time, we can treat these unobserved variables as fixed effects, and use panel data techniques to obtain consistent estimates of the parameter coefficients. This approach provides consistent estimates of the residuals in the Q regression, which we use to construct a test for correlation between managerial ownership and unobserved firm heterogeneity.

Our principal findings are threefold. First, proxies for the contracting environment faced by the firm (i.e., observable firm characteristics) strongly predict the structure of managerial ownership. We substantially extend the set of explanatory variables examined by Demsetz and Lehn, and we show that many of our results are robust to the inclusion of observed determinants of managerial ownership, industry fixed effects, or firm fixed effects. Second, we show that the coefficient on managerial ownership is not robust to the inclusion of fixed effects in the regression for Tobin's Q. Our formal statistical test rejects the null hypothesis of a zero correlation between managerial ownership and the unobserved determinants of Tobin's Q, thus supporting our conjecture that managerial ownership is endogenous in Q regressions. That is, managerial ownership and firm performance are determined by common characteristics, some of which are unobservable to the econometrician. Third, we explore the use of instrumental variables as an alternative to fixed effects to control for the endogeneity of managerial ownership in the Q regression. We find some evidence to support a causal link from ownership to performance, but this evidence is tentative because of the weakness of our instruments. We argue that future progress will require a more structural approach to the model.

Kole (1996) also argues that managerial ownership is endogenous; she further argues that causality operates in the opposite direction, from performance to ownership. Using a panel-data vector autoregression, we corroborate Kole's reverse causality evidence (results available upon request). Our research, however, supports the idea that both ownership and performance are determined by similar (observed and unobserved) variables in the firm's contracting environment. Thus, our interpretation is different from Kole's interpretation. That is, we find evidence endogeneity caused by unobserved heterogeneity as opposed to reverse causality.

C.P. Himmelberg et al. / Journal of Financial Economics 53 (1999) 353–384   357

The paper is organized as follows. In Section 2, we outline a simple model of managerial ownership and explain why it is difficult to estimate the relation between managerial ownership levels and firm performance, particularly in the context of cross-sectional data. Section 3 describes the sample selection criteria and the data we use in our empirical analysis of managerial ownership and firm performance. In Sections 4 and 5, respectively, we present empirical evidence on the determinants of managerial ownership and on the relation between managerial ownership and firm performance. Section 6 concludes.

2. An empirical framework for analyzing executive contracts

A common approach for estimating the impact of managerial ownership on firm value is to regress Tobin's Q on such variables as the percentage of equity held by managers. In this section, we argue that this regression is potentially misspecified because of the presence of unobserved heterogeneity. Specifically, if some of the unobserved determinants of Tobin's Q are also determinants of managerial ownership, then managerial ownership might spuriously appear to be a determinant of firm performance. To motivate our focus on the endogeneity of managerial ownership, we provide three examples of likely sources of unobservable heterogeneity, and in each case, we discuss their econometric consequences for cross-sectional regressions. We follow this discussion with a more formal exposition, in which we assume that the unobserved heterogeneity is a 'firm fixed effect', and we show how, under this assumption, panel data can be used to mitigate the endogeneity problem. In Section 5, we return to this model to describe a test for the endogeneity of ownership in regressions for Tobin's Q.

For our first example of unobserved heterogeneity, consider two firms that are identical except that the owner of one of the firms has access to a superior monitoring technology. Under the optimal contracting regime, the owners with access to the superior monitoring technology will choose a lower level of managerial ownership to align incentives, and this firm will have a higher valuation because fewer resources will be diverted to managerial perquisites. If measures of the quality of the monitoring technology are omitted from the specification, a regression of firm value on managerial ownership will spuriously (and falsely) indicate a negative relation, because ownership is a negative proxy for the quality of monitoring technology.

Intangible assets provide a second example of unobserved firm heterogeneity. Suppose two firms are identical except that one of the firms operates with a higher fraction of its assets in the form of intangibles. Under the optimal contracting regime, the owners of this firm will require a higher level of managerial ownership to align incentives because the intangible assets are harder to monitor and therefore subject to managerial discretion. This firm will also have a higher Q value because the market will value intangibles in the numerator (market value), but the book value of assets in the denominator will understate the value of intangibles (because Tobin's Q is measured as the ratio of the market value of the firm's outstanding debt and equity divided by the book value of assets). In this example, the unobserved level of intangibles induces a positive correlation between managerial ownership and Tobin's Q, but this relation is spurious, not causal.

A third example of unobserved heterogeneity is variation in the degree of market power. Suppose there are two firms competing in a market with differentiated products and that one firm enjoys a competitive advantage because (for some historical reason) it has been able to locate its products in such a way that confers more market power. If this market power insulates managerial decision-making from the discipline of competitive product markets, then the optimal contract for managers will call for higher levels of managerial ownership. Hence, unobserved heterogeneity in the form of unobserved differences in market power will (spuriously) induce a positive relation between ownership and performance. Alternatively, causation could run the other way; stockholders might design the manager's compensation to implicitly encourage collusive outcomes in the product market (Fershtman and Judd, 1987). Attempting to test this proposition using regressions of Tobin's Q on managerial ownership suffers from the same econometric problems we study here. The ownership decision is endogenous because of unobserved firm heterogeneity.

It is possible to generalize these examples in a simple analytical framework. We assume that within the general set of contracts agreed to by the firm, the owners of the firm choose a simple management compensation contract that includes a share of the firm's equity. This equity share (or 'managerial stake') is chosen to maximize the owners' equity return subject to incentive compatibility and participation constraints. For this purpose, we assume that gains from other means for reducing agency costs have been maximized, so that we examine the residual agency cost to be addressed by managerial ownership (we revisit this assumption in Section 5 below). Let x_{it} and u_{it}, respectively, denote observable and unobservable characteristics for firm i at time t related to the firm's contracting environment (including, e.g., proxies for the potential for moral hazard). In addition to unobserved firm characteristics, we implicitly assume a profitability shock that is observable to the manager, but not to outside shareholders. This shock cannot be contracted upon, giving rise to moral hazard.

The firm's owners must decide how much equity to give to managers in order to align incentives for value maximization. This equity share m_{it} depends on such factors as the potential for moral hazard and managers' exposure to risk, which we assume are partly measured by x_{it}, but are otherwise unobserved and

C.P. Himmelberg et al. / Journal of Financial Economics 53 (1999) 353–384   359

included in u_{it}. We assume that the functional relation is linear, and that $u_{it} = u_i$ is time-invariant for the firm, so that

$$m_{it} = \beta_1 x_{it} + \gamma_1 u_i + e_{it},$$ (1)

where e_{it} represents independent measurement error.

Faced with this contract, managers choose an optimal 'effort level', y_{it}, which could include a range of participation in non-value-maximizing activities. This effort choice depends on the managerial ownership stake, m_{it}, and, like the optimal contract itself, depends on both observed and unobserved character-istics of the firm, x_{it} and u_i. Assuming a linear functional form, we can represent the manager's effort choice by the following relation:

$$y_{it} = \theta m_{it} + \beta_2 x_{it} + \gamma_2 u_i + v_{it}.$$ (2)

Using firm value as a summary measure of expected firm performance, we assume that firm value depends on managerial effort plus the vector of observed and unobserved firm characteristics. Denoting the value of firm i at time t by Q_{it}, we assume that

$$Q_{it} = \delta y_{it} + \beta_3 x_{it} + \gamma_3 u_i + w_{it}.$$ (3)

We can now combine Eqs. (2) and (3) to derive the following relation among firm managerial ownership, firm characteristics, and firm performance:

$$Q_{it} = \delta\theta m_{it} + (\delta\beta_2 + \beta_3)x_{it} + (\delta\gamma_2 + \gamma_3)u_i + \delta v_{it} + w_{it}.$$ (4)

Simplifying the notation reveals the regression specification commonly used in the empirical literature:

$$Q_{it} = a_0 + a_1 m_{it} + a_2 x_{it} + \varepsilon_{it}.$$ (5)

In a cross-section of firms, as long as the error term, $\varepsilon_{it} = (\delta\gamma_2 + \gamma_3)u_i + \delta v_{it} + w_{it}$ – is uncorrelated with both m_{it} and x_{it}, one can consistently estimate the reduced-form coefficient on managerial ownership in the regression for firm value. However, because the choice of managerial ownership depends on unob-served firm characteristics, m_{it} depends on u_i, and is therefore correlated with ε_i. Specifically,

$$E(m_{it}\varepsilon_{it}) = E((\beta_1 x_{it} + \gamma_1 u_i)(\delta\gamma_2 + \gamma_3)u_i) = \gamma_1(\delta\gamma_2 + \gamma_3)\sigma_v^2.$$ (6)

In general, the expectation in Eq. (6) will be zero only in the unlikely event that the optimal contract does not depend on observed firm characteristics ($\gamma_1 = 0$), or in the event that neither effort nor Q_{it} do ($\gamma_2 = \gamma_3 = 0$). Hence one cannot estimate Eq. (5) using ordinary least squares. A natural solution to this problem would be to use instrumental variables for ownership, but this approach is difficult in practice because the natural instruments – the observed firm charac-teristics x_{it} – are already included on the right-hand side of the equation for firm valuation in Eq. (5). Hence it is difficult to identify instrumental variables that would permit identification of a_1. With panel data, however, one can use a fixed-effects estimator, assuming that the unobserved heterogeneity is constant over time.

In contrast to the model for Tobin's Q, the model for the optimal choice of managerial ownership levels in Eq. (1) is more easily identified because it requires only the much weaker assumption that the unobserved firm characteristics are uncorrelated with observed characteristics. Hence the focus of our results in Section 4 is on Eq. (1).

The above discussion suggests four lines of empirical inquiry. First, we explore whether the observed firm characteristics (proxies for the potential for moral hazard and risk) influence managerial ownership in ways that are consistent with theoretical predictions. Second, we investigate the importance of unobserved characteristics as determinants of managerial ownership. Third, we investigate the extent to which the empirical relation between managerial ownership and firm performance (measured by Tobin's Q) can be explained by the omission of observed and unobserved firm characteristics (i.e., by uncontrolled-for or unobserved heterogeneity). Fourth, we explore the possibility of using instrumental variables to recover the parameter values in Eq. (5). We describe these results in Sections 4 and 5 after describing our sample and data in Section 3.

3. The data

Our sample consists of firms from the Compustat universe. We restrict ourselves to firms that have no missing data (on sales, the book value of capital, and the stock price) over the three-year period 1982–1984. (We cannot avoid this conditioning because we cannot use firms with missing data or fewer than three years of data for the variables of interest.) We then select 600 firms by random sampling, and we collect data for all subsequent periods. Our panel is therefore balanced at 600 firms from 1982 through 1984, but the number of firms declines to 551 by 1985, and falls to a low of 330 by 1992, the last year in the sample. Because of this attrition from Compustat (principally due to mergers and acquisitions), our panel is systematically less random over time. However, we avoid exacerbating the scope for sampling bias by not requiring a balanced panel.

For this unbalanced panel of firms, we attempt to collect the following additional data for each firm-year observation: the number of top managers and directors (as reported in the proxy statement), the percentage of the firm's shares owned by those managers and directors, and the date of the proxy statement from which these two numbers are collected. For those observations for which we can locate proxy statements, we collect the managerial ownership variables and merge this information with the Compustat data. Because smaller firms (in

C.P. Himmelberg et al. / Journal of Financial Economics 53 (1999) 353–384   361

Table 1
Sample of Compustat firms by year

We start out with 600 firms randomly sampled from the universe of Compustat firms with data available over the period 1982–1984 on sales, book value of capital, and stock price. The number of firms declines after 1984, principally due to mergers and acquisitions. The number of available ownership observations represents firms for which we are able to obtain proxy statements with the number of top managers and directors and their collective percentage share ownership.

Year	Number of available Compustat observations	Number of available ownership observations
1982	600	398
1983	600	425
1984	600	427
1985	549	408
1986	518	385
1987	482	359
1988	442	330
1989	422	329
1990	396	300
1991	382	296
1992	330	293

terms of the number of shareholders) are not required to file proxies with the Securities and Exchange Commission, we are unable to obtain proxy information for all firms. We end up with managerial ownership information for about 70% of the Compustat firms. Table 1 summarizes the number of firms in our sample as a result of the sample selection process.

Despite the problems of attrition and proxy availability (which are not unique to our study), our sample provides several distinct advantages over datasets used in previous studies. First, in contrast to studies that focus on the Fortune 1000, our sample includes a much larger number of small firms and is more representative of the typical firm in Compustat. Second, we have a panel of firms rather than a single cross-section. This allows us to control for firm-level fixed effects. Third, we deliberately construct our panel in such a way that we can control for sample selection bias because of lack of data (for ownership) and attrition. In fact, it is possible to describe the significance of the bias imposed on the level of managerial ownership by a requirement that the panel be balanced; looking over the 1982–1992 period, the average ownership share varies from 16.2% to 19.4%, and for the balanced panel, for the firms removed by the balancing criterion, the ownership share varies between 22.4% and 25.3%. The availability of data on managerial ownership is well predicted by variables such as firm size and fixed

Table 2
Managerial ownership stakes by firm size, 1982

For the 398 Compustat firms for which we have data on sales, book value of capital, stock price, number of top managers and directors, and collective equity ownership of top managers and directors, we report the average number of managers and their average collective ownership stake by firm size.

Firm size class	Number of firms	Average number of managers per firm	Average total managerial ownership stake
Sales < $22 million	111	7.2	32.0%
$22 million ≤ Sales ≤ $188 million	147	12.4	25.4%
Sales > $188 million	140	22.3	13.4%

capital intensity, but as we explain in our discussion of empirical results, controlling for this 'missing data bias' does not qualitatively affect our results. While our sample design allows us to estimate and control for the effects of attrition bias, exit from Compustat due to mergers and acquisitions or bankruptcies is, in practice, difficult to predict using observable firm characteristics. A simple probit model for exit reveals that size is the principal explanatory variable; many more firms exit because of mergers than because of failure. When we include the inverse Mills ratio in our Q regressions, we find no statistically significant effect of selection bias. We therefore decide not to correct formally for attrition bias.

To illustrate differences between small and large firms, Table 2 shows, by size class, the average number of managers per firm and the percentage of shares outstanding owned collectively by those managers in 1982. The frequency distributions of managerial ownership and the number of managers are reported in Fig. 1. Note that the percentage of shares owned by insiders is much higher for small firms, measuring 32% on average for firms in (roughly) the bottom third of the size distribution of firms. By contrast, existing studies typically oversample large firms, and report average ownership shares of approximately 10%. This figure is consistent with the ownership stakes in firms in the top third of our size distribution (for comparison, the sales cutoff for Fortune 1000 firms is approximately $1 billion).

4. Determinants of managerial ownership: empirical evidence

4.1. Firm characteristics

The simple model outlined in Section 2 indicates the need to identify observable variables that relate to potential moral hazard and influence optimal

C.P. Himmelberg et al. / Journal of Financial Economics 53 (1999) 353–384   363

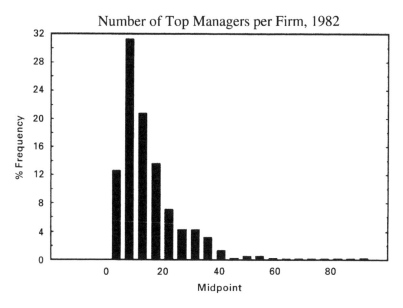

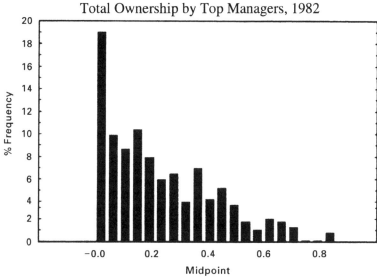

Fig. 1. Frequency distribution of managerial ownership and number of managers, 1982.

managerial stakes. If the scope for managerial discretion differs across firms according to observable differences in the composition of assets, then a prediction of the theory is that firms with assets that are difficult to monitor will have higher levels of managerial ownership. The specification used by Demsetz and Lehn (1985) to explain ownership concentration includes stock price volatility and industry dummies, but does not include proxies for the scope for managerial discretion (though managerial discretion is one interpretation offered for stock price volatility). We extend their specification by adding a large number of explanatory variables designed to proxy for the scope for managerial discretion, namely, size, capital intensity, cash flow, R&D intensity, advertising intensity, and gross investment rates. As we show below, this expanded variable set dramatically improves the R^2 statistic, and the coefficient estimates are all statistically different from zero with the predicted signs.

Size. Firm size has an ambiguous effect a priori on the scope for moral hazard. On the one hand, monitoring and agency costs can be greater in large firms, increasing desired managerial ownership. In addition, large firms are likely to employ more skilled managers, who are consequently wealthier, suggesting a higher level of managerial ownership. On the other hand, large firms might enjoy economies of scale in monitoring by top management and by rating agencies, leading to a lower optimal level of managerial ownership. We use the log of firm sales, $LN(S)$, and its square, $(LN(S))^2$, to measure size.

Scope for discretionary spending. To the extent that investments in fixed capital are observable and more easily monitored, firms with a greater concentration of fixed or 'hard' capital in their inputs will generally have a lower optimal level of managerial ownership (Gertler and Hubbard, 1988). We use the firm's capital-to-sales ratio, K/S, and its square, $(K/S)^2$, as measures of the relative importance of hard capital in the firm's technology.

Beyond hard capital, other firm spending is more discretionary and less easily monitored. The greater the role of these 'soft capital' inputs in the firm's technology, all else being equal, the higher is the desired level of managerial ownership. By including the capital-to-sales ratio, we have controlled (inversely) for soft capital, but some soft capital is 'softer' than others and hence more vulnerable to managerial discretion. To refine our proxies for the scope for discretionary spending, we use the ratio of R&D spending to capital, $(R\&D)/K$, the ratio of advertising spending to capital, A/K, and dummy variables for whether the firm reports R&D spending ($RDUM$) and advertising spending ($ADUM$) in that year. We include dummy variables when R&D and advertising are missing to control for the possibility that nonreporting firms are discretely different from reporting firms. By far the most common reason for not complying with the disclosure requirement is that the level of R&D or advertising expenditure is negligible. Simply eliminating observations with missing values for these variables is undesirable because it significantly reduces the sample size and biases the sample in favor of R&D-intensive and advertising firms.

C.P. Himmelberg et al. / Journal of Financial Economics 53 (1999) 353–384   365

As a proxy for the link between high growth and opportunities for discretionary projects, we use the firm's investment rate measured by the ratio of capital expenditures to the capital stock, I/K. Finally, we use the ratio of operating income to sales Y/S to measure market power or a firm's 'free cash flow' (the difference between cash flow and spending on value-enhancing investment projects). As suggested by Jensen (1986), the higher is a firm's free cash flow, all else being equal, the higher is the desired level of managerial ownership. While free cash flow is itself unobservable, it is presumably correlated with operating income.

Managerial risk aversion. Because higher managerial ownership levels, all else being equal, imply less portfolio diversification for managers, the optimal contract involves a tradeoff between diversification and incentives for performance. The higher is the firm's idiosyncratic risk, the lower is optimal managerial ownership. Demsetz and Lehn (1985) offer a second interpretation of this relation, suggesting that higher volatility indicates more scope for managerial discretion and thereby increases equilibrium managerial ownership levels. Unlike their specification, ours includes measures of intangible capital to control for managerial discretion. We therefore focus on the first interpretation of risk. As an empirical proxy for volatility, we use the standard deviation of the idiosyncratic component of daily stock prices (constructed from residuals from a standard CAPM regression), denoted by *SIGMA*, although our results are not qualitatively changed by the substitution of total stock return variance for our definition of *SIGMA*. Analogous to our treatment of missing values of $(R\&D)/K$ and A/K, we set missing values of *SIGMA* equal to zero, and then also include in the regression a dummy variable *SIGDUM* equal to unity when *SIGMA* is not missing, and zero otherwise.

To deal with zero-volume trading days in the daily data, we construct n-day returns by summing the Center for Research in Security Prices (CRSP) daily returns over the days in the period to create an approximate n-day return. We then divide this return (as well as n-day returns created by weekends and holidays) by the number of days in the period to obtain an average daily return. The variance of this average return will equal the variance of the daily return, and the same will be true for the idiosyncratic variance in a CAPM regression. Converting n-day returns to average daily returns thus removes the heteroskedasticity introduced by combining n-day-return observations with daily returns. Out of our initial universe of 600 firms for the 1984 period, the CRSP NYSE/AMEX and NASDAQ daily files contains 525 firms reporting returns in 1984. Of these, there are 502 firms with enough data to construct at least 20 observations on daily returns using only days for which trading volume is positive.

In addition to the problem of days with zero trading volume, there are days for which closing prices are not available, or days for which CRSP uses the average of the closing bid–ask spread instead of the closing price. This introduces nonclassical measurement error into the return calculation, which could bias our ordinary least squares (OLS) estimates of beta, return variance, and residual variance. To check the robustness of our results, we experiment with smaller samples that include only firms for which we can construct at least 20 observations based on (i) positive trading volume and (ii) transactions prices rather than the average of bid–ask prices. This substantially reduces the sample in 1984 to 328 firms (from 502). In practice, however, the results do not differ qualitatively from the larger sample. Hence, we report results in the paper using the larger sample, which, for many firms, relies on the closing average of the bid–ask spread rather than an actual closing price.

While we have addressed the most obvious examples of nonsynchronous trading (namely, days on which no trading occurs or on which CRSP cannot obtain a valid transaction price), there remain days on which CRSP calculates returns using the last price transacted rather than the closing price. As Scholes and Williams (1976), among others, point out, the inclusion of nonsynchronous trading days produces biased OLS estimates of beta. To check the robustness of our results against the possibility of biased beta estimates due to nonsynchronous trading days, we follow the approach recommended by Dimson (1979) by including leads and lags of the market return in the beta regression. These additional regressors are occasionally significant for some firms in some years, but using the alternative estimates of the idiosyncratic variance does not materially affect our results.

Summary. Combining these observable variables associated with moral hazard yields the following reduced-form expression for managerial ownership:

$$m_{it} = f(LN(S)_{it}, (K/S)_{it}, (R\&D/K)_{it}, RDUM_{it}, (A/K)_{it}, ADUM_{it}, (I/K)_{it},$$

$$(Y/S)_{it}, SIGMA_{it}, SIGDUM_{it}) + u_i + \eta_{it}, \tag{8}$$

where i and t represent the firm and time, respectively, u_i is a firm-specific effect, and η_{it} is a white-noise error term. Our list of variables is summarized in Table 3.

4.2. Evidence

Table 4A reports our estimates of the determinants of managerial stakes. The dependent variable in each case is $LN(m/(1 - m))$. Each of the specifications includes year dummies (not reported). In specifications including fixed firm effects, we control for the unobserved firm heterogeneity represented by u_i in Eq. (6).

The first column reports results from a baseline specification using pooled data for all firm-years. Increases in firm size, all else being equal, are associated with a reduction in managerial stakes. Increases in fixed capital intensity (which

C.P. Himmelberg et al. / Journal of Financial Economics 53 (1999) 353–384   367

Table 3
Variable descriptions

Q	Tobin's Q, that is, the ratio of the value of the firm divided by the replacement value of assets. For firm value, we use the market value of common equity plus the estimated market value of preferred stock (roughly estimated as ten times the preferred dividend) plus the book value of total liabilities, and for replacement value of assets we use the book value of total assets. This definition is closely related to the market-to-book ratio, which is easily seen by subtracting total liabilities from both the numerator and denominator
m	The total common equity holdings of top-level managers as a fraction of common equity outstanding
m^2	The square of m, included to allow for nonlinearities
$m1$	Equals m if $0.00 < m < 0.05$; 0.05 if $m \geqslant 0.05$
$m2$	Equals $m - 0.05$ if $0.05 < m < 0.25$; 0.00 if $m \leqslant 0.05$; 0.20 if $m \geqslant 0.25$
$m3$	Equals $m - 0.25$ if $0.25 < m < 1.00$; 0.00 if $m \leqslant 0.25$
e	The average common equity holdings per manager. This number is calculated as the market value of common equity times the fraction held by top managers divided by the number of top managers
$LN(S)$	The natural log of sales, used to measure firm size
$(Ln(S))^2$	The square of $LN(S)$, included to allow for nonlinearities in $LN(S)$
K/S	The ratio of tangible, long-term assets (property, plant, and equipment) to sales, used to measure the alleviation of agency problems due to the fact that such assets are easily monitored and provide good collateral
$(K/S)^2$	The square of K/S, included to allow for nonlinearities in K/S
Y/S	The ratio of operating income to sales, used to proxy for market power and measure the gross cash flows available from operations
$SIGMA$	The standard deviation of idiosyncratic stock price risk, calculated as the standard error of the residuals from a CAPM model estimated using daily data for the period covered by the annual sample
$SIGDUM$	A dummy variable equal to unity if the data required to estimated $SIGMA$ is available, and otherwise equal to zero (if $SIGMA$ is missing). To maintain sample size and reduce the risk of sample selection bias, we set missing observations of $SIGMA$ equal to zero, and then include this dummy variable to allow the intercept term to capture the mean of the $SIGMA$ for missing values
$R\&D/K$	The ratio of research and development expenditures to the stock property, plant, and equipment, used to measure the role of 'R&D capital' relative to other non-fixed assets
$RDUM$	A dummy variable equal to unity if R&D data were available, and otherwise equal to zero (see the definition of $SIGDUM$)
A/K	The ratio of advertising expenditures to the stock of property, plant, and equipment, used to measure the role of 'advertising capital' relative to other non-fixed assets
$ADUM$	A dummy variable equal to unity if R&D data were available, and otherwise equal to zero. For usage details, see the definition of $SIGDUM$
I/K	The ratio of capital expenditures to the stock of property, plant, and equipment

we associate with lower monitoring costs) also lead to a decline in managerial stakes. Among our proxies for discretionary spending (R&D, advertising, investment rates, and operating income relative to capital), R&D intensity appears to have a negative effect on ownership stakes, while advertising intensity, operating income, and the investment rate appear to have positive effects on ownership stakes. Increases in idiosyncratic risk, as measured by *SIGMA*, raise the cost of managerial ownership in terms of reduced portfolio diversification and also reduce managerial ownership.

Table 4

(A) Determinants of total equity ownership by top managers

The specifications reported in this table all model the fraction of common *equity held by top managers*, *m*, by regressing the transformed dependent variable $LN(m/(1-m))$ on the explanatory variables indicated below. Intercept terms and year dummies are included for all regressions, but not reported. Fixed effects at the industry or firm level are included where indicated, but not reported. Variable definitions for the acronyms are given in Table 3.

Variable	All firms (Pooled)	All firms (SIC3 effects)	All firms (Firm effects)	Fortune 500 (Firm effects)	Non-500 (Firm effects)
$LN(S)$	− 0.195 (0.050)	− 0.182 (0.053)	0.058 (0.095)	− 1.288 (0.697)	0.252 (0.121)
$(LN(S))^2$	− 0.027 (0.005)	− 0.027 (0.005)	− 0.038 (0.010)	0.040 (0.045)	− 0.067 (0.016)
K/S	− 1.131 (0.250)	− 0.826 (0.274)	− 0.826 (0.259)	− 1.05 (0.543)	− 0.448 (0.296)
$(K/S)^2$	− 0.023 (0.157)	− 0.011 (0.145)	0.301 (0.122)	0.440 (0.228)	0.143 (0.141)
$SIGMA$	− 5.20 (1.96)	− 3.84 (1.86)	− 5.13 (1.43)	− 0.707 (13.3)	− 4.84 (1.38)
$SIGDUM$	0.098 (0.098)	0.142 (0.092)	0.083 (0.111)	1.49 (0.568)	− 0.092 (0.090)
Y/S	0.143 (0.240)	− 0.020 (0.232)	0.219 (0.178)	0.683 (0.678)	0.191 (0.175)
$(R\&D)/K$	− 1.084 (0.197)	− 0.239 (0.206)	0.502 (0.284)	3.08 (1.21)	0.546 (0.289)
$RDUM$	− 0.191 (0.061)	− 0.056 (0.090)	0.332 (0.105)	0.665 (0.322)	0.242 (0.105)
A/K	0.227 (0.217)	0.953 (0.332)	0.184 (0.438)	3.60 (1.19)	− 0.067 (0.413)
$ADUM$	0.143 (0.061)	− 0.082 (0.067)	0.042 (0.072)	0.033 (0.215)	− 0.037 (0.077)
I/K	0.440 (0.156)	0.114 (0.152)	0.157 (0.099)	0.280 (0.191)	0.144 (0.106)
#Obs.	2630	2630	2630	764	1866
Adj. R^2	0.407	0.584	0.884	0.884	0.831

continued overleaf

Table 4. Continued.

(B) Determinants of average equity ownership per manager

The specifications reported in this table all model the *average equity owned by top managers, e,* by regressing the dependent variable *LN(e)* on the explanatory variables indicated below. Intercept terms and year dummies are included for all regressions, but not reported. Fixed effects at the industry or firm level are included where indicated, but not reported. Variable definitions for the acronyms are given in Table 3.

Variable	All firms (Pooled)	All firm (SIC3 effects)	All firm (Firm effects)	Fortune 500 (Firm effects)	Non-500 (Firm effects)
LN(S)	0.334	0.387	0.066	− 0.328	0.053
	(0.056)	(0.067)	(0.112)	(0.742)	(0.145)
$(LN(S))^2$	− 0.008	− 0.012	0.030	0.032	0.041
	(0.005)	(0.006)	(0.011)	(0.049)	(0.018)
K/S	1.044	1.629	0.830	0.510	0.888
	(0.255)	(0.302)	(0.300)	(0.600)	(0.355)
$(K/S)^2$	− 0.783	− 0.892	− 0.188	− 0.095	− 0.253
	(0.154)	(0.160)	(0.137)	(0.256)	(0.161)
SIGMA	− 18.5	− 18.3	− 14.5	− 24.6	− 12.6
	(2.14)	(2.12)	(1.68)	(15.3)	(1.67)
SIGDUM	0.089	0.915	0.598	1.63	0.412
	(0.101)	(0.100)	(0.115)	(0.526)	(0.107)
Y/S	1.58	1.14	1.80	4.63	1.56
	(0.326)	(0.335)	(0.242)	(0.830)	(0.235)
(R&D)/K	− 0.174	0.154	0.380	3.79	0.282
	(0.201)	(0.223)	(0.348)	(1.48)	(0.353)
RDUM	0.212	0.003	0.430	0.597	0.379
	(0.065)	(0.100)	(0.116)	(0.315)	(0.125)
A/K	− 0.139	0.834	0.235	3.34	0.121
	(0.225)	(0.418)	(0.658)	(1.08)	(0.662)
ADUM	0.314	− 0.080	0.030	0.276	0.012
	(0.067)	(0.076)	(0.082)	(0.261)	(0.090)
I/K	1.429	1.06	0.575	1.04	0.525
	(0.174)	(0.173)	(0.117)	(0.251)	(0.128)
#Obs.	2628	2628	2628	763	1865
Adj. R^2	0.300	0.446	0.818	0.838	0.770

Notes: Estimated standard errors (reported in parentheses) are consistent in the presence of heteroskedasticity. The adjusted R^2 statistics reflect the inclusion of fixed effects (where included).

The specifications reported in the second and third columns of Table 4A control for unobserved heterogeneity at the industry level and firm level, respectively. The second column includes fixed three-digit SIC effects; the third column includes fixed firm effects. Demsetz and Lehn (1985) included controls for certain (regulated) industries. By including fixed industry effects (and, in some cases, fixed firm effects), we control for industry influences generally. The inclusion of fixed effects changes the estimated coefficients significantly in some cases. For example, if we do not control for unobserved industry-level or firm-level heterogeneity, the estimated coefficients on size and investment rate are significantly larger in absolute value, and the estimated coefficient of the ratio of R&D spending to capital changes sign. These differences suggest that the unobserved firm characteristics are correlated with the observed characteristics, and therefore bias the estimated coefficients in a cross-sectional or pooled regression. For example, in a univariate regression, if there were a strong positive equilibrium relation between R&D intensity and managerial ownership, excluding firm fixed effects would bias downward the estimated coefficient on $R\&D/K$ in a pooled regression.

The fourth and fifth columns of Table 4A report results from splitting the sample according to whether the firm is in the Fortune 500 in the given year (including firm-level fixed effects). Some subsample differences emerge. The negative effect of idiosyncratic risk (measured by *SIGMA*) on ownership is traced to non-Fortune 500 firms, consistent with our earlier interpretation. Effects of capital intensity, operating income, R&D intensity, advertising intensity, and the investment rate are larger in absolute value for larger firms.

Because theoretical models generally emphasize managerial ownership levels relative to the managers' wealth and not simply the fraction of firm equity held by managers, we present in Table 4B results from the same models presented in Table 4A, but with the dependent variable being the log of managerial equity per manager. (We do not observe managerial wealth, so we focus only on managerial equity.) Broadly speaking, the patterns we identified in Table 4A carry over to the estimates in Table 4B. One difference is that the estimated coefficient on the capital-to-sales ratio is everywhere positive and statistically significantly different from zero. This could reflect the fact that capital-intensive firms employ relatively fewer workers and managers, but have higher levels of value added per worker, and hence derive larger incentive benefits from higher levels of managerial ownership.

Taken together, the results presented in Table 4A and B suggest strongly that observable firm characteristics in the contracting environment influence managerial ownership. In addition, unobserved firm characteristics are correlated with observed characteristics, making coefficients estimated using panel data more reliable than those estimated using cross-sectional data. The beneficial ownership data include options exercisable within 60 days, but omit recent awards that are not yet vested. Because we lack data on all of the stock options

C.P. Himmelberg et al. / Journal of Financial Economics 53 (1999) 353–384   371

granted to all top managers, we do not investigate the substitutability of direct
ownership stakes and stock options as mechanisms to align incentives for value
maximization. In the ExecuComp data over the 1992–1996 period, however, the
correlation between the pay-performance sensitivity for managers using the
'stock' definition and the pay-performance sensitivity using the stock plus
options definition exceeds 0.95.[1] Thus our focus on the beneficial ownership
data appears warranted.

5. Managerial ownership and firm performance

5.1. Evidence on the exogeneity of managerial ownership

Thus far, we have emphasized that managerial stakes are part of a larger set of
equilibrium contracts undertaken by the firm to align incentives for value
maximization, and we have shown that managerial ownership can be explained
by observable characteristics of the firm's contracting environment, such as
stock price volatility and the composition of assets, as predicted by the contracting view. These results also show, however, that even when industry dummies are
included, many important features of the firm's contracting environment remain
unobserved. Specifically, including firm-level fixed dummy variables raises the
adjusted R^2 from 0.584 to 0.884. These results cast doubt on the assumption that
managerial ownership is exogenous in regressions that attempt to measure the
impact of ownership on performance by regressing variables like Tobin's Q on
managerial ownership without controlling for fixed effects.

In this section, we use panel data techniques to investigate more directly the
question of whether managerial ownership can be treated as exogenous in the
performance regressions. We use Tobin's Q as our measure of firm performance,
but our results are robust to using return on assets as the dependent variable
(tables are available upon request). To investigate the impact of managerial
ownership on Q, we use variants of the reduced-form model in Eq. (3), in which
Q depends upon managerial ownership, m, observable firm characteristics, x,
and unobserved firm characteristics, u. We use two specifications of managerial
ownership in the Q regression. The first includes m and m^2 (see McConnell and
Servaes, 1990). The second includes three piecewise-linear terms in m (as in
Mørck et al., 1988). Specifically,

$$m1 = \begin{cases} \text{managerial ownership level} & \text{if managerial ownership level} < 0.05, \\ 0.05 & \text{if managerial ownership level} \geqslant 0.05; \end{cases}$$

---

[1] We are grateful to Andrew Samwick for this calculation.

372   *C.P. Himmelberg et al. / Journal of Financial Economics 53 (1999) 353–384*

$$
m2 = \begin{cases} \text{zero} & \text{if managerial ownership level} < 0.05, \\ \text{managerial ownership} & \text{if } 0.05 \leqslant \text{managerial ownership level} < 0.25, \\ \quad \text{level minus } 0.05 \\ 0.20 & \text{if managerial ownership level} \geqslant 0.25; \end{cases}
$$

$$
m3 = \begin{cases} \text{zero} & \text{if managerial ownership level} < 0.25, \\ \text{managerial ownership} & \text{if managerial ownership} \geqslant 0.25. \\ \quad \text{level minus } 0.25 \end{cases}
$$

For observable characteristics, we use the same vector of x variables used in the model for managerial ownership. We report results including and excluding arguably endogenous 'investment' variables (R&D, advertising, and fixed capital).

Our empirical analysis of the effects of managerial ownership and firm characteristics on Q is summarized in Table 5A and B. Table 5A reports estimated coefficients for cases in which managerial ownership is represented by m and m^2. Table 5B reports estimated coefficients for cases in which managerial ownership is represented by the piecewise-linear terms, $m1$, $m2$, and $m3$. For both of the above specifications, we report estimated coefficients for (1) regressions with managerial ownership alone (pooled, SIC3 industry effects, and firm effects), (2) the regressions including the full set of x variables (pooled, SIC3 industry effects, and firm effects), and (3) the regressions including the non-investment set of x variables. All specifications include year effects (not reported).

Turning first to the quadratic specifications of managerial ownership in Table 5A, we note that the managerial ownership variables are statistically significant only in the pooled model with no other variables and in the model with only industry effects. In other specifications, the managerial ownership coefficients are virtually never statistically significantly different from zero. (The Wald test for the joint significance of m and m^2 is reported at the bottom of the table.) Once we control for observed firm characteristics (x), or for unobserved firm characteristics (in the firm-fixed-effect version of u), there is no effect of changes in managerial ownership on Q. Though not reported in Table 5A, these results hold for both the Fortune 500 and non-Fortune 500 subsamples considered earlier.

Turning to the spline specifications for managerial ownership in Table 5B, the pooled results are consistent with those of Mørck et al. (1988), who find that the impact of m on Q increases at a decreasing rate, and thereafter declines. In contrast to the quadratic specification for managerial ownership, the Mørck–Shleifer–Vishny specification is robust to the inclusion of observable contracting determinants and industry dummies. Once we control for x variables and for u (via firm fixed effects), however, changes in managerial ownership levels have no statistically significant effect on Q. These results hold both for the Fortune 500 and non-Fortune 500 subsamples investigated earlier.

The results reported in Table 5A and B confirm the intuition of the contracting example sketched in Section 2. First, the results obtained when observed characteristics (x) are included suggest that previously asserted relations between Q and m in part reflect equilibrium relations among Q and firm characteristics in the firm's contracting problem. Second, to the extent that firm characteristics unobserved by the econometrician influence the firm's contracts and the equilibrium level of managerial ownership, the coefficient on m in a Q regression (when no attempt is made to incorporate the unobserved heterogeneity) is biased. Third, in keeping with our emphasis on contracting, the relations we estimate suggest that no inference can be made about the effect of 'exogenous' local increases in managerial ownership on firm performance.

One can formalize this evidence against the exogeneity of managerial ownership by testing for a correlation between the fixed effect and managerial ownership. We could use a Hausman (1978) test, but this test would tend to over-reject the null hypothesis of zero correlation because it would tend to reject if *any* of the explanatory variables were correlated with the fixed effect. To reduce this Type I error, we construct a more precise 'conditional moment' test, which is in the spirit of a Hausman test, but tends to reject only if managerial ownership is the source of the specification error (Greene, 1997, p. 534; Newey, 1985).

The test is constructed as follows. Let the performance model be

$$Q_{it} = \beta_0 + \beta z_{it} + u_i + \varepsilon_{it}, \tag{9}$$

where z_{it} includes the managerial ownership variables and the x variables described earlier, and u_i is the firm fixed effect. The formal hypothesis we want to test is whether the unobserved fixed effect, u_i, is correlated with managerial ownership, an element of z_{it}. That is, H_0: $E(m_{it} \cdot u_i) = 0$, where m_{it} is an $r \times 1$ vector of variables measuring the effect of managerial ownership. The idea of the test is to construct the simple analogue to the population moment, $s = E(m_{it} w_{it})$, and then to test whether it is statistically significantly different from zero.

Using a consistent 'within' estimator of β, we can construct consistent estimates of the residual $w_{it} = u_i + \varepsilon_{it}$. Our test statistic is $\hat{s} = \sum_{i=1}^{N} \sum_{t=1}^{T_i} m_{it} \hat{w}_{it} / NT_i$, where T_i is the number of observations for firm i. Under standard regularity conditions and under the null hypothesis that $E(m_{it} \cdot u_i) = 0$, $\sqrt{N}\hat{s}$ will be asymptotically distributed $N(0, \Sigma)$. Therefore the statistic $k = N\hat{s}\hat{\Sigma}^{-1}\hat{s}$ is asymptotically chi-squared with r degrees of freedom, where $\hat{\Sigma}$ is a consistent estimate of Σ (for more details, see Greene, 1997).

Table 5
(A) Determinants of firm value (Tobin's Q), quadratic specification

The specifications reported in this table all model firm value, Q, as a linear function of the explanatory variables indicated below. In this table, the influence of m enters as a quadratic function. Intercept terms and year dummies are included for all regressions, but not reported. Fixed effects at the industry or firm level are included where indicated, but not reported. Variable definitions for the acronyms are given in Table 3.

Variable	Pooled	SIC3 effects	Firm effects	Pooled	SIC3 effects	Firm effects	Pooled	SIC3 effects	Firm effects
m	0.539 (0.219)	1.25 (0.338)	0.573 (0.402)	−0.460 (0.218)	−0.031 (0.277)	0.125 (0.395)	−0.395 (0.234)	−0.061 (0.281)	0.293 (0.392)
m^2	−1.123 (0.317)	−1.649 (0.457)	−0.582 (0.559)	−0.062 (0.304)	−0.579 (0.393)	−0.438 (0.507)	−0.235 (0.317)	−0.571 (0.401)	−0.577 (0.522)
$LN(S)$	–	–	–	−0.251 (0.052)	−0.239 (0.062)	−0.890 (0.147)	−0.329 (0.053)	−0.260 (0.063)	−0.896 (0.152)
$(LN(S))^2$	–	–	–	0.015 (0.004)	0.010 (0.005)	0.073 (0.012)	0.021 (0.004)	0.012 (0.005)	0.075 (0.012)
K/S	–	–	–	0.621 (0.152)	0.277 (0.192)	−0.482 (0.289)	0.469 (0.155)	0.342 (0.208)	−0.504 (0.303)
$(K/S)^2$	–	–	–	−0.391 (0.084)	−0.420 (0.120)	0.040 (0.123)	−0.403 (0.087)	−0.454 (0.131)	0.048 (0.124)
$SIGMA$	–	–	–	−5.06 (1.25)	−4.82 (1.26)	−4.26 (1.28)	−4.47 (1.25)	−5.40 (1.27)	−4.62 (1.29)

continued overleaf

	(1)	(2)	(3)	(4)	(5)	(6)	(7)	(8)	(9)
$SIGDUM$	–	–	–	0.260 (0.051)	0.241 (0.056)	–0.044 (0.066)	0.258 (0.054)	0.275 (0.057)	–0.036 (0.067)
Y/S	–	–	–	0.652 (0.279)	0.713 (0.305)	1.44 (0.269)	0.782 (0.292)	0.664 (0.317)	1.43 (0.264)
$(R\&D)/K$	–	–	–	0.543 (0.227)	0.497 (0.271)	0.391 (0.410)	–	–	–
$RDUM$	–	–	–	0.156 (0.046)	0.264 (0.071)	0.191 (0.125)	–	–	–
A/K	–	–	–	–0.066 (0.125)	–0.423 (0.209)	0.082 (0.448)	–	–	–
$ADUM$	–	–	–	0.166 (0.041)	0.144 (0.056)	0.148 (0.095)	–	–	–
I/K	–	–	–	0.799 (0.121)	0.723 (0.115)	0.340 (0.103)	–	–	–
# Obs.	2630	2630	2630	2630	2630	2630	2630	2630	2630
Adj. R^2	0.012	0.127	0.584	0.130	0.213	0.630	0.073	0.178	0.626
p-value	–	0.038	0.194	–	0.008	0.156	–	0.008	0.084
Wald	20.125	13.142	2.501	23.254	15.599	1.897	36.348	15.034	1.588
pwald	–	0.001	0.286	–	–	0.387	–	0.001	0.452

Table 5. Continued.
(B) Determinants of firm value (Tobin's Q), spline specifications

The specifications reported in this table all model firm value, Q, a linear function of the explanatory variables indicated below. The influence of m enters as a spline function. Intercept terms and year dummies are included for all regressions, but not reported. Fixed effects at the industry or firm level are included where indicated, but not reported. Variable definitions for the acronyms are given in Table 3.

Variable	Pooled	SIC3 effects	Firm effects	Pooled	SIC3 effects	Firm effects	Pooled	SIC3 effects	Firm effects
$m1$	4.678 (1.127)	7.379 (1.727)	0.772 (1.820)	2.88 (1.34)	3.75 (1.53)	1.62 (1.73)	3.691 (1.334)	3.724 (1.555)	2.097 (1.736)
$m2$	-0.070 (0.312)	0.428 (0.365)	0.122 (0.395)	-0.587 (0.295)	-0.150 (0.338)	-0.214 (0.387)	-0.689 (0.314)	-0.201 (0.342)	-0.167 (0.386)
$m3$	-0.567 (0.167)	-0.546 (0.201)	0.171 (0.257)	-0.446 (0.168)	-0.703 (0.218)	-0.225 (0.247)	-0.636 (0.173)	-0.712 (0.228)	-0.152 (0.250)
$LN(S)$	–	–	–	-0.263 (0.054)	-0.247 (0.062)	-0.896 (0.147)	-0.345 (0.055)	-0.268 (0.064)	-0.903 (0.152)
$(LN(S))^2$	–	–	–	0.017 (0.005)	0.012 (0.005)	0.074 (0.012)	0.023 (0.005)	0.013 (0.005)	0.075 (0.012)
K/S	–	–	–	0.648 (0.154)	0.297 (0.193)	-0.475 (0.289)	0.492 (0.156)	0.359 (0.208)	-0.493 (0.304)
$(K/S)^2$	–	–	–	-0.395 (0.084)	-0.427 (0.120)	0.036 (0.123)	-0.404 (0.087)	-0.459 (0.130)	0.042 (0.125)
$SIGMA$	–	–	–	-4.83 (1.25)	-4.66 (1.24)	-4.24 (1.27)	-4.23 (1.25)	-5.24 (1.25)	-4.61 (1.28)

continued overleaf

SIGDUM	—	—	—	—	0.219	−0.044	0.242	0.254	−0.035
					(0.054)	(0.066)	(0.054)	(0.056)	(0.067)
Y/S	—	—	—	0.661	0.725	1.45	0.790	0.675	1.44
				(0.279)	(0.303)	(0.269)	(0.292)	(0.315)	(0.264)
(R&D)/K	—	—	—	0.551	0.499	0.384	—	—	—
				(0.225)	(0.268)	(0.409)			
RDUM	—	—	—	0.158	0.273	0.202	—	—	—
				(0.046)	(0.072)	(0.125)			
A/K	—	—	—	−0.046	−0.402	0.083	—	—	—
				(0.125)	(0.205)	(0.451)			
ADUM	—	—	—	0.159	0.142	0.144	—	—	—
				(0.041)	(0.055)	(0.095)			
I/K	—	—	—	0.776	0.713	0.339	—	—	—
				(0.123)	(0.115)	(0.103)			
# Obs.	2630	2630	2630	2630	2630	2630	2630	2630	2630
Adj. R^2	0.016	0.135	0.584	0.131	0.215	0.630	0.075	0.181	0.626
p-value	—	0.004	0.126	—	0.001	0.037	—	0.002	0.018
Wald	34.641	23.729	1.379	25.396	20.928	1.984	41.12	20.133	1.937
pwald	—	—	0.71	—	—	0.576	—	—	0.586

Note: Estimated standard errors (reported in parentheses) are consistent in the presence of heteroskedasticity. The adjusted R^2 statistics reflect the inclusion of fixed effects (where included). (The 'p-value' is the probability of observing the test statistic for endogeneity described in the text. Low p-values suggest that ownership is endogenous.) Wald and pwald, report, respectively, the Wald statistic and associated p-value for a test that the managerial ownership variables are jointly zero.

The *p*-values for this test statistic are reported in Table 5A and B. In both tables, the *p*-values tend to be lower for the tests based on industry-level fixed-effects estimator. This presumably reflects the higher test power generally implied by the greater efficiency of the slope estimates. The rejection of the null hypothesis of exogeneity of managerial ownership is particularly strong for the spline specification reported in Table 5B. These results strongly suggest that reported results using such a specification are subject to endogeneity bias.

An important caveat to all empirical work using fixed-effect estimators on panel data is that the 'within' estimator can, under a range of certain circumstances identified by Griliches and Hausman (1986), exacerbate the bias toward zero caused by measurement error. If our ownership variable were measured with classical error, then this would reduce the power of our Wald test for the joint significance of the ownership variables, and would invalidate the distributional assumptions for our test statistic due to the inconsistency of the residual estimates. While it is always possible to make an a priori case for measurement error, there is little empirical evidence that measurement error is a serious problem in our data. Table 4A and B show, for example, that the within variation in managerial ownership is significantly correlated with the explanatory variables, a result that does not square with serious measurement error. In addition, the within-firm point estimates of the ownership coefficients in Table 5A and B are not obviously biased toward zero, as measurement error would suggest. Finally, the conditions identified by Griliches and Hausman might not hold. If the variance of the measurement error were primarily cross-sectional rather than within, then the within estimator would actually tend to reduce the bias effects of measurement error. We nevertheless recognize the limitations of the within estimator, and in the next section, we report instrumental variables estimated as an alternative approach to deal with the endogeneity of ownership variables.

5.2. Toward a more structural interpretation of contracting relations

The strength of the empirical evidence against the exogeneity of managerial ownership suggests that more model structure is required to identify the impact of managerial ownership on firm value. A standard remedy would be to use an instrumental variable in the regression for firm value. In a related paper, Hermalin and Weisbach (1991) recognize a similar endogeneity problem and use lagged explanatory variables as instruments for managerial ownership. They find that the instrumental variable estimator increases the magnitude of the ownership effect on firm value. Hermalin and Weisbach report that a Hausman specification test rejects the exogeneity assumption. While this rejection provides evidence of endogenous ownership, it does not validate their choice of instruments. If omitted firm characteristics are the source of the endogeneity (as we have argued above), and if these unobserved firm characteristics change slowly over time (as we have also argued above), then lagged explanatory variables will suffer as much from the endogeneity problem as do contemporaneous ones.

Instrumental variables for managerial ownership are difficult to find. The basic problem is that for any variable that plausibly determines the optimal level of managerial ownership, it is also possible to argue that the same variable might plausibly affect Tobin's Q. For example, our results in Table 4A and B showed that market power (as measured by operating margins) is a candidate instrument. However, even though it is correlated with managerial ownership, it also determines the equilibrium value of Tobin's Q, and therefore must appear independently in this regression. Additional candidates suggested by these results, such as the capital-to-sales ratio, advertising, R&D, and fixed investment, are also invalid because of links between investment and Q and because intangible assets are conservatively valued on the balance sheet, therefore influencing the level of Tobin's Q.

A more plausible case can be made for using firm size and stock price volatility as instruments. It is possible to construct arguments under which either variable could be correlated with Tobin's Q. For example, suppose that high Q values reflect future growth opportunities. Such firms might generally be smaller (or larger), and might also have more volatile stock prices due to the greater uncertainty about future growth prospects. However, these arguments seem weaker than the arguments against operating margins, the capital-to-sales ratio, advertising, R&D, and investment. Moreover, in studies of fixed investment, it is generally argued that deviations of Tobin's Q from its equilibrium value are explained by the costs of adjusting the capital stock, and that these adjustment costs are proportional to the rate of investment. Therefore, the inclusion of advertising and R&D intensity and the investment rate should control for future growth opportunities. This argument eliminates the a priori case for including the size and volatility variables in the Q equation, and thus provides an argument for omitting these variables from the Q equation and using them as instruments for managerial ownership instead.

The results using $LN(S)$, $(LN(S))^2$, $SIGMA$, and $SIGDUM$ as instruments are reported in Table 6. We use the more parsimonious quadratic specification for managerial ownership to reduce the number of instruments required for identification. The first column of Table 6 reports the results of pooling without controlling for industry or firm effects. In contrast to Table 5A, these results confirm a large and statistically significant inverse-U relation between ownership and firm value. The coefficients of 6.29 and -10.8 on m and m^2, respectively, imply an inflection point of about 0.58. Given the distribution of managerial ownership shown in Fig. 1, Tobin's Q is generally an increasing, concave function of m.

The second and third columns of Table 6 show that these results are robust to the inclusion of three-digit industry effects, but not to firm effects. In both

Table 6
Ownership-performance model with instrumental variables

The specifications reported in this table all model firm value, Q, as a linear function of the explanatory variables indicated below. Intercept terms and year dummies are included. Instruments are $LN(S)$, $(LN(S))^2$, $SIGMA$, and $SIGDUM$. Fixed effects at the industry or firm level are included where indicated, but not reported. Variable definitions for the acronyms are given in Table 3.

Variable	Pooled	SIC3 effects	Firm effects
m	6.29	8.38	− 10.7
	(1.27)	(1.78)	(10.6)
m^2	− 10.8	− 12.3	− 4.88
	(2.61)	(3.48)	(10.8)
K/S	1.45	0.736	1.25
	(0.220)	(0.376)	(1.01)
$(K/S)^2$	− 0.738	− 0.587	− 0.611
	(0.119)	(0.171)	(0.396)
Y/S	0.414	0.603	1.003
	(0.273)	(0.300)	(0.637)
$(R\&D)/K$	0.739	0.718	0.687
	(0.242)	(0.339)	(1.11)
$RDUM$	0.178	0.256	− 0.230
	(0.049)	(0.115)	(0.805)
A/K	0.169	− 0.735	0.007
	(0.164)	(0.290)	(1.262)
$ADUM$	0.140	0.251	0.301
	(0.043)	(0.076)	(0.234)
I/K	0.990	0.937	0.478
	(0.140)	(0.151)	(0.202)
#Obs.	2630	2630	2630
Adj. R^2	− 0.197	− 0.057	0.192
Wald	67.576	55.659	1.310
pwald	–	–	0.519

Notes: Standard errors are in parentheses. *Wald* and *pwald* report, respectively, the Wald statistic and associated p-value for a test that the ownership variables are jointly zero.

specifications, the standard errors rise substantially, rendering the coefficients statistically indistinguishable from zero. However, this need not be interpreted as bad news for the results reported in the first column. One cannot reject the hypothesis that the firm effects are jointly zero, though one can reject that the industry effects are jointly zero (the p-values on the associated Hausman tests

C.P. Himmelberg et al. / Journal of Financial Economics 53 (1999) 353–384   381

arc 0.208 for the test of pooled versus the inclusion of firm effects and 0.00002 for the test of pooled versus the inclusion of industry effects). This conclusion has intuitive appeal because, by using instrumental variables, we have presumably controlled for the endogeneity that was the motivation for including firm fixed effects. However, it is more likely that the combined effect of using instrumental variables and controlling for fixed effects has reduced the precision of estimates to the point at which such a test would have little power. We believe that the results in Table 6 represent a promising step toward the construction of more complete models of the relation between managerial ownership and firm performance.

6. Conclusions

Firms are governed by a network of relations representing contracts for financing, capital structure, and managerial ownership and compensation, among others. For any of these contractual arrangements, it is difficult to identify the correspondence between the contractual choice and firm performance (e.g., measured by accounting rates of return or Tobin's Q) because contractual choices and performance outcomes are endogenously determined by exogenous and only partly observed features of the firm's contracting environment.

We confront this endogeneity problem in the context of the firm's compensation contract with managers. Because managerial equity stakes are an important and well-known mechanism used to align the incentives of managers and owners, we examine the determinants of managerial ownership as a function of the contracting environment. We extend the cross-sectional results of Demsetz and Lehn (1985) and use panel data to show that managerial ownership is explained by variables describing the contracting environment in ways consistent with the predictions of principal-agent models.

We find that a large fraction of the cross-sectional variation in managerial ownership is explained by unobserved firm heterogeneity. This unobserved heterogeneity in the contracting environment has important implications for econometric models designed to estimate the effect of managerial ownership on firm performance. Our empirical analysis shows that existing results are not robust to controls for endogeneity induced by time-invariant unobserved heterogeneity. Moreover, once we control both for observed firm characteristics and firm fixed effects, it becomes difficult to conclude that changes in firm managerial ownership affect performance. Our instrumental-variables results, however, suggest a promising step toward the construction of more complete models of the relation between managerial ownership and firm performance.

To take these observations one step further, we believe that the Q model results reported in Table 5A and B can be interpreted as supporting more generally the notion that the firm chooses among alternative mechanisms for minimizing agency costs. This is, of course, the concept articulated in Alchian (1969); Fama (1980); Fama and Jensen (1983) and Demsetz and Lehn (1985); more recently, see Crutchley and Hansen (1989) and Agrawal and Knoeber (1996).

Suppose, for example, that Q capitalizes the market's expectation of the effect of agency costs on firm value. The loss in value reflects residual agency costs, or agency costs remaining after corporate control mechanisms are chosen. In addition to managerial ownership choices emphasized here, alternative means of reducing agency costs include leverage (Jensen, 1986; Gertler and Hubbard, 1993), increased reliance on outside directors (American Law Institute, 1982; Baysinger and Butler, 1985; Millstein and MacAvoy, 1998), large shareholders (Shleifer and Vishny, 1986; Zeckhauser and Pound, 1990), institutional investors, dividend policy (Easterbrook, 1984), and radical changes in corporate control (Kaplan, 1989).

One can interpret the results in Table 5A, B, and 6 as reduced-form exercises in which the x variables and the firm fixed effects are determinants of the use of these mechanisms. For example, Gertler and Hubbard (1993) relate leverage in this context to the relative importance of firm-specific and aggregate risk and proxies for the scope for moral hazard (variables captured by R&D and advertising intensity, year dummies, and firm effects). Benefits from large shareholders likely depend on size or the relative importance of R&D (Zeckhauser and Pound, 1990); these channels are proxied through size, R&D intensity, and firm effects. Institutional shareholdings likely depend on firm size and whether the firm is listed on the New York Stock Exchange (variables accounted for in part by firm effects). The degree to which dividend policy can reduce agency costs depends on the importance of the scope for moral hazard (perhaps measured by idiosyncratic risk, R&D, or advertising) and the tax costs of paying dividends (measured in part by year and firm effects). Net benefits of a major restructuring also are reflected in proxies for moral hazard and firm effects.

Two other possible strategies are tasks for future research. The first involves identifying large, arguably exogenous changes in ownership levels arising from shifts in tax policy, regulation, or fixed costs in the market for corporate control (Kaplan, 1989; Hubbard and Palia, 1995; Cole and Mehran, 1997), though care must be taken because even certain 'natural experiments' are endogenous in that they affect performance directly. The second involves designing a dynamic structural model of firm contracting decisions, possibly permitting identification from economically reasonable assumptions about functional form (Margiotta and Miller, 1991). This strategy is particularly desirable given the lack of easily identified instrumental variables.

While our findings are consistent with the proposition that firms choose strategies to reduce agency costs optimally over the long run, at least two issues remain. First, the simultaneous choice of individual mechanisms or some subset

C.P. Himmelberg et al. / Journal of Financial Economics 53 (1999) 353–384   383

needs to be modeled; subsets of these choices have been considered in a reduced-form setting, as in Hermalin and Weisbach (1991); Jensen et al. (1992);
Moyer et al. (1992); Holthausen and Larcker (1993) and Agrawal and Knoeber
(1996). Second, the choice of mechanisms likely involves some fixed costs or
'costs of adjustment' so that firms are not always at their long-run contractual
optimum. Exploring these costs and how they might have changed over time for
different agency-cost-reducing mechanisms is a particularly interesting task for
future research.

References

Agrawal, A., Knoeber, C., 1996. Firm performance and mechanisms to control agency problems
    between managers and shareholders. Journal of Financial and Quantitative Analysis 31,
    377–397.
Alchian, A., 1969. Corporate management and property rights. In: Henry Manne, (Ed.), Economic
    Policy and Regulation of Corporate Securities. American Enterprise Institute for Public Policy
    Research, Washington, DC.
American Law Institute, 1982. Principles of Corporate Governance and Structure: Restatement and
    Recommendations. ALI, New York.
Baysinger, B., Butler, H., 1985. Corporate governance and the board of directors: performance
    effects of changes in board composition. Journal of Law, Economics, and Organization 1,
    102–123.
Berle, A., Means, G., 1932. The Modern Corporation and Private Property. Macmillan, New York.
Cole, R., Mehran, H., 1997. The effect of changes in ownership structure on performance:
    evidence from the thrift industry. Mimeograph, Board of Governors of the Federal Reserve
    System.
Crutchley, C., Hansen, R., 1989. A test of the agency theory of managerial ownership, corporate
    leverage, and corporate dividends. Financial Management 18, 36–46.
Demsetz, H., Lehn, K., 1985. The structure of corporate ownership: causes and consequences.
    Journal of Political Economy 93, 1155–1177.
Dimson, E., 1979. Risk measurement when shares are subject to infrequent trading. Journal of
    Financial Economics 7, 197–226.
Easterbrook, F., 1984. Two agency-cost explanations of dividends. American Economic Review 78,
    650–659.
Fama, E., 1980. Agency problems and the theory of the firm. Journal of Political Economy 88,
    288–307.
Fama, E., Jensen, M., 1983. Separation of ownership and control. Journal of Law and Economics 26,
    301–325.
Fershtman, C., Judd, K., 1987. Equilibrium incentives in oligopoly. American Economic Review 77,
    927–940.
Gertler, M., Hubbard, R.G., 1988. Financial factors in business fluctuations. Financial Market
    Volatility: Causes and Consequences. Federal Reserve Bank, Kansas City.
Gertler, M., Hubbard, R.G., 1993. Corporate financial policy, taxation, and macroeconomic risk.
    RAND Journal of Economics 24, 286–303.
Greene, W., 1997. Econometric Analysis. Prentice Hall, Upper Saddle River, NJ.
Griliches, Z., Hausman, J., 1986. Errors in variables in panel data. Journal of Econometrics 31,
    93–188.
Hausman, J., 1978. Specification tests in econometrics. Econometrica 46, 1251–1271.

Hermalin, B., Weisbach, M., 1991. The effects of board compensation and direct incentives on firm performance. Financial Management 20, 101–112.

Holderness, C., Kroszner, R., Sheehan, D., 1999. Were the good old days that good?: evolution of managerial stock ownership and corporate governance since the great depression. Journal of Finance 54, 435–469.

Holthausen, R., Larcker, D., 1993. Organizational structure and financial performance. Unpublished working paper. The Wharton School.

Hubbard, R.G., Palia, D., 1995. Executive pay and performance: evidence from the U.S. banking industry. Journal of Financial Economics 39, 105–130.

Jensen, G., Solberg, D., Zorn, T., 1992. Simultaneous determination of insider ownership, debt, and dividend policies. Journal of Financial and Quantitative Analysis 27, 247–263.

Jensen, M., 1986. Agency costs of free cash flow, corporate finance, and takeovers. American Economic Review 76, 323–329.

Jensen, M., Meckling, W., 1976. Theory of the firm: managerial behavior, agency costs and ownership structure. Journal of Financial Economics 3, 305–360.

Jensen, M., Warner, J., 1988. The distribution of power among corporate managers, shareholders, and directors. Journal of Financial Economics 20, 3–24.

Kaplan, S., 1989. Effects of management buyouts on operating performance and value. Journal of Financial Economics 24, 217–254.

Kole, S., 1995. Measuring managerial equity ownership: a comparison of sources of ownership data. Journal of Corporate Finance 1, 413–435.

Kole, S., 1996. Managerial ownership and firm performance: incentives or rewards? Advances in Financial Economics 2, 119–149.

Margiotta, M., Miller, R., 1991. Managerial compensation and the cost of moral hazard. Unpublished working paper. Carnegie Mellon University.

McConnell, J., Servaes, H., 1990. Additional evidence on equity ownership and corporate value. Journal of Financial Economics 27, 595–612.

Millstein, I., MacAvoy, P., 1998. The active board of directors and improved performance of the large publicly-traded corporation. Columbia Law Review 98, 1283–1322.

Mørck, R., Shleifer, A., Vishny, R., 1988. Management ownership and market valuation. Journal of Financial Economics 20, 293–315.

Moyer, R., Rao, R., Sisneros, P., 1992. Substitutes for voting rights: evidence from dual class recapitalization. Financial Management 21, 35–47.

Newey, W., 1985. Generalized method of moments specification testing. Journal of Econometrics 29, 229–256.

Scholes, M., Williams, J., 1976. Estimating betas from nonsynchronous data. Journal of Financial Economics 5, 309–327.

Shleifer, A., Vishny, R., 1986. Large shareholders and corporate control. Journal of Political Economy 94, 461–488.

Zeckhauser, R., Pound, J., 1990. Are large shareholders effective monitors?: an investigation of share ownership and corporate performance. In: Hubbard, R.G. (Ed.), Asymmetric Information, Corporate Finance, and Investment. University of Chicago Press, Chicago.

JOURNAL OF FINANCIAL AND QUANTITATIVE ANALYSIS　　　VOL. 31, NO. 1, MARCH 1996

Pension Fund Activism and Firm Performance

Sunil Wahal*

Abstract

This paper studies the efficacy of pension fund activism by examining all firms targeted by nine major funds from 1987 to 1993. I document a movement away from takeover-related proxy proposal targetings in the late 1980s to governance-related proxy proposal and nonproxy proposal targetings in the 1990s. For the vast majority of firms, there are no significant abnormal returns at the time of targeting. The subset of firms subject to nonproxy proposal targeting, however, experiences a significant positive wealth effect. There is no evidence of significant long-term improvement in either stock price or accounting measures of performance in the post-targeting period. Collectively, these results cast doubt on the effectiveness of pension fund activism as a substitute for an active market for corporate control.

I. Introduction

The involvement of large institutions in shareholder activism has been highly publicized and, in some circles, viewed as a natural response to the decline in the market for corporate control in the 1990s. Indeed, Pound (1992) and Black (1992) characterize institutional investor activism as an evolution away from market- and transactions-based systems of corporate governance (as exemplified by takeovers) to a political model of corporate governance. Pound (1992) suggests that the political model is preferable to the takeover model as a means of monitoring corporate performance due to its flexibility in addressing specific corporate mistakes and problems. In contrast, the takeover model offers only a drastic remedy, which

* Krannert Graduate School of Management, 1310 Krannert Building, Purdue University, West Lafayette, IN 47907-1310. This paper is derived from the first chapter of the author's Ph.D. dissertation at the University of North Carolina. The author is indebted to committee members Jennifer Conrad and Marc Zenner (co-chairs), Mustafa Gültekin, Henri Servaes, and Anup Agrawal for their guidance and support. The author also thanks Jonathan Karpoff (the editor), Ajay Khorana, Peggy Lee, Karen Van Nuys, and seminar participants at North Carolina, Purdue, Georgia, Notre Dame, and Case Western Reserve Universities for helpful comments and suggestions, as well as officials at Institutional Shareholder Services, the California Public Employee Retirement System, the California State Teachers Retirement System, the Colorado Public Employee Retirement System, the Florida State Board of Administration, the New York City Comptroller's office, the New York State Common Retirement System, the Pennsylvania Public School Employee Retirement System, the State of Wisconsin Investment Board, and TIAA-CREF for graciously providing data and insight into the activism process. The programming assistance of Doug McIntyre is gratefully acknowledged. Mehmet Ozbilgin provided excellent research assistance.

often is viewed with broad suspicion and subject to political retaliation in the form of antitakeover legislation.[1]

The increased interest in shareholder activism has prompted several academic investigations. For example, Karpoff, Malatesta, and Walkling (1995) and John and Klein (1994) examine firm-specific factors associated with the sponsorship of shareholder proposals by both institutions and individuals. In addition, several studies assess the impact of shareholder activism on firm performance by analyzing abnormal returns around proxy mailing, press announcement, and shareholder meeting dates for shareholder initiated proposals. Specifically, Karpoff, Malatesta, and Walkling (1995), and Gillan and Starks (1994) find small but statistically insignificant abnormal returns around these dates for proposals initiated by activist shareholders. On the other hand, Strickland, Wiles, and Zenner (1996) report a 0.9-percent abnormal return around the agreement date for resolutions sponsored by the United Shareholders Association. Additionally, Nesbitt (1994) and Smith (1996) find weak evidence that the long-term stock price performance of targets of the California Public Employee Retirement System (Calpers) improves in the post-targeting period.

This paper expands knowledge of shareholder activism by analyzing firms targeted by a comprehensive sample of activist pension funds from 1987 to 1993. The funds examined include the California Public Employee Retirement System, the California State Teachers Retirement System, the Colorado Public Employee Retirement System, the New York City Pension System, the Pennsylvania Public School Employee Retirement System, the State of Wisconsin Investment Board, the College Retirement Equities Fund, the Florida State Board of Administration, and the New York State Common Retirement System. These pension funds provide detailed data on the timing and nature of the targeting, which illuminate the activism process. Specifically, I document a secular movement away from takeover-related proxy proposal targetings in the late 1980s to governance-related proxy proposal and nonproxy proposal targetings in the 1990s. The evidence presented indicates that the success of pension funds in instituting confidential voting arrangements, changing the structure of corporate boards and redeeming poison pills is relatively high. For example, 40 percent of proxy proposals initiated by pension funds intended to change the governance structure of target firms were adopted by these firms.

If the changes engendered by pension funds are beneficial to firm performance, then targeting announcements should be associated with significant abnormal returns.[2] Consistent with both Karpoff, Malatesta, and Walkling (1995) and Gillan and Starks (1994), I find an approximately zero average abnormal return

---

[1] Roe (1994) provides a detailed account of the historical and legal reasons why takeovers (and, for that matter, concentrated ownership), have been viewed with suspicion by lawmakers and the popular press. Karpoff and Malatesta (1989) describe various types of takeover laws and examine their valuation effects.

[2] The notion that activism may be associated with positive wealth consequences has also attracted the attention of money managers. In July 1992, Robert Monks launched a money management firm (the Lens Fund) with the explicit intention of acquiring large positions in firms and becoming an active shareholder. Initially, Calpers planned to invest $200 million in the Lens Fund but subsequently declined the investment opportunity. Other money management firms, including Brown Brothers Harriman, Dillon Read, and Lazard Freres Asset Management, have also recently started "relationship investing" funds.

for targetings related to shareholder proposals. However, there is a significant positive abnormal return around the announcement of targeting for the subsample of firms subject to nonproxy proposal targetings. This result suggests that for a small subset of firms, the gains to shareholder activism are impounded at the time of targeting. In contrast, the vast majority of targeting announcements are not associated with significant abnormal returns. The lack of an announcement effect is surprising, given pension funds' success in obtaining negotiated agreements with management, particularly on governance issues.

Analysis of the stock price performance of sample firms over a two-year period prior to targeting also yields somewhat surprising results. Firms targeted by pension funds underperform the market. The industries, however, underperform the market over the same period. Thus, the general picture that emerges is that pension funds target poor performers, but do not discriminate between firm and industry performance.

Evidence on the post-targeting performance of these firms is mixed. On average, market-adjusted returns for targeted firms do not improve substantially. Industry-adjusted returns do not appear to improve either, despite the fact that the industries' returns improve. There is considerable cross-sectional variation in these returns, with a small subset of firms experiencing large returns reversals. Nonetheless, on average, pension fund activism does not improve the long-term stock price performance of targeted firms. Accounting measures of performance reinforce this conclusion; industry-adjusted operating and net income do not improve subsequent to targeting.

An examination of the holdings of activist pension funds in the sample of targeted firms shows that they do not systematically divest their shares. In contrast, two years after the first year of targeting, "inactive" institutions reduce their stakes by three percentage points. Further, the average number of inactive institutions holding equity in these firms declines substantially. In other words, activist pension funds continue to hold underperforming stock in their portfolios, while other institutions vote with their feet.

In general, the evidence supports conjectures by Romano (1993) and Murphy and Van Nuys (1994) that monitoring by active pension funds may be ineffective. These authors, as well as Admati, Pfleiderer, and Zechner (1994), recognize that there may be agency problems between the managers of pension funds (who make the monitoring decisions) and their residual claimants. They argue that these agency problems reduce the ability of pension funds to be effective monitors. Collectively, the results cast doubt on the effectiveness of shareholder activism as a substitute for an active market for corporate control.

The remainder of this paper is organized as follows. Section II provides a broad overview of the activism process. Section III describes the data and sample construction. Section IV discusses the empirical tests and results. Section V concludes. The Appendix provides details on the activism programs of the nine pension funds.

4   Journal of Financial and Quantitative Analysis

II.   Pension Fund Activism

In 1980, public pension funds held $44 billion in stock in their portfolios, representing 3.9 percent of the market capitalization of the New York Stock Exchange (NYSE). By 1990, their equity holdings had increased to $293 billion, approximately 10 percent of the market capitalization of the NYSE. Not only do pension funds hold large aggregate positions, but they also hold substantial stakes in individual firms. The size of these stakes renders them particularly sensitive to the performance of firms in their portfolios. Moreover, these stakes provide powerful incentives to pension funds to monitor firms.

Pension fund activism takes a variety of forms. These include active involvement in the regulation of institutional investors, litigation against firms deemed to engage in activities that are detrimental to shareholder interests, withholding votes or voting against management's nominees for boards of directors (also known as the "Just Vote No" campaign), and, finally, formally targeting firms. The last form of shareholder activism (i.e., the targeting of firms) is studied in this paper.[3]

Pension funds generally engage in two types of targeting. I refer to the first kind as proxy proposal targeting since it involves the submission of a shareholder proposal to be voted on at the firm's annual meeting. I refer to the second kind of targeting as nonproxy targeting since it does not involve the submission of a shareholder proposal. Nonproxy targeting is also referred to as "performance-based targeting" by pension funds. A broad, general characterization of both types of targeting is provided below.

A.   Proxy Proposal Targeting

Proxy proposal targeting can be divided roughly into four stages. The first stage involves target selection. Pension funds select targets from the portfolio of firms in which they own stock. In most cases, a fund's internal research analysts are asked to identify firms to be targeted. In some instances, however, outside consultants are also employed. Often funds look for a high level of institutional ownership (especially pension fund ownership) in target firms in the belief that institutions may be more likely to vote against management.[4] Poor performance (as measured by stock returns or various accounting measures) is often, but *not always,* part of the selection criteria. Indeed, targets may be selected exclusively on corporate governance criteria. For example, the presence of poison pills, blank check preferred stock provisions, or the lack of outsiders on the board can be sufficient to prompt targeting.

The second stage is to communicate with the target firm. Typically a letter is sent to the firm's management informing them of the selection and sometimes requesting dialogue. If the targeting is for a specific corporate governance issue,

---

[3]There are some prominent examples of shareholder activism that do not involve targeting. In the regulatory arena, for example, Calpers proposed changes to Rule 14(a) of the Securities and Exchange Act that allowed freer communication between large shareholders and reduced the disclosure burden. In 1992, some of these changes were adopted.

[4]In some cases, pension funds that have voted *with* management have raised the ire of other funds. For example, New York State Common Retirement System voted with management in the Texaco proxy contest in 1988.

such as the removal of a poison pill, it is identified in the letter. In some cases, the letter is publicized (as with Calpers) and is followed by a telephone call from the activist fund. Some funds choose not to publicize the letters, however, since they feel that the first step is to start a private and nonadversarial discussion with management.

The third stage, while common, is not universal. It involves the submission of a shareholder proposal to be voted on at the firm's annual meeting. These proposals are submitted under Rule 14A-8, which legally requires the firm to include the proposals in the proxy statement.

The fourth and final stage involves some sort of resolution between the firm and the pension fund. If agreement is reached on the issue prior to the shareholders' meeting, the fund's proposal is not submitted, or is withdrawn or voluntarily adopted by the firm without a vote (in other words, stage three does not occur). If agreement is not reached (and stage three occurs), however, the proposal is put to vote. Most proposals are advisory, rather than binding in nature. Thus, even if the proposal receives a majority of votes, it is rarely adopted (see Gordon and Pound (1993)). Unsuccessful resolutions of this type are often followed by the same firm being targeted in the following year. Negotiated agreements between the fund and the firm may also be reached subsequent to the annual meeting. Although many proposals eventually prompt a change in the company, many other proposals are simply ignored.

B. Nonproxy Targeting

Since nonproxy targeting does not involve shareholder proposals on specific issues, it is not convenient to characterize it in stages. The objective of this kind of targeting is merely to make management aware of the pension fund's dissatisfaction with the performance of the firm. The targeting is typically resolved either by the firm discussing its performance with the pension fund or by simply ignoring the fund. Since shareholder proposals are not involved, this type of targeting is not studied by Karpoff, Malatesta, and Walkling (1995) or John and Klein (1994).

While the activism process is similar for most pension funds, the specifics of the procedure vary across funds and have also changed over time. A brief description of the activism programs of each pension fund is provided in the Appendix.

III.   Data and Sample Construction

I obtained a list of active pension funds from Institutional Shareholder Services (ISS), a proxy voting agency for institutional investors. The list identifies the following pension funds as important shareholder activists. The abbreviations used for the funds and the assets of the funds at the end of 1994 (from the 1994 Money Market Directory of Pension Funds and their Investment Advisors) are reported in parentheses.

The California Public Employee Retirement System (Calpers, $77 billion)
The California State Teachers Retirement System (Calstrs, $47 billion)
The Colorado Public Employee Retirement System (Colpera, $13 billion)

6   Journal of Financial and Quantitative Analysis

> The New York City Pension Fund System, which includes the city's employees, teachers, police, and fire retirement systems as well as the board of education (NYC, $24 billion)
>
> The Pennsylvania Public School Employee Retirement System (PSERS, $24 billion)
>
> The State of Wisconsin Investment Board (SWIB, $24 billion)
>
> The Teachers Insurance and Annuity Association: College Retirement Equities Fund (TIAA-CREF, $125 billion)
>
> The Florida State Board of Administration (FSBA, $34 billion)
>
> The New York State Common Retirement System (NYSCR, $56 billion)

This list includes the most visible and active pension funds. With the exception of TIAA-CREF, all are public pension funds. Of the public funds, Calpers is the largest.

I obtained from each fund a list of the companies targeted by it between 1987 and 1993. The funds also were asked to identify, whenever possible, the dates on which targeting letters were sent, the issues targeted, the outcome of the targeting, and the date of the annual meeting. The sample identified consists of 356 independent targetings of 146 firms over the seven-year period. These targetings include both proxy proposals and nonproxy targeting.

Some pension funds provide detailed information on their activism programs while others do not. I use publicly available data sources to supplement the data provided by the funds. I searched the Wall Street Journal Index, Lexis/Nexis, and the Dow Jones News Retrieval Service for the first news announcement as well as the outcome of the targeting. For proxy proposal targetings, I read the proxy statements for all targeted firms over the seven-year period. From these proxy statements, I confirmed the name of the proposal's proponent and the proxy mailing date. When data on the final outcome of a shareholder proposal were not provided by the fund, I attempted to determine the outcome from three different sources. First, I read all 10Qs filed over the period to determine the number of votes for the proposal. Second, I looked at the "corporate events" section of Compact Disclosure to determine if the proposal was passed. Last, I read all newswire articles on the pension fund and the targeted firm to determine if a negotiated agreement was reached prior to, or after, the annual meeting. I also looked at all entries in the Wall Street Journal Index and Lexis/Nexis from 1985 to 1994 to determine the incidence and success of corporate control contests (both tender offers and proxy contests) and restructurings.

All returns and market value information are obtained from the 1994 CRSP NYSE, AMEX, and NASDAQ daily returns file. Accounting and SIC data come from the 1994 Active and Research Compustat files. Ownership data from 1988 to 1992 come from quarterly 13F filings by institutions to the SEC compiled by CDA/Spectrum and provided by Compact Disclosure. These data include the number of shares owned by each institution filing a 13F statement on a quarterly basis.[5]

---

[5]Institutional investors are required to report their portfolio holdings to the SEC under section 13F of the Securities Exchange Act of 1934 (Rule 13F-1). The institutional disclosure program under this section of the act requires all managers with investment discretion over $100 million in equity securities to report those holdings to the SEC. In the case of shared investment discretion, only one

IV.　Empirical Results

I use all available data for each of the following tests. Sample sizes vary across the tests because some tests are conducted on subsets of firms to ensure comparability between pre- and post-targeting statistics. It is also worth noting that there are many instances of the same firm being targeted several years in succession (by the same or another pension fund). These repeat targetings affect the tests in two ways. First, tests have to be conducted relative to the first or last year of targeting to avoid induced serial dependence due to overlapping observations. Second, the overlapping observations reduce the ability to perform cross-sectional tests with panel data since overlapping observations bias test statistics. I handle these empirical difficulties by performing a variety of robustness checks for each of the tests employed.

A.　Ownership Stakes and Incentives

Table 1 presents statistics on the holdings of each pension fund in the firms targeted by it over the sample period. The table also presents ownership statistics for "inactive" institutions, defined as all institutions except activist pension funds (generally banks, insurance companies, and money management organizations). Figures are presented as of the end of the year of targeting. Since 1993 ownership data are not available, 1993 targetings are not included in the reported figures. Both the percentage ownership and dollar value of equity are shown. The data are presented for the seven pension funds for which ownership data are available.

TABLE 1

Institutional Ownership of Firms Targeted by Activist Pension Funds between 1987 and 1993

Institution	Sample Size	Ownership (%)		Ownership ($)	
		Mean	Median	Mean	Median
Calpers	66	0.8%	0.6%	$　41M	$　56M
Calstrs	31	0.6	0.5	33	14
Colpera	12	0.1	0.1	8	14
SWIB	42	2.2	2.0	74	67
TIAA-CREF	43	1.1	1.0	86	63
NYSCR	8	0.9	0.9	50	27
FSBA	5	0.1	0.1	51	5
All Inactive Institutions	—	51	54	3,085	1,564
Average Ownership per Inactive Institution	—	0.3	0.3	14	7

The table presents statistics on the institutional ownership of 146 firms targeted by seven pension funds from 1987 to 1993. The percentage ownership and the dollar value of equity held are calculated as of the end of the calendar year of targeting. Inactive institutions are all institutional owners except the above listed pension funds. Figures for the average of inactive institutions are calculated by dividing the total institutional holdings of inactive institutions by the number of inactive institutions with holdings in that firm.

manager includes information regarding the securities held. For example, while the equity holdings of Calpers may be managed by many money managers, only aggregated holdings are reported by Calpers. This also serves the purpose of avoiding the problem of double counting. The law does provide certain institutions with the leeway not to file 13F reports even though their portfolio is larger than $100 million. The NYC pension system and PSERS, for example, do not file 13F reports and, thus, ownership data for them are unavailable.

As shown in Table 1, the average ownership position of activist pension funds in the firms that they target varies from a low of 0.1 percent to a high of 2.2 percent. Generally, pension funds own slightly less than 1 percent of targeted firms. It is worth noting that TIAA-CREF and SWIB hold more concentrated positions in the targeted firms than the other funds.

Looking at the dollar amount of equity held, it is clear that pension funds hold economically significant positions. Average ownership varies from $8 million to $86 million. These figures provide compelling evidence for the economic rationale behind pension fund activism. Consider, for example, a pension fund with a $25 million position in a targeted firm. If the announcement of a poison pill reduces stock prices by 1 percent (Malatesta and Walkling (1988)), the pension fund has an incentive to spend up to $250,000 to have the poison pill redeemed.

Inactive institutions also own significant positions in these firms. These institutions own approximately 51 percent of the targeted firms, an average stake of $3 billion. The average institution in this group owns 0.3 percent ($14 million) of targeted firms.

B. The Nature of Activism

Table 2 provides descriptive statistics on the shareholder activism programs of the nine pension funds examined in this study. As mentioned earlier, these pension funds targeted a total of 146 firms over the seven-year period from 1987 to 1993. The average number of times a firm was targeted was 2.15, while the maximum number of times a firm was targeted was 12. There are 48 cases where two or more funds target the same firm in the same year. These figures suggest clustering of targets in time and across firms, i.e., a firm may be targeted by several pension funds in any one year and also for several years in succession.

This table shows the frequency of issues targeted by activist pension funds. Several facts emerge from the data. First, despite the fact that Calpers is regarded as the progenitor of pension fund activism, it is not the most frequent sponsor of proposals or targeting in general. In fact, several other funds appear to be just as active over this period.

Second, there is considerable variation in the types of issues targeted. Common issues include the removal of blank check preferred stock, changing the structure of the board (requiring a greater percentage of outsiders or eliminating a classified board), separating the position of chairman and CEO, prohibiting greenmail payments, redeeming poison pills, requiring the firm to publish the names of shareholder proposal proponents, opting out of state antitakeover laws, establishing shareholder advisory committees and opposing targeted share placements. For some of these proposals it is not clear, a priori, that the passage of the proposal would be beneficial to shareholder interests. For example, while poison pills may decrease firm value on average (see Ryngaert (1988) and Malatesta and Walkling (1988)), the effects on firm value can be negligible or positive, depending on the time of adoption and board composition (see Comment and Schwert (1994) and Brickley, Coles, and Terry (1994)). Similarly, separating the position of chairman and CEO may not necessarily be in shareholder interests (see Brickley, Coles, and Jarrell (1994)). Moreover, Hansen and Lott (1996) argue that shareholder

TABLE 2

Distribution of Issues Targeted by Nine Activist Pension Funds between 1987 and 1993

	Calpers	Calstrs	Colpera	NYC	PSERS	SWIB	TIAA-CREF	NYSCR	FSBA	1987–1990	1991–1993	Total
Abstention	1	0	0	0	0	0	0	0	0	1	0	1
Board Composition	2	2	0	14	0	9	0	8	3	12	26	38
Separate Chairman and CEO	0	5	0	5	0	0	0	0	0	0	10	10
Compensation	5	1	0	5	0	1	0	0	0	3	9	12
Confidential Voting	11	9	0	78	0	8	16	0	2	62	62	124
Golden Parachute	0	2	0	0	0	1	0	0	0	2	1	3
Proponent Disclosure	0	0	0	5	0	0	0	0	0	0	5	5
Shareholder Committee	6	0	0	0	0	0	0	0	0	4	2	6
Governance-Related Targeting	25	19	0	107	0	19	16	8	5	84	115	199
Antitakeover Law	5	2	0	2	0	0	0	0	0	9	0	9
Blank Check Preferred	0	0	0	0	0	0	8	0	0	0	8	8
Greenmail	0	2	0	0	0	0	0	0	0	2	0	2
Poison Pill	25	10	0	1	0	30	21	0	0	73	14	87
Target Share Placement	0	0	0	0	0	0	1	0	0	1	0	1
Takeover-Related Targeting	30	14	0	3	0	30	30	0	0	85	22	107
Nonproxy Targeting (Performance-Targeting)	23	0	22	0	5	0	0	0	0	2	48	50
Total	78	33	22	110	5	49	46	8	5	171	185	356

The table shows the issues targeted by the nine activist pension funds listed above from 1987 to 1993. Proxy proposal targeting issues are classified into two categories: governance-related issues and takeover-related issues. Issues relating to abstentions, board composition, separating chairman and CEOs, compensation policies, confidential voting, golden parachutes, proponent disclosure, and shareholder committee formation are categorized as governance-related targetings. Issues relating to state antitakeover laws, blank check preferred stock, greenmail, poison pills, and targeted share placement are categorized as takeover-related targetings. The frequency of nonproxy targeting (commonly referred to as "performance-based targeting") is also shown in the table.

proposals can destroy shareholder value because they discourage managers from considering their firms' effects on other firms. In general, the implication of these arguments is that the average wealth effects of pension fund activism cannot be signed ex ante based on existing theoretical and empirical evidence.

Third, the data suggest that pension funds have clear preferences about the types of issues they target. For example, of the 110 issues targeted by the New York City pension system, the majority (78) relate to confidential voting of shares, followed by board composition (14). Colpera, on the other hand does not sponsor any shareholder proposals but focuses entirely on nonproxy targeting. SWIB and TIAA-CREF are important sponsors of proposals calling for the redemption of poison pills (30 and 21, respectively).[6]

Of the 356 targetings over the seven-year period, 124 (35 percent) relate to confidential voting. The second highest category is redemption of poison pills with 87 (24 percent) proposals submitted, followed by nonproxy targeting with 50 (14 percent), and board composition with 38 (11 percent). These figures are similar to those reported by Gordon and Pound (1993) for the 1990 proxy season.

For further tests, these issues are divided into three categories—governance-related targetings, takeover-related targetings, and nonproxy targetings. The details of the classification are provided in the table. While the classification is admittedly subjective, it does serve to highlight some important features of the data. Almost 56 percent of the issues targeted relate to governance structure. Takeover-related issues comprise 30 percent of the sample, while nonproxy targeting comprises the remaining 14 percent. Perhaps more interesting is the change

---

[6]Fifteen proposals relating to withdrawal of business from South Africa are deleted from the sample since these proposals are not attempts to increase shareholders' monetary returns.

in the types of issues over time. Of the 107 takeover-related targetings, more than 79 percent occur between 1987 and 1990. The corresponding figure for governance structure-related proposals for the same period is only 42 percent. The movement away from takeover-related issues is probably related to the decline in the takeover activity in the early 1990s. Also, of the 50 cases of nonproxy targeting, 48 (96 percent) took place after 1990. These figures suggest that the monitoring mechanisms employed by pension funds have changed over time, probably due to the decline in the market for corporate control.

C. Proxy Proposal Outcomes

The data description in Table 2 is useful in that it characterizes the form and manner in which pension funds monitor target firms. For proxy proposal targeting, the objective is clear (the adoption of the proposal) and, therefore, the "success" of the targeting can be judged by examining adoption rates. Accordingly, Table 3 presents statistics on the voting outcome and adoption rates of shareholder proposals initiated by these pension funds. Fifty nonproxy targetings are excluded from the sample since adoption rates are not meaningful. Also, 49 proxy proposal targetings for which the outcome could not be determined are excluded from the analysis. The second column of Table 3 shows the number of proposals sponsored. The third column shows the number of proposals adopted either prior to or after the shareholder vote. The fourth and fifth columns show the number of proposals that came to a shareholder vote and the percentage of votes for the proposal (excluding abstentions). Therefore, if a proposal was voted on and subsequently adopted, it appears in columns three and four. Note that the sample sizes in this table do not precisely match those in Table 2 because of incomplete information on the targeting outcome.

Panel A of the table shows that shareholder proposals sponsored by pension funds receive significant shareholder support, on average 34 percent of the votes cast. It is also evident that takeover-related proposals receive a greater percentage of votes for the proposal than governance-related proposals (37.7 percent vs. 32.5 percent, p-value $= 0.06$). In fact, on average, 38 percent of votes are cast in favor of proposals requiring poison pill redemptions vs. only 22.1 percent for changing board composition.

Although takeover-related proposals appear to receive greater support from shareholders, their adoption rates are somewhat lower than governance-related proposals. Of 83 takeover-related proposals for which data are available, only 24 (29 percent) were adopted. It is notable that 20 out of 67 (29 percent) poison pill redemption proposals were adopted by targeted firms. In contrast, out of 174 governance-related proposals, 71 (40 percent) were accepted. (The difference between the adoption rates of governance vs. takeover-related proposals is significant at the 0.05 level.) One interpretation of this is that management may be more willing to accept proposals that it regards as nonthreatening (such as confidential voting or proponent disclosure). Even for these proposals, however, the adoption rates are significantly lower than those for management-sponsored proposals (Brickley, Lease, and Smith (1988)) and proposals sponsored by the United Shareholders Association (Strickland, Wiles, and Zenner (1996)).

Governance and Ownership

TABLE 3

Outcomes of Shareholder Proposals Initiated by Activist Pension Funds between 1987 and 1993

Panel A. Outcome of Issues Targeted by Activist Pension Funds Classified by Type of Issue

	Proposals Sponsored	Proposals Adopted	Proposals Voted On	% Votes for Proposal
Board Composition	38	16	11	24.8
Separate Chairman and CEO	10	0	5	24.3
Compensation	12	11	n.a.	n.a.
Confidential Voting	124	35	83	34.5
Golden Parachute	3	1	2	29.0
Proponent Disclosure	5	3	2	20.4
Shareholder Committee	6	5	n.a.	n.a.
Governance-Related Targeting	199	71	103	32.5
Antitakeover Law	9	3	4	30.4
Blank Check Preferred	8	1	7	39.5
Greenmail	2	0	n.a.	n a.
Poison Pill	87	20	47	38.3
Target Share Placement	1	0	1	26.8
Takeover-Related Targeting	107	24	59	37.7
All Proposals	306	95	162	34.7

Panel B. Outcome of Issues Targeted by Activist Pension Funds Classified by Pension Fund

	Proposals Sponsored	Proposals Adopted	Proposals Voted On	% Votes for Proposal
Calpers	55	25	11	41.4
Calstrs	33	6	11	41.9
NYC	110	33	73	30.8
SWIB	49	21	20	39.4
TIAA-CREF	46	3	43	35.1
NYSCR	8	6	2	21.7
FSBA	5	1	2	35.0

The table presents information on outcomes of shareholder proposals sponsored by activist pension funds from 1987 to 1993, classified by type (Panel A) and sponsor (Panel B) of proposal. Proposals that are accepted by management or withdrawn by the pension fund because of a negotiated agreement are recorded as "accepted" in column three. Percentage votes for the proposal (column 5) excludes abstentions.

Since there are significant differences in the types of proposals sponsored by the different funds, I also examine adoption rates across funds. Calpers, SWIB, and the NYC funds are able to achieve high adoption rates. In general, it appears that pension funds are fairly effective in persuading firms to adopt the desired changes.

Several caveats are in order for the interpretation of the results presented in Table 3. First, the acceptance or rejection of shareholder proposals does not necessarily lead to improved firm performance. As argued earlier, it is not clear a priori that passage of these proposals should lead to increases in shareholder wealth. Second, the adoption rates presented may misstate the ability of pension funds to promote change at target firms. This is because, in many instances, pension funds herd in their targeting.[7] For example, while pressure from *many* institutions may be responsible for changing the board structure at a firm, only the sponsoring pension fund receives credit in the table. Finally, there may be instances where pension funds modify firm behavior without the passage of a specific proposal.

---

[7]Often these institutions coordinate their governance activities through the Council of Institutional Investors, an organization representing almost $600 billion in pension assets. Interestingly, the recent addition of corporate pension fund officials (often from targeted firms) has raised concerns about its effectiveness in serving as a coordinator.

Despite these caveats, the data presented in Table 3 suggest that pension funds are successful in getting many of their proposal items adopted.

D. Event Study Abnormal Returns

A direct way of gauging the impact of pension fund activism is by analyzing stock price reactions to targeting announcements. If the monitoring of these pension funds is expected by investors to be effective in reducing agency costs and improving firm performance, then the targeting announcement should be associated with positive abnormal returns. Accordingly, Panel A of Table 4 presents cumulative abnormal returns over a $-1,+5$ window for three sets of targetings dates: the letter date (i.e., the date on which the pension fund sent a letter to the targeted firm indicating that the firm had been targeted), the proxy mailing date (i.e., the date on which the proxy statement containing the shareholder proposal sponsored by the pension fund was mailed), and the press announcement date (i.e., the first press report of the targeting). Abnormal returns are calculated separately for each of these dates since they could contain different information. For example, CARs for proxy mailing dates may be biased downward because the market may interpret the sponsorship of a shareholder resolution as a sign that prior negotiations with the firm were unsuccessful at achieving the desired outcome. CARs are also presented for the earliest information date, which represents the earliest of the letter, proxy mailing, and press announcement dates. Abnormal returns are computed using standard event study methodology where a market model is estimated over the 240 trading days ending 10 days before the date of interest (day 0). Test statistics for the abnormal returns are calculated as in Brown and Warner (1980). The CRSP equally-weighted market index is used in the market model regression. A total of 295 letter, proxy mailing, and press announcement dates are available. Four observations are not included in the analysis because of confounding events such as earnings announcements and, in one case, a bankruptcy filing. Relatively wide windows are used for the abnormal returns since it is hard to pinpoint a single day where the information is released to the market.

For the full sample of targets, the average six-day CAR is insignificantly different from zero for the letter, proxy mailing, press announcement, and earliest information dates. An examination of the returns to firms targeted by the nine pension funds separately reveals that, for letter and earliest information dates, only firms targeted by Calpers experience a positive stock price reaction. While Calpers' targets experience a 2-percent (1-percent) abnormal return around the letter date (earliest information date), the returns to non-Calpers targets are not significantly different from zero. This suggests that the positive abnormal return for the full sample of targets (at least for the letter dates) may be driven by the Calpers subsample.

Table 2 showed that there is a fundamental change in the targeting strategy of pension funds after 1990. Institutions such as Calpers shifted focus from issues relating to the market for corporate control to governance-related and nonproxy targeting. To capture this change, Table 4 shows CARs for pre- and post-1990 targets. There is no wealth effect associated with targeting before 1990. There is some weak evidence, however, that targeting after 1990 may be associated with

TABLE 4

Abnormal Returns around Targeting by Activist Pension Funds between 1987 and 1993

Panel A. Cumulative Abnormal Returns (CARs) over − 1,+5 Window

	Letter Date	Proxy Mailing Date	Press Announcement Date	Earliest Information Date
All Targets	0.009	−0.003	0.003	−0.000
	(1.52) [*N* = 141]	(1.55) [*N* = 211]	(0.63) [*N* = 96]	(1.09) [*N* = 291]
Calpers	0.020	−0.007	−0.003	0.010
	(2.75) [*N* = 51]	(1.19) [*N* = 30]	(0.51) [*N* = 32]	(1.90) [*N* = 67]
Non-Calpers	0.002	−0.001	0.005	−0.000
	(0.22) [*N* = 90]	(1.11) [*N* = 181]	(1.13) [*N* = 64]	(0.96) [*N* = 224]
1987–1990 Targetings	0.010	−0.011	0.015	−0.003
	(1.32) [*N* = 60]	(1.21) [*N* = 119]	(1.60) [*N* = 34]	(1.41) [*N* = 145]
1991–1993 Targetings	0.008	0.008	−0.004	0.010
	(1.67) [*N* = 81]	(0.75) [*N* = 92]	(0.42) [*N* = 62]	(1.75) [*N* = 146]
Takeover-Related	0.010	−0.014	0.003	−0.004
	(1.22) [*N* = 33]	(1.16) [*N* = 76]	(0.02) [*N* = 28]	(1.03) [*N* = 88]
Governance-Related	−0.005	0.003	−0.000	−0.003
	(0.84) [*N* = 65]	(0.02) [*N* = 135]	(0.38) [*N* = 49]	(1.73) [*N* = 160]
Nonproxy	0.027	—	0.010	0.0186
	(3.29) [*N* = 43]		(1.75) [*N* = 19]	(2.02) [*N* = 43]

Panel B. Cross-Sectional Regressions of CARs on Explanatory Variables Related to Targeting

Intercept	−0.013	0.008	−0.009	0.006
	(−1.80)	(0.06)	(−1.35)	(0.72)
Calpers Dummy	0.018	−0.009	−0.016	−0.003
	(1.57)	(−1.05)	(−1.21)	(−0.42)
Post 90 Dummy	0.014	−0.017	0.031	0.001
	(1.42)	(−0.91)	(1.75)	(0.18)
Nonproxy Dummy	0.046	—	0.081	0.030
	(3.52)		(3.40)	(2.77)
Calpers ∗ Nonproxy Dummy	−0.029	—	−0.006	−0.021
	(−1.56)		(1.13)	(−1.32)
Letter Date Dummy	—	—	—	−0.007
				(−0.83)
Proxy Date Dummy	—	—	—	−0.012
				(−1.45)
Adjusted R^2	0.08	0.04	0.12	0.10
N	140	210	95	290

This table presents CARs for four dates: the letter date (the date on which the pension fund sent a letter to the firm); the proxy mailing date (the date on which the proxy statement containing the pension fund's shareholder proposal was mailed); the press announcement date (the first date on which the press reported the targeting); the earliest information date (the earliest of the letter, proxy mailing and press announcement dates). The variables employed in the cross-sectional regressions are defined as follows. The Calpers dummy is one if the targeting is by Calpers, zero otherwise. The post 90 dummy is one if the targeting takes place after 1990, zero otherwise. The nonproxy targeting dummy is one if the targeting is not associated with a shareholder proposal, zero otherwise. The letter date dummy is one if the letter date is the earliest information date, zero otherwise. The proxy date dummy is one if the proxy mailing date is the earliest information date, zero otherwise. *Z*-statistics are in parentheses in Panel A and heteroskedasticity consistent *t*-statistics are in parentheses in Panel B.

a small wealth effect. The six-day CAR for targetings between 1991 and 1993 is 0.8 percent for letter dates and 1 percent for the earliest information date; these CARs are significant at the 0.10 level.

The abnormal returns are not different for proposals that are adopted vs. those that are not (−0.5 percent vs. −0.1 percent, both insignificantly different from zero and also insignificantly different from each other). The CARs are, however, related to the issue being targeted. In general, takeover and governance-related targetings are not associated with significant wealth effects on letter, press announcement, or earliest information dates. In contrast, nonproxy targeting is associated with a significant wealth effect. Specifically, firms subject to nonproxy targeting experience a six-day CAR of 2.7 percent on the letter date, 1 percent on the press announcement date, and 1.86 percent on the earliest information date. All these CARs are significant at better than the 0.05 level. The abnormal returns reported above are not driven by outliers; median returns show similar patterns. Moreover, the results are robust to use of smaller windows (e.g., $-1,+1$) and market model estimation periods (e.g., estimation of market model parameters after the event period).

Since there is significant concentration of nonproxy targeting in the post-1990 period, and since a large number of Calpers's targeting in the post-90 period was nonproxy targeting, the CARs are also analyzed in a multivariate setting. Specifically, several specifications of cross-sectional regressions of CARs on dummy variables for the identity of the pension fund, the type of targeting (takeover- or governance-related vs. nonproxy targeting), and pre- vs. post-1990 targetings are estimated and presented in Panel B of Table 4. Separate cross-sectional regressions are estimated for letter, proxy mailing, press announcement, and earliest information dates. Heteroskedasticity consistent t-statistics (White (1980)) are presented in parentheses below the parameter estimates.

Dummy variables for Calpers vs. non-Calpers targetings, and for targetings after 1990 are included in all specifications. A nonproxy targeting dummy variable is also introduced in all regressions except for those for proxy mailing date CARs. Also, an interaction term between the Calpers dummy and nonproxy dummy is included in these regressions to determine if the positive wealth effect of nonproxy targeting is attributable entirely to Calpers. Finally, dummy variables for the letter and proxy mailing date are included in the regression using CARs computed from the earliest information date to reflect the potentially different information content of these dates.

Both the Calpers and post-1990 dummy variables are not statistically significant in any of the regressions. The nonproxy targeting dummy, however, is consistently positive across all regression specification. Further, the interaction term between the Calpers and nonproxy dummy variables is not significant, suggesting that the positive abnormal return to nonproxy targeting is not driven by the Calpers subsample.

Overall, these results show that there is approximately a zero average abnormal return for shareholder proposals and a positive abnormal return for attempts to influence target firms that did not employ shareholder proposals (i.e., nonproxy targeting). It is possible that the market anticipates improvements in the performance of these firms. For the overall sample, however, the empirical evidence is not strong enough to conclude that targeting announcements are associated with positive abnormal returns.

E. Long-Term Performance

Proponents of shareholder activism suggest that the benefits of activism occur through long-term improvements in the performance of targeted firms. This
performance improvement can be measured by long-term stock price performance
or by accounting measures of performance. Both are examined below.

1. Stock Price Performance

I analyze the abnormal holding period returns (AHPRs) of firms targeted by
these pension funds in Table 5. AHPRs are calculated as follows,

$$\text{AHPR}_{i,a,b} \;=\; \left[\prod_{t=a}^{b}\left(1 + R_{i,t}\right) - 1\right] - \left[\prod_{t=a}^{b}\left(1 + R_{p,t}\right) - 1\right],$$

where $R_{i,t}$ is the return of firm i for day t, and a and b define the interval over which
the return is compounded. $R_{p,t}$ refers to the return on the benchmark portfolio. For
market-adjusted returns, the value-weighted market index is used. For industry-
adjusted returns, the mean return for the corresponding three-digit SIC code is
used. A minimum of three firms in the three-digit SIC code (not including the
target firm) is required to compute the mean industry return.

AHPRs are appropriate return measures for two reasons. First, they represent
the returns to a buy and hold strategy (over a benchmark) and, consequently, are an
appropriate description of the returns actually earned by pension funds. Second,
as pointed out by Blume and Stambaugh (1983) and Conrad and Kaul (1993), they
avoid the cumulation of biases in arithmetic mean returns.

As mentioned earlier, sample firms are often targeted several years in succession, sometimes by the same or different pension funds. Therefore, inclusion of
all targetings in the computation of mean or median AHPRs would cause biased
t-statistics. Accordingly, Table 5 presents returns relative to the first and last year
of targeting. AHPRs are shown from two years before targeting to the year of
targeting ($\text{AHPR}_{-2,0}$) and for one year after targeting ($\text{AHPR}_{0,1}$). P-values for
standard t-tests for means and Wilcoxon sign tests (which require the assumption
of independence but not of symmetry) are presented in parentheses.

Panel A of the table shows market-adjusted AHPRs for targeted firms. The
mean return differs substantially from the median return for all horizons. In fact, the
Shapiro-Wilk statistic for normality easily rejects the null hypothesis. Therefore,
the discussion of the results focuses primarily on median returns.

The median $\text{AHPR}_{-2,0}$ for the full sample of firms is approximately -14
percent for returns computed relative to the first year of targeting and -13 percent
for returns computed relative to the last year of targeting. Both these returns are
significant at the 0.05 level. Thus, on average, targeted firms underperform the
market prior to targeting. It is worth noting, however, that there are important
outliers in the data. For example, GTE and Ford were targeted in 1989 and 1988
by TIAA-CREF and Calstrs, respectively. However, the two-year market-adjusted
AHPR for these firms prior to targeting was 67 percent and 80 percent. These
figures suggest that pension funds do not exclusively target underperforming firms.

Returns subsequent to the targeting continue to be negative; the median
$\text{AHPR}_{0,1}$ is -4 percent (p-value = 0.07) for returns computed relative to the first

16   Journal of Financial and Quantitative Analysis

TABLE 5

Long-Term Stock Price Performance of Firms Targeted by Activist Pension Funds between 1987 and 1993

	Relative to First Year of Targeting				Relative to Last Year of Targeting			
	$AHPR_{-2,0}$		$AHPR_{0,1}$		$AHPR_{-2,0}$		$AHPR_{0,1}$	
	Mean	Median	Mean	Median	Mean	Median	Mean	Median
Panel A. Target Firm Abnormal Holding Period Returns (Market-Adjusted)								
Full Sample	−0.086	−0.147	0.010	−0.040	−0.003	−0.130	−0.001	−0.026
(*N* = 135)	(0.07)	(0.02)	(0.71)	(0.07)	(0.95)	(0.05)	(0.94)	(0.44)
Overperformers	0.418	0.253	−0.048	−0.106	0.564	0.304	−0.016	−0.057
(*N* = 53)	(0.00)	(0.00)	(0.33)	(0.01)	(0.00)	(0.00)	(0.73)	(0.04)
Underperformers	−0.413	−0.358	0.047	0.027	−0.398	−0.346	0.007	0.10
(*N* = 82)	(0.00)	(0.00)	(0.18)	(0.33)	(0.00)	(0.00)	(0.78)	(0.84)
Panel B. Target Firm Abnormal Holding Period Returns (Industry-Adjusted)								
Full Sample	0.086	0.012	0.044	0.010	0 211	0.123	−0.089	−0.074
(*N* = 119)	(0.09)	(0.15)	(0.32)	(0.61)	(0.00)	(0.00)	(0.04)	(0.01)
Overperformers	0.498	0.326	−0.152	−0.094	0.638	0.409	−0.200	−0.118
(*N* = 44)	(0.00)	(0.00)	(0.00)	(0.03)	(0.00)	(0.00)	(0.00)	(0.00)
Underperformers	−0.326	−0.236	0.125	0.061	−0.373	−0.236	−0.012	−0.047
(*N* = 75)	(0.00)	(0.00)	(0.05)	(0.15)	(0.00)	(0.00)	(0.85)	(0.70)
Panel C. Industry Abnormal Holding Period Returns (Market-Adjusted)								
Full Sample	−0.100	−0.099	−0.030	0.003	−0.170	−0.198	0.092	0.103
(*N* = 119)	(0.00)	(0.00)	(0.36)	(0.50)	(0.00)	(0.00)	(0.00)	(0.00)
Overperformers	−0.171	−0.238	0.133	0.110	−0.259	−0.284	0.212	0.189
(*N* = 44)	(0.00)	(0.00)	(0.00)	(0.00)	(0.00)	(0.00)	(0.00)	(0.00)
Underperformers	−0.033	−0.020	−0.097	−0.038	−0.057	−0.068	0.012	0.062
(*N* = 75)	(0.48)	(0.32)	(0.02)	(0.02)	(0.20)	(0.29)	(0.80)	(0.24)

The table presents abnormal holding period returns (AHPRs) for targeted firms (Panels A and B) and for the industries of targeted firms (Panel C). Since firms are often targeted several years in succession by the same or different pension funds, returns are presented relative to the first or last year targeted. Year 0 refers to the year of targeting. Market-adjusted target firm AHPRs (Panel A) are computed by subtracting the buy-and-hold return for the equally-weighted CRSP market index from the buy-and-hold return for the firm. Industry-adjusted targeted firm AHPRs (Panel B) are computed by subtracting the buy-and-hold (mean) return for the industry (based on the three-digit SIC code and requiring a minimum of three firms in the industry) from the buy-and-hold return for the firm. Market-adjusted industry AHPRs (Panel C) are computed by subtracting the buy-and-hold return for the industry from the buy-and-hold return for the equally-weighted CRSP market index. The full sample of firms in Panel A is classified into under- and overperformers if $AHPR_{-2,0}$ (relative to the market index) is negative or positive, respectively. The sample of firms in Panels B and C is classified into under- and overperformers if $AHPR_{-2,0}$ (relative to the industry) is negative or positive, respectively.

year of targeting and −2 percent (*p*-value = 0.44) for returns computed relative to the first year of targeting.[8] Thus, on average, there are no dramatic improvements in the returns for targeted firms subsequent to targeting.

Given the cross-sectional variation in $AHPR_{-2,0}$, the full sample of firms is also separated into over- and underperformers based on this two-year return. Specifically, firms with positive (negative) $AHPR_{-2,0}$ are classified as overperformers (underperformers). The results indicate that *both* over- and underperformers experience returns reversals; for overperformers, $AHPR_{-2,0}$ is 25 percent and $AHPR_{0,1}$ is −10 percent. The returns of underperformers show similar characteristics. Therefore, it is hard to attribute any stock price improvement to pension fund targeting since both under- and overperformers show mean reversion in re-

---

[8] I also compute but do not report longer horizon returns ($AHPR_{0,2}$ and $AHPR_{0,3}$) for a subsample of firms. These returns are also generally negative and significant.

turns. These results are not qualitatively affected by the use of other benchmarks and standard risk adjustments. For example, using the S&P 500 or the equally-weighted market index does not change any of the inferences reported. Further, beta-adjusted returns also show similar patterns.

Panel B shows industry-adjusted AHPRs for the same firms. Relative to the first year of targeting, the median industry-adjusted AHPR over the two-year period prior to targeting is approximately 1 percent (p-value = 0.15); relative to the last year of targeting, however, the industry-adjusted $AHPR_{-2,0}$ is 12 percent (p-value = 0.00). This result suggests that while pension funds appear to target underperformers relative to the market, they do not discriminate between the firm and the industry. In fact, on average, target firms overperform their industry. Perhaps even more surprising is the fact that subsequent to targeting, industry-adjusted returns decline. The industry-adjusted sample is also truncated into over- and underperformers based on industry-adjusted $AHPR_{-2,0}$. Similar to market-adjusted returns, both under- and overperformers experience some degree of return reversals subsequent to targeting. For overperformers, the median industry-adjusted $AHPR_{-2,0}$ is 32 percent and $AHPR_{0,1}$ is −9 percent. Return reversals for underperformers are noticeably smaller and generally less statistically significant, particularly for returns computed relative to the last year of targeting.

The patterns in industry-adjusted returns suggest that looking at the returns to the industry as a whole might be worthwhile. Industry AHPRs are calculated as follows,

$$
\text{AHPR}_{ind;a,b} \; = \; \left[\prod_{t=a}^{b} \left(1 + R_{ind,t}\right) - 1 \right] - \left[\prod_{t=a}^{b} \left(1 + R_{m,t}\right) - 1 \right],
$$

where $R_{ind,t}$ is the mean return for the industry on day t, a and b define the interval over which the return is compounded, and $R_{m,t}$ refers to the value-weighted market index. Thus, these AHPRs represent the returns to a benchmark portfolio of the industry relative to the market index.

Panel C presents these market-adjusted industry AHPRs. The median two-year holding period return from year −2 to year 0 is −9 percent for returns computed relative to the first year of targeting and −19 percent for returns computed relative to the last year of targeting. This result indicates that pension funds target firms in poorly performing industries. Dividing this sample identically to panel B (i.e., based on targeted firm's industry-adjusted returns) also yields interesting results. Industries of both over- and underperformers experience some degree of return reversals subsequent to targeting, although once again, the reversals are stronger for overperformers than for underperformers.

Combining the information presented in all panels suggests that, on average, pension funds target underperforming firms but this is because the industry as a whole is performing poorly. In general, the evidence is not consistent with dramatic improvements in stock price performance subsequent to targeting.

2. Accounting Measures of Performance

Table 6 presents two accounting measures of performance for the sample of targeted firms. Panel A shows the ratio of operating income (Compustat data

18   Journal of Financial and Quantitative Analysis

item 13) to total assets (Compustat data item 6) and panel B shows net income (Compustat data item 172) divided by total assets from two years before to one year after targeting. In the interests of brevity, results are presented relative to the first year of targeting. Results relative to the last year of targeting are qualitatively similar. All figures are industry adjusted by subtracting the mean ratio for the industry (based on three-digit SIC codes) from the firm's ratio. The results are qualitatively similar for industry adjustments based on the median ratio for the industry. *P*-values for standard *t*-tests (for means) and Wilcoxon sign tests (for medians) are shown in parentheses.

TABLE 6

Long-Term Accounting Measures of Performance for Firms Targeted by Activist Pension Funds between 1987 and 1993

	Year −2		Year −1		Year 0		Year +1	
	Mean	Median	Mean	Median	Mean	Median	Mean	Median
Panel A. Industry-Adjusted Operating Income/Total Assets								
All Firms (*N* = 116)	−0.137	−0.11	−0.099	−0.077	−0.077	−0.044	−0.049	−0.034
	(0.00)	(0.00)	(0.00)	(0.00)	(0.00)	(0.00)	(0.00)	(0.00)
Overperformers over Years −2, 0 (*N* = 22)	0.032	0.012	0.044	0.022	0.072	0.067	0.068	0.063
	(0 05)	(0.01)	(0.00)	(0.00)	(0.00)	(0.00)	(0.00)	(0.00)
Underperformers over Years −2, 0 (*N* = 94)	−0.177	−0.159	−0 134	−0.092	−0.112	−0 085	−0.075	−0.060
	(0.00)	(0.00)	(0.00)	(0.00)	(0 00)	(0.00)	(0.00)	(0.00)
Panel B. Industry-Adjusted Net Income/Total Assets								
All Firms (*N* = 116)	−0 150	−0.126	−0 117	−0.084	−0 076	−0.045	−0.067	−0 036
	(0.00)	(0 00)	(0.00)	(0.00)	(0.00)	(0.00)	(0.00)	(0.00)
Overperformers over Years −2, 0 (*N* = 24)	0.012	0 007	0 034	0.029	0 061	0.047	0.022	0.002
	(0 67)	(0.90)	(0.03)	(0.01)	(0.00)	(0.00)	(0.13)	(0.09)
Underperformers over Years −2, 0 (*N* = 92)	−0.19	−0.162	−0.157	−0.119	−0 111	−0.009	−0 089	−0.056
	(0.00)	(0.00)	(0.00)	(0.00)	(0.00)	(0.00)	(0.00)	(0.00)

This table presents industry-adjusted operating income and net income (standardized by total assets) for firms targeted by nine activist pension funds from 1987 to 1993. These measures are presented from year −2 to year +1, where year 0 represents the year of targeting. Since firms are often targeted several years in succession, the figures are presented relative to the first year of targeting. The sample is divided into a sample of underperformers and overperformers based on the mean performance of the firm from year −2 to year 0. If the average industry-adjusted operating income for a firm is negative (positive), the firm is classified as an underperformer (overperformer). A similar procedure is employed for industry-adjusted net income. *P*-values from standard *t*-tests for means and nonparametric Wilcoxon sign tests for medians are shown in parentheses.

By both measures, firms targeted by pension funds underperform their industries from year −2 to year 0. In the year following the targeting, however, there does not appear to be any improvement in either operating or net income. For example, the average industry-adjusted operating income (standardized by total assets) in year +1 is −0.049 (*p*-value = 0.00).

Once again, however, there is considerable cross-sectional variation in the pretargeting performance figures. To better understand the distribution of these performance measures, I divide the sample into over- and underperformers. For each measure, the mean performance from year −2 to year 0 is computed. If the mean performance of a firm over this interval is negative (positive), it is classified as an underperformer (overperformer). On average, overperformers continue to overperform their industries and underperformers continue to underperform their industries. The patterns of performance for under- and overperformers are consistent for both panels.

In general, these results confirm the inferences drawn from the AHPRs, namely that there are no substantial improvements in the performance of these firms subsequent to targeting. I also compute but do not report industry-adjusted accounting measures for years +2 and +3 for a subsample of firms. The results for this subsample are qualitatively identical to those reported.

F. Voting with Their Feet

Table 7 shows level changes in institutional ownership subsequent to targeting. Changes are calculated by subtracting the ownership of institutions one, two, and three years after targeting from the end of the first year of targeting $\Delta IH_{0,+1}$ to $\Delta IH_{0,+3}$. Figures are presented for seven pension funds for which ownership data are available and for inactive institutions.[9] Sample sizes decline for $\Delta IH_{0,+3}$ since ownership data are available only through 1992. P-values for paired t-tests are shown in parentheses.

TABLE 7

Changes in Institutional Holdings Subsequent to Targeting

	$\Delta IH0, +1$	$\Delta IH0, +2$	$\Delta IH0, +3$	% Indexed
Calpers	−0.0009	−0.0017	−0.0036	53%
	(0.35) [N = 79]	(0.23) [N = 79]	(0.31) [N = 46]	
Calstrs	−0.0001	−0.0003	−0.0009	66
	(0.48) [N = 82]	(0.29) [N = 82]	(0.02) [N = 46]	
Colpera	−0.0006	0.0000	−0.0001	33
	(0.94) [N = 77]	(0.97) [N = 77]	(0.70) [N = 45]	
SWIB	−0.0016	−0.0041	−0.0029	8
	(0.28) [N = 67]	(0.05) [N = 67]	(0.43) [N = 41]	
TIAA-CREF	0.0001	0.0008	−0.0020	n.a.
	(0.83) [N = 81]	(0.48) [N = 81]	(0.01) [N = 46]	
NYSCR	−0.0007	−0.0012	−0.0007	67
	(0.06) [N = 77]	(0.01) [N = 77]	(0.06) [N = 77]	
FSBA	0.0004	0.0007	−0.0019	60
	(0.00) [N = 64]	(0.00) [N = 64]	(0.00) [N = 36]	
Inactive Institutions	−0.0230	−0.0300	−0.0312	n.a.
	(0.14) [N = 83]	(0.06) [N = 83]	(0.33) [N = 46]	

The table shows level changes in percent holdings of pension funds in targeted firms one, two, and three years after targeting. P-values for paired t-tests of differences in means from zero are shown in parentheses. The last column shows the percentage of the pension fund's equity portfolio that is indexed.

As can be seen from the table, there is very little variation in the holdings of Calpers, Calstrs, Colpera, SWIB, and TIAA-CREF. There is a decline in the holdings of NYSCR over the period; however, the decline is small, relative to the level of its holdings. Also, FSBA's stake in targeted firms increases marginally over the period studied. Overall, there is no evidence that activist pension funds sell their stock in targeted firms. These results are consistent with Wahal, Wiles, and Zenner (1995) who report that Calpers did not significantly reduce its holdings in firms that it unsuccessfully pressured to opt out of Pennsylvania's antitakeover law.

---

[9]Level changes are presented so that the statistics reported can be interpreted as the decline in the stake of the pension fund in the firm. Percentage changes provide similar inferences.

In contrast to the relatively stable holdings of pension funds, there is some evidence to suggest that inactive institutions do decrease their holdings in these firms. Inactive institutions' holdings decline by three percentage points two years after targeting. Further, the average number of inactive institutions owning equity in these firms declined from 186 to 173, a decrease of almost 7 percent. These statistics reinforce the notion that while pension funds may not vote with their feet, other institutions follow the "Wall Street Walk."

There are several possible explanations for why pension funds do not vote with their feet. First, since these firms are targeted, pension funds must anticipate improvements in their performance. Therefore, they do not reduce their stakes in these firms to capture the anticipated benefits of their monitoring activity. Second, the ownership positions of these funds in targeted firms are typically fairly large. Liquidating these positions can have a significant price impact. Chan and Lakonishok (1993), for example, shows that institutional trading is associated with price pressure. Third, the indexation policies of pension funds preclude them from divesting specific securities. The last column of Table 7 shows that with the exception of SWIB, the total equity holdings of the remaining six pension funds are heavily indexed.

V. Conclusions

This paper studies the efficacy of pension fund activism. I examine all firms targeted by the nine most active funds from 1987 to 1993. The evidence indicates that pension funds employ a variety of monitoring mechanisms in the activism process and are reasonably successful in changing the governance structure of targeted firms. For example, 40 percent of proxy proposals initiated by pension funds intended to change corporate governance structures were adopted by target firms. Despite this success, however, targeting announcement abnormal returns are not reliably different from zero, although a subset of firms subject to nonproxy targeting experiences significantly positive abnormal returns. The long-term abnormal stock price performance of targeted firms is negative prior to targeting and still is negative after targeting. Moreover, accounting measures of performance do not suggest improvements in operating or net income either; accounting measures of performance also are negative prior to and after targeting. Despite this weak performance, pension funds do not reduce their holdings in targeted firms. In contrast, other institutions reduce their stakes. These results cast doubt on the efficacy of pension fund activism in improving firm performance.

Appendix A

California Public Employee Retirement System (Calpers)

Calpers started its shareholder activism program in 1986 and is widely regarded as the progenitor of public pension fund activism. The target selection process in the late 1980s involved the identification of firms that implemented antitakeover devices without shareholder approval. Firms were then screened on the basis of the size of Calpers' stake and the aggregate level of institutional ownership. After 1989, however, the target selection process changed. Targets were selected on the basis of five-year returns. Firms were eliminated from the list if they had large employee stock ownership plans because Calpers believed that ESOPs are insider-controlled blocks. Overall, the most distinctive feature of Calpers' activism is its high profile and the visibility of the program's founder, Dale Hanson. Further details of Calpers' activism program can be found in Smith (1996).

California State Teachers Retirement System (Calstrs)

The Calstrs activism program was started in 1987. The activism process at Calstrs is similar to Calpers in many ways. In fact, in several cases, Calstrs cosponsored resolutions at target firms with Calpers. In the 1987–1989 period, most of the targeting related to the removal of antitakeover devices. Since 1990, however, Calstrs focused on governance-related (rather than takeover-related) issues. In 1992/1993, for example, five out of seven shareholder resolutions requested the separation of the Chairman/CEO position.

Colorado Public Employee Retirement System (Colpera)

Colpera's activism program was started in 1992. In 1992, 12 underperforming firms were selected as targets. Since then, 10 firms have been identified as targets annually. Unlike other pension funds, Colpera does not target specific issues. Rather, it identifies target firms as "underperformers" and sends a letter communicating this information to the CEO. Since 1993, it has also identified 10 good performing companies and sent them each a letter applauding their performance.

New York City Comptroller (NYC)

The New York City Comptroller's office controls the shareholder activism program of four New York City pension funds: the New York City Employee Retirement System (NYCERS), the New York City Teachers Retirement System (TRS), the New York City Police Pension Fund (Police), and the New York City Fire Department Pension Fund (Fire). NYC has been an extremely active pension fund since 1990, sponsoring more than 140 proposals. Its targeting has been primarily aimed at confidential voting provisions and changing the structure of the board of directors.

Pennsylvania Public School Employees Retirement System (PSERS)

Although celebrated for cosponsoring (but not initiating) the proxy solicitation against Honeywell in 1989 (see Van Nuys (1993)), PSERS is a relative newcomer to shareholder activism. Its formal activism program was started in 1993 by initiating discussions with five companies about their performance. Over the previous year, the PSERS board commissioned an independent study to identify companies that "possess significant potential to improve their profitability." Based on this study, five underperforming firms were targeted in 1993. PSERS does not target specific issues. In general, the approach is to initiate discussions in a nonadversarial setting.

State of Wisconsin Investment Board (SWIB)

SWIB's activism program was started in 1986. Two-thirds of SWIB's targets come from a $4 billion, internally managed portfolio of 300 medium-sized companies. Its larger than average equity stakes in target firms often carry more clout than other institutions. In the late 1980s, SWIB was the most frequent sponsor of proposals requiring shareholder vote on or rescinding of poison pills. In the 1990s, SWIB has focused more on changing the structure of the board of directors at target firms.

Teachers Insurance Annuity Association: College Retirement Equities Fund (TIAA-CREF)

TIAA-CREF started targeting firms in 1987. Its activism program has focused primarily on three issues: the removal of poison pills, the removal of blank check preferred stock, and confidential voting. Over a five-year period from 1987 to 1991, 10 firms were asked to remove or put to shareholder vote poison pills. If the fund was unsuccessful in removing a poison pill in the first year of targeting, the firm was often targeted again in subsequent years. Since 1991, CREF has targeted eight firms for removal of blank check preferred stock.

Florida State Board of Administration (FSBA)

FSBA's activism program differs from those of the other pension funds. FSBA rarely initiates shareholder proposals at targeted firms (although, in 1990, it sponsored three shareholder proposals at Kmart). Instead, it focuses its activism efforts through the Executive Committee of the Council of Institutional Investors and applies pressure on the management of firms targeted by other pension funds. In 1991 and 1992, FSBA voted against board nominees at five companies.

New York State Common Retirement System (NYSCR)

From 1989 to 1992, NYSCR withheld its votes on the election of directors in hundreds of companies. With each negative vote, a letter was sent, shortly before or after the meeting, to the Chairman of the Board, explaining the reason for the negative vote. There was no publication made of either the negative vote or the letters. In 1990, NYSCR initiated a nominating committee project where companies were contacted by the fund with the suggestion that the board establish a nominating committee of independent directors. Hundreds of companies were contacted as part of this project. From 1990 through 1991, eight companies were formally targeted with specific shareholder proposals regarding either the composition of the board or the creation of an independent nominating committee. NYSCR uses a computer-based corporate performance analysis system to identify underperforming firms in its portfolio for potential targeting.

References

Admati, A.; P. Pfleiderer; and J. Zechner. "Large Shareholder Activism, Risk Sharing and Financial Market Equilibrium." *Journal of Political Economy*, 102 (Dec. 1994), 1097–1130.

Black, B. "Institutional Investors and Corporate Governance: The Case for Institutional Voice." *Journal of Applied Corporate Finance* (Fall 1992), 19–32.

Blume, M., and R. Stambaugh. "Biases in Computed Returns: An Application to the Size Effect." *Journal of Financial Economics*, 12 (Nov. 1983), 387–404.

Brickley, J.; J. Coles; and G. Jarrell. "Corporate Leadership Structure: On the Separation of the Positions of CEO and Chairman of the Board." Working Paper, Univ. of Rochester (1994).

Brickley, J.; J. Coles; and R. Terry. "Outside Directors and the Adoption of Poison Pills." *Journal of Financial Economics*, 34 (June 1994), 371–390.

Brickley, J.; R Lease; and C. Smith, Jr. "Ownership Structure and Voting on Antitakeover Amendments." *Journal of Financial Economics*, 20 (Jan./March 1988), 267–291.

Brown, S., and J. Warner. "Measuring Security Price Performance." *Journal of Financial Economics*, 8 (Sept. 1980), 205–258.

Chan, L., and J. Lakonishok. "Institutional Trades and Intraday Stock Price Behavior." *Journal of Financial Economics,* 33 (April 1993), 173–200.

Comment, R., and W. Schwert. "Poison or Placebo? Evidence on the Deterrent and Wealth Effects of Modern Antitakeover Measures." *Journal of Financial Economics,* 34 (Sept. 1994), 3–45.

Conrad, J., and G. Kaul. "Long-Term Market Overreaction or Biases in Computed Returns?" *Journal of Finance,* 48 (March 1993), 39–64.

Gillan, S., and L. Starks. "Relationship Investing and Shareholder Activism by Institutional Investors: The Wealth Effects of Corporate Governance Related Proposals." Working Paper, Univ. of Texas at Austin (1994).

Gordon, L., and J. Pound. "Information, Ownership Structure, and Shareholder Voting: Evidence from Shareholder-Sponsored Corporate Governance Proposals." *Journal of Finance,* 48 (June 1993), 697–718.

Hansen, R., and J. Lott. "Externalities and Corporate Objectives in a World with Diversified Shareholders/Consumers." *Journal of Financial and Quantitative Analysis,* 31 (March 1996), 43–68.

John, K., and A. Klein. "Shareholder Proposals and Corporate Governance." Working Paper, New York Univ. (1994).

Karpoff, J., and P. Malatesta. "The Wealth Effects of Second-Generation State Takeover Legislation." *Journal of Financial Economics,* 25 (Dec. 1989), 291–322.

Karpoff, J.; P. Malatesta; and R. Walkling. "Corporate Governance and Shareholder Initiatives: Empirical Evidence." Working Paper, Univ. of Washington (1995).

Malatesta, P., and R. Walkling. "Poison Pill Securities: Stockholder Wealth, Profitability and Ownership Structure." *Journal of Financial Economics,* 20 (Jan./March 1988), 347–376.

Murphy, K., and K. Van Nuys. "State Pension Funds and Shareholder Inactivism." Working Paper, Harvard Univ. (1994).

Nesbitt, S. "Long-Term Rewards from Shareholder Activism: A Study of the Calpers Effect." *Journal of Applied Corporate Finance,* 6 (Winter 1994), 75–80.

Pound, J. "The Rise of the Political Model of Corporate Governance and Corporate Control." Working Paper, Harvard Univ. (1992).

Roe, M. *Strong Managers, Weak Owners: The Political Roots of American Corporate Finance.* Princeton, NJ: Princeton Univ. Press (1994).

Ryngaert, M. "The Effect of Poison Pill Securities on Shareholder Wealth." *Journal of Financial Economics,* 20 (Jan./March 1988), 377–418.

Romano, R. "Public Pension Fund Activism in Corporate Governance Reconsidered." *Columbia Law Review,* 91 (1993), 795–853.

Smith, M. "Shareholder Activism by Institutional Investors: Evidence from Calpers." *Journal of Finance* (forthcoming, 1996).

Strickland, D.; K. Wiles; and M. Zenner. "A Requiem for the USA: Is Small Shareholder Monitoring Effective?" *Journal of Financial Economics* (forthcoming, 1996).

Van Nuys, K. "Corporate Governance through the Proxy Process: Evidence from the 1989 Honeywell Proxy Solicitation." *Journal of Financial Economics,* 34 (Aug. 1993), 101–132.

Wahal, S.; K. Wiles; and M. Zenner. "Who Opts Out of State Antitakeover Protection? The Case Of Pennsylvania's SB 1310." *Financial Management,* 24-3 (Autumn 1995), 22–39.

White, H. "A Heteroskedasticity-Consistent Covariance Matrix Estimator and a Direct Test for Heteroskedasticity." *Econometrica,* 48 (June 1980), 817–838.

[8]

ELSEVIER   Journal of Corporate Finance 6 (2000) 71–110

Journal of
CORPORATE
FINANCE

www.elsevier.com/locate/econbase

Do occupational pension funds monitor companies in which they hold large stakes?

Mara Faccio [a,b,1], M. Ameziane Lasfer [b,*]

[a] *Università Cattolica del Sacro Cuore, Largo Gemelli, 1, 20123 Milan, Italy*
[b] *Centre for Empirical Research in Finance and Accounting, City University Business School, Barbican Centre, Frobisher Crescent, London EC2Y 8HB, UK*

Received 1 September 1998; accepted 1 October 1999

Abstract

In this paper we analyze the monitoring role of occupational pension funds in the UK. We argue that because of their objectives, structure and overall share holding, occupational pension funds are likely to have more incentives to monitor companies in which they hold large stakes than other financial institutions. By comparing companies in which these funds hold large stakes with a control group of companies listed on the London Stock Exchange, we show that occupational pension funds hold large stakes over a long-time period mainly in small companies. However, the value added by these funds is negligible and their holdings do not lead companies to comply with the Code of Best Practice or outperform their industry counterparts. Overall, our results suggest that occupational pension funds are not effective monitors. © 2000 Elsevier Science B.V. All rights reserved.

JEL classification: G30; G32; G35
Keywords: Corporate governance; Pension funds; Board structure; Performance

---

* Corresponding author. Tel.: +44-0-171-477-8634; fax: +44-0-171-477-8648; e-mail: m.a.lasfer@city.ac.uk
[1] Tel.: +39-02-7234-2436; e-mail: m.faccio@iol.it.

72   *M. Faccio, M.A. Lasfer / Journal of Corporate Finance 6 (2000) 71–110*

1. Introduction

It is now widely recognized that companies have to set a number of mechanisms to control the agency problems, which arise whenever managers have incentives to pursue their own interests at the expense of those of shareholders. In an extensive survey of corporate governance, Shleifer and Vishny (1997) show that legal protection alone is not sufficient to ensure investor protection and that other mechanisms, such as ownership concentration, could be the solution to these, so called, agency problems. However, the empirical evidence provided to date on the role and effectiveness of such alternative mechanisms is mixed. For example, Demsetz and Lehn (1985) find no cross-sectional relationship between the concentration of shareholdings and the accounting rates of return. Similarly, Agrawal and Knoeber (1996) show that the relationship between large institutional shareholding or blockholding and corporate performance as measured by Tobins Q is weak. [2] In contrast, other studies show that large shareholders play a significant role in top management turnover (e.g., Franks and Mayer, 1994; Kaplan and Minton, 1994; Kang and Shivdasani, 1995), in take-overs (Shleifer and Vishny, 1986; Agrawal and Mandelker, 1990; Sudarsanam, 1996), in the certification of initial public offerings (Lin, 1996) and that block purchases by large shareholders are typically followed by an increase in value, in top management turnover, in financial performance and in asset sales (e.g., Mikkelson and Ruback, 1985; Shome and Singh, 1995; Bethel et al., 1998). Other studies that specifically analyze shareholder activism also yield mixed results. [3] For example, while Strickland et al. (1996) show that monitoring by shareholders enhances firm value, Karpoff et al. (1996) do not find evidence that shareholder proposals increase firm value or influence firm policies.

The purpose of this paper is to extend previous research that documents the impact of large holdings on corporate performance by analyzing the monitoring role of occupational pension funds in the UK. We identify separately these funds from other financial intermediaries because of the large dimension of their overall stakes in the UK market, the particular structure of their portfolios and their investment objectives. As defined by Brickley et al. (1988; 1994), occupational pension funds are typical pressure-resistant institutions as opposed to other institutions, such as banks, investment and unit trusts and insurance companies, which are pressure-sensitive. Unlike previous studies (e.g., Strickland et al., 1996; Bethel et al., 1998) we do not analyze block purchases because of event date uncertainty and we do not concentrate on formal targeting by pension funds because we could

---

[2] Other studies suggest that the relationship between ownership, such as the fraction of shares held by insiders and performance is not linear but roof-shaped (e.g., Morck et al., 1988; Stulz, 1988; McConnell and Servaes, 1990).

[3] See Black (1998) and Karpoff (1998) for a survey of the shareholder activism literature.

M. Faccio, M.A. Lasfer / Journal of Corporate Finance 6 (2000) 71–110   73

not find any event where occupational pension funds in the UK target companies, i.e., make particular proposals at the company's annual meetings or negotiate privately some corporate governance issues (as in Carleton et al., 1998). Instead, we compare firms in which occupational pension funds hold large stakes against a control group of companies listed on the London Stock Exchange and test the hypotheses that monitoring increases with ownership concentration and, as a result, these funds reduce agency conflicts and lead companies to better performance.

Further research in this area is warranted for a number of reasons. First, the issue of involvement of pension funds in the running of companies is controversial. The popular belief is that pension funds are short-termists and impose their views on companies in which they invest. In particular, given their tax-exempt status, UK pension funds are criticized for making companies pay high cash dividends that could be used to finance growth opportunities (e.g., Hutton, 1995). [4] In contrast, other studies show that pension funds do not get involved in corporate monitoring because they find it easier and cheaper to sell their holdings, they do not want to sit on the board for fear of getting price sensitive information or because of the agency problems within the funds themselves. [5] At the same time, policy makers in the UK tend to rely on these institutions to promote corporate governance (e.g., Cadbury, 1992; Greenbury, 1995). [6] Second, previous studies were mainly undertaken under the US framework. Franks and Mayer (1997) show that, despite the fact that the US and the UK governance systems are both market-based, the two countries differ in two major respects: the US has more quoted companies than the UK and, while the largest category of shareholders in the UK is pension funds, most of the equity in the US is held by individuals (if each different type of institutional shareholder is treated as a different category). In addition, unlike US pension funds where investments and activism programs are

---

[4] Hutton (1995) argues that "pension funds...have become classic absentee landlords, exerting power without responsibility and making exacting demands upon companies without recognizing their reciprocal obligations as owners" (p. 304).

[5] For example, Drucker (1976) stipulates that "pension funds are not 'owners', they are investors. They do not want control...If they do not like a company or its management, their duty is to sell the stock" (p. 82). More recently, Porter (1997) argues that institutional investors, despite their substantial aggregate holdings, do not sit on corporate boards and have virtually no real influence on managements behavior because they invest nearly all their assets in index funds rather than directly in companies. Short and Keasey (1997) suggest that once pension funds are locked in, it is costly to get involved in monitoring and they cannot exit in case they are considered to trade on insider information. Murphy and Van Nuys (1994) argue that pension funds are run by individuals who do not have the proper incentives to maximize fund value.

[6] Cadbury (1992) notes that "Because of their collective stake, we look to the institutions in particular, with the backing on Institutional Shareholders' Committee, to use their influence as owners to ensure that the companies in which they have invested comply with the Code" (para. 6.16). The National Associate of Pension Funds also endorses such recommendations (NAPF, 1996b).

74   *M. Faccio, M.A. Lasfer / Journal of Corporate Finance 6 (2000) 71–110*

developed and implemented by fund staff then overseen and approved by trustees (Del Guercio and Hawkins, 1999), the UK pension funds, despite the size of their holdings, are not known for their monitoring and hardly vote at the annual general meetings (NAPF, 1996b; Financial Times, 1999). Thus, the testing of the empirical hypotheses in a pension fund dominated market such as the UK where corporate governance issues are debated and companies suffer from the same free cash flow problems as their US counterparts, will strengthen the evidence provided to-date. [7] Third, since our analysis is centered on pension funds that are tax exempt and hold large stakes, the evidence we provide should be of relevance to tax and market regulators and to policy makers involved in the growth of the UK economy.

We construct from the financial statements of all UK quoted non-financial companies a test sample of companies in which pension funds hold more than 3% of the issued share capital and a control sample by matching our test firms by industry and size. [8] We find that pension funds hold large stakes in 289 out of 1640 (18%) companies. These holdings are mainly in small companies and they did not change significantly over the 1992–1996 sample period. We show that our test companies are not more likely to restrain management compensation and/or adopt the Code of Best Practice, i.e., split the roles of chairman and CEO, have more non-executive directors and/or narrow the size of their board than our control firms. These results are not consistent with the recommendations of Cadbury (1992) and Greenbury (1995). In addition, we find that our test companies are not more profitable and do not pay higher dividends than the control firms despite the tax credit pension funds could claim during the sample period. We report weak and even negative relationship between occupational pension funds blockholdings and firm value, and, over a longer time period, our test firms do not overperform their peers. Our overall results are consistent with previous US evidence (e.g., Romano, 1994 and Wahal, 1996) and cast doubt on the effectiveness of UK occupational pension funds' monitoring role. At the same time, our results provide support to the proposition of Coffee (1991) and imply that pension funds do not follow an 'exit' policy which is increasingly more expensive because they must accept substantial discounts in order to liquidate their holdings. Thus, once "locked in", occupational pension funds avoid costly monitoring and refrain

---

[7] A number of studies document the free cash flow problem in the UK. For example, Franks and Mayer (1994) find that UK companies pay high dividends relative to German companies; Lasfer (1995) shows that debt mitigates the free cash flow problem; Lasfer (1997) provides evidence that firms with free cash flow problems pay scrip, rather than cash, dividends. The reports of Cadbury (1992) and Greenbury (1995) are a manifestation of the previous debate on the various wider corporate governance issues detailed in Charkham (1995), Stapledon (1996) and Keasey et al. (1997).

[8] Companies Act 1995, Sections 198 and 199 requires UK companies to disclose in their accounts the name of any investor who holds 3% or more of the issued share capital.

from selling their large stake for fear of losing from large discounts and/or conveying information to the market.

The rest of the paper is structured as follows. Section 2 presents the theoretical background. Section 3 describes the data. Section 4 presents the results. Conclusions are in Section 5.

2. Theoretical framework

In recent years, more than a third of all listed equities in the UK are held by pension funds. A large proportion of these holdings is concentrated in the portfolios of large funds. In this section we review the literature on the role of large shareholders, discuss the literature on pension funds activism, and analyze the structure of the UK occupational pension funds, the importance of equities in their portfolios, the relatively high concentration of their industry and the management approaches and objectives.

2.1. Review of the literature

Corporate governance deals with how companies are managed in the long-term interest of their shareholders. The literature has identified two main corporate governance systems that predominate in the developed economies: the *market-based* systems of the UK and the US characterized by liquid markets and unconcentrated company ownership, and the relationship-based systems of Japan and Germany where ownership is concentrated and markets are relatively illiquid. [9] The issue, although not trivial, has been considered in the literature only recently when agency theorists argue that public corporations suffer from excessive costs as managers pursue their own interests rather than the interests of shareholders (e.g., Jensen, 1986). As a result, there is a need for setting up mechanisms to make managers maximize shareholder wealth. These mechanisms include shareholding of managers, intermediaries and large blockholders (McConnell and Servaes, 1990; Morck et al., 1988), outside directors (Cotter et al., 1997), debt policy (Lasfer, 1995; McConnell and Servaes, 1995; Lang et al., 1996), the market for corporate control and incentive contracts (Hart and Holmstrom, 1987; Hart, 1995), large intermediaries (Diamond, 1984; Admati et al., 1994), and long-term relationships (Ayres and Cramton, 1993).

In theory, Diamond (1984) suggests that a large intermediary can represent a better solution to agency conflicts because of economies of scale and diversification. Admati et al. (1994) argue that when monitoring is costly, the intermediary will monitor only if this will result in a modification in firm's payoff structure and

---

[9] See Chew (1997) for a collection of papers dealing with these two corporate governance systems.

76   *M. Faccio, M.A. Lasfer / Journal of Corporate Finance 6 (2000) 71–110*

lead to net gains. When the intermediary does not hold all the firm's equity and the transaction costs are not excessive, the level of commitment will be sub-optimal even when optimal risk-sharing is attained. Maug (1998) extends this analysis and argues that liquid markets reduce large shareholders incentive to monitor because they can sell their holdings easily, but such markets make corporate governance more effective as it is cheaper and easier to acquire and hold large stakes. Kahn and Winton (1998) distinguish between liquidity, speculation and intervention and argue that intervention is a function of the size of the institution's stake, firm specific factors and institution's trading profit. Shleifer and Vishny (1997) and Agrawal and Knoeber (1996) suggest that large investors, because of the relevance of the resources invested, have all the interest and the power to monitor and promote better governance of companies.

Previous empirical studies show that institutions behave differently from individuals in sponsoring initiatives (Jarrell and Poulsen, 1987; Karpoff et al., 1996) and that the institutional behavior is not homogeneous as it depends on the sensitivity to managerial pressure (Brickley et al., 1988; Gordon and Pound, 1993). However, they disagree on the effectiveness of shareholder activism. [10] In particular, Wahal (1996) and Karpoff et al. (1996) find little evidence that operating performance of companies that are the target of pension funds proposals improves. These results are consistent, among other things, with the arguments of Murphy and Van Nuys (1994) and Romano (1994) that pension funds are not effective monitors because of the agency problems within the funds themselves. In contrast, Nesbitt (1994) and Smith (1996) find that companies targeted by large pension funds, such as CalPERS, increase significantly their performance. More recently, Del Guercio and Hawkins (1999) show that the monitoring effectiveness depends on the investment strategies of pension funds. They find that, unlike proposals sponsored by externally-managed funds, those made by internally managed funds are not associated with general increases in governance-related events at target firms. Other studies that looked at the characteristics of companies in which institutions hold large stakes find that the relationship between such holdings and firm value or accounting rates of return is weak (e.g., Demsetz and Lehn, 1985; Agrawal and Knoeber, 1996).

In sum, the primarily US-based studies provide mixed results on the monitoring role of pension funds. The testing of these hypotheses under a different institutional framework is, thus, warranted.

2.2. Institutional settings

In this section we describe the pension funds industry and the corporate governance system in the UK and set up the hypotheses.

---

[10] See Black (1998) and Karpoff (1998) for a survey.

2.2.1. The UK pension fund system

The UK pension fund system includes, in addition to the public pension scheme, occupational pension schemes, which are organized and sponsored by employers, and individual pension schemes offered by financial institutions. The occupational pension schemes are usually defined-benefits (DB) where the amount of benefits relates to the final salary of the member while individual pension schemes are defined-contribution (DC) where pension benefits depend on the contributions paid during the working life of the members and the returns realized on the investment (Blake, 1995). This difference has significant implications on these two schemes' investment policies. With defined contribution plans, individuals bear the investment risk and require a more cautious investment strategy. As a result, the proportion of shares relative to total assets of occupational pension schemes ranges between 70% and 80% while defined contribution pension plans usually hold no more than 25–30% of shares (NAPF, 1996b). In 1997 the overall value of individual pension schemes assets was £190 billion (ABI, 1998) while occupational pension funds assets (including insured schemes) reached £635 billion. [11]

The proportion of UK pension funds assets invested in equities is the highest amongst OECD countries (Davis, 1995). For example, in 1993, 78% of assets were invested in equities, 12% in fixed income securities and the remaining in cash and property (Business Monitor, 1997). This trend is likely to reflect the overall investments of all pension funds as Blake (1995) shows that asset structure is not significantly associated with the size of pension funds assets. The preference of equities over fixed income securities can be related to the tax-exempt status of pension funds who, like charities, are not subject to capital gains tax and claim back the tax credit, referred to as the advanced corporation tax, when they receive dividends. Lasfer (1996) shows that this tax credit discriminates in favor of dividends relative to capital gains.

In contrast, US pension funds invest a lower proportion of their assets in equities. For example, in 1990, out of the total assets of $2,491 billion, 38.6% are invested in equities (Charkham, 1995). Davis (1995) shows that the proportion of assets invested in equities has not changed over the 1970–1990 period. However, these investments are not evenly distributed but concentrated mainly in large firms (Charkham, 1995; Stapledon, 1996; Brancato, 1997).

In managing these assets, the UK pension funds are subject to trust law and implicitly follow the prudent-man concept. There is no explicit prudent-man rule and the pension trust law is very flexible. However, the duty of prudence to

---

[11] Similarly, in the US, the value of DC plans in 1993 was $1068 billion compared to $1248 billion for DB plans. However, DC schemes are growing at much faster rates of 19% per year, compared to 14% for DB plans (Jepson, 1998).

78   *M. Faccio, M.A. Lasfer / Journal of Corporate Finance 6 (2000) 71–110*

trustees can be interpreted as requiring the pension funds money to be invested for the sole benefit of the beneficiaries. The recent legislation for pension fund management (e.g., the 1995 Pension Fund Act) is similar to the American Employee Retirement Scheme Act with a basic view towards prudence. The legal barriers against institutional activism are weaker in the UK because active shareholders that hold a "block of shares" are not subject to any filing require-ments, such as the 13D Form with the SEC in the US, and they cannot be sued for breaching any duty of disclosure of their plans or proposals. This rule applies in the US to shareholders who act together (e.g., in the case of co-ordinated activism), and to investors who, *individually* or *jointly* hold 5% or more of a firm's equity (Black, 1998). Moreover, unlike in the US, UK pension funds have no legal duty to vote.

The pension fund industry is highly concentrated. For example, in 1994, the largest five in-house managed occupational pension funds managed assets worth £65.8 billion, 14.8% of all occupational pension funds assets (NAPF, 1996a) and British Telecommunications, accounted for £17.2 billion. The largest 68 schemes, whose assets value exceeds £1 billion in 1995, accounted for 57.3% of all occupational pension funds assets (Pension Funds and their Advisers, 1996). The industry of fund managers is also highly concentrated. At the end of 1996, the top 20 segregated fund managers managed assets worth £285.7 billion on behalf of occupational pension funds and, as a whole, managed assets of some £1029.2 billion (Financial Times, 1997a).

Over the last three decades, the aggregate share ownership in the UK has changed substantially. While in 1963 individuals were the main shareholders with 58.7% of all UK listed equities and pension funds held only 7%, by 1993 pension funds stakes increased to 34.7% (London Stock Exchange, 1995). In contrast, in the US, individuals held 50% in 1990 followed by pension funds with 20.1%, increasing to 25.4% in 1995 (Prowse, 1994; Brancato, 1997).

We use our sample firms (detailed below) to analyze further the ownership structure of UK companies. The results, reported in Fig. 1, show that managers and block shareholders (including occupational pension funds) own 53% of equity, implying a rather concentrated ownership structure. However, within these blocks, no single class of shareholders clearly dominates the others. Financial blockhold-ers account for 62% of block shareholdings by holding 24% of our firms' equity, while the remaining 38% are attributable to individuals and families, non-financial companies, public authorities, foreign investors and nominees. Internally managed occupational pension funds account for 14% of all financial blockholdings as they hold an average of 3% of equity. Externally managed occupational pension funds account for 9% by holding 2% of equity. The assets managed by external pension fund managers on behalf of clients other than pension funds represent 28% of these stakes, i.e., 7% of equity. Finally, all other financial institutions (including merchant banks, insurance companies, unit and investment trusts) wholly account for 48% of institutional holdings as they hold about 12% of equity.

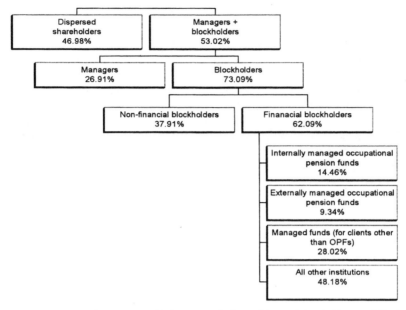

Fig. 1. Structure of block share ownership in our sample firms. *Dispersed shareholders* are defined as those owners who individually own less than 3% of ordinary shares, excluding managers. *Blockholders* are owners who individually own at least 3% of ordinary shares (excluding managers). *Non-institutional blockholdings* are block shareholdings attributable to individuals and families, non-financial companies, public bodies, foreign investors and nominees. *Institutional blockholdings* refer to block shareholdings held by financial institutions. *Internally managed occupational pension funds* are those pension funds whose assets are, wholly or in part, managed directly by the fund's trustees. *Externally managed pension funds* holdings refer to block shareholdings attributable to the largest 20 segregated pension fund managers, times the incidence of pension fund assets to the total asset managed by the segregated fund. *Managed funds (for clients other than OPFs)* refer to the residual proportion of block shareholdings managed by the top 20 segregated pension fund managers, once accounted for the assets managed on behalf of occupational pension funds (previous variable). Finally, *all other institutional holdings* are computed as residual item, and refer to block shareholdings held by merchant banks, unit and investment trusts, insurance companies, venture capital firms, and all other financial institutions. All percentages reported are computed assuming the relative upper line to be equal to 100%.

2.2.2. The UK corporate governance system

The importance of corporate governance in the UK has been emphasized by recent concerns about the way in which remuneration packages for senior executives have been determined, the spectacular collapse of a number of large companies and by the fraudulent use of the pension fund of Mirror Group Newspapers to finance an illegal scheme for supporting the share price of Maxwell Communications Corporation. These cases have highlighted instances where directors do not act in the best interest of shareholders.

80   *M. Faccio, M.A. Lasfer / Journal of Corporate Finance 6 (2000) 71–110*

In the train of these and other scandals, the Committee on the Financial Aspects of Corporate Governance (referred to as the Cadbury Committee after its chairman) was set up to look at the changes needed in corporate governance in the UK and published a report in December 1992 (Cadbury, 1992). The report is similar to the Statement on Corporate Governance released in September 1997 in the US by the Business Roundtable, an association of CEOs of large companies. At the heart of the report is the Code of Best Practice which details the role and composition of the board of directors, the appointment of non-executive directors, the disclosure of the remuneration of executive directors and the renewal of their contracts, and the way companies should report and audit their accounts. The main recommendation is that the offices of the chairman and the chief executive officer should be separated to prevent excessive concentration of power in boardrooms and that companies should appoint independent non-executive directors with high caliber so that their views will carry weight in board discussions. [12] The code defines the various roles non-executive directors should play. For example, they are to be in a majority on the nominating committee which is responsible for making recommendations for board membership, they should be the sole or majority members of the remuneration committee which makes recommendations to the board on the pay of executive directors, and of the audit committee whose function is to advise on the appointment of auditors, to insure the integrity of the company's financial statements and to discuss with the auditors any problems arising during the course of the audit. [13]

The report has also highlighted the responsibilities of institutional investors such as pension funds and suggests that such institutions should be encouraged to make greater use of their voting rights and to seek contacts with companies at a senior executive level. In particular, they should monitor boards where there is a concentration of power in the hands of the chief executive, seek to promote the influence of non-executive directors and they are expected to bring about changes in underperforming companies rather than dispose of their shares. Although the report recognizes that closer relations with managers can result in these investors gaining price sensitive information which makes them insiders, it does not go so far as to recommend the formation of shareholders' committees and the participation of shareholders in the appointment of directors and auditors.

This emphasis on institutions is driven by the size of their holdings but also by the fact that these institutions, such as pension funds, do not target companies and

---

[12] The report states that no "one individual has unfetted powers of decision. Where the chairman is also chief executive, it is essential that there should be a strong and independent element on the board, with a recognised senior member".

[13] The Code of Best Practice No 4.3 recommended an audit committee of at least three non-executive directors with written terms of reference and No 4.30 recommends the institution of a nomination committee as an internal committee within the board. This committee should be composed of majority of non-executive directors and chaired by the chairman of the board.

they rarely caste their vote at the annual general meetings, making them the object of public criticism (e.g., Mallin, 1997). This passive stance has not changed even after the advent of the Cadbury Report. More recently, commenting on the first major corporate governance action by pension funds, namely the ousting of the head of Mirror Group, a media company which has underperformed the market by 34% over the last 5 years, the Financial Times (1999) wrote:

> Unlike in the US, investor mutinies in Britain are still a relatively rare event. Complacency, reflected in the dismal attendance at annual general meetings, is the norm. This state of affairs has its critics. The Treasury, for example, has let it be known that it regards funds managers as a breed of idle ''fat cats'' who are partly to blame for the nations economic ills.

The main reservation of the code centers on the issue of compliance and enforcement. The corporate governance system in the UK has traditionally stressed the importance of internal controls and the importance of financial reporting and accountability as opposed to a large amount of external legislation. In this spirit, the Code of Best Practice is voluntary and lacks effective sanctions. Nevertheless, as a continuing obligation of listing, the London Stock Exchange requires all companies registered in the UK to state, after June 1993, whether they are complying with the code and to give reasons for any areas of non-compliance.

2.2.3. Pension fund management style and corporate monitoring

Del Guercio and Hawkins (1999) show that the level of monitoring by pension funds depends significantly on the way their assets are managed. In the UK pension funds assets can be managed in three different ways: self-managed, externally managed and insured. Within self-managed schemes, the trustees of the scheme define asset allocation, portfolio selection policies and directly invest pension fund assets. Within externally managed schemes, the investment power is wholly or in part delegated to one or few external managers. In the case of insured schemes, the funds are invested in insurance policies or managed through fund contracts taken out with an insurance company.

We expect internally managed occupational pension funds to have a stronger incentive to monitor than externally managed pension funds for a number of reasons. First, internally managed pension funds are larger than externally-managed and insured schemes (e.g., Minns, 1980; Blake, 1995; NAPF, 1996a). In addition, Stapledon (1996) reports that many large companies managed internally their pension schemes in the early 1990s. For example, in 1993, 14% of occupational pension schemes were managed wholly internally but these account for some 38% of the total assets invested. [14] Thus, following the arguments of Admati et al. (1994) and Diamond (1984), we would expect internally managed occupational

---

[14] The 99 in-house managed pension funds included in our study manage assets for some £150 billion, which correspond to 26.8% of all occupational pension funds' assets.

82   *M. Faccio, M.A. Lasfer / Journal of Corporate Finance 6 (2000) 71–110*

pension funds to be more active in corporate monitoring because of their size and the magnitude of their holdings. Their size and expertise minimize the monitoring costs. They are likely to understand when activism is necessary and they are large enough to make monitoring effective. Their large holdings are expected to alleviate the free-rider problem that makes atomistic shareholders' action non-rational and inefficient.

Second, internally managed occupational pension funds are expected to monitor companies in which they hold large stakes because they control directly or indirectly the investment and the voting decisions. Their objective is likely to maximize the value of funds in order to minimize the company's contributions and, possibly, use any pension fund surplus to inflate company's profits (Short and Keasey, 1997). In contrast, funds that delegate their investment functions to external managers effectively disconnect their activism efforts from their investment actions (Del Guercio and Hawkins, 1999). As a result, given that they will not be able to trade profitably on any private information that results from their activism, they are not likely to monitor or to publicize their activism efforts. The level of monitoring role of externally managed pension funds will depend on the content of the contract with the trustees and the level of competition among fund managers. Given that we do not have data on these contracts and on the investments made on behalf of pension funds, we cannot expect all externally managed funds to monitor.

Internally managed occupational pension funds may not monitor individual companies if they find it easier to sell, if they do not want to gain access to price sensitive information or if they themselves are subject to agency problems. In addition, given that these funds are defined benefits schemes, they are likely to be indexed and passive to minimize their management risk, transaction costs and to fit the needs of long-term pension investors (Tomlinson, 1998). Del Guercio and Hawkins (1999) argue that such passive management style will lead pension funds to monitor by promoting spill-over effects that boost the performance of the stock market overall rather than specific stocks. In our analysis we focus on internally-managed pension funds to test whether size and passive management styles define the level of monitoring activity but we control also for the monitoring roles of external pension funds and other blockholders.

The monitoring activity can take the form of selecting the board structure and/or improving performance. The monitoring of the board relates to the size of the board and its composition so that it becomes more accountable to the shareholders (Cadbury, 1992). [15] Jensen (1993) argues that as the size of the board

---

[15] The report summarizes the functions of the board as follows: "The responsibilities of the board include setting up the companys strategic aims, providing the leadership to put them into effect, supervising the management of the business and reporting to shareholders on their stewardship". As to the financial aspects of corporate governance, the report mentions: "The way in which boards set financial policy and oversee its implementation, including the use of financial controls, and the process whereby they report on the activities and progress of the company to the shareholders".

increases, its ability to control management decreases and the communication and co-ordination problems increase. Consistent with this proposition, Yermack (1996) and Eisenberg et al. (1998) find a negative correlation between board size and firm performance. Thus, if occupational pension funds are effective monitors, they are expected to mitigate this agency conflict by restricting the size of the board. At the same time, they will lead companies to adopt the Code of Best Practice defined by Cadbury (1992), i.e., to split the roles of chairman and chief executive officer, to have a high proportion of non-executive directors and to restrain executive pay. [16]

The monitoring of firm performance implies that companies in which occupational pension funds hold large stakes have a higher value than widely held companies and/or companies held by other blockholders. This level of monitoring is a function of the size of the pension funds and the relative importance of the amount of assets invested in these companies. We expect large pension funds and those with significant commitments to have a higher incentive to monitor companies in which they hold large stakes. In the long run, companies in which occupational pension fund carry on holding large stakes are expected to outperform their industry counterparts.

3. Sample construction and definition of proxy variables

We search all the 1640 non-financial companies quoted in the London Stock Exchange in 1995–1996 for those where occupational pension funds hold large stakes. We exclude financial companies because of the specificity of some of their ratios such as leverage, which cannot be related to the level of their risk and/or resolution of their agency conflicts. To avoid survivorship bias, our sample includes all companies for which the relevant data is available even if they are currently extinct. [17]

We started by gathering information on shareholding by category from the annual reports but we find that only a handful of companies disclose this information in their Analysis of Ordinary Shareholdings section of their accounts. This data would have been ideal but it would have given us only the aggregate holding of pension funds without distinguishing between funds that are internally managed from those that are externally managed. Instead, we rely on any

---

[16] See John and Senbet (1998) for an extensive survey of the monitoring role of corporate board of directors and Stapledon (1996, pp. 138–153), for the monitoring role of non-executive directors.

[17] The choice of 1995–1996 sample period is driven by data availability. The data on shareholding is inserted manually because Extel Financial provides only the latest data on shareholding in text format and this data is not available in machine-readable form. Other similar studies use also short time period (see Karpoff, 1998, for a review). We report below that the vast majority of companies (83% of our test firms) had large pension funds holdings in both 1992 and 1996 periods and the magnitude of their holdings has not changed significantly. Thus, our results are not likely to be sample-period dependent.

disclosed holding above 3% threshold in the accounts and reported in Extel Financial [18] and define these as occupational pension funds holdings or blockholders. All the holdings of directors are disclosed even if they are zero (Company Act 1985). Although this cut off point of 3% is constraining, it is the only data available. We, nevertheless, posit that the holding of 3% or above is significant to warrant monitoring and to allow us to test directly the Diamond (1984) and Admati et al. (1994) propositions. We searched for the keywords *pension, pension funds, retirement, superannuation and superannuation schemes* and for known pension funds, such as Hermes, to define the holdings of occupational pension funds. We identified 289 individual companies (18% of our total sample) with at least one occupational pension fund holding above 3%, and 356 large stakes held by 99 individual occupational pension funds. We split the other major disclosed holdings (other than managerial holdings) into externally managed pension funds, institutional and non-institutional blockholding depending on the identity of the shareholders. We compare the performance of our test firms against all other remaining companies and against a control group of companies with similar size and industry characteristics. We collect all the relevant accounting and financial data from Extel Financial and from each company's accounts.

Table 1 reports the proxy variables used to test our hypotheses. We use five definitions of pension fund holdings: (i) the first largest stake held by pension funds, LPF; (ii) the sum of all pension fund holdings, TPF, to analyze pension funds' individual and collective monitoring roles; (iii) the pension fund incidence, IPF, the ratio of pension fund investment in our test sample over their total assets to assess the magnitude of such investment in their portfolio; [19] (iv) the number of occupational pension funds in our test firms, NPF, and (v) the logged value of the largest pension fund's asset, LNPFA. Directors' ownership, Dir, is used to control for the managerial entrenchment hypothesis. [20] Any other large stake, Block, is used to control for the monitoring role of blockholders. This variable is split into institutional block shareholdings, IBlock, which includes all financial institutions' stakes (excluding internally- and externally-managed occupational pension funds' stakes), externally-managed pension funds, EPFM, i.e., the stakes held by the largest 20 external pension fund managers (either on behalf of occupational

---

[18] Extel Financial is a financial database microsystem. The database provides accounting as well as financial and reference data for all UK companies and many international companies.

[19] The ideal would be to exclude from the denominator of this ration other assets such as property, cash and fixed income securities, but the desegregated data on equity investment is not available.

[20] This variable includes directors holdings but excludes those of officers. UK quoted companies are required to disclose in their financial statements the proportion of shares held directly and indirectly by executive and non-executive directors (Companies Act 1985). However, no similar disclosure applies to officers. This legal disclosure requirement means that we had to define managerial ownership as ownership by members of the board of directors. Although this definition is consistent with that of Morck et al. (1988), it differs from that of McConnell and Servaes (1990) and Denis and Sarin (1999) as we do not include shares owned by corporate officers not members of the board.

Table 1

Description of proxy variables. Expected signs (E_{sign}) are for the Logit regressions

Variables	Definition	Proxying for (Hypotheses)	E_{sign}
LPF	Proportion of outstanding equity owned by largest occupational pension funds	Pension fund commitment to monitoring	+
TPF	The proportion of outstanding equity owned by all occupational pension funds	Pension fund commitment to monitoring	+
IPF	Occupational pension funds' holdings in test companies relative to their assets	Pension fund commitment to monitoring	+
NPF	Number of occupational pension funds holding large stakes in our test companies	Pension fund commitment to monitoring	+
LNPFA	Log of the asset value of the pension fund with the largest stake	Pension fund commitment to monitoring	+
Dir	Proportion of outstanding equity owned by directors	Management entrenchment	−
Block	Proportion of outstanding equity owned by other large shareholders	Blockholders' incentive to monitor	+
EPFM	Proportion of outstanding equity owned by the top 20 external fund managers	External managers' incentive to monitor	+
IBlock	Proportion of outstanding equity owned by financial institutions, other than internally and externally managed pension funds	Incentive to monitor by other financial companies	+
NIBlock	Proportion of outstanding equity owned by non-financial shareholders	Blockholders' incentive to monitor	+
Q	Market value of equity *plus* book value of debt over total assets	Firm value	+
M/B	Market value of equity over shareholders' funds	Firm value	+
M/S	Market value of equity *plus* book value of debt over sales	Firm value	+
P/E	Year-end share price over earnings per share	Growth opportunities	+
ROA	Profit before interest and tax over total assets	Firm performance	+
ROE	Earnings over shareholders' funds	Firm performance	+
ROS	Profit before interest and tax over sales	Firm performance	+
$R_{i,t-12\ to\ t}$	1-year share price return, adjusted for stock issues and dividends	Firm size	+
ME	Market value of equity at balance sheet date	Firm size	+
TA	Total assets	Firm size	+
Mlev	Long-term debt over long-term debt *plus* market value of equity	Monitoring role of debtholders	−
Blev	Long-term debt over long-term debt *plus* shareholders' funds	Monitoring role of debtholders	−
Dir rem./Sal	Directors' monetary pay (excl. options) over sales	Monitoring directors' pay	−
Nechair	Dummy = 1 if the role of Chairman is attributed to a non-executive director	Monitoring board composition	+
Split	Dummy = 1 if the role of Chairman is split from that of CEO	Monitoring board composition	+
#DIR	Number of directors (both executives and non-executives)	Monitoring board size	+
%NED	Proportion of non-executive directors	Monitoring board composition	+
Payout	Ordinary dividends over earnings	Monitoring of dividends	+

86   M. Faccio, M.A. Lasfer / Journal of Corporate Finance 6 (2000) 71–110

pension funds and other clients), and NIBlock, the holdings of individuals and families, non-financial companies, public bodies, foreign investors and nominees. [21]

As in Agrawal and Knoeber (1996), we compute Tobin's Q as the ratio of market value of equity *plus* book value of debt over total assets to measure firm value. The results are simulated using other measures of firm value such as market-to-book, M/B, and market-to-sales, M/S, ratios (Lins and Servaes, 1999). These variables are, however, ambiguous measures of value-added by pension funds investments, since they can also capture the value of future investment opportunities. As in Yermack (1996), we control for growth opportunities by using P/E ratio. In addition, we use various accounting rates of returns and a one year share price return, $R_{i,\,t-12\,\text{to}\,t}$, to measure performance and market value of equity, ME, or total assets, TA, to control for size. We follow previous literature (e.g., Lang et al., 1996) and use both the market value of leverage, Mlev, defined as long-term debt over market value of equity *plus* long-term debt, and the book value of leverage, Blev, defined as long-term debt over shareholders funds *plus* long-term debt, to test for the monitoring role of debtholders. We use Split (a dummy variable equal to 1 if the role of chairman and CEO are differentiated), Nechair (a dummy equal to 1 if the position of chairman is covered by a non-executive director), number of directors, #DIR, the proportion of non-executive directors in the board, %NED, and the relative remuneration of directors, Dir rem./Sal, to assess the pension fund role in monitoring board composition and compensation policy. Finally, payout ratio is used to test the hypothesis that pension funds prefer to invest in companies that pay high dividends.

4. Empirical results

4.1. Characteristics of occupation pension funds holdings

Table 2, Panel A, reports the distribution of companies with pension funds holdings. Out of 289 test companies, 175 (61%) reported an overall holding of

---

[21] Denis and Kruse (1999) and Denis and Sarin (1999) distinguish between unaffiliated and affiliated block shareholdings. Unaffiliated blockholders would be expected to perform an important monitoring role and make firms comply with the Code of Best Practice, while affiliated blockholders are more likely to be sensitive to managerial pressure or pursue goals other than share price maximization (Brickley et al., 1988, 1994). In this perspective, our internally managed occupational pension funds are clearly "unaffiliated shareholders". Since our data does not generally allow us to check for the intensity of the relationships between firms and shareholders, we consider together affiliated and unaffiliated shareholders in the category of blockholders. However, we distinguish between institutional and non-institutional blockholders, because these two categories of investors were shown to behave differently, i.e., when sponsoring initiatives (Jarrell and Poulsen, 1987; Karpoff et al., 1996).

M. Faccio, M.A. Lasfer / Journal of Corporate Finance 6 (2000) 71–110   87

Table 2

Distribution of pension funds holdings in test companies

The sample includes 289 test companies where occupational pension funds hold 3% or more of ordinary shares and 356 individual pension fund block shareholdings. LPF is the proportion of outstanding equity owned by largest occupational pension funds; TPF is the proportion of outstanding equity owned by all identified pension funds; IPF is the ratio of occupational pension funds holdings over their total assets; NPF is the number of occupational pension funds; EPFM is the proportion of shares owned by the largest 20 external pension fund managers, either on behalf of occupational pension funds or other clients; N_C is number of companies; and N_{Stakes} is for number of stakes; $N_{Pension\ funds}$ is the total number of pension funds.

(Panel A) Distribution of companies by total pension funds holdings ($N_C = 289$)

% holdings (TPF)	3–6%	6–10%	10–20%	+20%
Number of companies	175	70	36	8
% of total	60.6	24.2	12.5	2.8

(Panel B) Distribution of companies by number of pension funds' stakes ($N_C = 289$; $N_{Stakes} = 356$)

Number of pension funds' stakes (NPF)	1	2	3	4	5
Number of companies	238	40	8	1	2
% of total	82.3	13.8	2.8	0.3	1.0

(Panel C) Distribution of pension funds by number of stakes held ($N_{Stakes} = 356$; $N_{Pension\ funds} = 99$)

Number of stakes held	1	2–4	5–9	10–19	20–39	40+
Number of pension funds	68	18	4	4	3	2
% of total	68.7	18.2	4.0	4.0	3.0	2.0

(Panel D) Descriptive statistics of pension funds and block holdings %

	Mean	Median	Minimum	Maximum
LPF	6.01	4.70	3.00	56.90
TPF	6.96	5.06	3.00	56.90
NPF	1.23	1.00	1.00	5.00
IPF	0.15	0.03	0.01	14.75
EPFM	8.99	4.79	0.00	61.88

between 3% and 6%, and 70 (24%) had between 6 and 10%. Thus, more than 84% of our test companies have pension funds holdings between 3 and 10%. In 36 companies (12%) pension funds hold between 10% and 20% and in 8 companies (3%) the holdings exceed 20%. Although the pension fund deeds often set up upper limits of the proportion of shares that a fund is allowed to hold in an individual company, the law in force does not establish any limitations. The only limit is that a pension fund cannot invest more than 10% of its assets value in the sponsoring company's shares.

Table 2, Panel B, shows that 238 companies (82%) have only one pension fund interest; 40 companies (14%) have two relevant pension funds, 8 (3%) have three pension funds, 1 company had four pension funds and 2 reported five relevant pension funds holdings, a total of 356 stakes.

Table 2, Panel C, reports the distribution of the 99 pension funds that hold these 356 stakes. The vast majority of these funds hold a small number of stakes: 68 pension funds hold just one large stake, and 18 pension funds hold less than five large stakes. These 86 pension funds hold a total of 115 large stakes. Although not reported in the table, we find that the magnitude of the holdings is positively correlated with the size of individual occupational pension funds. The nine occupational pension funds that hold at least 10 large stakes, hold a total of 211 stakes (59% of our sample of stakes) and, with the exception of Mars Pension, the market value of their managed assets exceeds £4 billion. British Telecommunications-Post Office Pensions, the largest occupational pension fund in the UK, holds 53 stakes.

Table 2, Panel D, reports the descriptive statistics of occupational pension funds holdings and their incidence. On average, occupational pension funds hold individually 6% and collectively 6.96% of our test firms equities. Although these holdings range between 3 and 57%, the vast majority of our companies reported holdings of between 3 and 6% (Panel A). These holdings are relatively large comparing to those used in previous studies. For example, the average stake of institutional investors in target firms is 0.3% in Wahal (1996) and between 0.4% and 2.3% in Del Guercio and Hawkins (1999).

To assess the impact of these stakes on each individual pension fund assets, we compute Incidence on Pension Funds (IPF), the ratio of these investments over total assets of each pension fund. As stated above, the data on the portfolio of the assets managed is not available for all pension funds. The denominator of this ratio which includes other investments in fixed income securities, property, overseas equity and cash, is likely to be larger than pension fund equity investment. Thus, this ratio will understate the actual incidence level. [22] Keeping this drawback in mind, Table 2, Panel D shows that, on average, the investment of pension funds in our test companies represents 0.15% of their total assets, ranging between 0.01 to 14.75%. These proportions are larger than those reported by Del Guercio and Hawkins (1999) who show that pension funds holdings represent between 0.17 and 0.34% of their invested portfolio. However, given that, in our sample, 211 blocks out of 356 are held by only nine funds, the combination of the pension fund incidence statistics with this high concentration of holdings implies that the total, rather than the individual, incidence is likely to be high. In particular, the largest

---

[22] One possibility of overcoming this problem of lack of data of pension fund assets invested in UK equities would be to assume that all pension funds are homogeneous in their investment styles, i.e., the aggregate distribution of pension fund assets would apply to each fund. They would therefore hold an average of 53% of their assets in UK equities and the remaining 47% in fixed income securities, overseas equities, property and cash, as reported in NAPF (1996a). However, we consider that this assumption is not likely to hold as the average holding is not constant through time.

M. Faccio, M.A. Lasfer / Journal of Corporate Finance 6 (2000) 71–110   89

fund, British Telecommunications/Post Office pension fund, holds 53 large stakes, implying an average incidence of 7.95% (53 × 0.15%). Thus, while, the aggregate blocks may represent, individually, a small proportion of pension fund assets, for each pension fund the total stake may be substantial, suggesting that their monitoring role should be beneficial.

Overall, the results reported in Table 2 are striking and suggest that, despite their aggregate holdings, individually, internally-managed occupational pension funds hold large stakes in a small number of companies, most of these stakes are between 3 and 10%, the vast majority of our test firms report only one occupational pension fund holding and these holdings represent a relatively small proportion of pension funds' assets.

Table 2, Panel D, shows that external pension fund managers, EPFM, as a whole, hold, on average, 8.99% (median 4.79%) of our sample firms' equity, but these holdings are not statistically different from those of internally managed occupational pension funds (t-statistic of the difference in means = − 1.07). However, Financial Times (1997a) reports that only about 25% of these funds' assets are managed on behalf of occupational pension funds. This implies that the large stakes held by these external managers on behalf of occupational pension funds represent on average roughly 2.25% (8.99% ∗ 0.25) of firms' equity, assuming that these funds invest in the same way pension funds assets and other assets they manage. This suggests that the impact of these investors is likely to be marginal. Unfortunately, we do not have data on the way these stakes are allocated among the different clients, but we have included them in our analysis to assess the extent to which externally managed pension funds monitor companies.

In Table 3, Panel A and B, we report changes in the holdings of occupational pension funds in our test firms over the 1992–1996 period and the t-statistics of differences in means and medians. Data on pension fund stock ownership in 1992 is taken from the Hambros Company Guide and from the London Stock Exchange Yearbook, [23] since Extel Financial provides data only for the latest year. The table shows that 241 companies (83% of our test companies) reported large pension funds holdings in 1992 and 1996. On average, occupational pension funds held individually 6.21% of shares in 1992, 5.93% in 1995 and 6.09% in 1996. The difference in means and in median across these years is not statistically significant. We repeat the exercise using total pension fund holdings and number of pension funds and the results (not reported in Table 3) confirm that pension fund holding did not change over the 1992–1996 period. The results are consistent with WM

---

[23] Hambros Company Guide is a quarterly publication, which gives a summary financial data and shareholdings above 3% of UK companies. The Stock Exchange Yearbook is an annual publication of the London Stock Exchange. It provides a summary data of the activities, shareholdings and performance of UK listed companies.

Table 3
Annual changes in occupational pension fund holdings and list of occupational pension funds investing in their own companies

(Panel A) Distribution of occupational pension funds annual holdings

	Mean	Median	Minimum	Maximum
1992	6.21	5.00	3.00	41.6
1995	5.93	4.70	3.00	41.6
1996	6.09	4.60	3.00	56.9

(Panel B) t-statistics of annual differences in means and medians

	t-statistics of differences in means (p-value in parentheses)	Mann–Whitney p-value
1992 vs. 1995	− 0.80 (0.43)	0.193
1992 vs. 1996	− 0.32 (0.75)	0.149
1995 vs. 1996	− 0.44 (0.66)	0.844

(Panel C) The holdings of Pension fund in their parent company

Company	Proportion of equity held (%)
Ensor Holdings	4.70.
Eve group	4.48
Fuller, Smith and Turner	3.30
Garton Engineering	3.09
Gibbs and Dandy	10.86
Pension Trustees	
LPA Industries	4.82
Lucas Industries	6.11
MS International	10.90
Oliver Group	4.26
Rexmore	3.60
Walker, Thomas	5.11

(1996) findings and suggest that pension funds are long-term investors and that our analysis is not sample dependent.

We check whether pension funds invest in their own companies where they may have different objectives and monitoring roles than when they invest in other firms. Table 3, Panel C, lists the 11 companies (3.8% of our test firms) with such stakes. The number of these companies and the magnitude of their holdings are not substantial and the inclusion of these companies in our test sample did not alter our results.

4.2. Financial characteristics of our test companies

Table 4 reports the descriptive statistics of financial attributes of the test and control firms. We compute the t-statistics to test for differences in means and the

Table 4

Descriptive statistics on means of selected data on the test and control firms

This table provides the descriptive statistics of the proxy variables. The test sample includes all companies that reported pension fund holding above 3% in 1995–1996. In Panel A, the control sample includes all other quoted companies in the London Stock Exchange. In Panel B, the control sample includes industry and size matched firms. Block is the proportion of outstanding equity owned by blockholders other than directors and occupational pension funds; Dir is the proportion of outstanding equity capital owned by directors; ME is market value of equity at balance sheet date; TA is total assets; Q is the ratio of market value of equity plus book value of debt over total assets; M/S is the market value of equity plus book value of debt over sales; M/B is the market value of equity over book value of equity; $R_{i,\ t-12\ to\ t}$ is a 1-year stock return; P/E is the price-earnings ratio at the balance sheet date; Blev is the ratio of long-term debt over long-term debt plus shareholders funds; Mlev is the ratio of long-term debt over long-term debt plus market value of equity; Dir rem./Sal is the ratio of directors' remuneration over sales; Split is a dummy variable equals to 1 if the roles of chairman and CEO are split; #DIR. is the number of directors in the board; %NED is the proportion of non-executive directors; Payout is the ratio of dividends over earnings.

Variables	Test sample		Control sample		t-statistics of difference in means	Mann–Whitney p-value
	Mean	Median	Mean	Median		
Panel A: Size and other variables relative to all companies in the UK (N_{Test} = 586; $N_{Control}$ = 2702)						
ME (£ million)	96.7***	28.1***	534.10***	42.87***	−3.38	0.000
TA (£ million)	125***	33.4***	571.61***	49.54***	−2.41	0.000
Q	1.16	0.87	1.48	0.87	−1.32	0.520
ROA (%)	6.13	8.9	6.73	8.93	1.15	0.304
ROE (%)	−1.10	11.30	−24.97	11.72	0.75	0.960
Blev (%)	14.58***	9.90***	19.10***	14.60***	−3.88	0.001
Dir rem./Sal (%)	2.40	1.00***	2.56	0.79***	0.25	0.000
Payout (%)	31.78	33.0	36.03	33.55	−1.41	0.120
Panel B: Size and other variables relative to industry and size matched control firms (N = 586)						
Block	34.00	32.48	36.54	34.82	−1.29	0.135
Dir	14.53	6.02	14.01	7.38	0.32	0.875
ME (£ million)	96.7	28.1	121.1	31.1	−1.26	0.875
TA (£ million)	125	33.4	122	32.0	0.12	0.519
Q	1.16***	0.87***	1.61***	0.94***	−2.21	0.005
M/S	1.33*	0.60*	2.65*	0.65*	−1.68	0.051
M/B	2.78*	1.68***	3.44*	1.87***	−1.68	0.004
ROA (%)	6.13	8.90	4.10	8.70	1.03	0.550
ROE (%)	−1.10	11.30	11.95	12.00	−1.16	0.113
ROS (%)	5.49	6.80	−0.00	6.50	1.11	0.758
$R_{i,\ t-12\ to\ t}$ %	23.57	15.40	20.04	5.75	0.74	0.133
P/E	9.68	8.25	9.33	8.36	0.48	0.101
Mlev (%)	11.34***	5.80**	17.90***	12.75**	−3.21	0.012
Blev (%)	14.58***	9.90	21.01***	13.30	−3.08	0.458
Dir rem./Sal (%)	2.4	1.00	2.30	0.90	0.10	0.469
Split	0.84	1.00	0.88	1.00	−1.61	0.121
#DIR	5.92	6.00	5.80	6.00	0.85	0.382
% NED	0.40	0.40	0.38	0.40	1.31	0.334
Payout (%)	31.78	33.00	33.10	30.70	−0.40	0.399

Notes: *** Significant at 0.01 levels. ** Significant at 0.05 levels. * Significant at 0.10 levels.

Mann–Whitney *p*-value to test for differences in medians. [24] In Panel A, we test for a number of attribute differences between our test and all the remaining non-financial companies listed on the London Stock Exchange. Companies in which pension funds hold large stakes are, on average, very small. Their average (median) market value is £97 million (£28 million) compared to £534 million (£43 million) for the remaining sample. The test statistics of the differences in means and in medians are both significant at the 1% level, suggesting that, on average, our test firms are significantly smaller than all the remaining firms in the UK market. The results based on total assets as an alternative measure of size confirm that our test companies are substantially smaller than the control firms. However, our test companies are not all small. Out of the 289 test companies, 188 (65%) are part of the FTA All Share Index, the 800 most traded companies in the London Stock Exchange, with 8 companies (1.4% of our test sample) that are in the UK top 100 companies (FTSE 100 Index). The remaining 101 companies are from the mid-capitalization and the small companies indices. The findings that pension funds did not change their holdings over the 1992–1996 period reported above are not likely to be the result of illiquidity of our test companies. Bethel et al. (1998) report also a large number of small companies in their sample of firms in which large investor acquire large stakes. However, given that pension funds hold, at the aggregate, more than a third of the UK equity market and that our test companies are relatively small, we can tentatively conclude that the vast majority of companies in which pension funds invest (but without holding significant stakes) are large.

Panel A, Table 4, shows that our test companies have lower leverage but higher directors remuneration than other companies. Interestingly, the difference in payout ratios between our test and control firms is not statistically different. This comparison is, however, likely to be driven by size differences across the two samples. To overcome this bias we construct a control sample, by matching every test company with a similar company from the same industry and size, using year-end market value of equity.

Panel B, shows that compared to the industry and size-adjusted control group, the block and managerial holdings in our test firms are not statistically different. Blockholders hold an average of 34% in our test firms and 36.5% in our control sample. Insiders hold an average of 14.5% in our test firms and 14% in our control sample. The test statistics for differences in means and medians are not statistically significant at any confidence level. The results imply that our analysis is not affected by block or managerial ownership. However, compared to the results

---

[24] We exclude 58 companies with negative book value of equity due to goodwill write-offs when we use the market-to-book ratio, book leverage and return on equity. The inclusion of these companies did not, however, alter our reported results.

M. Faccio, M.A. Lasfer / Journal of Corporate Finance 6 (2000) 71–110 93

reported in Table 2, insiders and blockholders hold significantly larger stakes in our test firms than occupational pension funds, suggesting that these funds do not invest a large proportion of their assets in our test companies.

Table 4, Panel B, shows that the value of our test firms is significantly lower than that of our control group. The average Tobin's Q of our test firms is 1.16 while that of the control group is 1.62. The same conclusion is reached when we use market-to-book and market-to-sales as alternative measures of firm value. At the same time, our test companies have lower leverage than our control firms. However, in terms of accounting and market rates of return and P/E ratio, our test companies are not different from the control firms.

In terms of internal governance structure, our test and control companies have exactly the same number of directors of about 6, ranging between 2 and 15, and the same proportion of non-executive directors of about 40%. The proportion of our control companies that split the roles of chairman and CEO of 88% is higher than that of our test firms (84%). Finally, Table 4 shows that, our test firms do not exhibit lower directors' remuneration than the control firms. These results are striking and suggest that pension funds large holdings do not increase the likelihood of compliance with the Cadbury (1992) and Greenbury (1995) recommendations.

Table 4, Panel B, shows that our test firms pay an average of 32% of their earnings as dividends. This is not statistically different from the average payout ratio of 33% of our control firms. The results are not consistent with the short-termism arguments and indicate that occupational pension funds do not necessarily demand high payouts from companies in which they hold large stakes. Following Jensen (1986) arguments, the results also imply that pension funds are not monitoring these companies as they do not make them disgorge the free cash flow. The results are, nevertheless, consistent with previous studies who do not find dividend tax clientele in the UK (e.g., Lasfer, 1996).

4.3. Do pension funds affect firm value and board structure?

Table 5 reports the results of the Logit regressions where the various agency variables are considered simultaneously. The dependent variable is equal to 1 if company i is in the test sample and 0 if it is part of the control sample. The table shows that, with the exception of the variables that proxy for firm value that are significantly lower for our test firms, there is no statistical difference between our test and control firms. As shown in Table 4, companies in which occupational pension funds hold large stakes are not more profitable and do not pay higher dividends than the control firms. In addition, our test firms are not more likely to split the roles of chairman and chief executive officer, have less directors or more non-executive directors than our control group. These two last issues were the main focus of the recommendations of Cadbury (1992), which relied on pension funds for their implementation.

Table 5

Logit regressions of the probability that pension fund holdings exceeds 3% of shares 95–96

The dependent variable is equal to 1 for companies that reported pension fund holding above 3% in 1995–1996 and to 0 for industry and size matched control firms. M/S is market value of equity plus book value of debt over sales; Q is the ratio of market value of equity plus book value of debt over total assets; Blev is the ratio of long-term debt over long-term debt plus shareholders funds; $R_{i,t-12\ to\ t}$ is a 1-year share price return; Dir rem./Sal is the ratio of directors remuneration over sales; Split is a dummy variable equals to 1 if the roles of chairman and CEO are split; #DIR is the number of directors on the board; %NED is the proportion of non-executive directors in the board; Payout is the ratio of dividends over earnings; Dir is the proportion of outstanding equity held by directors; Block is the proportion of outstanding equity capital held by blockholders other than directors and occupational pension funds; χ^2, the chi-squared, is used to test that all slopes of the Logit regression are zero by comparing the restricted and the unrestricted log likelihoods. t-values are in parentheses.

	(1)	(2)	(3)	(4)	(5)	(6)
Constant	0.71*** (6.64)	0.61*** (6.69)	0.52*** (31.91)	0.52*** (32.16)	0.47* (1.84)	0.79*** (6.93)
Split	−0.014 (−0.27)	−0.017 (−0.31)				−0.005 (−0.09)
#DIR	0.011 (1.18)	0.016 (1.58)				0.008 (0.70)
%NED	0.04 (0.37)	0.042 (0.36)				−0.02 (−0.19)
Dir	−0.003 (0.28)	0.005 (0.53)				−0.00 (−0.00)
Block	−0.002 (−1.55)					−0.002* (−1.85)
Dirrem./Sal		0.123 (0.56)			0.001 (0.10)	0.005 (0.01)
Q			−0.01*** (−2.14)		−0.108* (−1.72)	−0.015*** (−2.20)
M/S				−0.01*** (−2.51)		
ROA			0.04 (0.92)	0.013 (0.75)	0.006 (0.03)	0.05 (0.64)
ROS						
$R_{i,t-12\ to\ t}$					−1.65*** (−3.48)	−0.025 (−0.95)
Blev						
Payout			0.006 (1.10)	0.006 (1.10)	−0.041 (−0.16)	−0.019 (−0.63)
χ^2	1.05	0.66	2.33*	2.81*	16.53***	1.42

*** Significant at the 0.01 level.
** Significant at the 0.05 level.
* Significant at the 0.10 level.

M. Faccio, M.A. Lasfer / Journal of Corporate Finance 6 (2000) 71–110 95

Column (6), Table 5, controls for differences in other monitoring mechanisms to account for the fact that these various mechanisms may be substitutes. The results show that the main difference between our test and control firms is the measure of firm value, Q, suggesting that our test firms have lower value than the control firms. [25] The coefficient of blockholding is also negative and significant at the 10% confidence level, suggesting that, after controlling for all other differences between our test and control firms, the test companies have lower blockholding than our control firms. No single pension fund-monitoring variable is significant at any confidence level. These results cast doubt on the monitoring role of pension funds in the UK. [26]

In Table 6 we analyze the causality in the relationship between board structure and occupational pension funds holdings. We run a set of regressions where the various dependent variables which proxy for board structure are measured in the 1996–1997 financial year and the explanatory variables such as pension funds holdings are in 1995–1996 financial year. We hypothesize that pension funds require companies in which they hold large stakes in 1995–1996 to adopt the Cadbury's (1992) board structure in 1996–1997, i.e., to split the roles of chairman and chief executive officer, to appoint a non-executive director as a chairman and to have a large proportion of non-executive directors on the board. In addition, we follow McConnell and Servaes (1995) and focus separately on low and high growth firms using E/P ratio as a proxy for growth opportunities. Firms with E/P ratio above (equal or below) the median are classified as low (high) growth. We expect a positive relationship between pension funds holdings and the adoption of the Cadbury (1992) recommendations on the composition of the board of low growth companies, which are more likely to suffer from the free cash flow problem.

The first three columns of Table 6 report the results of the Logit regression where the dependent variable is equal to 1 if the roles of CEO and Chairman are split and zero otherwise. The results show that the coefficients of the pension fund variables are positive but not significant except for pension fund size (LNPFA). When we split our sample into high and low growth companies none of the pension funds variables is significant. We tested for possible multicollinearity problem by running the regressions with each single variable. We find (but do not report) that the holdings of directors, Dir, and the coefficient of non-institutional block shareholders, NIBlock, are negative and significant. None of the occupa-

---

[25] The negative relationship between pension fund investments and Q has been widely documented in the investment literature. For example, Lakonishok et al. (1994) show that pension funds invest in glamour stocks (low book-to-market firms), which generally underperform value stocks (high book-to-market firms) because the previous success of the glamour stocks helps institutions justify their portfolio selection to their investors.

[26] The issue of director's pay system has just been considered by the National Association of Pension Funds through their call to vote on boardroom pay (Financial Times, 1997b).

Table 6
Determinants of board structure for low and high growth firms
In each regression the dependent variable is computed for the period 1996–1997, while all independent variables are 1-year lagged (i.e., 1995–1996). The regressions are run separately for all 250 companies, All, low-growth companies (119), and high growth companies (131). Growth opportunities are measured using the median E/P ratio. The first six columns are Logit regressions where Split or Nechair are equal to 1 if the company has split the roles of its chairman and chief executive officer or has a non-executive director as a chairman, and zero otherwise. In these regressions the Pseudo-R^2 measures the goodness of fit. In the last three columns we run OLS regression with the proportion of non-executive on the board %NED as the dependent variable. TPF is the proportion of outstanding equity owned by all identified pension funds; IPF is the ratio of occupational pension funds holdings over their total assets; LNPFA is the log of the asset value of the pension fund; Dir is the proportion of outstanding equity owned by the directors; EPFM is the proportion of equity held by external pension fund managers (either on behalf of pension funds or other clients); IBlock represents the proportion of equity overall held by institutional block shareholders other than (both internally and externally managed) pension funds; NIBlock is the proportion of equity held by non-institutional blockholders; $R_{i,\,t-12\ to\ t}$ is a 1-year stock return.

	Split			Nechair			%NED		
	All	Low growth	High growth	All	Low growth	High growth	All	Low growth	High growth
Constant	−2.974	−0.611	−6.447	0.091	−0.165	0.121	0.163	0.213	0.048
	(−0.68)	(−1.11)	(−1.11)	(0.02)	(−0.03)	(0.02)	(0.60)	(0.50)	(0.13)
Dir	−0.004	−0.019	0.002	−0.024**	−0.020	−0.019	−0.0002	−0.0001	−0.0004
	(−0.44)	(−0.88)	(0.19)	(−2.17)	(−1.42)	(−1.28)	(−0.24)	(−0.09)	(−0.46)
IBlock.	0.030	−0.010	0.028	0.039**	0.015	0.067**	0.0002	0.001	−0.002
	(1.13)	(−0.19)	(0.77)	(2.34)	(0.74)	(2.06)	(0.21)	(0.74)	(−1.25)
NIBlock	−0.011	−0.068*	0.000	−0.017	−0.025	−0.003	0.001	0.001	−0.00003
	(−0.96)	(−1.79)	(0.03)	(−1.46)	(−1.44)	(−0.18)	(0.73)	(1.00)	(−0.03)
TPF	0.02	0.10	0.03	0.05	0.03	0.05	0.002	−0.001	0.003
	(0.38)	(0.86)	(0.51)	(1.38)	(0.71)	(1.03)	(0.79)	(−0.36)	(1.9)

M. Faccio, M.A. Lasfer / Journal of Corporate Finance 6 (2000) 71–110   97

LNPFA	0.53** (2.15)	0.06 (0.12)	0.26 (0.94)	-0.01 (-0.01)	0.13 (0.50)	-0.05 (-0.17)	-0.01 (-0.64)	-0.01 (-0.01)	0.005 (0.27)
IPF	1.48 (1.26)	1.46 (0.46)	0.75 (0.45)	0.74 (0.94)	1.88 (1.13)	1.05 (0.77)	0.0005 (0.04)	-0.001 (-0.10)	0.10 (1.55)
EPFM	0.016 (0.43)	0.259 (1.10)	0.002 (0.05)	-0.004 (-0.25)	0.006 (0.28)	-0.001 (-0.05)	-0.0002 (-0.23)	-0.0001 (-0.04)	-0.001 (-0.35)
Blev	6.25** (2.17)	0.63 (0.32)	1.54 (0.63)	1.56 (1.61)	0.11 (0.10)	1.18 (0.78)	0.10* (1.70)	0.08 (0.99)	0.17 (1.61)
$R_{i,t-12\ to\ t}$	0.03 (0.08)	0.83 (1.23)	0.11 (0.07)	-0.21 (-0.82)	-0.02 (-0.06)	-0.34 (-0.94)	0.01 (0.76)	0.02 (0.83)	0.005 (0.18)
LN(TA)	-0.47 (-1.56)	0.09 (0.24)	0.07 (0.18)	-0.02 (-0.12)	-0.14 (-0.68)	-0.004 (-0.01)	0.02** (2.19)	0.02 (1.40)	0.01 (0.76)
Pseudo-R^2 or R^2	7.29%	15.92%	4.87%	15.27%	11.98%	19.82%	0.95%	0.00%	3.17%

*** Significant at the 0.01 level.
** Significant at the 0.05 level.
* Significant at the 0.10 level.

98   *M. Faccio, M.A. Lasfer / Journal of Corporate Finance 6 (2000) 71–110*

tional pension funds variables is significant. We find that the coefficient of the external pension fund managers variable, EPFM, is positive and significant for the whole sample, though it is not when the sub-samples of high and low growth firms are separated.

Columns 4 to 6 provide the results of the Logit regressions where the dependent variable is equal to 1 if the company has appointed a non-executive director as chairman and zero otherwise. Here again none of the coefficients of the pension fund variables are significant. However, when we run the regressions with a single independent variable, we find that the coefficient of pension funds incidence, IPF, is positive and significant (1.36 with $t = 1.71$) for the whole sample. For the low-Q companies, we find that the coefficient of total pension funds, TPF, is positive and significant (0.06 and $t = 1.93$). The coefficients of directors owner-ship, Dir, and non-institutional blockholders, NIBlock, are negative and significant while those of institutional blockholders and external fund managers are positive and significant.

The last three columns present the results of the OLS regressions where the dependent variable is the proportion of non-executive directors in the board. The results show that none of the pension fund variables is significant. When the regressions are run separately, we find that only size, Ln(TA), and leverage, Blev, are positive and significant.

The overall results do not provide strong support for the occupational and externally-managed pension fund monitoring of the board structure. At the same time, board structure is unrelated to market performance, suggesting that the recent trend towards the adoption of the Cadbury's prescriptions was not related to the presence of agency conflicts, but rather dictated by some "need of visibility" by companies. Franks et al. (1998) also report a similar relationship. We do, however, report some evidence consistent with monitoring role of other than pension funds institutional shareholders and of debtholders, at least with regards to the appoint-ment of non-executive directors within low growth firms. There is also some evidence that managerial ownership is used to entrench the position of incumbent managers as the coefficient of directors' ownership is, in most cases, negative and significant. Finally, our results are consistent with the hypothesis that institutional blockholders (other than pension funds) lead high growth firms to appoint a non-executive chairman. We simulated our results using growth in profits, market returns and Q as proxies for growth opportunities and/or presence of agency conflicts. The results are qualitatively similar to those reported in Table 6.

4.4. Pension funds investments and firm value

In this section we focus only on our test companies and test for the relationship between firm value and ownership structure. Table 7 reports the Pearson correla-tion matrix. The correlation between the various measures of occupational pension fund holdings and firm value is, in most cases, weak and negative. An exception is

Table 7

Pearson correlation coefficients between the variables used

The sample includes all companies that reported occupational pension fund holding above 3%. The dependent variables Q and M/S are measured in 1996–1997 financial year. LPF is the proportion of outstanding equity owned by largest occupational pension funds. TPF is the proportion of outstanding equity owned by all identified pension funds; IPF is the ratio of occupational pension funds holdings over their total assets; NPF is the number of occupational pension funds; Dir is the proportion of outstanding equity owned by the directors; EPFM is the proportion of equity held by external pension fund managers (either on behalf of pension funds or other clients); IBlock represents the proportion of equity overall held by institutional block shareholders other than (both internally and externally managed) pension funds; NIBlock is the proportion of equity held by non-institutional blockholders; ln(TA) is the log of total assets; Blev is the ratio of long-term debt over long-term debt plus shareholders funds; #DIR is the number of directors on the board; Split is a dummy variable equals to 1 if the roles of chairman and CEO are split; %NED is the proportion of non-executive directors in the board; P/E is the price–earnings ratio at the balance sheet date

	Q	M/S	TPF	IPF	NPF	LNPFA	EPFM	Dir	Dir²	IBlock	NIBlock	ln(TA)	Blev	No.Dir	Split	%NED
M/S	0.59															
TPF	-0.18	-0.07														
IPF	0.02	0.31	-0.03													
NPF	-0.12	-0.11	0.69	-0.04												
LNPFA	0.04	-0.08	0.04	-0.28	0.01											
EPFM	-0.10	-0.04	-0.01	0.02	0.04	0.16										
Dir	0.11	0.00	-0.05	-0.04	-0.04	-0.25	-0.34									
Dir²	0.11	-0.02	-0.09	-0.04	-0.08	-0.21	-0.29	0.95								
IBlock	-0.04	0.10	0.15	-0.01	0.00	0.04	0.02	-0.25	-0.23							
NIBlock	-0.02	-0.10	-0.04	-0.09	-0.05	-0.05	-0.27	-0.02	-0.06	-0.27						
ln(TA)	-0.07	0.07	-0.18	0.29	-0.01	0.22	0.36	-0.32	-0.25	-0.17	-0.25					
Blev	-0.06	-0.05	-0.04	0.13	-0.02	0.11	0.30	-0.21	-0.20	-0.10	-0.05	0.46				
No.Dir	0.09	0.07	0.01	0.01	0.05	0.18	0.07	-0.13	-0.12	-0.13	0.03	0.38	0.21			
Split	-0.11	-0.16	-0.02	0.05	-0.08	0.15	0.07	-0.21	-0.15	0.10	0.06	0.13	0.13	0.07		
%NED	0.06	0.04	-0.07	0.04	-0.11	0.07	0.10	-0.26	-0.17	0.13	-0.01	0.20	0.13	0.13	0.17	
P/E	0.37	0.26	-0.02	-0.01	-0.02	0.07	-0.04	-0.03	-0.02	0.03	-0.12	-0.06	-0.06	0.03	-0.04	-0.05

represented by the correlation between the market-to-sales ratio and the pension fund incidence variable. Similarly the correlation between firm value, blockholding and directors holdings is not significant. However, ownership variables are negatively correlated with size as measured by total assets, suggesting that occupational pension funds, directors, institutional blockholders (other than pension fund managers) and non-institutional blockholders hold large stakes mainly in small firms. However, the fund manager variable is positively related to size. Consistent with previous evidence (e.g., Lasfer, 1995), leverage is positively related to firm size but negatively correlated with firm value. The number of directors is positively correlated with occupational pension fund, externally-managed pension funds, non-institutional blockholding, leverage and size, while it is negatively correlated with institutional blockholders and directors' ownership.

The split dummy variable is positively related to leverage, block ownership, size and proportion of non-executive directors in the board, but negatively related to directors' holdings. This suggests that the larger the company and the higher the debt–equity ratio, blockholding and the proportion of non-executive directors in the board, the higher its propensity to split the roles of chairman and CEO. However, none of the occupational pension fund measure is statistically related to the split dummy, implying that pension funds, individually or collectively, do not push companies to split the roles of chairman and chief executive officer. Finally, directors' holdings are negatively related to the proportion of non-executive directors in the board, suggesting that such holdings exacerbate the potential agency conflicts between the board and the management.

In Table 8, columns (1) to (3), we report the results of the regressions of firm value, as measured by Tobin's Q in 1996/97, against various measures of occupational pension funds holdings in the 1995/96 financial year. These results show that, with the exception of total pension funds stakes, TPF, none of the various measures of pension funds holdings explain firm value. The total pension funds stakes variable, TPF, is actually, negative and significant, suggesting that pension funds collectively destroy value. Even after controlling for other monitoring mechanisms documented in the previous literature (e.g., Agrawal and Knoeber, 1996; Yermack, 1996), such as size and P/E, firm value is still negatively related to total pension funds holdings (3). Although the coefficient of pension fund incidence, IPF, and the size of pension fund, LNPFA, are positively related to firm value, they are not significant. The coefficient of external pension fund managers' stakes is negatively, though not significantly, related to firm value.

In contrast to previous studies (e.g., Yermack, 1996, and Eisenberg et al., 1998) we report a positive relationship between firm value and the number of directors. The difference in the results could be due to the fact that our companies are relatively middle-sized compared to the sample of small companies of Eisenberg et al. (1998) and that of large companies of Yermack (1996). Finally, the coefficients of the holdings of directors variable and its squared value are not significant suggesting that there is no linear or non-linear relationship between

M. Faccio, M.A. Lasfer / Journal of Corporate Finance 6 (2000) 71–110   101

Table 8
Relationship between firm value and pension fund holdings

The sample includes all companies that reported occupational pension fund holding above 3%. In columns (1) to (3) we use Q, the ratio of market value of equity plus book value of debt over total assets, as the dependent variable. In column (4) and (5) the results are simulated using the market value of equity to sales as dependent variable. The dependent variables are measured in 1996–1997 while the independent variables are measured in 1995–1996. TPF is the proportion of outstanding equity owned by all identified pension funds; IPF is the ratio of occupational pension funds holdings over their total assets; LNPFA is the log of the market value of the largest pension fund's asset; NPF is the number of occupational pension funds; EPFM is the proportion of equity held by external pension fund managers (either on behalf of pension funds or other clients); Dir is the proportion of outstanding equity owned by the directors; Dir² is its squared value; IBlock represents the proportion of equity overall held by institutional block shareholders other than (both internally and externally managed) pension funds; NIBlock is the proportion of equity held by non-institutional blockholders; #DIR is the number of directors; Split is a dummy variable equals to 1 if the roles of chairman and CEO are split; %NED is the proportion of non-executive directors; P/E is the price–earnings ratio at the balance sheet date. t-values are in parentheses.

	Q			M/S	
	(1)	(2)	(3)	(4)	(5)
Constant	−0.97 (−0.64)	0.62 (0.39)	0.57 (0.36)	0.07 (0.04)	0.97*** (2.80)
TPF	−0.033*** (−2.60)	−0.042*** (−3.07)	−0.049** (−2.57)	0.001 (0.06)	
IPF	0.034 (−0.46)	0.083 (1.34)	0.086 (1.38)	0.36*** (4.50)	0.372*** (5.41)
LNPFA	0.110 (1.62)	0.092 (1.46)	0.095 (1.50)	0.007 (0.09)	
NPF			0.09 (0.56)	−0.29 (−1.41)	−0.28** (−2.01)
EPFM		−0.003 (−0.51)	−0.003 (−0.53)	−0.001 (−0.18)	
Dir		0.004 (1.28)	0.004 (0.42)	0.010 (0.80)	
Dir²			0.000 (0.03)	−0.000 (−0.79)	
IBlock		−0.002 (−0.37)	−0.002 (−0.33)	0.013* (1.66)	0.013** (2.00)
NIBlock		−0.002 (−0.36)	−0.002 (−0.36)	−0.001 (−0.13)	
ln(TA)		−0.11* (−1.79)	−0.12* (−1.83)	0.03 (0.41)	
Blev		0.002 (0.01)	0.020 (0.04)	−0.619 (−1.09)	−0.512 (−1.02)
No.Dir		0.062* (1.86)	0.061* (1.85)	0.056 (1.32)	0.066* (1.71)
Split		−0.23 (−1.53)	−0.22 (−1.47)	−0.56*** (−2.92)	−0.57*** (−3.11)
%NED		0.67* (1.78)	0.69* (1.77)	0.40 (0.80)	
P/E		0.035*** (5.65)	0.035*** (5.62)	0.032*** (3.98)	0.031*** (4.08)
Adj. R^2%	2.21%	18.08%	17.43%	18.09%	20.63%
F	2.99**	4.84***	4.18***	4.31***	9.35***

Notes: * Significant at 10% level. ** Significant at 5% level. *** Significant at 1% level.

102   *M. Faccio, M.A. Lasfer / Journal of Corporate Finance 6 (2000) 71–110*

value and managerial ownership. These results are not consistent with the findings of McConnell and Servaes (1990; 1995).

We simulate these results using market value of the firm over sales as a proxy for firm value (Lins and Servaes, 1999). The results, reported in (4) and (5), show a positive relationship between value and pension fund incidence, but a negative relationship with the number of pension funds. The coefficient of externally-managed pension funds is negative but not significant while that of institutional block ownership is positive and significant. We also simulate our results by using sales as a measure of size and capital expenditure over total assets as a proxy for growth opportunities. The results, not reported for space reasons, are qualitatively similar to these reported in Table 8. Overall, our results suggest that pension funds do not add value to companies in which they hold large stakes.

4.5. Effects of pension fund holdings on firms' long-term performance

We analyze the long-term performance of our test firms by comparing the changes in accounting and stock price performance over the sample periods 1994–1995 and 1996–1997. As in Karpoff et al. (1996) and Del Guercio and Hawkins (1999), we investigate whether companies in which pension funds hold large stakes rebound more quickly from poor performance or maintain their good performance over a longer time period. We use return on assets (ROA) as a proxy for accounting performance. We follow Wahal (1996) and compute the 2-year industry-adjusted Cumulative Abnormal Return On Assets (CAROA) as

$$\text{CAROA}_{i,t,T} = \prod_{n=t}^{T}(1 + \text{ROA}_{i,n}) - \prod_{n=t}^{T}(1 + \text{ROA}_{s,n})$$

where $\text{ROA}_{i,t}$ is company i return on assets in year t and computed as

$$\text{ROA}_{i,t} = \frac{\text{Profit Before Interest and Tax}}{\text{Book Value of Total Assets}}.$$

$\text{ROA}_{s,t}$ is the industry s median return on assets in year t.

We simulate our results by computing in the same way Cumulative Abnormal Return On Equity (CAROE) and Cumulative Abnormal Return On Sales (CAROS). All measures of performance are adjusted by subtracting the industry median.

The abnormal performance is also evaluated using stock market returns. We compute the Share Price Return (SPR) from a buy-and-hold strategy over the sub-periods 1994–1995 and 1996–1997 as follows:

$$\text{SPR}_{i,t,T} = \prod_{n=t}^{T}\{1 + r_{i,n}\} - \prod_{n=t}^{T}\{1 + r_{c^*,n}\}$$

where

$$r_{i,n} = \frac{P_{i,n}}{P_{i,n-1}} - 1.$$

M. Faccio, M.A. Lasfer / Journal of Corporate Finance 6 (2000) 71–110 103

We adopt the Barber and Lyon (1997) methodology, and control for size (market capitalization) and market-to-book. We match each test company with a control company selected by identifying all firms with a market value of equity between 70% and 130% of that of the test company. Then, from this set of firms, we select the company with the market-to-book ratio closest to that of the test firm. We use the return of this company, $r_{c^*,n}$, as a benchmark.

This measure of performance accounts for the fact that occupational pension funds are long-term investors, as reported in Table 3, and does not suffer from cumulating biases observed in arithmetic mean returns (Conrad and Kaul, 1993; Wahal, 1996; Barber and Lyon, 1997). We eliminate survivorship bias by including dead companies in our sample. Out of our 289 test companies, 34 firms (11.76%) are excluded because they went public after 1995 and we could not compute the market performance for the first period.

The results reported in Table 9 show that the industry-adjusted return on assets (CAROA) has not changed significantly over the two sub-periods. Companies in which occupational pension funds hold large stakes underperform the industry average (though not significantly) by 3.38% in 1994–1995 and by 1.50% in 1996–1997. As in Wahal (1996), we split the sample into overperformers and underperformers. Companies with CAROA below (above) the median are classified as underperformers (overperformers). [27] The abnormal performance of the overperforming companies decreased from 11.62% to 6.44% and that of the underperformers has increased from -18.5% to -9.51%. The results are consistent with Wahal (1996) and indicate that both the under- and overperformers experience a convergence to industry means. The results are not qualitatively affected by the use of other measures of performance such as industry-adjusted return on equity (Panel B) or industry-adjusted return on sales (Panel C).

Panel D and E report the changes in firm value as measured by (the industry-adjusted) Tobin's Q and changes in abnormal returns. For the full sample, the industry-adjusted Q has decreased from 0.163 to 0.072. [28] The decrease in both the average and median firm value is statistically significant. The results suggest that, over time, the value of companies in which occupational pension funds hold large stakes decreases. As in the above panels, we split the sample into overperformers and underperformers. Overperforming (underperforming) companies are companies with Tobin's Q higher (lower) than the median. The overperforming companies have done worst over the two sample periods. Their average value has decreased from 0.67 to 0.48. The decrease in the mean median are statistically significant. In contrast, the average and the median Tobin's Q of the underperforming companies did not change significantly. These companies have underper-

---

[27] We have also split the sample into over- and underperformers on the basis of positive and negative CAROA or other variables used below but the results did not change.

[28] For both 1994–1995 and 1996–1997, the Q ratio is computed as arithmetic average.

Table 9

Pension funds holdings and long term accounting and stock price performance

The sample includes all companies that displayed (at least) one relevant pension fund holding. Industry-adjusted return on assets (CAROA) is the return on assets of each company in the sample less the median return on asset of the industry. Industry-adjusted return on equity and return on sales and Q are computed in a similar way. The control sample includes firms taken from the same SEC industry whose 1994–1995 performance is the closest to our test firm. Panel E reports the results based on the size and market-to-book adjusted share price returns using the Barber and Lyons (1997) methodology. The sample is dividend into a sample of underperformers and overperformers based on the median performance of the firm in 1994–1995. For example, if the industry-adjusted return on assets for a firm is lower (higher) than the median, the firm is classified as an underperformer (overperformer).

	N	1994–1995		1996–1997		t-statistic difference in means	Mann–Whitney p-value
		Mean	Median	Mean	Median		
(Panel A) Industry-adjusted return on assets CAROA%							
Full sample	255	−3.38	−0.584	−1.50	−0.31	−1.24	0.344
Overperformers	128	11.62***	6.48***	6.44***	3.56***	3.56	0.000
Underperformers	127	−18.50***	−10.30***	−9.51***	−4.76***	−3.59	0.000
(Panel B) Industry-adjusted return on equity CAROE%							
Full sample	255	−4.96	−1.412	−3.89	−0.53	−0.36	0.906
Overperformers	128	20.79***	10.31***	5.72***	2.13***	4.48	0.000
Underperformers	127	−30.90***	−16.50***	−13.56***	−6.91***	−3.94	0.000
(Panel C) Industry-adjusted return on sales CAROS%							
Full sample	255	−0.08	−0.67	0.33	0.00	−0.24	0.811
Overperformers	128	14.99***	7.13***	7.78***	4.92***	3.32	0.000
Underperformers	127	−15.27***	−7.57***	−7.19***	−4.75***	−3.35	0.000
(Panel D) Industry-adjusted firm value Q							
Full sample	255	0.163***	−0.082***	0.072***	−0.095***	2.72	0.009
Overperformers	128	0.674***	0.346***	0.480***	0.15***	3.22	0.000
Underperformers	127	−0.353	−0.322	−0.339	−0.306	−0.58	0.237
(Panel E) Size and market-to-book adjusted share price return SPR%							
Full sample	255	0.49	−3.85	−3.20	−8.76	0.42	0.916
Overperformers	128	68.22***	43.64***	−6.83***	−13.05***	6.62	0.000
Underperformers	127	−67.76***	−57.19***	0.45***	−2.09***	−7.01	0.000

* Significant at 10%, 5% and 1% respectively.

** Significant at 10%, 5% and 1% respectively.

*** Significant at 10%, 5% and 1% respectively.

formed in 1994–1995 period and carried on underperforming in the 1996–1997 period. These results are striking as they imply that companies in which occupational pension funds hold large stakes decrease in value through time, and those that are already underperforming do not improve. In sum, it appears that pension funds are passive investors: they do not make companies in which they hold large stakes improve their performance and they do not sell their holdings in companies that are underperforming.

Panel E reports the results based on the size and market-to-book adjusted share price returns using the Barber and Lyon (1997) methodology. For the full sample, companies have decreased their average performance from 0.49% to -3.2% and the median performance from -3.85% to -8.76%. However, this decrease is not statistically significant. The stock price performance of the sub-sample of the overperforming firms declined significantly from 68.22% to -6.83% (t-statistic of the difference in means $= 6.62$), while underperforming companies increased their performance from -67.76% to 0.45% (t-statistic of the difference in means $= -7.01$). As in Wahal (1996), our results are consistent with mean reversion hypothesis and cannot be attributed to pension funds investments. [29]

5. Discussion and conclusions

In this paper we analyze the performance of companies in which occupational pension funds hold large stakes and test the hypotheses that, because of their size, structure and objectives, these funds should be effective monitors of UK companies.

We compare the financial performance of companies in which occupation pension funds hold more than 3% of the issued share capital against all other non-financial and industry and size-adjusted control groups. We show that our test firms are small and have low value. These companies are also not likely to be more efficient and/or to pay higher dividends than the control group. However, our results show that these holdings constitute a small proportion of the occupational pension funds assets, suggesting that most of their funds are invested in large companies where they do not hold large stakes. We report that pension funds do not add value to the companies in which they hold large stakes. Our results cast doubt on the monitoring role of pension funds which are considered theoretically, on the one hand, to be the main promoters of corporate governance in the UK, and, on the other hand, to be short-termist and dictate their rules to companies. At the same time, we show that, despite the relatively poor performance of the companies in which they invest, occupational pension funds do not opt for the 'exit' strategy. We show that there is no apparent specific relationship between the funds and the companies in which they invest and these companies are not illiquid

---

[29] We obtained similar results either by using the industry median return as benchmark and, by matching our test firms by industry and prior performance. Also, for all accounting measures of performance, as well as firm value, the results were qualitatively similar when we compared the industry adjusted performance of 1990–92 to that of 1993–95. Similar results are obtained when we concentrate on survived companies, and exclude IPO firms.

to make it impossible to exit. One possibility is that pension funds choose to invest in low Q firms to benefit from return reversals on these securities. However, the lack of data on the investment styles of these funds does not allow us to explore this issue further. At this stage, our results suggest that, once 'locked in' pension funds find it difficult and costly to monitor or to sell their holdings for fear of selling at a discount or to convey information to the market.

Our results may not come as a surprise. There is a large debate in the UK about the lack of monitoring by pension funds and it is only recently that the National Association of Pension Funds considered seriously this issue (NAPF, 1996b). In addition, occupational pension funds may not have a material effect on the performance of companies in which they hold large stakes because these blocks tend to represent relatively small fractions of the total values of the funds' assets. The mean (median) block represents only 0.15% (0.03%) of the typical funds assets, and with such a small fraction, it is not clear that the gains to the funds of expending effort monitoring the sample firms would justify the costs. Thus, our results are consistent with Admati et al. (1994) proposition that, given that monitoring is costly, these funds will not monitor as this is not likely to result in a modification in the firms payoff structure and will not lead to net gains. They may also refrain from intervening publicly for fear of drawing to public attention the difficulties the company is facing and/or trading on insider information. However, our results could also imply that pension funds are passive investors, investing most of their funds in the index and these investments we analyzed in this paper are peripheral.

While our results are not consistent with the monitoring role of occupational pension funds, our study does not fill all the gaps in the literature. Our sample includes only companies in which occupational pension funds hold more than 3% of the issued share capital. A more desegregated and comprehensive data is not available. Similarly, because of data unavailability, we have not addressed the question of whether occupational pension funds sponsor initiatives, whether they meet with companies and whether there is a co-operation between various funds. The extent to which these additional factors will strengthen or alter our analysis is a matter of further investigation.

Acknowledgements

We are grateful to Yakov Amihud, Francesco Cesarini, John McConnell, Annette Poulsen (the editor), Jonathan Sokobin, Geof Stapledon, Sudi Sudarsanam, an anonymous referee, and seminar participants at Brunel University and the 1998 European Financial Management Association meeting in Lisbon for valuable insights and helpful comments. Faccio acknowledges a research grant from City University Business School. All errors are our responsibility.

References

ABI, 1998. Research update: How much in funded pensions in 1996? Insurance Trends 16, 27–29.

Admati, A.R., Pfleiderer, P., Zechner, J., 1994. Large shareholder activism, risk sharing, and financial market equilibrium. Journal of Political Economy 102, 1097–1130.

Agrawal, A., Knoeber, C.R., 1996. Firm performance and mechanisms to control agency problems between managers and shareholders. Journal of Financial and Quantitative Analysis 31, 377–397.

Agrawal, A., Mandelker, G.N., 1990. Large shareholders and the monitoring of managers: The case of antitakeover charter amendments. Journal of Financial and Quantitative Analysis 25, 143–162.

Ayres, I., Cramton, P., 1993. An agency perspective on relational investing. Working Paper, Stanford University, Stanford, CA.

Barber, B.M., Lyon, J.D., 1997. Detecting long run abnormal stock returns: The empirical power and specification of test-statistics. Journal of Financial Economics 43, 341–372.

Bethel, J.E., Liebeskind, J.P., Opler, T., 1998. Block share repurchases and corporate performance. Journal of Finance 53, 605–635.

Black, B.S., 1998. Shareholder activism and corporate governance in the United States. In: Newman, P. (Ed.), The Palgrave Dictionary of Economics and the Law.

Blake, D., 1995. Pension Schemes and Pension Funds in the United Kingdom. Clarendon Press, Oxford.

Brancato, C.K., 1997. Institutional Investors and Corporate Governance: Best Practice for Increasing Corporate Value. McGraw Hill, Chicago.

Brickley, J.A., Lease, R.C., Smith, C.W. Jr., 1988. Ownership structure and voting on antitakeover amendments. Journal of Financial Economics 20, 267–291.

Brickley, J.A., Lease, R.C., Smith, C.W. Jr., 1994. Corporate voting: Evidence from charter amendment proposals. Journal of Corporate Finance 1, 5–30.

Business Monitor, 1997. Central Statistical Office, London.

Cadbury, A., 1992. Report of the Committee on the Financial Aspects of Corporate Governance. Gee, London.

Carleton, W.T., Nelson, J.M., Weisbach, M.S., 1998. The influence of institutions on corporate governance through private negotiations: Evidence from TIAA-CREF. The Journal of Finance 53, 1335–1362.

Charkham, J., 1995. Keeping Good Company: A Study of Corporate Governance in Five Countries. Oxford University Press, Oxford.

Chew, D.H. (Ed.), 1997. Studies in International Corporate Finance and Governance Systems: A Comparison of the US, Japan and Europe. Oxford University Press, New York.

Coffee, J., 1991. Liquidity versus control: The institutional investor as corporate monitor. Columbia Law Review 91, 1277–1368.

Conrad, J., Kaul, G., 1993. Long-term market overreaction or biases in computed returns? Journal of Finance 48, 39–64.

Cotter, J.F., Shivdasani, A., Zenner, M., 1997. Do independent directors enhance target shareholder wealth during tender offers? Journal of Financial Economics 43, 195–218.

Davis, E.P., 1995. Pension Funds. Retirement-Income, Security and Capital Markets. An International Perspective. Clarendon Press, Oxford.

Del Guercio, D., Hawkins, J., 1999. The motivation and impact of pension fund activism. Journal of Financial Economics 52, 293–340.

Demsetz, H., Lehn, K., 1985. The structure of corporate ownership: causes and consequences. Journal of Political Economy 93, 1155–1177.

Denis, D.J., Kruse, T.A., 1999. Managerial discipline and corporate restructuring following performance declines. Working Paper, Purdue University, West Lafayette, IN.

Denis, D.J., Sarin, A., 1999. Ownership and board structures in publicly traded corporations. Journal of Financial Economics 52, 187–223.

Diamond, D.W., 1984. Financial intermediation and delegated monitoring. Review of Economic Studies 51, 393–414.

Drucker, P.F., 1976. The Unseen Revolution: How Pension Fund Socialism Came to America. Heinemann, London.

Eisenberg, T., Sundgren, S., Wells, M.T., 1998. Large board size and decreasing firm value in small firms. Journal of Financial Economics 48, 35–54.

Financial Times, 1997. FT Survey on Pension Fund Investment. May 9, 1997.

Financial Times, 1997. Pension Funds to Call for Votes on Boardroom Pay: NAPF Will Oppose Hampel Committees Findings. September 29, 1997, p. 20.

Financial Times, 1999. Fighting Fit. January 29, 1999, p. 17.

Franks, J.R., Mayer, C., 1994. The ownership and control of German corporations. Working Paper, London Business School, London.

Franks, J.R., Mayer, C., 1997. Corporate ownership and control in the UK, Germany, and France. Journal of Applied Corporate Finance 9, 30–45.

Franks, J.R., Mayer, C., Renneboog, L., 1998. Who disciplines bad managers? Working Paper, London Business School, London.

Gordon, L.A., Pound, J., 1993. Information, ownership structure, and shareholder voting: Evidence from shareholder-sponsored corporate governance proposals. Journal of Finance 48, 697–718.

Greenbury, R., 1995. Directors Remuneration: Report of a Study Group Chaired by Sir Richard Greenbury. Gee, London.

Hart, O., Holmstrom, B., 1987. The theory of contracts. In: Bewley, T. (Ed.), Advances in Economic Theory. Cambridge University Press, Cambridge, pp. 71–155.

Hart, O., 1995. Firms, Contracts, and Financial Structure. Oxford University Press, Oxford.

Hutton, W., 1995. The State We Are In. Vintage Press, London.

Jarrell, G.A., Poulsen, A.B., 1987. Shark repellents and stock prices: The effects of antitakeover amendments since 1980. Journal of Financial Economics 19, 127–168.

Jensen, M.C., 1986. Agency costs of free cash flow, corporate finance, and takeovers. American Economic Review 76, 323–329.

Jensen, M.C., 1993. The modern industrial revolution, exit, and the failure of internal control systems. Journal of Finance 48, 831–880.

Jepson, J., 1998. US Defined Benefits and Defined Contribution: Comparison and Implications. Paper presented at the 1998 NAPF Conference, Eastbourne, UK.

John, K., Senbet, L.W., 1998. Corporate governance and board effectiveness. Journal of Banking and Finance 22, 371–403.

Kahn, C., Winton, A., 1998. Ownership structure, speculation and shareholder intervention. Journal of Finance 53, 99–129.

Kang, J.K., Shivdasani, A., 1995. Firm performance, corporate governance, and top executive turnover in Japan. Journal of Financial Economics 38, 29–58.

Kaplan, S.N., Minton, B.A., 1994. Appointments of outsiders to Japanese Boards: Determinants and implications for managers. Journal of Financial Economics 36, 225–258.

Karpoff, J.M., 1998. Does Shareholder Activism Work? A Survey of Empirical Findings. Working Paper, University of Washington, Seattle, WA.

Karpoff, J.M., Malatesta, P.H., Walkling, R.A., 1996. Corporate governance and shareholder initiatives: empirical evidence. Journal of Financial Economics 42, 365–395.

Keasey, K.S., Thompson, S., Wright, M., 1997. Corporate Governance: Economic, Management, and Financial Issues. Oxford University Press, Oxford.

Lakonishok, J., Shleifer, A., Vishny, R.W., 1994. Contrarian investment, extrapolation, and risk. Journal of Finance 49, 1541–1578.

Lang, L.H.P., Ofek, E., Stulz, R.M., 1996. Leverage, investment, and firm growth. Journal of Financial Economics 40, 3–29.

Lasfer, M.A., 1995. Agency costs, taxes and debt: The UK evidence. European Financial Management 1, 265–285.

Lasfer, M.A., 1996. Taxes and dividends: The UK evidence. Journal of Banking and Finance 20, 455–472.

Lasfer, M.A., 1997. On the motivation for paying script dividends. Financial Management 26, 62–80.

Lin, T.H., 1996. The certification of large block shareholders in initial public offerings: The case of venture capitalists. Quarterly Journal of Business and Economics 35, 55–65.

Lins, K., Servaes, H., 1999. International evidence on the value of corporate diversification. Journal of Finance 54, 2215–2239.

London Stock Exchange, 1995. Survey on Share Ownership, Stock Exchange, London.

Mallin, C.A., 1997. Investors voting rights. In: Keasey, K., Wright, M. (Eds.), Corporate Governance: Responsibilities, Risks and Remuneration. Wiley: West Sussex.

Maug, E., 1998. Large shareholders as monitors: is there a trade-off between liquidity and control? Journal of Finance 53, 65–98.

McConnell, J.J., Servaes, H., 1990. Additional evidence on equity ownership and corporate value. Journal of Financial Economics 27, 595–612.

McConnell, J.J., Servaes, H., 1995. Equity ownership and the two faces of debt. Journal of Financial Economics 39, 131–157.

Mikkelson, W.H., Ruback, R.S., 1985. An empirical analysis of the interfirm equity investment process. Journal of Financial Economics 14, 523–553.

Minns, R., 1980. Pension Funds and British Capitalism: The Ownership and Control of Shareholders. Heinemann, London.

Morck, R., Shleifer, A., Vishny, R.W., 1988. Management ownership and market valuation: An empirical analysis. Journal of Financial Economics 20, 293–316.

Murphy, K., Van Nuys, K., 1994. State pension fund shareholder activism. Working Paper, Harvard Business School, Boston, MA.

NAPF, 1996. Year Book. National Association of Pension Funds, London.

NAPF, 1996. Good Corporate Governance. National Association of Pension Funds, London.

Nesbitt, S.L., 1994. Long-term rewards from shareholder activism: a study of the 'CalPERS effect'. Journal of Applied Corporate Finance 6, 75–80.

Pension Funds and their Advisers, 1996. London.

Porter, M.E., 1997. Capital choices: Changing the way American invests in industry. In: Chew, D.H. (Ed.), Studies in International Corporate Finance and Governance Systems: A Comparison of the US, Japan and Europe. Oxford University Press, New York, pp. 5–17.

Prowse, S., 1994. Corporate governance in an international perspective: A survey of corporate control mechanisms amongst large firms in the United States, the United Kingdom, Japan and Germany. BIS Economic Papers, No. 41, Bank of International Settlements, Basel.

Romano, R., 1994. Public pension fund activism in corporate governance reconsidered. Columbia Law Review 93, 795–853.

Shleifer, A., Vishny, R.W., 1986. Large shareholders and corporate control. Journal of Political Economy 94, 461–488.

Shleifer, A., Vishny, R.W., 1997. A survey of corporate governance. Journal of Finance 52, 737–783.

Shome, D.K., Singh, S., 1995. Firm value and external blockholdings. Financial Management 24, 3–14.

Short, H., Keasey, K., 1997. Institutional shareholders and corporate governance in the United Kingdom. In: Keasey, K.S., Thompson, S., Wright, M. (Eds.), Corporate Governance: Economic, Management, and Financial Issues. Oxford University Press, Oxford, 18–53.

Smith, M.P., 1996. Shareholder activism by institutional investors: evidence from CalPERS. Journal of Finance 51, 227–252.

Stapledon, G.P., 1996. Institutional Shareholders and Corporate Governance. Clarendon Press, Oxford.

Strickland, D., Wiles, K.W., Zenner, M., 1996. A requiem for the USA: Is small shareholder monitoring effective? Journal of Financial Economics 40, 319–338.

Stulz, R.M., 1988. Managerial control of voting rights: Financing policies and the market for corporate control. Journal of Financial Economics 20, 25–54.

Sudarsanam, S., 1996. Large shareholders, takeovers and target valuation. Journal of Business Finance and Accounting 23, 295–314.

Tomlinson, L., 1998. Should the Future Be All Passive? Paper presented at the 1998 NAPF Conference, Eastbourne, UK.

Wahal, S., 1996. Pension fund activism and firm performance. Journal of Financial and Quantitative Analysis 31, 1–23.

WM, 1996. UK Pension Fund Industry Results. WM, Edinburgh (various issues 1994–1996).

Yermack, D., 1996. Higher market valuation of companies with a small board of directors. Journal of Financial Economics 40, 185–211.

Influence and Intervention by Financial Institutions in their Investee Companies

John Holland

This article describes the corporate governance role of financial institutions in their portfolio companies during typical co-operative circumstances and during periods of corporate need and difficulty. The breakdown of relationships and the use of the market for control is also explored. Confidential case studies were prepared from interviews with senior directors and fund managers in UK based financial institutions. The implicit influence process was constrained by FI unwillingness to interfere in good performing companies and by limited FI power in co-operative circumstances. However, the case FIs were able to use their quasi insider knowledge advantage to diagnose problem areas in strategy, management quality, and the effectiveness of the board, and their negative impact on financial performance. They kept this diagnosis in reserve until circumstances arose where they could exercise much stronger influence. The article ends by exploring this extensive private influence process within institutionalist theory and by discussing the implications of this behaviour for policy changes.

Key words: financial institutions, private influence, insider knowledge.

Introduction

T his article begins by describing the corporate governance role of financial institutions in their portfolio or investee companies during typical co-operative circumstances. Confidential case studies were prepared from interviews with senior directors and fund managers in UK based financial institutions (FIs). The interviews were conducted in the period June 1993 to March 1994 and covered a period of change in Corporate Governance (CG) six months after the publication of the Cadbury Report. The case FIs constituted twenty seven of the thirty five largest UK FIs and included Life Insurance, Pension Fund, Unit trust and Investment trust FIs. The cases revealed a long term, private, programmed, set of regular interactions between FIs and companies in which

implicit FI 'relationship' influence was exercised and a two way flow of information occurred (Section 3).

The implicit influence process was constrained by FI unwillingness to interfere in good performing companies and by limited FI power in co-operative circumstances. FI influence was limited to informed questioning on matters of strategy and management change, with a more explicit influence on Cadbury style corporate governance matters. However, the case FIs were able to use their quasi insider knowledge advantage to diagnose problem areas in strategy, management quality, and the effectiveness of the board, and their negative impact on financial performance. They kept this diagnosis in reserve until circumstances arose where they could exercise much stronger influence. These include corporate requests for help, adverse corporate circumstances, corporate crisis, and the breakdown of institutional and company relationships. The latter refers to the form of FI-Co interactions evident in the ad hoc, intense, short period of a bid process. The paper also explores this extensive private influence process within institutionalist theory; and considers the implications of this behaviour for policy changes.

Corporate Governance and the Cadbury and Hampel Reports

Corporate governance is a broad and somewhat vague term for a range of corporate controls and accountability mechanisms designed to meet the aims of a range of corporate stakeholders. Tricker (1993) defined the boundary to the field of study as 'Corporate Governance covers the concepts, theories and practices of boards and their directors, and the relationships between boards and shareholders, top management, regulators and auditors, and other stakeholders'.

In the Cadbury report (December 1992), the stakeholders are primarily understood to be the shareholders of the firm. Even with this narrowing down on the 'financial aspects of corporate governance', there is some ambiguity about the term (Sir Adrian Cadbury, 1992). The Cadbury Report made many important recommendations on the role of the board. It also called on institutional investors to play a more active role in securing better corporate governance (s6.16), to take a positive interest in the composition of board (s6.11), to make positive use of their voting rights (s6.11) and to disclose their policies on the use of voting rights (s6.12). The committee saw the development of constructive relationships between companies and their owners as central to this process.

The Hampel committee produced its interim report in August 1997. Many recommendations were made to codify the recommendations of the Cadbury report (1992) and Greenbury report on remuneration (1995), to clarify the roles and responsibilities of directors, executive and non executive, and to disclose information on executive remuneration. The report reinforced the central role of shareholders in the corporate governance process and the importance of self regulation in the corporate governance process. It sought to highlight the importance of corporate wealth creation and its wider roles in creating national prosperity. Given the dominance of the large financial institutions in share ownership (Gaved, 1997), the insti-

tutions were effectively being asked to play the primary shareholder role in ensuring that companies were accountable for their wealth creation activities, their decisions on corporate executive pay, and corporate decisions on board structures.

A case study method was adopted to investigate the corporate governance role of FIs because of the scant prior work in this area. This research method allows rich insight into new research fields (Scapens 1990, Kaplan 1983). Patterns of relations concepts and governance methods have been identified from the full set of cases. However, generalisations should be restricted to the cases studied. Despite the coverage of the major UK FIs, the article does not claim to be a representative study of all UK FIs. The short cases and quotes have been edited to preserve confidentiality.

We begin by noting the relationship or implicitly contracting context for institutional and company interactions in the UK. The postwar concentration of share ownership in the hands of UK financial institutions has created a more concentrated form of institutional influence and control over UK companies (Holland 1995). This has reached the point in 1996 where up to 75% of major UK companies' shares are held by institutions, with UK institutions owning about 60% of shares in UK companies. Within this larger group of FIs is a further concentration of ownership. Gaved (1997) points out that in 1996 half of the UK equities in the UK stock market are owned by fifty financial institutions. This was relatively stable over the period 1989 to 1996. The top twenty own about a third of the market, the top ten about a quarter, with the largest, Mercury Asset Management owning 4% in 1996. The top fifty FIs dominated the shareholder bases of FTSE 100 companies and constituted the bulk of their core FIs. This has concentrated company and FI minds on each other and increased the significance of their direct relationships and other forms of contact. This has also created a much clearer target for FI research and for FI influence. Much of the case FI information collection and influence behaviour has been based on the growing institutional concentration of ownership and reflects the behaviour of the large UK case FIs.

The Private Information Agenda and Implicit Influence Processes

In private meetings with investee companies, the case FIs focused on information collection in the areas of corporate strategy, management qualities, and on the effectiveness of Cadbury style corporate governance mechanisms such as the board. The following 3 subsections explore how the case FIs linked information on strategy, management, the board and financial reporting to their understanding of historic and expected financial performance. These subsections also illustrate how the case FIs were then able to make informed judgments on how these ingredients of business performance had played a role in financial performance. This understanding provided the means to implicitly influence such linkages through probing questions.

The private dialogue was the means for the FIs to pre-condition and subtly influence companies in these fundamental areas based on their expertise and stable stakeholding. It was not used to provide strong advice to management. Such pre-conditioning and influencing concerning corporate strategy, management, and expected financial performance was designed so that investee companies internalised the interests of FI and aligned their policies and structures more closely to FI needs. Useem (1993) has argued that this has occurred in the US as US FIs have become more active. Such relationship influence was therefore normally exercised by the case FIs in a subtle semi covert manner, in the background, but understood by participants in a meeting or other interactions.

In contrast, the FIs exercised more explicit influence in the Cadbury defined area of corporate governance and used this as an indirect means to influence strategy and other fundamental performance areas. The case FIs restricted this explicit influence process to areas where they had expertise, such as dividends, return of capital, financing methods, and expected financial performance, and Cadbury style corporate governance issues. The dominant approach of the FIs with their relationship companies was to be pro-active on those performance and governance matters that had low intervention costs such as influencing attitudes to increasing shareholder wealth, boosting profits, cutting costs, separation of chairman and chief executive, or the quality of financial statements.

In Case S: 'In general we are careful to only attempt to influence a firm on matters of principle such as the corporate governance issue of separation of chairman and CE roles. Our influence is boosted here by the social and political significance of the issues. Financial performance of the firm

and financial management issues are areas where the financial institution can exercise influence based on its rights as an investor and its expertise in financial matters. In contrast, attempts to influence strategy involve the financial institution trying to second guess management in its own field of expertise. The financial institution should concentrate on listening and seeking clarification in these managerial domains. Financial institutions should conserve their firepower and restrict their influence to situations where there are clear cut principals, where they have something to offer and where they are likely to succeed.'

Such preconditioning on fundamental performance matters and overt influence on Cadbury governance issues was normally exercised with good performing companies in satisfactory relationships with core FIs. In section 6, we explore how this influence process became more active and explicit with changes in corporate problems and with increasing corporate resistance to FI influence.

Strategy and financial performance

The case FIs used private meetings to ask many specific questions about company strategy and how it was expected to maintain or improve corporate financial performance. Informed probing in this way was based on many prior contacts with the company and was a central means to implicitly exercise influence. These probing questions concerned prior strategic promises and performance promises, recent strategic changes, benchmark comparison with competitors and the industry, corporate innovation, 'good' management practice, and problems with strategy.

In FI case V:
'If we have met management before, the meeting is an opportunity to hear and discuss the company's strategy and to relate it to previous statements. We are hoping to hear a company story that demonstrates consistency and continuity. The discussion can focus around last year's set of stated objectives, how these have been achieved or how and why changes have occurred, and how the company is doing now in various geographic and business segments. Sometimes we take to this years meeting a copy of the slides they used last year. We ask questions about their disappointments over the year. Why are they in certain businesses, how do they

intend to improve ailing businesses, What are they going to do about specific problems. Very seldom do we get down to matters like the forecast range for earnings or other sensitive financial figures. This is more the domain of analysts. Asking this kind of question can give the wrong signal about our motives. We are more interested in getting information for our longer term investment decision and not for an immediate sale. Information about personalities in the company is very important, but information on the fundamentals is more important. The numbers must stack up. We are not insiders because most of the information is already publicly available. Other investors can ask the company for the same information if they are prepared to make the effort and expend their own resources in same way as us.'

Many questions were asked about innovation because of its central role in strategy and because of its financial performance and share value implications. The case FIs recognised that their portfolio companies had innovated in many ways. For example, distribution companies had innovated in warehousing, distribution and marketing channels to create significant shareholder wealth gains. In Life assurance and retail banking very large productivity gains had been made through the use of information technology to deliver financial services direct to customers and to bypass the branch network. Consumer companies had learnt how to manage and adapt a complex portfolio of brand names. Innovative 'stretching' of brand names had been combined with production innovations to create a very flexible product portfolio. They also recognised many examples where a company exploited quite complex new technology to create new products and services, without the company being a hi-tech company in its own right. Riley (1995) gives the example of BSkyB emerging as a new provider of TV and other leisure services by exploiting satellite technology. This has led to a dramatic increase in share value for this company. Technology exploiters and technology developer companies such as Cable and Wireless, Vodaphone, and Glaxo, formed a significant part of the FTSE 100 and thus the portfolios of the case FIs.

Good management practice was another element of the strategic agenda and was seen as central to good financial performance. The contemporary debate on excellence in companies and of 'good management' practice had an influence on the questions asked by

the case FIs during the private dialogue. For example, the ideas of writers such as Peters and Waterman (1982) were influential. These writers emphasised action over analysis, learning directly from customers, internal entrepreneurship, the work force as the root source of quality and productivity gains, direct observation by management of corporate activity, sticking to the core skills and markets, simple structures and lean staff, and simultaneous loose-tight controls. Other case FI sources of ideas on good management and good management practice lay in the wide range of organisational, production and managerial innovations associated with the rise of the Japanese economy. These include just-in-time, lean production, closely linked supply chains, and high company commitment by management and other employees.

The case FIs were aware that some of these ideas came in waves or fashions and required to be treated with some scepticism. The major example given was that the idea of conglomerates was fashionable in the 1970s and 1980s and was expressed best in the strategy of Hanson and BTR. The new fashion in the 1990s was focus and sticking to core strategic strengths. The key idea for case FIs was whether strategy was successful and made sense in the emerging global product-market environment.

The broader debate on these matters and the regular contact with many portfolio companies meant that the case FIs were in a unique position to learn how the character of innovation and management practices contributed to good financial performance in different ways across companies and industries. This provided them with a strong basis to ask informed questions about corporate innovation and management practices and to make comparisons with competitors. This could be an overt comparison during the meeting or it could be implicit in the questions. They were also in a good position to probe why certain innovations and management practices were and were not transferable between industries. Thus regular contact with leading corporate innovators or leading exponents of a new management practice provided the case FIs with an important means to influence the laggard corporate innovators and conservative management in their portfolio. This implicit influence process was a byproduct of fund management. However, it was a purposeful influence process in which the FIs sought to make their portfolio companies accountable for the use of FI risk capital. It therefore corresponded to the wider view of corporate governance as expounded by the Hampel interim report (1997).

Management quality, personality factors and impact on financial performance

Interpersonal interactions in meetings were seen as central to understanding how management personalities and management qualities contributed to financial performance. Information on these matters affected FIs' perception of the credibility of private strategic and financial information, and its usefulness in understanding financial performance and in valuing the company. Information on personalities of management also helped the case FIs assess whether they could influence the management teams through a creative dialogue or whether they would have to wait until the company needed help before significant influence was possible.

Thus the dominance of individuals and cohesiveness of management teams were observed and assessed. The personality characteristics of key managers, such as sense of purpose, honesty, integrity, reputation were very important in establishing FI trust, and confidence. These were assessed at the level of individuals and management teams.

FI case I:
'We can also create new information. For example, if the board and senior executives appear split during the meeting, this leads us to a closer analysis of our other sources and the financial figures to see if we have missed something. Often we have. We have many sources of information at our disposal, especially from other company contacts. This is very important for comparisons like this and for finding differences from what is generally known by the Financial Times reader. Meetings are about 'reading' the personalities in the company, interpreting the verbal nuances in the chairman's statements, and closely observing the behaviour of executives. These impressions are as important to us as a slide full of financial figures. In fact they are more important, because we generally know all the financial details … We can use the meeting to form a view on whether management are telling the truth or lies. We can confirm things management have said, or confirm information from other sources such as analysts. This raises our confidence in information that is often initially quite weak. It can make us happier about our sources and our investment decisions.'

Meetings were also seen as a key opportunity to collect information on the 'quality of management' as one of the most important ingredients in generating the required cor-porate financial performance. 'Management quality' was expressed as a fluid concept in the cases but seemed to consist of a complex combination of approved personality factors, trust, confidence, and reputation factors. It also included ideas of leadership, cohesiveness of management teams, successful track records in financial performance, an ability to deliver promises, and a responsiveness to new situations (expected, unexpected).

FI case V: 'Meetings are often the means to find out things such as whether the company is run by a dominant character. If a Chief Executive is continually exercising control over other managers in the meeting by direct verbal command or by eye contact then we have some idea how the company is actually run. We look out for this kind of thing and we try to avoid investing in "one man bands" and "The direct personal contact allow to assess individuals. We do not invest in 'get rich quick, flashy types'. We can often observe little details which tell us lot about individuals tendencies to consume perks, or to aggrandisement, or their staying power with the company" and "If we are unsure about the character of key executives or about gaps in their management history, we phone up the company broker to check out the background of managers. We also ask about individuals personalities, and see if the broker confirms our view of the individuals from the meeting."'

Thus a proven ability to generate growth, to innovate, and to manage growth were essential as was the clarity of strategy and the ability of management to articulate it. Managerial development plans and succession policies were important to see how 'management quality' might change over time. Information on consumption of perks, or of a 'get rich quick' attitude, was thought to be available only by direct observation.

The fund managers recognised that their ideas of 'management quality' were transient and fragile reflecting the contingent nature of the concept. However, they argued that they needed some feel for 'management quality' in their investee companies as one means for them to assess expected performance and to change management when needed. It was their understanding of management quality based on interactions with many portfolio companies over many years that formed the basis for their influence. This normally took the form of influencing the planned succession policy in their investee companies and pre-conditioning the new

Chairmen or new Chief Executives so that they knew what the FIs expected of them and were likely to be open to FI influence.

Donald Bryden (1993), Chairman of BZW Investment Management, explains the value of this pre-conditioning.

'Probably, the most important benefit is that it prevents nasty surprises. If you think of it from the perspective of the company's management, if they have a rough idea of the attitudes of their major shareholders, in advance, to many general issues I think that is beginning to condition their behaviour. A good example is the chairman who came to see us just a week ago and brought with him his successor, and went through a description of why he has chosen this man to be his successor and how the company was going to be run, but importantly wanted the new chairman to hear our views early so that he could then condition his behaviour to respond to his shareholders.'

Effectiveness of formal corporate governance mechanisms

The prevailing Cadbury (and the subsequent Greenbury and Hampel) debate on corporate governance was used by the case FIs as a stimulus to collect information on matters such as the separation of Chief Executive and Chairman roles, the number of non executive directors, planned executive succession, remuneration and other 'good practice' corporate governance matters. An active dialogue was a means to influence the company on these matters. It was also an indirect means to influence the strategic direction of the investee companies and their expected financial performance. A key connection identified by the case FIs was that corporate governance mechanisms such as Cadbury style board structures could play a central role in identifying, encouraging, and supporting good quality managers.

The case FIs also used the private meetings to observe if senior executives were implementing the full spirit and substance of the (more traditional) Cadbury and Greenbury corporate governance proposals or were adopting a superficial approach to the reforms. This form of probing went much beyond 'box ticking'. It allowed the case FIs to assess whether matters such as the separation of Chief Executive duties and Chairman duties had been implemented in a token manner by a powerful executive or had been implemented so that the two roles were distinct, complementary and substan-

tive. If it was the latter then this created more flexible points for future influence by the case FIs.

The FIs also observed unfavourable changes in management attitudes to shareholder wealth maximisation and to the consumption of perquisites. These observations alerted FIs to the potential threat to corporate financial performance that might emerge with a board and management team pursuing their own ends. This was a signal for the case FIs to begin to strengthen board structures and other aspects of 'good' corporate governance in the expectation that this would feed through into financial performance and into more flexible influence points. These data therefore reveal that implementing Cadbury was an important means for the case FIs to influence corporate performance to reflect their shareholder interests and to create new influence options. Smith (1996) has studied the effect of shareholder activism on corporate governance and its impact on shareholder wealth. He focused on one very large US FI, CalPERS, the Californian public employees pension fund. CalPERS targets companies that are poor financial performers or who adopt restrictive corporate governance practices. In the sample period 72% of the targets either adopted FI proposed governance practices or made changes sufficient to warrant a settlement. There was a significant stock price reaction for successful targeting events and a significant negative reaction for unsuccessful events. Thus activism was beneficial for CalPERS. This US evidence and the existence of an active UK influence process reveals the opportunities for the UK Hampel committee in extending FI influence in the interests of improved corporate governance and in boosting financial performance at the same time.

The case FIs also identified some formal corporate governance areas such as executive remuneration where they were careful and sometimes avoided influencing management. The case FIs provided a range of reasons why they preferred to avoid interfering in board decisions on remuneration. They argued that they appointed the board and top management as their agents to make a whole host of managerial decisions including pay. To interfere would undermine 'management's right to manage' and could involve the FIs in detailed managerial decisions outside their perceived area of competence. It appeared that the threat to their relationship advantages was a major issue in limiting the scope of FI interference. In some cases, other barriers to interference included the FI's need to secure pension fund management business from the corporate sector and the similarity of their own executive remuneration packages. Despite these FI comments, it may prove difficult in the political climate of the late 1990's for the case FIs to maintain the view that their corporate agents can determine the size and structure of their own remuneration.

Barker's (1996) survey results are similar to this case research in that he finds that formal and direct contacts with senior company management are the most important sources of information for fund managers, and that the report and accounts (especially the annual, though also the interim) are the second major source of information. Meetings with company executives were particularly important to allow fund managers to understand the strategy of the company, and to assess management's capacity to achieve the strategy.

Active Influencing of Companies During Difficult Problems and Conflict

The implicit influence process outlined in section 3 occurred simultaneously with information collection and knowledge acquisition. It focused on the same four areas of corporate performance of strategy, management qualities, accountability mechanisms, and financial performance. This influence was subtle and came out of the continuing dialogue on these matters. Areas of corporate strategy, long term succession plans, and the quality of management, were seen as management's strength and responsibility and the case FIs avoided explicitly intervening here during normal co-operative relationships with good performing companies.

The implicit influence process, was therefore constrained by FI unwillingness to interfere in good performing companies and by limited FI power in these co-operative circumstances. However, the case FIs were able to use their knowledge advantage to diagnose problem areas in strategy, management quality, the effectiveness of the board and of financial reporting, and their negative impact on financial performance. They kept this diagnosis of weaknesses in reserve until circumstances arose where they could exercise much more forceful and radical influence. The three major categories of circumstances encouraging explicit influence were, corporate requests for help, dramatic changes in strategy or adverse corporate circumstances, and the breakdown of institutional and company relationships.

As these circumstances arose, increasing case FI pressure and influence were exercised

via the board and senior management on problematic aspects of strategy, management quality, board structures and financial reporting, in the expectation that this would contribute to improved financial performance. The particular focus of FI influence depended on where the corporate performance problems were thought to lie. The prior diagnosis, based on the knowledge advantage was crucial to pinpointing these problems and to an effective, targeted influencing process. Public pressure in the form of media leaks and small but symbolic stock sales were used to intensify the pressure on reluctant executives. On occasion, the influence process failed, and the case FIs resorted to complete sales of stock or to the market for corporate control.

Management quality and succession was often a priority target for influence. This was because management were the medium to change other factors such as strategy, innovation, management quality, the quality of financial reports and the functioning of board committees. The FIs recognised that they had to go through management to change those factors affecting financial performance. Replacing management was also seen as a quick and cheap way of changing these fundamental performance factors if the case FIs were facing an obstructive management and board. As a result management quality and succession were the central focus of FI influence as corporate circumstances changed. As corporate circumstances changed from co-operative relations, to corporate need, to adverse circumstances, to hostile relations, then the nature of the influence and advice on management and management succession and change became more pro-active, forceful and explicit. This level of sophisticated influence concerning management quality and succession was dependent on long FI experience and knowledge of managers over their careers with many investee companies. The FIs argued that this influence focus meant that 'the market for corporate executives' was also a private market over which they exercised considerable influence.

In the following sub sections we explore these changes in the FI influence process in more detail as we move from co-operative relations, to corporate need, to going public, to hostile relations. These are categories of increasingly active and explicit FI influence but they do not necessarily imply a sequential change process. If FI influence is successful at one point then no further extension of influence may be required.

New pressure points for FIs

The case financial institutions made extensive use of various 'pressure points' to encourage substantive changes in corporate behaviour including fundamental performance and Cadbury style corporate governance areas. These pressure points, where most influence and pressure could be exercised, included situations where a company,

- had come to the market or to its major FI investors to ask for additional equity capital.
- sought to change or dilute FI ownership rights and required FI consent.
- asked questions, or asked for help and support during takeover situations or other uncertain situations.
- proposed a new financing method, a new voting structure, or new remuneration contracts for the board and top management.

In each situation, the case FIs bargained for more information and exercised a pro-active and explicit influence on companies. They were careful not to disrupt co-operative relationships. Depending on corporate need and FI perceptions of company problems, the FIs offered friendly and constructive advice on the relevant aspects of strategy, management, accountability mechanisms and their expected impact on financial performance. For example, this situation could create an opportunity to have a more open dialogue and to bargain on who should succeed in the key board and top management posts over time. These opportunities were rare and the case FIs waited for them to occur so that could bargain for desirable planned changes in management.

Case A below reveals an example of how a case FI tried to use company proposals as a pressure point to bargain on pay schemes and corporate performance,

Case

'A company may propose a new remuneration package for executives based on say an option scheme. We will respond by saying OK but what about the flow back or added value for us as a result of implementing this scheme. We would like to know how this scheme would produce improved corporate financial performance relative to some kind of sensible benchmark such as the sector's performance. Their proposal allows us to begin a dialogue with the corporate executives which we can use to pressure them to move towards financial performance aims consistent with the needs of the company and our needs. We are not too concerned about the specific forms of the remunerations scheme or the size of the benefits potentially coming to management as long as we have reasonable expectations that the scheme will create the climate for better than benchmark performance, we get a share of the additional benefits, and the company is creating enough internal capital for further investment and R&D. If the proposal improves the company's competitive edge and enhances stock market values and the extra 'cake' is shared out sensibly then we are all winners. We do not agree to remuneration contracts that contain rollover clauses for management that mean expensive compensation for managers having to depart for poor performance.'

Adverse circumstances

If adverse or unusual corporate circumstances occurred, then individual FI or core FI group intervention in an investee company could be stimulated, at the same time as corporate power to resist external influence declined. This could occur when, the company had been performing poorly for some time, board and management disputes had become serious and threatened the economic health of the company, and when the company had been blatantly ignoring all of the corporate governance guidelines and its financial performance had not been satisfactory. It could also occur when the FIs were seriously concerned about a major switch from a business strategy that management had promoted heavily in the recent past and which had been understood and agreed with the core FIs.

These circumstances encouraged the case FIs to offer strong advice and to exercise considerable explicit pressure on those aspects of strategy or of management where they thought the problem lay and where they thought action would boost financial performance. For example, this was the opportunity to negotiate changes in the existing management team or in succession plans.

Case S identifies how intervention can be stimulated by unacceptable managerial behaviour.

'Management needs are often a source of conflict with shareholders. Thus their requirements for income, for perks, for incentive schemes, for power, for independence of owners, can all create major conflict in relations and stimulate active intervention by us.'

Holberton (1990) reports the views of a top manager of one of Britain's biggest investors,

'Our strength increases the weaker the company's position is. Until the company's strategy has been proved wrong all one is doing is exchanging opinions. You need to be pretty sure of your position before you can push things through. The chance of doing something when the situation is quite clear is pretty good. But that means that the situation has been deteriorating for some time. It is much more difficult when you express your views at an earlier stage, especially if the non executive directors are prepared to back their executive colleagues.'

In these circumstances the FI can demand rather than bargain for extra information and can dramatically alter strategy, board composition, and the occupants of chief executive, chairman and finance director positions. In case C we see the significance of FI power and benefits of intervention:

'In general, if you are going to intervene in a company make sure you enter to win and also ensure that you are well within your rights when you go in there. If you don't have this sense of purpose the probability of failure is high.'

and in Case G: 'In the confrontational situations where we kick out the bad management or the Board this gives a very strong signal to companies not to get into such circumstances. This can affect the whole of our portfolio of investee companies. In the case of cooperative relationships we may be voting against the company's AGM proposals or refusing to take up the rights issue when the company requests that we do so. Again this acts as a very clear signal to the individual company and to the rest of our portfolio companies as to what our policy is. Too much activity and intervention here can, of course, disrupt relationships in the long run and we have to be fairly careful as to what we're doing in this respect.'

Combining with other institutions was another means for boosting FI influence. However, there were problems here. Whittington (1993) argued that UK institutional arrangements for pooling shareholder voting power were weak and informal. The case institutions supported this view and case G illustrates the difficulties of co-ordination.

'In the case of the companies with very poor financial performance we have to consider sometimes getting together a group of financial institutions to coordinate action against the company. One of the problems here is secrecy. How many financial institutions can you get together and ensure that the matters can be conducted behind closed doors. We think the limit is two or maybe three financial institutions. Ideally we would need up to 25%/30% cumulative stake in the company to ensure we have as strong as possible an influence. Once we have established this kind of influence we can then establish what to change. This could be the management itself, the Board and the management or just a change to the strategy, or perhaps all three. In these circumstances we have to have a powerful enough group to make a clear decision as to what we want. We look at the company's share register and see who the other top institutions are. We then phone around to try and secure as much support as we can from the key institutional shareholders. In one case recently a leading financial institution got eleven to twelve institutions around the table to deal with a company. It was very difficult to coordinate this large group with very different needs. It was also the case that some fund managers were not senior enough to pledge their votes and support collective action. There was also conflict in the group in that one or two of the financial institutions did not want to pay a share of the legal fees and were acting as free riders. There was also conflict because some of them had the authority but did not wish to pledge the use of their votes in a collective action. They therefore weakened the collective action.'

The transition to public conflict

The transition from strong private advice (normally in adverse corporate circumstances) to open public conflict between institutions and companies was somewhat problematic. Several examples were identified in the cases. These included, continued corporate requests for help and very difficult corporate circumstances, several years of poor quality relationship contacts combined with poor financial performance in one period, and consistently poor financial performance combined with an incoherent strategy. When these coincided with the company ignoring strong FI advice then public, open disputes arose between company and FIs.

Confrontations were seen as unusual and only occurred two to three times a year in the experience of individual case FIs. However, on rare occasions a private confrontation became a very public conflict and because of this appeared to be the dominant pattern of FI-Co interaction. In practice it was the public 'tip of the private iceberg' of long term FI attempts to influence the company.

For example, Ross Goobey, a top fund manager at Postel (now Hermes) publicly wrote to the chairmen of the top 100 UK companies informing them that Postel expected its investee companies to get rid of long term rolling contracts which can lead to poor performing managers receiving large pay offs. He said (1993),

'We haven't stopped talking to people about the subject of rolling contracts and remuneration packages'. He argued that much is going on behind the scenes concerning these and other corporate governance issues. 'There is a point when going public can be useful. But those occasions are very rare... It doesn't mean nothing's been happening'. In terms of going public on some these issues he says 'There is a point when, if the company tells you its none of your business, you have to gather support for your view amongst other shareholders, and ultimately you may have to go public on it. The media can be useful in getting a point of view across to other shareholders, maybe small shareholders and institutions who may not be aware of what is happening, and getting a groundswell of opinion to put more pressure on management'. (Hosking, 1994, p. 8)

Some recent public examples of public FI conflict with investee companies include Farnell (1996), Forte (1996), British Gas (1995), Saatchi and Saatchi (1994), Pentos (1993), Amstrad (1992), Pegasus (1992), Hanson (1992) and Lonrho (1992). In these situations, the FIs assumed a quasi management role. Their primary target was normally the poor performing or resistant management but it could be a major strategic issue. The FIs abandoned negotiation and used selective stock sales to encourage board action and they leaked information to the media suggesting that senior executives had lost their confidence and should resign. When this did not unseat senior executives, the potential existed to stimulate the market for corporate control and to change the whole management team.

In Case X: 'If the company refuses to listen to our individual "behind the scenes" influence, then group financial institution action and the use of public pressure mechanisms such as the media may be employed. The last resort may be to fall back on the stock market and the market for managerial control. This ranking of intervention policies reflects a UK preference for a "private club" solution rather than a public confrontation. Of course all methods of intervention may be present in varying degrees in a particular situation.'

Stimulating the market for corporate control

The case FIs argued that a bid could result from the core FIs complaining about the company within a broader institutional-corporate network of contacts. In turn, this may provide the necessary information for a predator company (A) to identify a company (B) with weak institutional support. Despite this, the case FIs denied direct involvement in putting a 'company into play'. They argued that if company A already had strong support and positive sentiment amongst its core FIs and the City, and was more adept in managing its own FI-Co relationships in a pro-active manner then it could be able to exploit weaknesses in company B's relations with its FIs to create a takeover opportunity.

Direct FI activation of a bid crisis for a poorly performing company (B) was not observable in the FI cases. However, the cases FIs were pre-conditioning investee companies on what they would expect if a bid ever occurred. This included preferred financing terms, and bid terms. It also seemed probable from the case data that a company B could 'put itself into play' by generating a poor reputation within the wider FI-corporate network. The network transmitted the failure of the direct contact corporate governance mechanism and stimulated the market for corporate control as a replacement corporate governance mechanism. For example, Cohen (1996) notes the following institutional investor comment on the Forte-Granada case during the December 1995 to January 1996 takeover battle.

'Shareholders are almost incapable of influencing mediocre managements in spite of the introduction of a vast array of measures designed to improve corporate governance, one of the UK's leading institutional investors said yesterday. 'We have found it very difficult in the UK to weed out poor management,' said Mr Robin Morgan, the chief executive of M&G, the UK's largest independent unit trust company. 'It is very difficult to address things unless there is a crisis.' Mr Morgan said that the only really effective mechanism for forcing strategic or managerial change remained the take-over bid. 'In the Granada-Ford bid, that was an expensive mechanism,' he said, noting £150 million in advisers' fees. 'There was no mechanism to change the management in a cheaper way.'

Morgan implies that FIs may have to wait for the crisis to occur. In contrast, Glasberg (1989) argues that banks and other financial institutions have the capacity to define and construct 'crises' and 'problems' in their borrower or investee companies. They can therefore ignore problems or exercise controlled private pressure if they think the management team can deal with them or they can activate a 'crisis' if they wish to make major changes in policy or in the composition of the management team. Private disputes within the management team and followed by public 'washing of this dirty linen' increased the likelihood of public FI action.

In the City of London, a small number of institutions such as MAM, the Pru or Standard Life, with common, large stakeholdings in both predator company A and target company B, can dominate the institutional influencing and decision making process before, during and after the merger. This overlapping group of core stakeholders for both companies A and B has the strongest pre bid influence on the thinking of the predator and they can become insiders if so desired. They become the focus for intensive private and public corporate communications during the merger as both parties seek to gain their support, their share buying/selling and eventual voting can sway the whole decision, and their post merger monitoring can ensure that the predator keeps its promises. If not then company A may become a bid target itself. Throughout this takeover process these FIs are exploiting their knowledge advantage concerning companies A and B and probably have a stronger advantage here at the end of the process. During the Granada-Forte bid there was considerable speculation that Forte was put into play by major institutional shareholders such as Mercury Asset Management who held large stakes in both Forte and Granada long before the bid was announced. For example Connon (1996) noted

'Little known outside the City but a legend within it, MAM owns 14.5% of Granada and 15% of Forte. It has nine days left in which to choose whether to back Gerry Robinson's £3.8 billion bid for Sir Rocco Forte's empire. But is it a coincidence that MAM is in this position? or did MAM deliberately put Forte into play? Those who believe it did argue that even Robinson, one of Galley's (MAM fund manager) favourite businessmen, would not dare launch such a bid without prior discussion with it and Forte's largest shareholder. Others say such an active role is not MAM's style – and besides, Granada hardly seems to be behaving as if it has Forte in the bag. In practical terms, it hardly matters. The City believes that MAM's presence on a share register is tantamount to an invitation to bid.'

The overt or covert placing of company B 'in play' by FIs for takeover by another company A can be seen as one way of bringing the 'market for control' into operation when private relationship corporate governance influence fails with that company B. This can also be interpreted as private FI-Co corporate governance working well for company A and creating takeover opportunities for the company. These arise in part because the company A is well connected into the FI network and into the wider company-FI network. They also arise because of FI dissatisfaction with B.

After management change had occurred through a takeover, the case FIs argued that they returned to their pre-conditioning influence process. They stabilised their equity holding in company A and they sought to support their new nominee managers. They also encouraged new remuneration packages in which executive pay was aligned with FI wealth creation aims.

Theoretical Discussion of the 'Behind the Scenes' Corporate Governance Process

Current theorising and empirical work on the corporate governance role of financial institutions emphasises publicly observable events such as voting behaviour, unexpected and planned managerial departures and appointments, public rebukes by FIs, and listings of poor performing companies by FIs. These public corporate governance events are investigated by a range of research methods such as questionnaire surveys of voting behaviour (Mallin 1996), or by market based methods of the price impact of such events (for example see Smith, 1996). In addition, the media focuses on newsworthy public events such as an open dispute between the board and the institutions, subsequent management departures and appointments, and public statements on strategy changes. Such finance based academic work and media attention gives the strong impression that it is the public institution-company (FI-Co) interactions that are the main activity. However, this article on FI influence, Holland's (1997) research concerning company communications to FIs, Gaved (1997), Marston (1993), and Barker (1996), all reveal that private company and institution interactions are a systematic and pervasive feature of the UK financial system. There is the possibility that the use of public data alone to study or report FI intervention misses the primary FI influence phenomena and only provides insights on a residual public process as the visible output of an extensive private influence process. In contrast, the approach adopted in this article has generated data on private processes and the opportunity to link up the private and public influence processes. This creates the opportunity to extend the theoretical framework for understanding the corporate governance role of financial institutions.

Institutionalism is a theoretical development in sociology that emphasises the idea that organisations are deeply and essentially embedded in a wider institutional framework (Scott and Meyer, 1994). In a UK context, institutionalism suggests that the UK City and Corporate environment consisting of City networks or social connections can be seen as a relevant organisation template already available in this UK environment for the design of rationalised FI-Co relations and for legitimising their role in Cadbury style and the broader Hampel view of corporate governance.

The existing networks of City and corporate relations have played a central role in fashioning recent UK developments in corporate governance. The major UK FIs, corporations, and their representative bodies all have a heavy concentration of major offices and HQs in or near the City of London and use the physical proximity to maintain their influence in the City network. In the period 1991 to 1997, FI bodies such as the Association of British Insurers (ABI), the National Association of Pension Funds (NAPF), or their joint Institutional Shareholders Committee (ISC), lobbied and advised the Government on its proposed legislation on company law, on corporate governance, and insider information, and many other matters that impinged on their relationships with investee companies. Corporate bodies such as the IOD, the CBI, and 100 group of Finance

Directors have also played an important lobbying role. All of these groups lobbied hard from 1991 to 1997 to influence the Cadbury Report and the subsequent Greenbury and Hampel reports. Many of these groups were represented on these three committees and have helped produce the three reports. It is therefore no surprise to note that the Cadbury, Greenbury and Hampel reports all reflected a negotiated balance between the vested interests of these groups.

The City club environment has also made it easy and necessary for FIs and companies to use close relations as their 'normal' transacting and influence channels and it treats organisations that have them and use them as by definition more legitimate than others (Meyer, 1994, p. 122). Thus the stable organising of FI-Co relations and their role in corporate governance, requires and results from external legitimation. FI-Co relations observed in the cases conformed to organising patterns considered acceptable in the City and corporate environment. The environment patterns that drive organising of FI-Co relations and their role in corporate governance, work through linkages that go beyond 'hard wired' controls and can be seen as shared corporate and City meaning systems. These meaning systems determine what FI-Co relations and corporate governance processes look like. Thus in the UK financial system, hidden, 'behind the scenes', social control processes are a common cultural feature (see Streek and Schmitter (1985), Birkinshaw et al (1990)). This article illustrates that the micro 'behind the scenes' influence process reflects the wider 'behind the scenes' patterns to be observed in UK capitalism. These networks and the shared vested interests of City and corporate members can also be seen as a source of collective FI power (Scott 1993) and of some of the barriers to good corporate governance as perceived by other corporate stakeholders.

The environmental patterns that create FI-Co relations are both rationalised and rationalising. The City and corporate sociocultural environment encourage the use of means-ends (transaction based) FI-Co relationships and of standardised systems of corporate governance control for FI shareholders. More specifically, fund managers have established core corporate holdings as a means of acquiring stable investment opportunities and rich information flows on individual companies, industries and the economy. They have also invested resources in relationships contacts to maintain these information advantages. The modernising and rationalising culture in the UK has also created extensive legal rights for investors and these have in the 1990s been tied to notions of 'good' corporate governance. This has created a new non transacting role for FI-Co relations in which these channels are seen as a convenient, rational and culturally consistent means to encourage 'good' corporate governance. Companies have also rationalised their core FIs as part of a cost efficient and effective City influence and communication activity (Holland 1995).

This institutionalist view that the environment has a strong influence on interactions between companies and FIs and on corporate governance has also been expressed by Colin Mayer (1995, 1994). He argues that corporate governance in the UK and its problems are a direct function of UK legal and market structures which ease the transfer of ownership in the UK, of the dispersed nature of ownership, and of the trading orientation of the City of London. This has two consequences. It lowers the commitment of investors to other stakeholders in the firm than is the case in Germany or Japan and it reduces UK FI incentives to monitor firms compared to German (see Edwards and Fischer 1994) and Japanese shareholders with much larger stakes. It is therefore more difficult in the UK for dispersed FI shareholders to establish implicit contracts and long term relations with other corporate stakeholders such as suppliers, senior management, employees and purchasers. Disrupting implicit contracts with one of these stakeholders in Japan and Germany can create major reputational costs for the large (bank or institutional) shareholder. No such discipline applies in the UK. However, this article indicates that UK FI shareholder influence appears more extensive than Mayer (1995) would suggest. The large case FIs are not the dispersed shareholders assumed by Mayer and others. The increasing concentration of UK share ownership means that they hold stable stakes (Gaved, 1997), and act as core shareholders, employing close corporate relationships to identify problems, to intervene early, to prevent a company from sliding into poor performance and to make adjustments at an early stage. This behaviour reveals that large UK financial institutions have developed an early warning system that is similar in substance but different in practice to the German lead or Haus Bank. The latter is present on German company boards and is thus far more visible than its UK equivalent as a monitoring and governance mechanism and this may explain its importance in the literature compared to UK FI-Co relations.

This research finds that the UK business and financial environment does encourage a UK variant of implicit contracting between FIs and the top management group of investee firms. The factors identified by Mayer are likely to play a role in undermining this specific sub set of implicit contracts in the UK compared to say France, Germany or Japan. However, the (information, influence, and capital exchange) benefits, especially for the top 50 UK financial institutions and top 250 UK listed UK companies, appear to outweigh the problems created by a trading oriented City and by unsupportive ownership structures. In the absence of major changes to UK ownership patterns and to the trading orientation of the City, it appears that the implicit FI-Co contracts discussed here offer a home grown mechanism for effecting corporate governance change. The growth of this mechanism out of existing UK organisational structures appears to offer an available, and relatively low cost mechanism to bring about change. Its central weakness lies in the exclusion of other stakeholders. This problem has been magnified by the management remuneration debate in 1994–97 where FIs have been much criticised for their ineffective corporate governance role especially with the privatised utilities. The route to wider legitimation of FI-Co relations as a corporate governance mechanism may lie in FIs reflecting the corporate governance views of a wider UK community including small investors, employees, suppliers and customers. This could occur through these other stakeholders exercising pressure through their pension funds and their investment management decisions. Alternatively, it could arise through companies and FIs recognising that the wider corporate stakeholder base plays a significant role in creating corporate wealth and it is therefore in FI and corporate executive interests to reflect the concerns of these stakeholders.

New Questions on the Role of Financial Institutions

The implicit FI influence process outlined in this article and its transition to a more active influence process indicate that the idea of 'separation of ownership and control' (Berle and Means, 1967) may no longer be relevant in the UK. The case FIs invested in relationships with investee companies to increase their ability to influence the company. This was not the full control of a majority holding but it was a higher level of control and influence than possible with an 'arms length' approach to the company. As a result, separation of ownership and control may be a myth in the 1990s where concentrated capital in the form of major UK institutions can now have direct influence on internal strategy formulation and also communicate their views on strategy to operational managers.

This development has been fortunate for the UK corporate governance debate. The concentration of control in the hands of UK FIs now offers many opportunities for using relationship channels to encourage 'good' corporate governance (Holland 1995). However, the question remains, Who governs the governors? The interests of small investors are not explicitly recognised in the private information collection and influence process outlined in this article. There is a possibility that the gains of the private exchange process could just be shared between company managers and their core FI fund managers. Increased transparency of this private process will be required to allay such fears. For example, one proposal could be to replace private FI-Co interactions with say a quarterly public meeting where the company reports on all qualitative matters. The view of the case FIs was that if the meetings were open, many of the relationship advantages would be lost. If they were public, they would certainly be lost to the parties and thus the public meeting would probably not release any extra useful information. It would be like a frequent AGM. The parties would probably find other ways of establishing contact to bypass the public system and to exchange private information and influence. As an example of this resistance to the change, the Myners report (DTI, 1995) does not suggest that 1:1 FI-Co meetings become public or more transparent in some way. The report does suggest improved company public disclosures in the financial report, public announcements, and in terms of more active FI involvement in public AGMs. However, the privacy of the 1:1 meeting is clearly too valuable to suggest that it becomes more open.

Privacy and the joint acquisition of knowledge and confidence advantages are key sources of power for the relationship parties. This power can be used relative to other FIs, investors and companies. It will not be easy to persuade these parties to relinquish this source of power by making the meetings more transparent. These network based influence and information exchange systems are endemic to the UK variant of capitalism. They are legitimised in a wider 'club' system and can be seen as part of shared corporate and institutional meaning systems (Scott 1993). This is likely to be the major barrier to radical change in the area of relationships and the corporate governance role of financial institutions.

The relationship model could also be applied to representatives of small investors. In the case of small investors, we have seen that institutions have privileged access to information and unique learning opportunities. The institutional relations model described here suggests how other non privileged investors could acquire similar benefits. For example, small shareholder associations could demand similar access to companies and similar information and learning opportunities as the major financial institutions. They would then be responsible for quickly placing their record of meetings in the public domain so that it was available to small shareholders in general. An Internet Web page or the use of TV CEEFAX pages would be appropriate.

However, extensive legislation requiring FIs to be more transparent on company meeting and influence, or to require FIs to influence companies for corporate governance, financial performance, investment or other 'national interest' aims may be short-sighted if they threaten working relationships with companies. If FIs are seen as social or economic 'police' by companies then the fruitful exchange of information and influence may wane, and this may not be in the broader public interest. Legislation may also 'signpost' behaviour to 'swerved around' as management and FIs pursue their own personal interests. Trustees may also be concerned that returns may fall or risks increase and their savers or pensioners suffer the losses. They will have to be persuaded that maximising financial returns for a given level of risk can be shortsighted and lead to major social problems.

Summary

This article has sought to illustrate the corporate governance role of relationships between financial institutions and their portfolio companies. Large FIs as core shareholders employed close corporate relationships to identify problems, to intervene early, to prevent a company from sliding into poor performance and to make adjustments at an early stage. This possibility indicated that the UK financial institutions had developed an early warning system that was similar in substance but different in practice to the German lead or Haus Bank. The 27 case studies provided considerable insight into how co-operative relations were used for corporate governance purposes. This corporate governance process was illustrated in some detail by case studies. The overall set of FI cases reveals that there are many circumstances in which FIs can intervene and influence their investee companies concerning corporate governance issues. The circumstances range from co-operative relations, corporate need, adverse company circumstances, to a breakdown in relations. The article therefore reveals part of a hidden or 'behind the scenes' corporate governance mechanism. Finally, the article has explored the broader significance of FI-Co corporate governance mechanisms and discussed some policy implications arising from the research.

References

Accounting Standards Board 1995, Exposure Draft Statement of Principles for Financial Reporting (ASB, London).

Barker, R.G. 1996, *Financial Reporting & Share Prices: The Finance Director's View*, published by Price Waterhouse: London.

Berle, A.A. and Means, G.C. 1967, *The modern corporation and private property*, revised edition, New York.

Birkinshaw, P., Harden, I. and Lewis, N. 1990, *Government by moonlight*, Unwin Hyman: London.

Bryden, D. 1993, BBC Radio 4, 10th June.

Cadbury, A. 1992, *The Observer*, 6th December, p. 36.

Cohen, N. 1996, *Financial Times*, February 9th, 'Big investor criticises lack of shareholder power'.

Connon, H. 1996, *The Observer, the Business*, p. 1, 14th January, 'Whose bid is it anyway? Did investment guru Galley put Forte into play? Dancing to MAM's tune'.

Easterby-Smith, M., Thorpe, R. and Lowe, A. 1991, *Management Research – An introduction*, Sage: London.

Edwards, J. and Fischer, K. 1994, *Banks, Finance and Investment in Germany*, Cambridge University Press: Cambridge.

'Financial Aspects of Corporate Governance' (The Cadbury report), December 1992, London.

The Greenbury committee on Corporate Governance (Remuneration issues), July, 1995, London.

The interim Hampel report on corporate governance, August 1997, London.

Gaved, M. 1997, *Closing the communications gap: Disclosure and Institutional Shareholders*, ICAEW: London.

Glasberg, D.S. 1989, *The power of collective purse strings*, University of California Press.

Goobey, R. 1994, quoted in Hosking, Patrick, *Independent on Sunday*, 30 January, p. 8.

'Guidance on the dissemination of price sensitive information', London Stock Exchange, February 1994.

Holberton, S. 1990, *Financial Times*, 4th July.

Holland, J.B. 1995, 'The Corporate Governance role of Financial Institutions in their investee companies', Chartered Association of Certified Accountants, Research Report No. 46 (65 pages), November.

Holland, J.B. 1996, 'Self Regulation and the Financial Aspects of Corporate Governance', *The Journal of Business Law*, March, pp. 127–164.

Holland, J.B. 1996, 'Corporate and institutional control over the dissemination of price sensitive information', *European Journal of Finance*, v2, pp. 77–102.

Holland, J.B. and Stoner, G. 1996, 'Dissemination of price sensitive information and management of voluntary corporate disclosure', *Accounting and Business Research*, Vol 26, No 4, Autumn, pp. 295–313.

Holland, J. 1997, *Corporate Communications to Institutional Shareholders*, ICAS: Edinburgh, November.

Holland, J. 1998, 'Private corporate disclosure, financial intermediation, and market efficiency', *Journal of Business Finance and Accounting*, forthcoming January–March.

Kaplan, R.S. 1983, 'Measuring manufacturing performance: A new challenge for managerial accounting research', *The Accounting Review*, October, pp. 686–705.

Mallin, C. 1995, *Voting: The Role of Institutional Investors in Corporate Governance*, ICAEW: London.

Marston, C. 1993, *Company communications with analysts and fund managers*, PhD: Glasgow.

Mayer, C. 1994, 'Stock markets, financial institutions, and corporate performance' in N.H. Dimsdale and M. Prevezer (eds), *Capital Markets and Corporate Governance*, Clarendon Press: Oxford, p. 179.

Mayer, C., Chairman of working group, 1995, 'Developing a Winning Partnership: How companies and institutional investors are working together', DTI Report of the joint City/Industry working group, February.

Peters, T. and Waterman, R. 1982, *In Search of Excellence*, Harper and Row: London.

Riley, B. 1995, 'Bursting the technobubble', *Financial Times*, p. 1 section 2, 22nd October.

Royal Society of Arts (RSA) 1995, Enquiry on 'Tomorrow's Company', London.

Scapens, R. W. 1990, 'Researching Management Accounting practice: The role of case study methods', *British Accounting Review*, Vol 22, pp. 259–281.

Scott, J. 1993, 'Corporate groups and network structures', chapter 16 in *Corporate Control and Accountability*, eds. McCahery, J., Picciotto, S. and Scott, C. Clarendon Press: Oxford.

Scott, W.R. and Meyer, J.W. 1994, *Institutional environments and organizations*, Sage.

Streeck, W. and Schmitter, P.C. 1985, 'Community, Market, State – and Associations?' Ch. 1, pp. 1–29, in Streeck, W. and Schmitter P.C. (eds), *Private Interest Government: beyond market and state*, London: Sage.

Smith, M.P. 1996, 'Shareholder activism by Institutional Investors: Evidence from Calpers', *Journal of Finance*, Vol 51, No 1, pp. 227–252.

Tricker, R.I. 1993, Editorial, *Journal of Corporate Governance*, pp. 1–3, Vol 1, No. 1, January.

Useem, M. 1993, *Executive defense*, Harvard University Press.

Whittington, G. 1993, 'Corporate governance and the regulation of financial reporting', *Accounting and Business Research*, Vol 23, No 91A, pp. 311–319.

John B. Holland, BSc, MBA, PhD, Professor and Head of Department, Department of Accounting and Finance, University of Glasgow. Teaching and research interests in 'International Financial Management', 'Financial Markets and Financial Institutions', and 'Governance and Disclosure issues at the boundaries between companies, financial institutions and financial markets'.

Part III
Ownership, Managerial Succession and Corporate Restructuring

[10]

ELSEVIER

Journal of Financial Economics 52 (1999) 187–223

JOURNAL OF
Financial
ECONOMICS

Ownership and board structures in publicly traded corporations[☆]

David J. Denis[a],*, Atulya Sarin[b]

[a]*Krannert Graduate School of Management Purdue University, West Lafayette, IN 47907, USA*
[b]*Leavey College of Business and Administration, Santa Clara University, Santa Clara, CA 95053, USA*

Received 10 February 1997; received in revised form 11 May 1998; accepted 1 January 1999

Abstract

We examine the equity ownership structure and board composition of a sample of 583 firms over the ten-year period 1983–1992. Our evidence suggests that a substantial fraction of firms exhibit large changes in ownership and board structure in any given year. These changes are correlated with one another and are not reversed in subsequent years. Ownership and board changes are strongly related to top executive turnover, prior stock price performance, and corporate control threats, but only weakly related to changes in firm-specific determinants of ownership and board structure. Furthermore, large ownership changes are typically preceded by economic shocks and followed by asset restructurings. © 1999 Elsevier Science S.A. All rights reserved.

JEL classification: G32; G34

Keywords: Ownership structure; Board composition

---

* Corresponding author. Tel.: + 1-765-494-4434; fax: + 1-765-494-9658.

E-mail address: daviddenis@mgmt.purdue.edu (D.J. Denis)

☆We are grateful for helpful comments received from John Chalmers, Diane Denis, Jon Garfinkel, Stacey Kole (the referee), Tim Kruse, John McConnell, Wayne Mikkelson, Greg Niehaus, G. William Schwert (the editor), Henri Servaes, Anil Shivdasani, Sunil Wahal, Mike Weisbach, Marc Zenner, finance workshop participants at Loyola University at Chicago, Michigan State University, and Notre Dame, and participants at the Western Finance Association Meetings in San Diego. Sarin acknowledges support from a Leavey Research Grant.

188   *D.J. Denis, A. Sarin / Journal of Financial Economics 52 (1999) 187–223*

1. Introduction

Corporate ownership and board structures have received considerable attention from financial economists in recent years. Studies in this literature include
those that examine the cross-sectional relation between ownership and board
characteristics and measures of firm performance (e.g. McConnell and Servaes,
1990; Morck et al., 1988; Yermack, 1996), those that examine the influence of
ownership and board characteristics on specific decisions (e.g. Brickley et al.,
1994; Byrd and Hickman, 1991; Weisbach, 1988), and those that compare
ownership and board characteristics across countries (e.g. Roe, 1993).[1]

Despite the volume of research on these topics, surprisingly little is known
about how ownership and board structures evolve in individual firms. Kole and
Lehn (1997a,b) observe that studies in the corporate governance literature have
historically been static in nature, with theory generating predictions that relate
governance structure to attributes of the firm's monitoring environment, and
empirical work providing cross-sectional tests of these predictions. Several such
studies find that ownership and board structures are correlated with one
another and are related to observable firm characteristics.[2] Because these
characteristics tend to change slowly over time, it is commonly believed that
ownership and board structures also change very slowly (if at all) over time.
However, to date there is little systematic evidence on how frequently the
ownership and board structures of a given firm change, what causes these
changes, and to what extent changes in ownership and board structure are
interrelated.

We provide evidence on these issues by conducting a time-series analysis of
equity ownership structure and board composition in a random sample of 583
publicly traded firms over the 10-year period 1983–1992. Because there is little
formal theory underlying many of our tests, our study is best viewed as
exploratory data analysis, rather than as testing of formal hypotheses. Our
primary goal is to establish a set of empirical regularities that will enhance the
understanding of how ownership and board structures evolve in public corporations. Such an understanding is important for several reasons. First, it represents
an important input into assessing the relative efficiency of alternative governance structures. Second, knowing how ownership and board structures are
formed can be useful in evaluating recent proposals for corporate governance
reform in the United States, such as those that call for smaller, outsider-
dominated boards (e.g. Lipton and Lorsch, 1992), and those that call for greater
equity holdings by managers and other board members (e.g. Stewart, 1990).

---

[1] See Shleifer and Vishny (1997) for a survey of the corporate governance literature.

[2] See, among others, Demsetz and Lehn (1985), Agrawal and Knoeber (1996), and Himmelberg
et al. (1998).

D.J. Denis, A. Sarin / Journal of Financial Economics 52 (1999) 187–223 189

Finally, a more complete understanding of the evolution of ownership and board structures is relevant to the interpretation of cross-sectional associations between ownership and board characteristics and measures of firm performance.

We first analyze the stability of equity ownership structure and board composition in the sample firms over time. This analysis indicates that a substantial fraction of the sample firm-years are characterized by large changes in either ownership structure or board composition. Specifically, 12% of the sample-firm-years exhibit changes in ownership by officers and directors exceeding 5% of the firm's shares, 4% exhibit changes in the fraction of outsiders on the board exceeding 0.2, and 13% exhibit a change in board size of more than two members. These changes in equity ownership and board structure are significantly correlated with one another and are not reversed in the three years following the change. More strikingly, 65% of the sample firms exhibit at least one of the large changes in ownership or board structure described above. Taken together, these findings suggest that substantial changes in ownership structure and board composition are not uncommon and are not transitory changes in corporate governance structures.

We next examine the factors associated with large changes in equity ownership and board composition. We hypothesize that such changes are related to changes in firm-specific or owner-specific determinants of ownership and board structure, to prior firm performance, or to external corporate control threats. Our findings suggest that changes in ownership structure and board composition are most strongly related to top executive changes, and are also significantly associated with corporate control threats and prior stock price performance. In contrast, changes in ownership and board structure are only weakly related to changes in firm-specific attributes such as the size of the firm, stock return variance, leverage, and growth opportunities.

Finally, we supplement our large-sample evidence with detailed case analyses on subsets of our sample firms. The principal advantage of this approach is that it allows us to assess directly the sequence of events that bring about the documented changes in ownership and board structure. We find that large changes in ownership and board structure are typically preceded by fundamental changes in the business conditions facing the firm and followed by large-scale asset restructurings. Moreover, among those firms having large changes in ownership and board structure in the same year, we find that, typically, ownership changes directly cause changes in the top management team and in board structure These findings collectively suggest that ownership and board changes are part of a process that reallocates assets to different uses and to different management teams in response to a change in business conditions. This view closely resembles Mitchell and Mulherin's (1996) characterization of takeovers as a response to industry shocks.

Overall, our findings suggest that the determination of ownership and board structure is a considerably more dynamic process than previously understood.

190   *D.J. Denis, A. Sarin / Journal of Financial Economics 52 (1999) 187–223*

Ownership and board structures are not as stable as is commonly believed. Rather, fundamental changes in the nature of the firm's business appear frequently to lead to changes in the decision rights governing the management of the firm's assets, as well as changes in the assets themselves. These findings provide new insights into how firms arrive at the ownership and board structures that exist at a particular point in time, and have several implications for researchers conducting empirical studies using ownership and board data. We discuss these implications in the paper's conclusion.

The remainder of the paper is organized as follows. Section 2 describes our sample selection process and reports descriptive statistics for the sample firms in the first year that they enter the sample. We also provide cross-sectional evidence on the joint distribution of equity ownership and board composition in our sample firms. Section 3 documents the stability of equity ownership and board composition over time. Section 4 presents evidence on why ownership and board structures change. Section 5 concludes and discusses the implications of our findings.

2. Sample selection and description

We first select a random sample of 692 firms listed on the Center for Research in Security Prices (CRSP) data files for NYSE, Amex, and Nasdaq firms in 1983. As depicted in Table 1, bankruptcies, takeovers, and other delistings reduce the number of publicly traded firms from 692 in 1983 to 382 in 1992. We search for proxy statements for each year that each firm is listed on CRSP. Of the 5401 possible firm-years, we are able to locate proxy statements for 4563 firm-years, corresponding to 583 of the original 692 firms. From the proxy statements for each firm-year, we collect data on the firm's equity ownership structure, board composition, and whether or not the top executive is the firm's founder. We obtain financial data from the Compustat files and the year of incorporation from *Moody's Manuals*.

By design, our sample exhibits a survivor bias in that, for any given calendar year, the sample includes only those firms that have remained publicly traded since 1983. This reflects our desire to examine the evolution of ownership and board structures in individual firms over time. One limitation of this approach, however, is that it does not allow us to address how, on average, the distribution of ownership structure and board composition has changed over time.[3] Moreover, if delisting events such as bankruptcies and takeovers produce large changes in ownership and board structure, our data will understate the incidence of such large changes in a random set of firms because firms that go

---

[3] For evidence on how average managerial ownership has changed since 1935, see Holderness et al. (1998).

D.J. Denis, A. Sarin / Journal of Financial Economics 52 (1999) 187–223 191

Table 1
Time profile of the sample. The sample consists of a random set of 692 firms listed on CRSP as of year-end 1983. Of these, 583 firms have at least one available proxy statement over the years 1983–1992. For each year, we list the number of firms that are listed on CRSP, the number for which we have available proxy data, and the fraction of total firm-years represented by that calendar year

Year	Number of CRSP-listed firms	Number of firms with available data	Fraction of firm-years
1983	692	506	0.111
1984	692	520	0.114
1985	666	522	0.114
1987	542	495	0.108
1988	514	473	0.104
1989	464	447	0.098
1990	432	421	0.092
1991	409	389	0.085
1992	382	287	0.063
Total	5401	4563	1.000

bankrupt or are taken over disappear from the sample. We do, however, follow the ownership structure and board composition of the sample firms for as long as they remain publicly traded. Furthermore, because an unusually large fraction of firms were delisted during this time period, our ability to generalize our findings to other time periods is potentially limited. We address this issue in Section 3.5.

2.1. Descriptive statistics

Panel A of Table 2 reports descriptive statistics for the ownership structure and board composition of the sample firms in the first year that they enter the sample.[4] On average, officers and directors hold 15.7% of the firm's equity, approximately half of which is held by the chief executive officer. These fractional stakes are higher than those documented in McConnell and Servaes (1990) and Morck et al. (1988), who study samples of large firms. Our ownership numbers are more comparable to those documented in Mikkelson and Partch (1989) who, like us, study a random set of firms.[5]

---

[4] Because of missing proxy statements, 77 firms enter the sample at some point following 1983.

[5] McConnell and Servaes (1990) report an average ownership of 13.9% for all officers and directors in a sample of 1,173 *Value Line* firms in 1976 and 11.8% in a sample of 1,093 firms in 1986. Although McConnell and Servaes do not report firm size characteristics for their sample, the 1984 *Value Line* sample used in Denis et al. (1997) has an average market value of equity of $1,334 million (median = $421 million), substantially larger than the average of $435 million (median = $59 million) for our sample firms. Morck et al. (1988) report an average ownership of 10.6% for all directors in a sample of 371 Fortune 500 firms. Mikkelson and Partch (1989) report an average 19.6% ownership for all officers and directors in a random sample of New York and American Stock Exchange firms.

Table 2

Descriptive statistics for the 583 sample firms as of the first year that the firm enters the sample. Ownership and board characteristics are obtained from corporate proxy statements. Firm age is defined as the number of years that the firm has been incorporated as stated in *Moody's Manuals*. Financial data are obtained from Compustat

	Mean	Minimum	25th percentile	Median	75th percentile	Maximum
A. Equity ownership and board structure						
CEO ownership (%)	7.22	0.00	0.00	0.30	8.80	80.2
Ownership of officers and directors	15.74	0.00	0.40	8.08	24.90	86.38
Number of directors	9.35	3	7	9	11	30
Fraction of independent outsiders	0.40	0.00	0.25	0.43	0.56	0.89
Fraction of inside directors	0.39	0.08	0.25	0.35	0.50	1.00
Fraction of affiliated outsiders	0.20	0.00	0.10	0.20	0.29	0.83
Fraction with outside-dominated boards[a]	0.40	n.a.	n.a.	n.a.	n.a.	n.a.
B. Other characteristics						
Fraction of firms in which founder is the CEO	0.13	n.a.	n.a.	n.a.	n.a.	n.a.
Tenure of CEO (years)	6.37	0	0	4	5	37
Age of Firm	24.39	2	11	19	25	127
Market value of equity (millions)	434.61	0.72	16.76	58.87	245.18	14481.25
Total debt/total assets	0.56	0.01	0.42	0.55	0.66	1.29
R&D/total assets (%)	1.58	0.00	0.00	0.00	2.21	19.88

[a]Outside-dominated boards are those boards in which at least 50% of the board members are independent outsiders.

D.J. Denis, A. Sarin / Journal of Financial Economics 52 (1999) 187–223   193

We follow the convention in the literature of labeling directors as insiders if they are currently employees of the firm, as affiliated outsiders if they have substantial business relations with the firm, are related to insiders, or are former employees, and as independent outsiders if they are neither insiders nor affiliated outsiders. On average, the board of directors consists of nine members, of which 40% are insiders, 20% are affiliated outsiders, and 39% are independent outsiders. Independent outsiders hold a majority of the board seats in 40% of the sample firms. Both the number of directors and the fraction of independent outsiders on the board are smaller than those documented in Yermack's (1996) study of Forbes 500 firms. Again, this is likely due to the presence of smaller firms in our sample.

Panel B of Table 2 reports other characteristics of the sample firms in the first year for which we have proxy data. Thirteen percent of the firms list the firm's founder as its top executive, nearly double the percentage reported by Denis et al. (1997) for *Value Line* firms. On average, the firms have been incorporated for 24.4 yr, while the firm's top executive has held that position for an average of 6.4 yr. The market value of the firm's equity averages $435 million, while the ratio of total debt to total assets averages 0.56. On average, research and development expenditures amount to 1.6% of total assets.

2.2. The cross-section of equity ownership and board composition

Previous studies have documented significant cross-sectional correlations between ownership and board attributes. The data presented in Table 3 confirm these correlations within our sample. Although these correlations are consistent with interdependence among ownership and board characteristics, the data in Table 3 also indicate that other factors, such as the presence of a founder on the top management team, the age of the firm, and the market value of the firm's equity are correlated with both ownership structure and board composition. Thus it is not clear whether correlations between ownership and board characteristics are due to interdependencies or to these other factors.

To provide further evidence on this issue, we estimate cross-sectional regressions relating ownership and board characteristics to firm-specific and owner-specific variables and to the other ownership and board characteristics. Our approach is similar to that employed by Smith and Watts (1992) in their examination of financing, dividend, and compensation policies. We note, as they do, that the independent variables are most probably partially endogenous themselves. Like Smith and Watts (1992), however, we require only that the right-hand side variables be predetermined, not completely exogenous. Also, because theory provides little guidance as to the exact structure of the underlying simultaneous system of equations, we do not estimate structural models specifying interdependencies between the various ownership and board characteristics. Rather, we simply estimate ordinary least-squares models in which we

194   D.J. Denis, A. Sarin / Journal of Financial Economics 52 (1999) 187–223

Table 3
Correlation matrix for various equity ownership and board charactersitics as of the first year that
each of the 583 sample firms enters the sample. P-values are reported in parentheses below

	Officers/ directors	Founder	Number of directors	Fraction of outsiders	Firm age	CEO tenure	Market value of equity
CEO ownership	0.77 (0.00)	0.17 (0.00)	− 0.33 (0.00)	− 0.31 (0.00)	− 0.11 (0.00)	0.20 (0.00)	− 0.17 (0.00)
Officers and directors		0.18 (0.00)	− 0.33 (0.00)	− 0.36 (0.00)	− 0.16 (0.00)	0.08 (0.12)	− 0.22 (0.00)
Founder			− 0.14 (0.00)	− 0.20 (0.00)	− 0.07 (0.08)	0.28 (0.00)	− 0.07 (0.11)
Number of directors				0.37 (0.00)	0.21 (0.00)	− 0.10 (0.05)	0.37 (0.00)
Fraction of outsiders					0.10 (0.02)	− 0.09 (0.07)	0.18 (0.00)
Firm age						− 0.01 (0.78)	0.17 (0.00)
CEO tenure							− 0.01 (0.81)

first orthogonalize each ownership and board characteristic with respect to the
other independent variables, then include the orthogonalized value of the
ownership and board characteristic as a separate independent variable in the
cross-sectional regressions.[6]

Prior research suggests that ownership concentration is related to the variance of stock returns, firm size, leverage, the firm's investment opportunity set,
the age of the firm, the firm's extent of diversification, the tenure of the CEO, and
the presence of a founder in the top management team. These variables capture
the costs and benefits of monitoring managerial behavior, the costs to managers
of holding large equity stakes, and nonpecuniary benefits of managerial equity

---

[6] By orthogonalizing the governance variables in this manner, we potentially bias the coefficients
on the other independent variables. To gauge the importance of this potential bias, we compare the
coefficient estimates in Table 4 for the nongovernance variables with coefficent estimates from
models in which the governance variables are not included. Because the significance levels of the
coefficients are nearly identical, we conclude that the orthogonalizing procedure does not impart
a meaningful bias on the coefficients of the other independent variables.

D.J. Denis, A. Sarin / Journal of Financial Economics 52 (1999) 187–223   195

ownership.[7] We hypothesize that these same factors will be related to other corporate governance attributes such as board composition. We also include industry dummy variables for each two-digit SIC industry for which there are at least ten sample firms (not reported); we obtain nearly identical results if we define industry at the 3-digit SIC level. (No more than two industry dummy variables are significant in any of the regression models.) Standard errors for all regression estimates use White's (1980) correction for heteroskedasticity.

The cross-sectional regression results reported in Table 4 suggest that ownership and board characteristics are related to common factors. In general, as first implied by the results in Table 3, larger firms are characterized by lower inside ownership, larger boards, and a greater fraction of independent outsiders on the board. In addition, firms with higher leverage are characterized by lower managerial ownership and by larger boards with a larger fraction of independent outsiders, firms with greater growth opportunities (as measured by the industry's median market/book ratio) have smaller boards, consisting of a smaller fraction of outsiders, and firms in which the top executive is the firm's founder have higher inside ownership and lower outsider representation on the board.

The regression results also suggest that, after controlling for the above endogenous determinants of ownership structure and board composition, ownership and board characteristics are interrelated. Specifically, inside ownership is negatively related to the fraction of independent outsiders on the board of directors and board size is positively related to the fraction of independent outsiders. To gauge the relative importance of the ownership and board variables, Table 4 also reports adjusted R-squareds for regression models that include all of the independent variables except the ownership and board variables. The results indicate that the governance variables account for a relatively small fraction of the explanatory power of the regressions in which inside ownership and the number of directors are the dependent variables, but for nearly 50% of the explanatory power in the regression in which the fraction of outsiders on the board is the dependent variable.

Our cross-sectional evidence thus confirms that ownership and board characteristics are related to common firm-specific and owner-specific characteristics. Moreover, after controlling for these common determinants, different aspects of ownership and board structure are correlated with one another. Such evidence is limited, however, in that it says nothing about how ownership and board characteristics evolve over time. Therefore, in order to provide a richer understanding of the dynamics of ownership and board structures, we focus our analysis on the time-series properties of the data.

---

[7] See Agrawal and Knoeber (1996), Chaplinsky and Niehaus (1993), Crutchley and Hansen (1989), Demsetz and Lehn (1985), Denis and Denis (1994), Friend and Lang (1988), Holderness et al. (1998) and Holthausen and Larcker (1993) for further discussion of how these variables are likely to influence insider ownership.

196   *D.J. Denis, A. Sarin / Journal of Financial Economics 52 (1999) 187–223*

Table 4
Estimates of cross-sectional regressions relating each ownership and board characteristic to firm- and owner-specific characteristics, and to other characteristics of ownership and control. Other ownership and board characteristics are orthogonalized with respect to the other independent variables prior to their inclusion in the model. Industry dummy variables are included in the models, but are not reported in the table in order to conserve space. The sample consists of 583 firms for the first year that they enter the sample. Coefficient estimates are reported with heteroskedasticity-consistent t-statistics in parentheses below

Independent variables	Dependent variable		
	Ownership of officers/ directors	Percent of independent outsiders	Log (number of directors)
Intercept	1.84	0.21	1.67
	(8.19)	(3.54)	(19.33)
Log (market value of equity)	−3.64	0.03	0.11
	(−6.81)	(5.23)	(11.81)
Stock return variance (× 100)	−0.77	0.01	−0.02
	(−1.09)	(1.08)	(−1.64)
Industry median market value of firm/book value of total assets	1.49	−0.03	−0.08
	(1.18)	(−2.22)	(−3.63)
Total debt/total assets	−6.65	0.07	0.10
	(−2.08)	(1.92)	(1.85)
Log (firm age)	−0.99	−0.00	0.04
	(−0.94)	(−0.35)	(2.37)
CEO tenure	−1.35	0.00	−0.02
	(−1.80)	(0.28)	(−1.36)
Founder dummy	7.29	−0.07	0.01
	(3.14)	(−2.68)	(−0.32)
No of reported segments	−0.00	0.01	0.01
	(−0.01)	(0.77)	(0.95)
Ownership of officers/directors		−0.01	−0.00
		(−3.33)	(−1.04)
Percentage of independent outsiders on board	−13.83		0.32
	(−3.33)		(4.66)
Log (number of directors)	−3.01	0.15	
	(−1.04)	(4.66)	
Adj. R^2	0.24	0.19	0.48
Adj. R^2 (without governance variables)	0.19	0.11	0.45

D.J. Denis, A. Sarin / Journal of Financial Economics 52 (1999) 187–223 197

3. The stability of equity ownership structure and board composition

Although it is widely believed that the ownership structure and board composition of individual firms change very little over time, there is little time-series evidence on this issue.[8] In this section, we first examine whether, on average, ownership and board structure change from the first year a firm enters our sample to the last year. Second, we document the frequency distribution of changes in ownership structure and board composition for individual firm-years. Third, we document the correlation between changes in different aspects of ownership structure and board composition. Fourth, we report evidence on the permanence of large changes in ownership and board structure. Finally, we present and discuss data on the generality of our findings.

3.1. Average changes in ownership and board structure over time

Fig. 1 plots median levels of ownership structure and board composition variables for the first year and the last year that firms enter the sample. We limit this analysis to those 430 of the 583 sample firms that remain in the sample for more than five years.[9] We divide the sample into ownership and board categories as of the first year that a firm enters the sample, then compare the median ownership and board level within a given category for the first year to the median level for that same set of firms in the last year that the firm is present in the sample. Panel A depicts the data for the ownership of officers and directors, panel B the fraction of directors that are independent outsiders, and panel C the number of directors.

From panel A, the ownership of officers and directors appears fairly stable, on average, among low ownership firms. For those firms in which insiders own less than 15% of the shares in the first year, median ownership is virtually identical in the last year that they appear in the sample. The pattern is somewhat different for firms with high insider ownership. These firms reduce median insider ownership from the first to the last year that they appear in the sample. In each ownership category above 15%, inside ownership is reduced by about five percentage points. This reduction is statistically significant at the 10% level

---

[8] One exception is the study of Kole and Lehn (1997b) mentioned previously. Kole and Lehn examine how governance structures of U.S. airlines evolve over a 22-yr period that includes the Airline Deregulation Act of 1978. They thus provide evidence on how firms adapt governance structures to structural changes in the business environment.

[9] For these firms, the average (median) number of years that they remain in the sample is 8.9 (9). The distribution is as follows: 10 years – 200 firms, nine years – 93 firms, eight years – 57 firms, seven years – 40 firms, six years – 40 firms. Our results are not sensitive to this choice. For example, we obtain nearly identical results if we limit our analysis to those firms that remain in the sample for the entire 10-year period.

198   D.J. Denis, A. Sarin / Journal of Financial Economics 52 (1999) 187–223

Panel A: Percentage Ownership of Officers and Directors

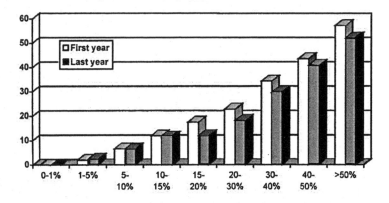

Panel B: Fraction of Board Members that are Independent Outsiders

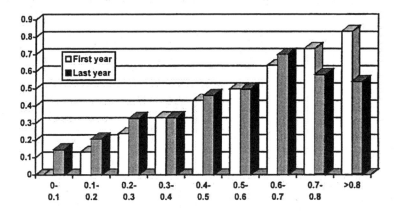

Panel C: Number of Directors

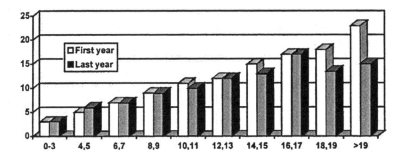

D.J. Denis, A. Sarin / Journal of Financial Economics 52 (1999) 187–223   199

(using a pairwise Wilcoxon signed-ranks test) in all categories except the 40–50% group. A possible explanation for this is that these firms tend to be younger firms. Mikkelson et al. (1997) document large declines in inside ownership in the first ten years following the time a firm first goes public. We explore the link between firm age and changes in ownership and board structure in Section 4.

The fraction of directors that are independent outsiders exhibits some mean reversion. Firms with low outsider representation increase the fraction of outsiders on the board, while those with high outsider representation tend to decrease the fraction of outsiders. Significant increases in outsider representation are observed for firms in which fewer than 30% of the directors are outsiders in the first sample year. Significant decreases are observed for firms in which the percentage of outsiders in the first sample year exceeds 70%. Nevertheless, the changes are fairly small, so that the ordering of outsider representation across categories is preserved.

Board size remains fairly constant with the exception of those firms with a large number of directors in their first sample year. The decline in the median number of directors from the first to the last sample year is statistically significant at the 10% level for firms in which the number of directors exceeds seventeen in the first sample year.

3.2. Frequency distribution of yearly changes in ownership and board structure

Although informative with respect to systematic tendencies, the data depicted in Fig. 1 are limited in the sense that they capture only the changes for the median firm in each category. The data do not indicate the frequency or magnitude of changes in ownership and board structure for individual firms. For example, it may be the case that many firms exhibit large changes, but increases and decreases offset one another. To address this issue, we examine the frequency distribution of changes in ownership structure and board composition for the full sample of 4563 firm-years. We divide ownership and board changes into five categories reflecting small changes, medium increases and decreases, and large increases and decreases. Large changes are defined as changes in percentage equity ownership of more than 5%, changes in the fraction of independent outsiders on the board of more than 0.2, or changes in the number of directors of at least two members.

Fig. 1. Median levels of ownership structure and board composition for the first year and the last year that a firm appears in the sample. Firms are grouped according to their ownership and board structure in the first sample year. The sample is restricted to those 437 firms for which we have at least five years of proxy statement data.

Our definitions of large changes are admittedly arbitrary, but are based on existing empirical evidence that changes of this magnitude have material impacts on firm value.[10] As a result, we are confident that our categorization of large changes correctly identifies economically meaningful changes in governance structure. However, we recognize that our procedures may label some changes as being of small or medium magnitude when they are, in fact, economically meaningful. For example, a change in percentage equity ownership from 0.1% to 2% in a large firm represents a substantial change in the dollar investment in the firm's shares. Our findings will thus understate the incidence of large changes in ownership structure and board composition.

Panel A of Table 5 reports the frequency distribution of annual changes in the fractional ownership of officers and directors. The data indicate that the majority of firms exhibit only small changes in ownership structure from year to year. In approximately 62% of the firm-years, the absolute change in the percentage ownership of officers and directors is less than 1%. Nonetheless, a large fraction of the sample firm-years exhibit substantial changes in ownership structure. The absolute change in the ownership of officers and directors is greater than 5% in 12% of the firm-years. In addition, the data in panel A indicate that the stability of equity ownership structure is much greater in low ownership firms. Among those firm-years in which officers and directors own less than 10% of the firm's shares, the fraction of firm-years in which the absolute change in insider ownership is less than 1% is 0.79. In contrast, this fraction is only 0.52 for those firm-years in which officers and directors own between 10% and 20% and 0.42 for firm-years in which officers/directors own more than 20% of the shares. Nevertheless, among those firms with ownership of less than 10%, more than five percent of the firm-years exhibit a change in ownership of at least 5% of the firm's shares.

In panels B and C, we conduct a similar analysis of the fraction of outsiders on the board and the number of directors. As is the case with ownership structure, the majority of firms exhibit only minor changes in board composition from year to year. In approximately 84% of the sample firm-years, the fraction of directors that are independent outsiders changes by less than 0.1. Similarly, in about 61% of the firm-years, the total number of directors does not change. Nevertheless, there is again a large number of firm-years in which there are substantial changes in the composition of the board of directors. In approximately 4% of the firm-years, the change in the fraction of outsiders on the board is

---

[10] See, for example Wruck (1989) for the stock price effects of changes in the ownership of officers and directors in the context of private equity sales, Mikkelson and Ruback (1985) for the the the stock price effects of changes in block ownership, Rosenstein and Wyatt (1990) for the stock price effects of the addition of an outsider to the board, Weisbach (1988) for the effects of board composition on the relation between CEO turnover and firm performance, and Yermack (1996) for the stock price effects of changes in the number of directors.

D.J. Denis, A. Sarin / Journal of Financial Economics 52 (1999) 187–223   201

Table 5
The frequency of annual changes in ownership structure and board composition. Ownership and
board data are obtained from corporateproxy statements for each of the 4563 firm-years. The table
reports the percentage of firm-years having a given change in ownership structure or board
composition

Panel A: Ownership structure

Change in percentage ownership	Previous ownership of officers and directors			
	All firms	0–10%	10–20%	> 20%
Less than − 5%	6.6	0.6	5.9	16.3
− 5% to − 1%	14.0	8.0	22.5	18.5
− 1% to 1%	62.3	79.4	51.5	42.0
1% to 5%	11.3	7.2	15.0	15.4
Greater than 5%	5.8	4.7	5.1	7.9

Panel B: Fraction of independent outsiders on board[a]

Change in fraction of outsiders	Previous fraction of outsiders on board			
	All firms	0–0.4	0.4–0.6	> 0.6
Less than − 0.2	1.8	1.2	1.6	3.5
− 0.2 to − 0.1	4.1	3.1	6.0	7.1
− 0.1 to 0.1	84.4	83.0	87.3	81.8
0.1 to 0.2	7.4	8.8	4.0	6.5
Greater than 0.2	2.3	5.1	2.7	4.6

Panel C: Number of directors

Change in number of directors	Previous number of directors			
	All firms	0–6	6–10	> 10
Less than − 2	6.9	1.0	5.2	11.0
− 2 to − 1	14.8	5.9	13.4	19.6
No change	60.7	72.6	63.9	52.6
1 to 2	11.9	12.3	12.4	11.2
Greater than 2	5.7	8.3	5.1	5.6

[a]Directors are classified as insiders if they are currently employees of the firm, as affiliated outsiders if
they have business relations with the firm, are related to insiders or are former employees, and as
independent outsiders otherwise.

greater than 0.2. This fraction is slightly greater among firms having a high
fraction of outsiders on the board to begin with. Similarly, in 13% of the
firm-years, the number of directors on the board changes by more than two
members.

202   *D.J. Denis, A. Sarin / Journal of Financial Economics 52 (1999) 187–223*

Because several papers find that board independence may be more important than the fraction of outsiders on the board,[11] we also examine (but do not report in a table) changes in board independence, where boards are classified as independent if the percentage of independent outsiders on the board is at least 50%. We find that boards change from nonindependent to independent in 4.4% of the firm-years and from independent to nonindependent in 3.9% of the firm-years. In other words, boards maintain their independence classification in 92% of the firm-years.

It is also possible that the composition of the board changes substantially without any change in either the number of directors or the fraction of outsiders on the board. Therefore, we also examine (but again do not report in a table) the frequency distribution of the fraction of directors that change in any given firm-year. We find that this fraction is less than 0.1 in 71% of the sample firm-years. The composition of the board changes by more 20% in 11% of the sample firm-years.

Taken together, the findings in Table 5 suggest that substantial changes in ownership structure or board composition are not uncommon. To provide further perspective on this issue, we compute the fraction of the sample firms that exhibit at least one large change in ownership or board structure over the course of the sample period. We again define a large change to be a change of more than 5% in the ownership of officers of directors, a change of more than 0.2 in the fraction of outsiders on the board, or a change in the number of directors of more than two members. Of the full sample of 583 firms, 381 (65%) exhibit at least one large change in ownership or board structure. This percentage is 66% for the firms that remain in the sample at least five years, and 62% for the firms that remain publicly traded over the entire ten-year sample period. In other words, approximately two out of every three firms listed in 1983 experience a large change in ownership or board structure over the following ten-year period. Such a finding is notable when viewed in light of the valuation effects typically associated with 'large' changes in ownership and board structure.

3.3. Correlations between changes in ownership structure and board composition

Table 6 reports a correlation matrix for changes in ownership structure and board composition. As was the case cross-sectionally, there are significant correlations between changes in various aspects of ownership and control.[12] Changes in the equity ownership of officers and directors are negatively correlated with changes in the fraction of outsiders on the board and positively

---

[11] See, for example, Brickley et al. (1994) and Cotter et al. (1997).

[12] We obtain similar results when we examine correlations between changes in ownership and board structure over the entire sample period rather than over individual firm-years.

D.J. Denis, A. Sarin / Journal of Financial Economics 52 (1999) 187–223 203

Table 6
Correlation matrix for changes in equity ownership structure and board composition. The sample consists of 4563 years for the 583 sample firms over the period 1983–1992. *P*-values are reported in parentheses below

	Officer/directors	Fraction of outsiders	Number of directors
CEO ownership	0.38	− 0.07	− 0.07
	(0.00)	(0.00)	(0.00)
Officers and directors		− 0.03	0.02
		(0.08)	(0.12)
Fraction of independent outsiders[a]			0.04
			(0.02)

[a]Directors are classified as insiders if they are currently employees of the firm, as affiliated outsiders if they have business relations with the firm, are related to insiders or are former employees, and as independent outsiders otherwise.

correlated with changes in board size. Not surprisingly, changes in the ownership of all officers and directors are also strongly associated with changes in the ownership of the CEO ($\rho = 0.38$). In short, the results in Table 6 suggest that changes in ownership structure and board composition tend to occur contemporaneously.

3.4. The permanence of large changes in ownership and board structure

A final issue surrounding the stability of ownership and control concerns the permanence of changes in equity ownership and board composition. It is possible that the data in Table 5 overstate the importance of large changes in ownership and control because such changes are only temporary. Alternatively, the importance of large changes may be understated if the data in Table 5 represent the beginning of a longer-run trend. To provide evidence on these possibilities, Fig. 2 (panels A–C) plots the median cumulative change in ownership structure and board composition from the year prior to each large change in ownership and board structure (year − 1) through the third year following the year of the large change (year + 3). There are 234 firms represented in panel A, 83 firms in panel B, and 129 firms in panel C. (Because those firms with no change in ownership or board structure in year 0 also have no change, on average, over the subsequent three years, they are not plotted in Fig. 2.)

As depicted in Fig. 2, large changes in ownership and board structure persist, in general through year + 3. There is evidence of a small reversal following large increases in the ownership of officers and directors; however, the median

204   *D.J. Denis, A. Sarin / Journal of Financial Economics 52 (1999) 187–223*

Panel A: Percentage Ownership of Officers and Directors

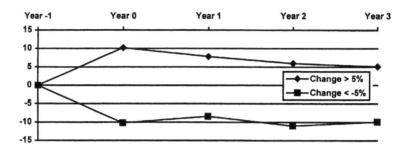

Panel B: Fraction of Independent Outsiders on Board

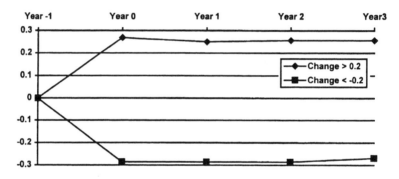

Panel C: Number of Directors

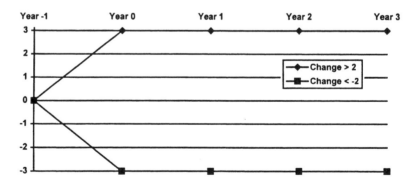

increase in ownership through year + 3 is still over 5%. Similarly, large changes in board structure are not reversed in the three years following the initial board change. These findings, taken together with the correlations reported in Table 6, suggest that large changes in ownership and board structure represent discrete shifts in the governance structures of the sample firms.[13]

3.5. Generality of results

As mentioned earlier, one concern with our findings is that we examine a time period, 1983–1992, that is characterized by an unusually high rate of takeover activity. As documented in Table 1, 45% of the sample firms are delisted from CRSP over the 10-year sample period. This delisting frequency is comparable to the delisting rate for the CRSP universe over the same time period (47%), but is higher than the 37% delisting frequency for the CRSP universe over the previous 10-year period, 1973–1982. If ownership and board changes are linked with delisting events such as takeovers and bankruptcies, our findings will overstate the incidence of ownership and board changes during a period of more typical takeover activity.

We address this issue by dividing our sample firm-years into two subperiods according to the percentage of firms delisted per year. The first subperiod contains firm-years between 1983 and 1988, with annual delisting frequencies ranging from a low of 10.7% in 1988 to a high of 16.4% in 1986. The second subperiod, 1989–1992, exhibits delisting frequencies ranging between 6.5% (1992) and 9.5% (1989). The delisting frequency for this second subperiod is more comparable to that for the CRSP universe during the 1973–1982 (median = 6.8%) period and that during the 1993–1996 period (median = 10.8%). We then compare the frequency distribution of ownership and board changes between the 1983–1988 and 1989–1992 subperiods.

Our results (not reported in a table) indicate that the frequency distributions are quite similar in the two subperiods. For example, during the 1983–1988 period, 13% of the sample firm-years exhibit a change in the ownership of officers and directors exceeding 5% of the firm's shares. This occurs in 12.2% of

---

[13] These results are not sensitive to the inclusion of multiple observations from the same firm. When we include only one (at most) observation for each firm, our findings are nearly identical.

Fig. 2. Median cumulative changes in ownership structure and board composition from the year prior to large changes (year − 1), through three years following the large change (year + 3). Large changes are defined as changes in the equity ownership of officers and directors, unaffiliated blockholders, or affiliated blockholders exceeding 5% of the firm's shares, changes in the fraction of independent outsiders exceeding 0.2, and changes in the number of directors exceeding two members. The are 234 firms in panel A, 83 in panel B, and 129 in panel C.

the firm-years in the 1989–1992 period. The difference is statistically insignificant. Similarly, the percentage of firm-years for which there is a change in the
fraction of independent outsiders of more than 0.2 and the percentage of
firm-years in which the number of directors changes by more than two are not
statistically different in the two sub-periods.

As a second check on the influence of delistings, we compare the frequency
distribution of ownership and board changes between those firms that remain
listed over the entire sample period and those firms that are delisted at some
point. We find weak evidence that large ownership changes are more common in
firms that are ultimately delisted. Specifically, among delisted firms, 13.5% of
the firm-years exhibit a change in the ownership of officers and directors
exceeding 5% of the firm's shares. This change occurs in 11.2% of the firm-years
among firms not delisted; the difference in proportions is significant at the 0.05
level. In contrast, the percentage of firm-years for which there is a change in the
fraction of independent outsiders of more than 0.2 and the percentage of
firm-years in which the number of directors changes by more than two are not
statistically different in the two subsamples. Overall, these findings suggest that
our results are not due solely to the unusually high rate of takeover activity in
the first part of our sample period and, consequently, can be generalized to other
time periods.

4. Why do ownership and board structures change?

The evidence in the preceding section indicates that a nontrivial fraction of
firms, particularly those firms with high managerial ownership, exhibit large,
discrete changes in governance structure that are sustained well beyond the
initial year of the change. Why do such discrete changes in ownership and
control take place? One possibility is that changes in ownership and board
structure are caused by changes in the firm-specific attributes that determine
optimal ownership and board structure. For example, changes in a firm's
growth opportunities, firm size, leverage, or information asymmetries can all
plausibly lead to endogenous adjustments in equity ownership and the composition of the board of directors. More generally, Mitchell and Mulherin (1996)
argue that economic shocks to an industry are likely to alter the allocation of
resources within industry firms. It is possible that changes in governance
structures are part of this process of restructuring. Consistent with this view,
Kole and Lehn (1997b) report significant changes in the corporate governance
structures of U.S. airlines following deregulation of the industry in 1978.

Alternatively, changes in ownership and control may be closely linked with
changes in the attributes of specific owners of the firm rather than with any
firm-specific attributes. For example, Fama and Jensen (1983) and DeAngelo
and DeAngelo (1985) discuss how ownership and board structures can be due in

D.J. Denis, A. Sarin / Journal of Financial Economics 52 (1999) 187–223 207

part to the presence of individual owner-managers who possess valuable firm-specific knowledge or who derive large private benefits from control of the firm.[14] To the extent that there is a change in the managerial involvement of such individuals, ownership and board structure are likely to change. Examples of changes in owner-specific attributes include changes in the status of a founder/manager and changes in the identity of the top executive.

A third possibility is that changes in ownership structure and board composition occur in response to changes in firm performance. For example, firms that are performing well may experience an increase in insider ownership as a result of the exercise of executive stock options. Conversely, firms that are performing poorly may place additional outsiders on the board for additional monitoring (Hermalin and Weisbach, 1988), or experience changes in ownership and board structure as a result of financial distress (Gilson, 1990).

Finally, ownership and board changes may be linked with external corporate control threats. The threats themselves may produce the changes, such as when a potential bidder purchases a block of shares and obtains board seats. Alternatively, changes in ownership and control may result from managers' response to the takeover threat. For example, managers may repurchase shares as a defensive adjustment in ownership structure (Dann and DeAngelo, 1988; Denis, 1990) or to encourage a more prominent ownership and board role for affiliated blockholders (Denis and Serrano, 1996).

In this section, we provide evidence on these potential determinants by first documenting the factors associated with changes in ownership and board structure. We note that the above mentioned determinants of ownership and board changes are not mutually exclusive. As just one example, a change in business conditions can lead to poor firm performance, which in turn could lead to corporate control activity and to a CEO change. We then supplement this large-sample evidence with data from detailed case analyses of subsets of the sample firms.

4.1. Factors associated with large changes in equity ownership structure and board composition

Table 7 reports univariate comparisons of selected characteristics across subsamples grouped by the magnitude of changes in ownership structure or board composition. We group firm-years by the size of the change in the fractional ownership of all officers and directors in panel A, by the change in the fraction of

---

[14] DeAngelo and DeAngelo (1985) provide some empirical support for this view in their study of firms with dual-class equity ownership structures. Denis and Denis (1994) empirically document the importance of owner-specific attributes in the choice of majority ownership as an organizational form.

Table 7

Average changes in firm-specific and owner-specific characteristics, stock price performance over the prior year, and the incidence of corporate control threats for the sample of 4563 firm years over the period 1983–1992. The sample is partitioned by changes in the fractional ownership of officers and directors (OWN) in panel A, by changes in the fraction of independent outsiders on the board (OUT) in panel B, and board size (BOARD) in panel C. P-values (reported in italics) denote the significance of an F-test for the equality of means across groups

	N	ΔR&D	ΔVAR	ΔFirm size	ΔTotal debt/total assets	Age of firm	Fraction with new CEO	Fraction in which founder leaves	Prior year's market-adjusted stock return	Fraction with control threats
A. Ownership of officers/directors										
ΔOWN < −5%	252	−0.0178	0.0031	18.94	0.044	21.81	0.155	0.012	0.163	0.047
−5% < ΔOWN < 5%	3296	0.0003	0.0013	83.85	0.020	32.97	0.082	0.005	0.127	0.040
5% < ΔOWN	200	0.0015	−0.0002	−6.89	0.040	21.80	0.205	0.010	0.001	0.080
p-value		*0.00*	*0.03*	*0.05*	*0.29*	*0.00*	*0.00*	*0.29*	*0.00*	*0.03*
B. Fraction of independent outsiders on board[a]										
ΔOUT < −0.2	48	0.0120	0.0035	−163.13	1.211	21.10	0.396	0.042	−0.075	0.021
−0.2 < ΔOUT < 0.2	3647	−0.0009	0.0014	78.95	0.013	31.85	0.087	0.005	0.127	0.043
0.2 < ΔOUT	54	−0.0002	0.0019	27.14	−1.144	26.24	0.296	0.0185	0.064	0.074
p-value		*0.27*	*0.52*	*0.03*	*0.00*	*0.00*	*0.00*	*0.00*	*0.01*	*0.39*
C. Number of directors										
ΔBOAR < −2	100	−0.0006	0.0036	118.71	0.035	30.62	0.350	0.010	−0.064	0.060
−2 < ΔBOARD < 2	3581	−0.0008	0.0014	72.45	0.022	31.76	0.086	0.005	0.127	0.040
2 < ΔBOARD	68	0.0003	0.0001	188.73	0.062	26.06	0.132	0.029	0.168	0.132
p-value		*0.98*	*0.16*	*0.23*	*0.49*	*0.15*	*0.00*	*0.03*	*0.00*	*0.00*

[a] Directors are classified as insiders if they are currently employees of the firm, as affiliated outsiders if they have business relations with the firm, are related to insiders or are former employees, and as independent outsiders otherwise.

D.J. Denis, A. Sarin / Journal of Financial Economics 52 (1999) 187–223   209

· directors that are independent outsiders in panel B, and by the change in the number of directors in panel C. We compare contemporaneous changes in firm-specific and owner-specific characteristics, stock price performance over the prior calendar year, and the incidence of corporate control threats during the firm-year. For the continuous variables, we report average changes, but the results using medians are qualitatively similar.

The firm-specific characteristics that we examine are the same as in Table 4 – growth opportunities, as measured by the ratio of research and development expenditures to total assets (R&D), the standard deviation of daily stock returns (VAR), firm size, measured as the market value of equity, the ratio of total debt to total assets, and the age of the firm.[15] As owner-specific characteristics, we consider the fraction of firms experiencing a change in top executive during the calendar year and the fraction of firms in which a founding owner/manager relinquishes management responsibilities. We measure stock price performance as the cumulative market-adjusted stock returns over the prior year, and corporate control threats as any takeover offers, rumors, threats, proxy contests, or blockholder pressure over the year as reported in the *Wall Street Journal Index*.

The results in Table 7 provide only weak evidence that changes in firm-specific characteristics are important determinants of changes in ownership structure and board composition.[16] There is some evidence of a relation between changes in the ownership of officers and directors and changes in research and development spending, stock return variance, and firm size. In addition, there is evidence that large changes (both increases and decreases) in the ownership of officers and directors are more common in younger firms. However, there is no evidence that changes in the fraction of outsiders on the board or the number of directors are related to changes in firm-specific characteristics.

In contrast, large changes in ownership structure and board composition are strongly associated with changes in the identity of the top executive. Among those firms with either large increases or decreases in the ownership of officers and directors, the fraction of outsiders on the board, and board size, the rate of top executive turnover is over double that of firms with small changes in ownership and board structure. Turnover rates for firms with small changes in ownership and board structure are similar to those documented in previous studies. For example, Weisbach (1988) documents a CEO turnover rate of 7.8%

---

[15] Recall that growth opportunities were measured in Table 4 as the median industry market-to-book ratio, where industry is defined at the two-digit SIC level. We employ R&D expenditures here so as not to confuse the change in growth opportunities with stock price performance. Our results in Table 4 are not sensitive to the choice of growth opportunity measure.

[16] We obtain qualitatively similar results if we measure percentage changes in the firm-specific variables rather than the raw changes reported in Table 7.

210   *D.J. Denis, A. Sarin / Journal of Financial Economics 52 (1999) 187–223*

in a sample of large firms, while Denis and Denis (1995) document a 9.3% top executive turnover rate in a sample of *Value Line* firms over the period 1985–1988. Thus, firms experiencing small ownership and board changes exhibit normal turnover rates while firms experiencing large ownership and board changes exhibit unusually high turnover rates.

Large changes in ownership and board structure are also associated with market-adjusted stock returns over the prior year. Changes in the ownership of officers and directors are negatively related to prior stock price performance. In other words, lower stock price performance is more likely to be followed by an increase in ownership concentration, while higher stock price performance is associated with subsequent decreases in ownership concentration. Surprisingly, market-adjusted returns appear to be higher among those firms that subsequently increase the fraction of outsiders on the board. Hermalin and Weisbach (1988) find that firms are more likely to add outsiders to the board following poor performance. Market-adjusted returns are also higher in those firms that increase board size than in firms that decrease board size.

Finally, large changes in ownership and board structure are associated with a higher incidence of corporate control activity. Among the firms that increase (decrease) inside ownership by more than 5%, 8.0% (4.7%) experience some corporate control threat during the same year, as compared to 4.0% of the firms with small changes. Among the firms with large increases in the fraction of outsiders on the board, 7.4% experience some corporate control threat, as compared to 4.3% of the firms with small changes and 2.1% of the firms with large decreases in the fraction of outsiders on the board. Among firms that decrease (increase) board size by more than two members, 6.0% (13.2%) are subject to some control threat, as compared to only 4.0% of the firms that change board size by less than two members.

In sum, although there is some evidence that changes in firm-specific characteristics are associated with changes in ownership structure and board composition, the predominant factors associated with ownership and control changes appear to be top executive changes, prior stock price performance, and corporate control threats. These findings are broadly consistent with the theoretical predictions of Hermalin and Weisbach (1998). In their model, board structure is endogenously determined as the result of bargaining between the CEO and the board. Their model thus predicts long-term stability in corporate governance except when there is a change in the relative bargaining strength of the CEO versus the board. CEO changes, prior stock price performance, and corporate control threats arguably represent such shifts in bargaining power.

4.2. Direct evidence from case histories

A shortcoming of the evidence in Table 7 is that it provides no direct evidence on the direction of causality in the association between various factors and

D.J. Denis, A. Sarin / Journal of Financial Economics 52 (1999) 187–223   211

changes in ownership and board structure. Moreover, the cross-sectional associations offer little insight into either the nature of the correlation between large
changes in ownership and board attributes or the possible interactions among
the factors that produce the changes.

Evidence of this type requires precise data on the timing of the ownership and
changes relative to the timing of other possible causes of the changes. These data
are often difficult to obtain and are not easily summarized in large-sample
evidence. Therefore, we offer further insights into why ownership and board
structures change and how such changes are interrelated by conducting a detailed examination of subsamples of our sample firms. We first analyze those
eighteen firms exhibiting a change in the ownership of officers and directors
exceeding 5%, a change in the fraction of outsiders on the board of directors
exceeding 0.2, and a change in the number of directors of at least two members
in a given year. In other words, we examine a set of firms experiencing large
changes in ownership and board structure in a single year. Such a subsample has
at least two advantages. First, because the changes in ownership and board
structure are relatively large, we are more likely to uncover information in press
reports about why the ownership and board changes took place. Second,
because the firms exhibit large changes in both ownership and board structure,
this subsample allows us to investigate how changes in ownership and board
structure are interrelated. An obvious caveat, however, is that these eighteen
firms represent extreme cases, thereby limiting our ability to generalize the
findings from this set of firms to the population of ownership and board
changes. Thus, we later supplement this analysis with the examination of two
additional subsamples.

The appendix provides brief case histories for each of the 18 cases. The data
are obtained from corporate proxy statements and from press reports during the
period surrounding the ownership and board changes. Although the sample size
is relatively small, it comprises a fairly broad cross-section of ownership and
board changes. Both large increases and decreases are present in the subsample,
and there is a wide range of starting values for the ownership and board
structure variables.

Several interesting observations emerge from the case descriptions. First, like
Mitchell and Mulherin's (1996) findings for takeovers, it is apparent that
ownership and board changes often follow some fundamental change in the
business conditions of the firm. In twelve of the eighteen cases, the owner-
ship/board changes are preceded by a sharp decline in operating profitability,
frequently caused by an industry-wide shock. In several of these firms, poor
financial performance is clearly the impetus for the purchase of large blocks of
shares and the corresponding changes in board composition and top management (see, for example, the appendix entries for Astradyne, Datapower,
Geodyne, Ideal Basic, E.M. Smith, and Tierco). In the remaining six cases, the
ownership and board changes are due either to the sale of a large block of shares

212   D.J. Denis, A. Sarin / Journal of Financial Economics 52 (1999) 187–223

(five cases) or to the death of a controlling blockholder (one case). In these cases, large blockholders assert their control over the firm by revamping the board of directors and the top management team in the absence of any clear signs of financial difficulty (see, for example, the appendix entries for Electronic Research, Evergreen, and Nevada National).

Second, the ownership and board changes typically involve the same individual(s). In the most common case, a change in the blockholdings of a single or small group of shareholders simultaneously results in a change in board composition. In some cases, the block purchase of shares results in complete turnover of the board of directors. As a representative example, consider the case of Enterra Corporation. In this case, large blockholder Shamrock Holdings purchased a 23% stake in the firm, installed its representative as chairman of the board, and filled two other board seats with individuals affiliated with Shamrock. Subsequently, Enterra's CEO resigned as did three other board members. Thus, Shamrock's block purchase produced large changes in both ownership structure and the composition of the board of directors.

Third, the ownership and board changes are typically followed by large-scale restructurings of the firm's assets. In 13 of the 18 cases, the firm sells assets, closes down operations, or initiates cost-cutting efforts either following or coincident with the ownership and board changes. These asset restructurings are typically a direct response to the decline in profitability which preceded the ownership/board changes.

Viewed collectively, these findings imply that large ownership and board changes are part of a process that reallocates assets to different uses and to different management teams in response to a change in business conditions. A plausible interpretation of the evidence is that the ownership/board changes help facilitate the restructuring process by altering the structure of decision rights within the firm.

As noted earlier, one problem with analyzing those 18 firms with large changes in ownership and board structure is that they may not be representative of the typical ownership and board structure change. To address this concern, we examine a subsample of 30 firms having a large change in just one ownership or board structure attribute. Specifically, from the set of firm-years exhibiting a change in the ownership of officers and directors exceeding 5%, a change in the fraction of outsiders on the board of directors exceeding 0.2, or a change in the number of directors of at least two members in a given year, we randomly select 10 firm-years having a large ownership change, ten firms having a large change in the fraction of outsiders on the board, and ten firms with a large change in the number of directors. We require that the firm have a large change in only one ownership or board attribute. Thus, if a firm had a change in the ownership of officers and directors that exceeded 5% and a change in the number of directors of more than two members, we would not include it in this subsample. We then conduct a detailed examination of proxy statements and

D.J. Denis, A. Sarin / Journal of Financial Economics 52 (1999) 187–223   213

press reports identical to that conducted for the 18 firms described in the appendix.

Our findings for this subsample (not reported separately) are remarkably similar to our findings reported earlier. In 19 of the 30 cases, the ownership or board change is preceded by a sharp decline in profitability. In 12 of these 19 cases, the ownership or board change is followed by a large-scale asset restructuring. In two other cases, the decline in profitability and ownership or board change is followed by a change in control of the firm. Thus, as was the case with the eighteen firms having large changes in ownership and board structure, this second subsample of ownership and board changes appear to be part of a process that reallocates assets to different uses and to different management teams following a decline in performance.

Finally, to provide further perspective on these subsamples of ownership and board change, we examine a third subsample consisting of a random sample of 30 firm-years, in which there was no change in ownership or board structure. For each of these thirty firm-years, we examine press reports and proxy statements over the three years centered on the selected firm-year for evidence of changes in business conditions and restructuring similar to those documented above for firms exhibiting changes in ownership and board structure. Our analysis indicates that firms with no change in ownership and board structure exhibit a much lower incidence of declines in performance and corporate restructuring events. For only two of the thirty firm-years is there evidence of a decline in operating profitability, and only six of the thirty firm-years are followed by large restructurings. We thus conclude that the incidence of changes in business conditions and corporate restructuring activity is unusually high among firms exhibiting large changes in ownership and board structure. This finding supports our earlier interpretation that ownership and board changes are part of a process that reallocates assets to alternative uses following fundamental changes in business conditions.

5. Summary and implications

Using a panel of 583 publicly traded firms over the 10-year period 1983–1992, we conduct a time-series examination of ownership structure and board composition in individual firms. Our analysis indicates that a nontrivial subset of the sample firms experience substantial changes in ownership and board structure in individual firm-years. These changes are correlated with one another and represent discrete shifts in ownership structure and board composition. Furthermore, changes in ownership and board structure are strongly related to top executive turnover, prior stock price performance, and corporate control threats, but are only weakly related to changes in firm-specific determinants of ownership and board structure. We also find that large changes in ownership

214   *D.J. Denis, A. Sarin / Journal of Financial Economics 52 (1999) 187–223*

and board structure are typically preceded by fundamental changes in the business conditions facing the firm and followed by large-scale asset restructurings. These findings collectively suggest that ownership and board changes are part of a process that reallocates assets to different uses and to different management teams in response to a change in business conditions.

Overall, these findings provide new insights into how ownership and board structures evolve in public corporations. Previous work on this topic has focused on how ownership and board characteristics vary cross-sectionally with the firm's asset structure and investment opportunities. Our findings suggest that the determination of ownership and board structures is a more dynamic process than previously understood. Ownership and board structures adjust frequently to economic shocks, leading observed ownership and board structures to be considerably less stable than commonly believed. Having documented the extent of this instability, we believe that much more can be learned by studying the dynamics of large shifts in governance structure. Important recent contributions along these lines are Hermalin and Weisbach's (1998) theoretical analysis of the evolution of board structure and Kole and Lehn's (1997a,b) analysis of the effects of industry deregulation on governance structure.

Our findings also have several implications for the design of research studies involving corporate governance characteristics. First, the fact that different aspects of ownership and control are strongly interdependent suggests that researchers must take great care in isolating the impact of individual governance characteristics. Second, because a nontrivial fraction of firm-years exhibit large changes in ownership structure or board composition, and because these changes are typically associated with CEO changes, corporate control events, and prior firm performance, researchers need to be cognizant of systematic biases that can result from assuming constant ownership and board structure over time. Our findings suggest that the magnitude of such biases will depend on the particular sample being studied. Third, to the extent that changes in ownership and control are linked with events that typically have significant valuation consequences (e.g. CEO changes and corporate control events), tests relating firm performance to governance characteristics can be biased even if ownership and board structure are, on average, relatively stable. Moreover, because changes in equity ownership and board composition are related to prior performance, the predominant direction of causality in governance-performance associations is not clear.[17]

---

[17] Recent empirical studies attempting to discern the direction of causality in the relation between ownership structure and performance include Himmelberg et al. (1998) and Kole (1996). Other studies providing relevant evidence on this issue include Hermalin and Weisbach (1991) and Wruck (1989).

D.J. Denis, A. Sarin / Journal of Financial Economics 52 (1999) 187–223 215

Appendix A

This appendix presents case summaries of those 18 firms experiencing large changes in ownership structure and board composition in a given year. Large changes are defined as a change of at least 5% in the equity ownership of officers and directors, a change in the fraction of independent directors on the board of at least 0.2, and a change in the number of directors of at least two members. For each case, we report the actual changes in ownership and board structure and provide additional details based on our reading of the relevant proxy statements and press reports during the period surrounding the changes.

Company name	Ownership of officers and directors	Fraction of independent outsiders on the board	Number of directors	Description
1. Astradyne Computer Industries Inc.				
1985	20.9%	0.44	9	The firm's account-managment subsidiary had been experiencing operational problems which resulted in a severe cash drain on Astradyne. Blockholder Candace Weir (11.3%) obtained a seat on the board of directors in 1985. Following SEC charges that the company had filed misleading reports on the finances of the cash-short subsidiary, the firm replaced the CEO, installed a new director as board chairman, and removed a vice-president and the company's lawyer from the board.
1986	33.6%	0.71	7	
2. Banker's Note Inc.				
1985	40.36%	0.00	2	Equity ownership increased primarily through the private placement of a 14% block of shares with S.K. Chow, who was also then named a director. In addition, three other independent outsiders were added to the board of directors. At the time of the sale, the company was experiencing record earnings and press reports stated that the proceeds of the sale were to be used for working capital. In the following year, the company experienced earnings declines due to 'lower-than-anticipated sales' and downsized from 75 to 66 stores.
1986	51.63%	0.33	6	

216   *D.J. Denis, A. Sarin / Journal of Financial Economics 52 (1999) 187–223*

Appendix A. Continued.

Company name	Ownership of officers and directors	Fraction of independent outsiders on the board	Number of directors	Description
3. Cheezem Development Corporation				
1984	41.5%	0.22	9	Founder and chief executive Charles Cheezem sold his 41.5% stake in the company to Rodney L. Propps and G. Dale Murray. All nine of the firm's directors ended their service with the firm. The new board consisted of Propps (who was also named CEO), Murray, and three others from the real estate firm owned by Propps and Murray. The new management team rapidly expanded the development of real estate properties. However, continued hard times in the Miami condominium market resulted in 'an excessive amount of non-income producing property'.
1985	60.4%	0.00	5	
4. Circle K. Corporation				
1983	36.1%	0.29	7	In 1983, the company was placed on Credit Watch and was given a BB- rating on its subordinated debt. American Financial Corp. and its chairman Carl Lindner acquired a 13.4% stake in the company and Lindner became a member of the board of directors. The company then appointed director Karl Eller as its CEO and adopted a new policy of having a majority of outsiders on the board of directors. As a result of this new policy, three other outsiders were named to the board of directors. Under Eller, the company expanded from 1300 stores to 4650 stores over the next six years. This expansion was financed primarily through the issuance of below-investment grade debt. However, the new stores did not produce enough operating income to service the large debt burden and the firm filed for Chapter 11 bankruptcy in 1990.
1984	56.6%	0.67	9	
5. Datapower Inc.				
1986	32.6%	0.20	5	After incurring large net losses due to weaknesses in the personal computer market, the company defaulted on its bank debt. Subsequently, Datapower entered into an agreement with the Revere fund in which a $2.5 million note held by Revere was
1987	45.7%	0.67	3	

D.J. Denis, A. Sarin / Journal of Financial Economics 52 (1999) 187–223 217

converted into convertible preferred stock. Following conversion of this and another note, Revere's stake was increased to 44.1% of the firm's equity. All five of the firm's directors ended their service with the firm. The new board consisted of the new chief executive, a representative of Revere, and a representative of Datapower's other main creditor. The company ceased operations in 1988.

REFAC Technology Development Corp. purchased 27% of the firm's shares, installed its president as chairman of the board, its former executive vice-president as CEO, and a vice-president as the other board member. All five previous directors of Electronic Research Associates (ERA) ended their service with the firm. REFAC hoped to merge ERA with its REFAC Electronics unit so as to produce synergies by combining ERA's products with REFAC's manufacturing system. The merger was approved in 1990 and the combined firm reported sharply higher earnings.

Enterra reported losses in 1983 and 1984 which it attributed to a downturn in the oil industry. The company also eliminated its dividend in 1984. Shamrock Holdings began purchasing shares in early 1985, eventually raising its stake in the firm to 23% of the shares outstanding. Shamrock stated in an SEC filing that it might attempt to influence Enterra management or even seek control of it. Eventually, Shamrock's CEO, Stanley Gold, was installed as Enterra's chairman of the board. Enterra's CEO resigned, as did three other members of the board of directors. In addition to Gold, two other individuals affiliated with Shamrock were named to the Enterra board. In 1987 and 1988, Enterra sold several units and acquired CRC-Evans Pipeline International.

Two individuals, James C. Ryan and John J. Ryan of Barfield Oil Corporation, purchased a combined stake of 17.3% in the firm. James Ryan became the company's chief executive, John Ryan became a vice-president and three others affiliated with Barfield were named to Evergreen's board of directors.

6. Electronic Research Associates			
1987	0.9%	1.00	5
1988	27.1%	0.67	3
7. Enterra Corporation			
1985	3.9%	0.60	10
1986	26.4%	0.38	8
8. Evergreen Resources Inc.			
1988	7.7%	0.50	5
1989	22.1%	0.14	7

continued overleaf

Appendix A. Continued.

Company name	Ownership of officers and directors	Fraction of independent outsiders on the board	Number of directors	Description
9. Geodyne Resources Inc.				In conjunction with a reorganization plan to aid this financially distressed firm, Paine Webber Group agreed to inject $7.4 million of equity capital into the firm in return for the right to elect a majority of the board of directors. In addition, Geodyne's CEO (and main shareholder) was removed from office. The capital infusion allowed Geodyne to expand its purchase of oil and gas properties for its limited partnerships.
1986	46.2%	0.25	4	
1987	3.4%	0.89	9	
10. Ideal Basic Industries Inc.				The firm faced deteriorating profitability and its debt was downgraded due to unfavorable conditions in the cement and potash markets. Ideal had launched a $500 million capital spending program in the early 1980's based on forecasts that cement prices would be $100 per ton by the mid-1980s. However, prices in late 1985 were less than one-half that amount. The firm suspended interest and principal payments on its unsecured debt held by banks and insurance companies and implemented a shareholder-approved financial restructuring in which 125 million common shares were issued to the company's bank and insurance lenders. Holdernam Inc. purchased a 67% stake in the firm from Ideal Basic's lenders, ousted the firm's CEO and CFO, and installed its own representative as the new CEO. Five others affiliated with Holdernam were also added to the board of directors. The company sold its Canadian potash operations and took a $200 million write-down on an idled cement plant.
1986	22.0%	0.57	7	
1987	86.2%	0.24	11	

D.J. Denis, A. Sarin / Journal of Financial Economics 52 (1999) 187–223   219

11. Lancer Orthodontics

Year			
1988	57.4%	0.78	9
1989	25.7%	0.50	6

Four directors sold their shares to Biomerica Inc. and resigned from the board of directors in 1988. Biomerica's CEO was named Chairman of the Executive Committee of Lancer. Also, investor Merrill Barthomeley purchased a 4.5% stake in Lancer and was named to the board of directors. The company incurred net losses in 1989 and 1990, leading the new management team and board of directors to initiate a restructuring involving staff reductions and a refocusing on the company's most profitable products.

12. Nahama and Weagant Energy Co.

Year			
1987	39.8%	0.43	7
1988	30.0%	0.20	5

In 1986, the company closed 20 of its 22 oil wells due to declining oil prices. The company was controlled by the firm's two founders, who owned approximately 27% of the shares. In 1987, two outside directors, one of whom owned 7.6% of the firm's shares, were removed from the board. This reduced both the number of directors and the fraction of independent outsiders on the board. The company retained First Arcadia Corp. to help it expand its base of operations by acquiring entities with producing reserves and cash flow. As stated by one of the founders, 'The fact is, it's cheaper to buy a barrel of oil than to look for it'.

13. Nevada National Bancorporation

Year			
1984	0.4%	0.78	9
1985	31.9%	0.20	5

Louis Farris Jr. acquired a large stake in the firm and was named chairman of the board of directors and chief executive officer. In addition, two others affiliated with Farris were elected to the board of directors. Seven previous directors of the firm were not re-elected. Problems with bad real estate loans contributed to a net loss in the first nine months of 1986. In addition, Farris defaulted on several of his bank loans, leading him to lose his ownership position in various companies. NNB agreed in late 1986 to be acquired by Security Pacific Corp.

continued overleaf

Appendix A. Continued.

Company name	Ownership of officers and directors	Fraction of independent outsiders on the board	Number of directors	Description
14. Oppenheimer Industries Inc.				The company was performing poorly due to a large amount of non-income-producing land. H.G. Oppenheimer (chairman and CEO) and four other directors resigned in a move coinciding with the firm's decision to restructure and pursue a possible sale of the company. Two of the other ex-directors had been large blockholders, owning approximately 15% of the firm's shares. As part of the restructuring, the firm sold two of its subsidiaries and 350,000 acres of land that it owned in New Mexico and California, but still posted a large loss in 1990. The company filed for Chapter 11 in late 1990.
1989	23.3%	0.42	12	
1990	2.2%	0.71	7	
15. E.M. Smith International				Between 1983 and 1985 the company incurred losses totaling $221 million due primarily to declining oil and gas prices. The firm filed for bankruptcy in 1986. As part of this process, the president of the company resigned and left the board of directors. Industrial Equity Ltd., a securities firm, purchased a 15% stake in the company and placed one of its representatives on the board of directors. In addition, two other new independent outsiders were named to the board, one of whom replaced the incumbent CEO/Chairman in 1987. The company emerged from Chapter 11 in late 1987, and posted net profits in the third and fourth quarters of 1987 which were attributed to higher product prices and cost-cutting efforts.
1986	3.5%	0.29	7	
1987	18.5%	0.67	9	
16. Tierco Group Inc.				In the wake of large operating losses, large blockholder Windcrest Partners increased its stake in the firm and installed its representative as chairman of the board. Two other outsiders, both affiliated with Windcrest, were named to the board of directors, while six other directors were not nominated for re-election. The company sold its 26% stake in FPA Corp. to FPA's chairman for $18 million.
1984	22.9%	0.78	9	
1985	47.8%	0.50	6	

D.J. Denis, A. Sarin / Journal of Financial Economics 52 (1999) 187–223   221

17. Vicon Industries Inc.

1986	14.3%	0.40	5
1987	19.4%	0.67	9

Vicon posted losses in 1985 which the chairman blamed on 'sluggish sales, product development costs, fourth-quarter write-downs on inventories of older products, and a sizable foreign exchange translation loss'. In October 1986, Vicon received an unsolicited tender offer for all of its shares from Sensormatic Electronics Corp. As part of its defensive strategy, the company nominated four new outside directors, one of whom was the president of Thomson McKinnon, Vicon's financial advisor. The firm also enacted staggered boards, a supermajority provision, and golden parachute contracts for its top three officers. Also, Vicon's chief executive and founder increased his stake from 8.8% to 11.1%, and the company sold 10.8% of its shares to Chugai Boyeki Co., a Japanese trading company with whom Vicon had formed an exclusive distribution arrangement.

18. Wrather Corporation

1985	27.2%	0.36	11
1986	20.9%	0.00	6

Following the death of the firm's founder, J.D. Wrather, the founder's son took over as chief executive, the founder's wife became chairman of the board, and two new executive vice-presidents were named to the board. All former outside directors were removed from the board. The decrease in ownership reflects the fact that the former outside directors collectively owned 6.7% of the firm's shares, while the new directors owned negligible amounts of stock. The company experienced losses due to the poor performance of its home building unit. This unit was sold in 1985, as were the firm's television and motion-picture properties. Nevertheless, the firm was in technical default of its revolving loan agreement with Security Pacific National Bank in early 1987. Later that year, the firm agreed to be acquired by a new concern that would be owned 50% by Walt Disney and 50% by Industrial Equity, a Hong Kong investment firm. Disney later purchased the shares held by Industrial Equity.

222 *D.J. Denis, A. Sarin / Journal of Financial Economics 52 (1999) 187–223*

References

Agrawal, A., Knoeber, C.R., 1996. Firm performance and mechanisms to control agency problems between managers and shareholders. Journal of Financial and Quantitative Analysis 31, 377–398.

Brickley, J.A., Coles, J.L., Terry, R.L., 1994. Outside directors and the adoption of poison pills. Journal of Financial Economics 35, 371–390.

Byrd, J., Hickman, K., 1991. Do outside directors monitor managers? Evidence from tender offer bids. Journal of Financial Economics 32, 195–221.

Chaplinsky, S., Niehaus, G., 1993. Do inside ownership and leverage share common determinants?. Quarterly Journal of Business and Economics 32, 51–65.

Cotter, J.F., Shivdasani, A., Zenner, M., 1997. Do independent directors enhance target shareholder wealth during tender offers?. Journal of Financial Economics 43, 195–218.

Crutchley, C.E., Hansen, R.S., 1989. A test of the agency theory of managerial ownership, corporate leverage, and corporate dividends. Financial Management 18, 36–46.

Dann, L.Y., DeAngelo, H., 1988. Corporate financial policy and corporate control: a study of defensive adjustments in asset and ownership structure. Journal of Financial Economics 20, 87–128.

DeAngelo, H., DeAngelo, L.E., 1985. Managerial ownership of voting rights: a study of public corporations with dual classes of common stock. Journal of Financial Economics 14, 33–71.

Demsetz, H., Lehn, K., 1985. The structure of corporate ownership: causes and consequences. Journal of Political Economy 93, 1155–1177.

Denis, D.J., 1990. Defensive changes in corporate payout policy: share repurchases and special dividends. Journal of Finance 45, 1433–1456.

Denis, D.J., Denis, D.K., 1994. Majority owner-managers and organizational efficiency. Journal of Corporate Finance 1, 91–118.

Denis, D.J., Denis, D.K., 1995. Performance changes following top management dismissals. Journal of Finance 50, 1029–1058.

Denis, D.J., Denis, D.K., Sarin, A., 1997. Ownership structure and top executive turnover. Journal of Financial Economics 45, 193–221.

Denis, D.J., Serrano, J.M., 1996. Active investors and management turnover following unsuccessful control contests. Journal of Financial Economics 40, 239–266.

Fama, E.F., Jensen, M.C., 1983. Separation of ownership and control. Journal of Law and Economics 26, 301–326.

Friend, I., Lang, L.H.P., 1988. An empirical test of managerial self-interest on corporate capital structure. Journal of Finance 43, 271–282.

Gilson, S., 1990. Bankruptcy, boards, banks, and blockholders: evidence on changes in ownership and control when firms default. Journal of Financial Economics 27, 355–388.

Hermalin, B.E., Weisbach, M.S., 1988. The determinants of board composition. Rand Journal of Economics 19, 589–606.

Hermalin, B.E., Weisbach, M.S., 1991. The effect of board composition and direct incentives on firm performance. Financial Management 20, 101–112.

Hermalin, B.E., Weisbach, M.S., 1998. Endogenously chosen boards of directors and their monitoring of the CEO. American Economic Review.

Himmelberg, C.P., Hubbard, R.G., Palia, D., 1998. Understanding the determinants of managerial ownership and the link between ownership and performance. Journal of Financial Economics, forthcoming.

Holderness, C.G., Kroszner, R.S., Sheehan, D.P., 1998. Were the good old days that good? The evolution of managerial stock ownership since the great depression. Journal of Finance, forthcoming.

Holthausen, R.W., Larcker, D.F., 1993. Organizational structure and financial performance. Working paper, The Wharton School, University of Pennsylvania.

Kole, S., 1996. Managerial ownership and firm performance: incentives or rewards?. Advances in Financial Economics 2, 119–149.

Kole, S., Lehn, K., 1997a. Deregulation, the evolution of corporate governance structure, and survival. American Economic Review 87, 421–425.

Kole, S., Lehn, K., 1997b. Deregulation and the adaptation of governance structure: the case of the U.S. Airline industry. Journal of Financial Economics, forthcoming.

Lipton, M., Lorsch, J., 1992. A modest proposal for improved corporate governance. The Business Lawyer 48, 59–77.

McConnell, J.J., Servaes, H., 1990. Additional evidence on equity ownership and corporate value. Journal of Financial Economics 27, 595–613.

Mikkelson, W.H., Partch, M.M., 1989. Managers' voting rights and corporate control. Journal of Financial Economics 25, 263–290.

Mikkelson, W.H., Partch, M.M., Shah, K., 1997. Ownership and operating performance of companies that go public. Journal of Financial Economics 44, 281–308.

Mikkelson, W.H., Ruback, R.S., 1985. An empirical analysis of the interfirm equity investment process. Journal of Financial Economics 14, 523–553.

Mitchell, M.L., Mulherin, J.H., 1996. The impact of industry shocks on takeover and restructuring activity. Journal of Financial Economics 41, 193–229.

Morck, R., Shleifer, A., Vishny, R., 1988. Management ownership and market valuation: an empirical analysis. Journal of Financial Economics 20, 293–316.

Roe, M., 1993. Some differences in corporate structure in Germany, Japan, and the United States. The Yale Law Review 102, 1927–2003.

Rosenstein, S., Wyatt, J.G., 1990. Outside directors, board independence, and shareholder wealth. Journal of Financial Economics 26, 175–192.

Shleifer, A., Vishny, R.W., 1997. A survey of corporate governance. Journal of Finance 52, 737–783.

Smith, C.W., Watts, R., 1992. The investment opportunity set and corporate financing, dividend, and compensation policies. Journal of Financial Economics 32, 263–292.

Stewart, G.B., 1990. Remaking the public corporation from within. Harvard Business Review 68 (4), 126–137.

Weisbach, M.S., 1988. Outside directors and CEO turnover. Journal of Financial Economics 20, 431–460.

White, H., 1980. A heteroskedasticity-consistent covariance matrix estimator and a direct test for heterskedasticity. Econometrica 48, 817–838.

Wruck, K.H., 1989. Equity ownership concentration and firm value: Evidence from private equity financings. Journal of Financial Economics 23, 3–28.

Yermack, D., 1996. Higher market valuation of companies with a small board of directors. Journal of Financial Economics 40, 185–212.

[11]

ELSEVIER

Journal of Corporate Finance 5 (1999) 341–368

Journal of
CORPORATE
FINANCE

www.elsevier.com/locate/econbase

Management succession and financial performance of family controlled firms

Brian F. Smith *, Ben Amoako-Adu

Clarica Financial Services Research Centre, School of Business and Economics, Wilfrid Laurier University, Waterloo, Ontario, Canada N2L 3C5

Received 1 November 1997; accepted 1 February 1999

Abstract

This paper examines the immediate and long-term impacts on financial performance of 124 management successions within Canadian family controlled firms. When family successors are appointed, stock prices decline by 3.20% during the 3-day (-1 to $+1$) event window, whereas there is no significant decrease when either non-family insiders or outsiders are appointed. However, a cross-sectional analysis indicates that the negative stock market reaction to family successors is related to their relatively young age which may reflect a lack of management experience rather than their family connection per se. Investors are uncertain about the "management quality" of family successors who have less established reputations than more seasoned non-family insiders and outsiders. Non-family member appointments tend to follow periods of poor operating performance implying that there might be more scope for improvement when a non-family successor is appointed. Unlike the US sample in McConaughy et al. [McConaughy, D.L., Walker, M.C., Henderson, G.V., Mishra, C.S., 1998. Founding family controlled firms: efficiency and value, Review of Financial Economics 7, 1–19.], which indicates that the median percentage of votes held by controlling families is less than 15%, the Canadian sample indicates a more concentrated ownership with the median percentage of family controlled votes exceeding 51%. Of the firms in our sample, 62% use dual class capitalization to maintain control within the family. © 1999 Elsevier Science B.V. All rights reserved.

JEL classification: G39

Keywords: Succession; Financial performance; Family firms

* Corresponding author. Tel.: +1-519-884-0710, ext. 2953; fax: +1-519-884-0201; E-mail: bsmith@wlu.ca

342   *B.F. Smith, B. Amoako-Adu / Journal of Corporate Finance 5 (1999) 341–368*

1. Introduction

Despite the prevalence of family controlled firms in many countries, finance research has not extensively examined how corporate decision-making and financial performance is influenced by family control. [1] The special concern of firms controlled by families is that family interests may be furthered at the expense of outside shareholders. One corporate decision that may bring family and outside shareholder interests into conflict is the appointment of a family member to a senior management position. [2]

This study examines several fundamental questions related to the controlling family's decision as to whether to appoint as a successor, a family member, non-family insider or an outsider. [3] What factors, including poor financial performance lead to succession by a family member, a non-family insider or an outsider? How do the three types of successors differ in terms of age and experience? What is the impact of an appointment of each of the three types of successors on shareholder wealth and post-succession corporate performance?

We analyze 124 management successions in Canadian family firms listed on the Toronto Stock Exchange (TSE) and draw the following conclusions. Those firms with multiple family members occupying senior management positions and without outside blockholders are more likely to appoint a family member as successor. There is some evidence that poor corporate performance leads to the appointment of a non-family insider or an outsider rather than a family member. Family successors tend to be younger than non-family insiders and are nearly always related by direct bloodline to the incumbent. The stock market reacts negatively to the appointment of family member successors but the effect is attributed to the fact they are younger and have less established reputations rather than their family connection per se. Furthermore, the operating performance of firms with non-family and outside successors is significantly below the industry median but improves after succession. The operating performance of firms with

---

[1] Zingales (1994), Kunz and Angel (1996), Rydqvist (1996), and Taylor and Whittred (1998) document evidence of concentrated ownership by families in European and Australian markets.

[2] DeAngelo and DeAngelo (1985) note that an important goal of some owner/managers is to ensure that their children succeed them to control their firms. Hence, they resort to the issuance of dual class shares whereby the family holds fully franchised voting shares and outsiders hold shares with less voting power per share. Dual class shares have been criticized that they insulate management from the market for corporate control. Smith and Amoako-Adu (1995) describe the market for dual class shares in Canada.

[3] The definition of each of the three kinds of possible successors is (a) a family successor is one who is a blood or non-blood relative of the family which holds at least 10% of the votes, (b) a non-family insider is a person unrelated to the incumbent family, but is in a senior management position prior to the retirement or death of the founder or predecessor, (c) an outsider is a newly appointed replacement person who is neither a family member nor a corporate insider prior to the retirement or death of the founder or predecessor.

B.F. Smith, B. Amoako-Adu / Journal of Corporate Finance 5 (1999) 341–368   343

family successors is not significantly below the industry median before succession but worsens after succession.

Our results contrast with those of McConaughy et al. (1998) who find that US descendent controlled firms are more efficient than founder controlled firms. One aspect of our study focuses on the period immediately surrounding succession whereas McConaughy et al. (1998) do not. Thus, the difference in the findings may reflect the special challenges that family successors face in the transition period. In addition, the median ownership by families in our study exceeds 51% whereas that of McConaughy et al. (1998) is less than 15%. Thus, outside investors in family firms may have greater influence on appointment decisions in the US than in Canada.

The paper is organized as follows. Section 2 of the paper reviews the literature on family succession and corporate performance. Section 3 describes hypotheses, data and methodology. Research findings and conclusions are presented in Sections 4 and 5, respectively.

2. Family succession and corporate performance

2.1. Factors related to family firm successions

As discussed in Furtado and Karan (1990) and Denis and Denis (1995), there is considerable evidence that poor corporate performance is followed by senior management turnover in widely held firms. However, this relationship is found to be weak or absent in closely held firms, including family controlled firms. Allen and Panian (1982) find that there is no relationship between performance and managerial succession in firms directly controlled by families during periods of low profitability. Morck et al. (1988a) show that firms that are managed by members of the founding family are less likely to experience a complete management turnover or a hostile takeover.

Given that previous research has not demonstrated a clear link between corporate performance and succession per se in a family firm, there is no strong a priori support for corporate performance to be a significant factor in the decision to appoint as a successor a family member, non-family insider or outsider. While a non-family insider is an "insider" on the basis of previous employment with the company, a family insider is considered more of an "insider" because of the family relationship. It is argued by Vancil (1987) that appointing an insider to the CEO position is not an appropriate method to turn around a company's performance. Thus, a poorly performing family firm looking for a turnaround would rank its choice of successors as first being an outsider, second a non-family insider and third a family member. However, in family firms, management appointments are also affected by family interests that may supersede standard corporate objectives, such as maximization of shareholder wealth.

The extent of family interests is related to a number of factors. The most obvious factor is the availability of qualified family members. Another factor is the concentration of votes among family members which is enhanced by the use of dual class shares. Typically, the class of shares with greater votes per share is owned by the family and the other class is owned by non-family outsiders. With such a dominant voting position, family interests are entrenched.

Control by a family is weakened in the presence of an outside blockholder. Megginson (1990) and Bergstrom and Rydqvist (1992) discuss how two or more blockholders generally act in concert to control corporations through shareholder agreements. However, these coalitions may break down when disagreements arise and the coalition members subsequently vie for control of the firm. [4]

2.2. Is succession by family members value enhancing?

The question of whether a family firm should appoint a family member, a non-family insider or an outsider to a senior management position is one that may pit corporate against personal interests. Some argue that the appointment of family members to senior posts is a form of nepotism that reflects a deep personal bias on the part of the founder and his descendants. The selection process may be so circumscribed that individuals more competent than the chosen family member are not considered. This will have a negative impact on the value of the firm given less than optimal decision making by the successor family members and a lack of interest of non-family members in occupying management positions given the limited opportunities for promotion. Other problems associated with family succession include sibling rivalry and social pressures to provide perquisites to the family. [5]

Succession by a non-family insider or an outsider may suggest that the firm is "in play" for a takeover. Morck et al. (1988a) report that firms with a family member as CEO are less likely to be the target of a hostile takeover than other firms. Because of the lower probability of a takeover, shareholders may react negatively to the appointment of a family member. Another factor that may have a detrimental impact on a firm's stock price is the expectation that greater "quality

---

[4] In 1995, Andrew and Wallace McCain, the Canadian brothers who founded and controlled McCains Foods which was the largest producer of frozen french fries in the world, publicly fought over whose sons should succeed them in management of the company. One of the brothers eventually left the company to establish a new firm which he vowed would compete with and eventually overtake McCains in the food processing industry.

[5] These issues have been raised in case studies of family firms such as Barnes and Hershon (1976) and Mace (1986) as well as in the popular financial press. For example, at the 1996 shareholders' meeting, Catherine Beck was appointed president of Noma Industries, a family controlled firm which specialized in the manufacture of electrical equipment. At the meeting, outside shareholders accused the company of nepotism. Beck's father and grandmother had founded the firm and controlled over 90% of the votes. See "Noma Names President", *Globe and Mail*, June 19, 1996.

B.F. Smith, B. Amoako-Adu / Journal of Corporate Finance 5 (1999) 341–368   345

uncertainty" surrounds the appointment of a family member than a non-family insider or an outsider. [6] As evidence in this paper indicates, non-family insiders and outsiders are typically older than family members and are more likely to have extensive management experience and an established reputation. The negative stock price reaction expected with this "quality uncertainty" should be distinguished from a market assessment of the family member's true managerial skills.

There are several arguments advanced in support of the appointment of family members. First, family members are said to have a special interest in the firm's success given that the firm represents the legacy of its founder and the social status of the family is likely tied to the performance of the firm. The close link between family and corporate identity is reflected in the widespread use of the family surname in the corporate name. Examples include Ford, Molson and Bombardier. Failure of the firm may mean social sanctions are applied against family managers by non-management family members who are dependent on the firm for income. A second defence of the appointment of family members is that they have excellent knowledge of the firm, given their long-standing relationship with the senior management of the firm. In addition, some family firms institute succession plans which include training for successors. [7] In larger family firms, a reason why the appointment of family members may not reduce corporate value is that such firms are able to appoint a number of non-family members to senior management to act to offset any shortcomings of family members. Reinganum (1985) finds that smaller firms have a more significant response to external appointments than larger firms.

Empirical evidence on the impact of family succession on corporate performance is limited. Morck et al. (1988b) find that Tobin's Q for older firms is lower when the firm is managed by a member of the founding family than when it is run by an officer unrelated to the founder. In contrast, among newer firms, the presence of a member of the founding family raises Tobin's Q. They suggest that founders with long tenures and their descendants thwart value maximization whereas newer founders offer special entrepreneurial talents. Morck and Strangeland (1994) document that firms controlled by heirs of the founder have lower profitability than other firms in the industry. Thus, one would expect that the succession by family members would lower corporate performance.

In contrast, evidence provided in McConaughy et al. (1998) indicates that family controlled firms are more efficient and valuable than other firms because family relationships improve monitoring while "providing incentives that are associated with better firm performance". Furthermore, they find that the descendant-controlled family firms are more efficient than founder-controlled firms. They

---

[6] We thank an anonymous reviewer for providing this insightful argument.

[7] Trow (1962) finds that only organizations that plan for succession show profitability in subsequent periods in his study of 108 small manufacturing firms.

346   *B.F. Smith, B. Amoako-Adu / Journal of Corporate Finance 5 (1999) 341–368*

argue that descendants are in a "position to consolidate advantages passed on to them by the founder".

3. Hypotheses, data and methodology

3.1. Hypotheses

The paper tests three hypotheses related to different aspects of family firm succession and corporate performance. The null hypotheses are as follows:
- Prior corporate performance has no impact on whether a family member, non-family insider or outsider is appointed as a senior management successor.
- The appointment of a family member, non-family insider or outsider as a senior management successor has no differential impact on shareholder wealth.
- The appointment of a family member, non-family insider or outsider as a senior management successor has no differential relationship to subsequent corporate performance.

It is our expectation that there will be a pecking order of effects, with those of the non-family insiders lying between those of family and outsider successors.

3.2. Data

The research is based on a sample of actively managed family firms which were listed on the TSE between 1962 and 1996 and which underwent a succession in which a family member, non-family insider or an outsider was appointed to the position of president and/or CEO. There are 124 such appointments in the study. An actively managed family firm is defined as (1) a corporation in which a person or a group related by family ties holds the largest voting block and holds at least 10% of the total votes, and (2) the president and/or CEO is a family member before the succession. [8] The reason the definition of family firm includes cases where only one person owns a significant voting interest relates to the fact that such individuals are generally assumed to operate on a non-arms length basis with their families. Thus, other family members usually have some significant influence over the firm. For example, family interests manifest themselves when the controlling shareholder dies and the estate is left to other family members. The inclusion of only actively managed family firms is based on the argument that family members closely involved in the operation of a firm are in a better position to use corporate resources for family reasons than family members who are not managers.

---

[8] The 10% ownership threshold is consistent with the Ontario Securities Act definition of a corporate insider.

The compilation of a set of family firms starts with an extensive review of copies of the annual *Financial Post Survey of Industrials* and *Financial Post Survey of Mines* which lists significant shareholders and senior management of all TSE listed firms. Secondary sources include *Financial Post 500* and *Canadian Business 500*. Firms which meet the above definition of actively managed family firms are identified. Then we identify successions by comparing the president and CEO of these firms over time. In total, we find 136 successions. Cases in which the succession coincides with a takeover of the family firm are excluded as we want to isolate the impact of management succession from changes in ownership. Twelve such cases are identified, leaving a final sample of 124 successions. To identify the exact date of announcement of the succession, we examine *Canadian Business and Current Affairs* CD-ROM and its predecessor, the *Canadian Business Periodical Index*, for relevant newspaper stories.

For each family firm, biographical information on the resigning and incoming senior executive is obtained from the *Blue Book of Canadian Business* and *Directory of Directors*. In addition, the year of birth and the existence and nature of family relation between the resigning and incoming senior executive are recorded from newspaper account or by contacting the company directly. We obtain common stock and TSE 300 Total Return Index returns from the Canadian Financial Markets Research Centre stock database. Financial statement data are obtained from the *Financial Post Survey of Industrials* and *Financial Post Survey of Mines*.

3.3. Research methodology

The impact of prior corporate performance and other factors on the likelihood of a company choosing a particular successor type is estimated with a multinomial logit model. The estimation of this model involves two dependent binary variables. The first dependent variable will have a value of one for those cases in which the successor is a family member and zero otherwise. The second dependent variable has a value of one for those cases in which the successor is an outsider and zero otherwise. In addition to prior period abnormal performance, independent variables include the number of family members within senior management and percentage of votes controlled by the family. [9] Both of these additional variables should have a positive impact on the likelihood of a family member successor. The size of the firm as measured by the logarithm of total assets is included to account for the argument that a larger family firm may be inclined to look outside the family for a manager because of the greater scale of operations. Given this

---

[9] The number rather than the proportion of managers who are family members is expected to be a better predictor of whether the firm will appoint a family member successor as it is the availability of such members that is considered to be most important.

348   *B.F. Smith, B. Amoako-Adu / Journal of Corporate Finance 5 (1999) 341–368*

argument, it is expected that size is negatively related to the appointment of a
family member. A final explanatory variable is the other significant blockholder
variable which is expected to have a negative relationship with the appointment of
a family member successor. [10]

Probability(family member successor)

= f(firm performance, number of senior officers who are family

members, vote ownership by family, size, other significant

blockholder).

Abnormal performance is measured in two ways as shown below. First, it is
measured by the market-adjusted model. In this model, abnormal stock return is
measured by the difference between the monthly return of the company stock and
the TSE 300 Total Return Index over the four years ending before the announcement of the resignation. The standard market model is not used as the long tenure
of the resigning family member company presidents does not provide us with an
uncontaminated period for estimating the regression parameters. [11] The second
measure of corporate performance is the average difference between the company's
annual return on assets less the median return on assets of the industry for the four
years prior to the succession.

Market-Adjusted Model of Abnormal Monthly Stock Return:

$$AR_{it} = R_{it} - R_{mt} \qquad (1)$$

where R_{it} is the monthly stock return inclusive of dividends for security i in
month t and R_{mt} is the monthly return on the TSE 300 Total Return Index in
month t.

Industry-Adjusted Return on Assets: $AROA_{it} = ROA_{it} - IROA_{it}$ \qquad (2)

where ROA_{it} is the annual return on asset of company i for year t and $IROA_{it}$ is
the median annual return on assets of the firms with the same four-digit SIC codes.

---

[10] The multinomial logit model is specified as

$$p_{i0} = 1 / \left[1 + \sum_{j=1}^{2} \exp(x_i' \beta_j) \right],$$

$$p_{ij} = \exp(x_i' \beta_j) / \left[1 + \sum_{j=1}^{2} \exp(x_i' \beta_j) \right] \qquad \forall j = 1,2,$$

where p_{i0}, p_{i1} and p_{i2} are the probability that a non-family insider, a family member and an outsider,
respectively, will be appointed in firm i, β_j is a vector of unknown parameters to be estimated and x_i
is a vector of the explanatory variables.

[11] The alpha and beta are constrained to be zero and one, respectively. Brown and Warner (1985)
compare different methods of measuring excess daily stock returns, including the market-adjusted
method and conclude that alternative measures exhibit similar ability to detect abnormal performance.

B.F. Smith, B. Amoako-Adu / Journal of Corporate Finance 5 (1999) 341–368   349

The median returns are extracted from the Dun and Bradstreet Key Business Ratios for Canadian Companies with assets in excess of $1 million.

To examine the hypothesis that the choice of successor from within and outside the family affects corporate performance, several tests are conducted. First, the immediate impact on shareholder wealth from the succession announcement is measured using cumulative abnormal residuals (CARs) of the company's common stock. The abnormal residuals are based on the daily stock return less that of the TSE 300 Total Return Index. The CARs of the firms announcing successions over the period -40 to $+20$ days relative to the announcement day $t = 0$ are compared across the three types of successors. CARs are also compared over five sub-periods such as days -1 to $+1$ to capture the immediate impact of the news. Second, to control for other factors, a cross-sectional regression is conducted with the CARs (-1 to $+1$ days) as the dependent variable and a set of explanatory variables measuring whether the successor is a family member or outsider, the age of the successor, the number of years of experience in senior management of the successor, the size of the company and whether the predecessor is a founder.

$$CAR_i = f(\text{family successor, outside successor, age of successor,}$$

$$\text{number of years of experience in senior management of successor,}$$

$$\text{firm size, founder})$$

where $CAR_i = \sum_{t=-1}^{1} AR_{it}$, $AR_{it} = R_{it} - R_{mt}$, $R_{it} =$ daily return on stock, and $R_{mt} =$ daily return on TSE 300 Total Return Index.

The age of the successor is a measure of the extent to which managerial reputation has been established. The number of years of experience of the successor within senior management of the company should be positively related to the performance of the company if this factor is a strong measure of the human capital of individual managers. The size variable is used to control for the argument of Reinganum (1985) that a successor can have a bigger impact on a smaller firm than a larger firm. Finally, founder is a binary variable with a value of one if the founder is the predecessor and zero otherwise. Based on the research of McConaughy et al. (1998), the founder coefficient should be positive as the descendent-controlled firms tend to be more efficient than founder-controlled firms. Furthermore, given that Johnson et al. (1985) find that there is a significantly positive response to the death of a founder, it is possible that the coefficient on this variable will be positive, even in cases in which the founder resigns, instead.

One potential weakness of the CAR analysis is that the succession announcement may not convey new information to investors. Vancil (1987) and Booth and Deli (1996) note that CEO successors are typically selected several years prior to the CEO's departure and groomed for the top position over a period of time. Thus, the identity of the successor may not be a surprise to investors and, therefore, stock prices may not react to this event upon announcement.

To test whether long-term corporate performance is affected by the type of successor, the change in annual return on assets of the company less that of the industry over the four years before to the four years after is calculated for each firm. The changes in performance for cases of family, non-family insider, and outside successors are compared and tested for statistical significance. The change in corporate performance is measured using nonparametric test statistics. Barber and Lyon (1996) recommend the use of nonparametric test statistics for accounting based figures because of the problem of outliers. Long-term performance is also measured using monthly abnormal stock returns. In examining post-succession performance, we identify cases in which the family sold its controlling interest. In such cases, the post-succession performance is measured only with data up to the date of the ownership change.

4. Empirical analysis

4.1. Sample characteristics

Tables 1–9 provide descriptive statistics for the sample of 124 appointments of presidents and chief executive officers. These tables demonstrate that family firms are different from other publicly listed firms. In addition, they show that there are significant differences among family firms that appoint family members, non-family insiders and outsiders.

Panel A of Table 1 shows the industry classification of the family firms in the sample. Approximately one-third of the firms are in the wholesale and retail sectors and one-third are involved in manufacturing. In contrast, only 7.5% and 22.8% of all TSE listed companies are in these industries. Thus, there is a strong family affiliation of many firms in these sectors. On the other hand, only 8.1% of the sample is in the natural resource industry compared to 45.4% of all companies listed on the TSE. Panel B of Table 1 illustrates that the mean (median) asset size of the total sample of firms is $805.6 ($131.0) million. Thus, most family firms tend to be relatively small but there are a few large firms that skew the distribution of asset size.

The ownership of the family firms in the sample is described in Table 2. On average, for the whole sample, families control 53.52% of the votes. The ownership of votes varies significantly at the 5% level according to type of successor. Firms which appoint family members are most closely controlled with almost 60% of the votes controlled by family members whereas those firms that appoint outsiders are least closely controlled. In such firms, family members hold an average of 46% of total votes. For firms that appoint non-family insiders, the degree of ownership by family members lies between that of the family and outside successor firms.

B.F. Smith, B. Amoako-Adu / Journal of Corporate Finance 5 (1999) 341–368   351

Table 1

Industry classification and size of family firms with appointments of presidents/CEOs

Panel A classifies by industry the sample of family firms involving 124 appointments of presidents and CEOs. A family firm is a corporation in which: (1) a family is the largest shareholder; (2) the family holds at least 10% of the votes; and (3) a family member was a president and/or CEO before the succession. The family firms were listed at some time during the period 1962 to 1996 on the Toronto Stock Exchange. The percentage of Toronto Stock Exchange Stocks is calculated as the number of companies in the industry divided by the total number of companies listed on the Toronto Stock Exchange as at December 31, 1987, a median date for the announcements in the sample. Panel B provides descriptive statistics on the total asset size of the sample of family firms as of the year of the appointment of presidents and CEOs.

Panel A: Industry distribution

Type of industry	Companies which appointed family members	Companies which appointed non-family insiders	Companies which appointed outsiders	Number (% of total sample)
Manufacturing	15	18	13	46 (37.1)
Wholesale and retail	18	19	3	38 (32.3)
Communications[a]	9	1	2	12 (9.7)
Natural resources	4	4	2	10 (8.1)
Financial	4	2	0	6 (4.8)
Real estate	0	3	2	5 (4.0)
Transportation	2	3	0	5 (4.0)
Total	52	50	22	124 (100.0)

Panel B: Total assets in $ millions in year of succession

	Companies which appointed family members	Companies which appointed non-family insiders	Companies which appointed outsiders	All firms in sample
Mean	$1285.0[b]	$600.0[b]	139.9[b]	$805.6
Median	120.0[c]	199.0[c]	63.0[c]	131.0
Standard deviation	4760.8	937.6	201.7	315.4

[a] Broadcasting and newspapers.

[b] The means of the total assets of the groups of successors are not significantly different. The F-test statistic is 1.20 which is less than $F_{0.10,2,121} = 2.35$.

[c] The Kruskall–Wallis test for the equality of the location of the three populations is 10.48 which is significant at the 1% level.

Given previous findings by researchers such as DeAngelo and DeAngelo (1985), that firms using dual class shares are generally closely held by families, it is not surprising that 62% of family firms in the total sample employ such a dual class share structure. Dual class shares are an effective measure to prevent a hostile takeover and ensure an intergenerational transfer of control. Consistent with this purpose, the use of restricted shares is highest among firms with family successors.

A difference between the ownership of family firms that appoint family members as successors and those that appoint non-family insiders and outsiders is

352 *B.F. Smith, B. Amoako-Adu / Journal of Corporate Finance 5 (1999) 341–368*

Table 2
Ownership characteristics of family firms with appointments of presidents/CEOs
This table provides descriptive statistics concerning the ownership of a sample of family firms involving 124 appointments of presidents and CEOs. Ownership by family is measured by the percentage of total votes that are held by the family with the largest percentage of votes of the firm.

	Companies which appointed family members	Companies which appointed non-family insiders	Companies which appointed outsiders	Total
Ownership of votes by family				
Mean[a]	59.36%	50.59%	46.36%	53.52%
Median[b]	59.30%	50.87%	40.96%	51.55%
Standard deviation	22.92%	21.00%	16.77%	21.64%
Dual class shares[c]				
Number (percentage of total)	35 (67%)	31 (62%)	11 (50%)	77 (62%)
Number (percentage) of cases where				
(i) Control by single family[d]	50 (96%)	37 (74%)	18 (82%)	105 (85%)
(ii) Control by family and other large blockholder[e]	2 (4%)	13 (26%)	4 (18%)	19 (15%)
Total	52 (100%)	50 (100%)	22 (100%)	124 (100%)

[a] The means of the family ownership of votes are significantly different at the 5% level. The F-statistic is 3.71 which exceeds $F_{0.05,2,121} = 3.07$.
[b] The Kruskall–Wallis test statistic is 3.87 which is less than $\chi^2_{0.10,2} = 4.61$. Thus, the locations of the three populations are not significantly different.
[c] The χ^2 test statistic for differences in proportions across the three groups is 1.97 which is not significant at even the 10% level.
[d] Number of cases where one family either has legal control (owns more than 50% of votes) or only one has effective control (owns more than 10% of votes, but less than 50%). The χ^2 test statistic for differences in proportions across the three groups is 9.81. This is significant at the 1% level.
[e] Number of cases where family and other blockholder each hold between 10% and 50% of votes.

whether control lies within a single family or is held by the family and another significant blockholder. Of the 52 cases of appointments of family members, only two family firms have significant other blockholders. In contrast, 26% and 18% of the cases of appointments of non-family insiders and outsiders, respectively, involve firms with another significant blockholder. The three proportions are significantly different at the 1% level. Thus, large blockholders appear reluctant to appoint the family's offspring and a non-family member is selected as an acceptable alternative.

The high degree of family involvement in the sample of firms is evidenced by the number of family members who are directors and senior managers as shown in Table 3. In cases of family member appointments, the average numbers of directors and senior managers who are family members are 3.06 and 2.67, respectively. These figures are significantly different at the 1% level from the

B.F. Smith, B. Amoako-Adu / Journal of Corporate Finance 5 (1999) 341–368   353

Table 3

Extent of family involvement in family firms at time of succession

This table shows the number of members of the board of directors at the time of the appointment who are members of a family that owns at least 10% of the firm. The table also shows the number of senior managers who are family members. Senior managers are those executives who are listed in the *Financial Post Survey of Industrials.*

	Companies which appointed family members	Companies which appointed non-family insiders	Companies which appointed outsiders	*F*-statistic of equality of means
Number of directors who are family members[a]				
Mean	3.06	2.00	1.73	13.35***
Standard deviation	1.23	1.34	0.94	
Number of senior managers who are family members				
Mean	2.67	1.56	1.32	19.34***
Standard deviation	1.29	0.99	0.32	

*** Significant at the 1% level, given $F_{0.01,2,121} = 4.61$.

[a] St. Pierre et al. (1996) report that the mean (median) number of directors for their sample of 88 Canadian companies was 9.68 (9.00). Thus, the above numbers represent large percentages of the total board of directors.

samples of non-family and outside appointments. This finding is not surprising as a larger number of family members who are senior managers increases the size of the pool of candidates for the family to draw upon.

Table 4 describes the positions held by the incumbent senior manager. In most cases, the incumbents hold considerable power in the family firms with most holding multiple senior management positions. In 85 of 124 cases, just prior to succession, the incumbent serves in at least two of the positions of president, CEO and chair of the board. Furthermore, after their resignation from the role as president and/or chief executive officer, most incumbents continue their direct involvement in managing the firms. Of the 124 cases, there are 91 in which the incumbent serves as chair of the board and in half of these cases, the incumbent also acts as chief executive officer. Nineteen other incumbents serve in other positions in the firm while only nine retire completely and five die while in office. The paucity of cases of death triggering succession makes the study different from those of Johnson et al. (1985) and Slovin and Sushka (1993). In the latter study, death of a large inside blockholder leads to a break-up of control blocks which, as shown in Table 9, occurs relatively infrequently in our sample.

As indicated in Table 5, for the family member appointments, the mean age of the incumbent manager is 62.5 years whereas those of the cases of non-family insiders and outside appointments are 59.7 and 56.4 years, respectively. The three ages are significantly different at the 5% level which implies incumbents with family member successors are significantly older than those with non-family successors. The maximum age of the incumbent is 86 years which indicates that

Table 4
Corporate position of incumbent senior manager

	Companies which appointed family members	Companies which appointed non-family insiders	Companies which appointed outsiders	Total
Prior position of incumbent				
President only	23	11	5	39
President and chief operating officer	5	1	0	6
President and chief executive officer	5	11	5	21
President and chief financial officer	0	1	0	1
President, chief executive officer and chair of board	7	13	7	27
President and chair of board	4	4	3	11
Chief executive officer and chair of board	8	9	1	18
Chief executive officer and vice-chair	0	0	1	1
Total	52	50	22	124
New position of incumbent				
Chair only	21	14	8	43
Chief executive officer and chair	13	27	8	48
Vice chair only	4	0	1	5
Director only	4	2	0	6
Vice president	0	2	1	3
Other position	2	1	2	5
Retired	5	3	1	9
Deceased	3	1	1	5
Total	52	50	22	124

some individuals in family firms are able to maintain their senior posts well beyond the normal retirement age. This finding is reinforced by the long tenure of the incumbents. The incumbents have an average tenure of approximately 13 years.

The incumbent is a founder of the firm in 89 cases out of the sample of 124 companies. A further 27 appointments involve descendants of the founder. Only eight of the cases involve an incumbent not related to the original founder of the firm. Thus, most of the firms in the sample are controlled by either the founder or the direct descendent of the founder.

From Table 6, well over half of the family and non-family successors are vice-presidents and thus are clearly being groomed within the firm for the position

B.F. Smith, B. Amoako-Adu / Journal of Corporate Finance 5 (1999) 341–368   355

Table 5

Characteristics of incumbent president and/or CEO

This table presents descriptive statistics concerning the incumbent president and/or CEO. The sample includes 124 appointments of presidents and/or CEOs in family firms with the exception of the age statistics which are based on 116 cases. Ages in nine cases were not available.

	Companies which appointed family members	Companies which appointed non-family insiders	Companies which appointed outsiders	F-statistic of equality of means
Age of incumbent at time of appointment of successor				
Mean	62.5	59.7	56.4	4.40**
Median[a]	64.1	60.0	56.0	
Standard deviation	7.5	6.6	11.4	
Minimum	44.0	46.0	43.1	
Maximum	75.0	75.0	86.0	
Number of years incumbent with firm as senior executive prior to appointment				
Mean	13.77	13.42	11.23	0.60
Standard deviation	10.32	7.85	9.18	
Relationship of incumbent to founder (number of cases)				
Founder	36	40	13	
Descendent of founder	10	10	7	
Not related to founder	6	0	2	
Total	52	50	22	

**Significant at 5% level.

[a]The Kruskall–Wallis test statistic is 12.97 which is significant at the 1% level. Thus, the locations of the three populations are significantly different.

of president and/or CEO. Only three of the successors who are family members, hold positions outside the firm at the time of the succession. Even in the 22 cases of appointments of an outsider, six successors have ties to the firm in their roles as outside directors. Table 6 also shows that almost all successors hold the new position of president, often in conjunction with another title. Thus, the successors are in a position to significantly influence operations of their firms and set corporate strategy.

The characteristics of the successors are described in Table 7. The successors who are family members are significantly younger than non-family inside and outside successors. The mean (median) age of the family members is 45.7 (43.0) years whereas that of the outsiders is 52.3 (52.0). Most of the family members are direct descendants of the incumbent. Of the 52 appointments, 32 are sons and four are daughters. There are nine brothers who are successors and four cases in which a founder is reappointed and one case in which a fellow founder from another controlling family is appointed. The large proportion of sons becoming family successors remains a historical practice where parents tend to groom their sons to succeed them in business. There are only two cases, a son-in-law and a spouse,

Table 6
Position of successor before/after appointment

	Companies which appointed family members	Companies which appointed non-family insiders	Companies which appointed outsiders	Total
Prior position with firm				
Vice-president	31	33	0	64
President and chief operating officer	6	5	0	11
President of subsidiary	1	8	0	9
President	1	2	0	3
Chair and chief executive officer	2	1	0	3
Other executive	6	1	0	7
Director only	2	0	6	8
Position with other firm	3	0	16	19
Total	52	50	22	124
New position with firm				
President	23	12	4	39
President and chief executive officer	9	15	14	38
President and chief operating officer	10	21	4	35
President, chair and chief executive officer	5	2	0	7
President and chair	1	0	0	1
Chief executive officer and chair	4	0	0	4
Total	52	50	22	124

where the successor is not a direct bloodline of the incumbent. Thus, the story of marriage as a path to the president's office appears to be largely a myth, at least in the case of publicly traded firms.

Table 8 shows the extent of the work experience of successors. For cases in which the successor is currently employed as a senior officer of the firm, the average number of years of experience is about eight years for both family and non-family insiders. Thus, the mean age of 45.7 from Table 7 suggests that the family members who become successors entered the ranks of senior management in their mid-thirties, a relatively young age. The tenure of successors who are family members is almost twice as long as that of outsiders. For cases of appointments before 1989, the family member successors have a mean tenure of 9.11 years and outsiders have a tenure of only 4.40 years. Thus, successors who are tied to the firm through familial and ownership links have a significantly longer tenure than others. Anecdotal evidence suggests non-family members acting

B.F. Smith, B. Amoako-Adu / Journal of Corporate Finance 5 (1999) 341–368   357

Table 7

Age and relationship of management successor

This table presents descriptive statistics concerning management successors. The sample includes 124 appointments of presidents and CEOs in family firm with the exception of the age statistics which are based on 112 cases. Ages in 12 cases were not available.

	Companies which appointed family members	Companies which appointed non-family insiders	Companies which appointed outsiders	F-statistic of equality of means
Age of successor at time of appointment				
Mean	45.7	47.6	52.3	3.33**
Median[a]	43.0	49.0	52.0	
Standard deviation	11.2	7.0	6.7	
Minimum	26.1	32.1	41.0	
Maximum	75.1	62.9	70.0	
Relationship of successor to incumbent				
Son	32	0	0	
Brother	9	0	0	
Daughter	4	0	0	
Son-in-law	1	0	0	
Spouse	1	0	0	
Reappointment of founder	4	0	0	
Appointment of fellow founder	1	0	0	
Unrelated to family	0	50	22	
Total	52	50	22	

** Statistically significant at the 5% level.

[a] The Kruskall–Wallis test statistic of 16.01 rejects the equality of the locations of the three populations at the 1% level.

as president often run into conflict with family members presiding over them as CEO or Chair of the Board of Directors. [12]

Table 9 provides evidence on whether succession in family-owned firms is associated with changes in control, not coincident with, but over the five years subsequent to the succession. Only three (14%) of the firms which appoint outsiders, five (10%) of the firms which appoint non-family members and two (4%) of the firms which appoint family members experience changes in control. The chi-squared test statistic for these percentages is 2.22 which is not significant at the 10% level. Thus, any observed difference in post-succession performance is not due to a change in control.

---

[12] There are newspaper accounts of outside successors quitting within three years of being hired as president because of apparent disputes with controlling family members. Cases include Electrohome in 1982, Denison Mines in 1985, SICO in 1991, Peoples Jewellers in 1992 and Firan in 1996. A recent discussion of the dismissal of an outsider is provided in ''Frame Back in the Game'', *Globe and Mail*, February 17, 1997.

Table 8
Employment experience of successors

	Companies which appointed family members	Companies which appointed non-family insiders	Companies which appointed outsiders	F-statistic of equality of means
Number of years successor previously with firm as senior executive[a]				
Mean	8.68	7.80	not applicable	
Standard deviation	6.35	5.96		
Number of years successor with firm in new position				
All cases				
Mean	5.98	3.92	3.23	4.15**
Standard deviation	5.23	3.78	3.01	
Excluding appointments after 1989				
Mean	9.11	5.96	4.40	4.95***
Standard deviation	5.17	4.46	3.89	

**Significant at the 5% level.
***Significant at the 1% level.
[a]Includes only cases where the successor has previous experience with firm. *T*-statistic for difference in means is 0.70 which is insignificant.

4.2. Results of multinomial logit analysis

To test whether prior corporate performance affects the choice of a successor, a multinomial logit analysis is conducted. The results of this analysis are shown in Table 10. The first and third columns of Table 10 indicates that prior corporate performance, as measured by the industry adjusted return on assets and monthly abnormal stock return, is not significantly related to the likelihood of a family successor. That is, stronger performance will not necessarily lead to the appointment of a family member and poorer performance will not necessarily lead to the appointment of an outsider. [13]

As expected, columns (2) and (4) of Table 10 show that the number of senior officers who are family members has a positive relationship, at the 5% significance level, with the likelihood of the appointment of a family member. In addition, cases in which there is another large blockholder with ownership in excess of 10% of votes have a significantly lower likelihood at the 5% level of

---

[13] An alternative explanation for the lack of a significant link between operating performance and selection of an outsider when other dependent variables are added to the logit analysis is offered in the findings of Murphy and Zimmerman (1993). They identify an endogeneity problem with corporate performance leading to a change in accounting treatment which other researchers had mistakenly attributed to a new CEO. In our paper, it is possible that poor financial performance led family members not to seek senior management positions in the years before the succession. Thus, the lack of family members prior to the announcement of a CEO successor could be a symptom rather than a cause of hiring an outsider.

B.F. Smith, B. Amoako-Adu / Journal of Corporate Finance 5 (1999) 341–368   359

Table 9
Changes in control during 5 years subsequent to appointment of senior manager

	Companies which appointed family members	Companies which appointed non-family insiders	Companies which appointed outsiders	Total
(a) Acquired by outsiders	2	5	1	8
(b) Family acquired shares	0	0	2	2
Total number of changes of control	2	5	3	10
Percentage of total cases[a]	4%	10%	14%	8%

[a]The chi-square test statistic for the percentage of total cases involving changes in control is 2.22 which is less than the critical value of $\chi^2_{0.10,2} = 4.61$.

appointing a family member than firms controlled by a single family. However, the vote ownership by the family and size have no significant impact on the likelihood of a family member being appointed as successor. Overall, the evidence suggests that family members are more likely to be appointed where more family members are senior executives of the firm and the firm is controlled by a single family. Controlling for these factors, poor corporate performance does not generally affect the type of successor appointed.

4.3. Results of abnormal returns analysis

The remainder of the test results described in the paper focus on whether the appointment of a family member significantly affects shareholder wealth and the company's financial performance. Fig. 1 and Table 11 present the cumulative abnormal returns surrounding the announcement of successions for the firms in the sample. Fig. 1 suggests that shareholders of firms that appoint outsiders experience a cumulative abnormal return of about 9.0% versus a cumulative abnormal return of approximately −1.6% for firms that appoint family members and non-family insiders over the period from 40 days before to 20 days after the announcement. Table 11 indicates that over the period from the day before to the day after the announcement, the abnormal return of firms with family successors is −3.20%. The three groups of CARs are significantly different from each other at the 1% level. To control for ancillary factors, a cross-sectional analysis shown in Table 12 of the three day event window (−1, +1) CARs is conducted.

Table 12 indicates that the CARs of firms at the time of succession announcements are not significantly related to whether the successor is a family member or an outsider when other factors are considered. The age variable is positively related to CAR at the 10% significance level. This indicates that investors favour the appointment of older and likely more seasoned executives with established reputations. Thus, the negative CARs for companies which appoint family successors in Table 11 reflects the fact that these successors tend to be younger than

Table 10
Multinomial logit analysis of determinants of type of successors in family firms

This table shows the results of multinomial logit analyses. The models measure the probability of belonging to one of three alternatives, $j = 0$, 1 or 2, where $j = 0$ is a non-family insider, $j = 1$ is a family successor and $j = 2$ is an outsider. The table shows the estimated coefficients and their corresponding t-statistics in parentheses. The analysis is conducted using prior performance as the only explanatory variable in models (1) and (3) and using an expanded set of explanatory variables in models (2) and (4). Prior performance is measured using industry-adjusted return on assets which is calculated as the mean of the difference between the company's return on assets and that of the industry median over the four years prior to the year of the succession. The industry median return on assets is extracted from the Dun and Bradstreet Key Business Ratios for Canadian companies with the same four-digit SIC code and assets in excess of $1 million. The abnormal monthly stock return is the mean of the difference between the logarithm of one plus the company's monthly stock return and that of the logarithm of one plus the Toronto Stock Exchange 300 total return index over the 48 months prior to the month of the succession. The variable, other significant blockholder, has a value of one if the family and another blockholder each hold between 10% and 50% of votes. The variable, firm size, equals the logarithm of the total assets in $ millions in year of succession.

| | Prior performance measured by industry-adjusted return on assets | | | | Prior performance measured by abnormal monthly stock returns | | | |
| | (1) | | (2) | | (3) | | (4) | |
	Family successor	Outsider	Family successor	Outsider	Family successor	Outsider	Family successor	Outsider
Constant	0.10	−0.82	−0.30	4.29	0.01	−0.81	−0.12	4.30
	(0.48)	(2.81)***	(0.28)	(2.98)***	(0.06)	(3.14)***	(0.13)	(2.96)***
Prior performance	5.25	1.18	1.18	−0.10	−9.00	−4.77	−17.12	−2.67
	(1.38)	(0.30)	(0.36)	(0.03)	(0.92)	(0.38)	(1.51)	(0.21)
Number of senior officers who are family members			0.88	−0.61			1.00	−0.54
			(3.69)***	(1.37)			(4.00)***	(1.25)
Other significant blockholder(s)			−2.23	−0.79			−2.32	−0.79
			(2.54)**	(1.14)			(2.79)***	(1.12)
Percentage of votes controlled by family members			−0.01	−0.01			−0.01	−0.01
			(0.60)	(0.79)			(1.08)	(1.00)
Firm size			−0.15	−0.72			−0.18	−0.72
			(1.02)	(3.34)***			(1.34)	(3.29)***
Likelihood ratio test (number of degrees of freedom)	2.25 (4 d.f.)	2.25 (4 d.f.)	51.79*** (12 d.f.)	51.79*** (12 d.f.)	0.88 (4 d.f.)	0.88 (4 d.f.)	56.11*** (12 d.f.)	56.11*** (12 d.f.)
Number of cases	119	119	119	119	122	122	122	122

* Significant at 10% level.
** Significant at 5% level.
*** Significant at 1% level.

B.F. Smith, B. Amoako-Adu / Journal of Corporate Finance 5 (1999) 341–368   361

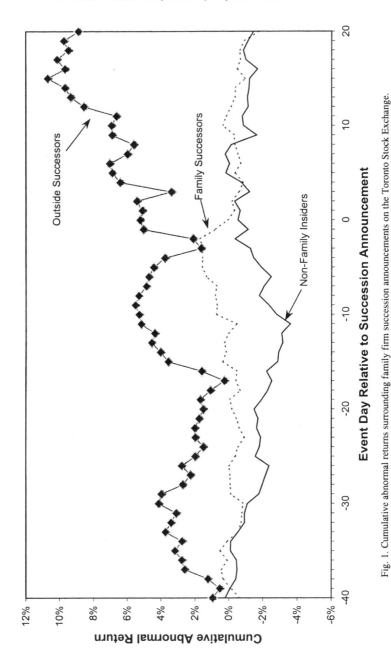

Fig. 1. Cumulative abnormal returns surrounding family firm succession announcements on the Toronto Stock Exchange.

Table 11

Cumulative abnormal returns surrounding announcements of family firm successions on the Toronto Stock Exchange from 1963 to 1996

This table shows the cumulative abnormal returns (CARs) over the period −40 to +20 days for a set of family firms in which a family member, non-family insider or outsider is appointed as president and/or chief executive officer. The number of cases varies over different sub-periods because firms with any daily observations missing are not included in the calculation of CAR.

Days relative to announcement day	(1) Companies which appointed family successors			(2) Companies which appointed non-family insiders			(3) Companies which appointed outsiders			F-statistic for equality of means
	Number of cases	Cumulative abnormal return (%)	t-test	Number of cases	Cumulative abnormal return (%)	t-test	Number of cases	Cumulative abnormal return (%)	t-test	
−40 to −2	30	1.68	0.67	35	−0.88	0.34	13	1.10	0.18	0.22
−1 to 0	34	−1.73	3.11***	41	−0.32	0.45	15	3.77	1.21	4.26**
0	35	−0.70	1.74*	42	0.50	1.43	15	0.44	0.70	2.79*
−1 to +1	34	−3.20	5.03***	41	−0.50	0.58	15	3.54	1.49	7.31***
+2 to +20	33	−1.53	0.95**	39	−0.65	0.28	13	4.14	0.90	0.91
−40 to +20	30	−1.64	0.43	34	−1.60	0.54	13	8.75	1.27	1.43

* Significant at the 10% level.
** Significant at the 5% level.
*** Significant at the 1% level.

Table 12
Cross-sectional analysis of cumulative abnormal returns at time of announcement of successions of CEOs and/or presidents in family firms

This table shows the results of a cross-sectional regression in which the dependent variable is the cumulative abnormal return over the event window from the day before to the day after the announcement of the succession. The explanatory variable, family successor, is a dummy variable with a value of one if a member of a controlling family is the successor and zero if a non-family member is the successor. The variable outside successor is a dummy variable with a value of one if the successor is an outsider and zero otherwise. The variable founder is a dummy variable with a value of one if a predecessor is a founder of the company. Age is the age of the successor. Firm size is measured by the logarithm of the total assets in $ millions in the year of the succession. The sample includes 90 announcements of successions in family firms in the Toronto Stock Exchange, 15 of which involve the appointment of an outsider, 41 of which involve a non-family insider, and 34 of which involve the appointment of a family member. The t-statistics are shown in parentheses beside the estimated coefficients. The standard errors have been corrected for potential heteroskedasticity using heteroskedastic-consistent covariance matrix estimation of White (1980).

Constant	-0.078 $(1.96)^*$
Family successor	-0.012 (1.06)
Outside successor	0.021 (0.98)
Founder	-0.012 (1.01)
Age	0.001 $(1.76)^*$
Number of years successor was senior executive at company	-0.002 (1.23)
Firm size	0.008 $(2.12)^{**}$
Adjusted R^2	0.09
Number of observations	90

* Significant at the 10% level.
** Significant at the 5% level.

other successors and there is greater uncertainty over their management quality. As the size coefficient is significantly positive at the 5% level, CARs at larger companies are more positive than those of small companies when successions are announced. This may be related to the fact that smaller companies find successions more challenging and value reducing. As shown in Table 12, the explanatory variables, founder and number of years successor was senior executive at the company have no significant impact on CAR. This suggests that whether or not the predecessor was a founder has no impact on shareholder wealth. This differs from Johnson et al. (1985), who find significant positive CARs at the death of the founder likely because only 4% of our sample includes founders who die at the time of succession. As shown in Table 5, most incumbents in our sample of companies remain in some senior position with the firm.

4.4. Analysis of long-term performance

Table 13 shows the results for tests as to whether the appointment of family members has an effect on long-term financial performance. Column 1 of Panel A of Table 13 indicates that for the sample of family successor firms, there is a significant decrease, at the 10% level, in the median industry-adjusted return on

Table 13

Impact of successions on performance during pre and post four-year period

This table shows the change in financial performance from the four years before to the four years after the succession of presidents and CEOs in family firms listed on the Toronto Stock Exchange. In Panel A, the median of the industry adjusted return on assets is shown. The industry adjusted return on assets is calculated as the four-year average of the company's annual return on assets less the median return on assets of firms with the same four-digit SIC codes. The median returns for the industry are extracted from the Dun and Bradstreet Key Business Ratios for Canadian Companies with assets in excess of $1 million. In Panel B, the abnormal stock return is calculated as the average of 48 months of the logarithm of one plus stock return less the logarithm of one plus the return on the TSE 300 Total Return Index. The pre-succession period includes the 48 months preceding the announcement. The post-succession period includes the 48 months following the announcement. The month of the announcement is excluded from each period. The figures in parentheses in columns (1), (2) and (3) are standardized Wilcoxon Signed Rank Sum test statistics. The figure in column (4) shows the Kruskall–Wallis test statistic for the equality of the location of the three populations.

	(1) Family successor	(2) Non-family inside successor	(3) Outside successor	(4) Kruskall–Wallis test statistic
Panel A: Median industry adjusted return on assets				
Number of cases	42	39	19	
(1) Pre-succession industry adjusted return on assets	−0.25% (424)	−2.30% (122)***	−3.20% (39)**	10.55***
(2) Post-succession industry adjusted return on assets	−0.60% (343)	−1.10% (280)	−0.10% (91)	0.57
Change in industry adjusted return on assets (2)–(1)	−1.45% (312.5)*	0.60% (278.5)	1.10% (53)*	6.65**
Panel B: Median monthly abnormal stock return				
Number of cases	49	49	19	
(1) Pre-succession abnormal stock return	−0.31% (450)	−0.46% (502)	−0.70% (44)**	2.28
(2) Post-succession abnormal stock return	−0.20% (502)	−0.52% (464)	−1.15% (36)**	3.48
Change in abnormal stock returns (2)–(1)	0.49% (568)	−0.23% (542)	−0.56% (74)	1.53

* Significant at the 10% level.
** Significant at the 5% level.
*** Significant at the 1% level.

assets of family firms from before to after the succession. On the other hand, the third column of Panel A of Table 13 indicates that there is a significant increase in the industry-adjusted return on assets for the outside successor sample. The non-family insider group has a positive but not significant impact on operating profits.

We attribute the increase in profitability for the non-family insider and outside successor firms relative to the family successor firms to the fact that the non-family successor firms underperform in the pre-succession period. Thus, there is greater

B.F. Smith, B. Amoako-Adu / Journal of Corporate Finance 5 (1999) 341–368   365

scope for improvement. Unlike Table 10, Table 13 indicates that the pre-succession performance of the non-family and outsider successor firms is significantly lower than that of the family successor firms. The Kruskall–Wallis test indicates that the three group pre-succession operating performances are significantly different at the 1% level. While the pre-succession median industry-adjusted return on assets for firms that appoint family members is not significantly different from zero, the median industry-adjusted return on assets for firms that appoint non-family insiders and outsiders is significantly negative at the 1% level. In interpreting the results of Table 10 versus Table 13 concerning pre-succession performance, we note that Barber and Lyon (1996) recommend the use of nonparametric test statistics when analysing accounting based data because of the problem of outliers. Thus, we place more weight on the findings of Table 13 and conclude that family firms are sensitive to corporate performance when selecting a type of successor. For the post-succession period, the industry-adjusted return on assets for all three groups of firms is not significantly different from zero.

Panel B of Table 13 provides evidence on the impact of successions on the monthly abnormal stock return. For the pre-succession period, the results for the abnormal stock returns are consistent with those of the industry-adjusted return on assets for the family successor and outside successor firms. The family firm abnormal stock returns are not significantly different from zero whereas the outside successor abnormal stock returns are significantly less than zero. However, unlike the pre-succession industry-adjusted return on assets, the pre-succession abnormal stock returns of the non-family insiders is negative but not significantly less than zero. In the post-succession period, we do not expect the abnormal stock return to be significantly different from zero. This is because the market impact of the announcement is likely impounded in the stock price in the days immediately surrounding the announcement. These days are not included in the monthly return analysis because the month of the announcement is excluded from the analysis. While the family and non-family insider groups have post-succession abnormal stock returns not significantly different from zero, the outsider group has post-succession abnormal stock returns significantly less than zero. Thus, firms which appoint outsiders tend to experience negative abnormal stock returns in the four years following a succession which offset the positive CARs at the time of the announcement. This is not surprising given the high rate of management turnover in these firms.

5. Conclusions

Management literature on family firms suggests that the goal of shareholder wealth may be influenced by family interests at the time of president and/or CEO succession. This research is designed to test directly the impact of family succession on corporate value by comparing appointments from within the family with non-family insider or outside successor. The sample comprises 124 announcements of the appointments of presidents and CEOs in Canadian firms in which members of the controlling family actively participate in management. Family controlled firms are characterized by a high concentration of votes held by family members, dual class capitalization and long tenured family member CEOs and presidents. These characteristics hold less for firms that appoint either non-family insiders or outsiders. Family successors tend to be appointed at a younger age than non-family insiders and outsiders. Family appointments are dominated by direct bloodline relations, such as children and siblings. Appointments of spouses and in-laws are the exception.

The study provides some limited evidence that poor corporate performance affects the firm's selection of a family member versus a non-family insider and an outsider as a successor. Over a four-year pre-succession period, the median industry-adjusted return on asset for companies with non-family insiders and outsiders appointed as the new CEO/president is significantly negative. The pre-succession monthly abnormal stock return is also significantly negative for the outside successor firms. On the other hand, the firms which appoint family successors do not have significantly negative pre-succession performance. Thus, there is some evidence that poor corporate performance leads to the appointment of non-family members, especially outsiders. However, multinomial logit analysis indicates that the only significant factors that lead to the choice of a family member as successor are a high number of family members in senior management and the absence of another large blockholder. The latter variable may reflect disagreements between the family and the blockholder as to whose members should assume the senior executive position.

Analysis of stock prices indicates that the appointment of family members results in a significant loss to shareholders of -3.20% over days $(-1, 1)$ surrounding the announcement whereas there is no negative reaction to appointment of non-family insiders and outsiders. However, a cross-sectional regression indicates that the age of the successor and size of the company are significantly related to the stock price reaction whereas the family connection of the successor is not. We argue that shareholders react negatively to the appointment of a family member because of greater uncertainty over the management quality than arises with the appointment of non-family insiders and outside successors who tend to be older. As reported above, non-family insiders and outside successors are more often appointed to poorly performing firms in which there is greater scope for improvement. This poorer pre-succession condition is consistent with the finding that long-term industry adjusted return on assets improves significantly more with the appointment of non-family insiders and outsiders than family members. Finally, outside successor firms have negative long-term stock performance post-succession which is consistent with the high level of turnover of senior management that these firms experience after succession.

Acknowledgements

We gratefully acknowledge the financial support of the Social Sciences and Humanities Research Council of Canada and the research assistance of Dan Dankyi, Kari Gough, Jennifer Hayes, A. Raman Krishnaprasad, Neil Mohammed, Mark Noronha, and Jovan Stupar. An earlier version of this paper was discussed at the 1997 Southern Finance Meeting in Baltimore.

References

Allen, M.P., Panian, S.K., 1982. Power, performance, and succession in the large corporation. Administrative Science Quarterly 27, 538–547.

Barber, B.M., Lyon, J.D., 1996. Detecting abnormal operating performance: The empirical power and specification of test statistics. Journal of Financial Economics 41, 359–399.

Barnes, L.B., Hershon, S.A., 1976. Transferring power in the family business. Harvard Business Review 54, 105–114.

Bergstrom, C., Rydqvist, K., 1992. Differentiated bids for voting and restricted voting stock in public tender offers. Journal of Banking and Finance 16, 97–114.

Booth, J.R., Deli, D.N., 1996. Factors affecting the number of outside directorships held by CEOs. Journal of Financial Economics 40, 81–104.

Brown, S.J., Warner, J.B., 1985. Using daily stock returns: The case of event studies. Journal of Financial Economics 14, 3–31.

DeAngelo, H., DeAngelo, L., 1985. Managerial ownership of voting rights: A study of public corporations with dual class classes of common stock. Journal of Financial Economics 17, 33–69.

Denis, D.J., Denis, D.K., 1995. Performance changes following top management dismissals. Journal of Finance 50, 1029–1057.

Furtado, E.P.H., Karan, V., 1990. Causes, consequences, and shareholder wealth effects of management turnover: A review of the empirical evidence. Financial Management 19, 60–75.

Johnson, W.B., Magee, R.P., Nagarajan, N.J., Newman, H.A., 1985. An analysis of the stock price reaction to sudden executive deaths: Implications for the managerial labor market, Journal of Accounting and Economics, 151–174.

Kunz, R.M., Angel, J.J., 1996. Factors affecting the value of the stock voting right: Evidence from the Swiss equity market. Financial Management 25, 7–20.

Mace, M.L., 1986. Directors: Myth and Reality. Division of Research, Harvard Business School Press, Boston.

McConaughy, D.L., Walker, M.C., Henderson, G.V., Mishra, C.S., 1998. Founding family controlled firms: Efficiency and value. Review of Financial Economics 7, 1–19.

Megginson, W.L., 1990. Restricted voting stock acquisition premiums and the market value of corporate control. Financial Review 25, 175–198.

Morck, R.K., Strangeland, D.A., 1994. Corporate performance and large shareholders, Working paper no. 4-94, Institute for Financial Research, Faculty of Business, University of Alberta, Edmonton.

Morck, R., Schleifer, A., Vishny, R.W., 1988a. Characteristics of targets of hostile and friendly takeovers. In: Auerbach, A. (Ed.), Corporate Takeovers: Causes and Consequences. National Bureau of Economic Research, Cambridge, MA. pp. 101–134.

Morck, R., Schleifer, A., Vishny, R.W., 1988b. Management ownership and market valuation: An empirical analysis. Journal of Financial Economics 20, 293–316.

Murphy, K.J., Zimmerman, J.L., 1993. Financial performance surrounding CEO turnover. Journal of Accounting and Economics 16, 273–315.

Reinganum, M.R., 1985. The effect of executive succession on corporate wealth. Administrative Science Quarterly 30, 46–60.

Rydqvist, K., 1996. Takeover bids and the relative prices of shares that differ in their voting rights. Journal of Banking and Finance 20, 1407–1425.

Slovin, M.B., Sushka, M.E., 1993. Ownership concentration, corporate control activity, and firm value: Evidence from death of inside blockholders. Journal of Finance 48, 1293–1321.

Smith, B.F., Amoako-Adu, B., 1995. Relative prices of dual class shares. Journal of Financial and Quantitative Analysis 30, 223–239.

St. Pierre, J., Gagnon, J.-M., Saint-Pierre, J., 1996. Concentration of voting rights and board resistance to takeover bids. Journal of Corporate Finance 3, 45–73.

Taylor, S., Whittred, G., 1998. Security design and the allocation of voting rights: Evidence from the australian IPO market? Journal of Corporate Finance 4, 107–131.

Trow, D.B., 1962. Executive succession in small companies. Administrative Science Quarterly 7, 228–239.

Vancil, R.F., 1987. Passing the baton: Managing the process of CEO succession, Harvard Business School Press, Boston, MA.

White, H., 1980. A heteroskedasticity — consistent covariance matrix estimator and a direct test for heteroskedasticity. Econometrica 48, 817–838.

Zingales, L., 1994. The value of the voting right — a study of the Milan Stock Exchange experience. Review of Financial Studies 7, 125–148.

[12]

Journal of Management Studies 32:4 July 1995
0022-2380

MANAGERIAL AND OWNERSHIP SUCCESSION AND CORPORATE RESTRUCTURING: THE CASE OF MANAGEMENT BUY-INS*

KEN ROBBIE
MIKE WRIGHT

University of Nottingham

ABSTRACT

This paper addresses the effects on corporate restructuring of changing management and ownership. First, it synthesises a number of perspectives on corporate restructuring which involve managerial succession, voluntary restructuring, agency theory, incentives and entrepreneurship, to obtain insights into the relative impact of simultaneously changing either, neither or both management and ownership. Second, it uses case study evidence from management buy-ins to examine the effects of changing both management and ownership. The evidence suggests that whilst management may be adequately incentivized, problems may arise in respect of information asymmetries, difficulties in matching entrepreneurs to the context and monitoring by venture capitalists, and implementation of strategies.

INTRODUCTION

The corporate restructuring debate has increasingly drawn attention to the importance of changes in management and ownership as part of enhancing management control (Bowman and Singh, 1989; Singh, 1993). These two aspects of control directly raise the importance of managerial incentives, managerial skills and capabilities and the monitoring devices imposed on managers. However, the debate so far has not addressed systematically the expected and actual effects of changing management and ownership. As a result, it has not been possible to disentangle the relative impact on the efficacy of corporate restructuring of simultaneously changing either, neither or both management and ownership. This point raises issues which concern, for example, whether the introduction of appropriate incentives for incumbent management with ownership remaining the same is likely to be more effective than changing either management only, changing ownership only, or changing both management and ownership. In turn, issues are raised which concern both the nature of managerial capabilities and the contexts in which each category of change may be appropriate.

The aim of this paper, therefore, is to develop understanding of the effects of restructuring organizations through changes in ownership and management. First it develops a framework to analyse the effects on corporate restructuring of

Address for reprints: Ken Robbie, Centre for Management Buy-out Research, University of Nottingham, University Park, Nottingham NG7 2RD, UK.

changing management and ownership. Second, the empirical material presented focuses on one aspect of this framework which has hitherto received little systematic attention: that is, the case of simultaneously changing both management and ownership through a relatively new form of organization, the management buy-in.

Two of the most prominent types of managerial and ownership change which have developed in the last decade concern management buy-outs and management buy-ins. Both have been proposed as means of reducing the agency costs of control in organizations since they combine equity incentives for managers with monitoring by financiers (Jensen, 1989; Thompson and Wright, 1991). In a management buy-out, incumbent managers obtain significant equity stakes – typically in smaller transactions, a majority – whereas before the transaction they held zero or negligible amounts of equity. In a management buy-in, a team of outside managers/entrepreneurs as individuals rather than as part of an already existing group, come together to acquire shares in a company and subsequently manage it. As in a management buy-out, the equity incentive for managers is complemented by control mechanisms (such as the use of equity ratchets, whereby management's stake will increase or decrease according to whether performance targets are met; commitments to meet external finance servicing costs, etc.) and control processes (such as board representation). Initial evidence, as will be seen below, showed that these forms of transactions were typically highly effective means of undertaking corporate restructuring. However, the problems which have subsequently emerged in the more difficult economic circumstances of the early 1990s suggests a need for careful analysis of their contribution to the restructuring of organizations.

The structure of the paper is as follows. The following section reviews the corporate restructuring literature relating to the relationships between managerial and ownership succession. Then we outline the data sources and the methodology employed in the study. The fourth section presents the results from the case studies as they relate to issues concerning: the nature of pre-buy-in problems and asymmetric information, the problems involved in implementing planned strategies, financial incentive and control mechanisms, control processes used by financiers, and the control actually exercised by financiers, refinancings and the effects on managerial incentives. In the light of the earlier literature review, the next section discusses the contribution of the case studies to an understanding of the importance of managerial and ownership succession in the corporate governance debate and attempts some conclusions.

MANAGERIAL AND OWNERSHIP SUCCESSION AND CORPORATE RESTRUCTURING

Recent developments in corporate restructuring have emphasized that adaptation to appropriate control systems, strategies and enhanced performance are linked to the structures and processes of ownership and management (Singh, 1993). In essence the combination of managerial and ownership influences can be categorized as in Figure 1. Each of the four quadrants has implications for the nature of managerial and entrepreneurial skills, managerial incentives, monitoring mechanisms and organizational contexts. The agency cost perspective, which has been at

	No management change	Management change
No ownership change	*Quadrant 2* Voluntary restructuring	*Quadrant 1* Managerial succession
Ownership change	*Quadrant 3* MBO	*Quadrant 4* MBI

Note. Acquisition of one company by another may or may not involve replacement of incumbent management.

Figure 1. Managerial and ownership change typologies

the forefront of much of the recent literature on corporate restructuring, emphasizes the role of managerial incentives and monitoring devices as mechanisms for aligning the interests of managers and shareholders in organizations where previously there was a divorce between ownership and control (Jensen, 1986; Jensen and Meckling, 1976). However, the mere alignment of such interests may not necessarily and effortlessly bring about improvements in efficiency.

Using an eclectic approach, two particular themes can be argued to inform the effectiveness of the agency cost approach as a framework for analysis. The first concerns the literature on managerial and entrepreneurial characteristics and competencies. The second relates to the organizational context in which managers find themselves. Organizations typically involve complex internal norms, processes and relationships which may frustrate efforts by even well-incentivized managers to effect change (Armstrong, 1991; Bartlett, 1989). The relative importance of these issues are discussed in what follows.

Consider first quadrant 1, which concerns the causes and consequences of managerial succession without changes in the overall ownership of the organization. A review of the management succession literature by Virany and Tushman (1986) found little consensus amongst studies – new top executives can have positive, neutral or disruptive effects on organizational performance. Virany and Tushman show that it is necessary to consider the characteristics of the new top executives, the strategic actions they take and the organizational context at the time the succession occurs. They find that lower performing firms replace executives in response to crisis but often recruit top executives who do not fit the changing competitive conditions in the industry, whereas higher performing firms make replacements with executives who do fit the environment. The need for a fit between the characteristics of the new management and the situation faced by the firm has also been identified by Norburn (1986) and Zimmerman (1991).

Replacement of management may be by internal appointments or external recruitment, although in practice both forms are utilized (Grinyer et al., 1988; Slatter, 1984). A major issue is whether external recruitment will result in superior performance. Bibeault (1982) and Hofer (1980) have argued that external management are necessary for successful corporate turnaround. Hofer argues that incumbent management have a strong set of beliefs about how to run the company, many of which must be wrong for the current problems to have occurred. Hoffman (1989) notes that change of chief executive stimulates change, provides new views of the situation and creates the levels of stress or tension required to stimulate organizational change. Evidence from the USA does not generally support this view (e.g. Dalton and Kesner, 1985; Furtado and Karan, 1989; Warner et al., 1988). One problem that may be faced by new management from outside is resentment from remaining internal management, which may produce resistance to change and depressed performance at least in the short term. In addition, it may also be necessary to consider whether incumbent management had adequate incentives to perform and whether an appropriate monitoring (or governance) system was also in place.

The literature in respect of managerial succession has tended not to highlight either the incentive structures available to managers or monitoring arrangements. In quadrant 2, performance improvements are achieved voluntarily by incumbent managers and without managerial succession. Donaldson (1990), shows that voluntary restructuring without managerial or ownership changes can be achieved in the presence of management who are adequately incentivized to focus on financial performance and not just growth, where there are sufficient internal disciplines to engender change and where there is an unambiguous and persistent signal of danger. Donaldson notes that such change tends to take place less rapidly than change triggered by other mechanisms. In an examination of Ford US, Starkey and McKinlay (1993) also demonstrate that increased pressure from Japanese competition led incumbent management to embark upon major change and restructuring, including a shift from a management style which had become synonymous with the company.

Quadrant 3 focuses on changes in ownership and hence governance structures without changes in management. Incumbent managers undertaking a buy-out are, or at least ought to be, familiar with the real strengths and weaknesses of the firm, whereas external managers may acquire such knowledge only after they have taken over. In a detailed case study approach, Jones (1992) shows that the effect of changing ownership with incumbent management not changing but becoming equity owners is to lead to an improved match between control systems and organizational contexts. Indeed, there is now extensive evidence of improved organizational effectiveness following a management buy-out, at least in the short term and using data relating primarily up to the mid-1980s (for reviews of the literature see, for example, Palepu, 1990; Wright, 1994). Green (1992) finds using case studies of buy-outs, that owner-control and debt-control have positive effects on managerial motivation, organizational decision making and implementation of cost-reduction strategies, but negative effects on fundamental changes in strategy; that is, owner-managers did not become more innovative partly because of concern that they might lose their own money and partly because of the restraining effect of high leverage. More recently, studies have suggested that a somewhat modified perspective of buy-outs is appropriate. For example, US evidence shows that those buy-outs funded in the late 1980s with certain financial instruments such as junk bonds, those funded in riskier industries, and those which were unable to complete planned asset sales were highly vulnerable to failure (Kaplan and Stein, 1993). UK evidence shows that buy-outs display a heterogeneous life-cycle, some change ownership structure again very quickly (see, for example, Green and Berry, 1991) whilst the majority last for considerable periods, which is influenced by the objectives of management and funding institutions and the market conditions faced by a particular buy-out (Wright et al., 1994).

Changes in both management and ownership, as portrayed in quadrant 4 of Figure 1, may involve a hostile takeover bid by an existing group or LBO organization, or an agreed takeover by a management buy-in. In the latter case the enterprise remains as an independent entity. The literature concerning the workings of the market for corporate control places special emphasis on the role of the takeover mechanism, especially hostile takeovers, in removing under-performing managers (Jensen and Ruback, 1983). Franks and Mayer (1993) show that changes of top management are associated with takeover in only a quarter of cases, although it is possible that the changes resulting from boardroom and shareholder disputes may be undertaken in order to avoid the emergence of a hostile takeover bid. Other evidence suggests that with or without a takeover, higher levels of management succession are associated with poor performance (e.g. Fredrickson et al., 1988; Schwartz and Menon, 1985). Murphy and Zimmerman (1993) provide some evidence that incoming management take steps to change accounting policies so as to report reductions in initial performance as a means of blaming outgoing management. There does, however, remain some debate in the case of acquisitions as to whether and when managers depart is related to their performance (Walsh and Ellwood, 1991). It is also far from clear whether, even in hostile bids, a better management team replaces an under-performing one (Singh, 1993).

Evidence relating to traditional takeovers also draws attention to the problems in integrating acquisitions, emphasizing that such integration typically takes significantly longer than initially planned, and when turnrounds are involved may be particularly difficult (Haspeslagh and Jemison, 1991; Jemison and Sitkin, 1986; Singh, 1993). Jones (1985) has highlighted the problems which may arise where an independent company is acquired and becomes the subsidiary of a larger group, notably pressure to conform to parental control systems which may be inappropriate for the subsidiary.

The importance of managers in corporate restructuring is evident in each of the four quadrants of Figure 1. An agency cost perspective emphasizes the importance of enhancing incentives for managers and monitoring systems. Hence in quadrants 1 and 2, it may be expected that management may be incentivized to effect improvements through a closer link between performance and remuneration, whether through profit-related pay or stock options (see, for example, Jensen and Murphy, 1990). However, such an approach fails to capture the complexities of the restructuring phenomenon (Singh, 1993). At the very least it also seems necessary to take account, firstly, of differences in the characteristics of varying types of entrepreneurs and managers which in turn are likely to influence their objectives and behaviour, and secondly of the organizational context.

There has, of course, been considerable debate as to the differences between individuals who are entrepreneurs and those who are managers (e.g. Cooper and Dunkelberg, 1986; Cooper et al., 1989; Low and Macmillan, 1988; Woo et al., 1991). In comparison to managers, entrepreneurs have been seen as having a high need for achievement, an internal locus of control, tolerance for ambiguity, and being prepared to accept a certain degree of risk. In Figure 1, it is the managers in quadrants 3 and 4 who may be expected to more closely resemble entrepreneurs. Though they do not create a new venture in the classical entrepreneurial sense, they are risk-takers in the sense that their own funds are partially used to acquire the enterprise, and they may be considered to have identified an entrepreneurial opportunity in seeking to acquire an enterprise and improve its performance (see, for example, Bull, 1989). It has been suggested that entrepreneurs can broadly be dichotomized into opportunists and craftsmen.

Opportunists are viewed as being more adaptive to change and more flexible, seeking more diverse sources of external finance, having a managerial orientation, adopting formal plans, and having a more balanced attention to different tasks. Craftsmen, in contrast, are more likely to run their business for intrinsic satisfaction than financial gain or growth. The development of different kinds of organizations such as management buy-outs and buy-ins introduce notions of a more subtle blend of entrepreneurial and managerial skills. But there may also be important differences between buy-outs and buy-ins.

The buy-in entrepreneur has to deal with an entirely new combination of factors whereas the buy-out team leader is able to operate with many familiar factors. The buy-in entrepreneur has to identify a suitable target company whereas the buy-out entrepreneur as an incumbent may be reacting to corporate restructuring opportunities in the organization. An attempt, using the sample described below, to identify types of buy-in entrepreneurs on the basis of motivational and demographic factors (Ennew et al., 1994) finds that buy-in entrepreneurs can be classified into three distinct clusters: opportunistic, craftsman, and a small proportion who were 'pushed' into the buy-in. The majority (68 per cent) were identified as opportunistic, with 27 per cent being craftsmen and the balance 'pushed'. In contrast, management buy-out entrepreneurs are more likely to be craftsmen (77 per cent of the sample) than opportunists (12.8 per cent) or 'pushed' (10.2 per cent) (Robbie, 1993).

The decision whether or not to invest in a buy-out or buy-in raises important adverse selection issues (Stiglitz and Weiss, 1981). As Amit et al. (1993) also point out in respect of entrepreneurs in general, while the entrepreneur's familiarity with the industry, personal characteristics and track record can provide some insight, these criteria are at best partial predictors of future success. In the case of a management buy-out proposal, financiers need to take funding decisions on the basis of observed managerial performance in post, expectations about whether improving managerial incentives will improve performance and management's willingness to take on the risk of a buy-out in order to secure the fruits of their human capital.

Management buy-outs may typically arise for defensive reasons and with management wishing to develop their own strategy away from the constraints imposed by group head office. Frequently, incumbent management have attempted a management buy-out but have been unable to obtain financial support from venture capitalists who consider that on the basis of previous performance they do not possess the requisite skills to own and manage an independent business.

In contrast, management buy-ins appear to be more proactive with incoming managers aiming to build successful businesses, achieve growth and be innovative (Robbie et al., 1992). Management buy-ins have typically been focused on enterprises which require turnround and restructuring, but where the parties involved consider that there is significant potential for growth which has not been realized by incumbent management. The problem of matching buy-in managers to an appropriate enterprise context is reported to be one of the major problems for investing institutions (3i, 1992), a view consistent with the evidence on top executive turnover by Virany and Tushman (1986) referred to above. Whilst such a match may be desirable, problems of asymmetric information, both in relation to the true skills of the entrepreneur and the enterprise context as viewed from outside, may make it difficult to achieve.

It is not immediately clear whether buy-in owner-managers are necessarily better entrepreneurs than buy-out owner-managers, or whether they are merely willing to accept higher risks. Moreover, in a buy-in the investing institution has not had the opportunity to observe the manager in post. Amit et al. (1993) show that where venture capitalists are unable to assess private information about an entrepreneur's capabilities, low ability entrepreneurs will accept the venture capitalist's price offer while high ability entrepreneurs do not. Moral hazard problems are also raised since after the entrepreneur has been funded it may be difficult to distinguish between the effects of low entrepreneurial ability and adverse environmental conditions. Financing institutions may engage in more rigorous scrutiny of buy-in managers and seek more extensive post-transaction monitoring than for buy-outs. However, even with such scrutiny, asymmetric information problems relating both to the entrepreneur and the organizational context remain over and above those which might be expected in a management buy-out.

The discussion in this section identified major differences between types of corporate restructuring involving insiders and outsiders which related to issues concerning managerial and organizational characteristics and competencies, incentives and monitoring systems. Three principal propositions in respect of management buy-ins, the focus of the empirical evidence in subsequent sections, emerge from this discussion.

The first relates to asymmetric information issues whereby an incumbent management team is better placed to know the true state of a company as well as venture capitalists being able to assess their capabilities in situ and may be divided into two parts:

Proposition 1a: The managerial and organizational characteristics of management buy-ins indicates that in contrast to management buy-outs and voluntary restructurings, they are likely to be particularly susceptible to the problems of asymmetric information and consequent problems for implementing restructuring strategies. Such considerations may lead to under-recognition in the due diligence process of the size of the turnround task and the type of restructuring actions required.

In addition, it is important to find a match between managerial and entrepreneurial skills and the organizational context of the management buy-in, but in this form of restructuring there may be particular difficulties for the venture capitalist in identifying the entrepreneur's skills *ex ante*. This gives rise to Proposition 1b:

Proposition 1b: Major problems will emerge in the stability of buy-ins which result from the problems of asymmetric information relating to the true skills of the entrepreneur and the enterprise context as viewed by outside stakeholders (such as institutional investors).

534   KEN ROBBIE AND MIKE WRIGHT

The background to this proposition leads on to the second and third propositions, which stem from the suggestion above that there is a need for buy-in
structures to include a combination of appropriate monitoring and control
mechanisms by the venture capitalist as well as having sufficient managerial
incentives. Hence:

Proposition 2: In management buy-ins there is a need for greater monitoring by
investors than in the other forms of ownership and managerial change identified here, notably in comparison with management buy-outs. This monitoring
will include board representation by the venture capitalist and regular reporting procedures.

Proposition 3: Management buy-in teams will be heavily incentivized through
ratchets on their equity holdings and be influenced by the debt bonding of
relatively highly leveraged financial structures.

The following section outlines the data and methodology used to examine these
propositions.

DATA AND METHODOLOGY

The evidence presented here is part of a wider study of management buy-ins,
which has involved both the establishment of a comprehensive database of all
identifiable buy-ins completed in the UK, a questionnaire survey of 59 buy-ins
and detailed case study analysis. Management buy-ins emerged as a significant
element in the transfer of ownership and control in the UK only from the mid-
1980s. From 1988 onwards there have been at least 100 management buy-ins
per year in the UK, compared with some 400 or more management buy-outs
(Chiplin et al., 1993).

Quantitative results from the questionnaire survey have been reported elsewhere (Robbie et al., 1992) and revealed substantial restructuring following
management buy-in. For example, in 95 per cent of cases administrative and
financial systems were reorganized, in 84 per cent of cases new products were
introduced, in 73 per cent of cases average periods of credit for debtors were
reduced, and in 59 per cent of cases stock levels were reduced. However, despite
such changes, which were significantly more extensive than found in buy-outs
(Wright et al., 1992), buy-ins frequently had difficulty in meeting performance
targets in the period after the transactions were completed.

Examination of the propositions outlined in the previous section may help to
identify the underlying reasons for these problems. The depth of analysis
required focuses on the need to utilize a detailed case study approach. The
evidence from the case studies also provides insights which may be useful in
theory-building in relation to corporate governance, to which we return in the
conclusion. The role of case studies is the subject of considerable debate (see, for
example, Eisenhardt, 1989; Scapens, 1990, 1992; Llewellyn, 1990). Several
authors have drawn attention to the importance of case studies in understanding
corporate restructuring (e.g. Green, 1992; Jensen, 1992; Baker and Wruck, 1989);

Green (1992) in particular discusses the applicability of case study research to buy-outs, pointing out that quantitative studies have difficulty in capturing the complexity of the managerial and organizational changes which take place following such transfers of ownership. He also emphasizes the importance of gaining evidence on managers' interpretations of the issues, since it is such perceptions which reflect managers' actions and, in this particular case, the problems involved in effecting corporate restructuring.

The five case studies analysed in this paper were selected from the respondents to the questionnaire survey on the basis that they broadly represented the range of issues raised in the above theoretical discussion. The interviews were conducted with the buy-in team leader using a semi-structured checklist and lasted between one and three hours. Findings have been cross-checked with the respondents. In order to preserve confidentiality, the names of buy-ins are not reported here. In addition, interviews were held with the officers of the financing institution who were directly responsible for the investment and its subsequent monitoring. These interviews provided a means of triangulating the findings from the interviews with managers and helped to check for biases in the study and the conclusions drawn by the researchers.

The main features of the case studies in terms of the nature of the buy-in team, the nature of the target company and the details of the transaction are summarized in Table I. Case A was a divestment of loss-making part of a small, privately owned company which operated franchises with a team of three who had experience in a closely related business. Case B was a £2.6 million divestment of a moderately profitable subsidiary by an overseas controlled group to a buy-in team who had unsuccessfully attempted a management buy-out earlier elsewhere. Case C, an industrial distribution company, was a marginally loss-making privately owned company where the family had lost interest in running it. The relatively large management team undertaking the buy-in, as in Case B, were required to relocate to a new region. Case D was a moderately profitable manufacturing subsidiary of a large acquisitive group which was under increasing financial pressure. The team leader had extensive Group experience. Case E, the largest of the sample, was a buy-in of a poorly performing buy-out and was linked to the acquisition of another privately owned company. One of the joint managing directors had extensive entrepreneurial experience. In none of the five cases did existing incumbent management join the buy-in in an equity owning capacity; that is, the cases exclude hybrid buy-in-buy-outs. Cases A, B and D were completed near the peak of the market in 1989.

THE ISSUES

This section uses the five case studies to provide empirical evidence on the propositions outlined above. The issues raised by the propositions are addressed in terms of: the nature of pre-buy-in problems; transfer of ownership and asymmetric information; implementation of strategies; financial incentive and control mechanisms; control processes; the link between entrepreneurs and context; and control by financiers, refinancings and effects on incentives.

Table 1. Characteristics of the MBI Cases

	A	B	C	D	E
Team formation					
Composition	Three	Three	Four	Two	Five
Previous relationship	Worked together	Worked together	Worked together	Group relationship	Worked together to varying degrees
Entrepreneurial experience	None	Failed buy-out attempt	None	None	Strong
Management experience	General, financial	General	General	General, sales, finance	General, sales
Skills gap	No	Financial	Financial	Finance	Finance
Education	Professional qualifications	University	University	Professional qualifications	University
Age	26–35	41–45	41–45	41–45	41–45
Previous employer	Top 500	Private	Private	Top 500	Top 500
Target company					
Method of identification	Earlier take-over analysis	Personal knowledge as competitor	Industrial contact	Group company	Financial institution
Vendor motivation for sale	Poor prospects, lack of profitability	Cash requirements, poor profits	Next generation not interested	Redefinition core activities, finance requirement	Poorly performing MBO with no other exit option
Employees	4*	30	44	182	175
Previous ownership	Private	Overseas controlled	Private	PLC	MBO
Competition for target	None	Yes	None	Yes	Yes
Turnover	£500k	£4.7m	£4.7m	£6.2m	£15m
Operating profit	(£75k)	£0.4m	(£38k)	£400k	£2m
Deal value	£303k	£2.571m	£964k	£3.7m	£17.4m
Characteristics	Stable cash flow, stable demand, growing industry, no import completion	Highly positive cash flow, low import exposure, reasonable industry growth	Significant cash requirements, low import competition, stable industry demand	Reasonably positive cash flow	Moderately declining size of industry
Transaction completion					
Date of completion	10/1989	7/1989	8/1987	6/1989	7/1988
Due diligence	Inadequate a/c info	Inadequate a/c info	No obvious problems	No problems at time as prior operating knowledge	Warning signals
Financial structuring					
Management share	75%	60%	60%	65%	n/a
Management contribution	£150k	£75k, 60	£68k	£100k	£1.82m
Ratchet	No	Yes, 60 65%	Yes, down to 51%	Yes, 49% to 75%	Yes
Gearing	1.3	20.5	2.6	2.9	1.6
Presence of non-executive director	None	One	One	One	Two

*Franchisees not counted as employees.

The Nature of Pre-buy-in Problems, Transfer of Ownership and Asymmetric Information
Although the backgrounds of the five case studies and the nature of previous ownership showed diversity, the incoming management's view of the target company and the reasons for previous owners wishing to hive down assets had similarities. A common underlying theme in the cases was the belief that the targets were not performing as well as they should and that the new management would be able to bring about the transformation which was required. Although only one firm was actually loss making in the latest audited period prior to buy-in, they were all considered by the buy-in team to be underperforming. Team leaders considered that they had the ability to improve performance and had worked out an appropriate strategy to effect this; both the vendor and the venture capitalists who funded them recognized the merits in the various business plans. Both the venture capitalists and buy-in teams had felt confident that the reasons for underperformance were identifiable and could be corrected. The lack of profitability was seen to be a common and important reason for the previous owner seeking a sale in all five cases.

As seen in the previous section, three of the cases (A, B and D) arose on sales of subsidiaries from larger groups. In these cases there were also some similarities with the reasons often cited for divestment to a management buy-out (Green and Berry, 1991; Wright, 1994, ch. 1). In all three cases, poor growth prospects of the entity concerned in the context of the redefinition of the parent group's core activities were seen as important or very important reasons for the hive down of assets. There was evidence, particularly in respect of the vendor of Case D, that the parent considered that more attractive opportunities were available elsewhere, so that whilst subsidiaries were being divested acquisitions of other activities were being undertaken.

Having decided to divest the assets, the vendor had also to decide between sale to a buy-in team and sale to another type of purchaser. In two of the cases (A and B) the buy-in team emerged as the only serious bidders and in none of the cases was there a buy-out team bidding. There was thus evidence that a serious buy-in bid would succeed in the absence of competition from internal management or a trade purchaser. Other factors were also relevant as to why a buy-in should be successful, the not least of which was a belief that the new management team would be able to make the assets work more effectively than when under the vendor's control. Thus, for example in Case A with the previous owner exiting from the particular sector niche, the team's proven skills in a similar field with a competitor was seen as an important factor.

The incoming teams expected major improvements in financial returns from the assets employed. Company A's team took the view that considerable sectoral growth could be achieved, with additional enhancement of profitability coming from better support for franchises and an expansion of the franchise network which was still relatively geographically limited. The company was seen to have problems of poor control and service. Company B's business plan involved a considerable expansion of its mining and contracting activities with the team believing it had the specific expertise and contacts to generate new business in addition to some contribution from its existing plant hire activities. Company C was seen to be adversely affected by the loss of interest by the current generation of family owners, which had *inter alia* resulted in a decline in quality of customer service. Company D's team leader envisaged profitability improvements coming from three main sources – reorganization and cost cutting leading to higher operational efficiency; expansion of the organic business through expanding customer networks and entering different market sectors; and through selective acquisitions with activities purchased being relocated to the company's existing premises. Company E involved the initial creation of a group involved in sales broking to the fast-moving consumer goods market as well as the manufacture and distribution of fragrances. The team intended to develop into major broker-age to the chemist and drug store markets as well as operating on behalf of higher margin toiletry, personal care and fragrance manufacturers in the grocery trade assigned to previous low margin food items.

Although all five teams had worked out a mixture of strategic and operating actions to effect a turnround in the businesses being purchased, they all experienced significant unforeseen problems. In Company A, the franchise network was in an unexpectedly poor state and evidence also emerged that a previous audit had been flawed. For Company B, contracts were awarded more slowly than expected and its plant hire business collapsed. Company E experienced the adverse effects of inadequate warranties. Company D experienced the problems resulting from changes in local education authority purchasing systems.

A major difficulty reported in the case interviews related to the ability to obtain adequate up-to-date information concerning the target company, especially in relation to management accounts, indications of current trading positions and the status of major contracts. Thus in Companies B and C, it became clear that the level of business actually being transacted was significantly less than that indicated to the new management and there were serious declines in profitability during the course of the negotiations. There were also concerns as to the robust-ness and accuracy of previous audited accounts which led to the consideration of legal action (Company E) and actual legal action as well as representations to the appropriate professional institute (Company A). Appropriate assessment of valua-tion of stock and fixed assets had not taken place in either Company B or C. Contact turned out to have been made with only the better performing members of the franchise network in Company A.

In theory the process of due diligence must be rigorously applied. In practice, if deals are to be completed, management and their financial backers may have to make realistic decisions which may leave some exposure to future risk. In retro-spect, there was a general perception in the cases that insufficient thoroughness was exercised in the due diligence process considering the extent of asymmetric problems which are widely assumed to exist in management buy-ins. This was especially true in the smaller companies where such fees could represent a high proportion of the deal value. In one case, Company D, the risk had been largely reduced because of the team leader's previous head office relationship with the firm. Even so, a warning in the due diligence report concerning the stability of local education authority purchasing arrangements had been considered but dis-counted, leading to considerable problems in the second year of the buy-in.

Implementation of Strategies
The ability of management to implement their planned strategies for turnround was restricted partly because of the onset of recession during this period, but also

as a result of other factors such as the reliability of the audit, the state of accounting control systems and problems which arose from management coming from outside.

The problems of due diligence were discussed above and resulted in considerable diversion of management time and resources. As a result, strategic actions such as the development of new brands and entry into new markets were reported as effectively being delayed by at least a year while management devoted time and efforts to operational matters. The deepening recession also adversely affected the later buy-ins, making it difficult to implement strategic actions and with much attention having to be placed on operating actions such as debtor and creditor control as well as overhead cost control. However, changes to original strategy were clearly not the result of just the deteriorating macro economic and financial conditions.

Both the two earlier cases, C and E, experienced considerable initial problems with the businesses being less strong than originally expected. In Case C, activities and customer relationships had been run down considerably more than expected while unexpected problems had been found in stock valuation. In Case E, accounting procedures for previous year's accounts had not been robust while there were considerable operational problems and a need to implement new control procedures. Original plans were effectively delayed. The other three cases, as well as suffering from the timing of transactions coinciding with interest rate rises and deteriorating economic indicators, also experienced initial problems which were greater than expected. Company A's franchise network was worse than expected and major flaws were found with earlier accounts; fixed asset valuations were faulty in B's case while the plant hire activities had collapsed; and D had a number of problems, although initially on a lesser scale than the other cases. Subsequently companies B, D and E were further affected by failure to develop strategy as planned. Company B failed to obtain the number of new mining and contracting contracts necessary to generate adequate profitability; privatization resulted in D's dominant customer being replaced by a multitude of small purchasers involving very different logistics and significantly delayed sales; and a major acquisition by E was made at an excessive price involving over-leveraging at a time when E's profitability had not been sufficiently established.

A major issue is whether failure to analyse correctly the type and extent of necessary strategies was a reflection on the composition and skills of the team and whether there was inadequate information available to venture capitalists on the abilities of the team members. No evidence was found to suggest that those buy-ins with looser relationships were less likely to succeed than those with much closer working experience. Indeed, mistakes were identified in respect of team selection among those who were working together immediately prior to the buy-in, implying that team leaders' judgement concerning fellow team members was important as well as the problems of asymmetric information which the venture capitalist backers may have experienced in assessing the team.

Issues were raised in particular which concerned the abilities of team members, the existence of skills gaps, the appropriateness of previous experience and the size of the team. In Company C, the venture capitalist had been keen to accept a team of four, larger than the team leader had felt was strictly required. In the event two of the extra members of the team failed to perform adequately and had to be removed at considerable expense. The team member responsible for warehousing and transport was asked to leave after six months, because of his failure to adapt to the changed circumstances and a lack of ability at this level which only became evident after the buy-in. The sales director survived two years but it was considered that his skills were not appropriate to an environment which required an emphasis on field sales as opposed to being an inside salesman. In Company E, poor performance led eventually to the venture capitalist forcing the resignation of one of the joint team leaders, recruiting finance and other specialists and taking a greater interest in controlling the company.

In four out of the five cases team leaders identified specific financial skills gaps. The absence of these skills at the planning and due diligence stages was considered to have contributed significantly to the problems experienced by Companies B and C. Only the team leader in Company E had prior entrepreneurial experience, although the management of Company B felt that they had gained valuable experience from a failed buy-out attempt. In the case of Company D in particular, there appeared to be problems in making the adjustment from working in one of the UK's Top 500 companies to being an owner-manager in a relatively small buy-in. The aim of Company B to achieve a phased expansion through diversification into new markets was frustrated by the relocation of the business. Management were operating in a geographical region which was new to them and in which they lacked initial credibility having no effective track record. In addition, the business lacked financial credibility since as a new company it did not possess a realistic accounting track record. Problems also arose in appraising the skills of non-team members and making the necessary changes at the right point. This was particularly evident in the case of Company D. Although it was initially recognized that the accountant could best be viewed as a 'bookkeeper' rather than having the capabilities of a finance director, it was decided to retain him and defer the appointment of a finance director as the incumbent was only a short period from retirement. This decision led to considerable problems when a restructuring plan had to be formulated, the team leader having to write the plan in conjunction with external financial advisers.

Some team leaders commented that relatively high levels of gearing caused problems in developing the business, such as difficulties in obtaining credit status (limiting ability to win contracts) as well as providing reduced flexibility in the context of economic downturn and high interest rates. In particular, the leader of the Company C buy-in considered that the stability of the company had been threatened by high gearing. The experiences of Companies D and E also illustrated that pressures put on financial structures by poor performance were exacerbated by difficult economic and financial conditions. In Case E, where overpayment (and over-leverage) of both the initial business and major acquisition were belatedly recognized and other mistakes had been identified and actions taken, the venture capitalist took the view that the business was basically sound but performance benefits would not be immediate and would take time to come through.

Financial Incentive and Control Mechanisms
As seen above, it is the combination of incentive elements such as managerial equity stakes, control mechanisms and processes which provide both the incentive

and the monitoring which are important in achieving enhanced performance and appropriate internal control systems. In four of the cases incoming management obtained equity stakes of at least 60 per cent. Only the smallest management buy-ins did not involve an equity ratchet. Management reported that they had encouraged the negotiation of ratchets which would give them higher equity stakes and felt that the conditions attached to them were realistic, at least at the time of the buy-in. However, by the time of the case study interviews, the prospects of the original ratchet targets being achieved had become highly unlikely. Companies B, D and E all had produced disappointing operating performance despite the determination of managers to introduce corrective measures. These findings in respect of buy-ins stand in stark contrast to the position in respect of buy-outs (Hatherly et al., 1994). Whilst some of the problems in buy-ins are recession related, whereas the findings from buy-outs relate to pre-recession conditions, as noted in the discussion above, the differences in access to internal information by managers in the two types of transaction also have an important impact on the ability to set realistic targets where ratchets are used.

Debt bonding did appear to be effective. For example, in the restructuring of Company D, the trigger for urgent action was the pressure put on it by the bank threatening to call in receivers as a series of banking covenants were broken. In another case, the breaking of a banking covenant was seen by the institutional investor to be an important warning signal. However, the institutional investor's reaction took into account the company's performance relative to that of its sector, which was also badly affected by economic conditions. In contrast, management in Company A considered that the real bonding effect was not in relation to corporate covenants but rather the commitment in respect of their personal financing such as the second mortgages which had been taken out. The disproportionately high amount of equity provided by the team in the smaller transactions was seen by the investing venture capitalist as a means of countering less thorough due diligence procedures which may occur because of the disproportionately high cost of undertaking full due diligence in deals of this size.

Control Processes
In addition to incentive and control mechanisms, buy-ins involve a more subtle array of control processes. The framework for such processes is typically written into the Shareholders' Agreements and Articles of Association at the time of the buy-in. Basic monitoring in the form of monthly submission of accounts was carried out in all cases but the form of regular contact varied. All team leaders interviewed considered that it was advantageous not only to provide the basic level of information required under the monitoring agreements (this was felt to be a useful internal management tool which they would have wanted to introduce in any case) but also to keep the venture capitalists informed of developments through regular telephone and personal contact. Team leaders were convinced that their interests were better served by increasing the level of information available to the venture capitalist in this way especially if acquisition proposals were being considered.

Not all venture capitalists adopted an active board representation strategy. In one case, Company A, despite having the right to appoint non-executive directors in the Articles of Association of the company, the venture capitalist had not

542   KEN ROBBIE AND MIKE WRIGHT

done so, the small size of the company again being a factor. The team leader adopted the approach of having informal contact with the local office of the venture capitalist on a four-monthly basis. The lead investor in Company C held direct representation, regularly attending board meetings and meeting informally with the team leader beforehand. Where independent directors were appointed great care appeared to have been taken initially to ensure that the external non-executive directors were acceptable to the buy-in team.

The general lack of interest in exercising control at board level was somewhat surprising in view of the discussion above and may contribute to an explanation as to why performance was disappointing. In the case of Company D, the more indirect control by the lead venture capitalist may have made it more difficult to obtain a rapid appreciation of the options available when the company encountered severe difficulties despite the venture capitalist considering that he had spent more time than normal controlling the investee company and discussing performance with the team leader. Any concern by the team leader about the venture capitalist and the possibilities for divergent views when more than one venture capitalist is involved, may make restructuring highly problematical. Indeed, Company D's leading venture capitalist has subsequently changed its policy on board representation and now includes non-executives in transactions of this size.

The presence of extensive monitoring by venture capital firms and the appointment of non-executives with relevant sector experience does not, of course, by itself mean financial success will necessarily be achieved. Company E, for example, had an apparently robust process of monitoring and board representation. However, it still managed to make an excessively costly acquisition which led to very considerable later problems despite having gone through an extensive screening process to obtain the incremental finance it required in order to make the purchase.

The Link Between Entrepreneurs and Context
On the basis of the results in Ennew et al. (1994), the team leaders in companies A, D and E could be classified as opportunistic entrepreneurs, with the team leaders in companies B and C being identified as craftsman-type entrepreneurs.

The evidence from the cases suggests that the craftsman entrepreneurs in companies B and C had initially intended to use their skills and experience in a similar context but that this became problematical in the light of events. In company B difficulties were experienced in obtaining the new contracts which were necessary to implementation of the strategy. The circumstances facing the company also changed quite dramatically, which craftsman entrepreneurs appeared unable to deal with. In company C problems arose because the context in which some of the entrepreneurs were attempting to use their skills was considerably different from their experience.

Two of the opportunistic team leaders (D and E) exhibited a highly expansionary and acquisitive strategy in the early days of the buy-in. All three opportunistic cases, to varying degrees, experienced problems in implementing strategies as the circumstances under which they entered the buy-in changed significantly or were not what they had initially seemed. Hence the anticipated basis for strong turnround was absent.

Given the difficulties encountered in the early days of the buy-ins, all teams including the opportunists had to take rectifying actions. There was no evidence in cases A and D that the team leaders were not able to adapt to this role, although Case D's team leader was clearly hindered by his failure to appoint an appropriate finance director and he found it necessary to lean on advice from his venture capitalists and professional accounting adviser. In Case E, the need to change strategy and produce more operational control led to the resignation of one of the joint managing directors, the appointment of a new finance director and general management and control strengthening.

Control by Financiers, Refinancings and Effects on Incentives
The general failure of performance to meet targets, raises questions which concern the control actually exercised by financiers. The case studies emphasize the difficulties provoked by the nature of the control mechanisms and processes noted already in relation to the manner and timing of intervention by financiers and the issues involved in maintaining equity incentives.

The team leader in Company D, for reasons described earlier, was highly critical of the degree of support offered by the venture capitalists in restructuring the company. The nature of the problem was perceived to be to provide financial support for an interim period of restructuring until demand recovered and more regular debtor patterns emerged. An action plan was worked out with accounting advisers. Although the venture capitalists were keen to support the company, efforts to buy businesses from the receiver which could then be relocated to the company's site were unsuccessful. In addition, a key condition of the restructuring plan, which was to obtain agreement of leasing facilities, could not be met. The team leader had to find new sources of finance which involved accepting a much reduced equity stake. In such difficult circumstances where further venture capital support is effectively withdrawn, management ascribed their lack of support to the low level of earlier involvement and understanding of the business as well as possible differences between the venture capitalists involved. However, the venture capitalist took the view that a disproportionately high amount of time and cost had been spent in trying to achieve a satisfactory restructuring but at the end the risk factors were too high to justify further investment.

An example of the need to maintain incentives when restructuring occurs was seen in the case of Company C. The departure of team members involved the sale of their shares, but remaining members lacked the financial resources to increase their holdings. The shares were purchased by the venture capitalists, further increasing their influence. The reluctance of the venture capitalist, given the company's poor performance, to support an expansion plan proposed by management led to the trade sale of the company. The exit was carefully engineered so that management would not incur a financial loss as long as they met new performance targets. While the team leader took the view that venture capitalists were only prepared to take the long-term view when things go well, the venture capitalist felt that the nature of the company's market was such as to generate unsatisfactory long-term returns. Direct representation of the venture capitalist on this board enabled them to take a proactive stance and protected their financial position.

In the case of funds being required to enable expansion via acquisition, the Company E management team recognized the inevitability of equity dilution. They were prepared to accept equity dilution on the basis that a smaller share in a larger company would be worth more than a larger share of a smaller one. Subsequently, extremely poor performance led to the banker effectively taking control of the equity of the company after a survival plan had been agreed by management, the venture capitalist and the bank. Both management and the venture capitalist were given options by the bank under the new equity structure should the company be sold.

DISCUSSION AND CONCLUSIONS

The case study evidence presented in the previous section sheds light on the impact of changing both ownership and management. The interpretations of managers and financiers presented in this paper indicate considerable support for Proposition 1a, that many problems emanated from issues relating to asymmetric information, the nature of the buy-in team and the monitoring and control exercised by financiers. There did appear to be a need to improve management in the case study firms, but the due diligence process was typically unable to reveal the full extent of problem areas, making it necessary for incoming management and financial institutions to make the acquisition decision on the basis of at best partial information. It is notable that these problems arose even where incoming management had prior knowledge of the company through various industry contacts. Post-buy-in, the need to deal with unanticipated problems, frequently frustrated the ability of incoming management to implement planned strategies. In cases where further finance was required there was evidently a point beyond which the venture capitalists would refuse to support the strategy any further. In several of the cases, the venture capitalists engineered an exit even though it involved them taking a loss. Asymmetric information difficulties also extended to problems in assessing the competencies of internal management. The case studies emphasized problems in the nature and skills of the incoming management team as a whole, particularly where a team has not worked together before.

The case study evidence supported the need to ensure that managerial and entrepreneurial abilities were matched to the context of the buy-in (Proposition 1b). Some teams were not able to react successfully to problems which arose because the target company's environment was different from that of the predecessor company thereby aggravating poor performance and resulting in changes in team composition.

The need to deal with unanticipated problems placed emphasis on the efficacy of the institutional monitoring process and the incentives and controls put on management. Whilst there is some evidence to support Propositions 2 and 3, in that financing institutions exercised greater influence than in buy-outs, the case studies indicated a number of areas of weakness. Control mechanisms were problematical in the light of unanticipated difficulties arising from shortcomings in the due diligence process, since they did not allow sufficient flexibility. The use of equity ratchets, which have been over-generous in terms of the risk-reward trade-off in buy-outs which over-achieve their targets, were seen in buy-ins to raise

opposite difficulties as enterprises failed to meet targets, thus throwing doubt on
the second proposition. Gearing levels were seen as being restrictive but the early
warning signal attached to the breaking of bank covenants was useful in triggering corrective action in at least one case. The process of control, notably through
board representation, did not appear to be as effective in dealing with problems
as might have been anticipated. Thus although the theoretical framework of
control appeared to exist to support Proposition 2, in practice venture capitalists
were not in all cases implementing all the control possibilities until crisis situations were imminent. Moreover, asymmetric information problems often meant
that although venture capitalists may have invested what they considered to be
huge efforts in monitoring it was very difficult to effect corrective action. Where
major post-buy-in restructuring was required, the need to maintain incentives
was considered to be highly important, even though management's initial equity
stakes were heavily diluted. This evidence suggests that Proposition 3 oversimplifies the role of incentives. The level of managerial incentives *per se* is not as
important as the need to match such incentives to the particular circumstances of
a buy-in and the need to provide for sufficient flexibility in the operation of
incentives when factors outwith the manager's control, such as the problems
associated with asymmetric information and general adverse macroeconomic
conditions, emerge.

The cases must also be seen in the context of transactions which were completed when the phenomenon of buy-ins was relatively young and venture capitalists had relatively little experience of them. Follow-up interviews in December
1993 with the venture capital case officers involved in these deals indicate major
policy changes by the venture capitalists, including more active board representation and smaller teams as well as an unwillingness to invest in a number of
industries and hesitation over proposals for small transactions.

The case study findings relating to buy-ins serve to crystallize a number of
points of comparison with other forms of managerial and ownership succession.
This comparison can be summarized by elaborating the four categories identified
in Figure 1 and as shown in Figure 2.

In voluntary restructurings and management buy-outs, incumbent management remain in place and have the benefit of knowing the 'true' state of affairs
in their enterprise. Management buy-ins resemble traditional acquisitions and
managerial succession in respect of difficulties in accessing internal information.
As with managerial succession, the effects of a management buy-in can be varied.
In both cases, evidence shows that problems arise where insufficient attention is
addressed to the match between the new incoming management, both top
owner-managers and other new management, and the company environment
that is involved.

The study found that managers in a buy-in may be well-incentivized and that
there may be systematic and responsive monitoring in place, but that the efficacy
of these mechanisms may be swamped by problems which arise when the
business context *ex post* was not what it appeared to be *ex ante*. This result
suggests that suitably incentivized and capable managers in Quadrants 2 and 3
may be better placed than those in Quadrants 1 and 4 to deliver enhanced performance.

The similarities and differences between buy-outs (Quadrant 3) and buy-ins

	No management change	Management change
No ownership change	*Quadrant 2* Voluntary restructuring • good management, incentivized to improve performance • internal governance and pressures, clear and persistent environmental signals • relatively slow	*Quadrant 1* Managerial succession • replace poor managers • incoming management do not have insider knowledge
Ownership change	*Quadrant 3* MBO • management now incentivized to improve performance • removal of inappropriate parental control • benefits of internal information • important role of financing institutions • management may be reactive and limited by set beliefs	*Quadrant 4* MBI • external managers, incentivized to improve performance replace inadequate internal managers • important role of financing institutions • incoming management do not have insider knowledge

Note: Acquisition of one company by another may or may not involve replacement of incumbent management.

Figure 2. Summary of managerial and ownership change typologies and expected impact on performance

(Quadrant 4) should not, however, be forgotten. Green and Berry (1991) in a detailed case study analysis of management buy-outs provide evidence of similarities and contrasts between buy-outs and buy-ins in these respects. In terms of similarities they note, in particular, the importance of aligning the aims of owner-managers and institutional investors, and the need to have appropriate flexibility in the financial instruments used in structuring and controlling the new forms of organization. They also point out the risks in buy-outs which depend on major turnrounds and/or large increases in market share. In both buy-outs and buy-ins there is evidence of the restrictive effect of high gearing levels. Where these factors are not well addressed, buy-outs may experience similar problems to buy-ins. The freedom and incentives provided in a buy-out, compared to the previous ownership and control structure, has been found (Green and Berry, 1991) to enable management to undertake actions which appeared desirable because of their insider knowledge, but which they were previously constrained from doing, and to prove their effectiveness as owner-managers. In contrast, the evidence presented here suggests that asymmetric information is one of the major problems faced by buy-in managers. As a result, although they may already have a track record as effective managers and be highly incentivized, they are in a comparatively weak position to take appropriate restructuring action.

Such conclusions are indicative only and there would appear to be scope for a direct study of the comparative effects on management control and organizational effectiveness of changing management and ownership. There appears also to be a need to examine the longer-term impact of the changes in management and ownership, the effects of such changes when buy-ins occur in non-recessionary periods, and a test of whether subsequent development of the buy-in type of transaction has been accompanied by a learning process which has helped to mitigate some of the problems alluded to here.

NOTES

*Financial support from BZW Private Equity Limited and Touche Ross Corporate Finance is gratefully acknowledged. Thanks to Chris Ennew, David Hatherly, Ken Starkey, Steve Thompson and Pauline Wong, the editors, an anonymous *JMS* referee and several venture capitalists involved in funding management buy-ins for comments on an earlier draft.

REFERENCES

AMIT, R., GLOSTEN, L. and MULLER, E. (1993). 'Challenges to theory development in entrepreneurship research'. *Journal of Management Studies*, **30**, 5, 815–34.
ARMSTRONG, P. (1991). 'Contradictions and social dynamics in the capitalist agency relationship'. *Accounting, Organizations and Society*, **16**, 1, 1–25.
BAKER, G. and WRUCK, K. (1989). 'Organizational change and value creation in leveraged buy-outs: the case of O. M. Scott & Sons'. *Journal of Financial Economics*, December, 163–90.
BARTLETT, R. (1989). *Economics and Power*. Cambridge: Cambridge University Press.
BIBEAULT, D. (1982). *Corporate Turnaround*. New York: McGraw-Hill.
BOWMAN, E. and SINGH, H. (1989). 'Corporate restructuring: trends and consequences'. In Rock, R. (Ed.), *Corporate Restructuring*. New York: McGraw-Hill.
BULL, L. (1989). 'Management performance in leveraged buy-outs: an empirical analysis'. *Journal of Business Venturing*, **4**, 263–79.
CHIPLIN, B., WRIGHT, M. and ROBBIE, K. (1993). *Management Buy-outs in 1993: The Annual Review from CMBOR*. Nottingham: CMBOR.
COOPER, A. and DUNKELBERG, W. (1986). 'Entrepreneurship and paths to business ownership'. *Strategic Management Journal*, **7**, 53–68.
COOPER, A., WOO, C. and DUNKELBERG, W. (1989). 'Entrepreneurship and the initial size of firm'. *Journal of Business Venturing*, **4**, 317–32.
DALTON, D. and KESNER, I. (1985). 'Organisational performance as an antecedent of inside/outside chief executive succession: an empirical assessment'. *Academy of Management Journal*, December, 749–62.
DONALDSON, G. (1990). 'Voluntary restructuring: the case of General Mills'. *Journal of Financial Economics*, **27**, 117–41.
EISENHARDT, K. (1989). 'Building theories from case study research'. *Academy of Management Review*, **14**, 4, 532–50.
ENNEW, C., ROBBIE, K., WRIGHT, M. and THOMPSON, S. (1994). 'Small business entrepreneurs and performance: evidence from management buy-ins'. *International Small Business Journal*, **12**, 4, 28–44.
FRANKS, J. and MAYER, C. (1993). 'European capital markets and corporate control'. In Bishop, M. and Kay, J. (Eds), *European Mergers and Merger Policy*. Oxford: OUP.
FREDRICKSON, J., HAMBRICK, D. and BAUMRIN, S. (1988). 'A model of CEO dismissal'. *Academy of Management Review*, **13**, 2, 255–70.
FURTADO, E. and KARAN, V. (1989). 'Causes, consequences and shareholder wealth effects of management turnover: a review of the empirical evidence'. *Financial Management*, Summer, 60–75.

GREEN, S. (1992). 'The impact of ownership and capital structure on managerial motivation and strategy in management buy-outs: a cultural analysis'. *Journal of Management Studies*, **29**, 4, 513–35.

GREEN, S. and BERRY, D. (1991). *Cultural, Structural and Strategic Change in Management Buy-outs*. London: Macmillan.

GRINYER, P. H., MAYES, D. and McKIEMAN, P. (1988). *Sharpbenders: The Secret of Unleashing Corporate Potential*. Oxford: Basil Blackwell.

HASPESLAGH, P. and JEMISON, D. (1991). *Managing Acquisitions*. New York: Free Press.

HATHERLY, D. et al. (1994). 'An exploration of the MBO–financier relationship'. *Corporate Governance*, **2**, 1, 20–9.

HOFER, C. (1980). 'Turnaround strategies'. *Journal of Business Strategy*, Summer, 19–31.

HOFFMAN, R. (1989). 'Strategies for corporate turnarounds'. *Journal of General Management*, **14**, 3, 46–66.

JEMISON, D. and SITKIN, S. (1986). 'Corporate acquisitions: a process perspective'. *Academy of Management Review*, **11**, 1, 145–63.

JENSEN, M. C. (1986). 'Agency costs of free cash flow, corporate finance and takeovers'. *American Economic Review*, May, 326–9.

JENSEN, M. (1992). 'Foreword'. In Green, S. and Berry, D., *Cultural, Structural and Strategic Change in Management Buy-outs*. London: Macmillan.

JENSEN, M. C. (1989). 'Eclipse of the public corporation'. *Harvard Business Review*, September/October.

JENSEN, M. and MECKLING, W. (1976). 'The theory of the firm: managerial behavior, agency costs, and ownership structure'. *Journal of Financial Economics*, **3**, 305–60.

JENSEN, M. and MURPHY, K. (1990). 'Performance pay and top-management initiatives'. *Journal of Political Economy*, **98**, 2, 225–64.

JENSEN, M. C. and RUBACK, R. S. (1983). 'The market for corporate control'. *Journal of Financial Economics*, **11**, 5–50.

JONES, C. S. (1985). 'An empirical study of the role of management accounting systems following takeover or merger'. *Accounting, Organizations and Society*, **10**, 177–200.

JONES, C. S. (1992). 'Accounting and organizational change: an empirical study of management buy-outs'. *Accounting, Organizations and Society*, **17**, 2, 151–68.

KAPLAN, S. and STEIN, J. (1993). 'The evolution of buy-out pricing and financial structure in the 1980s'. *Quarterly Journal of Economics*, **CVIII**, 2, 313–59.

LLEWELLYN, S. (1990). 'The role of case study methods in management accounting research: a comment'. *British Accounting Review*, **24**, 17–31.

LOW, M. and MACMILLAN, I. (1988). 'Entrepreneurship: past research and future challenges'. *Journal of Management*, **14**, 2, 139–61.

MURPHY, K. and ZIMMERMAN, J. (1993). 'Financial performance surrounding CEO turnover'. *Journal of Accounting and Economics*, **16**, 273–315.

NORBURN, D. (1986). 'GOGOS, YOYOS and DODOS: company directors and industry performance'. *Strategic Management Journal*, **7**, 2, 110–17.

PALEPU, K. (1990). 'Consequences of leveraged buy-outs'. *Journal of Financial Economics*, **27**, 247–62.

ROBBIE, K., WRIGHT, M. and THOMPSON, S. (1992). 'Management buy-ins in the UK'. *Omega*, **20**, 4, 446–56.

SCAPENS, R. (1990). 'Researching management accounting practice: the role of case study methods'. *British Accounting Review*, **22**, 259–81.

SCAPENS, R. (1992). 'The role of case study methods in management accounting research: a personal reflection and reply'. *British Accounting Review*, **24**, 369–83.

SCHWARTZ, K. and MENON, K. (1985). 'Executive succession in failing firms'. *Academy of Management Journal*, **28**, 3, 680–6.

SINGH, H. (1993). 'Challenges in researching corporate restructuring'. *Journal of Management Studies*, **30**, 1, 147–72.

SLATTER, S. (1984). *Corporate Recovery: Successful Turnaround Strategies and their Implementation*. Harmondsworth: Penguin Books.

STARKEY, K. and McKINLAY, A. (1993). *Strategy and the Human Resource: Ford and the Search for Competitive Advantage*. Oxford: Blackwell.

STIGLITZ, J. and WEISS, A. (1981). 'Credit rationing in markets with imperfect information'. *American Economic Review*, **71**, June, 393–410.

THOMPSON, S. and WRIGHT, H. (1991). UK managemnet buy-outs: debt, equity and agency cost implications. *Managerial and Decision Economics*, **12**, 1, 15–26.

3I, (1992). *The MBI Phenomenon*. London: 3i.

VIRANY, B. and TUSHMAN, M. (1986). 'Top management teams and corporate success'. *Journal of Business Venturing*, **1**, 261–74.

WALSH, J. and ELLWOOD, J. (1991). 'Mergers, acquisitions and the pruning of managerial deadwood'. *Strategic Management Journal*, **12**, 201–17.

WARNER, R., WATTS, R. and WRUCK, K. (1988). 'Stock prices and top management changes'. *Journal of Financial Economics*, March, 461–92.

WOO, C. Y., COOPER, A. and DUNKELBERG, W. (1991). 'The development and interpretation of entrepreneurial typologies'. *Journal of Business Venturing*, **6**, 93–114.

WRIGHT, M., THOMPSON, S. and ROBBIE, K. (1992). 'Venture capitalist and management-led, leveraged buy-outs: a European perspective'. *Journal of Business Venturing*, **7**, 47–71.

WRIGHT, M. (Ed.) (1994). *Readings in Management Buy-outs*. International Library of Management, Dartmouth Publishing.

WRIGHT, M., ROBBIE, K., THOMPSON, S. and STARKEY, K. (1994). 'Longevity and the life-cycle of management buy-outs'. *Strategic Management Journal*, **15**, 3, 215–27.

ZIMMERMAN, F. (1991). *The Turnaround Experience*. New York: McGraw-Hill.

[13]

ELSEVIER Journal of Corporate Finance 6 (2000) 55–70

Journal of
CORPORATE
FINANCE

www.elsevier.com/locate/econbase

Managerial ownership, board structure, and the division of gains in divestitures

Robert C. Hanson [a,*], Moon H. Song [b]

[a] *Department of Finance and CIS, College of Business, Eastern Michigan University, Ypsilanti, MI 48197-2201, USA*
[b] *Department of Finance, College of Business Administration, San Diego State University, San Diego, CA 92182-8236, USA*

Received 1 December 1997; accepted 1 August 1999

Abstract

This study shows that shareholders of a firm that divests assets receive gains that are significantly related to stock ownership by the firm's managers and to the proportion of outside directors on the firm's board when the divestiture produces positive total dollar gains. Our results agree with the notions that higher levels of ownership give managers the incentive to sell assets that create negative synergies, the incentive to negotiate the best price for shareholders, and that outside directors fulfill their responsibilities as effective monitors and advisors to management. © 2000 Elsevier Science B.V. All rights reserved.

JEL classification: G34; G32
Keywords: Divestitures; Managerial ownership; Board structure

1. Introduction

Corporate governance has emerged as an important ingredient in the theory and practice of finance. Theory suggests that managerial stock ownership and the board of directors, two aspects of corporate governance, are effective internal mechanisms to reduce agency costs (Jensen and Meckling, 1976; Fama and Jensen, 1983). Stock ownership provides managers the economic incentive to act

---

* Corresponding author. Tel.: +1-734-487-9747; fax: +1-734-487-1941; e-mail: robert.hanson@emich.edu

56   *R.C. Hanson, M.H. Song / Journal of Corporate Finance 6 (2000) 55–70*

in concert with the interests of outside shareholders, while monitoring by the board of directors helps to assure that managers will not make decisions that stray too far from these interests. Consistent with these arguments, in recent years boards of directors at firms such as General Dynamics, Sears, IBM, and Compaq have facilitated changes in strategy or management to enhance shareholder wealth. At the same time, many firms have adopted governance provisions that reduce the effectiveness of the market for corporate control as an external monitoring mechanism (Danielson and Karpoff, 1998), thus making internal control systems more important to shareholders. In this paper, we study the relation between two internal control mechanisms, managerial stock ownership and the board of directors, and the wealth consequences of the decision to divest assets.

One facet of finance theory suggests that managers divest assets when the sale will increase shareholder wealth (Hite et al., 1987). Within this view, transferring assets from one firm to another creates gains for both sellers and buyers. Sellers benefit by capturing gains from buyers that derive more value from the assets or by getting the buyer to overpay. Sellers also benefit if the sale corrects agency problems or removes assets that cause negative synergies, such as assets that are more valuable to managers than shareholders or assets unrelated to the firm's core business. Buyers of divested assets benefit from better fit when these assets complement existing operations, and when a superior organizational form or other comparative advantages allow the buyer to operate the assets more efficiently.

A competing and more sceptical view presented by Lang et al. (1995) argues that managers pursue their own objectives and initiate asset sales to raise capital. Here, managers use asset sales to avoid exposure to the capital markets, perhaps because of the costs of managerial discretion, rather than primarily as a means to increase shareholder wealth. In their view, managers value control and firm size and have incentives to use the proceeds of the sale in ways that do not benefit shareholders. Moreover, agency problems could lead the buyer to waste rather than create value if hubris (Roll, 1986) or excessive free cash flow (Jensen, 1986) motivates the purchase. In this competing view, agency concerns rather than value maximization play the prominent role in explaining why some firms divest assets and whence the gains.

Taken together, these competing views suggest that divestitures could either alleviate or aggravate agency problems, or, irrespective of agency problems, could create gains through the more efficient use of assets. Theory suggests that, to the extent that agency costs of managerial discretion are important, gains from divestitures should be conditional on the effectiveness of internal mechanisms intended to control agency costs. Thus, although earlier studies show that divestitures produce small gains on average (for example, Hite et al., 1987), these gains should vary cross-sectionally when agency considerations are important. In this paper, we explore the cross-sectional relation between gains to the selling firm and measures of the effectiveness of internal control mechanisms. We use managerial stock ownership and the fraction of unaffiliated outside directors on the board as

R.C. Hanson, M.H. Song / Journal of Corporate Finance 6 (2000) 55–70 57

proxies for the effectiveness of internal control mechanisms and the resolution of agency problems.

In our analysis of a pair-wise sample of divestitures from 1981 through 1995, we find that sellers exhibit a trend toward smaller boards with a higher percentage of unaffiliated outside directors consistent with the growing importance of internal control mechanisms. Cross-sectional regressions show that, even though gains on average are small, when total dollar gains are positive, managerial ownership and independent outside directors play a significant role in increasing returns to the divesting firm. Our evidence is consistent with the notion that gains to the divesting firm arise in part from the resolution of agency problems. Our results contribute to the growing body of evidence that documents a significant cross-sectional relation between corporate governance mechanisms and the shareholder wealth effects of managerial decisions.

2. Synergy gains, ownership, and board structure

The division of gains between seller and buyer, and the extent that gains represent wealth transfers or resolution of agency problems, will depend on the selling firm's ownership and board structure. In this view, we extend to divestitures similar analysis of tender offers by Stulz et al. (1990) and Byrd and Hickman (1992), and management buyouts by Lee et al. (1992).

2.1. Ownership structure and gains

Theory suggests that stock ownership by the divesting firm's managers will affect shareholder gains in several ways. First, higher levels of ownership will force managers to bear the costs related to negative synergies and, thus, provide incentives to sell assets that reduce firm value and to improve operations afterwards. Second, the wealth consequences of ownership will provide managers an incentive to be tough bargainers when they negotiate a price for the divested assets. This argument parallels the work of Song and Walkling (1993) who argue that ownership by target firm managers gives them incentive to negotiate a higher price once the decision to merge has been made. In takeovers, control of voting rights and the prospective loss of incumbency give managers the power and incentive to strike a hard bargain. In asset sales, however, the incentive is purely pecuniary. The incentive to bargain hard derives solely from a manager's claim on the firm's residual cash flow. Moreover, in asset sales, where multiple bids are unusual (Jain, 1985; Sicherman and Pettway, 1992), sellers must rely on their own skills to bargain away gains created by the buyer, and to ensure that internally generated gains stay within the firm. Thus, we expect a positive relation between the divesting firm's gains and the stock ownership of its managers.

58   *R.C. Hanson, M.H. Song / Journal of Corporate Finance 6 (2000) 55–70*

2.2. Board structure and gains

Directors play an important role in the corporate governance process (Fama and Jensen, 1983). As part of their responsibility, directors monitor and assess managerial performance, decide compensation levels of senior managers, provide advice, and provide links to other organizations. But their primary responsibility involves resolving agency conflicts that arise between shareholders and managers. [1] Outside directors, who are otherwise unaffiliated with the firm, have the most independence to credibly arbitrate these conflicts.

Recent research provides mixed evidence about the effectiveness of boards in fulfilling their responsibilities as monitors and arbiters. For example, Baysinger and Butler (1985) find a significant non-contemporaneous relation between board composition and firm performance, although Hermalin and Weisbach (1992) find no relation between board composition and Tobin's q. Weisbach (1988) shows that outside directors influence executive turnover in poorly performing firms. Rosenstein and Wyatt (1990) find a significant positive market response to the appointment of additional outside directors, suggesting that the market expects better performance from firms with more outside directors. Research by Byrd and Hickman (1992), Lee et al. (1992), Brickley et al. (1994), and others show that board composition matters and that outside directors provide effective monitoring. These studies find significantly higher returns at announcements of tender offers, management buyouts, and poison pills when outside directors dominate the board.

In this study, we hypothesize that outside unaffiliated directors will have a positive effect on resolving agency problems and motivating managers to sell assets that produce negative synergies. The board will normally give managers wide latitude to run the company, but, along the lines of Warther (1998), at some point when losses in a business segment or division become too severe to ignore, the board will recommend divestiture. The threshold where the board overcomes its normal passivity and coalesces to recommend change will likely be lower and be reached earlier, the greater the proportion of independent outside directors on the board. In this context, the board will promote asset sales that increase corporate focus and reduce diversification and overinvestment. In addition, when industry overcapacity requires exit and traditional compensation schemes do not provide the proper incentives (Dial and Murphy, 1995), the board could provide managers the necessary impetus to downsize. Outside directors, for example, will motivate managers to sell in a more timely manner assets that they are reluctant to sell (Boot, 1992), or assets that are part of an unsuccessful acquisition (Kaplan and Weisbach, 1992), or remove assets that benefit managers more than shareholders

---

[1] See the Continental Bank Roundtable on the Role of Corporate Boards in the 1990s (1992) for anecdotal evidence of the board's involvement in corporate restructuring.

(Shleifer and Vishny, 1989), or remove assets with manager-specific returns (Weisbach, 1995). Moreover, when assets are sold to raise capital that will be retained for general corporate use, the board will provide effective monitoring to insure that managerial discretion over the use of these funds does not harm shareholders. Thus, we expect a positive relation between the degree to which outside directors influence the board and the gains earned by the selling firm.

3. Data and methods

We collect our sample from *Mergers and Acquisitions* and select transactions occurring from 1981 through 1995 that were classified as divestitures, have a value listed, and were also announced in the *Wall Street Journal*. These criteria, for the most part, eliminate divestitures by small firms and low value divestitures by small and large firms that do not get mentioned in the press, along with asset sales to private investors and to foreign corporations. We further require that both buyer and seller have stock returns on the Center for Research on Security Prices (CRSP) files, and that information about the seller's board structure and managerial stock ownership for the year of the divestiture be available from Q-file proxy statements or the SEC's Edgar database. Our final sample consists of 326 matched buyer and seller pairs.

Following the scheme used by Baysinger and Butler (1985), Byrd and Hickman (1992) and Brickley et al. (1994) among others, we classify the selling firm's directors based on their economic or personal ties to the firm. Directors are classified as *inside* if they are current or past employees or are related to the firm's chief executive or part of the founding family. Directors fall into the *gray* area if they have a close but indirect relation with the firm such as consultants, lawyers, or executives of firms with a business relationship with the firm. The following are deemed independent *outside* directors — executives of unrelated firms, private investors, or directors from outside the business community.

We calculate announcement period excess returns using the market model with the CRSP value weighted index and estimate parameters over a 240-day period ending 60 days before the divestiture was reported in the *Wall Street Journal*. We report cumulative excess returns for the 3 days surrounding the *Wall Street Journal* announcement. In our tests for statistical significance, for consistency with tests of dollar returns, we calculate t-statistics from cross-sectional standard errors. The conclusions do not change if we test excess returns for significance using z-statistics following the technique described by Dodd and Warner (1983). Dollar returns for each firm are found by multiplying the 3-day excess return by the market value of equity 30 trading days prior to the initial announcement.

The discussion in Section 2 suggests that the gains received by the seller from removing negative synergies should depend on the firm's ownership and board structure. Moreover, gains captured from (or transferred to) the buyer through the bargaining process should also depend on the seller's ownership structure. But this division of gains makes sense only when there are positive gains to allocate between buyer and seller. Stated differently, if the divestiture increases the combined certainty equivalent cash flows, then how the present value of the increased cash flow is allocated between buyer and seller will depend on the bargaining effort of each side. On the other hand, if the divestiture reduces the combined certainty equivalent cash flows below pre-divestiture levels, then it makes no sense to talk about allocating the present value of now non-existent cash flows. Thus, to address the division of gains in our regression analysis, we follow the approach of Stulz et al. (1990) and consider the relation between the seller's gain and its ownership and board structure when total gains are positive.

4. Empirical results

4.1. Sample description

Table 1 presents descriptive statistics for our sample of divestitures; all dollar values are adjusted to constant 1981 dollars using "Indexes for Major Expenditure Classes" as our price index. We report results for the 1980s and 1990s to facilitate comparison with earlier studies and to highlight differences between decades. Even though our sample is concentrated in the 1990s, with 66% of the divestitures announced since the end of 1989 and 82% announced since the end of 1987, our pre-1988 divestitures (in nominal dollars) produce results similar to earlier studies (e.g., Sicherman and Pettway, 1992). Divested assets were valued at US$169 million on average, while the median transaction was only US$68 million. Our transactions range in size from Wal Mart's 1988 sale of its Helen's Arts and Crafts to Michaels Stores for a reported US$2.3 million to the 1994 sale by McKesson of

Table 1
Descriptive statistics about a sample of 326 divestitures from 1981 to 1995
Value is the reported price paid for the divested assets. Seller's and buyer's equity are market values 30 days preceding the divestiture announcement. Relative value is value of transaction divided by seller's equity value. Dollar values are in constant 1981 dollars.
Medians are in square brackets.

	All years	1980s	1990s
Value of transaction (US$ millions)	168.8 [67.7]	246.9 [94.9]	127.9*** [56.3]***
Seller equity value (US$ millions)	4,172.8 [1,407.3]	3,071.0 [1,308.0]	4,749.4*** [1,421.2]
Buyer equity value (US$ millions)	2,991.5 [758.2]	3,009.2 [860.4]	2,982.2 [710.3]
Relative value of transaction	0.275 [0.069]	0.332 [0.106]	0.246 [0.057]***
Number of divestitures	326	112	214

Asterisks indicate that *t*-tests (means) or Kruskal–Wallis tests (medians) show that the 1990s value differs from the 1980s value at the 1% (***), 5% (**) or 10% (*) level of significance.

R.C. Hanson, M.H. Song / Journal of Corporate Finance 6 (2000) 55–70   61

its PCS Health Systems to Eli Lilly for a reported US$4 billion. Transactions were smaller in the 1990s than in the 1980s, US$128 million (median US$56 million) vs. US$247 million (median US$95 million). Large differences between mean and median values show that the distribution is highly skewed, thus medians may better represent typical values. By comparison, in nominal terms, the median value of the transactions in our sample (US$100 million) is about 3 times larger than the value reported by Lang et al. (1995), but half as large as the sample of John and Ofek (1995). Table 1 also shows that sellers are larger than buyers in the 1990s. The differences in means and medians are significant at the 0.01 level. Sellers, but not buyers, were significantly (mean $p = 0.01$, median $p = 0.11$) larger in the 1990s than in the 1980s. By comparison, John and Ofek (1995) report buyers and sellers having similar values of about US$4.7 billion for their 1986–1988 sample. Sicherman and Pettway (1992) report that buyers were 7.38 times larger than sellers for their 1981–1987 sample. The relative size of the transaction is quite large on average, 27.5% of the seller's equity value for the entire period, while the median value is quite small, only 6.9%. For the 1980s, our mean (33.2%) and median (10.6%) relative values are slightly smaller than the 39.4% and 15.3% reported by John and Ofek (1995). In the 1990s, our median relative size (5.7%) is significantly less than the 1980s value, reflecting smaller transactions by larger sellers.

4.2. Ownership and board structure

Table 2 describes the ownership and board structure of the divesting firm. Panel A shows that officers and directors of the divesting firm own 7.27% of the firms stock while the CEO controls on average 2.90% of the shares. These levels of ownership are lower than the 13% reported by Lang et al. (1995), but not unexpectedly so given the larger firms in our sample. Inside directors own 5.68% of the shares while outside directors own 1.01%. Comparing decades, median ownership is significantly lower in the 1990s for officers and directors (10% level) and gray directors (1% level), but insignificantly higher for outside directors. Average ownership is lower for officers and directors, inside directors, and outside directors, although not significantly lower. Lower ownership perhaps merely reflects the larger size of the selling firms. Average and median CEO ownership are higher in the 1990s, but not significantly higher.

Panel B shows the board structure of the selling firm. Outside directors make up 52.5% of the average board. During the 1980s, the fraction was 45.9%, but the value is a significantly higher 55.9% in the 1990s. Our 1980s result contrasts with Lee et al. (1992) who find that outside directors dominate the board in their samples of going private (59%) and management unit buyout (60%) transactions. But our value is higher than the 39% reported by Byrd and Hickman (1992) for acquirers and the 38% reported by Brickley et al. (1994) for firms adopting poison pills. The higher 1990s value in our sample could be a consequence of an

62   *R.C. Hanson, M.H. Song / Journal of Corporate Finance 6 (2000) 55–70*

Table 2
Descriptive statistics about the divesting firm's ownership and board structure for a sample of 326
divestitures from 1981 to 1995
Medians are in square brackets.

Period	All years	1980s	1990s
Number of cases	326	112	214
Panel A: Ownership			
Officers and Directors (%)	7.270 [1.255]	8.368 [1.710]	6.696 [0.950]*
CEO (%)	2.899 [0.275]	2.631 [0.235]	3.040 [0.305]
Inside directors[a] (%)	5.679 [0.860]	6.412 [1.220]	5.296 [0.770]
Gray directors[b] (%)	0.582 [0.010]	0.561 [0.020]	0.592 [0.000]***
Outside directors[c] (%)	1.009 [0.030]	1.395 [0.020]	0.807 [0.040]
Panel B: Board structure			
Number of inside directors	3.78 [3.0]	4.56 [4.0]	3.38*** [2.0]
Number of gray directors	2.02 [2.0]	2.45 [2.0]	1.80*** [1.0]
Number of outside directors	6.57 [7.0]	6.31 [6.0]	6.71 [7.0]
Total number of directors	12.38 [12.0]	13.32 [13.0]	11.89*** [12.0]
Fraction of outside directors (%)	52.5 [54.2]	45.9 [46.5]	55.9*** [57.5]***
Percentage of boards with outside directors > 50%	55.5	43.8	61.7***

[a]Inside directors are current or past employees or are related to the chief executive.
[b]Gray directors have a close but indirect relation with the firm.
[c]Outside directors have no other relationship with the firm.
Asterisks indicate that *t*-tests (means) or Kruskal–Wallis tests (medians) show that the 1990s value
differs from the 1980s value at the 1% (***), 5% (**) or 10% (*) level of significance.

increased focus on corporate governance issues and concerns about board independence by institutional investors (e.g., Skowronski and Pound, 1993; Nesbitt,
1994). Our results suggest that the 1990s have witnessed changes in ownership
and board structure, especially a trend toward smaller boards with fewer inside
directors. To the extent that divestitures represent value maximizing behavior on
the part of managers, smaller boards are consistent with the inverse relation
between board size and firm value found by Yermack (1996). Moreover, the trend
toward smaller boards dominated by outside directors is consistent with the
suggestions of Jensen (1993) for revitalizing internal control systems.

4.3. Synergy gains

Table 3 reports percentage and dollar synergy gains (in constant 1981 dollars)
for the entire sample period and by decade. In panel A, we show, like earlier
studies (e.g., Rosenfeld, 1984; Jain, 1985; Hite et al., 1987; Sicherman and
Pettway, 1992), that divestiture announcements produce significantly positive
cumulative excess returns on average. Divesting firms receive 3-day excess returns
of 0.602% ($t = 2.39$), buyers receive 0.477% ($t = 2.23$), and the value-weighted

R.C. Hanson, M.H. Song / Journal of Corporate Finance 6 (2000) 55–70 63

Table 3

Percentage and dollar synergy gains for a sample of 326 divestitures from 1981 to 1995

Excess returns are cumulated from 1 day before to 1 day after the initial announcement. Total cumulative excess return is the value weighted average of the seller and buyer returns. Dollar excess returns, synergy gains, are cumulative excess returns times dollar value of equity 30 days before the announcement. Dollar values are in constant 1981 dollars.

Median values are shown in square brackets. *t*-Statistics calculated from cross-sectional standard errors are shown in parentheses.

	Seller	Buyer	Total
Panel A: All years			
Cumulative excess returns (%) Days −1 to +1	0.602 [0.282] (*t* = 2.39)**	0.477 [0.221] (*t* = 2.23)**	0.269 [0.047] (*t* = 1.69)*
Dollar excess returns (US$ millions)	8.700 [0.568] (*t* = 0.91)	11.332 [0.213] (*t* = 1.51)	20.032 [0.298] (*t* = 1.66)*
Number of divestitures	326	326	326
Panel B: 1980s			
Cumulative excess returns (%) Days −1 to +1	0.561 [0.303] (*t* = 1.50)	0.282 [0.250] (*t* = 0.72)	0.070 [0.097] (*t* = 0.27)
Dollar excess returns (US$ millions)	17.005 [0.890] (*t* = 0.92)	22.575 [0.214] (*t* = 1.36)	39.580 [0.458] (*t* = 1.63)
Number of divestitures	112	112	112
Panel C: 1990s			
Cumulative excess returns (%) Days −1 to +1	0.623 [0.125] (*t* = 1.89)*	0.579 [0.221] (*t* = 2.28)**	0.373 [0.002] (*t* = 1.86)*
Dollar excess returns (US$ millions)	4.353 [0.262] (*t* = 0.40)	5.848 [0.213] (*t* = 0.73)	9.801 [0.236] (*t* = 0.74)
Number of divestitures	214	214	214

Asterisks indicate that *t*-tests (means) are significant at the 1% (***), 5% (**) or 10% (*) level.

64   *R.C. Hanson, M.H. Song / Journal of Corporate Finance 6 (2000) 55–70*

total return is a marginally significant 0.269% ($t = 1.69$). Dollar excess returns show, interestingly, that on average buyers receive insignificantly more gains than sellers even though sellers are larger and receive higher percentage gains. Median dollar gains suggest a more conventional distribution of gains. Sellers receive median dollar returns of US$0.568 million, more than double the US$0.213 received by buyers. Median total dollar gains are US$0.298 million.

The significant percentage returns are not driven by outliers. Indeed, both seller and buyer excess returns have fairly symmetric distributions without extreme observations. The selling firm's 3-day excess returns range from −16.45% to +19.64% with 53% of the returns being positive. The buying firm's returns range from minus −14.35% to +17.00% with 52% of the returns being positive. However, dollar gain distributions are skewed, as indicated by mean and median values, because of large selling (equity value of US$19 billion) and buying (equity value of US$54 billion) firms creating large dollar synergy gains (US$1.5 and US$1.3 billion, respectively).

Panels B and C report gains for the 1980s and 1990s. In all cases, percentage and dollar gains are positive but significant (percentage) returns occur only in the 1990s. Interestingly, mean and median constant dollar returns are higher in the 1980s than in the 1990s. Even without adjusting for inflation, mean and median (except median buyer) dollar returns are higher in the 1980s. However, none of these differences between decades is statistically significant. As in panel A, panels B and C show that buyers receive insignificantly higher dollar gains on average than sellers, although median gains are higher for sellers. By way of comparison, John and Ofek (1995) find significantly positive returns to sellers and positive but not statistically significant returns to buyers. Sicherman and Pettway (1992) find positive percentage and dollar returns to both buyers and sellers of transactions when the transaction price was disclosed. Buyers in their sample received about twice the dollar gains as sellers, compared to US$22.6 million (nominal US$29.5) for buyers and US$17.0 million (nominal US$17.2) for sellers in our 1980s sample.

4.4. Regression results

Our main hypothesis involves the cross-sectional relation between gains and agency concerns. That is, if divestitures resolve or exacerbate agency problems, then the gains to the selling firm should depend on its managerial ownership and board structure. Moreover, as described in Section 3, this relation makes sense when the divestiture generates non-negative total gains. In Table 4, we present results from cross-sectional regressions that test this hypothesis. In regressions using the divesting firm's cumulative excess return as the dependent variable, we use a dummy variable, *gain dummy*, that equals one when total dollar gains are positive to create interactive terms that isolate the effects of managerial ownership and board structure on gains to the divesting firm when total gains are positive.

R.C. Hanson, M.H. Song / Journal of Corporate Finance 6 (2000) 55–70   65

Table 4
Regression analysis of seller's cumulative excess returns on managerial ownership and board of director composition
Gain dummy equal one when total synergy gain is positive. Ownership is by officers and directors as a group. Gain dummy equals one if total synergy gain is positive. Normalized total gain is total dollar gain divided by market value of the selling firm's equity. Normalized total gain if positive equals the normalized total gain times the gain dummy. Normalized total gain if negative equals the normalized total gain times one minus the gain dummy. Decade dummy equals one if 1990s. Relative value is transaction value divided by seller's equity value.
t-Statistics are in parentheses.

Explanatory variable	Dependent variable: Seller's excess returns				
	1	2	3	4	5
Constant	0.0034 (1.20)	0.0041 (1.47)	0.0055 (0.69)	0.0039 (0.53)	−0.0012 (−0.16)
Ownership (×10⁻²) (Officers and Directors)	0.0144 (0.80)	−0.0287 (−1.27)	0.0129 (0.68)	0.0013 (0.06)	−0.0147 (−0.66)
Ownership × gain dummy (×10⁻²)		0.1045 (3.15)***		0.0529 (1.64)*	0.0521 (1.67)*
Fraction outside directors			−0.0038 (−0.28)	−0.0287 (−2.20)**	−0.0288 (−2.21)**
Fraction outside directors × gain dummy				0.0580 (6.57)***	0.0579 (6.76)***
Normalized total gain if positive	0.0134 (2.49)**		0.0133 (2.46)**		
Normalized total gain if negative	−0.0011 (−0.12)		−0.0014 (−0.14)		
Normalized total gain		0.0033 (0.68)		−0.0008 (−0.18)	−0.0063 (−1.35)
Decade dummy (1990s = 1)					0.0031 (0.62)
Relative value of transaction					0.1677 (4.66)***
Adjusted R^2	0.02	0.04	0.01	0.15	0.20
F-test p-value	0.04	0.00	0.08	0.00	0.00

Asterisks indicate significance at the 10% (*), 5% (**), or 1% (***) level.

We use ownership by officers and directors as a group for our measure of ownership and the fraction of independent outside directors on the board for our measure of board structure. [2] We control for the decade with a dummy variable that equals one if the divestiture was announced in the 1990s, and we also control for the size of the transaction and the total gain, both normalized by the market value of the selling firm's equity.

Regressions 1 and 3 in Table 4 show that the seller's gain is significantly related to normalized gains only when gains are positive, consistent with arguments made in Section 3. The coefficient of the managerial ownership variable (regression 1) is, however, not significant. But our main interest is the explanatory power of this variable when total gains are positive. We test this in regression 2 where we use the interactive term *ownership × gain dummy* to isolate cases of positive total gains. The coefficient of the interactive term is positive and highly significant ($t = 3.15$), which shows that ownership by officers and directors has a significantly larger impact on returns to the divesting firm when total gains are positive. When total gains are negative, ownership has a negative but insignificant ($t = -1.27$) impact on the sellers returns. The combined coefficients of the ownership variable and the interactive term is significantly positive ($t = 3.13$) suggesting that managerial ownership has a positive effect on gains to the selling firm when total gains are positive. [3] This is consistent with our argument that stock ownership motivates managers to sell assets that created negative synergies and provides incentives to negotiate a better price for the assets.

In regressions not reported, we assess the robustness of the ownership results by using CEO ownership in place of ownership by officers and directors. CEO ownership provides further insight by tying the wealth effects of the sale to the individual with the decision making responsibility. Moreover, by examining just CEO ownership, we can reduce co-mingling the impact on gains that result from incentives provided by managerial ownership and the monitoring provided by outside directors. [4] In a regression similar to regression 2, for example, the coefficient of the interactive term *CEO ownership × gain dummy* is significant at the 5% level ($t = 2.22$) while the coefficient for the CEO ownership variable is insignificant ($t = -0.35$). These estimates further support the notion that when

---

[2] A continuous measure of board structure is beneficial because it allows for the prospect that outside directors need not dominate the board to be effective as long as they can form coalitions with gray directors and sympathetic inside directors, consistent with the bandwagon effect in the Warther (1998) model of board effectiveness.

[3] The combined coefficient is $[0.0758(= 0.1045 - 0.0287)] \times 10^{-2}$ with an implied t-statistic of $t = 3.13$. The t-statistic was found by dividing the combined coefficient by an estimated standard error calculated using the two variance and two covariance terms from the variance–covariance matrix of regression coefficients.

[4] The correlation between ownership by officers and directors as a group and the fraction of outside directors on the board is -0.31 ($p = 0.00$), while the correlation between CEO ownership and the fraction of outside directors is -0.20 ($p = 0.00$).

R.C. Hanson, M.H. Song / Journal of Corporate Finance 6 (2000) 55–70 67

total gains are positive, stock ownership by the CEO, or officers and directors as a group, has a significant positive effect on gains to the divesting firm's shareholders.

In regression 4, we assess whether outside directors influence the selling firm's gains when total gains are positive. We include the fraction of outside directors as an explanatory variable and an interactive term that controls for the case of positive total dollar gains. As before, the combined coefficients of the managerial ownership variables remains significant ($t = 2.29$). The coefficient for the fraction of outside directors variable is significantly negative (-0.0287, $t = -2.20$), while the interactive term *fraction outside directors $\times$ gain dummy* is positive and highly significant (0.0580, $t = 6.57$). The combined coefficient is significantly positive ($t = 2.20$). From regression 4 we see that when total dollar gains are positive, the seller's gain is significantly increased as the fraction of outside directors increase. The significantly positive coefficient supports the view that the board provides effective monitoring, perhaps by providing reluctant managers the impetus to sell assets that were part of a failed acquisition, or assets that benefit managers more than shareholders.

In regression 5, we control for the decade with a dummy variable that equals one for the 1990s and control for the size of the transaction normalized by sellers' equity value. The coefficients for the interactive terms *ownership $\times$ gain dummy* and *fraction outside directors $\times$ gain dummy* remain significantly positive, consistent with regression 4. The date dummy is insignificant, thus supporting the univariate results shown in Table 3 that gains do not differ between decades. The coefficient of the relative size variable is highly significant (0.1677, $t = 4.66$). Thus, larger asset sales produce larger gains, which supports the notion that divestitures reduce overinvestment.

The regression specifications in Table 4 could raise concerns because the right-hand side measure of total synergy gain is functionally related to the dependent variable, the selling firm's excess return. We conduct sensitivity analysis to assess whether the relation that we find between selling firm excess returns and managerial ownership truly reflects the impact of ownership on the division of gains. Ideally, we would like regress the selling firm's share of the total gain on our managerial ownership and board structure variables. But statistical inference from these regressions would be problematic because the dependent variable would be the ratio of two normal distributions and, thus, distributed as a Cauchy distribution. Alternatively, we estimate separately two regressions using measures of the seller's gain (the numerator in the selling firm's share of the gain) and total gain (the denominator in the selling firm's share of the gain) as the dependent variable. The former regressions using percentage excess returns as the dependent variable are reported in Table 4. In the later regressions, we use as a measure of total gain the value-weighted average of the selling and buying firms' excess returns as the dependent variable. In these regressions, neither managerial ownership nor the fraction of independent directors on the board have significant

68   *R.C. Hanson, M.H. Song / Journal of Corporate Finance 6 (2000) 55–70*

explanatory power. The absence of a relation between total gain and managerial ownership suggests that the significant relation between selling firm excess returns and ownership shown in Table 4 is not merely a proxy for a relation between ownership and total synergy gains. Thus, these explanatory variables help explain the selling firm's gain, but not the total gain. In other tests where we restrict the sample to cases with positive total synergy gains, our regressions show a significant ($p = 0.09$) relation between the selling firm's excess returns and CEO ownership but not to ownership by non-CEO officers and directors. Although these tests provide additional evidence that managerial ownership influences the selling firm's share of the total gain, interestingly, these tests do not show a significant relation between independent outside directors and the selling firm's gain.

In sum, regression estimates in Table 4 show that managerial ownership and board structure significantly and positively influence the gains to the divesting firm, given that the divestiture produces overall positive dollar synergy gains. These results are consistent with the notions that the value created from divestitures arise from removing negative synergies, reducing overinvestment, or by resolving agency problems.

5. Conclusions

Theory suggests that agency concerns influence the decision to divest assets and the gains that result. We examine the cross-sectional relation between gains to divestitures and measures of the effectiveness of internal control mechanisms intended to resolve agency problems. In our sample of divestitures from 1981 to 1995, we find that buyers and sellers on average receive significant positive percentage returns, although significant returns only occur in the 1990–1995 period. Significant percentage returns are consistent with the views that divestitures create value by moving assets to the buyer's more efficient operating environment and that divestitures resolve agency problems. But when divestitures resolve agency problems, gains will depend on the effectiveness of the firm's internal control mechanisms.

Our cross-sectional regressions show that the divesting firm's managerial ownership and board structure influence gains to the selling firm's shareholders. When the divestiture creates positive total dollar gains, the divesting firm's returns are directly and significantly related to managerial ownership, as measured either as ownership by officers and directors as a group or by CEO ownership, and by the percentage of unaffiliated outside directors on the board. These results agree with the notions that higher levels of ownership give managers incentive to sell assets that create negative synergies, that ownership provides managers negotiating incentives to retain these gains within the selling firm, or bargain away gains from the buyer. Our results also support the view that outside directors fulfill their responsibilities as effective monitors and advisors to management.

References

Baysinger, B., Butler, H., 1985. Corporate governance and the board of directors: Performance effects of changes in board composition. Journal of Law Economics and Organization 1, 101–124.

Boot, A., 1992. Why hang on to losers? Divestitures and takeovers. Journal of Finance 47, 1401–1424.

Brickley, J.A., Coles, J.L., Terry, R.L., 1994. Outside directors and the adoption of poison pills. Journal of Financial Economics 35, 371–390.

Byrd, J., Hickman, K., 1992. Do outside directors monitor managers? Evidence from tender offer bids. Journal of Financial Economics 32, 195–221.

Continental Bank Roundtable on the Role of Corporate Boards in the 1990s, 1992. Journal of Applied Corporate Finance 5, 58–77.

Danielson, M.G., Karpoff, J.M., 1998. On the uses of corporate governance provisions. Journal of Corporate Finance 4, 347–371.

Dial, J., Murphy, K., 1995. Incentives, downsizing, and value creation at General Dynamics. Journal of Financial Economics 37, 261–314.

Dodd, P., Warner, J., 1983. On corporate governance: A study of proxy contests. Journal of Financial Economics 11, 401–438.

Fama, E., Jensen, M., 1983. Separation of ownership and control. Journal of Law and Economics 26, 301–325.

Hermalin, B.E., Weisbach, M.S., 1992. The effects of board composition and direct incentives on firm performance. Financial Management 20, 101–112.

Hite, G.L., Owers, J., Rogers, R., 1987. The market for interfirm asset sales, partial sell-offs and total liquidations. Journal of Financial Economics 18, 229–252.

Jain, P., 1985. The effect of voluntary sell-off announcements on shareholder wealth. Journal of Finance 40, 209–224.

Jensen, M., 1986. The agency costs of free cash flow: Corporate finance and takeovers. American Economic Review 76, 323–329.

Jensen, M., 1993. The modern industrial revolution, exit, and the failure of internal control systems. Journal of Finance 48, 831–880.

Jensen, M., Meckling, W., 1976. Theory of the firm: Managerial behavior, agency costs, and ownership structure. Journal of Financial Economics 3, 305–360.

John, K., Ofek, E., 1995. Asset sales and increase in focus. Journal of Financial Economics 37, 105–126.

Kaplan, S., Weisbach, M., 1992. The success of acquisitions, evidence from divestitures. Journal of Finance 47, 107–139.

Lang, L., Poulsen, A., Stulz, R., 1995. Asset sales, firm performance, and the agency costs of managerial discretion. Journal of Financial Economics 37, 3–37.

Lee, C.I., Rosenstein, S., Rangan, N., Davidson, W.N. III, 1992. Board composition and shareholder wealth: the case of management buyouts. Financial Management 21, 58–72.

Nesbitt, S., 1994. Long-term rewards from shareholder activism: a study of the "CALPERS effect". Journal of Applied Corporate Finance 6, 75–80.

Roll, R., 1986. The hubris hypothesis of corporate takeovers. Journal of Business 59, 197–216.

Rosenfeld, J., 1984. Additional evidence on the relation between divestiture announcements and shareholder wealth. Journal of Finance 39, 1437–1448.

Rosenstein, S., Wyatt, J.G., 1990. Outside directors, board independence, and shareholder wealth. Journal of Financial Economics 26, 175–192.

Shleifer, A., Vishny, R., 1989. Management entrenchment: The case of manager-specific investments. Journal of Financial Economics 25, 123–139.

Sicherman, N., Pettway, R., 1992. Wealth effects for buyers and sellers of the same divested assets. Financial Management 21, 119–128.

Skowronski, W., Pound, J., 1993. Building relationships with major shareholders: A case study of Lockheed. Journal of Applied Corporate Finance 6, 39–47.

Song, M., Walkling, R., 1993. The impact of managerial ownership on acquisition attempts and target shareholder wealth. Journal of Financial and Quantitative Analysis 28, 439–457.

Stulz, R., Walkling, R., Song, M., 1990. The distribution of target ownership and the division of gains in successful takeovers. Journal of Finance 45, 817–833.

Warther, V., 1998. Board effectiveness and board dissent: A model of the board's relationship to management and shareholders. Journal of Corporate Finance 4, 53–70.

Weisbach, M., 1988. Outside directors and CEO turnover. Journal of Financial Economics 20, 431–460.

Weisbach, M., 1995. CEO turnover and the firm's investment decisions. Journal of Financial Economics 37, 159–188.

Yermack, D., 1996. Higher market valuation of companies with a small board of directors. Journal of Financial Economics 40, 185–211.

[14]

ELSEVIER Journal of Corporate Finance 5 (1999) 103–117

Journal of
CORPORATE
FINANCE

www.elsevier.com/locate/econbase

Institutional ownership and firm performance: The case of bidder returns

Rakesh Duggal [a], James A. Millar [b,*]

[a] College of Business, Southeastern Louisiana University, Hammond, LA 70401, USA
[b] College of Business Administration, University of Arkansas, Fayetteville, AR 72701, USA

Received 1 July 1993; accepted 1 March 1998

Abstract

We employ corporate takeover decisions to investigate the impact of institutional ownership on corporate performance. The OLS regressions of bidder gains on institutional ownership indicate a positive relation between the two. However, we find institutional ownership to be significantly determined by firm size, insider ownership and the firm's presence in the S&P 500 index. Thus, when bidder gains are regressed on the predicted values of institutional ownership in two-stage regressions, the recursive estimates do not confirm the relationship shown by the OLS regressions. Furthermore, we do not find any evidence that active institutional investors (e.g., CalPERS) as a group enhance efficiency in the market for corporate control. These findings cast doubt on the superior selection/monitoring abilities of institutional investors. © 1999 Elsevier Science B.V. All rights reserved.

JEL classification: G32

Keywords: Bidder returns; Corporate performance; Institutional ownership

1. Introduction

Institutional investors are rapidly replacing individual investors in the stock market. According to one estimate, institutional investors may now be holding up to 46.5% of the outstanding common stock of U.S. corporations. [1] Such a high

---

* Corresponding author. E-mail: jamilla@comp.uark.edu

[1] See 'Small Investors Continue to Give up Control of Stocks,' *The Wall Street Journal*, May 11, 1992, C1.

level of institutional ownership of corporations raises an important question: Do institutional investors enhance, diminish or have no impact on corporate efficiency?

Previous studies have addressed the above question within the context of such corporate events as antitakeover amendments, and proxy fights and have reported contradictory evidence. While Pound (1988) finds that institutional investors contribute to managerial entrenchment by supporting incumbent managers in proxy fights, both Brickley et al. (1988) and Agrawal and Mandelker (1990) find that institutional investors monitor managers in the adoption of antitakeover amendments. More recently, some studies have focused on the monitoring effectiveness of pension funds and have also reported inconsistent findings. Nesbitt (1994) finds that companies targeted for monitoring by California Public Employees' Retirement System (CalPERS) outperform S&P index by 41% over the subsequent five-year period. While Smith (1996) detects a positive stock price reaction to the news of a settlement between CalPERS and a targeted firm on a shareholder proposal, he fails to notice any improvement in the firm's operating performance subsequent to the settlement. Finally, although Wahal (1996) notices an impressive success rate of 40% for corporate governance proposals sponsored by pension funds, he reports no change in the abnormal stock price performance of these firms. We test the hypotheses concerning the institutional behavior within the context of takeover decisions.

Extant evidence indicates the existence of agency costs in takeover decisions. For example, Amihud and Lev (1981) find that managers resort to takeovers to reduce firm risk, and Morck et al. (1990) report that bad managers acquire growing firms to enhance their reputations. Further, Jensen (1988) also cites evidence to support his theory that managers use takeovers as a device to maintain control over free cash flows. Takeovers that further the above managerial objectives are unlikely to be in stockholders' interests. The fact that some managers successfully accomplish such takeovers indicates inefficiency in corporate decision making, resulting most likely from managerial entrenchment. What role, then, do institutional investors play in managerial entrenchment and sub-optimal takeover decisions?

Before we can answer the above question, we need to address a methodological issue. Some recent merger studies have used OLS regressions with control variables to test the hypotheses of interest (Lang et al., 1989; Morck et al., 1990). However, unlike those studies our main variable of interest, namely, institutional ownership, is likely to be an endogenous variable; therefore, Two-Stage Least Squares procedures are more appropriate for our purposes than one-step OLS regressions. However, we provide results based on both methodologies to suggest that OLS results may be spurious when an endogenous variable, such as institutional ownership, is involved.

Employing OLS regressions, we find a positive relation between the bidders' gains and institutional ownership. However, the first stage of the two-stage

R. Duggal, J.A. Millar / Journal of Corporate Finance 5 (1999) 103–117   105

regressions reveals that institutional ownership in bidders is significantly determined by bidder size, insider ownership and whether or not the bidder is in the
S&P 500 index. Regressions of bidder gains on the predicted estimates of
institutional ownership in the second stage do not show the positive relationship
yielded by the OLS regressions. Furthermore, we do not find any evidence that
active institutional investors have better selection/monitoring abilities. The rest of
the paper is organized as follows. Section 2 contains a discussion of the hypotheses, which is followed by Section 3 describing the sample selection procedures,
methodology and variables. Results and conclusions are presented in Sections 4
and 5.

2. The hypotheses

2.1. The efficiency-augmentation hypothesis

Institutional supporters argue that institutional investors enhance corporate
efficiency in two ways. First, institutional investors perform quality research in
order to identify efficient firms for investing funds, thus directing scarce capital to
its most efficient use. Given the evidence of Lang et al. (1989) and Servaes (1991)
that efficient bidders gain more than inefficient bidders, a positive relation
between the bidders' gains and institutional ownership in bidding firms may be
expected.

Second, according to institutional supporters, large institutional stakes in public
corporations provide strong economic incentives for institutional investors to
monitor managers. [2] This vigilant institutional monitoring enhances managerial
efficiency and the quality of corporate decision making. Institutional monitoring
may involve holding discussions with management on corporate plans and performances, supporting (opposing) the management's wealth enhancing (reducing)
policies and decisions, and active participation in board elections and other voting

---

[2] The underlying case for institutional monitoring is that the relatively large equity positions of
institutions renders research and monitoring expenditures cost effective for them. Furthermore, there
may exist scale economies in research and monitoring activities so that the marginal cost to
institutional investors of monitoring their relatively small equity holdings may be small. Thus,
relatively large aggregate institutional ownership of a firm, even comprising a number of small
institutional stakes, may indicate a closer firm monitoring than low aggregate institutional ownership.
See Shleifer and Vishny (1986) for the monitoring incentives of large investors and Pound (1988),
Brickley et al. (1988) and Agrawal and Mandelker (1990), for institutional investors.

106   *R. Duggal, J.A. Millar / Journal of Corporate Finance 5 (1999) 103–117*

issues. [3] If institutional investors are indeed monitoring investors, then takeovers undertaken by bidders with high levels of institutional ownership may be expected to be more wealth enhancing than those effected by bidders with low institutional ownership.

2.2. The efficiency abatement hypotheses

These hypotheses hold that institutional investors are incapable of monitoring managers due to their passivity, myopic goals, conflict of interests or legal constraints.

It is argued that institutional investors are passive investors who are more likely to sell their holdings in poorly performing firms than to expend their resources in monitoring and improving their performance. It is further argued that many institutional investors take a myopic view of their investments, guided solely by the short-term goal of outperforming some benchmark in the current quarter. This short-term perspective leads to overreaction to information and excessive trading, and renders these investors incapable of monitoring managers. [4] Furthermore, many institutions, such as insurance companies, may currently (or potentially in the future) have business relations with firms whose stock they also own. These business relations may prevent institutional investors from being active corporate monitors.

One school of thought blames mistrust of powerful financial institutions for a number of federal and state laws and regulations that restrict institutional ownership of public corporations and discourage institutional monitoring of managers. [5] For example, the Investment Company Act of 1940 prohibits diversified investment companies from investing more than 5% of their assets in securities issued by one issuer and from owning more than 10% of the voting securities of one issuer (§6(a)(1), p. 13, Public No. 768, 76th Congress). A mutual fund violating these restrictions can be subjected to regulatory and tax penalties. [6] In addition,

---

[3] Recently, the financial press has been reporting about increased institutional activism in corporate affairs. The Council of Institutional Investors, the principal trade group for pension funds, and other institutional investors are reportedly opposing the adoption of poison pills and lucrative pay packages of top managers of large corporations. Furthermore, these investors are also asking for – and in many cases succeeding in – installing independent directors on corporate boards. See 'The Battle for Corporate Control', *Business Week*, May 18, 1987, 101–109; and 'More Directors are Recruited from Outside', *The Wall Street Journal*, March 20, 1991, B-4.

[4] See Jarrell et al. (1985) for a discussion of the short-term hypothesis.

[5] See Roe (1990) for a discussion of the motivations behind various laws and regulations that restrict the institutional role in the stock market.

[6] Many other institutional investors face similar restrictions (Roe, 1990).

R. Duggal, J.A. Millar / Journal of Corporate Finance 5 (1999) 103–117   107

various SEC rules under Section 14 of the Securities and Exchange Act of 1934 serve to discourage institutional investors from having even informal word-of-mouth discussions with other investors prior to detailed filings with the SEC (Pound, 1991). [7] It is argued that these restrictions result in sub-optimal allocations of resources and a lack of institutional monitoring.

In summary, the efficiency-abatement hypotheses predict a positive relation between institutional ownership and managerial entrenchment and, consequently, a negative relation between the bidders' gains and institutional ownership in bidding firms.

3. Sample selection, methodology and variables

3.1. Sample selection

Using the COMPUSTAT Research File, a sample is constructed by identifying the bidders of target firms that were deleted from the COMPUSTAT data base in the 1985–1990 period. In some cases, however, first acquisition bids for targets precede deletions from COMPUSTAT by one calendar year. Consequently, the sample includes some acquisitions that were initiated in 1984.

This period of 1985–1990 is chosen for two reasons: (1) a tremendous growth in the equities portfolios of institutional investors in recent years, and (2) a reported rise in institutional activism in this period due perhaps to a change in the public and regulatory perception of their role in the equities market (see Footnote 3). The sample includes only the acquisitions that are reported by the *Wall Street Journal*. The sample is restricted to the bidding firms listed on either the New York Stock Exchange or the American Stock Exchange. Over The Counter (OTC) firms are not included in order to avoid a potential bias because, as Agrawal and Mandelker (1990) point out, OTC firms have low institutional ownership. To avoid noise in the findings, the sample further excludes the observations where the market value of the target equity is less than one percent of the market value of the bidder equity (see Morck et al., 1990). In all, 143 observations are available for analysis. The stock price data are unavailable for seven firms. Information on institutional ownership and insider ownership is unavailable for 13 and 14 firms, respectively. In addition, 16 observations are lost because of missing values

---

[7] In October 1992, the SEC relaxed these rules, allowing institutional investors not seeking control to communicate with other shareholders without filing extensive documentation with the SEC. See 'SEC to Allow Investors More Room to Talk,' *The Wall Street Journal*, October 15, 1992, C1.

108   *R. Duggal, J.A. Millar / Journal of Corporate Finance 5 (1999) 103–117*

needed for calculating the *q*-ratio. Thus, depending on the model employed, non-availability of data reduces the sample to between 108 and 120 observations.

3.2. Event study methodology

Standard event study methodology is employed to estimate wealth changes for the bidding firms around the publication of first takeover proposal by the successful bidder in the *Wall Street Journal* ($t = 0$). The market model is employed to generate the benchmark returns:

$$R_{jt} = A_j + B_j R_{mt} + E_{jt} \qquad (1)$$

where R_{jt} = return on the *j*th stock on day *t*; R_{mt} = return on the CRSP equally-weighted portfolio on day *t*; A_j, B_j = ordinary least squares parameters for security *j*, and E_{jt} = the residual term for security *j* on the day *t*.

The market model parameters, A_j and B_i, are estimated for each security *j*, by regressing the security's post-event period daily stock returns for the 250-day period ($t = +21$ to $t = +270$) on the corresponding CRSP returns. The post-event returns are used because takeovers may change the risk of bidding firms, in which case the use of pre-event data for estimating market model parameters may bias the results. [8] The estimated equation for each security is employed to predict the benchmark returns for the event date *t* ($t = -20$ to $t = +1$). The benchmark returns are then subtracted from the actual stock returns to yield daily abnormal returns (AR_{jt}):

$$AR_{jt} = R_{jt} - \left(\hat{A}_j + \hat{B}_j R_{mt} \right). \qquad (2)$$

The daily abnormal returns are cumulated over the 22-day period $[-20, +1]$ to yield an estimate of the bidder's gain from the takeover ($GAINS_j$):

$$GAINS_j = \sum_{t=20}^{t=+1} AR_{jt}. \qquad (3)$$

$GAINS_j$ is employed as the dependent variable in cross-sectional regressions to test the hypotheses. [9]

---

[8] See Copeland and Mayers (1982) for the use of post-event data to generate benchmark returns. Also see Brown and Warner (1985) for details of event study methodology.

[9] The robustness of the findings reported in Tables 2, 4 and 5 was checked by estimating the bidders' gains over longer intervals, e.g., $[-60, +1]$ or $[-50, +1]$, with essentially similar results. The results are not reported here but are available from the authors on request.

R. Duggal, J.A. Millar / Journal of Corporate Finance 5 (1999) 103–117   109

4. Models and empirical evidence

4.1. OLS models

We use percentage of bidder common stock owned by institutional investors (INST) one quarter preceding the bid as the main independent variable in the OLS regression models. [10] Information on institutional ownership is gathered from *Spectrum 3*.

The following independent variables are included in the regressions as control variables. The control variables represent factors that have been found by previous studies to explain bidder gains.

IN: Percentage of bidder common stock owned by managers one quarter preceding the bid, as reported by *Value Line*. There is prior evidence of a positive relation between insider ownership and the bidder's gains (Lewellen et al., 1985).

AVALUE: Market value of bidder equity one quarter preceding the bid. AVALUE is employed as a proxy of firm size and is estimated using COMPUS-TAT. It may be argued that large bidders have the resources to identify the right target and to put together an optimal takeover proposal. Furthermore, the large size of the bidder may deter other small bidders from entering the competition, thus ensuring a larger premium for the bidder.

FORM: A dummy variable, assigned the value of 1 if the takeover involves at least some cash and 0, otherwise. Extant evidence shows that bidders' gains are higher in cash financed takeovers than in stock financed ones (Servaes, 1991).

COMPETE: A dummy variable, assigned the value of 1 if there is a single bidder involved and 0 if there are multiple bidders. Previous studies have found that multiple bidders for a target reduce the takeover gains for the successful bidder (Morck et al., 1990).

Information on FORM and COMPETE is gathered from the *Wall Street Journal Index*.

SIZE: The ratio of the market value of target equity to the market value of bidder equity one quarter preceding the bid. Asquith et al. (1983) find that the bidders' gains rise with the size of acquisition.

TOBIN: Lang et al. (1989) and Servaes (1991) find that efficient bidders – Tobin's q being the measure of efficiency – gain significantly more than inefficient bidders. The q-ratio is estimated for the year immediately preceding the takeover proposal. We use both the firm's actual q-ratio as well as a dummy variable (the value of 1 is assigned to a firm with the q-ratio of greater than 1 and

---

[10] Institutional ownership in individual corporations may fluctuate significantly from quarter to quarter if institutional investors are short-term investors, thus causing a bias in the findings. Therefore, institutional ownership in the bidding firms was averaged over four quarters preceding the bids and employed in the models. However, no material difference in the findings was detected.

110   R. Duggal, J.A. Millar / Journal of Corporate Finance 5 (1999) 103–117

0, otherwise) in the regression models with identical results (only results based on actual q-values are reported here).

TINST: Institutional ownership in the target firms. Stulz et al. (1990) report higher gains to targets in tender offers when a larger proportion of the target stock is held by institutional investors. Being in low tax-brackets, institutional investors have incentives to tender their shares earlier in the tender offer process, thus causing a lower (higher) return to targets (bidders).

4.1.1. OLS results

Table 1 contains univariate statistics of interest. On average, the bidding firm stockholders experience a wealth loss of approximately 1.20% (significant at the 0.10 level) around the takeover announcement. This finding is consistent with earlier evidence that takeovers on average do not enhance the wealth of bidding stockholders (Servaes, 1991). The average institutional ownership of approximately 46% in the bidding firms is close to the reported institutional ownership of 46.5% for all US corporations. About 71% of the bidding firms in the sample pay some cash for the acquisitions. Further, about 76% of the bidders face no competition in the takeovers. The average size of the target, as measured by the market value of equity, is only 37% of the bidder size. The average q-ratio of 84.35% for our sample is almost identical to the 84.5% reported by Lang et al.

Table 1
Descriptive statistics for a sample of bidder firms in takeovers initiated during the 1984–1990 period

Variable (N)[a]	Mean	Median	Standard deviation	Minimum	Maximum
GAINS (136)	− 1.202%	− 1.476%	8.219%	− 21.682%	27.890%
INST (130)	45.976%	45.800%	16.028%	0.800%	78.000%
IN (129)	9.169%	2.000%	13.904%	0.200%	73.000%
AVALUE[b] (143)	2822.683	1373.063	3996.264	61.763	30,023.320
FORM (143)	70.629%	1.000	47.706%	0.000	1.000
COMPETE (143)	76.224%	1.000	42.721%	0.000	1.000
SIZE (143)	37.047%	16.414%	54.479%	11.373%	3.791
TOBIN (127)	84.351%	75.800%	47.941%	9.200%	2.580
TINST (136)	31.377%	29.750%	18.165%	0.000%	73.300%

The data are the means, medians, standard deviations and minimum and maximum values for the sample variables at the time of takeover offers. The variables are GAINS (22-day-announcement period abnormal returns), INST (percent of bidder stock owned by institutional investors), IN (percent of bidder stock owned by insiders), AVALUE (market value of bidder equity one quarter preceding the bid), FORM (a dummy variable with the value of 1 if the takeover offer involves at least some cash and 0, otherwise), COMPETE (a dummy variable with the value of 1 if there is a single bidder in the takeover contest and 0, otherwise), SIZE (the ratio of the market value of target equity to the market value of bidder equity), TOBIN (the ratio of the firm's market value to its replacement value), and TINST (institutional ownership in target firms).
[a]N is not uniform across all the variables due to non-availability of stock price and ownership data.
[b]In millions of dollars.

(1989) for their sample of tender offers. Finally, the average institutional ownership in the targets is 31.37%.

Table 2 contains the regression results from different models with unique
combinations of independent variables. The first model contains the two ownership variables, namely, INST (institutional ownership) and IN (insider ownership).
The coefficient of INST is significant at the 0.03 confidence level. The coefficients of INST in the models in columns (2) and (3) are significant at the 0.02
level. The only other variable with a significant coefficient is COMPETE (at 0.06
level). Our findings confirm the earlier evidence that bidder gains are lower when
there is competition in the market for corporate control. [11]

We also test two additional hypotheses relating to institutional ownership. First,
if institutional investors are better monitors of managers due to the large size of
their stock ownership, then a greater concentration of the bidding firms' stock in
the hands of a few institutional investors might result in closer institutional
monitoring and higher gains to the bidding firms. We construct an ownership
concentration index (HINDEX), by summing up the squared values of the percent
ownership of the largest ten investors (see Agrawal and Mandelker, 1990). The
results are displayed in column (4) of Table 2. Institutional ownership concentration does not appear to explain bidder gains in a significant way. We recalculate
HINDEX using institutional ownership of the largest five, 15 and 20 investors, but
these different measures of concentrations do not yield different findings (results
of these regressions are not reported here).

Second, it is plausible that some institutional investors are more active – and
therefore better monitors – of public firms. Based on various news reports and
prior research (Wahal, 1996), we identify the following active investors who
targeted public firms in the 1984–1990 period to either redress a specific firm
action (e.g., poison pill defense) or elevate the firm performance in general: The
California Public Employee Retirement System (CalPERS); The California State
Teachers Retirement System; The Colorado Public Employee Retirement System;
Florida State Board of Administrators; New York State Common Retirement
System; The New York State Teachers Retirement System; Pennsylvania Public
School Employee Retirement System; State of Wisconsin Investment Board;
Teachers Insurance Annuity Association-College Retirement Equities Fund
TIAA-CREF).

These active institutions owned an average of 2.58% of the bidder common
stock, with a minimum of 0% to a maximum of 7.96%. Column (5) of Table 2

---

[11] It may be argued that the relationship between institutional ownership and the incentives to
monitor managers is nonlinear. To test this hypothesis, the five models of Table 2 were re-estimated by
taking the log values of the ownership variables. Following Demsetz and Lehn (1985), the ownership
values were transformed in the following way to convert them into unbounded forms: OWNERSHIP =
log{percentage ownership/(1-percentage ownership)} The transformations do not enhance the models.
The results (not reported here) are essentially similar to the results in Table 2.

112   R. Duggal, J.A. Millar / Journal of Corporate Finance 5 (1999) 103-117

Table 2
Results from the regressions of bidder gains (dependent variable) on institutional ownership and control variables for a sample of bidding firms in takeovers initiated during 1984–1990. The bidder gains are computed based on a model derived from the post announcement period stock returns (from $t = +21$ to $t = +270$, where $t = 0$ is the *Wall Street Journal* publication date for the takeover offer)[a]

Variable	(1)	(2)	(3)	(4)	(5)
INTERCEPT	−0.0672 (0.02)	−0.0537 (0.11)	−0.0861 (0.02)	−0.0362 (0.26)	−0.0513 (0.14)
INST	0.1130 (0.03)	0.1225 (0.02)	0.1279 (0.02)	–	–
HINDEX	–	–	–	−0.1408 (0.83)	–
ACTINST	–	–	–	–	0.3350 (0.48)
IN	0.0667 (0.25)	0.0695 (0.29)	0.0630 (0.35)	0.0023 (0.97)	0.0137 (0.83)
AVALUE[b]	–	0.0111 (0.57)	0.0174 (0.39)	0.0168 (0.42)	0.0182 (0.38)
SIZE	–	0.0168 (0.26)	0.0233 (0.14)	0.0165 (0.29)	0.0197 (0.21)
FORM	–	−0.0039 (0.82)	−0.0083 (0.66)	−0.0000 (0.99)	−0.0013 (0.95)
TOBIN	–	−0.0196 (0.23)	−0.0214 (0.21)	−0.0207 (0.23)	−0.0200 (0.25)
COMPETE	–	–	0.0371 (0.06)	0.0434 (0.03)	0.0482 (0.01)
TINST	–	–	−0.0144 (0.75)	0.009 (0.83)	0.0032 (0.94)
N	120	113	108	108	109
R^2	0.04	0.07	0.12	0.08	0.09

The main independent variables are INST (percent of bidder stock owned by institutional investors) and HINDEX (sum of the squared values of the largest ten institutions). The control variables are: IN (percent of bidder stock owned by insiders), AVALUE (market value of bidder equity one quarter preceding the bid), SIZE (the ratio of the market value of target equity to the market value of bidder equity), FORM (a dummy variable with the value of 1 if the bid involves at least some cash and 0, otherwise), COMPETE (a dummy variable with the value of 1 for a single bidder in the takeover contest and 0, otherwise), TOBIN (q-ratio of the firm's market value to its replacement value), and TINST (institutional ownership in targets). The data are regression coefficients and t-probabilities (in parentheses).
[a] Bidder gains were also estimated using pre-event stock returns ($t = -270$ to $t = -21$) and using a combination of pre-event and post-event stock returns. The regression results based on these gains were not different from those presented here.
[b] $\times 10^{-4}$.

contains the results of a regression of bidder gains on ownership of active institutions (ACTINST). The regression coefficient is statistically insignificant.

The above divergent findings – a positive relation between bidder gains and institutional ownership but an absence of a relation between ownership concentration or active institutional ownership and bidder gains – raise doubts about the robustness of the OLS results. [12,13]

---

[12] We can only conjecture as to why, unlike prior studies, we did not discover any significant relationship between bidders' gains and such variables as the q-ratio, bidder's size, form of payment and insider ownership. Some of the possible explanations lie in the differences in the sampling and statistical procedures, model constructions, and the periods of study.

[13] We also tested the monitoring incentives of three categories of institutional investors, as classified by Brickley et al. (1988), but failed to find any relation between the type of investor and the gains to bidding firms (the results are not reported here).

R. Duggal, J.A. Millar / Journal of Corporate Finance 5 (1999) 103–117 113

4.2. Two-stage least squares models

Demsetz and Lehn (1985) argue that ownership concentration is determined by several industry and firm-specific factors, so that the resulting concentration is value-maximizing for the firm. If ownership concentration is in fact determined by exogenous factors, then the above evidence of a positive relationship between bidder gains and institutional ownership must be spurious and misleading. There is evidence that institutional ownership in firms vary systematically with many factors. We hypothesize that the following factors may determine institutional ownership:

S&P Index (SP): Many institutional investors either offer fund choices to their clients that merely mimic the S&P index, or, in their effort to match or beat these indices, end up investing mostly in the firms included in these indices. Therefore, a higher institutional stake in S&P 500 firms may be expected. A dummy variable SP is used whose value is 1 if the firm is in the S&P 500 index and 0, otherwise.

Firm Size (SIZE): A positive relation between firm size and institutional ownership may be expected due to legal and liquidity reasons. As mentioned before, the Investment Company Act of 1940 prohibits diversified funds from investing more than 5% of their assets in the securities of a firm, thus driving funds to larger companies. Furthermore, larger firms offer greater trading liquidity to institutions. We test both ASSET (book value of the firm's assets) and AVALUE (market value of the firm's equity) as proxies of the bidder size in the model (the results are similar, therefore we report only the results based on ASSET).

Insider Ownership (IN): A higher insider ownership entails a lower magnitude of agency costs, thus reducing the need for institutional monitoring. Also, a higher insider ownership reduces the size of available stock to institutions, resulting in a negative relation between the two.

Size of Debt (DEBT): The higher the size of a firm's debt, the closer the firm monitoring by creditors, reducing the need for institutional monitoring of the firm. Grier and Zychowicz (1994) find a negative relationship between institutional ownership of a firm and the firm's debt size. The firm's book value of long-term debt is divided by the sum of the market value of equity and the book value long-term debt.

Regulatory Monitoring (REGUL): Demsetz and Lehn (1985) find a negative relation between institutional ownership concentration and the presence of regulatory monitoring. We use a dummy variable called REGUL with the value of 1 for a financial or utility firm and the value of zero otherwise.

Variability of Return (SDA): Following Demsetz and Lehn (1985) – who find a positive relationship between a firm's variability of return and institutional ownership, due to a greater profit potential for the firm from increased monitoring – we use two measures of variability: the standard deviation of monthly stock market returns of the 60 months before the acquisition (SDM), and the standard deviation

114   *R. Duggal, J.A. Millar / Journal of Corporate Finance 5 (1999) 103–117*

of annual accounting profit rates of the five-year period preceding the acquisition (SDA). (The results are identical, therefore only the results based on the accounting rate are presented here).

Timing (YEAR): Institutional ownership in public firms has been increasing with time, reflecting many trends. For example, small investors are investing in the stock market in larger numbers than ever before and they are increasingly investing through mutual funds and pension plans. We use the calendar year in which an acquisition is initiated as a value for YEAR to capture these trends affecting institutional ownership.

We first build a model using the above independent variables to predict institutional ownership in the bidders. We then regress bidder gains on the predicted estimates of institutional ownership to see if the previously observed positive relation holds.

4.2.1. Two-stage regression results

Table 3 contains univariate statistics on the above independent variables for the first-stage regressions. The average bidder has a debt ratio of 31% and the standard deviation of the five-year annual accounting returns of 6%. Further, 66% of the bidders are included in the S&P index, while 89% of them are in unregulated businesses.

We construct two prediction models, one for institutional investors in general (INST) and the other for active institutional investors (ACTINST). The results are

Table 3
Descriptive statistics of the variables employed to predict institutional ownership in bidding firms

Variable (N)	Mean	Median	Standard deviation	Minimum	Maximum
ASSET (113)	8201.16	2428.31	19,178.19	74.26	173,597.00
DEBT (129)	0.31	0.27	0.22	0.01	0.88
SDA (128)	0.06	0.03	0.11	0.00	0.69
SP (131)	0.66	1.00	0.48	0.00	1.00
REGUL (134)	0.11	0.00	0.32	0.00	1.00
YEAR (143)	86.18	86.00	1.17	84.00[a]	90.00

The data are the means, medians, standard deviations and minimum and maximum values of the variables. The variables are ASSET (book value of assets in millions of dollars), SP (a dummy variable with the value of 1 if the bidder is in an S&P index and 0, otherwise), REGUL (a dummy variable with the value of 1 if the bidder firm is regulated and zero, otherwise), SDA (standard deviation of annual accounting rates of return for preceding five years), DEBT (long-term debt/(long-term debt + market value of equity)), and YEAR (1984–1990, calendar year of acquisition initiation).

[a]Although the sample includes bidders whose targets were deleted from COMPUSTAT in 1985–1990, a small number of acquisitions whose targets were deleted in 1985 were actually initiated in 1984. We use the acquisition initiation year, not the deletion year, as the reference year for data gathering and analyses in this study.

Table 4
Regression coefficients (probabilities in parentheses) from regressions of INST (institutional owner-ship) and ACTINST (percent ownership of active institutional investors) on IN (insider ownership), ASSET (book value of bidder's assets), SP (a dummy variable with the value of 1 if the bidder is in S&P index and 0, otherwise), REGUL (a dummy variable with the value of 1 if the firm is regulated and 0, otherwise), SDA (standard deviation of the five-year annual accounting rates of return), DEBT (ratio of the book value of debt to the sum of the value of debt and market value of equity), and YEAR (acquisition initiation year 1984–1990)

Independent variables	Dependent variable	
	INST	ACTINST
	(1)	(2)
INTERCEPT	−1.0736 (0.25)	−0.4908 (0.00)
IN	−0.3617 (0.00)	−0.0217 (0.05)
ASSET[a]	0.0201 (0.02)	0.0006 (0.52)
SP	0.1042 (0.00)	0.0102 (0.00)
REGUL	−0.0744 (0.23)	−0.0138 (0.04)
SDA	−0.0732 (0.66)	−0.0088 (0.62)
DEBT	−0.0614 (0.43)	0.0018 (0.83)
YEAR	0.0176 (0.11)	0.0060 (0.00)
N	117	118
R_2	0.36	0.37

[a] $\times 10^{-4}$.

presented in Table 4. Column (1) shows that institutional ownership is positively and significantly related to the size of the bidder, as measured by its assets, and whether or not it is in the S&P index. The coefficients of ASSET and SP are

Table 5
Results from regressions of bidder gains on the predicted estimates of INST (institutional ownership) and ACTINST (ownership of active institutions). Also included in the model are the following control variables: SIZE (the ratio of the market value of target equity to the market value of bidder equity), FORM (a dummy variable with the value of 1 if the bid involves at least some cash and 0, otherwise), COMPETE (a dummy variable with the value of 1 for a single bidder in the takeover contest and 0, otherwise), TOBIN (q-ratio of the firm's market value to its replacement value), and TINST (institutional ownership in targets). The data are regression coefficients and t-probabilities (in parentheses)

Variables	(1)	(2)	(3)	(4)
INTERCEPT	−0.0235 (0.55)	−0.0755 (0.14)	0.0033 (0.88)	−0.0401 (0.27)
INST	0.0333 (0.69)	0.0795 (0.37)	–	–
ACTINST	–	–	−0.4082 (0.58)	0.0447 (0.96)
SIZE	–	0.0171 (0.26)	–	0.0142 (0.34)
FORM	–	0.0012 (0.95)	–	0.0028 (0.88)
COMPETE	–	0.0482 (0.01)	–	0.0461 (0.02)
TOBIN	–	−0.0189 (0.26)	–	−0.0181 (0.29)
TINST	–	0.0079 (0.86)	–	0.0119 (0.79)
N	115	109	115	109
R^2	0.00	0.09	0.00	0.08

significant at the 0.02 and 0.00 confidence levels, respectively. Further, institutional ownership and insider ownership are negatively and significantly related at the 0.00 level. Ownership of active institutions (ACTINST) rises significantly with YEAR, but falls with insider ownership. Further, ACTINST is significantly higher when the bidder is in the S&P index and lower when the bidder is regulated. The R-squared values of the two models are fairly high (36% and 37%, respectively), which compare favorably with the range of R-squared values (16%–23%) reported by Demsetz and Lehn (1985) for their prediction models.

The bidders' gains are regressed on the predicted values of INST (see columns (1) and (2) of Table 5) and ACTINST (columns (3) and (4)). The coefficients of INST are positive but statistically insignificant at the conventional confidence levels. The coefficients of ACTINST are not significant, either. Moreover, the sign of the regression coefficients of ACTINST is not stable. The above findings cast doubts on our earlier finding of a positive relation between institutional ownership and bidder gains using OLS regressions.

5. Conclusion

In light of the contradictory evidence on whether institutional investors enhance or diminish corporate efficiency, we provide further evidence on this subject from an important corporate event, namely, takeovers. In particular, we examine the relation between the bidders' gains and institutional ownership in bidding firms to determine the impact of institutional ownership on corporate performance.

Using OLS regressions we find a positive relation between the bidder gains and institutional ownership. However, we find that institutional ownership is significantly determined by firm size, insider ownership and the firm's presence in the S&P 500 index. Thus, when the bidder gains are regressed on the predicted values of institutional ownership in two-stage regressions, we detect no relationship between the two variables. Furthermore, neither the OLS nor two-stage regressions reveal any significant role played by active institutional investors in the takeover market. Together, these results suggest that institutional investors do not enhance efficiency in the market for corporate control. These results also conform with the argument of Demsetz and Lehn (1985) that ownership concentration is determined by specific factors and that, once these factors are accounted for, no relation may exist between ownership concentration and firm performance.

References

Agrawal, A., Mandelker, G.N., 1990. Large shareholders and the monitoring of managers: The case of antitakeover amendments. Journal of Financial and Quantitative Analysis 25, 143–161.
Amihud, Y., Lev, B., 1981. Risk reduction as a managerial motive for conglomerate mergers, Bell Journal of Economics Autumn, 605–617.

R. Duggal, J.A. Millar / Journal of Corporate Finance 5 (1999) 103–117   117

Asquith, P., Bruner, R., Mullins, D. Jr., 1983. The gains to bidding firms from merger. Journal of Financial Economics 11, 121–140.

Brickley, J., Lease, R., Smith, C., 1988. Ownership structure and the monitoring of managers. Journal of Financial Economics 20, 267–291.

Brown, S.J., Warner, J.B., 1985. Using daily stock returns: The case of event studies. Journal of Financial Economics 14, 3–31.

Copeland, T.E., Mayers, D., 1982. The Value Line enigma (1965–1978): A case study of performance evaluation issues. Journal of Financial Economics 10, 289–321.

Demsetz, H., Lehn, K., 1985. The structure of corporate ownership: Causes and consequences. Journal of Political Economy 93, 1155–1177.

Grier, P., Zychowicz, E.J., 1994. Institutional investors, corporate discipline and the role of debt. Journal of Economics and Business 46, 1–11.

Jarrell, G., Lehn, K., Marr, W., 1985. Institutional ownership, tender offers and long-term investments, Office of the Chief Economist, Securities and Exchange Commission, Washington, DC.

Jensen, M.C., 1988. Takeovers: Their causes and consequences. Journal of Economic Perspectives 2, 21–48.

Lang, L.H.P., Stulz, R.M., Walkling, R.A., 1989. Managerial performance, Tobin's q and the gains from successful tender offers. Journal of Financial Economics 24, 137–154.

Lewellen, W., Loderer, C., Rosenfeld, A., 1985. Merger decisions and executive stock ownership in acquiring firms. Journal of Accounting and Economics 7, 209–231.

Morck, R., Shleifer, A., Vishny, R., 1990. Do managerial objectives drive bad acquisitions? Journal of Finance 45, 31–48.

Nesbitt, S., 1994. Long-term rewards from shareholder activism: A study of the CalPERS effect. Journal of Applied Corporate Finance 6, 74–79.

Pound, J., 1988. Proxy contests and the efficiency of shareholder oversight. Journal of Financial Economics 20, 237–265.

Pound, J., 1991. Proxy voting and the SEC: Investor protection versus market efficiency. Journal of Financial Economics 29, 241–285.

Roe, M.J., 1990. Political and legal restraints on ownership and control of public companies. Journal of Financial Economics 27, 7–41.

Servaes, H., 1991. Tobin's q and the gains from takeovers. Journal of Finance 46, 409–419.

Shleifer, A., Vishny, R., 1986. Large shareholders and corporate control. Journal of Political Economy 94, 461–488.

Smith, M.P., 1996. Shareholder activism by institutional investors: Evidence from CalPERS. Journal of Finance 51, 227–252.

Stulz, R., Walkling, R.A., Song, M.H., 1990. The distribution of target ownership and the division of gains in successful takeovers. Journal of Finance 45, 817–834.

Wahal, S., 1996. Public pension fund activism and firm performance. Journal of Financial and Quantitative Analysis 31, 1–23.

[15]

ELSEVIER   Journal of Financial Economics 51 (1999) 125–166

An analysis of value destruction and recovery in the alliance and proposed merger of Volvo and Renault[1]

Robert F. Bruner*

Darden Graduate School of Business Administration, University of Virginia, Charlottesville, VA 11906, USA

Received 20 August 1996; received in revised form 6 February 1998

Abstract

Volvo's attempt to merge with Renault in 1993 temporarily destroyed SEK 8.6 billion (US$ 1.1 billion) in Volvo shareholder wealth. This study traces the destruction to hubris, managerialism, and the escalation of commitment – elements suggested in previous research. In addition, the case suggests path dependence as a source of wealth destruction in mergers. An elaborate structure of cross-shareholdings, joint committees, and a poison pill made it difficult for the strategic allies (Volvo and Renault) to follow any strategic path other than merger if they wanted to exploit economies more fully. Activism by institutional investors was instrumental in halting the destruction of shareholder wealth and redirecting the firm. This study reveals significant positive abnormal returns associated with the institutional activism. Consistent with Shleifer and Vishny (1986), institutional 'jawboning' is valuable. An analysis of the voting premium between Volvo's 'A' and 'B' shares suggests that the value created by institutional voice derived from the strategic change in the firm's direction rather than the power of the coalition of institutional investors to expropriate wealth. © 1999 Elsevier Science S.A. All rights reserved.

JEL classification: G34; G20; L33; L90

Keywords: Mergers; Acquisitions; Alliances; Institutional investors; Privatization

---

* Corresponding author. Tel.: 804 924 4802; fax: 804 243 7678; e-mail: rfb9k@virginia.edu.

[1] I thank many people for helpful comments and contributions, most notably Karl-Adam Bonnier, Susan Chaplinsky, Ken Eades, Bob Harris, Mike Jensen (editor), Krishna Palepu (referee), Kristian Rydqvist, Sven-Ivan Sundqvist, Anjan Thakor, and seminar participants at Virginia and Indiana. My colleague, Robert Spekman, assisted in some of the later research interviews as part of our parallel research on strategic alliances. I gratefully acknowledge the cooperation of Volvo, Renault, and 20 interviewees, as well as the financial support of a Citicorp Global Scholarship, the Darden School Foundation, and the Darden Partnership Program. Some interviewees requested anonymity, a request respected here. Others were willing to speak for the record and are identified in the text of the article. I am solely responsible for interpretations herein and any errors that may remain.

126   *R.F. Bruner/Journal of Financial Economics 51 (1999) 125–166*

1. Introduction

On December 2, 1993 the directors of AB Volvo withdrew their proposal to merge the firm's automotive business with Renault, a French state-owned enterprise. This set in motion changes in the firm's governance, ownership structure, and strategy and ended a major strategic alliance between Volvo and Renault. The resignations of the firm's executive chairman, Pehr Gyllenhammar, and four directors accompanied the board's action. While many groups and individuals ultimately influenced the board's decision, almost all observers and participants agree that the main impetus for this change was a rebellion against the merger by a handful of Swedish financial institutions holding a minority of the firm's shares.

The collapse of the Volvo–Renault merger warrants attention for at least two reasons. First, the profitability of alliances and mergers is a question of enduring interest, and this case can shed light on hypotheses about the origins of value destruction in mergers. These hypotheses include hubris, bad judgment, entrenchment, escalation of commitments, and path dependence. The case also illuminates the efficacy of remedies to these problems, including changes in management, strategy and governance.

Second, this case illuminates the types and wealth effects of institutional 'voice' (i.e., influence without control). There are no previous scientific case analyses of institutional activism, and this episode is remarkable for its size and drama, even by American standards. In Europe, this case is arguably the most prominent example of institutional investors' activism to date.

Section 2 summarizes the research objectives and methodology of this study. Section 3 presents the history of the episode and discusses the abnormal returns and voting premiums associated with main events. Section 4 summarizes the study and offers several conclusions.

2. Research objectives and methodology

2.1. Research objectives

My study examines the failed Volvo–Renault merger to illuminate three aspects of interest to financial economists.

2.1.1. The economic profitability of alliances and mergers

Harrigan (1988) and Levine and Byrne (1986) suggest that 60% of alliances fail to achieve their economic promise. A broad test of profitability is beyond the scope of this study, but this case does afford the opportunity to determine the extent to which investors anticipate failure. Bleeke and Ernst (1995) have also suggested that alliances are often precursors to acquisition. This study

R.F. Bruner/Journal of Financial Economics 51 (1999) 125–166   127

illuminates why alliances may be linked with acquisition, and the effect of this linkage on shareholders' wealth. Volvo's commitment to an alliance with Renault in 1990 created a *path dependence* that contributed to the destruction of wealth in the merger attempt. This case illustrates other hypothesized sources of wealth destruction in mergers, such as hubris (Roll, 1986), managerial entrenchment (Morck et al., 1988), Jensen (1986), bad judgment (Morck et al., 1990), and the escalation of commitment (Lys and Vincent, 1995).

2.1.2. The value of institutional voice

Hirschman (1970) contrasts voice with exit as possible actions by a principal who disagrees with an agent's actions. In the context of institutional investors, exit corresponds to the 'Wall Street Rule' (i.e., if you do not like management, sell your shares). Voice, on the other hand, entails a process of exhortation to management and coalition-building among investors and directors to influence a firm's board and managers in response to what Hirschman calls 'an objectionable state of affairs'. Shleifer and Vishny (1986) discuss voice or 'jawboning' along with tender offers and proxy fights as means by which a large minority shareholder can monitor management. They show that the choice of jawboning will depend on the balance of costs and benefits associated with each option.

Black (1992a,b) has argued that institutional voice is potentially valuable because someone must monitor corporate managers. It can add value by increasing the independence of corporate directors, discouraging bad takeovers, encouraging more efficient governance rules, discouraging cash hoarding, and establishing a more arms-length process for setting CEO pay. Gilson (1994) suggests that corporate governance may be linked to economic performance through its ability to monitor and discipline management and to create sufficient stability for a firm to honor implicit contracts necessary to realize internal business transformations through strategies based on lean manufacturing, total quality management, alliance networks, and so on. Stability is one of the purported benefits of the German and Japanese 'relational investing'. Franks and Mayer (1990) argue that implicit contracts are better supported by systems of inside, as opposed to market-style, ownership.

The empirical evidence in support of the value-adding role of institutional monitoring remains relatively scanty, although the evidence is consistent with the hypothesis that voice is valuable. Nesbitt (1994) finds that intervention by CalPERS, a large pension fund, is associated with excess returns of 41% over the five years following intervention. Smith (1996) uncovers significant positive excess returns associated with activism by CalPERS, but no significant effect on operating performance. The Gordon Group (1992) suggests excess returns from institutional activism of up to 30%. Agrawal and Mandelker (1990) show that companies with high institutional ownership experience event returns that are much more positive in response to antitakeover amendment proposals, and

128 *R.F. Bruner/Journal of Financial Economics 51 (1999) 125–166*

McConnell and Servaes (1990) conclude that institutional ownership correlates with Tobin's q and with accounting measures of profitability. Pound (1988), Jarrell and Poulsen (1987), Brickley et al. (1988) and Gordon and Pound (1993) give evidence that institutional ownership is associated with a higher probability of dissidents winning proxy contests, with lower adoption of value-decreasing antitakeover proposals, and with the success of shareholder-sponsored proposals to change corporate governance structures. Yet the direction of association implicit in these findings is unclear. Corporate performance may improve because of institutional holdings or institutions may tend to concentrate their investment in the shares of well-run companies. Moreover, there may be a selection bias in such research, as the research may ignore bad proposals that were forestalled by watchful institutional investors. As Black (1992b) notes, further study of the association between institutional monitoring and value is 'badly needed'. My study offers evidence about the value of institutional voice.

2.1.3. The value of remedies to 'objectionable states of affairs'

Institutional activists have a variety of remedies, including changes in governance, management, and strategy. It is interesting to consider shareholders' reactions to these types of remedies. Some studies find gains associated with replacing the executives of underperforming firms. Warner et al. (1988) find a significant association between poor stock performance and the frequency of management turnover, but no significant excess returns to shareholders at the announcement of management change; they note that 'the unimpressive magnitude [of abnormal returns at announcement] raises questions about the gains from such an endeavor' (p. 488). Other studies by Bonnier and Bruner (1989), Furtado and Rozeff (1987), and Weisbach (1988) show significantly positive returns when management changes. Yet none of these studies focus specifically on instances of investor activism, nor do they resolve the question whether the gains derive from a change in the individual (consistent with hypotheses of hubris, managerialism, or behaviorism) or a change in the firm's strategy (consistent with the hypothesis of path dependence).

2.2. Field research

The research for this study entailed field interviews of 20 individuals, including senior managers at both Volvo and Renault, institutional investors, journalists, bankers, and the two CEOs who founded the strategic alliance, Pehr Gyllenhammar and Raymond Lévy. These interviews are supplemented by examination of domestic and English-language publications and as well as television news reports. I employed field research to reconstruct the history of the alliance and merger proposal and to understand the motives and perspectives of the various participants.

R.F. Bruner/Journal of Financial Economics 51 (1999) 125–166   129

2.3. Analysis of abnormal returns

To assess the wealth effect associated with institutional voice over this period, I compute abnormal returns for Volvo's 'A' and 'B' shares using market-adjusted returns over the time periods of the alliance, merger proposal, and redirection of the firm. The market adjusted return for day t is calculated as the total percentage return on the Volvo share (change in price plus dividend) at day t, less the total return on the Affärsvarlden Index, a value-weighted index of all shares listed on the Stockholm Stock Exchange, at day t. I focus on the major events – the founding of the alliance, the negotiation of the merger, the response of institutions, and the strategic redirection – and calculate abnormal returns in two-day windows (the day before and the day of publication) in which each event is reported in the press or associated with a press release or conference (in which case I used the day of release and day after). My main source of press dates is the *Financial Times of London*. Spot checking suggests that publication of news in the Financial Times was contemporaneous with publication in the Swedish and French financial press. The date of press release is preferred to the press date on the assumption that it is more closely associated with the arrival of news in the capital markets. Each abnormal return accumulated from day K to day L was tested by $t = AR_{KL}/SD_{KL}$. Following Ruback (1982) the estimate of the standard deviation adjusts for the autocovariance of returns:

$$SD_{KL} = (T*VAR(AR_t) + 2(T - 1) \, COVAR \, (AR_t, AR_{t-1}))^{1/2}, \qquad (1)$$

where $T = L - K + 1$. I estimate VAR and COVAR from a 202-day hold-out period beginning December 31, 1988 and ending October 10, 1989, just before the first announcement regarding the strategic alliance. The variance and autocovariance of abnormal returns for Volvo's 'A' shares are 0.0000758 and 0.0000078, respectively. For Volvo's 'B' shares, the variance and autocovariance are 0.0001115 and 0.0000030.

The observation period of abnormal returns runs from October 12, 1989, when rumors of an impending alliance were first published, until October 19, 1994, when Volvo sold a block of its shareholdings in Renault. I divide this observation period is into several sub-periods, as indicated in Fig. 1. These segments correspond to major phases in the episode and are identified by the nature of the information released to investors.

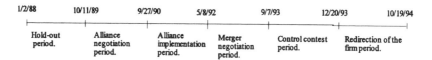

Fig. 1. Observation sub-periods.

2.4. Analysis of the voting premiums

The dual-class structure of Volvo's common equity can help illuminate the nature of the value associated with institutional voice. Studies of firms that have two classes of common stock outstanding show that the class with superior voting rights trades at a material premium relative to the other class. Based on a sample of Swedish firms, Rydqvist (1992a) estimates a premium of 15%. Using data on companies in the United States, Lease et al. (1983) find a premium of 5.44%. From a sample of Israeli companies, Levy (1982) finds a premium of 45.5%; Biger (1991) also uses an Israeli sample and estimates a premium of 74%. With a sample of 133 British firms, Megginson (1990) finds a premium of 13.3%. Using data on Canadian firms, Amoaku-Adu and Smith (1991) estimate a premium of 10%. Zingales (1994) finds a premium of 80% for a sample of Italian firms. Horner (1988) finds a premium of over 10% for and a sample of Swiss companies, Finally Kunz and Angel (1996) find premiums of about 18% after controlling for various factors. About 80% of all companies listed on the Stockholm Stock Exchange have a dual-class structure like Volvo's.

Lease et al. (1983) argue that two classes of stock, which have the same explicit payoff per unit of investment and differ only in voting rights, should trade at the same price, unless the class with superior voting rights could receive some incremental benefits that are not available to the other class. From this perspective, the magnitude of the voting premium should vary as the power of one class to appropriate incremental benefits rises or falls. Megginson (1990) and Rydqvist (1992b) extend this argument to the arena of takeovers, predicting that (1) the voting premium will be related to the probability of takeover, (2) the premium will be larger in actual takeover contests, and (3) the premium will be higher in firms with dispersed ownership of votes than in firms with concentrated ownership where hostile takeovers are less likely or may not occur at all if majority control exists. Megginson, however, concludes that the typically observed voting rights premium is too large relative to the expected value of some future takeover premium. Moreover, none of the studies to date considers the exercise of institutional voice as opposed to outright change of control.

If control over Volvo is valuable, it should have been reflected in the price premium between Volvo's two classes of common stock. These classes are similar except for voting rights: the 'A' shares carry voting rights equal to one vote per share, while the 'B' shares carry only one-tenth vote per share.

To assess the behavior of the voting premium in Volvo shares during the control contest a price premium is calculated as follows:

$$\pi_t = \frac{P_{A,t} - P_{B,t}}{P_{B,t}}, \tag{2}$$

where $P_{A,t}$ is the price of an 'A' share and $P_{B,t}$ is the price of the 'B' share on day t. I estimate daily changes in the voting premium, $\Delta\pi_t$, and a t-statistic on these

R.F. Bruner/Journal of Financial Economics 51 (1999) 125–166   131

changes. As in Eq. (1), the estimate of the standard deviation of $\Delta\pi_t$ from day K to day L adjusts for the autocovariance of $\Delta\pi_t$:

$$SD_{KL} = (T*VAR(\Delta\pi_t) + 2(T - 1)\, COVAR(\Delta\pi_t, \Delta\pi_{t-1}))^{1/2}, \qquad (3)$$

where $T = L - K + 1$. VAR and COVAR are estimated from a 202-day hold-out period beginning December 31, 1988 and ending October 10, 1989, just before the first announcement regarding the strategic alliance. The variance and autocovariance of $\Delta\pi_t$ are 0.00035815 and $-$ 0.00000883, respectively.

3. Overview of the episode

3.1. Strategic background

In the early 1990s, three developments seemed to indicate a fundamental shift in competition in the worldwide automobile industry. First, growth in unit demand was slackening, reflecting in part the economic recession that began in North America in 1990 and in Europe in 1992. While cyclicality has always been a fact of life in the automobile industry, many observers feared that this recession revealed the increasing saturation of demand in the mature auto markets of the world. Beginning in the mid-1980s in Europe and the U.S., there was little net growth in the number of automobiles in service. Increasingly, new cars were purchased simply to replace old ones. European economic integration and deregulation narrowed the returns to commercial operators of automotive equipment. This reduced demand for trucks and buses, and sharpened price competition. Profitability in the automotive industry fell sharply between 1989 and 1992.

Second, the industry's capacity utilization was declining. In 1993, capacity utilization in Europe was 66%; worldwide it was 73%. High rates of profitability are ordinarily associated with utilization rates of 80% or higher. The lower utilization reflected automakers' strategies of 'building where one sells'. Thus, manufacturers were opening new plants in the high-growth markets of Latin America and Asia, while refusing to reduce capacity in the mature markets. Lower capacity utilization worldwide contributed to declining profitability.

Third, competition increasingly was being decided on the bases of quality, research breakthroughs,[2] new product cycle times, and new forms of organization. Volume producers exploited 'lean' manufacturing techniques to achieve

---

[2] Between 1979 and 1989, Volvo's annual expenditure on truck research and development (R&D) rose from SEK 300 million to SEK 1250 million. Similarly, for cars, the annual R&D expenditure rose from SEK 600 million to SEK 4300. These increases arose from tightening environmental regulations, and increasing competition, which made product enhancement an important competitive tool.

132   *R.F. Bruner/Journal of Financial Economics 51 (1999) 125–166*

cost and quality advantages. These techniques emphasized the reduction of unnecessary assets and time in the production process, along with continuous improvement in product quality. Successful application of these techniques gave the lean manufacturers cost advantages. For various reasons, smaller manufacturers had been slow to adopt these techniques or resisted adopting them altogether.

In 1993, Maryann Keller, a leading auto industry analyst, published an assessment of the leading automobile manufacturers, concluding that 'these companies and others will increasingly collide with each other . . . . Too many countries [are] employing the same systems and technology to produce an excess of the same kinds of products for markets that are not growing fast enough to accommodate them all' (Keller, 1993, p. 213).

Volvo is a small player in the global automotive industry. With an annual output of around 208,000 cars, it ranked 27th in the world. In comparison, General Motors had a 1993 output of 4.3 million units, Toyota about 3 million; and Ford with about 3 million; Renault's output in 1993 was 1.26 million units (Ward's Automotive Yearbook, 1994, p. 55). Although the firm had enjoyed a niche franchise in the market based on safety and engineering, other manufacturers (notably Toyota and Chrysler) were making inroads to this segment. Volvo's car sales were heavily concentrated in Scandinavia, the United Kingdom, and the United States. In trucks and buses, Volvo ranked number two in the world on the basis of a volume of 33,191 units.

Gyllenhammar argued that Volvo was strategically vulnerable and needed a sizable partner with whom it could obtain advantageous purchasing arrangements, over whose volume of output it could amortize rising new product development costs, and whose deeper financial pockets could sustain Volvo through a moderately severe recession such as it had experienced in 1992. Although Volvo's CEO never discussed other strategic alternatives, he probably faced at least two possibilities:

- *Exiting the automobile business.* The firm could have concentrated its resources on the profitable trucks segment, where it was a leader, and discontinued the cars business. It is not clear whether the two segments could have been separated or whether trucks would have been viable without cars. Gyllenhammar believed that the Volvo brand-name in cars was valuable and that it was a serious asset for use in a potential alliance or merger. Moreover, exiting that business would signify a retreat and reduction in the scale of the firm. He appealed to Swedish national pride in arguing that the Volvo marque should be saved.
- *Forming a network of smaller, highly focused alliances.* Instead of cutting a large and comprehensive deal with one partner, Volvo could have remained independent and sought to tailor alliances around specific needs. New

R.F. Bruner/Journal of Financial Economics 51 (1999) 125–166   133

product development could have been financed by selling of non-automotive assets. In essence, this is Volvo's strategy in the mid-1990s. Gyllenhammar showed a proclivity toward large and dramatic deals and had been the architect of Volvo's conglomerate diversification. A strategy based on smaller, focused alliances would have required a major redirection of Gyllenhammar's style and strategy.

Volvo's predicament suggested that some strategic initiative would be necessary, if not immediately, then over the medium term. However there is relatively little to suggest that a single, comprehensive partnership necessarily dominated other alternatives.

3.2. The alliance that predated the merger proposal

Volvo and Renault had a relatively long history of association, beginning with a components swap agreement in 1971, and deepening with Renault's purchase of a minority equity interest in Volvo in 1980. Renault sold those shares at the time of its near-bankruptcy in 1985. With the installation of new Renault management in 1986, Pehr Gyllenhammar offered to acquire Renault's truck-manufacturing business. Renault's CEO, Raymond Lévy, demurred at the time, saying that, as a new executive, he wanted to settle into his new job before deciding on any such proposals. The two CEOs resumed discussions in earnest in the fall of 1989. In an interview, Raymond Lévy told me that initially the CEOs explored the concept of a cross-border merger along the lines of Royal Dutch and Shell. For political reasons, a merger was not an option then. The possibility of a merger, however, appears to have colored the thinking of managers in both companies as they implemented the strategic alliance. In January 1990, Gyllenhammar and Lévy announced a letter of intent for a 'joint venture'. The details of this association did not emerge until September 1990, when it became apparent that this was to be a far-ranging strategic alliance.

The alliance agreement was a complex engagement of the two firms–indeed, Lévy called it a 'marriage'. Fig. 2 gives a diagram of the cross-shareholdings: not only would each ally own a minority interest in the other ally, but each would own a large minority interest in the other's auto and truck manufacturing units. Renault purchased 8.8% of AB Volvo, 25% of Volvo's automobile business, and 45% of Volvo's truck business. Volvo purchased a 20% interest in Renault S.A. and a 45% interest in Renault's truck business. Shortly after the merger announcement, Renault increased its equity interest to 10%. Its interests in Volvo's auto and truck businesses were unchanged from 1990. At the time of the merger proposal, Renault was Volvo's single largest equityholder. The CEOs argued that the direct stakes in each other's manufacturing units would align the firms with each other's fortunes and promote industrial cooperation. Not indicated in

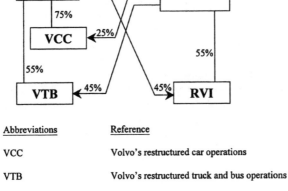

Abbreviations	Reference
VCC	Volvo's restructured car operations
VTB	Volvo's restructured truck and bus operations
Renault SA	Parent company of the Renault Group, following conversion to a capital stock company
RVI	Renault Véhicules Industriels SA

*Renault had acquired 8.24% of Volvo's shares and 10% of the votes.

Fig. 2. Structure of strategic alliance and cross-shareholdings of Volvo and Renault as of September, 1993. This figure gives the cross-shareholdings between Volvo and Renault and their subsidiaries. A cross-shareholding is indicated by an arrow (←) that emanates from the investor to the investee. Ownership of a subsidiary is indicated by a simple line (i.e., with no arrow). The percentages on the lines and arrows indicate the portion of total shares owned by the investor in the investee. For instance, the top-most arrow shows that Renault S.A. owns 8% of AB Volvo's shares. (AB Volvo, 1990 and 1993b, p. 40)

the diagram was a complex poison pill provision which would make it costly[3] for either party to seek to unwind the alliance. The exact terms of the provision have not been disclosed publicly, so it is not possible to know whether the size of the payment was to reflect a recovery of costs and investments, or whether the payment was simply an arbitrary penalty to the departing firm. In toto, this agreement constituted a significant escalation of commitment between the two firms and dedicated them to the path of intimate industrial cooperation. Commitment escalated again in 1993 when the two firms proposed to merge. This pattern bears some similarities to the escalation of commitment described in Lys

---

[3] At the conclusion of this episode, Volvo paid Renault SEK 5.2 billion under the terms of the poison pill provision.

R.F. Bruner/Journal of Financial Economics 51 (1999) 125–166   135

and Vincent's (1995) study of the destruction of value in ATT's acquisition of NCR.

The alliance between Volvo and Renault sought to exploit economies of scale. Volvo estimated that the undiscounted value of economies available through the alliance would amount to SEK 30 billion between 1994 and 2000. With joint purchasing power of FF 200 billion per year, the two firms looked forward to exploiting purchasing economies. They also contemplated developing a range of new car models off of a common platform. Volvo had spent SEK 7 billion and taken 8 years to introduce the Model 850; as a comparatively tiny automobile manufacturer, it could not afford to introduce new models with any regularity. Finally, it was believed that Renault's truck operation would benefit from association with Volvo, the second-ranked heavy truck manufacturer in the world.

The firms consummated the alliance with cross-acquisition of shares in January 1991. Over the next two years their endeavor showed modest success. Although slow to gain momentum, purchasing benefits could be foreseen more clearly by 1993. By most accounts, however, the joint automobile project and rationalization of truck manufacturing were stalling. Interviewees point to many causes, including French protectionism, Swedish-French cultural conflicts, a ponderous alliance bureaucracy of 21 committees, and distant senior leaders. Worse, Volvo's principal market, North America, slid into recession in late 1991, prompting one of the worst declines in reported financial performance in the firm's history.

In general, events surrounding the founding of the strategic alliance (see Table 1, line 4) are associated with significant positive excess returns of 20.27% ($t = 8.78$) for 'A' shares and 11.27% ($t = 4.27$) for 'B' shares. These results are due mainly to returns at two events, October 12, 1989, when newspapers published unconfirmed reports of alliance negotiations (8.54% and $t = 6.47$ for 'A' shares; 4.21%, $t = 2.77$ for 'B' shares) and February 23, 1990, when the companies announced the signing of a letter of intent to negotiate a strategic alliance (9.96% and $t = 7.72$ for 'A' shares; and 7.50% and $t = 4.97$ for 'B' shares).

The actual implementation of the alliance is associated with negative returns. Across all the events during the implementation of the strategic alliance (line 11, Table 1), abnormal returns are − 5.83% ($t = − 1.94$) for the 'A' shares and − 7.79% ($t = − 2.28$) for the 'B' shares. The returns on November 8, 1990 (line 7), when Renault announced its first purchase of Volvo shares; are especially noteworthy: the returns to the 'A' shares are significantly negative, − 4.23% ($t = − 3.22$).

Volvo's voting premium had been in the high teens during the hold-out period in 1988 and 1989, consistent with Rydqvist's finding of an average voting premium in Swedish dual-class shares of 15%. The voting premium stood at 36.99% on September 27, 1990 when Volvo announced the details of the

Table 1
Abnormal returns related to the alliance and proposed merger of Volvo and Renault

Line number	Event date	Volvo A Shares		Volvo B Shares		$L - K + 1$	Event description
		Abnormal return	t-statistic	Abnormal return	t-statistic		
Events leading to implementation of strategic alliance							
1	12 Oct. 1989	8.54%	6.47	4.21%	2.77	2	News report that Volvo and Renault are discussing a combination of their automotive businesses.
2	19 Oct. 1989	1.77%	1.40	−0.44%	−0.28	2	Report that both firms confirm negotiations to found a joint venture.
3	23 Feb. 1990	9.96%	7.72	7.50%	4.97	2	Company announcement: of letter of intent for strategic alliance.
4		20.27%	8.78	11.27%	4.27	6	Cumulative abnormal returns, only specific events in this period.
5		3.86%	0.25	−18.15%	−1.06	251	Cumulative abnormal returns, all trading days 10/11/89 to 9/25/90.
Events during implementation of alliance but before merger discussions							
6	27. Sep. 1990	−0.72%	−0.43	−2.38%	−1.58	2	Company announcement: detailed agreement to implement letter of intent.
7	8 Nov. 1990	−4.23%	−3.22	−2.58%	−1.71	2	Company announcement: Renault has acquired 6.2% of Volvo votes and 4.23% of Volvo capital.
8	9 Jan. 1991	−1.54%	−1.19	0.90%	0.60	2	Company announcement: Renault has increased holdings to 6.78% of Volvo votes and 5.7% of Volvo capital.
9	18 Jan. 1991	1.94%	1.50	−2.45%	−1.63	2	Company announcement: alliance is implemented with exchange of shares in operating units.
10	29 Aug. 1991	−1.28%	−0.99	−1.28%	−0.85	2	Company announcement: Renault has increased holdings to 7.52% of votes and 6.62% of capital.

continued overleaf

No.	Date					N	Event
11		−5.83%	−1.94	−7.79%	−2.28	10	Cumulative abnormal returns, only specific events in this period.
12		8.46%	0.43	37.61%	1.69	421	Cumulative abnormal returns, all trading days 9/26/90 to 5/7/92.
Events during merger negotiation period							
13	8 May 1992	4.10%	3.17	2.95%	1.94	2	Report that Volvo and Renault agree to merger, but political hurdles prevent implementation.
14	14 June 1992	11.74%	9.27	14.07%	9.09	2	Report that French Minister encourages merger.
15	4 June 1993	4.70%	3.59	4.72%	3.09	2	Report that French Minister of industry supports merger.
16	18 June 1993	0.87%	0.68	0.39%	0.26	2	Report that Volvo and Renault discuss merger terms.
17	8 July 1993	1.80%	1.39	1.57%	1.04	2	Report that French official says merger will be announced before August.
18	26 Aug. 1993	3.98%	3.07	4.22%	2.76	2	Report that Volvo and Renault are near to announcing merger terms.
19		27.19%	8.27	27.92%	7.45	12	Cumulative abnormal returns, all specific events in this period.
20		23.21%	7.74	23.70%	6.93	10	Cumulative abnormal returns, specific events in this period.
21		−4.87%	−0.27	−7.48%	−0.37	347	Cumulative abnormal returns, all trading days 5/8/92 to 9/6/93.
Events from announcement to withdrawal of merger terms							
22	7 Sept. 1993	−6.04%	−4.72	−6.64%	−4.46	2	Report of announcement of merger terms.
23	14 Sep. 1993	−3.03%	−2.35	−2.58%	−1.70	2	Report of appointments of managers to run RVA.
24	22 Sep. 1993	−1.33%	−1.02	−0.61%	−0.40	2	Company announcements: Renault has increased Volvo holdings to 9.98% of votes and 8.27% of capital.
25	23 Sep. 1993	3.58%	2.76	3.84%	2.52	2	Announcement that the fourth Found will vote 'yes' unless there is no new information.
26	7 Oct. 1993	−2.45%	−1.90	−2.45%	−1.62	2	Report of a 'stormy' Volvo board meeting in London-terms of golden share are clarified to directors. Small Shareholders Association opposes merger.

Table 1. Continued.

Line number	Event date	Volvo A Shares		Volvo B Shares		$L - K + 1$	Event description
		Abnormal return	t-statistic	Abnormal return	t-statistic		
27	12 Oct. 1993	−5.18%	−4.06	−5.20%	−3.48	2	Report that Small Shareholders Association calls for 2/3 votes on merger.
28	12–13 Oct. 1993	−3.73%	−2.90	−3.97%	−2.64	2	Volvo meets with 10 largest institutional investors, and issues press release clarifying golden share and privatization.
29	26 Oct. 1993	4.27%	3.28	4.77%	3.13	2	Merger prospectus is distributed-it contains no additional explanation of synergies or merger terms. Two unions issue press release opposing merger. Two influential newspapers publish editorials against merger.
30	28 Oct. 1993	5.43%	4.15	4.50%	2.96	2	Report that the 92–94 Fund opposes merger. Skandia insurance delays decision. Qviberg and Hagstromer call for Gyllenhammar's resignation.
31	29 Oct. 1993	1.60%	1.24	−0.45%	−0.29	2	Announcement that SPP Insurance opposes merger.
32	2 Nov. 1993	−1.83%	−1.42	−2.10%	−1.38	2	Report that Volvo delays shareholder meeting to Dec. 7.
33	4 Nov. 1993	3.00%	2.32	2.30%	1.53	2	Volvo's managers give unauthorized release of 9-month profits in trucks.
34	10 Nov. 1993	0.92%	0.71	0.68%	0.45	2	Report that Wasa Forsakring Fund will vote 'no' Soren Gyll acknowledges strong shareholder opposition to the deal.
35	11 Nov. 1993	0.23%	0.18	−0.24%	−0.16	2	Report that Volvo reopens merger negotiations with France.
36	12 Nov. 1993	−1.21%	−0.93	−1.45%	−0.96	2	Report that, without merger, Volvo will require a large rights offering of equity. Skandia Insurance threatens to vote 'no'.

continued overleaf

37	18 Nov. 1993	4.47%	3.43	1.84%	1.21	2	Report that the Swedish prime minister doubts that shareholders will approve the merger. Press release of 9-month profits for entire company.
38	25 Nov. 1993	-2.10%	-1.62	-0.91%	-0.60	2	Report that the 10 largest institutional investors visit Renault in Paris. The Fifth Fund opposes merger.
39	26 Nov. 1993	-2.92%	-2.27	-0.78%	-0.51	2	Report that the Fourth Fund and the Folksam Fund support merger.
40	29 Nov. 1993	-0.52%	-0.40	-2.24%	-1.48	2	Report that Foreningsbanken opposes merger.
41	30 Nov. 1993	4.45%	3.43	2.51%	1.73	2	Report that Skandia Insurance opposes merger.
42	2 Dec. 1993	7.37%	5.60	7.32%	4.76	2	Report that S-E Banken opposes merger and that the Fourth Fund will reconsider support.
43	3 Dec. 1993	1.14%	0.98	-0.21%	-0.08	2	Report that the Volvo board has withdrawn merger proposal; Gyllenhammar and four directors resign.
44		-0.03%	0.00	-2.08%	-0.32	36	Cumulative abnormal returns, all specific events in this period.
45		5.52%	0.67	4.25%	0.46	74	Cumulative abnormal returns, all trading days 9/7/93 to 12/19/93.
Period 1: Announcement of merger to publication of proxy, 26 Oct.							
46		-15.02%	-4.38	-17.62%	-4.52	13	Cumulative abnormal returns, all specific events in this period.
47		-22.81%	-4.04	-23.11%	-3.61	35	Cumulative abnormal returns, all trading days 9/7/93 to 10/25/93.
Period 2: Publication of proxy to withdrawal of proposal							
48		10.73%	2.35	10.76%	2.07	23	Cumulative abnormal returns, all specific events in this period.
49		28.33%	4.75	27.36%	4.05	39	Cumulative abnormal returns, all trading days 10/26/93 to 12/19/93.
Cumulative abnormal returns partitioned by institutional support or opposition							
50		0.66%	0.35	3.06%	1.42	4	All reports of institutional support.
51		14.85%	4.51	11.40%	3.04	12	All reports of institutional opposition.

Table 1. Continued.

Line number	Event date	Volvo A Shares		Volvo B Shares		L − K + 1	Event description
		Abnormal return	t-statistic	Abnormal return	t-statistic		
Events associated with unwinding the alliance and redirection of the firm							
52	20 Dec. 1993	2.76%	2.13	3.62%	2.38	2	Announcement that institutions representing 40% of votes propose a new board of directors.
53	19 Jan. 1994	−2.39%	−1.83	−1.79%	−1.18	2	Report that Volvo will focus on automotive business and sell unrelated assets.
54	20 Jan. 1994	−3.38%	−2.62	−2.94%	−1.96	2	Report of special shareholders meeting: new board elected.
55	29 Jan. 1994	3.71%	2.85	3.57%	2.35	2	Report that Volvo and Renault will dismantle joint purchasing arrangement.
56	2 Feb. 1994	−0.75%	−0.55	−0.33%	−0.20	2	Company announcement that Renault has reduced holdings to 8.76% of votes and 3.45% of capital.
57	11 Feb. 1994	−0.12%	−0.08	0.18%	0.12	2	Report that Volvo sells an investment unrelated to autos.
58	17 Feb. 1994	0.89%	0.69	−0.13%	−0.09	2	Company announcement that Volvo and Renault agree to terminate alliance.
59	11 Mar. 1994	0.06%	0.05	−1.22%	−0.81	2	Report that Volvo will pay SKR 5.2 bn under terms of poison pill to unwind alliance.
60	25 Mar. 1994	0.18%	0.14	0.02%	0.01	2	Report that Volvo sells investment unrelated to autos.
61	14 Sep. 1994	−0.28%	−0.20	−0.98%	−0.65	2	Report that France will partially privatize Renault. Volvo will sell its 3% stake in Volvo Trucks.
62	19 Oct. 1994	−0.84	−0.64	−0.14%	−0.09	2	Report that the privatization sale is implemented.
63		3.10%	0.71	2.79%	0.56	21	Cumulative abnormal returns, all specific events in the period.
64		23.52%	1.67	25.86%	1.62	218	Cumulative abnormal returns, all trading days in this period, 12/20/93 to 10/19/94.

continued overleaf

Summary of entire period: 12 Oct. 1989 to 19 Oct. 1994

No.						Description
65	24.43%	2.88	20.83%	2.16	79	Cumulative abnormal returns, all specific events in the entire episode.
66	31.75%	0.92	38.77%	0.99	1310	Cumulative abnormal returns, all trading days in the entire episode.
						Cumulative abnormal returns associated with announcements of changes in Renault shareholdings in Volvo
67	−6.44%	−2.15	−6.01%	−1.76	10	Increases in holdings by Renault.
68	−1.03%	−0.55	−1.31%	−0.61	4	Decreases in holdings by Renault.
						Cumulative abnormal returns associated with announcements about alliance or merger
69	43.02%	13.08	37.67%	10.06	12	Announcements about concept of alliance or merger.
70	−14.03%	−4.27	−20.48%	−5.47	12	Announcements about specific terms of alliance or merger.
						Cumulative abnormal returns associated with announcements about dissolution
71	6.47%	3.46	7.18%	3.34	4	Divorcing Renault.
72	−6.01%	−2.41	−3.58%	−1.25	7	New strategy: independence and focus on auto business.

strategic alliance agreement. It peaked at 46.55% on November 8, 1990, when Renault announced its first acquisition of Volvo shares. The voting premium declined to 2.27% by January 21, 1991 the day after Renault and Volvo exchanged share interests in their operating units. The -34.72% decline in the voting premium over the 83 trading days is significant ($t = -2.06$). Of this change, a decline of -7.39% is associated with two specific events, November 8 and January 9, when Renault announced increases in Volvo shareholdings. This equates to a loss of SEK -2.6 billion of equity value for the 'A' shares, a decline in value of about 25% for the holders of those shares. The loss is estimated as the value of the change in the voting premium divided by the market value of 'A' shares ex ante. The value of the change in voting premium equals -34.72%, times the price of the 'B' share at September 27, 1990, SEK 292, times the number of 'A' shares outstanding at September 27, 25.3 million. The market value of all 'A' shares outstanding equals the 'A' share price, SEK 400, times the number of shares, 25.3 million, or SEK 10.12 billion. This loss in the premium helped motivate investor activism in the autumn of 1993.

The significant drop in the voting premium is consistent with a decline in the probability of a takeover for Volvo. The alliance entailed substantial blocking minority interests in the respective firms and their operating units, as well as a sizable poison pill. As Megginson (1990) and Rydqvist (1992b) suggest, the voting premium is a function of the probability of takeover, which the changes in ownership almost certainly affected.

3.3. The merger proposal and its motives

Against this backdrop, Gyllenhammar and Louis Schweitzer (appointed CEO of Renault upon Lévy's retirement in 1992) secretly began negotiating a merger of the two businesses in the fall of 1992. Unfortunately, the French Socialist Party, which was in power at the time, would not consider privatization of the country's largest state-owned enterprise. When the conservatives came to power in the elections of March 1993, negotiations between the two firms reopened. These talks culminated in the merger proposal announced on September 6, 1993.

During the negotiation period, abnormal returns at announcements about a potential merger are uniformly positive. For instance, the sum of announcement returns during this period (Table 1, line 19) is 27.19% ($t = 8.27$) for the 'A' shares and 27.92% ($t = 7.45$) for the 'B' shares. The report on August 27 of surprisingly strong second-quarter earnings for Volvo, however, possibly confounded the return on August 26. The strong earnings are associated with the recovery of demand in the North American auto market in the spring of 1993. Excluding the August 26 event return gives (line 20) a return of 23.21% ($t = 7.74$) for the 'A' shares and 23.70% ($t = 6.93$) for the 'B' shares. Adjusting for the confounding event does not change the conclusion that shareholder returns associated with the merger negotiation are positive.

The Volvo merger prospectus pointed to three main reasons for the merger: (a) increasing competitive advantages, (b) improving financial strength and the ability to meet new capital requirements (estimated in Volvo's case to amount to between SEK 5 and 8 billion), and (c) exploiting operating efficiencies in procurement, research and development, and production. Gyllenhammar projected these merger economies to amount to SEK 16.4 billion on an undiscounted basis between 1994 and 2000, over and above those expected from the alliance alone (see AB Volvo 1993b,c).

The proposed governance of the new firm included three important elements. First, the new entity, Renault–Volvo Automotive (RVA), would be directed by a management board under the guidance of a supervisory board. The supervisory board would have extended powers and would be called upon to decide major financial issues. Pehr Gyllenhammar, Volvo's executive chairman, would be nominated chairman of RVA's supervisory board. The management board would have overall management responsibility for the running of Renault–Volvo RVA and would report periodically to the supervisory board. The French government would nominate the chairman of the management board and the CEO of RVA, the likely nominee was Louis Schweitzer, CEO of Renault.

Second, the French state would own 65% of RVA, and Volvo 35%. AB Volvo would directly own 17.85% of RVA's shares. The French government would directly own 47.15% of the shares, including the 0.79% share attributable to Renault employees who had been issued non-voting share certificates. A holding company, RVC, would own 35% of RVA. Renault S.A. (a holding company organized by the French government) would in turn own 51% of RVC, and AB Volvo would own 49%. Volvo's 35% holding is the sum of the direct holding, 17.85%, and the indirect holding through RVC (49% times 35%). Fig. 3 shows the structure of ownership interests. The complexity of this structure is impressive, and, as my interviews revealed, contributed to the difficulty in understanding the deal. RVC would not have an operational role; its purpose was to 'secure the fundamental interests of its shareholders and ensure the stability of their investment in Renault–Volvo RVA. It will be called upon to decide on major issues ... such as capital increases' (AB Volvo, 1993a, p. 3). The shareholder's agreement governing RVC would be valid for 25 years, although each side would have the right to terminate the agreement after the eighth year. The French government and AB Volvo agreed not to sell or pledge their respective holdings in RVC until the privatization of Renault-Volvo RVA. Each also agreed to give the other a right of first refusal on the sale of shares, and not to sell shares to a competitor. Gyllenhammar told me that RVC would have given AB Volvo a stronger voice in the control of RVA, and that a similar holding company structure had been used in other major cross-border mergers, such as the merger of Asea and Brown-Boveri. Ultimately, however, RVC left

144   *R.F. Bruner/Journal of Financial Economics 51 (1999) 125–166*

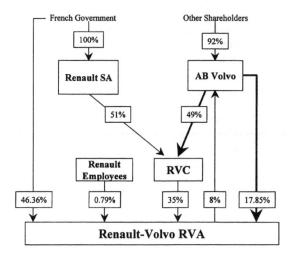

Fig. 3. Proposed structure of ownership of Rnault-Volvo RVA following merger of the automotive business. The projected shareholdings in the operating company, Reanult Volvo RVA, and in the holding company, RVC, after the proposed transation is completed. A shareholding is indicated by an arrow (←) that emanates from the investor to the investee. The percentage on the arrows indicate the portion of total shares owned by the investor in the investee. For instance, the right most arrow shows that AB Volvo would own 17.85% of RVA's shares directly. (AB Volvo, 1993a, p. 3.)

the balance of control unchanged, since France would retain a majority of votes on the RVC board.

Third, the French government announced that it intended to privatize Renault–Volvo RVA in 1994, and that it would sell its shares principally to a *noyau dur* (or 'hard core') of investors. Observers believed that leading candidates for this hard core included Matra-Hachette (a French industrial firm and co-producer with Renault of the *Espace* minivan) and French state-owned banks and insurance companies. The French government would retain an unusual right, an *action specifique* (popularly called a 'golden share') that reserved for the government the ability to prevent an investor from acquiring (or voting) more than a 17.85% direct interest in RVA.[4] Like a poison pill or control share antitakeover amendment, the golden share could change the voting power of certain (i.e., powerful) shareholders. The French had discretion in using the golden share, however, as the limitation was not automatic. Golden shares are now a common feature in the privatization of state-owned enterprises.

---

[4] Later, in a letter to the Swedish prime minister, the French prime minister stated that the 'golden share' would not be used against Volvo as long as Volvo's participation in Renault–Volvo RVA did not exceed a total of 35%. This letter appeared to relax the original golden-share limitation.

R.F. Bruner/Journal of Financial Economics 51 (1999) 125–166   145

Their origin is difficult to ascertain, although many observers cite the wave of British privatizations in the 1980s as the first in Europe to include golden shares. This right would last indefinitely.

In summary, the merger proposal offered Volvo's shareholders participation in the benefits of potential new synergies in exchange for a short position in a bundle of control options (i.e., the golden share, a privatization option concerning the timing and magnitude of any public offering of RVA shares, as well as a *noyau dur* option concerning the targeted purchasers of any shares offered). Collectively, these options granted the French state significant rights to determine RVA's equity clientele and its voting. By virtue of these control options, the merger would escalate the commitment between Volvo's investors and the French government.

At the time of the merger announcement, 19.1% of Volvo's votes were presumed to support the merger. The 'committed' camp included Renault, which owned 10% of Volvo's votes, and two investment companies that had sizable cross-shareholdings with Volvo. Gyllenhammar's task was to increase the supporting coalition to over 50%. Table 2 shows that the 17 largest investors in Volvo held 65.4% of the votes. Of this total, 46.3% were held by 14 uncommitted groups. The remainder, 34.6%, was relatively widely dispersed. Curiously, Gyllenhammar was slow to approach the institutional investors for their support, and many of the meetings that ultimately did occur happened at the initiative of the institutions. He seemed inclined to let the deal speak for itself, rather than to be an advocate. Many interviewees suggest that this was consistent with Gyllenhammar's leadership style of being a grand strategist and visionary.

3.4. Reaction to the merger proposal

We may divide the period in two from the announcement of the merger terms to their withdrawal by Volvo's board: the first seven weeks of relative quiet information-gathering and growing opposition by institutional investors, and then a five-week period of vociferous opposition by institutions.

3.4.1. The first seven weeks: opposition gathers

Volvo's share prices fell dramatically following the announcement of the merger proposal. Abnormal returns on September 6–7 (Table 1, Line 22) are -6.04% ($t = -4.72$) for the 'A' shares, and -6.64% ($t = -4.46$) for the 'B' shares. Over the following seven weeks, abnormal returns accumulate to -22.81% ($t = -4.04$) for the 'A' shares and -23.11% ($t = -3.61$) for the 'B' shares (see Line 47). This cumulative abnormal return represents a decline in equity value of about SEK 8.6 billion (US$ 1.1 billion). I estimate the loss by summing the losses for 'A' and 'B' shares. For the 'A' shares, the loss is estimated as the product of the number of shares (25.3 million), the stock price per share (SEK 485), and cumulative abnormal return (-22.81%), or SEK -2.799

Table 2
Voting strength in AB Volvo represented by major groups on September 6, 1993

Institution	Percent votes owned
Major investors committed to the merger as of Sept. 6, 1993	
Renault S.A.	10.0
Investment AB Cardo, an investment company	4.8
Protorp Förvaltnings AB, an investment company	4.3
Subtotal, Committed to Merger on Sept. 6, 1993	19.1
Major investors uncommitted as of Sept. 6, 1993	
Fourth Fund, a pension fund	7.5
Skandinaviska Enskilda Banken, a bank	5.8
Svenska Handelsbanken, a bank	5.0
SPP Insurance, an insurance company	4.5
Skandia Insurance, an insurance company	3.7
Folksam Fund, a pension fund	3.6
Parcitas Investments SA, an investment company	3.3
Skandinaviska Banken pension fund	2.6
92–94 Fund, a pension fund	2.5
AMF Pensionsförsäkringar AB, a pension fund	2.5
Nordbanken, a bank	1.9
Trygg-Hansa, an insurance company	1.4
Fifth Fund, a pension fund	1.3
Foreningsbanken, a bank	0.7
Subtotal, Uncommitted on Sept. 6, 1993	46.3
Grand total, committed and uncommitted blocks	65.4

Sources: AB Volvo (1992, 1993d), interviews; newspaper accounts.

billion. For the 'B' shares, the loss is the product of 52.3 million shares, a price of SEK 483, and a cumulative abnormal return of − 23.11%, or SEK − 5,838 billion. The conversion to U.S. dollars is at the exchange rate of 7.83, prevailing on September 6, 1993.

A large portion of this wealth destruction is associated with the release of detailed information about the merger terms. Information was released at four events: the announcement day, Sept. 6, (an abnormal return of − 6.04%, Line 22), appointment of specific managers to run RVA (− 3.03%, Line 23), the clarification of the golden share terms to Volvo's board[5] (− 2.45%, Line 26),

---

[5] Though nominally a private gathering, Sundqvist (1994) reports that the substance of the Volvo board meeting in London on October 6, 1993 leaked quickly to the financial community and set a confrontational tone for the meeting with institutional investors on October 12. As Sundqvist describes it, the board meeting broke into an 'uproar' when Gyllenhammar read to the directors a letter from the French Minister of Industry outlining the terms of the golden share. These detailed terms were not explained to the directors in early September when they were asked to approve the deal.

R.F. Bruner/Journal of Financial Economics 51 (1999) 125–166   147

and a press release containing further clarification of the golden share and privatization intentions of the French (− 3.73%, Line 28). These aggregate to − 15.25%, or about three-quarters of the cumulative abnormal return over the seven weeks following the announcement. The negative abnormal returns at the release of new information about the terms of merger is consistent with investors' growing clarity about the value transfer implicit in the French control options, and with their incredulity at the projected synergies. The Appendix presents an analysis that suggests that if one accepts Gyllenhammar's forecast of synergies, the control options were worth at least SEK 3.12 billion, or 8.3% of AB Volvo's market value of equity just before the merger announcement.

Other parties fanned the growing dissent of the institutional investors. Two Swedish tabloids immediately condemned the merger, largely on nationalistic grounds. The Swedish Small Stockholders Association, a shareholder advocacy group roughly similar to the United Shareholders Association in the U.S., requested information and met with Volvo's management twice following the merger announcement. The Association voiced opposition to the merger on October 7, and solicited proxies from its members. Several publications held that the Swedish Small Shareholders' Association accounted for 7–10% of Volvo's votes, but Lars-Erik Forsgårdh states that in the final event, the Association could muster proxies for only 2% of the votes. It also threatened to sue Volvo's directors. The Association argued that the bylaws of AB Volvo dictated that the firm should be primarily engaged in the automotive industry, and that changes in the bylaws required a two-thirds majority vote of shareholders. Volvo retained a prominent attorney who opined that the merger would require only a simple majority for approval. The Association replied that it would sue the directors to invalidate any simple majority approval of the merger. In late November, the opposition coalition accounted explicitly for about one-third of Volvo's votes. This eliminated any chance for a clear larger-than-two-thirds majority and ensured that the directors would have to deal with a lawsuit. Volvo's blue-collar union expressed support for the merger, believing that the deal would preserve their jobs and possibly seeing some benefit in allying with the Confederation Générale du Travail, Renault's communist-led trade union, but this support for the deal repelled, rather than attracted, the institutional investors. Volvo's white-collar union, representing 5000 employees, voiced opposition, as did the union of Volvo's engineers, representing 900 employees. Three former senior executives of Volvo wrote newspaper columns opposing the deal. Until the end of October, however Volvo's institutional investors offered no public comments.

In mid-October, Swedish investors witnessed the spectacle of a management coup at Air France, another French state-owned enterprise. The CEO, Bernard Attali, had sought to cut wages and jobs and change work rules at France's worst-performing state ward. The unions struck and began to pressure the government to sack Attali. Swedish investors viewed this confrontation as an acid test of the French government's resolve to run state enterprises in a businesslike fashion, a crucial condition for them to realize acceptable returns from RVA. When Attali was fired on October 16, investors' doubts about the French connection gained momentum.

3.4.2. The final five weeks: active opposition by institutional investors

The institutional investors remained silent until they saw the formal merger prospectus, published on October 26. Several institutional investors had hoped that the prospectus would present a detailed justification for the projected merger synergies, and that it would value Renault and Volvo's automotive assets as a foundation for justifying the share exchange ratio in the merger. The prospectus gave no information beyond what was already in the public domain, however, and the institutions would contain their impatience with the merger no longer.

Within three days, two institutions, the 92–94 Fund (2.5% of Volvo's votes) and SPP Insurance (4.5%), declared their opposition to the deal, and a third, Skandia Insurance indicated that it would delay its decision. Two of Stockholm's leading investment managers, Mats Qviberg and Sven Hagstromer, published a newspaper article condemning the deal and calling for Gyllenhammar's resignation. They wrote, 'We don't like the proposed Renault agreement, and we don't like the way Volvo has been abused over the years' (quoted in Bartal and Hardin, 1993). Reeling from the tide of institutional opposition, Gyllenhammar agreed to postpone the shareholder meeting by one month in order to give the institutions added information and time for them to assess it.

On November 4, Volvo's operating managers, at a golf outing in Marbella, Spain, told journalists that nine-month profits in Volvo's truck segment would be up sharply, indicating a strong recovery from a year earlier. This was confirmed at the formal release of nine-month figures on November 18. These revelations triggered a fresh round of accusations from the institutions that the merger had been negotiated when Volvo was at a cyclical low in cash flows and that now, in the face of a buoyant recovery, the automotive business was being given away. Abnormal returns on the 'A' shares of 3.00% and 4.47% at both dates (Table 1, Lines 33 and 37) are significant. More importantly, the buoyant reports turned the merger debate toward the central issue of valuation. One commentator wrote:

> Volvo and Renault have refused to break down the values placed on their respective assets, or give detailed performance forecasts, leaving many Swedes suspicious that Volvo, once again profitable, will in effect be milked by Renault which is suffering falling profits. (Carnegy, 1993a).

R.F. Bruner/Journal of Financial Economics 51 (1999) 125–166   149

An institutional investor was quoted as saying,

> Renault is basically making a bid for Volvo's cars and trucks and paying with its shares. As Volvo shareholders, we cannot assess what those Renault shares are worth until Renault has a market value. (quoted in Carnegy and Ridding, 1993).

Lars-Erik Forsgårdh, president of the Swedish Small Shareholders Association said, 'The fundamental point is that Volvo has not succeeded in showing that this deal is good for its shareholders'. (quoted in Brown-Humes, 1993).

In mid-November, Volvo undertook two efforts to strengthen institutional support for the merger. First, Volvo tried to reopen its merger negotiations with France, only to be rejected. The French minister of industry did issue a letter guaranteeing that the government would not exercise its golden share against Volvo as long as Volvo's equity interest in RVA did not exceed 35%. This letter was unsatisfactory to the institutions. Second, Volvo said that the company would initiate a large (SEK 5 billion) rights offering if the merger was not approved. The institutions viewed this as an attempt to intimidate them, as it ignored the possibility of selling non-automotive assets to finance the car and truck segments.

Two more funds expressed their opposition on November 24 and 29, and on November 30 Skandia Insurance announced that it would vote against the proposal. Volvo's largest institutional investor, the Fourth Fund, announced that it would vote for the deal. Six days later, however, the Fourth Fund, announced that it would reconsider its previous commitment to vote in favor. The Fourth Fund's board had barely approved its support for the deal, with a vote of 8-to-6, and only after very heavy lobbying by Volvo's blue-collar union representatives on the board.

As Volvo's board meeting approached on December 2, the largest bank in Scandinavia, S-E Banken (SEB) announced that it would vote 'no'. In explaining SEB's opposition, the CEO said,

> The information was not up to the standard we like to have in such an important case as this ... [Also] we are very concerned about the doubts among Volvo's personnel, especially the engineers. If you don't have your employees with you going into a merger like this it will be very damaging. (quoted in Carnegy, 1993b).

In a surprise move on December 2, 25 senior managers informed the board of their opposition to the merger, leaving Pehr Gyllenhammar, Volvo's executive chairman, isolated in his own company. On that date, the board withdrew the proposal; Gyllenhammar and four directors resigned.

The significance of certain institutional announcements in the final days before the board meeting is worth noting. S-E Banken was the largest bank in

150   *R.F. Bruner/Journal of Financial Economics 51 (1999) 125–166*

Scandinavia, on whose board Gyllenhammar served as a director. Skandia Insurance was the largest insurance company in Scandinavia, and a firm with which Gyllenhammar had personal ties. Gyllenhammar's father had been CEO of Skandia, as had Gyllenhammar himself in his early 30s. Gyllenhammar's inability to sway these two 'lead steer'[6] institutions may have signaled to Volvo's board the strong hostility of institutional investors to the deal.

The reaction to the news of the first[7] institutional opposition on 28 October (see Table 1, Line 30) is positive and significant for both classes of shares: 5.43% ($t = 4.15$) for the 'A' shares and 4.5% ($t = 2.96$) for the 'B' shares. None of the other announcements of opposition is significantly positive until those of Skandia Insurance and S-E Banken on 30 November and 2 December (see lines 41 and 42). Skandia's announcement of opposition is associated with an abnormal return on 'A' shares of 4.45% ($t = 3.43$); S-E Banken's announcement is associated with a 7.37% return ($t = 5.60$).

From publication of the proxy statement to the withdrawal of the proposal the period when institutions expressed their 'voice' the returns are significantly positive. The abnormal return on 'A' shares over all trading days is 28.33% ($t = 4.75$) (see Table 1, Line 49); specific events are associated with an abnormal return of 10.73% ($t = 2.35$) (see Table 1, Line 48). Abnormal returns associated with published news of institutional opposition (see Table 1, Line 51) account for 14.85% ($t = 4.51$) for the 'A' shares and 11.40% ($t = 3.04$) for the 'B' shares. Reaction to announcements of institutional support for the merger (Table 1, Line 50) is insignificantly positive, although the only truly definitive statement of support (Table 1, Line 39) is significantly negative, -2.92% ($t = -2.27$) for the 'A' shares. When the Fourth Fund announced on September 23 a preliminary expression of support for the merger, the return was significantly positive 3.58% ($t = 2.76$) (see Table 1, Line 25).

In general, investors' reactions during this period are consistent with the hypothesis that institutional voice is valuable; opposition to the merger terms is, on average, positive. Reaction to news of initial opposition and 'lead steer' opposition is significantly positive; the only expression of definitive support for the merger (Table 1, Line 39) is significantly negative.

It is surprising that the voting premium barely changes during the control contest. The premium rises as high as 3.08% on November 8, 1993 when the Swedish prime minister publicly doubted that the merger would be approved. In

---

[6] In the parlance of Wall Street, a lead steer is an investor that by virtue of special expertise, size, or investment record is a closely-watched opinion leader. See Stern (1989) for a discussion of this concept. S-E-Banken and Skandia Insurance were, respectively, the second and fifth largest independent institutional investors in Volvo.

[7] This study used the conventional definition of an institutional investor as a professional group engaged in fiduciary or proprietary money management. The Swedish Small Shareholders Association, which had expressed its opposition to the merger on October 6, did not fit this definition.

R.F. Bruner/Journal of Financial Economics 51 (1999) 125–166   151

general, however, the voting premium behaves as if there were no control contest, averaging only 1.00% over the entire period. During the period of institutional silence (September 6 to October 25), the voting premium averages 0.51%. Over the period of institutional activism (October 26 to December 19), the premium averages 1.45%.

3.5. Unwinding the alliance, and redirection of the firm

Volvo's share prices recovered dramatically in the weeks following the withdrawal of the merger proposal, nearly doubling by the annual meeting in April 1994. The French government partially privatized Renault in October 1994. Three key actions characterize this period.

First, a coalition of the activist Swedish institutional investors jointly nominated a new board of directors in December 1993 and called for a special shareholders' meeting, which elected them in January 1994. Second, Volvo's management negotiated a dissolution of the strategic alliance with Renault. This reversed the cross-shareholdings in the two firms' operating units. Third, Volvo's management announced a new strategy for the firm that entailed focusing on the automotive industry. Volvo would sell investments in other businesses and use the proceeds to finance the development of new products. In addition, Volvo would remain independent, possibly exploiting small highly-focused alliances but avoiding mergers and complex far-ranging alliances.

During the final period of redirecting the firm, abnormal returns are positive but not significant (see Table 1, Lines 63 and 64). Yet, as line 71 shows, abnormal returns are significantly positive at news of the unwinding of the alliance with Renault (6.47% and $t = 3.46$ for the 'A' shares; and 7.18% and $t = 3.34$ for 'B' shares.) In contrast, abnormal returns are significantly negative at news associated with the new strategy of independence and the focus on automobiles, -6.01% ($t = -2.41$) for 'A' shares (see Table 1, Line 72). The results on these two dates are consistent with hypotheses that the proposed merger with Renault would have destroyed the wealth of Volvo's shareholders, and that the new strategy failed to resolve Volvo's strategic predicament. In other words, neither strategy was economically attractive.

Across the entire six-year period (see Table 1, Lines 69 and 70), Volvo shareholders receive positive and significant returns associated with all news about the *concept* of alliance or merger – for the 'A' shares, the cumulative return is 43.02% ($t = 13.08$). This cumulative result is the aggregate of two-day returns at six events: initial rumors of an alliance (Line 1), announcement of a letter of agreement to be allies (Line 3), the agreement in principle to merge thwarted by politics (Line 13), the support of a French minister for merger (Lines 14 and 15), and the announcement that Volvo and Renault were near to announcing a merger agreement (Line 18). When specific terms of alliance or merger were

152   R.F. Bruner/Journal of Financial Economics 51 (1999) 125–166

announced, however, the reaction of investors was negative: Line 70 shows that the cumulative effect of six events for the 'A' shares was $- 14.03\%$ ($t = -4.27$). The six events are the announcement of the detailed terms of alliance (Line 6), the exchange of shares for the alliance (Line 9), the announcement of merger terms (Line 22), the appointment of managers to run RVA (Line 23), and the clarification of the golden share to directors (Line 26) and to the institutional investors (Line 28).

In short, investors applauded the concept of the alliance and merger but regretted the actual terms. Several interviewees cite this pattern of expectation and disappointment as a recurring feature of Gyllenhammar's relationship with investors.

The voting premium did not change after the control contest. During the entire final period under observation (December 20, 1993 to October 19, 1994), the voting premium does not exceed 3.5%, and averaged only 0.05%.

4. Discussion and conclusions

My study analyzes the governance changes, shareholder returns and voting premiums associated with Volvo's strategic alliance and attempt to merge with Renault. The findings shed light on why firms undertake value-destroying combinations, whether institutional activism is valuable, and why such activism is valuable.

4.1. Why the merger proposal and alliance failed

The interviews and analysis of returns suggest that the merger proposal and alliance failed because of factors with which the literature of financial economics is acquainted: hubris (Roll, 1986) managerial entrenchment (Jensen, 1986; Morck et al., 1988), managerialism (Morck et al., 1990), and the escalation of commitment and endowment effect (Lys and Vincent, 1995).

No interviewee or published source disputes Gyllenhammar's strategic rationale for the alliance or merger. In an industry characterized by scale economies, the small producer will have a cost disadvantage and therefore an incentive to increase size through alliances and mergers. In other words, the merger did not fail for want of a sound strategic motive.

Gyllenhammar himself explained the failure of the merger proposal in behavioral terms: irrationality, Swedish cultural chauvinism, or an envious vendetta against him. In April 1993 the Swedish Small Shareholders Association compelled Gyllenhammar to reveal that his compensation was SEK 9.5 million, revealing that he was the highest-paid executive in Scandinavia at a time when Volvo reported losses and was closing plants. As Dial and Murphy (1995) describe in the case of the restructuring of General Dynamics, CEO

R.F. Bruner/Journal of Financial Economics 51 (1999) 125–166   153

compensation is a lightning-rod for criticism. Gyllenhammar created the impression that he was the victim a 'gigantic power play' by the Wallenberg interests, the only other Swedish industrial group of size and significance comparable to Volvo, which sought to 'cut Volvo down to size' (Carnegy, 1994c). The chairman of Volvo's newly-elected board, Bert-Olaf Svanholm, was an executive with Asea, in which the Wallenberg family is a large minority shareholder, an association which appeared to support Gyllenhammar's claims. Several interviewees, however, discount the significance of this fact. Sundqvist (1994) argues that over time Gyllenhammar had amassed enough enemies in the Swedish business community that he had no base of support with which to confront the opposition. This suggests that the merger failed because of psychology or politics. Yet such an explanation is ultimately unsatisfying, for it sheds little light on the roots of opposition to *this* deal. For instance, if the merger of Renault and Volvo were to have created shareholder value, it seems doubtful that the supposed jealousy and megalomania of Gyllenhammar's opponents would have successfully defeated the proposal.

A counter-assessment, offered by Swedish institutional investors in interviews and by Sundqvist (1994), explains the failure to merge as follows. Volvo's shares materially underperformed the Swedish stock market over the term of Gyllenhammar's leadership (see Fig. 4). Gyllenhammar led the firm into a number of alliances and diversifying acquisitions that failed to deliver the performance

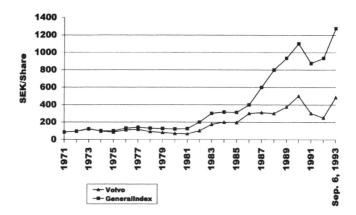

Fig. 4. Share price performance: Volvo vs. Swedish stock market index. This figure gives the time-series of AB Volvo's share prices and the GeneralIndex, the Swedish stock market index, from 1971 (the year of Pehr Gyllenhammar's appointment as CEO of Volvo) to September 6, 1993 (the date of announcement of the merger proposal). For comparability, the market index is pegged at the beginning of the time series to Volvo's share price. Source of data used in this figure: 'PG sitter kvar,' Affarsvärlden, December 8, 1993, page 7 (in Swedish).

improvements investors expected.[8] The strategic alliance with Renault that Gyllenhammar personally crafted was not going well, and institutional investors surmised that otherwise Gyllenhammar would not have advocated merger. In 1993 the merger proposal was a bad deal, presented badly: the control provisions were confusing, and the projected synergies were not justified. Eventually it was learned that the synergies were estimated not by Volvo's staff, but by Credit Suisse First Boston and Booz Allen and Hamilton, who were advising Gyllenhammar. Rather than lending the credibility of objective outside advisers, this revelation served to heighten suspicions that Gyllenhammar was manipulating his investors and employees. Eventually, the investors discounted the merger synergies and concluded that the control rights represented an expropriation of Volvo equity value by the French state. From this perspective, the deal failed on its economics.

An internal study (reported in Carnegy, 1994b) by Volvo supports this view. It claims that the golden share and uncertainty about the privatization of Renault were the key drivers of the collapse of the merger proposal. Reflecting on the predicted synergies, the author of the study, Arne Wittlov, is quoted as saying, 'People quite simply did not believe in the benefits of co-operation'.

The centerpiece of the counter-assessment is *managerial entrenchment*. Morck, Shleifer, and Vishny (1988, p. 293) explain: 'When managers hold little equity in

---

[8] It is beyond the scope of this study to examine the profitability of Gyllenhammar's individual alliances and acquisitions predating Volvo-Renault. These included eight major transactions of which five represented efforts to diversify out of the automobile industry:

- Attempted merger with Saab-Scania, Sweden's other major car manufacturer. Plans for merger were announced in May 1977 but abandoned in August when opposition to the merger developed.
- Attempted investment in the Norwegian oil industry. In August 1977 Gyllenhammar initiated discussions with Norway's prime minister to exchange Volvo's shares for a 40% interest in Norway's North Sea oil fields. The proposal was abandoned after a majority of Volvo's shareholders opposed the plan.
- Acquisition of Beijerinvest Group in late 1977. Gyllenhammar was attracted by Beijerinvest's oil-trading firm, although the firm also operated food, engineering, and other businesses.
- In 1979, sale of a 9.9% share interest in Volvo to Renault. Renault sold its shares in 1985 as part of a restructuring program.
- In the early 1980s, Volvo acquired a number of minority interests in consumer foods manufacturers.
- In 1986, Gyllenhammar negotiated the sale of Volvo's pharmaceutical businesses to Fermenta AB, and the acquisition of 20 percent of Fermenta's shares This deal broke down when it appeared that Fermenta's CEO had engaged in fraud.
- In 1986, Volvo acquired 25% interests in each of two pharmaceutical companies, Pharmacia and Sonesson.
- In 1991, Volvo organized NedCar B.V. as a joint venture between Volvo, Mitsubishi, and the Dutch Government. The objective of this joint venture was to manufacture car models in the medium-size segment for sale under the Volvo and Mitsubishi names.

R.F. Bruner/Journal of Financial Economics 51 (1999) 125-166   155

the firm and shareholders are too dispersed to enforce value maximization, corporate assets may be deployed to benefit managers rather than shareholders'. Indeed, Gyllenhammar's weak alignment with shareholders emerged as an issue in the debate over the merger. He owned about 10,000 shares, 0.10% of the total shares outstanding. Gyllenhammar's shareholding in Volvo is reported in Sundqvist (1994, p. 247). At the market values prevailing on the date of the merger announcement, this holding equaled about SEK 4.85 million, or about half of his annual compensation in 1995. Several interviewees contend that Gyllenhammar had stacked the board with his friends and supporters. Jensen (1986), Shleifer and Vishny (1989), and others have argued that, in the absence of significant ownership stakes, managers will undertake wealth-destroying strategies to pursue their own goals to the detriment of the firm's owners. Shleifer and Vishny (1989) suggest that a manager may diversify a firm in a way that increases the firm's demands for his or her particular skills. Amihud and Lev (1981) indicate that diversification may be pursued to reduce the firm's total risk since managers cannot efficiently diversify their risk of employment. Jensen (1986, p. 328) writes: 'The [free cash flow] theory implies managers of firms with unused borrowing power and large free cash flows are more likely to undertake low-benefit or even value-destroying mergers. Diversification programs generally fit this category, and the theory predicts they will generate lower gains'. Critics point toward Gyllenhammar's program of unrelated diversification, several spectacularly poor deals, and generally his long-term managerial record of financial underperformance.

Despite the evidence of entrenchment, there is one important inconsistency: Gyllenhammar's departure is not associated with significant positive abnormal returns, as one would expect if he were associated with expected destruction of shareholder wealth (see Table 1, line 43). Indeed, this fact suggests an alternative hypothesis: the destruction and recovery of value are associated with policies, rather than an individual. The policy of alliance and merger was costly to shareholders: at the announcements of progressively deeper engagement, abnormal returns are significantly negative, returns are significantly positive at announcements of the unwinding of that engagement.

Path dependence may explain a tendency of managers to undertake value-destroying mergers. Bleeke and Ernst (1995) suggest that alliances can set a path dependent strategy toward merger. Extensive cross-shareholdings and a poison pill dictate a costly exit if the allies grow dissatisfied with their partnership. When the CEOs of Volvo and Renault grew dissatisfied with the progress of their alliance, the path pointed toward deeper integration and merger. This case suggests that one of the key roles for institutional voice is to break the grip of value-destroying path dependence through changes in management, the board, the strategy, and the governing coalition of investors.

Path dependence as an explanation for bad mergers complements, rather than excludes, other hypotheses. The failed merger of Volvo and Renault is consistent with these other hypotheses as well. Roll (1986) argues that hubris, the mistaken belief in takeover gains, drives unprofitable acquisitions. Gyllenhammar plainly believed in takeover gains from a merger with Renault but could not get the institutions to accept them. Repeatedly, in previous acquisitions, he had projected financial gains and then failed to deliver. Numerous interviewees used adjectives to describe Gyllenhammar that suggest a leader who does not shed mistaken beliefs easily: 'emperor', ambitious, domineering, dictatorial, and having no particular passion for the products or customers of his firm, but rather for financial deal-doing. Gyllenhammar's small stake in the firm and a board dominated by his friends insulated him from the consequences of his mistaken beliefs.

Morck et al. (1990, p. 33) hypothesize that 'bad managers may make bad acquisitions simply because they are bad managers'. They hold that bad managers pursue managerial objectives, such as size maximization and unrelated diversification. The lengthy list of costly diversifying acquisitions by Volvo, Volvo's long-term underperformance relative to the Swedish stock market, and Gyllenhammar's own stated objectives for the merger (e.g., 'to become a player of size') are broadly consistent with the managerial objectives hypothesis.

Lys and Vincent (1995, p. 375) offered behavioral hypotheses for value-destroying mergers, including an endowment effect and a tendency to escalate commitments: 'once a decision maker takes action, there are powerful psychological, environmental, and structural pressures to continue the course, regardless of subsequent information to the contrary'. The historical relationship of the two firms reveals an increasing commitment between them from 1971 to 1993. Path dependence and escalation of commitments are similar but not identical: a poison pill and cross-ownership of shares in the alliance committed both firms to a path, and rendered other paths (i.e., exits) costly. The decision to merge (i.e., to proceed farther down that path) was an escalation of commitment.

In short, this case is generally consistent with a range of explanations for bad mergers: path dependence, hubris, entrenchment, pursuit of managerial objectives, and a tendency to escalate commitments.

4.2. The value of institutional voice

It is remarkable that Volvo's board, management, and corporate strategy changed without a formal proxy contest or takeover attempt. Shleifer and Vishny (1986) cite 'jawboning' as an alternative to influence a board of directors to abandon a value-destroying course of action. Black (1992a) and others hypothesize that institutional voice is valuable, and this case is consistent with their hypothesis.

First, the contest over the merger terms illustrates the many forms that voice may take:

Asking questions/demanding more information. Press reports and interviews reveal numerous requests for more information about the golden share, merger

R.F. Bruner/Journal of Financial Economics 51 (1999) 125–166   157

synergies, and French intentions for privatizing RVA. The Swedish Small Shareholders' Association is widely credited with asking initial questions that eventually led to a cascade of inquiry by the institutions.

Direct communication with the board of directors. It is not possible to reconstruct a history of informal conversations among opponents of the merger, Volvo's board, or the boards of institutional investors. In the close-knit Swedish business society, however, director interlocks are widespread. One can show the representation of several interested parties on the boards of Volvo and of the institutional investors, where, it is reasonable to assume, the voice of direct opposition was heard.[9] Gunnar Johansson, former CEO of Volvo and outspoken critic of the merger, and Peter Nygards, head of the while-collar union (which announced its opposition to the merger) sat on the board of the Fourth Fund, Volvo's largest independent institutional investor. Soren Gyll, Volvo's CEO, was a director of Trygg Hansa SPP, one of the earliest institutional opponents of the merger. Gyllenhammar was a director of S-E Banken, whose CEO publicly criticized the merger and Gyllenhammar, and which opposed the merger. Three of Volvo's outside directors, Ulf Laurin, Bo Rydin, and Sven Ågrup, represented Svenska Handelsbanken, which took no public stand in opposition, but which Gyllenhammar cites in an interview with me as one of the leading organizers of opposition.

Announcements of deferral of support. Volvo was never able to develop a 'bandwagon effect' in part because lead-steer institutions (such as Skandia Insurance) announced that they were not yet ready to give their support. Usually these announcements followed the release of additional information by Volvo.

Announcements of opposition. Committing the institution to vote against the proposal signaled the investor's attitude to the board, Volvo's management, and the other institutions. Public expressions of opposition are extremely rare in the Swedish business community, which makes the vocal opposition in this case especially notable.

Threats to sue. The 92–94 Fund and the Swedish Small Shareholders Association publicly threatened to sue the Volvo directors if the merger were implemented without a two-thirds majority vote. There was no precedent in Swedish business history of large investors suing to invalidate a shareholder vote.

Demand for renegotiation of the merger terms. Several institutions called publicly for Gyllenhammar to reopen negotiations with the French. Bjorn Wolrath, CEO of Skandia Insurance, was a leading advocate of renegotiation. In fact, this was tried, but to no avail.

---

[9] I am indebted to Sven-Ivan Sundqvist and Kristian Rydqvist for assistance in the identification of these linkages.

Demand for the resignation of the chairman and/or the board. Influential leaders in the Swedish financial community published commentaries or gave interviews that called for Gyllenhammar's resignation. Mats Qviberg and Sven Hagstromer, prominent Stockholm investors, demanded resignation of the entire board. Pehr Thelin, CEO of S-E Banken, demanded Gyllenhammar's resignation. These were extremely strong expressions of sentiment in the Swedish business community.

Second, the case illustrates the value associated with institutional voice. The loss of value at the announcement of the merger and over the initial seven weeks following is material and significant. Abnormal returns associated with institutional activism are positive and significant during the period of active opposition, and they are positive and significant at announcements of opposition by 'lead steer' institutions. Returns are negative and significant at the announcement of institutional support for the merger. The abnormal returns associated with specific reports of institutional opposition (Table 1, Line 51) equate to increases in Volvo equity value of SEK 4.7 billion (US$ 600 million). I estimate the gain by summing the gains for 'A' and 'B' shares. For the 'A' shares, the gain is estimated as the product of the number of shares (25.3 million), the initial stock price per share (SEK 485), and the cumulative abnormal return (14.85%), or SEK 1.822 billion. For the 'B' shares, the gain is the product of 52.3 million shares, a price of SEK 483, and a cumulative abnormal return of 11.40%, or SEK 2.879 billion. The conversion to U.S. dollars is at the exchange rate of 7.83, prevailing on September 6, 1993.

4.3. Sources of value recovered by institutional voice

The analysis of abnormal returns yields insights into the sources of value recovered by institutional activism. Hubris, managerialism, and the escalation of commitment were reversed by changing managers and the board. Path dependence in this case was changed by unwinding the merger and alliance. A new management, new board, and new strategy committed the firm to a new path. Contrary to Gyllenhammar's assertion that the opposition to the merger was really opposition toward him personally, the abnormal returns suggest that the opposition was focused on the path down which he was taking the firm. In short, the source of value recovered in this case was the redirection of Volvo from its path-dependent alliance with Renault.

It is also interesting that the gains from jawboning are not reflected in a widening of the voting premium in Volvo's shares. The voting premium declines sharply at the beginning of the strategic alliance, consistent with the hypothesis that the terms of the alliance effectively blocked other existing or potential control parties. The premium remains small throughout this episode, both in absolute terms and relative to typical premiums found in other research. Moreover, events that marked changes in the political landscape during the control contest had a relatively immaterial effect on the changes in the voting premiums. The theory of the voting premium, summarized in Rydqvist (1992b), suggests that the recovery of value associated with institutional voice did not derive from the institutions' power to expropriate value – if that were the case, the premium would have risen – but rather from a fundamental redirection of the firm. The redirection reduced the firm's probability of a hostile takeover.

4.4. Implications for further research

The hypothesis of path dependence suggested by this case invites further study. Path dependence can complement hypotheses about bad mergers that originate from managers themselves. This new hypothesis merely recognizes that decisions managers have made in the past may constrain their choices in the present. Of course, it may be that bad decisions in the past originated in hubris or bad judgment. The hypothesis of path dependence invites researchers to look farther back in time than the first announcement of a merger to build a deeper understanding of the origins of bad deals.

As this study and other clinical studies (e.g., Lys and Vincent, 1995) suggest, scholars should work with *joint hypotheses* about wealth effects in mergers. This case also illustrates the slow-building chorus and wide variety of voice or jawboning in institutional activism. The nature of the chorus and variety invites further research.

Appendix A. Valuing the French control options

The control options to be granted to the French government were essentially rights to influence the strategy of RVA. Transfer of these rights from public shareholders to France would affect shareholder wealth. A rational investor would support the merger terms if his or her wealth were greater after the merger (and the transfer of rights) than ex ante. Using this insight along with data supplied by the merger prospectus, it is possible to estimate a minimum value for the control options.

After the merger, the Volvo investor's interest in the automotive business would be equal to this aggregate value:

$$\text{Value}_{\text{after merger}} = [(\text{Vo} + \text{AS} + \text{MS} + R) * 0.35] - \text{CO}, \qquad (A.1)$$

where Vo is the value of Volvo's automotive business on a stand-alone basis, before the effect of any alliance or merger synergies, AS the value of alliance synergies, derived from the alliance with Renault of 1990, MS the value of incremental new *merger* synergies, and CO the value of the bundle of control options.

If the merger were rejected, it was unclear ex ante whether the alliance would stand or dissolve. Gyllenhammar and Schweitzer (the CEO of Renault) said on more than one occasion that the alliance would continue, but with the benefit of hindsight, one must question this. One must assume some probability, p, that the alliance would stand if the merger proposal were rejected, and a probability, $(1 - p)$, that the alliance would be dissolved. If the merger were rejected but the alliance continued to stand, one must assume that Volvo would receive its share, k, of the alliance synergies, AS. If the alliance were dissolved, alliance synergies would disappear. One must also assume costs if the alliance were dissolved–these costs would include payments under the poison pill that would be triggered by dissolution. We now know the costs were material. Inserting an assumption about dissolution costs only amplifies the size of the golden-share value, so the value estimated here is probably biased downward. Accordingly, the value of the Volvo investor's interest in the automotive business would be

$$\text{Value}_{\text{merger rejected}} = p*[(0.75*\text{Vo}*W_{\text{Volvocar}}) + (0.55*\text{Vo}*W_{\text{Volvotruck}})$$

$$+ (0.20*\text{Ro}*W_{\text{Rencar}}) + (0.45*\text{Ro}*W_{\text{Rentruck}})$$

$$+ (\text{AS}*k)] + (1 - p)*(\text{Vo} - \text{UC}), \qquad (\text{A.2})$$

where Ro is the equity value of Renault's car and truck businesses on a stand-alone basis, apart from the benefit of any alliance or merger synergies, p the probability that the alliance would stand if the merger were rejected, W_{Volvocar} the proportion of Vo attributable to Volvo's car business, $W_{\text{Volvotruck}}$ the proportion of Vo attributable to Volvo's truck business, W_{Rencar} the proportion of Ro attributable to Renault's car business, W_{Rentruck} the proportion of Ro attributable to Renault's truck business, and UC the present value of costs associated with unwinding the alliance, should it dissolve.

In short, the rational investor would reject the merger proposal if

$$\text{Value}_{\text{merger rejected}} > \text{Value}_{\text{after merger}}. \qquad (\text{A.3})$$

Inserting the respective formulas and rearranging to isolate the value of the bundle of control options, CO, the decision rule of the Volvo investor becomes to reject the merger proposal if

$$\text{CO} > [(\text{Vo} + \text{AS} + \text{MS} + \text{R})*0.35] - p*[(0.75*\text{Vo}*W_{\text{Volvocar}})$$

$$+ (0.55*\text{Vo}*W_{\text{Volvotruck}}) + (0.20*\text{Ro}*W_{\text{Rencar}})$$

$$+ (0.45*\text{Ro}*W_{\text{Rentruck}}) + (\text{AS}*k)] - (1 - p)*(Vo - UC). \qquad (\text{A.4})$$

R.F. Bruner/Journal of Financial Economics 51 (1999) 125–166   161

We can derive the values for the variables in this equation directly from public information, or infer them from public statements by Gyllenhammar and others.[10]

MS	Merger synergies were estimated at SEK 17.95 billion. The merger prospectus (p. 4) presents a graph of the time distribution of SEK 16.43 billion in savings spread over six years. Taxing these savings (at 35%) including a terminal value for the savings (estimated as the final year's savings capitalized at 10%), and discounting them at 10% to obtain a present value yields SEK 17.95 billion.
AS	Alliance synergies were estimated to be SEK 44.66 billion. The merger prospectus (p. 4) gives a forecast for the realization of SEK 41.07 billion in alliance synergies over six years. As with the merger synergies, the alliance synergies are adjusted for taxes and terminal value and discounted to the present.
p	The probability that the alliance will survive despite a rejection of the merger proposal is estimated to be 1.0, based on public statements by Gyllenhammar and Schweitzer in the fall of 1993. We know that the probability was considerably less than 1.0. The first derivative of CO (the value of control options) with respect to p is negative: assuming certainty biases the resulting estimate of CO downward.
k	Volvo's share of the alliance synergies was estimated to be 0.50. The merger prospectus hypothesizes equal sharing in the benefits of the strategic alliance. Using this value in our analysis here assumes that the division of gains does not change after the merger.
Ro	The equity value of Renault's car and truck businesses on a stand-alone basis, apart from the benefit of any alliance or merger synergies, is estimated to be SEK 37.67 billion. The value of Renault's equity was estimated in September 1993 by analysts to vary between SEK 55 billion (Carnegie International, 1993) and 60 billion (Barclays, 1993). Using the SEK 60 billion figure and backing out Renault's assumed 50% share in the alliance synergies of SEK 44.66 billion yields SEK 37.67 billion. We now

---

[10] Some quantities are expressed by Volvo and outside observers in French francs, and others in Swedish Kroner. For simplicity of exposition, all quantities are discussed here in Kroner, translated from Francs at 1.369 SEK/FRF, the rate prevailing on the date of merger announcement, September 6, 1993.

know that Renault was partially privatized in October 1994 (a year after the episode discussed in this study) at share prices valuing Renault's equity at SEK 58 billion. The first derivative of CO with respect to R is positive; using the 'perfect foresight' value of Renault's equity (SEK 58 billion) would increase the implied value of CO.

Vo   The equity value of Volvo's car and truck businesses on a stand-alone basis, apart from the benefit of any alliance or merger synergies is estimated to be SEK 2.67 billion. In September 1993, analysts estimated that the equity value of Volvo's car and truck businesses was SEK 23.3 billion (Carnegie International, 1993) to 25 billion (Barclays, 1993). Using the SEK 25 billion estimate and deducting Volvo's share (50%) of the expected alliance synergies (SEK 44.66 billion) yields a stand-alone equity value of SEK 2.67 billion.

$W_{volvocar}$ and $W_{Volvotruck}$ The proportions of Volvo's stand-alone equity value attributable to its automobile and trucks segments are assumed to be 0.50 each. In September 1993, Barclays (1993) published a valuation analysis of AB Volvo that attributed half the equity value of its automotive business to cars, and half to trucks.

W_{Rencar} and $W_{Rentruck}$ The proportions of Renault's stand-alone equity value attributable to its automobile and trucks segments are assumed to be 0.86 (cars) and 0.14 (trucks). There exist no estimates of the distribution of Renault's equity value across its car and truck businesses, but an informational document published by AB Volvo (1993b, p. 5) projects the stand-alone sales of the Renault car and truck businesses through the year 2000. Using the distribution of sales as a proxy for the distribution of equity values yields these weights for cars and trucks. The first derivative of CO with respect to W_{Rencar} is negative. Thus, if the use of the sales-based proxy overestimates the proportion of Renault's equity in cars, the resulting estimate of CO would be biased downward.

UC   The costs of unwinding the alliance are estimated to be SEK 5.2 billion. This estimate looks to the actual cost that AB Volvo announced it would incur to terminate the alliance (reported in Carnegy, 1994a). It is impossible to tell how much of this amount was a true cash outlay (i.e., as opposed to an accrual), although Volvo did imply that a substantial portion was a cash payment from Volvo to Renault. Using this figure implies perfect foresight on the part of investors in September 1993. Assuming certain survival of the alliance after a rejection of the merger, however reduces the impact of UC to nil.

Completing the model by inserting assumed values into (A.4) yields

$$CO > [(2.67 + 44.66 + 17.95 + 37.67)*0.35] - 1.0*[(0.75*2.67*0.50)$$

$$+ (0.55*2.67*0.50) + (0.20*37.67*0.86) + (0.45*37.67*0.14)$$

$$+ (44.66*0.50)] - (1 - 1.0)*(2.67 - 5.2).$$

The calculation reveals that rejection of the merger is consistent with a value for the control options that is greater than SEK 3.12 billion (or about US $398 million using the September 6, 1993 exchange rate). On September 6, 1993, the total market value of AB Volvo's equity was about SEK 37.5 billion. Thus, the implied conservative estimate of the value of the control options was 8.3% of AB Volvo's equity value.

Sensitivity analysis of this model reveals that the implied minimum control option value is sensitive to variations in R, Renault's equity. For a 10% variation in Renault's equity value, the resulting control option estimate will vary in the same direction by 14%. It is also sensitive to the probability of the alliance survival. This analysis assumes a 100% probability that the alliance will survive. If the probability is reduced to 50%, the implied value of the control options is SEK 20.8 billion. The estimated value of the control options is sensitive to variations in AS and MS, the alliance and merger synergies as well. Since the forecast of these synergies emanated from the company (Gyllenhammar) and could have been seen as self-serving, one could discount them, as some interviewees suggested. If the forecasted synergies are discounted to 75% of Volvo's estimate, the resulting implied value of the control options is SEK 2.19 billion. At discounts to 50% and 25% of Volvo's synergy estimate, the implied control option values are SEK 1.26 and 0.33 billion, respectively. This sensitivity analysis suggests an association between forecast optimism and the size of the wealth transfer from Volvo's shareholders to Renault's owner, the French government.

In his public statements, Gyllenhammar seemed to minimize the importance of the control options in the deal. Yet, if he truly believed in the synergy forecasts that Volvo published, the implied value of the control options would be material. This internal inconsistency supports the claims of Sundqvist (1994) and various interviewees that the proposed merger of Volvo and Renault failed in no small part because of doubts about the credibility of its chief advocate. Almost as an epitaph to the entire episode, Gyllenhammar said in an interview with me, 'I did not take the golden share seriously'.

References

AB Volvo, 1990. Information on the alliance between Volvo and Renault.
AB Volvo, 1992. 1992 Annual report.

AB Volvo, 1993a. Information to Volvo shareholders, Sept. 9, 1993.

AB Volvo, 1993b. Merger of Volvo's automotive operations with Renault: information prior to extraordinary general meeting of shareholders in AB Volvo, November 9, 1993.

AB Volvo, 1993c. Merger of Volvo's automotive operations with Renault: supplementary information to the shareholders.

AB Volvo, 1993d. 1993 Annual report.

Affarsvärlden, PG setter kvar, Dec. 8, 1993, p. 7 (in Swedish, no author attributed).

Agrawal, A., Mandelker, G., 1990. Large shareholders and the monitoring of managers: the case of antitakeover charter amendments. Journal of Financial and Quantitative Analysis 25, 143.

Amihud, Y., Lev, B., 1981. Risk reduction as a managerial motive for conglomerate mergers. Bell Journal of Economics 12, 605–617.

Amoaku-Adu, B., Smith, B.F., 1991. Relative prices of dual class shares with preferential property and takeover rights: evidence from the Toronto stock exchange. Unpublished manuscript, Wilfrid Laurier University.

Barclays de Zoete Wedd Securities. Volvo Company Report, September 3, 1993, electronically retrieved through Investext, Thomson Financial Networks.

Bartal, D., Harbin, I., Pressure mounts on car chief. The European, Nov. 9, 1993, p. 14.

Biger, N., 1991. Market recognition of the value of control. Unpublished manuscript, University of Haifa.

Black, B.S., 1992a. Agents watching agents: the promise of institutional investor voice. UCLA Law Review 39, 811–892.

Black, B.S., 1992b. The value of institutional investor monitoring: the empirical evidence. UCLA Law Review 39, 895–939.

Bleeke, J., Ernst, D., 1995. Is your strategic alliance really a sale? Harvard Business Review 73, 97–106.

Bonnier, K.-A., Bruner, R., 1989. An analysis of stock price reaction to management change in distressed firms. Journal of Accounting and Economics 11, 95–106.

Brown-Humes, C. Volvo urged to drop Renault deal. Financial Times, Nov. 5, 1993, p. 27.

Brickley, J., Lease, R., Smith, C.W., 1988. Ownership structure and voting on antitakeover amendments. Journal of Financial Economics 20, 276–299.

Carnegie International. Volvo - Company Report, September 9, 1993, electronically retrieved through Investext, Thomson Financial Networks.

Carnegy, H., 1993a. Hostile chorus to Volvo deal reaches crescendo. Financial Times, Nov. 1, 1993, p. 19.

Carnegy, H., 1993b. Sinking in a sea of opposition. Financial Times, Dec. 2, 1993, p. 30.

Carnegy, H., 1994a. Volvo pays the cost of a failed merger. Financial Times, March 11, 1994, p. 19.

Carnegy, H., 1994b. Volvo finds key to merger failure. Financial Times, August 19, 1994, p. 21.

Carnegy, H., 1994c. Gyllenhammar switches to banking after Volvo debacle. Financial Times, September 10, 1994, p. 22.

Carnegy, H., Ridding, J., 1993. Time-out called as strains start to show. Financial Times, Nov. 3, 1993, p. 24.

Dial, J., Kevin, J.M., 1995. Incentives, downsizing, and value creation at General Dynamics. Journal of Financial Economics 37, 261–314.

Franks, J., Mayer, C., 1990. Capital markets and corporate control: a study of France. Germany and the U.K. Economic Policy 10, 189.

Furtado, E.P.H., Rozeff, M.S., 1987. The wealth effects of company initiated management changes. Journal of Financial Economics 18, 147–160.

Gilson, R.J., 1994. In; Isaksson, M., Skog, R. (Eds.), Corporate governance and economic efficiency, Aspects of Corporate Governance, Juristförlaget, Stockholm, pp. 131–141.

Gordon, L.A., Pound, J., 1993. Information, ownership structure, and shareholder voting: evidence from shareholder-sponsored corporate governance proposals. Journal of Finance 68, 697–718.

Gordon Group, 1992. Active investing in the US equity market: past performance and future prospects, December 2, 1992, working paper, cited in Robert A.G. Monks and Nell Minow, 1995, Corporate Governance, Basil Blackwell, Cambridge.

Harrigan, K., 1988. Strategic alliances and partner asymmetries. Management International Review 28, 53–72.

Hirschman, A.O., 1970. Exit, Voice and Loyalty, Harvard University Press, Cambridge.

Horner, M.R., 1988. The value of the corporate voting right: evidence from Switzerland. Journal of Banking and Finance 12, 69–83.

Jarrell, G.A., Poulsen, A., 1987. Shark repellants and stock prices: the effects of antitakeover amendments since 1980. Journal of Financial Economics 19, 127–168.

Jensen, M.C., 1986. Agency costs of free cash flow, corporate finance, and takeovers. American Economic Review 76, 323–329.

Keller, M., 1993. Collision: GM, Toyota, Volkswagen and the race to own the 21st century, Doubleday, New York

Kunz, R.M., Angel, J.J., 1996. Factors affecting the value of the stock voting right: evidence from the Swiss equity market. Financial Management 24, 7–20.

Lease, R.C., McConnell, J.J., Mikkelson, W.H., 1983. The market value of control in publicly-traded corporations. Journal of Financial Economics 11, 439–471.

Levine, J.B., Byrne, J.A., 1986. Corporate odd couples. Business Week, July 21, 1986, 100–106.

Levy, H., 1982. Economic evaluation of voting power of common stock. The Journal of Finance 38, 79–93.

Lys, T., Vincent, L., 1995. An analysis of value destruction in AT&T's acquisition of NCR. Journal of Financial Economics 39, 353–378.

McConnell, J., Servaes, H., 1990. Additional evidence on equity ownership and corporate value. Journal of Financial Economics 27, 595.

Megginson, W.L., 1990. Restricted voting stock, acquisition premiums, and the market value of corporate control. The Financial Review 25, 175–198.

Morck, R., Shleifer, A., Vishny, R., 1988. Management ownership and market valuation: an empirical analysis. Journal of Financial Economics 20, 293–315.

Morck, R., Shleifer, A., Vishny, R., 1990. Do managerial objectives drive bad acquisitions? Journal of Finance 65, 31–48.

Nesbitt, S.L., 1994. Long-term rewards from shareholder activism: a study of the 'CalPERS effect'. Journal of Applied Corporate Finance 6, 75–80.

Pound, J., 1988. Proxy contests and the efficiency of shareholder oversight. Journal of Financial Economics 20, 237–266.

Roll, R., 1986. The hubris hypothesis of corporate takeovers. Journal of Business 59, 197–216.

Ruback, R., 1982. The effect of discretionary price control decisions on equity values. Journal of Financial Economics 10, 83–106.

Rydqvist, K., 1992a. Takeover bids and the relative prices of shares that differ in their voting rights, unpublished manuscript, Stockholm School of Economics.

Rydqvist, K., 1992b. Dual-class shares: a review. Oxford Review of Economic Policy 8, 3, 45–57.

Shleifer, A., Vishny, R., 1986. Large shareholders and corporate control. Journal of Political Economy 94, 461–488.

Shleifer, A., Vishny, R., 1989. Management entrenchment: the case of manager-specific investments. Journal of Financial Economics 25, 123–139.

Smith, M.P., 1996. Shareholder activism by institutional investors: evidence from CalPERS. Journal of Finance 51, 253–278.

Stern, J., 1989. Lead steer roundtable, Journal of Applied Corporate Finance 2, 24–44.

Sundqvist, S.-I., 1994. Exit PG, Bokförlaget T. Fischer and Co., Stockholm, Sweden (in Swedish).

Ward's Automotive Yearbook, 1994. Ward's Communications, Southfield.

Warner, J.B., Watts, R.L., Wruck, K.H., 1988. Stock price and top management changes. Journal of Financial Economics 20, 461–492.

Weisbach, M., 1988. Outside directors and CEO turnover. Journal of Financial Economics 20, 431–460.

Zingales, L., 1994. The value of the voting right: a study of the Milan Stock Exchange experience. Review of Financial Studies 7, 125–148.

Part IV
Ownership, Executive Compensation and Corporate Decision Making

[16]

ELSEVIER   Journal of Financial Economics 38 (1995) 163–184

Executive compensation structure, ownership, and firm performance

Hamid Mehran

Wallace E. Carroll School of Management, Boston College, Chestnut Hill, MA 02167-3808, USA

(Received October 1991; final version received February 1994)

Abstract

An examination of the executive compensation structure of 153 randomly-selected manufacturing firms in 1979–1980 provides evidence supporting advocates of incentive compensation, and also suggests that the form rather than the level of compensation is what motivates managers to increase firm value. Firm performance is positively related to the percentage of equity held by managers and to the percentage of their compensation that is equity-based. Moreover, equity-based compensation is used more extensively in firms with more outside directors. Finally, firms in which a higher percentage of the shares are held by insiders or outside blockholders use less equity-based compensation.

Key words: Compensation structure; Ownership; Directors; Blockholders
JEL classification: G32; J33; L22

1. Introduction

Despite widespread public attention and a surge in research interest, the relationships among executive compensation structure, ownership structure and control, and firm performance are still little understood. For example, Jensen and Murphy (1990a) suggest that equity-based rather than cash compensation

The author would like to acknowledge the helpful comments of Timothy Mech, Ram Ramanan, Betty Strock Bagnani, and Kenneth Wiles. Special thanks are due Clifford Holderness, Michael Jensen (the editor), Kevin Murphy (the referee), and Robert Taggart. I also benefited from the comments of participants in seminars at Boston College and the London School of Economics. An earlier version of this paper entitled 'The Determinants of the Structure of Executive Compensation' was presented at the 1990 Financial Management Association meeting.

gives managers the correct incentive to maximize firm value, but there is little empirical evidence on whether corporations whose executive compensation is more equity-based actually perform better. Little is known, either, about whether the ownership of the company's stock by insiders versus outsiders or the composition of the board of directors affects executive compensation structure.

This study presents empirical evidence on the relationship between the structure of executive compensation and firm performance. It is exploratory in that executive compensation, ownership structure, and board composition are ultimately part of a simultaneous system that determines the corporation's value and the allocation of that value among various claimants. As a result, the associations reported here are not necessarily causal ones. Nevertheless, empirical regularities in the structure of executive compensation should help guide future research.

This study differs from previous work on compensation in two ways. First, it focuses on the structure rather than the level of compensation. Second, it investigates executive compensation in the context of the firm's ownership structure and the composition of its board of directors. I use 1979–1980 compensation data for 153 randomly-selected manufacturing firms. An important feature of the sample is that it focuses on small as well as large firms, thus providing the variation necessary to conduct statistical tests. In addition, the sample is constructed separately for CEOs, for top executives, as well as for all officers and directors as a group.

My primary findings on compensation structure are as follows: (1) firms with more outside directors have a higher percentage of their executive compensation in equity-based form; (2) the percentage of executive compensation that is equity-based is inversely related to their percentage of equity holdings; and (3) firms in which a higher percentage of the shares are held by outside blockholders use less equity-based compensation. My findings on firm performance, as proxied by Tobin's Q and by return on assets, are as follows: (1) firm performance is positively related to the percentage of executive compensation that is equity-based; and (2) firm performance is positively related to the percentage of equity held by managers. These findings support tying executive compensation more closely to firm performance (as measured by stock price or other indicators); they also suggest that the form, rather than the level, of compensation is what motivates managers to increase firm value.

Section 2 of the paper presents possible relationships among the composition of executive pay packages, ownership structure, board composition, and firm performance. Section 3 describes the sample selection procedure and method. The empirical results and their interpretation are presented in Section 4. Section 5 summarizes the key findings.

H. Mehran/Journal of Financial Economics 38 (1995) 163–184 165

2. Agency theory, executive compensation structure, and firm performance

Jensen and Meckling (1976) argue that ownership structure, executive compensation structure, and board composition are determined by each other and by the nature of a firm's business (e.g., business risk, nature of real assets, cash flow pattern, and firm size). They suggest that these variables also influence a firm's performance. Although aspects of this potentially complex simultaneous relationship have been examined by researchers, only limited research has been done on the structure of executive compensation.[1] Moreover, the empirical relationship between executive incentive plans and firm performance has not been established. What work has been done, however, provides some guidance for the empirical investigations that are the primary focus of this paper.

Top managers, like most individuals, are portrayed in the literature as being risk-averse. This implies, as Harris and Raviv (1979) explain, that managers will want their compensation structured so that they bear less personal risk. Given a certain level of compensation, managers should prefer fixed cash compensation over equity-based compensation. The latter, of course, is tied to the firm's stock return and is to some degree beyond managers' control. This preference is reinforced because the value of a manager's human capital will also vary with the firm's stock performance. In order to reduce their compensation risk, managers may engage in activities which reduce the firm's risk (Jensen and Meckling, 1976; Amihud and Lev, 1981). These activities in turn can adversely affect shareholders' wealth.

Shareholders, on the other hand, are considered risk-neutral because they can diversify firm-specific risk simply by holding a diversified portfolio. Moreover, shareholders will anticipate that managers will attempt to avoid risks in ways that can reduce firm value. While there are several ways to reduce this conflict over risk, previous research suggests that tying managers' compensation to firm

---

[1] Brickley and Dark (1987), among others, have shown that ownership structure is related to business risk and firm size. Other studies provide empirical evidence on the relationship between insiders' ownership and firm performance, although the evidence is mixed. While Demsetz and Lehn (1985) find no significant relationship between various measures of insider ownership and accounting profit, Morck, Shleifer, and Vishny (1988), McConnell and Servaes (1990), and Hermalin and Weisbach (1991) find a nonlinear relationship between the fraction of company stock held by insiders and Tobin's Q. These studies also examine the relationship between the nature of the firm's business and firm performance, again with mixed results. Several researchers have studied factors influencing board composition. Brickley and van Drunen (1987) document a positive relationship between the percentage of outside directors and firm size. They find a similar relationship between the percentage of outside directors and the firm's stock return variance. Weisbach (1988) finds a negative relationship between the percentage of outside directors and insiders' ownership. He argues that monitoring by outside directors and the direct incentive created by insiders' ownership may be substitute methods of controlling agency costs. However, no significant relationship has been found between board composition and firm performance (Hermalin and Weisbach, 1991).

performance motivates them to make more value-maximizing decisions (e.g., Holmstrom, 1979; Harris and Raviv, 1979; Grossman and Hart, 1983). Other studies suggest that one specific way to tie pay to performance is by making a greater percentage of a manager's compensation equity-based, such as through incentive stock options (e.g., Jensen and Murphy, 1990a). Other researchers have formally shown that incentive-compensation plans motivate managers to take on more risk (e.g., Hirshleifer and Suh, 1992). For these reasons, shareholders should prefer (holding the level of compensation constant) that managers' pay packages contain more equity-based forms of compensation, although it may not be optimal to tie all of the components of these pay packages to the firm's stock price (Paul, 1992; Sloan, 1993).

Shareholders, of course, do not set executive compensation. They elect directors, who have the exclusive right under corporate law to manage the corporation. Among the most important of directors' tasks is to set the level and structure of the compensation of top executives (e.g., Fama and Jensen, 1983), which raises the issue of how the composition of the board affects the structure of executive compensation. There is a growing body of evidence that outside directors (those who do not work for the company) are more independent of top management and thus better represent the interests of shareholders than do inside directors. For example, Rosenstein and Wyatt (1990) find that the appointment of outside directors produces a positive stock price response, on average. Weisbach (1988) documents that poor stock-price performance increases the probability that the CEO will be replaced; this probability increases further with the percentage of outside directors.

In light of these empirical findings, I hypothesize that outsider-dominated boards are likely to make greater use of equity-based compensation. In contrast, insider-dominated boards are likely to be more responsive to the interests of top management and will thus use proportionately more fixed cash compensation. I investigate these possibilities by examining the relationship between the composition of the board and the structure of executive compensation. I also investigate whether the presence of certain types of outside directors on the board, particularly investment bankers and top managers from other firms, is associated with greater use of equity-based compensation.[2]

In addition, I examine whether boards consider the managers' total incentives (e.g., their stock options outstanding and their direct equity holdings) in setting compensation packages. I hypothesize that boards will use more equity-based compensation when the managers own a small fraction of the firm or when they

---

[2]The role of investment bankers in LBOs and venture capitalists in startups and IPOs is more than that of outside directors who give advice. Since they supply capital, they are large blockholders, and thus can exercise substantial influence on compensation policy, as well as on other policies in these organizations.

do not have a significant amount of unexercised stock options or other equity-based compensation plans.

Many have argued, starting with Jensen and Meckling (1976), that agency problems typically will be controlled by several mechanisms, including the market for corporate control (e.g., Jensen and Ruback, 1983), the managerial labor market (e.g., Fama, 1980), and product market control (e.g., Hart, 1983). Thus, the structure of executive compensation is unlikely to be determined by the composition of the board alone. Several papers indicate that large outside blockholders play a role in management decisions (e.g., Shleifer and Vishny, 1986), raising the possibility that the use of equity-based compensation will increase with the presence of outside blockholders. Alternatively, if outside blockholders are substitutes in part for monitoring activities by the board, then the use of equity-based pay would decline as a result of their presence.

There is some anecdotal evidence that outside blockholders have influenced executive compensation.[3] For example, a number of major shareholders questioned a proposal by General Motors to increase its executives' pensions (White, 1990). The plan would have increased the annual retirement pay of the CEO, who was scheduled to retire in 75 days, to $1.2 million. Among the opposition was Michigan's state treasurer, who indicated that he would vote the state's 8.8 million GM shares against the plan. GM's board could have proceeded with the plan even if a majority of shareholders voted against it, but instead assured the shareholders that it would abide by their wishes. In general, however, there is little empirical evidence on the relationship between the firm's compensation structure and the presence of outside blockholders.

An issue related to, but separate from, the determinants of the structure of executive compensation is the relation between compensation structure and firm performance. Simply put, is the greater use of equity-based compensation associated with improved firm performance? Murphy (1985) finds a statistically significant relationship between the level of pay and performance. Jensen and Murphy (1990b) also find a statistically significant relationship between the level of pay (measured by changes in executive wealth) and performance (measured by changes in firm value), but they are surprised by the lack of a strong economic relationship between changes in executive wealth and changes in firm value. They suggest that there may be a stronger relationship between equity-based compensation and firm performance. They also suggest that most firms could increase value by using more equity-based compensation (Jensen and Murphy 1990a). In this paper I explore these possibilities.

---

[3]Of course, small shareholders can propose equity-based compensation plans for managers (see for example, the shareholders' proposal in relation to stock option plans, GAF Corporation's 1979 proxy statement). In most cases, the board recommends a vote against adoption of the shareholder proposal.

3. The methodology and sources of data

3.1. Method

The hypotheses established in Section 2 are tested cross-sectionally using ordinary least-squares (OLS) analysis. Eq. (1) describes the model used to test the relationships between compensation structure and variables for ownership structure and control:

Compensation structure

$$= f \text{(percentage of equity held by managers, percentage of equity held by all outside blockholders, percentage of outside directors, and control variables)} \qquad (1)$$

Fq. (2) describes the relationships between firm performance and variables for compensation structure, ownership structure, and control:

Firm performance

$$= f \text{(compensation structure, percentage of equity held by managers, percentage of equity held by all outside blockholders, percentage of outside directors, and control variables)} \qquad (2)$$

3.2. Data sources and time

The sample consists of 153 randomly-selected manufacturing firms (of the initial random sample of 170 firms, five firms were dropped because of missing proxy statements, six were excluded because of their foreign origin, and six firms were deleted because their stocks traded infrequently). Each firm has a complete record for selected data items for 1973–1983 on the COMPUSTAT Annual Industrial File. I collected the following items for 1979 and 1980: (1) salary, (2) bonus, (3) performance shares and units, (4) restricted stocks, (5) phantom stocks, (6) dividend units, (7) number of options granted and their exercise prices, (8) number of options held and their weighted average exercise price, (9) saving plans, (10) properties and insurance, (11) number of shares held by executives and their immediate families, (12) number and identity of outside blockholders and their equity investment in the firm, (13) number and affiliations of board members, (14) age of the CEO, and (15) number of top managers employed by the firm. Items (1)–(14) come from proxy statements and item (15) from Moody's Manuals. The exercise price and maturity on the components of stock options outstanding for 1979 and 1980 were collected from 1975–1977 proxy statements. I collected compensation data [items (1)–(10)] and insiders' ownership data [item (11)] separately for the highest-ranking executive and the group of top executives whose compensation is explicitly defined in the proxy statements, as

H. Mehran/Journal of Financial Economics 38 (1995) 163–184   169

well as for all officers and directors as a group. I measure most of the variables as the averages for the years 1979–1980, but different proxies of business risk require longer periods, the longest being 1973–1983.

3.3. Measurement of variables

Compensation structure: I use three measures of compensation: (1) percentage of total compensation in grants of new stock options, with the options valued by the Black–Scholes formula, (2) percentage of total compensation that is equity-based, and (3) percentage of total compensation in salary plus bonus. Total compensation is the sum of the dollar values of salary, bonus, dividend units, saving plans, properties, insurance, and the value of the awards from grants of new stock options, phantom stocks, restricted stocks, performance shares, and performance units. The percentage of total compensation that is equity-based is measured as the ratio of the sum of the value of awards from grants of new stock options, restricted stocks, phantom stocks, and performance shares to total compensation. Finally, the cash percentage of total compensation is the ratio of salary plus bonus to total compensation.

In analyzing the effect of compensation structure on firm performance, I only considered expected rather than realized compensation. Thus, the measurement of stock options exclude the change in the value of the accrued stock of outstanding options during the sample period. The reason is that there is a mechanical relation between firm performance and realized executives' wealth. As an example, consider two firms that pay salaries of X and that made a one-time-only stock option grant of 1,000 shares several years ago (with no subsequent grants). Suppose one of these firms turns out to be a high performer, while the other one is low performer. The low-performing firm will have a zero realized option value, while the high performer (with high appreciation) will have a large realized option value. Thus, a regression of firm performance on realized stock options will yield a positive mechanical correlation, and will not allow inferences about the effectiveness of stock options. Measurement of compensation is discussed further in the appendix.

Ownership structure: The percentage of equity held by managers is measured using the sum of their direct share ownership and their stock options outstanding plus share ownership by their immediate families. The percentage of equity held by all outside blockholders is measured using the sum of the percentages of equity held by individual investors, institutional investors, and corporations who own at least 5% of the common stock of the company. I choose 5% (as many researchers do) because this ownnership level triggers mandatory public filing under SEC regulation.

Percentage of outside directors: Outside directors are members of the board who are neither top executives, retired executives, or former executives of the company nor relatives of the CEO. Outside corporate lawyers who are

170   H. Mehran/Journal of Financial Economics 38 (1995) 163–184

employed by the firm and also serve on the board are considered insiders since many have conflicts of interest (e.g., Vancil, 1987). I also measure the percentage of outside directors employed by manufacturing firms, savings and loans and banks, investment banking firms, venture capital firms, and insurance companies.

Firm performance: The proxies for firm performance in Eq. (2) are Tobin's Q, measured by the ratio of the market value of the firm's securities to the replacement cost of its tangible assets, and return on assets (ROA), measured by the ratio of net income to the book value of the firm's total assets. The Qs are from the R&D Master File (Cummins, Hall, Laderman, and Mody, 1985), and net income and total assets are from the COMPUSTAT Annual Industrial File.

Whether Q and ROA are correct proxies for firm performance is a subject of continuing debate in the literature. In addition to well-known measurement problems associated with Q, many have argued that Q is a better proxy for the firm's growth opportunity than its performance. Others argue that ROA (and other accounting rates of return) conveys little information about economic rates of return (e.g., Fisher and McGowan, 1983; Benston, 1985). An argument for using ROA is that accounting returns are highly important in determining executive compensation (e.g., Antle and Smith, 1986; Jensen and Murphy, 1990b; Ely, 1991). Paul (1992) argues that accounting returns provide information to the board about the value added to the firm by the CEO. Therefore, executives have incentives to make major corporate decisions and/or report income in such a way as to affect ROA and, thus, their compensation (e.g., Defeo, Lambert, and Larcker, 1989). Other measures, such as stock return, have also been suggested in the literature. Stock return as a proxy for firm performance is most appropriate, however, for all-equity firms. While the three proxies have their own shortcomings, they are highly correlated (Jacobson, 1987; Landsman and Shapiro, 1989), and the qualitative nature of the results should not be affected by the choice of the proxy. Therefore, to be consistent with the literature, I have chosen Q and ROA.

Control variables: Control variables introduced in Eq. (1) are growth opportunities, leverage ratio, business risk, and firm size (see Smith and Watts, 1992, or Lewellen, Loderer, and Martin, 1987, for a discussion of the relationship between these variables and executive compensation). Eq. (2) contains an additional control variable to capture the portion of firm value in assets in place. The source of data for these variables is the COMPUSTAT Industrial Annual File. The proxy for growth opportunities is research and development as a percentage of sales. The proxy for the portion of the firm's value in assets in place is the ratio of inventory plus gross plant and equipment to total assets. The proxy for leverage is the ratio of long-term debt to total assets. Size is measured by the log of the book value of assets. The proxies for growth opportunities, assets in place, leverage, and size are measured over 1979–1980. Business risk is measured by the standard deviation of the percentage of change in operating income, where the latter is measured with annual data over 1973–1983.

4. Empirical results

4.1. Sample characteristics

Compensation structure and insider ownership: Summary statistics for the structure of various CEO compensation plans over 1979–1980 are presented in panel A of Table 1. Nearly 74% of the CEOs' total compensation is in salary and bonus. New stock options granted account for only 6.9%, whereas equity-based compensation accounts for 12.7% of CEOs' total compensation.[4] Panel B of

Table 1
Summary statistics

Panel A: Distribution of percentages of CEOs' total compensations in salary plus bonus, new stock options granted, and equity-based compensation for the average of 1979–1980 data for 153 randomly-selected manufacturing firms. Total compensation is the sum of the dollar values of salary, bonus, dividend units, saving plans, properties, insurance, and the value of the awards from grants of new stock options, phantom stocks, restricted stocks, performance shares, and performance units. Equity-based compensation is the sum of values of the awards from grants of new stock options, phantom stocks, restricted stocks, and performance shares.

Variables	Mean	Med.	Min.	Max.
% of compensation in salary & bonus	74.3%	79.0%	3.4%	100.0%
% of compensation in grants of new stock options	6.9	0.0	0.0	57.9
% of compensation in all equity-based plans	12.7	2.4	0.0	92.1

Panel B: Distribution of age of CEOs, percentage of shares and stock options outstanding held by CEOs plus shares held by their immediate families, and percentage of CEOs' voting power for 153 manufacturing firms for the average of 1979–1980 data.

Variables	Mean	Min.	1st quart.	Med.	3rd quart.	Max.
Age of CEO	57	42	53	58	61	80
% of shares and stock options outstanding held by CEOs plus shares held by their immediate families	5.9%	0.0%	0.1%	1.2%	6.6%	45.5%
CEOs' voting power (in percent)[a]	9.0%	0.0%	0.3%	1.8%	11.2%	62.2%

[a] CEOs' voting power is measured by the sum of the percentage of shares that CEOs and their immediate families beneficially own and the percentage of shares over which CEOs have the sole or shared power to direct the voting (such as being a co-trustee of employees' trust or a co-trustee of a charitable foundation trust) plus CEOs' stock options outstanding.

[4]Ninety-two sample firms granted options to their CEOs, 124 firms granted options to their top executives, and 130 to their officers and directors. Bennett (1987) reports that 82% of manufacturing firms have option plans for their executives, exactly the percentage found in this study.

Table 1 shows CEO age, the percentage of the CEOs' ownership of equity and stock options outstanding in the firm, and their voting power. CEOs' voting power is the sum of the percentage of shares that CEOs and their immediate families beneficially own, CEOs' stock options outstanding plus the percentage of shares over which CEOs having the sole or shared power to direct the voting (such as being a co-trustee of an employees' trust or a co-trustee of a charitable foundation trust). The average age of a CEO in the sample is 57. CEOs hold on average 5.9% in the form of equity and stock options outstanding in their firms (median = 1.2%), and CEOs' voting power exceeds their direct ownership on average by 3.1%.[5]

Outside blockholders: Outside blockholders' investment in the firm varies with their identity. The number of firms in the sample reporting the presence of individual investors, institutional investors, and corporations holding at least 5% of their firms is 20, 46, and 20, respectively.

Size of the board and its composition: Table 2 shows the size and composition of the board of directors. Each board, on average, has 10.4 members. Nearly 56% of the directors are outsiders. These directors are either retired from or currently employed in the following industries: 32.7% are from manufacturing firms, 3.6% are from savings and loans or banks, 3.4% are investment bankers, 1.6% are venture capitalists, and 1.1% are from insurance companies. The remainder of outside directors are academics, former government and military employees, consultants, clergy, and employees of nonprofit organizations.

4.2. Regression results

Regression estimates for the structure of compensation appear in Table 3. The results are reported separately for CEOs, top executives, and all officers and directors as a group. The estimates for performance are presented in Table 4. Following Eaton and Rosen (1983), the reported results in all the tables are based on the averages of variables over 1979 and 1980, except for the proxy for business risk, which is measured over 1973–1983. I use this approach to account for unusual changes that may have occurred in the variables.

4.2.1. Compensation structure
Table 3 shows the regression results for the equity-based percentage of total compensation. The coefficients of percentage shares and stock options outstanding held by CEOs, top executives, and all officers and directors have the

---

[5]Percentages of equity and stock options outstanding held by top executives and all officers and directors are 9.3 and 15.1, respectively.

Table 2

Distributions of the size of the board of directors, percentage of outside directors, percentage of outside directors employed by or retired from manufacturing firms, bank-like institutions, investment banking firms, venture capital institutions, and insurance companies for the average of 1979–1980 data for 153 randomly-selected manufacturing firms. The remaining outside directors are academics, former government and military employees, consultants, clergy, and employees of nonprofit organizations.

Variables	Mean	Med.	Min.	Max.
Size of the board	10.6	10.0	3.0	19.0
% of outside directors	55.0	57.1	4.2	91.3
% of outside directors employed by manufacturing firms	32.7	29.2	11.0	87.5
% of outside directors employed by bank-like institutions	3.6	0.0	0.0	40.0
% of outside directors employed by investment banking firms	3.4	0.0	0.0	37.5
% of outside directors employed by venture capital institutions	1.6	0.0	0.0	21.4
% of outside directors employed by insurance companies	1.1	0.0	0.0	16.0

predicted signs and are statistically significant, which suggests that firms with higher managerial ownership have less equity-based compensation in their executive compensation packages. I also find significant negative relationships between percentage of shares held by the above groups (relationships not reported here) and their respective equity-based compensations. The coefficient of the percentage shares held by all outside blockholders is negative and significant in the regression equation in which the dependent variable is the percentage of equity-based compensation for CEOs, suggesting that CEOs of firms in which a larger percentage of shares held by outside blockholders have less equity-based compensation in their compensation packages. The coefficient of the percentage of outside directors is significant, suggesting that firms with more outside directors have more equity-based compensation in their executive pay packages. The coefficient of the ratio of research and development to sales is positive and statistically significant, supporting Smith and Watts (1992), who argue that firms with larger investments in growth opportunities use incentive plans more extensively. Other studies also find this positive relationship (e.g., Eaton and Rosen, 1983; Lewellen, Loderer, and Martin, 1987; Clinch, 1991).

The results for cash compensation (not reported here) are the opposite of those for equity-based compensation. I find a positive relationship between the percentage of total compensation in cash (salary and bonus) and the percentage of shares held by managers. I also find a positive relationship between the

174   H. Mehran/Journal of Financial Economics 38 (1995) 163–184

Table 3
Ordinary least-squares estimates of percentage of CEOs', top executives', and all officers' and directors' total compensation in equity-based forms on percentages of their respectives shares and outstanding stock options holdings, percentage of shares held by all outside blockholders, percentage of outside directors, and proxies for growth opportunities, debt ratio, business risk, and size. Sample is 153 randomly-selected manufacturing firms in 1979–1980. Standard deviation of the percentage change in operating income is measured over 1973–1983. Other variables are averages for the years 1979 and 1980 (t-statistics in parentheses).

Independent variables	Dependent variable: % equity-based compensation for		
	CEOs	Top executives	All officers and directors
Intercept	0.106	0.099	0.096
	(1.097)	(0.991)	(0.964)
% shares and stock options outstanding held by CEOs	− 0.225		
	(− 2.224)**		
% shares and stock options outstanding held by top executives		− 0.268	
		(− 2.229)**	
% shares and stock options outstanding held by all officers and directors			− 0.256
			(− 2.222)**
% shares held by all outside blockholders	− 0.156	− 0.171	− 0.165
	(− 1.681)*	(− 1.612)	(− 1.553)
% of outside directors	0.899	0.887	0.897
	(2.321)**	(2.294)**	(2.284)**
R&D/sales	1.127	1.188	1.236
	(1.975)**	(2.098)**	(2.195)**
Long-term debt/total assets	− 0.099	− 0.093	− 0.040
	(− 0.658)	(− 0.626)	(− 0.325)
Standard deviation of the percentage change in operating income	− 0.011	− 0.011	− 0.011
	(− 0.733)	(− 0.754)	(− 0.770)
Log of total assets	0.014	0.014	0.013
	(1.396)	(1.408)	(1.349)
Adjusted R^2(%)	14.0	14.1	13.9
F-statistics	4.558	4.564	4.515

Asterisks indicate significance at 0.05 (**) and 0.10 (*) levels, two-sided test.

percentage of total compensation in cash and the percentage of shares held by all outside blockholders in the regression equation for CEOs. On the other hand, I find a negative relationship between the percentage of total compensation in cash and both the percentage of outside directors and the ratio of R&D to sales. Although the relationship between managers' equity-based compensation and the firm size is not statistically significant, I find that the percentage of compensation in salary and bonus is inversely related to firm size, consistent with Eaton and Rosen's finding.

The age of the CEO was also regressed against types of compensation. The argument for including this variable is that older CEOs may prefer cash compensation because of their shorter employment horizon. The conflict of interest between managers and shareholders due to employment horizon may be reduced, however, if managers own a large percentage of their company's shares. I find the coefficient of age to be significant at the 10% level in the regression equation for cash. Regressions were also run on the percentage of outstanding shares held by individual investors, institutional investors, and corporations and the percentage of outside directors employed by manufacturing firms, bank-like institutions, investment banks venture capital institutions, and insurance companies, but the results were not significant.

4.2.2. Firm performance

Panels A and B of Table 4 show the results of regressing firm performance on equity-based CEO compensation. Panel A uses Tobin's Q to proxy for firm performance, and panel B uses return on assets (ROA). Column (1) in both panels contains the basic model, in which Q and ROA are regressed against equity-based CEO compensation. The coefficients of the variable in both panels are positive and significant. The results indicate that companies in which CEO compensation is relatively sensitive to firm performance tend to produce higher returns for shareholders than companies in which the relationship between CEO pay and performance is weak.

Column (2) shows the regression results for the percentage of shares and stock options outstanding held by CEOs. The coefficient of the percentage of shares and stock options outstanding held by the CEO is positive and statistically significant. I also find a significant positive relationship (which is not reported here) between the percentage of shares held by the CEO and firm performance.[6] These findings support Jensen and Meckling (1976), who suggest that managers' incentive to work harder and smarter increases as their stake in the firm rises.

The regressions of proxies for performance on equity-based CEO compensation together with ownership are presented in column (3). Both are significant

---

[6]As in McConnell and Servaes (1990), I regressed Q and ROA on the square of CEOs' ownership together with CEOs' ownership to test for nonlinearity. The coefficient of the square term, however, was not significant.

and together they explain much larger cross-sectional variations in Q and ROA. Finally, additional explanatory variables are introduced to test the sensitivity of previous findings to their inclusion. The results are reported in column (4). The coefficients of equity-based compensation and equity ownership remain positive and significant in both panels.

Table 4
Regression of firm performance on CEO compensation

Panel A: Ordinary least-squares estimates of Tobin's Q on percentage of CEOs' equity-based compensation, percentage of shares and stock options outstanding held by CEOs, percentage of shares held by all outside blockholders, percentage of outside directors, and proxies for growth opportunities, assets in place, debt ratio, business risk, and size. Sample is 153 randomly-selected manufacturing firms in 1979–1980. Standard deviation of the percentage change in operating income is measured over 1973–1983. Other variables are averages for the year 1979 and 1980 (*t*-statistics in parentheses).

	Dependent variable: Tobin's Q			
Independent variables	(1)	(2)	(3)	(4)
Intercept	0.752	0.866	0.698	1.393
	(11.228)***	(11.634)***	(8.809)***	(2.684)***
% of CEOs' equity-based compensation	2.486		0.521	0.361
	(4.85)***		(4.391)***	(3.500)***
% of shares and stock options outstanding held by CEOs		2.035	2.263	1.876
		(2.160)**	(2.571)**	(2.323)**
% of shares held by all outside blockholders				0.261
				(0.469)
% of outside directors				0.075
				(0.513)
R&D/sales				14.279
				(5.938)***
(Inventory + gross plant and equipment)/total assets				− 0.351
				(− 1.472)
Long-term debt/total assets				− 0.054
				(− 0.995)
Standard deviation of the percentage change in operating income				− 0.113
				(− 1.965)
Log of total assets				− 0.107
				(− 2.144)**
Adjusted R^2(%)	13.0	2.9	15.5	43.2
F-statistics	23.568	4.664	12.320	11.381

Table 4 (continued)

Panel B: Ordinary least-squares estimates of return on assets on percentage of CEOs' equity-based compensation, percentage of shares and stock options outstanding held by CEOs, percentage of shares held by all outside blockholders, percentage of outside directors, and proxies for growth opportunities, assets in place, debt ratio, business risk, and size. Sample is 153 randomly-selected manufacturing firms in 1979–1980. Standard deviation of the percentage change in operating income is measured over 1973–1983. Other variables are averages for the years 1979 and 1980 (*t*-statistics in parentheses).

	Dependent variable: Return on assets			
Independent variables	(1)	(2)	(3)	(4)
Intercept	21.325	21.043	19.442	33.193
	(23.898)***	(20.171)***	(19.360)***	(4.561)***
% of CEOs' equity-based compensation	19.853		6.320	8.394
	(2.852)***		(3.682)***	(3.982)***
% of shares and stock options outstanding held by CEOs		12.501	18.442	11.664
		(2.248)**	(2.642)**	(2.115)**
% of shares held by all outside blockholders				8.454
				(1.117)
% of outside directors				0.613
				(0.308)
R&D/sales				42.126
				(1.223)***
(Inventory + gross plant and equipment)/total assets				4.257
				(1.306)
Long-term debt/total assets				− 1.225
				(− 1.712)
Standard deviation of the percentage change in operating income				− 3.493
				(− 4.445)
Log of total assets				− 0.735
				(− 1.041)**
Adjusted R^2(%)	4.4	3.2	14.2	30.0
F-statistics	8.136	5.054	11.172	6.842

Asterisks indicate significance at 0.01 (***), 0.05 (**), and 0.10 (*) levels, two-sided test.

I also find that both Q and ROA are inversely related to the percentage of CEOs' total compensation in cash (not reported here). This inverse relationship holds even after controlling for the firm's growth opportunities, assets in place, leverage ratio, business risk, and size. The explanatory variables in general explain more of the variation in the firm's performance when the latter is measured by Q. The F-statistics of the regression equations are all significant at 1% critical values or better.

4.2.3. Other results

Regressions similar to those in Table 4 were run separately for top executives and all officers and directors. Firm performance is positively related to both groups' percentage of equity-based compensation and negatively related to their total compensation in cash. In addition, performance is positively related to the percentage of equity held by top executives. The relationship between the equity holdings of all officers and directors and the firm's performance, however, is not statistically significant.

Regressions were run on managers' voting power, but this did not alter the results. Regressions were also run on other measures for outside blockholders. These measures are the percentage of shares held by the largest individual investor, the largest institutional investor, and the largest corporation, and the percentage of shares held by the three largest individual, institutional, and corporate investors. The identity of major shareholders may be relevant if motivations of outside blockholders differ (Holderness and Sheehan, 1988, p. 323). I constructed two proxies for each investor group, since the largest investor may not be the one that monitors the firm. The previous results did not change with these measures of outside blockholders.

In addition, I tried variables other than the percentage of outside directors in Eq. (2). One variable I used is the percentage of equity held by outside directors. The justification for using this variable is that the directors who have an incentive to monitor management and take strong positions on the board may be those with large ownership positions (Baum and Byrne, 1986). Morck, Shleifer, and Vishny (1988) bolster this argument by documenting a nonlinear relationship between Tobin's Q and the percentage of equity held by outside directors. Similar to Morck, Shleifer, and Vishny (1988), I introduce a number of zero–one dummy variables for different levels of outside directors' ownership to test for the presence of nonlinearity. Overall, I find a positive relationship between Tobin's Q and the percentage of equity held by outside directors and I do not find evidence of nonlinearity.

Other measures tried instead of the percentage of outside directors are the percentage of inside board members, board size, and the number of top managers employed by the firm. The justification for these variables is that subordinate managers may have an incentive to monitor their superiors, particularly when there is competition for promotion (e.g., Fama, 1980). It has also been argued that a larger internal managerial labor market gives rise to more intense monitoring (e.g., Comment, 1985). By constraining top managers' freedom to act, this monitoring increases organizational efficiency. None of these variables show any significant influence.

H. Mehran/Journal of Financial Economics 38 (1995) 163–184   179

I also tried other proxies for growth opportunities, assets in place, business risk, and size. For example, I used capital expenditures as a percentage of total assets for growth opportunities. In place of inventory plus gross plant and equipment to total assets, I used the ratio of intangible assets to total assets. Rather than using the log of the book value of assets, I used the log of sales. In place of the standard deviation of the percentage change in operating income, I used the standard deviation of the return on investment over 1973–1983, and the 60-month return variance (using the Center for Research in Security Prices monthly returns tape) over 1973–1978. These proxies did not change the general character of my results. Finally, I estimated coefficients of the regression equations by calculating heteroskedastically consistent standard errors (White, 1980). The test was not significant, indicating that the model is not subject to heteroskedasticity.

5. Summary and conclusions

One way to mitigate the conflict of interest between managers and shareholders in the corporate form of organization might be through compensation contracts. For many years organization theorists have recognized the importance of compensation in motivating top managers (e.g., Finkelstein and Hambrick, 1988). There has been little research, however, on how managers should be rewarded and on the relationship between the structure of executive compensation and firm performance. Likewise, little empirical evidence exists on the influence of various corporate claimants in designing executive compensation.

This paper provides empirical evidence on the determinants of executive compensation structure and the relationship between executive compensation structure and firm performance. I find a negative relationship between the percentage of executives' equity-based compensation and their percentage equity holdings, indicating that the board considers executives' total incentives in designing pay packages. In addition, I find that firms with more outsiders on the board make greater use of equity-based compensation. Equity-based compensation, however, is unrelated to outside directors' industry representation. A possible interpretation is that compensation structure is determined collectively, with no single industry group of outside directors exerting a dominant influence. Moreover, I find that firms with a larger percentage of their shares held by outside blockholders use less equity-based compensation, suggesting that monitoring by outside blockholders may be a substitute for incentive pay for executives.

The results on firm performance indicate that both Tobin's Q and return on assets are positively related to both the percentage of executives' total compensation that is equity-based and the percentage of shares held by top managers.

Thus compensation does affect CEO incentives in ways that have a measurable impact on corporate efficiency. The evidence presented in this paper supports advocates of incentive compensation.

In a finding consistent with Hermalin and Weisbach (1991), I observe no relationship between firm performance and board composition. This lack of correlation has been interpreted by previous researchers as implying that boards are forsaking their obligations to shareholders (e.g., Wade, O'Reilly, and Chandratat, 1990). Directors, however, can design more efficient compensation packages that include equity-based compensation. Contracts that link executives' compensation to the outcome of their actions reduce the effort and expertise required of directors for effective oversight.

I also find no significant relationship between firm performance and outside directors' equity holdings. This result contrasts with the finding of Morck, Shleifer, and Vishny (1988). Their sample is limited to large firms, which could explain the difference in results, since it has been documented that the percentage of outside directors increases with firm size. In addition, outside directors' equity ownership in general is not significant enough to give them an incentive to monitor the firm. Those directors who do have a large stake in the firm are most often blockholders who gained a seat (or seats) on the board through proxy contests. Also, a vast majority of outside directors are paid a fixed fee for their services. A study of 532 manufacturing firms shows that less than 9% have stock option plans for their outside directors (*Wall Street Journal*, March 17, 1987, p. 1), and the percentage of the outside directors' compensation for those firms that report the presence of such plans is not significant (Crystal, 1991). Thus outside directors rarely become owners of a significant percentage of the firm's equity by exercising their options. Unless a substantial component of outside directors' compensation is tied to the firm's performance (e.g., through stock options), their capital risk may not be large enough to motivate them to monitor the management team.

In addition, I find no support for a relationship between firm performance and blockholders' stockholdings (consistent with McConnell and Servaes, 1990). Similarly, I find no support for a relationship between firm performance and the percentage of shares held by different groups of outside blockholders, i.e., individual investors, institutional investors, and corporations. One explanation for the lack of correlation between performance and the percentage of shares held by institutional investors could be that this study does not distinguish between institutions which buy and sell securities for short-term profit and those which hold shares for a long period — e.g., the College Retirement Equities Fund (CREF). It has been suggested that institutions with a longer holding period have more incentive to monitor managers (Nussbaum and Dobrzynski, 1987). Another possibility is that some of the institutional investors may not monitor the management team because they transact business with the firm (e.g., Brickley, Lease, and Smith, 1988). In addition, financial institutions face

H. Mehran/Journal of Financial Economics 38 (1995) 163–184 181

substantial legal barriers in their efforts to hold large blocks of stock in public corporations, thus limiting their ability to control managers (e.g., Roe, 1990). Finally, Barclay and Holderness (1991) have shown that the effect of large blockholders on firm value also depends on the specific skills the blockholders bring to the firm.

An important area for future research is which forms of equity-based compensation matter. We also need to understand why board composition is unrelated to firm performance, and what relationship there is, if any, between performance and the form in which outside directors are compensated.

Appendix: Measurement of executive compensation

As in Larcker and Balkcom (1984), Antle and Smith (1986), and Ely (1991), this paper attempts to measure total compensation. The estimates of executives' annual compensation in this study exclude pension plans because of difficulties in estimating their value. The valuation procedures for each element of compensation are discussed in turn.

Salary and bonus consist of dollar amounts for regular salary and bonuses earned annually during the 1979–1980 period. The annual bonus is adjusted if the bonus for one year was paid in the subsequent fiscal year. For example, in a number of cases bonuses for 1980 were reported in 1981 proxy statements. These bonuses are added to those in 1980.

Dividend units are valued as the number of units held by an executive multiplied by the present value (at the risk-free rate) of the dividend stream over the life of the dividend unit, assuming that the dividends per share declared and paid in the 1979–1980 period will continue over the life of the dividend unit.

Stock options are measured by the value of options granted during the sample period. The new grants can be calculated by applying a variation of Black–Scholes suggested by Noreen and Wolfson (1981), allowing for continuous dividend payments (see below). Stock appreciation rights (SARs) are typically granted along with stock options (i.e., either the option or the SAR could be exercised). Since the option and the SAR should have similar values, SARs granted in tandem with options are assumed to provide zero additional remuneration to the executive.

Restricted stocks are valued as the number of restricted shares granted times the stock price at the grant date. Phantom stocks are valued the same way as restricted stock plans. Performance shares are valued as the number of shares times the stock price at the grant date. Performance units are valued as the number of units times the dollar value assigned to each unit in the year granted.

182   *H. Mehran/Journal of Financial Economics 38 (1995) 163–184*

Valuation of stock options

The value of each executive stock option granted is calculated using the following formula:

$$C = S\, e^{-dT}\, \phi(Z) - X\, e^{-rT}\, \phi(Z - \sigma\sqrt{T}),$$

where

C = price of option,

S = common stock price on the date of the grant (data source: proxy statement),

X = exercise price (data source: proxy statement),

$\phi(.)$ = cumulative standard normal distribution function,

T = time to expiration (data source: proxy statement),

r = continuous risk-free interest rate, measured as $\ln(1 + R)/12$, where R is the annual five-year and ten-year average market yield on U.S. Government securities (data source: Federal Reserve Bulletin).

d = continuous dividend yield defined as $\ln[1 + (\text{dividend per share}/\text{closing stock price})]/12$ (data sources: COMPUSTAT and the Center for Research in Security Prices),

σ = estimated monthly stock return variance for the sixty-month period preceding the first day of the current fiscal year (data source: Center for Research in Security Prices monthly returns tape),

Z = $[\ln(S/X) + (r - d + \sigma^2/2)]\,(T/\sigma\sqrt{T})$.

References

Amihud, Yakov and Baruch Lev, 1981, Risk reduction as a managerial motive for conglomerate mergers, Bell Journal of Economics 12, 605–617.

Antle, Rick and Abbie Smith, 1986, Measuring executive compensation: Methods and an application, Journal of Accounting Research 23, 269–325.

Barclay, Michael J. and Clifford G. Holderness, 1991, Negotiated-block traders and corporate control, Journal of Finance 46, 861–878.

Baum, Laurie and John A. Byrne, 1986, The job nobody wants, Business Week, September 8, 56–61.

Bennett, Amanda, 1987, Executives see stock options drop in value, Wall Street Journal, October 21, 39.

Benston, George J., 1985, The validity of profits-structure studies with particular reference to the FTCs Line of Business Data, American Economic Review 75, 37–67.

Brickley, James A. and Frederick H. Dark, 1987, The choice of organizational form: The case of franchising, Journal of Financial Economics 18, 401–420.

Brickley, James A. and Christopher James, 1987, The takeover market, corporate board composition, and ownership structure: The case of banking, Journal of Law and Economics 30, 161–180.

Brickley, James A. and Leonard D. van Drunen, 1987, Residual claims, decision rights and board structure, Working paper (William E. Simon Graduate School of Business Administration, University of Rochester, Rochester, NY).

H. Mehran/Journal of Financial Economics 38 (1995) 163–184 183

Brickley, James A., Ronald C. Lease, and Clifford W. Smith, 1988, Ownership structure and voting on antitakeover amendments, Journal of Financial Economics 20, 267–292.

Clinch, Greg, 1991, Employee compensation and firms' research and development activity, Journal of Accounting Research 29, 59–78.

Comment, Robert, 1985, The effects of firm-specific human capital on management equity investment and turnover, Unpublished doctoral dissertation (University of Michigan, Ann Arbor, MI).

Crystal, Graef, 1991, Do directors earn their keep?, Fortune, May 6, 78–80.

Cummins, Clint, Bronwyn H. Hall, Elizabeth S. Laderman, and Joy Mody, 1985, The R&D master file: Documentation, NBER paper.

Defeo, Victor J., Richard A. Lambert, and David F. Larcker, 1989, The executive compensation effects of equity-for-debt swaps, Accounting Review 64, 201–227.

Demsetz, Harlod and Kenneth Lehn, 1985, The structure of corporate ownership: Causes and consequences, Journal of Political Economy 93, 1155–1177.

Eaton, Jonathan and Harvey Rosen, 1983, Agency delayed compensation, and the structure of executive remuneration, Journal of Finance 5, 1489–1505.

Ely, Kirsten M., 1991, Interindustry differences in the relation between compensation and firm performance variables, Journal of Accounting Research 29, 37–58.

Fama, Eugene F., 1980, Agency problems and the theory of the firm, Journal of Political Economy 88, 288–325.

Fama, Eugene F. and Michael C. Jensen, 1983, Separation of ownership and control, Journal of Law and Economics 26, 301–325.

Finkelstein, Sydney and Donald C. Hambrick, 1988, Chief executive compensation: A synthesis and reconsideration, Strategic Management Journal 9, 543–558.

Fisher, Franklin M. and John J. McGowan, 1983, On the misuse of accounting rates of return to infer monopoly profits, American Economic Review 73, 82–97.

Grossman, Sanford J. and Oliver D. Hart, 1983, An analysis of the principal agent problem, Econometrica 51, 7–45.

Harris, Milton and Arthur Raviv, 1979, Optimal incentive contracts with imperfect information, Journal of Economic Theory 20, 231–259.

Hart, Oliver D., 1983, The market mechanism as an incentive scheme, Bell Journal of Economics 14, 366–382.

Hermalin, Benjamin E. and Michael S. Weisbach, 1991, The effects of board composition and direct incentives on firm performance, Financial Management 20, 101–112.

Hirshleifer, David and Yoon Suh, 1992, Risk, managerial effort and project choice, Journal of Financial Intermediation, forthcoming.

Holderness, Clifford G. and Dennis P. Sheehan, 1988, The role of majority shareholders in publicly held corporations: An exploratory analysis, Journal of Financial Economics 20, 317–346.

Holmstrom, Bengt, 1979, Moral hazard and observability, Bell Journal of Economics 10, Spring, 74–91.

Jacobson, Robert, 1987, The validity of ROI as a measure of business performance, American Economic Review 77, 470–478.

Jensen, Michael C. and William H. Meckling, 1976, Theory of the firm: Managerial behavior, agency costs and ownership structure, Journal of Financial Economics 3, 305–360.

Jensen, Michael C. and Kevin J. Murphy, 1990a, CEO incentives – It's not how much you pay, but how, Journal of Applied Corporate Finance, 36–49.

Jensen, Michael C. and Kevin J. Murphy, 1990b, Performance pay and top-management incentives, Journal of Political Economy 98, 225–264.

Jensen, Michael C. and Richard S. Ruback, 1983, The market for corporate control, Journal of Financial Economics 11, 5–50.

Landsman, Wayne R. and Alan C. Shapiro, 1989, Tobin's q and the relationship between accounting ROI and economic return, Accounting working paper no. 89-3 (Anderson Graduate School of Management, University of California at Los Angeles, Los Angeles, CA).

Larcker, David F. and John E. Balkcom, 1984, Executive compensation contracts and investment behavior: An analysis of mergers, Working paper (Northwestern University, Evanston, IL).

Lewellen, Wilbur, Claudio Loderer, and Kenneth Martin, 1987, Executive compensation and executive incentive problem, Journal of Accounting and Economics 9, 287–310.

McConnell, John J. and Henri Servaes, 1990, Additional evidence on equity ownership and corporate value, Journal of Financial Economics 27, 595–612.

Morck, Randall, Andrei Shleifer, and Robert W. Vishny, 1988, Management ownership and corporate performance: An empirical analysis, Journal of Financial Economics 20, 293–316.

Murphy, Kevin J., 1985, Corporate performance and managerial remuneration: An empirical analysis, Journal of Accounting and Economics 7, 11–42.

Noreen, Eric and Mark Wolfson, 1981, Equilibrium warrant pricing models and accounting for executive stock options, Journal of Accounting Research 19, 384–398.

Nussbaum, Bruce and Judith H. Dobrzynski, 1987, The battle for corporate control, Business Week, May 18, 102–109.

Paul, Jonathan M., 1992, On the efficiency of stock-based compensation, Review of Financial Studies 5, 471–502.

Roe, Mark J., 1990, Political and legal restraints on ownership and control of public companies, Journal of Financial Economics 27, 7–42.

Rosenstein, Stuart and Jeffrey G. Wyatt, 1990, Outside directors, board independence, and shareholder wealth, Journal of Financial Economics 26, 175–191.

Shleifer, Andrei and Robert W. Vishny, 1986, Large shareholders and corporate control, Journal of Political Economy 95, 461–488.

Sloan, Richard G., 1993, Accounting earnings and top executive compensation, Journal of Accounting and Economics 16, 55–100.

Smith, Clifford W. and Ross L. Watts, 1992, The investment opportunity set and corporate financing, dividend, and compensation policies, Journal of Financial Economics 32, 263–292.

Vancil, Richard F., 1987, Passing the baton: Managing the process of CEO succession (Harvard Business School Press, Boston, MA).

Wade, James, Charles A. O'Reilly, and Ike Chandratat, 1990, Golden parachutes: CEOs and the exercise of social influence, Administrative Science Quarterly 35, 587–603.

Weisbach, Michael S., 1988, Outside directors and CEO turnover, Journal of Financial Economics 20, 431–460.

White, Halbert, 1980, A heteroskedasticity-consistent covariance matrix estimator and a direct test for heteroskedasticity, Econometrica 48, 817–838.

White, Joseph B., 1990, GM's plan to boost executives' pensions draw fire; one big holder is to say 'no', Wall Street Journal, May 14, A3.

[17]

© Academy of Management Journal
1998, Vol. 41. No. 2, 200–208.

THE EFFECT OF INSTITUTIONAL INVESTORS ON THE LEVEL AND MIX OF CEO COMPENSATION

PARTHIBAN DAVID
Nanyang Technological University

RAHUL KOCHHAR
Purdue University

EDWARD LEVITAS
Texas A&M University

This study investigated the influence of institutional investors on CEO compensation policy. Results suggest that institutional owners that have only an investment relationship with a firm influence compensation in accordance with shareholder preferences to (1) lower its level and (2) increase the proportion of long-term incentives in total compensation. However, institutions that depend on a firm for their own business are not able to influence compensation in this manner. This study extends prior research by supporting the viewpoint that the nature of ownership in a firm is an important determinant of CEO compensation.

Considerable research has examined the effect of ownership structure on chief executive officer (CEO) compensation policy (see Gomez-Mejia [1994] for a review). Essentially, the conclusion of this research has been that owners with large blocks of shares (typically, more than 5 percent of a firm's total shares) influence CEO compensation as per the interests of all shareholders. Although prior research has provided significant insights on the relationship between the *size* of ownership stakes and CEO compensation, it has failed to consider the effect of the *nature* of corporate ownership. Specifically, the role of an increasingly important shareholder group, institutional investors, has not been adequately studied (Gomez-Mejia, 1994).

Institutional investors own more than half the equity of U.S. corporations (Useem, 1996). Although institutional investors may individually have small holdings, their large aggregate ownership provides them power over a firm's management (Davis & Thompson, 1994). Institutional investors are a heterogeneous group of organizations, including banks, public and private pension funds, mutual funds, and insurance companies, and they have potentially divergent predilections toward exercising influence (O'Barr & Conley, 1992). As own-

ers, all institutions have an obligation to exercise a governance role; however, some institutions may not effectively perform this role because of conflicts of interest resulting from business relationships with firms in which they invest (Heard & Sherman, 1987). Our study addresses this question by examining the influence of different types of institutional investors on CEO compensation. As a firm's compensation policy has the potential to affect its performance (Gerhart & Milkovich, 1990), it becomes important to examine the impact of institutional investors on CEO compensation.

OWNERSHIP STRUCTURE AND CEO COMPENSATION

According to a political perspective, organizational outcomes are shaped by a struggle for dominance among coalitions with possibly opposing goals (Mintzberg, 1983; Pfeffer, 1981). Managers and owners represent two major coalitions at the apex of a firm with opposing preferences as regards compensation policy, and the level and mix of compensation is likely to reflect the preferences of the group that gains the preponderance of power (O'Reilly, Main, & Crystal, 1988; Tosi & Gomez-Mejia, 1989). In the absence of strong owners, CEOs may gain power to extract higher pay than is justified by market considerations (for instance, the level of the CEOs' human capital, their expected

We have greatly benefited from the comments of Michael Hitt, Javier Gimeno, Albert Cannella, and two anonymous reviewers.

marginal product vis-à-vis the competitive price set by the market for CEO talent, and the level of firm performance [Finkelstein & Hambrick, 1988]). Prior research has generally supported this viewpoint: CEOs of owner-controlled firms—firms in which at least one owner possesses more than 5 percent of the shares—have been shown to have lower levels of pay than those of manager-controlled firms, which are characterized by more diffuse ownership (Dyl, 1988; Hambrick & Finkelstein, 1995).

The compensation mix, or the proportion of long-term incentives in a compensation contract, may serve to align the interests of managers with those of shareholders by rewarding CEOs only if shareholder returns are enhanced (Beatty & Zajac, 1994; Gomez-Mejia, 1994; Zajac & Westphal, 1994). As long-term incentives lessen the need for vigilant monitoring (Beatty & Zajac, 1994; Zajac & Westphal, 1994), shareholders often favor them. However, CEOs may prefer to minimize this long-term component as they can benefit only if performance improves (Gomez-Mejia, Tosi, & Hinkin, 1987; Westphal & Zajac, 1994). The portion of CEO pay linked to long-term performance is vulnerable to factors beyond managerial control, such as aggregate market demand and stock market fluctuations, that increase the riskiness of compensation (Hill & Phan, 1991). Furthermore, long-term incentives granted in the form of stock increase a CEO's firm-specific investment and, consequently, his or her associated risk (Beatty & Zajac, 1994). CEOs would presumably prefer to retain control over their pay by getting compensated through cash, thereby limiting the extent to which their income is exposed to risk. Consistent with these arguments, research has shown that incentive alignment is greater in owner-controlled than in manager-controlled firms (Tosi & Gomez-Mejia, 1989) and that, when CEOs gain power—as they do, for instance, when they also hold the board chairperson title—the compensation mix reflects CEO preferences for minimizing the long-term component of pay (Beatty & Zajac, 1994; Zajac & Westphal, 1994).

THEORY AND HYPOTHESES

The Role of Institutional Investors

Institutional investors have recently emerged as an important group of shareholders with the potential to check managerial hegemony. Institutional investors increased their aggregate ownership stakes in U.S. equity markets from 16 percent in 1965 to 57 percent by 1994 (Useem, 1996). Even when single institutional investors do not own large blocks of shares, they may nevertheless seek a more active governance role than individual shareholders. Unlike individuals, institutions essentially invest "other people's money," and they thus have a legal fiduciary obligation to take proactive actions, such as actions influencing CEO pay, to protect their investments against erosion in value (Krikorian, 1991). Additionally, their high aggregate ownership makes it difficult for institutional investors to sell off their shares in response to poor firm performance, as their doing so may adversely affect the stock price. Moreover, it is difficult for institutional investors to find appropriate alternate investments, considering that they already own significant stakes in most firms in the economy. The difficulty of exit provides these investors with the incentive to exercise voice to influence the level and mix of CEO compensation (David & Kochhar, 1996). Ownership in hundreds of firms provides institutional investors the opportunity to gain economies of scale in monitoring compensation policy (Black, 1992). Through their interactions with various companies in their portfolios, institutions can likely develop the ability to determine if the compensation policy of a firm is appropriate.

It has been suggested that the rise in institutions' power arising from the increase in their aggregate equity holdings constitutes a new social movement (Davis & Thompson, 1994). Although single institutional investors may not have large blockholdings, they can gain power from coordinated action through their joint holdings to influence CEO compensation. The formation of shareholder organizations such as the Council of Institutional Investors has conferred a shared identity on institutional investors and provided a springboard for collective action (Davis & Thompson, 1994). Institutions are increasingly resorting to activism to press their demands. Their involvement in setting compensation policy is most visible in poorly performing firms, where these investors seek to initiate change by negotiating with the boards, demanding the nomination of independent compensation committees, voicing public criticism, and sometimes even voting against board nominees proposed by management (Useem, 1996). These pressure tactics have been successful at firms such as Champion International and Advanced Micro Devices, both of which changed compensation packages in response to institutional demands (Star, 1993). In most cases, institutional investors with far less than 5 percent ownership have initiated such actions (Wahal, 1996). However, the groundswell of support from various institutional investors with high aggregate ownership has forced managers to respond to their demands (Useem, 1996). Thus, it appears that ownership stakes can provide institutional investors the power to influence compensation.

Differences among Institutional Investors

As noted, institutional investors are a diverse set of organizations, including banks, public and private pension funds, mutual funds, and insurance companies, among others (O'Barr & Conley, 1992). The power to monitor managers and the predilection for doing so may differ across these organizations, and not all institutional investors may have the means or the inclination to influence compensation. The relationship between institutional investors and firms can be described along two dimensions. First, equity ownership in a firm provides institutions with an *investor relationship*. All institutional investors have this relationship to the firms they invest in and, as owners, they have a fiduciary responsibility to safeguard their investments (O'Barr & Conley, 1992). Thus, institutional investors will attempt to influence the level and mix of CEO compensation in the firms they invest in to safeguard the value of their ownership stakes, as discussed previously.

An institutional investor, however, may also have a *business relationship* with a firm in which it invests. For such an institution, the power gained from the ownership stake (Finkelstein, 1992) may be partially negated by dependence on the firm for business (Cook, 1977; Levine & White, 1961). Firm managers can, presumably, take advantage of the business relationship to co-opt institutional investors by penalizing them if they oppose managerial preferences (Heard & Sherman, 1987). Thus, it appears that the two relationships—investor and business—may pose counteracting pressures on institutional investors (Heard & Sherman, 1987). Ownership represents a source of power that can be used to either support or oppose managers (Salancik & Pfeffer, 1980). Institutions without business relationships can use their ownership power to oppose managers' preferences for more generous compensation. In contrast, the presence of business relationships may constrain institutional investors. To safeguard such business relationships, institutional investors may be reluctant to use their ownership power against managers and may even support managers' efforts to obtain more generous compensation. Thus, ownership stakes may not automatically signify better governance, and it becomes necessary to examine the *nature* of ownership to determine whether owners are likely to safeguard shareholder preferences or be coopted to support managerial preferences.

Brickley, Lease, and Smith (1988) developed a taxonomy for classifying institutional investors in terms of the extent to which business relationships can reduce ownership power and, hence, the ability to effectively influence firm policies. Institutional investors with business relationships with firms in which they might invest include banks, insurance companies, and nonbank trusts. For instance, insurance companies sell insurance policies to firms, and banks derive interest income by lending to firms. These investors are susceptible to influence exercised by firm managers and are termed *pressure-sensitive* (Brickley et al., 1988). *Pressure-resistant* institutions, on the other hand, do not have business relationships with firms and, accordingly, do not face conflicts with their investor relationship. These institutions, such as public pension funds, mutual funds, and endowments and foundations, can intervene in corporate governance without fear of retribution from corporate managers. Previous research has shown that pressure-resistant institutions are more effective in influencing managers than are pressure-sensitive institutions. Brickley and colleagues (1988) found that when voting on antitakeover amendments, pressure-resistant institutions were more likely to oppose firm managers than pressure-sensitive institutions. Similarly, pressure-resistant institutions were found to positively influence firm innovation, but pressure-sensitive institutions had no effect (Kochhar & David, 1996).

A third-category, *pressure-indeterminate* institutions, includes those whose relationships with the firms they invest in cannot be so clearly defined.

CEO compensation is an outcome of a political power struggle between CEOs who attempt to extract the most favorable pay packet and owners who would like to limit the level of compensation and increase the proportion of long-term incentives. The extent to which owners are successful in influencing pay is a function of the power they have to exercise over CEOs. Although all institutional investors have the fiduciary obligation to exercise influence, there may be differences in their ability and incentive to do so. Pressure-resistant institutions are not susceptible to managerial influence and should therefore be able to use the power gained from their ownership stakes to counteract managerial dominance and influence the level and mix of CEO compensation, per shareholders' preferences.

Hypothesis 1a. Pressure-resistant institutional ownership is negatively associated with the level of CEO compensation.

Hypothesis 1b. Pressure-resistant institutional ownership is positively associated with the proportion of long-term incentives in total CEO compensation.

The influence of pressure-sensitive institutions is less clear-cut. As owners, they have the fiduciary obligation to influence compensation, just like pressure-resistant institutions. However, business relationships may pose conflicts of interests, mitigating the extent of their influence. Hence, pressure-sensitive institutions may get coopted and be reluctant to influence compensation. Alternately, they may support managers in their quest for more generous compensation to cement cordial business relationships. However, the extent of such cooptation is difficult to predict. At the very least, we expected pressure-resistant institutions to be more capable than pressure-sensitive institutions of influencing CEO compensation in a direction consonant with shareholder preferences.

Hypothesis 2a. The effect of pressure-resistant institutions on the level of CEO compensation is more consistent with shareholder preferences than the effect of pressure-sensitive institutions.

Hypothesis 2b. The effect of pressure-resistant institutions on the proportion of long-term incentives in CEO compensation is more consistent with shareholder preferences than the effect of pressure-sensitive institutions.

METHODS

Sample and Analyses

Sample firms were identified from the *Fortune* compensation survey of the 200 largest U.S. corporations during 1992, 1993, and 1994. CEO compensation in these firms was tracked for the period 1990–94. A total of 125 firms for which compensation and other data were available for all five years were included in the sample. We lagged data on independent and control variables by one year. As lagged compensation was one of the independent variables, the analyses were carried out on a sample of 500 observations (125 firms, four years). The data were longitudinal, with both cross-sectional and time series elements, and a random effects pooling model was estimated using generalized least squares (Greene, 1993).[1]

---

[1] This data structure enabled us to make both between-firms and within-firm comparisons, thus controlling for the effects of any unobserved variables. A one-year lag addresses how compensation policies respond to changes in institutional ownership. Yet limiting the data to four years ensured that policies remained relatively stable over time.

Variables

The two dependent variables used were (1) the level of CEO compensation and (2) the proportion of long-term incentives in total CEO compensation. The *level of compensation* was the sum of total salary, bonus, and long-term compensation (grants of restricted stock, stock options, stock appreciation rights, and performance plans) in a year. We obtained compensation data from proxy statements and valued long-term compensation using the Black-Scholes options-pricing model (Cannella & Gray, 1996). The *proportion of long-term incentives* was the ratio of long-term compensation to total compensation. As the distribution of this variable was skewed, we applied a logarithmic transformation. Use of this transformation is consistent with prior research (Zajac & Westphal, 1994).

The independent variables of interest described ownership by the different types of institutional investors. Detailed information on institutional ownership was obtained from the database Compact Disclosure. We used the *Money Market Directory, Moody's Bank and Finance Manual,* and *Nelson's Directory of Investment Managers* to classify a total of 1,622 institutional investors. The percentage of aggregate ownership held by each of the following three types of institutional investors was computed: (1) *pressure-resistant* institutions were public pension funds, mutual funds, and endowments and foundations, (2) *pressure-sensitive* institutions were insurance companies, banks, and nonbank trusts, and (3) *pressure-indeterminate* institutions, a residual category, were investors such as corporate pension funds, brokerage houses, and investment counselors, whose motives and actions could not be clearly defined. For example, a corporate pension fund does not depend on other firms for business, but it may be unwilling to intervene actively in their affairs as its sponsoring corporation may not like to be the target of similar efforts on the part of its institutional investors.

We included several control variables in the model to account for other factors that might affect CEO compensation policy. Blockholders (shareholders with greater than 5 percent ownership) provide better governance in setting compensation policy than do smaller investors (Hambrick & Finkelstein, 1995; Tosi & Gomez-Mejia, 1989). Following the cited prior research, we used a dummy variable to capture the effect of blockholders. The variable noninstitutional blockholders was coded as one when at least one blockholder, other than an institutional investor, was present in a firm and as zero otherwise. Outside directors may provide better governance and thus influence CEO compensation, and CEO duality (one person is both a firm's CEO and chairperson of its board) may provide CEOs undue influence over compensation (Westphal & Zajac, 1994). Accordingly, we controlled for the proportion of outside directors on a board and for CEO duality. A dummy variable was used to code CEO duality (1 = CEO also the chair, 0 = otherwise). Data on blockholders and boards were obtained from Compact Disclosure.

Older CEOs may, by virtue of their experience, receive higher compensation. Also, older CEOs may be more risk-averse and prefer a smaller proportion of long-term incentives. Accordingly, we controlled for CEO age. Hambrick and Finkelstein (1995) suggested that CEOs' compensation is affected by both (1) their accession to a new position and (2) changes over the course of their tenure. New CEOs are likely to receive higher salaries than they received formerly and, over time, they can expect annual salary increases. Furthermore, CEOs with greater tenure accumulate power over their boards (Finkelstein, 1992), and this may help them obtain higher levels of compensation (Finkelstein & Hambrick, 1989; Hill & Phan, 1991) and limit the proportion of long-term incentives (Westphal & Zajac, 1994). We controlled for the appointment of a new CEO by introducing a dummy variable valued one in a year of appointment and zero otherwise. CEO tenure was measured as an individual's number of years of service as the CEO of a given firm. Data on CEO characteristics were obtained from Compact Disclosure.

Firm performance may drive the level (Jensen & Murphy, 1990a) and mix of compensation (Westphal & Zajac, 1994). As there is some debate in the literature about the preferred measure (Weiner & Mahoney, 1981), we used both an accounting measure, return on assets (ROA), and a market measure, Jensen's alpha. CEO compensation is strongly influenced by firm size (Gomez-Mejia, 1994; Lambert, Larcker, & Weigelt, 1991). Therefore, we used the logarithm of firm assets to control for size. Compensation may need to be tailored to firm risk (Gomez-Mejia, 1994). CEOs in firms with high risk may demand a higher level of compensation (Hill & Phan, 1991) and a lower proportion of long-term incentives (Westphal & Zajac, 1994). We controlled for a firm's systematic risk, defined as the variance of its stock price relative to that of a market portfolio. Data to calculate performance, size, and risk were obtained from COMPUSTAT and Center for Research in Security Prices (CRSP) files.

CEO pay is likely to be set in line with prevailing industry norms (Hambrick & Finkelstein, 1995). To control for possible variations in compensation policies across industries, we included two variables for industry pay. Industry pay was determined by computing the mean level of pay and the mean proportion of long-term incentives received by all CEOs in each two-digit Standard Industrial Classification (SIC) code represented in the sample in each year (Hambrick & Finkelstein, 1995; Hill & Phan, 1991). Finally, CEO compensation in prior time periods may affect current compensation. Accordingly, we introduced lagged values in the model as controls.

RESULTS

Table 1 presents the descriptive statistics, including means, standard deviations, and correlations, of the variables used in this study. Table 2 presents the results of the regression analyses. A negative and statistically significant association between pressure-resistant ownership and level of CEO compensation would provide support for Hypothesis 1a. A positive and statistically significant association between pressure-resistant ownership and the proportion of long-term incentives in CEO pay would support Hypothesis 1b. We observed that pressure-sensitive ownership had a positive and significant effect on compensation level but a positive and nonsignificant effect on the proportion of long-term incentives. We evaluated support for Hypotheses 2a and 2b using a *t*-test of the difference between the coefficients for pressure-resistant and pressure-sensitive institutional ownership. The difference in coefficients for the level of compensation was statistically significant, indicating that pressure-resistant ownership reduced pay more than pressure-sensitive ownership. Thus, with respect to the level of pay, pressure-resistant institutions upheld shareholders' interests better than pressure-sensitive institutions, supporting Hypothesis 2a. With respect to long-term incentives, however, the difference between pressure-resistant and pressure-sensitive ownership was not statistically significant, thus failing to support Hypothesis 2b.[2]

---

[2] To test the sensitivity of our results, we ran the analyses using alternative measures of ownership structure. A Herfindahl measure that weighted large ownership stakes more than smaller ownership stakes gave the same results. This finding suggests that institutional investors with small stakes also play an important role. Our classification of institutional investors is a slight modification of that adopted by Brickley and colleagues (1988). Those authors classified all institutions with less than 1 percent ownership as pressure-indeterminate, arguing that this level of ownership might not be sufficiently high to provide investors the incentives or the power to influence decisions. Our sample consisted of very large firms, and a small stake in such firms may be of very high value. Furthermore, institutional

1998   David, Kochhar, and Levitas   205

TABLE 1
Descriptive Statistics and Correlations[a]

Variable	Mean	s.d.	1	2	3	4	5	6	7	8	9	10	11	12	13	14	15	16	17	18
1. Level of compensation[b]	3.72	5.10																		
2. Proportion of long-term incentives	2.55	3.01	.24																	
3. Pressure-resistant ownership	22.02	10.74	−.02	.07																
4. Pressure-sensitive ownership	17.71	7.39	.11	.08	.36															
5. Pressure-indeterminate ownership	16.02	7.97	.02	.08	.49	.31														
6. Noninstitutional blockholder ownership	0.26	0.44	−.03	−.10	.02	−.06	−.04													
7. CEO duality	0.92	0.27	.05	.04	.03	.05	.06	.02												
8. Proportion of outside directors	75.72	11.61	.08	.16	.10	.09	.04	−.06	.00											
9. New CEO	0.09	0.28	−.03	.05	−.00	−.07	.01	−.06	−.15	−.06										
10. CEO tenure	7.76	7.00	.01	−.25	.06	.01	.03	.15	.03	−.08	−.30									
11. CEO age	58.99	5.37	.05	.01	.04	.04	.16	.02	−.03	−.04	−.07	.42								
12. ROA	0.04	0.06	.12	−.09	−.11	.16	−.01	.03	−.10	−.10	−.08	.12	−.01							
13. Jensen's alpha	0.00	0.02	.15	.08	.09	.00	.14	−.05	−.03	.06	−.05	−.02	.00	.18						
14. Size	9.51	1.26	.11	.24	.04	−.11	.06	−.09	.01	.03	.06	−.02	.06	−.32	.05					
15. Firm risk	1.05	0.49	.01	−.03	.17	−.05	.03	.13	−.04	−.04	.05	.03	−.12	.02	−.01	.06				
16. Lagged level of compensation	4.08	7.91	.37	.04	−.06	.05	−.01	.03	.03	−.00	−.04	.01	.00	.16	.10	.05	.02			
17. Industry level of compensation	3.72	1.58	.31	.20	.03	.14	.12	.09	−.11	−.02	.02	.00	.05	.02	.03	.24	.11	.07		
18. Lagged proportion of long-term incentives	2.54	3.06	.13	.41	.03	.08	.08	−.05	.03	.15	.05	−.23	−.02	−.06	.06	.23	.00	.19	.11	
19. Industry proportion of long-term incentives	2.55	1.20	.16	.40	−.03	.05	.02	−.00	−.06	.08	.08	−.17	.04	−.05	.13	.40	.09	.03	.50	.22

[a] Correlations greater than .18 are significant at $p < .001$; r's $> .11$ are significant at $p < .01$; r's $> .09$ are significant at $p < .05$; and r's $> .07$ are significant at $p < .10$. $N = 500$ (125 firms, four years).

[b] Millions of dollars.

DISCUSSION AND CONCLUSIONS

We found that institutional investors influenced CEO compensation, but their effect depended on the nature of their relationships with firms. The presence of pressure-resistant institutions that had an exclusively investment relationship with firms and did not depend on the firms for business reduced the level of their CEOs' pay and increased the proportion of long-term incentives in CEO compensation. The direction of this influence is congruent with the principles of shareholder wealth maximization. The presence of pressure-sensitive institutions, however, had no effect on the mix of

---

investors have not hesitated to exercise their influence on compensation even when their individual ownership has been lower than 1 percent (Wahal, 1996). Thus, we preferred to classify all institutions, including those with less than 1 percent ownership, as pressure-sensitive or pressure-resistant. We then reanalyzed the data using the Brickley et al. (1988) approach and found the same results. Again, this pattern suggests that small ownership stakes held by institutional investors are important in affecting CEO compensation.

CEO compensation and, in fact, appeared to be associated with higher CEO compensation. The divergence between pressure-resistant and pressure-sensitive institutions with respect to their influence on the level of CEO compensation illustrates the political nature of executive pay. Presumably, managers use threats that they will discontinue business relationships to coopt pressure-sensitive institutions or, alternatively, these investors may choose to favor generous pay packages for CEOs in order to cement valued business relationships. The absence of business relationships enables pressure-resistant institutions to favor reduced CEO compensation, in accordance with shareholder preferences. This result is consistent with the viewpoint that institutional investors are owners who actively influence firm outcomes (Jensen, 1993) and with prior research suggesting that institutional investors influence firm strategy (Kochhar & David, 1996) and performance (Nesbitt, 1994). Although prior researchers have mainly considered the effect of the *size* of ownership stakes, our results suggest

TABLE 2
Results of Pooled Cross-Sectional Time Series Regression Analysis of Institutional Ownership on CEO Compensation[a]

Independent Variable	Level of Compensation		Proportion of Long-Term Incentives	
	Parameter Estimate	Standardized Estimate	Parameter Estimate	Standardized Estimate
Intercept	−6.84*** (0.91)		−0.76 (0.62)	
Pressure-resistant ownership	−0.02*** (0.01)	−0.04***	0.01* (0.00)	0.03*
Pressure-sensitive ownership	0.04*** (0.01)	0.05***	0.01 (0.01)	0.01
Pressure-indeterminate ownership	−0.02* (0.01)	−0.03*	0.01 (0.01)	0.02
Noninstitutional blockholder ownership	−0.40*** (0.10)	−0.04***	−0.18* (0.07)	−0.03*
CEO duality	0.91*** (0.20)	0.05***	0.31* (0.13)	0.03*
Proportion of outside directors	0.03*** (0.01)	0.06***	0.01** (0.00)	0.03**
New CEO	0.12 (0.16)	0.01	−0.07 (0.12)	−0.01
CEO tenure	−0.02* (0.01)	−0.03*	−0.05*** (0.01)	−0.12***
CEO age	0.04*** (0.01)	0.05***	0.01 (0.01)	0.02
ROA	5.35*** (1.00)	0.06***	−0.48 (0.59)	−0.01
Jensen's alpha	14.80*** (1.90)	0.06***	−1.88 (1.53)	−0.02
Size	0.17*** (0.05)	0.04***	0.04* (0.03)	0.02*
Firm risk	0.09 (0.08)	0.01	−0.04 (0.07)	−0.01
Lagged level of compensation	0.10*** (0.02)	0.16***		
Industry level of compensation	0.75*** (0.04)	0.23***		
Lagged proportion of long-term incentives			0.36*** (0.03)	0.36***
Industry proportion of long-term incentives			0.45*** (0.05)	0.18***
Logarithmic likelihood	−917.6***		−779.3***	
Buse R^2	0.65		0.43	
t^b	3.26***		0.31	

[a] $N = 500$ (125 firms, four years). Standard errors are in parentheses.
[b] Test of difference between pressure-resistant and pressure-sensitive ownership.
 * $p < .05$
 ** $p < .01$
 *** $p < .001$

that the *nature* of ownership is also an important determinant of CEO pay.

The divergence between pressure-resistant and pressure-sensitive institutions with respect to long-term incentives was less marked. The presence of pressure-resistant institutions increased the proportion of long-term incentives in CEO pay, thus exhibiting influence consistent with shareholder preferences. However, pressure-sensitive institutions appeared neither to exercise governance to increase long-term incentives nor to get coopted by managers to reduce long-term incentives. Also, their effect was not significantly different from that of pressure-resistant institutions, suggesting that pressure-sensitive institutions may find it difficult to justify a reduction in long-term incentives. In recent years, academics have called for an increase in the use of such incentives, arguing that they are important in aligning the interests of managers and shareholders and are far more relevant to shareholders than the level of compensation per se (Jensen & Murphy, 1990b). In the face of the growing popularity of such incentives, supporting their

reduction could be interpreted as a violation of institutional investors' fiduciary duty.

Shareholders holding large blocks have been the focus of prior research examining the effects of ownership structure on CEO compensation. Our measure of noninstitutional blockholders differs from the measure previously used for owner control (at least one shareholder owning more than 5 percent of a firm's shares) in that it excludes institutional investors. Noninstitutional blockholders, including family owners and other corporations, are expected to influence CEO compensation to uphold the interests of owners. We found that, like pressure-resistant institutions, noninstitutional blockholders reduced the level of CEO pay. This finding is consistent with prior research showing that the presence of large blockholders reduced pay levels (e.g., Dyl, 1988; Hambrick & Finkelstein, 1995). With respect to the proportion of long-term incentives in CEO pay, however, we found that noninstitutional blockholders had an effect opposite to that of pressure-resistant institutions. This result is consistent with prior findings of a negative association between long-term incentives and blockholder ownership (Beatty & Zajac, 1994; Mehran, 1995; Zajac & Westphal, 1994). Thus, large blockholders may be reducing the agency conflict by monitoring managerial action themselves (Shleifer & Vishny, 1986). As firms with large blockholders are likely to be adequately monitored, there is less need for their boards to grant long-term incentives to align managers with shareholders. In contrast, institutional investors, who typically have holdings in numerous firms, may not be able to devote much attention to an individual firm. Hence, these investors rely on bonding mechanisms, such as compensation policies, to reduce agency problems. In other words, the nature of ownership may also be an important determinant of the choice of alternate forms of governance devices.

According to agency theory, mechanisms that align the interests of managers with those of shareholders increase the value of a firm (Jensen & Meckling, 1976). Pressure-resistant institutions can reduce agency costs by monitoring and influencing compensation. By decreasing excessive pay, pressure-resistant institutions limit the extent of managerial expropriation, thereby improving firm performance. By fostering long-term incentives, pressure-resistant institutions induce managers to pursue appropriate strategies that benefit shareholders with increased returns and benefit managers with increased long-term compensation. However, it should be noted that if the long-term incentives received by CEOs are provided in addition to their base pay, they may prefer lower-risk strategic choices to protect their base compensation (Wiseman & Gomez-Mejia, 1998). In contrast, restructuring total managerial compensation to include a greater proportion of contingent pay is more likely to lead to desirable actions (Wiseman & Gomez-Mejia, 1998). Hence, institutional investors need to pay careful attention to managerial risk preferences when influencing CEO compensation policies.

Attention also needs to be paid to the various components of long-term incentives. In this study, we included all forms of long-term compensation in one variable. Some scholars have pointed out that the diverse components may not all have similar effects in altering the risk-taking behavior of and the benefits available to managers (Gomez-Mejia, 1994; Gomez-Mejia, Paulin, & Grabke, 1990; Gomez-Mejia & Wiseman, 1997). For instance, some stock options are offered free or at very favorable prices. It is possible that our nonsignificant result for Hypothesis 2b may be due to the aggregation of various components. This possibility provides an interesting avenue for future research.

The differences among institutional investors on CEO pay and the potential performance implications of those differences suggest the importance of understanding the underlying process by which the influence of these owners is exercised in firms (Gomez-Mejia, 1994: 193). Future researchers would benefit by examining the power interplay between managers and institutional investors. What actions do pressure-resistant institutions take to gain power, and how do managers influence pressure-sensitive institutions to support grants of generous CEO compensation?

REFERENCES

Beatty, R. P., & Zajac, E. J. 1994. Managerial incentives, monitoring, and risk bearing: A study of executive compensation, ownership, and board structure in initial public offerings. *Administrative Science Quarterly*, 39: 313–335.

Black, B. S. 1992. Agents watching agents: The promise of institutional investor voice. *UCLA Law Review*, 39: 811–893.

Brickley, J. A., Lease, R. C., & Smith, C. W., Jr. 1988. Ownership structure and voting on antitakeover amendments. *Journal of Financial Economics*, 20: 267–291.

Cannella, A. A., Jr., & Gray, S. R. 1996. *Measuring executive compensation: The case of stock options.* Paper presented at the AMJ Special Issue Conference on Managerial Compensation and Firm Performance, Tilburg, the Netherlands.

Cook, K. S. 1977. Exchange and power in networks of interorganizational relations. *Sociological Quarterly*, 18: 62–82.

David, P., & Kochhar, R. 1996. Barriers to effective governance by institutional investors: Implications for theory and practice. *European Management Journal*, 14: 457–466.

Davis, G. F., & Thompson, T. A. 1994. A social movement perspective on corporate control. *Administrative Science Quarterly*, 39: 141–173.

Dyl, E. A. 1988. Corporate control and management compensation. *Managerial and Decision Economics*, 9: 21–25.

Finkelstein, S. 1992. Power in top management teams: Dimensions, measurement, and validation. *Academy of Management Journal*, 35: 505–538.

Finkelstein, S., & Hambrick, D. C. 1988. Chief executive compensation: A synthesis and reconciliation. *Strategic Management Journal*, 9: 543–558.

Finkelstein, S., & Hambrick, D. C. 1989. Chief executive compensation: A study of the intersection of markets and political processes. *Strategic Management Journal*, 10: 121–134.

Gerhart, B., & Milkovich, G. T. 1990. Organizational differences in managerial compensation and firm performance. *Academy of Management Journal*, 33: 663–691.

Gomez-Mejia, L. R. 1994. Executive compensation: A reassessment and a future research agenda. In G. R. Ferris (Ed.), *Research in personnel and human resources management*, vol. 12: 161–222. Greenwich, CT: JAI Press.

Gomez-Mejia, L. R., Paulin, G., & Grabke, A. 1990. Executive compensation: Research and practical implications. In G. R. Ferris, S. D. Rosen, & D. T. Barnum (Eds.), *Handbook of human resource management:* 548–569. Cambridge, MA: Blackwell.

Gomez-Mejia, L. R., Tosi, H., & Hinkin, T. 1987. Managerial control, performance, and executive compensation. *Academy of Management Journal,* 30: 51–70.

Gomez-Mejia, L., & Wiseman, R. M. 1997. Reframing executive compensation: An assessment and outlook. *Journal of Management,* 23: 291–374.

Greene, W. H. 1993. *Econometric analysis.* New York: Macmillan.

Hambrick, D. C., & Finkelstein, S. 1995. The effects of ownership structure on conditions at the top: The case of CEO pay raises. *Strategic Management Journal,* 16: 175–193.

Heard, J. E., & Sherman, H. D. 1987. *Conflicts of interest in the proxy voting system.* Washington, DC: Investor Responsibility Research Center.

Hill, C. W. L., & Phan, P. 1991. CEO tenure as a determinant of CEO pay. *Academy of Management Journal,* 34: 305–360.

Jensen, M. C. 1993. The modern industrial revolution, exit, and the failure of internal control systems. *Journal of Financial Economics,* 48: 830–880.

Jensen, M. C., & Meckling, W. H. 1976. Theory of the firm: Managerial behavior, agency cost, and ownership structure. *Journal of Financial Economics,* 3: 305–360.

Jensen, M. C., & Murphy, K. J. 1990a. Performance pay and top management incentives. *Journal of Political Economy,* 98: 225–264.

Jensen, M. C., & Murphy, K. J. 1990b. CEO incentives—It's not how much you pay, but how. *Harvard Business Review,* 68(3): 138–149.

Kochhar, R., & David, P. 1996. Institutional investors and firm innovation: A test of competing hypotheses. *Strategic Management Journal,* 17: 73–84.

Krikorian, B. L. 1991. Fiduciary standards: Loyalty, prudence, voting proxies, and corporate governance. In A. W. Sametz, & J. L. Bicksler (Eds.), *Institutional investing: Challenges and responsibilities of the 21st century:* 257–277. Homewood, IL: Business One Irwin.

Lambert, R. A., Larcker, D. F., & Weigelt, K. 1991. How sensitive is executive compensation to organizational size? *Strategic Management Journal,* 12: 395–402.

Levine, S., & White, P. E. 1961. Exchange as a conceptual framework for the study of interorganizational relationships. *Administrative Science Quarterly,* 5: 583–601.

Mehran, H. 1995. Executive compensation structure, ownership, and firm performance. *Journal of Financial Economics,* 38: 163–184.

Mintzberg, H. 1983. *Power in and around organizations.* Englewood Cliffs, NJ: Prentice-Hall.

Nesbitt, S. 1994. Long-term rewards from shareholder activism: A study of the CalPERS effect. *Journal of Applied Corporate Finance,* 6 (Winter): 75–80.

O'Barr, W. M., & Conley, J. M. 1992. *Fortune and folly: The wealth and power of institutional investing.* Homewood, IL: Business One Irwin.

O'Reilly, C. A., Main, B., & Crystal, G. 1988. CEO compensation as tournament and social comparison: A tale of two theories. *Administrative Science Quarterly,* 33: 257–274.

Pfeffer, J. 1981. *Power in organizations.* Boston: Pitman.

Salancik, G. R., & Pfeffer, J. 1980. Effects of ownership and performance on executive tenure in U.S. corporations. *Academy of Management Journal,* 23: 653–664.

Shleifer, A., & Vishny, R. W. 1986. Large shareholders and corporate control. *Journal of Political Economy,* 94: 461–488.

Star, M. G. 1993. Governance issues fill '93 proxies. *Pensions & Investments,* April 5: 16–20.

Tosi, H. L., & Gomez-Mejia, L. 1989. The decoupling of CEO pay and performance: An agency theory perspective. *Administrative Science Quarterly,* 34: 169–189.

Useem, M. A. 1996. *Investor capitalism: How money managers are changing the face of corporate America.* New York: Basic Books.

Wahal, S. 1996. Pension fund activism and firm performance. *Journal of Financial and Quantitative Analysis,* 31: 1–23.

Weiner, N., & Mahoney, T. 1981. A model of corporate performance as a function of environmental, organizational, and leadership influences. *Academy of Management Journal,* 24: 453–470.

Westphal, J. D., & Zajac, E. J. 1994. Substance and symbolism in CEOs' long-term incentive plans. *Administrative Science Quarterly,* 39: 367–390.

Wiseman, R. M., & Gomez-Mejia, L. 1998. A behavioral agency model of managerial risk taking. *Academy of Management Review,* 23: 133–153.

Zajac, E. J., & Westphal, J. D. 1994. The costs and benefits of managerial incentives and monitoring in large U.S. corporations: When is more not better? *Strategic Management Journal,* 15: 121–142.

Parthiban David is a lecturer at Nanyang Technological University, Singapore. He received his Ph.D. degree in strategic management from Texas A&M University. His current research interests are focused on corporate governance and its links with corporate strategy and performance.

Rahul Kochhar (Ph.D., 1995, Texas A&M University) was an assistant professor of management in Purdue University's Krannert School until his death in the fall of 1997. In his short tenure as a professor, Rahul established an outstanding research record, having published in outlets such as the *Academy of Management Journal, Strategic Management Journal, Journal of International Management, European Journal of Management,* and *Journal of Financial and Strategic Decisions.* More importantly, Rahul was a caring friend, a trustworthy advisor, and a calming influence during otherwise stressful times. His many coauthors and friends deeply mourn his passing.

Edward Levitas is a doctoral student at Texas A&M University. His current research interests are focused on knowledge diffusion, strategic alliances, and corporate governance.

[18]

Managerial Incentives, Monitoring, and Risk Bearing: A Study of Executive Compensation, Ownership, and Board Structure in Initial Public Offerings

Randolph P. Beatty
Southern Methodist University
Edward J. Zajac
Northwestern University

We argue in this study that a resolution of the ambiguity and conflict surrounding executive compensation and corporate control practices requires a more unified perspective on top management compensation, ownership, and corporate governance. Drawing from agency and organizational research, the study develops and tests a contingency perspective on how organizations seek to ensure appropriate managerial behavior through a balancing of trade-offs between incentive, monitoring, and risk-bearing arrangements. We suggest that (1) the ability of firms to use executive compensation contracts to address managerial incentive problems is hampered by risk-bearing concerns that stem from the risk aversion of top managers, (2) this problem is particularly severe for riskier firms, and (3) firms seek to address this problem by structuring their boards of directors to ensure sufficient monitoring of managerial behavior, given the magnitude of the agency problem. This contingency perspective is then tested using a large sample of initial public offering firms. The findings and their implications for the debates about ownership and control and executive pay for performance are discussed.[•]

INTRODUCTION

Organizational theorists have increasingly drawn on agency theory (Ross, 1973; Jensen and Meckling, 1976) to generate an extensive body of research on topics such as executive compensation and corporate governance (e.g., Tosi and Gomez-Mejia, 1989; Zajac, 1990; Davis, 1991; Westphal and Zajac, 1994). In applying or adapting agency theory to these organizational issues, however, it is useful to distinguish between what Jensen (1983: 334–335) referred to as two "almost entirely separate" agency literatures: a normative principal-agent literature that emphasizes the design of compensation contracts with optimal risk-sharing properties (see Levinthal, 1988, for a review) and a positive, empirically based, agency literature that focuses primarily on questions relating to the separation of corporate ownership and control and the role of boards of directors (Fama and Jensen, 1983; Weisbach, 1988; Morck, Shleifer, and Vishny, 1989).

The positive versus normative split in the agency literature has important implications for organizational researchers seeking to explain phenomena such as incentive compensation for top executives. For example, while the positive agency literature highlights the value of placing greater amounts of managerial compensation and managerial wealth at risk by tying it closer to firm performance (e.g., Jensen and Murphy, 1990), the normative agency literature stresses the need to consider the potential disadvantages of forcing managers to bear excessive compensation risk (Holmstrom, 1979, 1987; Shavell, 1979; Stiglitz, 1987; Fama, 1992).

Eisenhardt (1989) noted that organizational research using agency theory has tended to draw from the positive rather than the normative agency literature. One implication of this is that organizational research has generally placed greater emphasis on the importance—from an incentive and control

•

Both authors contributed equally to the paper. The comments of Sanjai Bhagat, Jeanne Brett, Jerry Davis, Ron Dye, Peter Easton, Eugene Fama, John Hand, Steven Kaplan, Joe Moag, Jay Ritter, Abbie Smith, Robert Vishny, and three anonymous *ASQ* reviewers are greatly appreciated. Todd Glass and Jeffery Nguyen provided valuable research assistance. An earlier version of this paper received the Best Paper Award of the Business Policy and Strategy Division of the Academy of Management.

standpoint—of imposing strong pay-for-performance linkages, rather than the possible disadvantages of imposing risk bearing in managerial compensation contracts. The lack of debate in the recent organizational literature on this issue is somewhat surprising, given that the organizational behavior literature on compensation has historically recognized that different forms of compensation, such as pay for performance, vary in their attractiveness to individuals and therefore vary in their appropriateness as incentives and motivational tools (Lawler, 1971; Mahoney, 1979).

A similar, if more subtle divergence has also occurred in the agency-based discussions of monitoring as a means for controlling managerial behavior. Both the normative and positive agency literatures have addressed the relationship between managerial incentives and monitoring. The former examines abstractly the costs and benefits of monitoring as a second-best solution when optimal compensation contracts cannot be written; the latter discusses the benefits, but not necessarily the costs, of the monitoring technology observed in modern corporations (cf. Fama and Jensen, 1983). Again, organizational research has tended to draw more from the positive agency literature in focusing on the effectiveness or ineffectiveness of boards of directors as monitors of top management, without considering explicitly the possible cost-benefit trade-offs between using incentives and using monitoring as alternative sources of controlling managerial behavior.

We argue that resolving the ambiguity and conflict about executive pay-for-performance relationships and corporate control requires a more unified perspective on top management compensation, ownership, and corporate governance. To achieve this goal, we examine both of the potential trade-offs mentioned above and develop hypotheses about the organizational and personal contingencies that may lead to differences across firms in how these trade-offs are addressed. By proposing and testing this contingency perspective with a large sample of initial public offering (IPO) firms, we hope to extend and unify the growing literature on top management compensation, ownership, and corporate governance.

The study is distinctive in a number of ways. Conceptually, it provides an analysis of the relationship between firm risk (an organizational contingency) and the form of top executive compensation, and it considers jointly the structuring of top executive compensation, ownership, and corporate governance mechanisms. The study examines these issues empirically using the entire top management team, rather than only the chief executive officer (CEO), and our sample comprises firms "going public" (i.e., about to sell their stock to the general investing public for the first time), rather than the large, established corporations typically studied.

Financial economists have recently invoked organizational theories in discussing compensation questions, arguing that aspects of top executive compensation and corporate control in large corporations may often be the result of historical tradition and bureaucratization (cf. Baker, Jensen, and

Managerial Incentives

Murphy, 1988). Thus, studying newer firms that are considering a wider variety of alternative internal control mechanisms, such as whether to introduce stock options for top managers or how to structure the board of directors to monitor managers, may provide a particularly clear test of the agency-based, contingency perspective offered here.

In addition, the range of riskiness in a sample of IPO firms should be much wider than for larger, established firms and should provide sufficient variation in key risk-bearing aspects of management compensation contracts. Furthermore, given that smaller and less well-established firms seeking to go public may be particularly dependent on the existing top management team, such vulnerable firms may be more sensitive to managerial preferences for minimizing risk bearing than would larger firms.

Although most agency-based empirical studies have focused on large firms in which ownership is dispersed across many individuals and managers own little equity, agency theory's applicability is not limited to large firms. Jensen and Meckling's (1976: 312) original discussion of agency costs began with an analysis of the problems that arise, and of the value of monitoring, when a 100-percent owner/manager reduces his equity holdings to 95 percent. Agency approaches can apply not only in situations in which managers own little equity, but in all situations in which there is no single 100-percent owner/entrepreneur who bears the full cost of his or her actions. Thus, our IPO setting is well-suited to providing an empirical analysis that complements the traditional focus on large firms typically found in the existing literature.

Finally, given that newly formed corporations are more likely to have active investors (Finnerty, 1986) involved in monitoring top management activities, our findings may have bearing on future governance relationships for large corporations currently facing increased investor activism. Taken together, these issues suggest that studying firms that are undertaking an IPO can provide a unique opportunity to examine compensation arrangements and governance relationships that become formalized when an organization becomes an open corporation (Fama and Jensen, 1983; Fama, 1992) and its stock is openly traded for the first time.

Managerial Incentives and Risk Bearing

While Jensen and Meckling (1976) originally defined the magnitude of the agency problem in terms of the degree of separation between the interests of owners and managers, subsequent clarifications suggest that linking a manager's compensation too closely to firm performance might lead to risk-avoiding behavior on the part of the manager. This argument, as summarized in Fama (1992) and Holmstrom (1987), stresses the fact that while contingent compensation may seem to have desirable incentive and motivational properties relative to noncontingent forms of compensation, it also has undesirable risk-bearing properties. Such a compensation contract would cause a manager to bear risk that could be more efficiently borne by diversified stockholders. The underlying assumption is that the manager, unlike the owners, has already invested most of his or her nondiversifiable and nontradable human capital in the firm and that the agent is relatively risk averse, while the principal is relatively risk neutral. It follows that agents would be reluctant to bear this risk of firm performance and that it is therefore difficult and costly for the principal to have the agent bear this risk. This issue is summarized succinctly by Myron Scholes in a recent roundtable debate on the question of whether there should be a tightening of the pay-for-performance contingency for top management (*Journal of Applied Corporate Finance,* 1992: 123):

Managers are more likely to attach significantly more value to a given level of cash than to the same expected level in stock or options because they can use that cash to buy a diversified portfolio of common stocks, bonds, or whatever. But, as you force managers to reduce their cash compensation while making a larger investment in their own firm, you're asking them to bear more risk—risk that cannot be diversified away by holding other stocks and bonds. And because that risk cannot be diversified, companies will be forced to pay their executives disproportionately more in total compensation to compensate them for bearing this nondiversifiable risk.

The key issue here is not whether, in an absolute sense, the incentive benefits outweigh the risk-sharing costs of heavy incentive-based compensation but, rather, the need to recognize the potential trade-off between incentives and risk sharing and begin to identify contingencies that could affect the trade-off. This study focuses first on one such organizational contingency, i.e., firm risk, that may increase the riskiness of contingent compensation contracts and therefore may make managers particularly reluctant to accept such contracts. Thus cross-sectional variation in firm risk is associated with the costs of using incentive compensation, since it can influence managers' willingness to accept compensation contracts that include a risk-bearing component. Given that the most significant risk-bearing component in executive compensation contracts is typically stock options, we hypothesize:

Hypothesis 1: The riskier the firm, the less likely it is that top managers will have stock options in their compensation contracts.

Since an economic definition of incentives theoretically encompasses all financial rewards that are contingent on firm performance, the next two hypotheses extend the notion of incentives to include not only contingent compensation, such as executives' stock options, but also the change in value of the managers' equity holdings, which varies with firm performance. This represents a more complete calculation of a manager's income that is at risk, in that it is directly related to a firm's equity value. This suggests that top managers in riskier firms will have (1) a lower level of equity holdings in their firms and (2) a smaller proportion of noncash incentives—incentive compensation from stock options plus changes in equity value based on stock ownership—relative to their total compensation (i.e., noncash incentives + cash compensation):

Hypothesis 2: The riskier the firm, the smaller the equity holdings of its top managers.

Hypothesis 3: The riskier the firm, the smaller the noncash incentive portion of its top managers' total compensation.

Managerial Incentives

While the discussion thus far has treated both contingent compensation and income change due to equity holdings as resulting from managerial choices, for firms about to go public it is possible to consider equity ownership as an independent variable, rather than as a variable whose level is simultaneously determined with the compensation variable. Specifically, the legal and institutional restrictions on equity trading for firms that are not publicly traded, such as limits on interstate equity transfers or limits on the number of shareholders, may create transaction costs that have prevented top managers from reducing or increasing their equity holdings to a desired level. Therefore, the magnitude of the existing equity positions held by top managers may influence their willingness to accept further risk bearing, such as stock options, in their compensation contracts. This argument is consistent with our earlier discussion of risk bearing and incentives but with an added emphasis on the specific differences in risk exposure facing top management that is attributable to the variation in the amount of equity they hold in their respective firms. Whereas the earlier hypotheses considered an organizational, firm-specific contingency (i.e., firm risk) that can affect compensation contracts, the following hypothesis considers an individual, manager-specific contingency (i.e., managerial equity holdings):

Hypothesis 4: The larger the equity stakes held by top managers, the less likely it is that top managers will have stock options in their compensation contracts, ceteris paribus.

The same hypothesis is also suggested by another explanation that is consistent with our study; namely, that firms whose top managers have low equity positions face a more severe agency incentive problem, making it more likely that such firms will need to use stock options in their executive compensation contracts. Such an explanation considers only the incentive component of the agency problem, rather than the incentive and risk-bearing components addressed in the present study.

Monitoring and Incentives

Both the normative and positive agency literatures have also addressed the relationship between managerial incentives and monitoring. The former examines more abstractly the role and costs of monitoring when optimal compensation contracts cannot be written, while the latter discusses the monitoring technology observed in modern corporations (e.g., Fama and Jensen, 1983). Both literatures generally stress the primacy of incentive contracting as a first-best solution to the agency problem and emphasize that the optimal level of monitoring would be based on the magnitude of the incentive gap between principal and agent. For example, a higher level of monitoring by boards of directors would be required when a manager does not accept any compensation risk tied to firm performance than when a manager's incentives are tied to the performance of the firm. Strong monitoring is therefore particularly appropriate when managerial incentives are only weakly tied to firm performance, and the benefits of monitoring would outweigh the costs. Thus the desired level of monitoring is contingent on the magnitude of the incentive aspect of the agency problem.

For positive agency theorists, the magnitude of the incentive problem has traditionally been defined, in part, by the level of a top management group's equity interest in the firm (Jensen and Meckling, 1976; Jensen and Murphy, 1990). When the top management group holds only a minor equity position in the firm, firms need to increase monitoring. There are several governance design features that firms may use to increase the level of monitoring of top management by the board of directors. The board of directors is generally acknowledged to be an important, if imperfect formal mechanism for monitoring top managers (Fama, 1980; Fama and Jensen, 1983; Weisbach, 1988). Although the degree to which boards of directors are effective monitors of top management has been the subject of continued debate (cf. Mace, 1971; Lorsch and MacIver, 1989), for our purposes, one need not assume fully effective board monitoring to posit that there may be cross-sectional differences in firms' level of monitoring (as measured by aspects of board structure) that are contingent on the differences in top management incentive problems that firms face. One need only assume that boards engage in some non-zero, positive level of monitoring.

One governance design issue involves the proportion of outside directors on the board. Fama (1980) and Fama and Jensen (1983) viewed outside directors as professional referees and experts in internal organizational control. Even if one disputed this characterization of outside directors and viewed them, instead, as often coopted by top management (Wade, O'Reilly, and Chandratat, 1990), a heavy use of insider directors who are from top management still suggests relatively weak monitoring. Insider-dominated boards imply problematic self-monitoring and particularly weak monitoring of the CEO, since the CEO is likely to be in a position to influence an inside director's career advancement within the firm.

A second mechanism for dealing with this monitoring problem is choosing outside directors who also hold equity interests in the firm. Outside directors who are also owners would seem likely to be more vigilant in their monitoring role (Morck, Shleifer, and Vishny, 1988). The logic of vigilant monitoring based on ownership interest can be extended to a third mechanism for monitoring: the presence of a shareholder with large equity holdings who, for whatever reason, is not on the board but is a blockholder (Huddart, 1993). Such large-scale owners are more likely to be keen monitors of managerial behavior. Finally, the logic of vigilant monitoring can also be extended to a fourth mechanism that is particularly relevant when an IPO firm is financed by venture capital: Venture capitalists are also likely to engage in active monitoring.

A fifth potential mechanism for ensuring adequate monitoring involves choosing whether the CEO should also serve as chairman of the board of directors. Recent calls for changes or reforms in corporate governance structure have emphasized the importance of the increased monitoring

Managerial Incentives

afforded by the separation of CEO and chairman roles (Lorsch and MacIver, 1989). The presence of an outside board chairman who is not also CEO can represent an additional monitor of managerial behavior.

The expected relationship between the magnitude of the agency incentive problem (i.e., the level of top management equity ownership in the firm) and the level of monitoring can be phrased in terms of the following hypotheses, each corresponding to one of the five specific governance mechanisms discussed above:

Hypothesis 5a: The smaller the equity stakes held by top managers, the greater the levels of firm monitoring, as represented by a larger percentage of outside directors.

Hypothesis 5b: The smaller the equity stakes held by top managers, the greater the levels of firm monitoring, as represented by a larger percentage of outside director-owners.

Hypothesis 5c: The smaller the equity stakes held by top managers, the greater the levels of firm monitoring, as represented by a major non-board-member blockholder.

Hypothesis 5d: The smaller the equity stakes held by top managers, the greater the levels of firm monitoring, as represented by venture capital backing.

Hypothesis 5e: The smaller the equity stakes held by top managers, the greater the levels of firm monitoring, as represented by separate CEO and board chairman positions.

We can also extend the definition of the magnitude of the agency incentive problem to include not only managerial equity holdings but also the incentive component of managers' compensation contracts. Consistent with the earlier discussion, managers who have a lower proportion of their total compensation contingent on firm performance (through stock options and equity stakes) create a more severe incentive problem for firms, which may be addressed by increasing the level of monitoring. This suggests the following related hypotheses:

Hypothesis 6a: The smaller the noncash incentive portion of top managers' total compensation, the greater the levels of firm monitoring, as represented by a larger percentage of outside directors.

Hypothesis 6b: The smaller the noncash incentive portion of top managers' total compensation, the greater the levels of firm monitoring, as represented by a larger percentage of outside director-owners.

Hypothesis 6c: The smaller the noncash incentive portion of top managers' total compensation, the greater the levels of firm monitoring, as represented by a major non-board-member blockholder.

Hypothesis 6d: The smaller the noncash incentive portion of top managers' total compensation, the greater the levels of firm monitoring, as represented by venture capital backing.

Hypothesis 6e: The smaller the noncash incentive portion of top managers' total compensation, the greater the levels of firm monitoring, as represented by separate CEO and board chairman positions.

METHOD

Data

The data used in the empirical analysis are the 435 of 535 initial public offering (IPO) firms from 1984 for which we had complete data. The primary data source for the variables is IPOs' registration statements on file at the Securities and Exchange Commission (SEC) reading room, supplemented by *The Venture Capital Yearbook,* and Howard and Co.'s *Going Public: The IPO Reporter.* IPO registration statements disclose information on the riskiness, ownership, management compensation, and monitoring structures of a firm, along with other details relevant to potential investors, regulators, and other interested parties. To check for representativeness, we compared our 1984 sample firms with all IPOs from 1975 to 1984 in terms of industry classification (Ritter, 1991). The 1984 sample and 1975–1984 industry frequency distributions were similar, with two exceptions: The 1984 sample had fewer oil and gas firms and financial institutions. In addition, Ibbotson, Sindelar, and Ritter (1988) reported that average initial returns and total gross proceeds are 11.52 percent and $3.9 billion for 1984, compared with 16.37 percent and $3 billion for the 1960–1987 period. Although there is no "typical" IPO year, these descriptive results suggest that 1984 is not an atypical IPO market and that results derived from 1984 sample firms are unlikely to be produced by highly anomalous market conditions.

Risk Measures

Firm risk can be measured in a number of ways, and there is a considerable literature on assessing firm risk for IPO firms. We measured firm risk in four ways. The first proxy for risk is the number of risk factors described in the IPO registration statement, where top management must explicitly list and discuss the risk factors facing the IPO firm. Since personal legal liability stemming from the Securities Act of 1933 is imposed on top management's presentation of risk factors in the registration statement, differences in the number of risks described in the registration statements capture fundamental differences in the riskiness of IPO firms (Feltham, Hughes, and Simunic, 1991). As Perez (1984: 44–45) noted, for investment bankers involved in the IPO process, "willful failure to include all material information in the offering documents constitutes criminal fraud, for which the penalties are severe," and as a result, "extensive analysis" is conducted to ensure that "when the investment banker brings out an issue of common stock in a small, relatively new company, the offering prospectus will contain complete, unbiased disclosure of all material facts . . . ."

The second risk measure concerns the choice of a best-efforts or firm-commitment offering contract in the IPO underwriting. After a company seeking to go public files its registration statement with the SEC, it employs underwriters to assist in the IPO process. This can take two forms: (1) the underwriters can purchase the shares directly from the IPO firm, thus guaranteeing the firm the sale of a specified number of shares at a specified price, or (2) as Finnerty (1986: 465) noted, "in the case of riskier offerings, best efforts underwriting" is used, in which underwriters make their best efforts but do not make a firm commitment or guarantee. Ritter (1987) showed that firms choosing best-efforts contracts are riskier relative to those choosing

Managerial Incentives

firm-commitment contracts. The measure takes the value of 1 for firm commitment, 0 for best efforts.

A third measure of firm risk is derived from the reported profitability or unprofitability of the IPO firm (0 = profitable, 1 = unprofitable). If a firm has a reported profit, products or services with measured net inflow of resources have been produced and sold. This documented minimum inflow from operating activities suggests that firm risk will be lower than for firms that did not report any measured earnings. Also, the use of profitability/unprofitability as a measure of risk is suggested by numerous studies of financial distress (e.g., Beaver, 1966; Altman, 1968; Zmijewski, 1984). It should be noted that because many of the firms are quite young, we could not use a continuous measure of profitability trends as a measure of firm risk. Similarly, firm risk for IPOs cannot be measured in terms of the variation in a firm's stock returns, since this variation only occurs after the IPO. It is possible, however, to create an expected or predicted value, which we did for our final risk measure.

The fourth risk measure was constructed by regressing the actual after-market standard deviation from the post-IPO market on the three previous risk measures (profitability indicator, number of risks disclosed, and type of underwriting contract) for all firms. The expected after-market standard deviation is the predicted value of this cross-sectional regression, capturing an element of market expectations. Specifically, the predicted aftermarket standard deviation is .03 + .01 (Profit) + .001 (Number of Risks) + .01 (U-type). T-statistics for the intercept and coefficients are 5.82, 2.85, 3.26, and 2.29, respectively. Thus the measure reflects the composite of the three risk measures described earlier, along with the actual variability of share price for the post-IPO firm. Higher levels of this value suggest higher levels of firm risk. Analyses were run separately for each of the four measures of risk to assess whether the test of the relationship between firm risk and the introduction of incentives hinges on any single measure of firm risk or is robust across measures.

Compensation and Ownership Measures

Three measures of management compensation and ownership were used in the analyses. First, we used a dichotomous measure of executive compensation to indicate whether stock options were used to compensate the top management group (1 = yes; 0 = no). We began with this measure for several reasons. First, our detailed reading of the 435 registration statements led us to conclude that, for our sample of firms, the decision to offer stock options to top managers is a major decision made by the board of directors: Typically, a board committee is created and made responsible for granting options to top managers. Also, the presence or absence of options has the advantage of being reliably measurable for our sample of firms because it is explicitly discussed in every firm's registration statement with the SEC. Our reading of firms' registration statements also revealed that the granting of stock options was almost always limited to the top management group. This implies that the board, when deciding whether to offer options, expects that options can influence top management behavior.

To the extent that firms may use other aspects of compensation to address agency problems (e.g., retirement plans, deferred compensation, stock bonuses, low- or no-interest loans, and other idiosyncratic fringe benefits), the stock options measure can be viewed as a conservative measure of incentive compensation. The measure is also conservative in that while having options increases the undiversifiable risk that managers must bear, the valuation of those options is positively related to the riskiness of the stock.

We calculated two additional continuous measures of financial managerial incentives. One is the percentage of total executive compensation derived from noncash sources, which captures the amount of a manager's total income that is at risk, because it includes the gain or loss attributable to the shares of stock held by the manager, as well as options held. This variable thus summarizes the incentive components of managers' total compensation that are directly related to equity value. The measure was constructed as follows: (the value of managers' stock options + the change in value of stock held by the manager in the pre-IPO year) / (cash compensation + the value of managers' stock options + the change in value of stock held by the manager in the pre-IPO year). Stock options were valued using the Black-Scholes (1973) option pricing model. No adjustment was made for dividend yield because IPO firms rarely pay dividends. In fact, many firms specifically state that dividends are unlikely to be paid in the near term. The risk-free rate was estimated with the average market yield on government securities of similar maturity to the option. Consistent with prior IPO research, the variance of stock price was estimated using the 20-day after-market standard deviation (Ritter, 1987; Berry, Muscarella, and Vetsuypens, 1991; Schultz, 1993). The managers' equity value change was estimated by computing the difference between the first-day bid price and the contributed capital per share divided by the age of the firm multiplied by the number of equity shares held by the managers.

While other compensation studies (e.g., Jensen and Murphy, 1990) have also considered the income gain or loss attributable to the shares of stock held by the manager as a component of a manager's total incentive compensation, one could consider such stock-based gains and losses as investment income. From an incentive/motivational standpoint perspective, we believe that managers' compensation and shareholding gains, when taken together, represent a more complete calculation of a manager's total income that is at risk by being directly related to a firm's equity value. Because there is no consensus about how narrowly or broadly incentives should be defined (cf. Lambert and Larcker, 1987: 93), we have assessed incentive compensation both ways, excluding and including incentives from equity shares held (hypotheses 1 and 3, respectively).

Finally, we also measured the percentage of IPO firms' equity held by the top management group. The individuals in

Managerial Incentives

the top management group and their equity holdings before the IPO are explicitly identified in the IPO registration statements.

Monitoring Measures

We used five measures of monitoring, all of which are straightforward. The first monitoring measure is the ratio of the number of outside directors to total directors (i.e., inside and outside directors), a measure commonly used by researchers to measure corporate control (e.g., Morck, Shleifer, and Vishny, 1988; Weisbach, 1988). The second measure is the proportion of outside owner-directors (e.g., directors who are also shareholders) to total directors. The third monitoring measure is the presence (1 = yes; 0 = no) of a shareholder with large equity holdings (>5 percent; 0 otherwise) who is not on the board (i.e., a blockholder). The fourth monitoring measure captures whether the IPO firm is venture-backed (1 = yes; 0 = no). The fifth monitoring measure is the dichotomous CEO/chairman variable, indicating whether the CEO position is separated from the chairman of the board position (1 = yes; 0 = no).

The five measures of monitoring used in this study all emphasize either IPOs' boards of directors or significant nondirector equity investors. To the extent that these measures do not capture other forms of monitoring that may exist to address agency problems (e.g., debt covenants, bank relationships), our reliance on the five board-related and investor-related measures represents a conservative test of the hypothesized trade-off between monitoring and incentives.

Control Variables

Several control variables were also used. Sales revenue, total equity (i.e., market capitalization), and firm age provide controls for the size of the IPO firm; firm age also controls more for the experience or "sophistication" of the IPO firm. Because size and experience may be related to our measures of compensation, ownership, and monitoring structures, we controlled for the effects of size on our findings. We considered various transformations [i.e., 1n(1 + sales)] of the size variables to assess the influence of possible outliers on the estimated regressions. The results of these unreported tests were consistent with the results described below. Also, we controlled for the mean age of the members of the top management group. A top management group comprising older executives might be expected to have different preferences for contingent versus noncontingent forms of compensation than would younger executives and may also be less sensitive to discipline from the managerial labor market, thus presenting a more severe agency problem (Lewellen, Loderer, and Martin, 1987). Finally, we also controlled for industry effects to ensure that the compensation and monitoring structures observed are not simply outcomes of industry practices or traditions. We included 13 dummy variables—each at the three-digit Standard Industry Classification code level—in all multivariate analyses. Given the large number of variables included in each analysis, however, the coefficients for industry dummy variables are not reported in Tables 3–7 below.

Means, medians, and standard deviations for all variables are shown in Table 1. Table 2 displays the correlation matrix.

Table 1

Means, Medians, and Standard Deviations

Variable	Mean	Median or %*	S.D.
Risk			
(Un)profitability		58%	
Number of risks	12.43	13.00	8.17
Contract type		34%	
Predicted after-market s.d.	.04	.04	.01
Compensation and ownership			
Stock option plans		33%	
Percentage of executive compensation from noncash			
sources	79%	93%	32%
Proportion of equity ownership by top management	55%	56%	30%
Monitoring			
Ratio of outside directors/total directors	.39	.40	.22
Ratio of outside owner-directors to total directors	.17	.14	.19
CEO/chairman split		62%	
Non-director blockholder		48%	
Venture capital backing		9%	
Control variables			
Equity value (in thousands $)	154981	4684	2954047
Sales revenue (in thousands $)	23649	893	109373
Firm age	6.56	3.00	10.55
Mean age of top managers	37.91	38.29	6.28

* Percentages are reported for 1/0 indicator variables.

Analysis

Given that ordinary least squares (OLS) regression assumes a linear model with error terms that are "continuous, homoskedastic or normally distributed" (Aldrich and Nelson, 1984: 15), probit models were estimated when the dependent variables of interest were dichotomous. For the other analyses, OLS regressions were estimated, and the variance-covariance matrix was computed employing the

Table 2

Correlation Matrix for All Variables*

Variable	2	3	4	5	6	7	8
1. (Un)profitability	.59	.34	.78	−.11	−.07	−.18	.14
2. No. of risks		.60	.92	−.23	.00	.01	.17
3. Contract type			.76	−.27	−.05	.09	.13
4. Predicted after-market s.d.				−.25	−.04	−.03	.18
5. Stock options					.01	−.11	−.05
6. Noncash portion of compensation						.48	−.15
7. % of equity held by top management							−.26
8. Separate CEO/chair							
9. % of outside directors							
10. % of outside owner-directors							
11. Blockholder							
12. Venture capital							
13. Equity value							
14. Sales revenue							
15. Firm age							
16. Manager age							

* All correlations >.11 (or ≤.11) are statistically significant at the .01 level.

Managerial Incentives

White (1980) adjustment, thus correcting for possible heteroskedasticity.

RESULTS

Risk-bearing and Incentives

Tables 3–5 show the results relating to the hypothesized trade-offs between risk bearing and managerial incentives. For each of the four risk proxies, probit regressions were used to test the predicted inverse relation between the level of firm risk and the probability of observing stock options in top management compensation. Our motivation for estimating separate probit regressions for each measure of risk was to show that the test of the relation between firm risk and the introduction of incentives does not hinge on any single measure of firm risk. The results in Table 3 show that for each of the four measures of risk, riskier firms are significantly less likely to include stock options in their executive compensation contracts, consistent with hypothesis 1. Logit analyses were also conducted, with consistent results. Finally, to supplement the probit regressions predicting the use of stock options, we estimated a regression in which the dependent variable was the percentage of contingent compensation (i.e., the value of the options, using the Black-Scholes option pricing model) relative to total compensation (i.e., options value plus cash compensation). Again, the direction and significance of the relationship between risk and the percentage of contingent compensation is consistent with the results reported in Table 3. Where the dependent variables were measured in terms of percentages, logarithmic transformation of these variables was also considered (Demsetz and Lehn, 1985). In each instance, the results of these unreported tests were consistent with the results reported here.

Table 4 examines the relationship between firm risk and incentive compensation in greater detail by measuring incentive compensation in terms of the proportion of total managerial compensation (i.e., cash compensation +

Table 2 (continued)

9	10	11	12	13	14	15	16
−.15	.17	.13	−.17	−.06	−.21	−.41	−.28
−.31	.10	.07	−.33	−.08	−.28	−.44	−.41
−.30	−.01	.01	−.21	.04	−.15	−.30	−.35
−.31	.11	.08	−.29	−.07	−.27	−.47	−.42
.19	.08	−.01	.20	−.03	.02	.06	.15
−.14	.05	−.16	−.02	−.12	−.25	−.08	−.06
−.36	−.29	−.35	−.13	−.09	−.14	−.01	−.15
.01	−.01	.07	−.09	−.06	−.04	−.09	−.09
	.44	.09	.20	.08	.19	.14	.53
		.17	.14	−.04	−.11	−.10	.16
			.16	−.05	.00	−.09	.03
				−.01	.03	.01	.09
					.80	.14	.10
						.33	.25
							.37
							−

Table 3

Probit Models of the Relationship between the Use of Stock Options and Measures of Firm Risk and Management Equity Holdings*

$$\text{STOCK OPTIONS}_i = a + b_1\text{SALES}_i(\times10^{-3}) + b_2\text{EQUITY VALUE}_i(\times10^{-3}) + b_3\text{ FIRM AGE}_i + b_4\text{MGT. AGE}_i + b_5\text{MGT. OWN}_i + b_6\text{ RISK}_i + e_i$$

Risk measure	Estimated coefficients							χ^2	% correct
	a	b_1	b_2	b_3	b_4	b_5	b_6		
(Un)profitability	−.836	.212	−.051	−.001	.020	−.472**	−.254**	35.70***	69
	(.524)	(1.059)	(.090)	(.007)	(.012)	(.231)	(.153)		
No. of risks	−.203	−.471	−.034	−.004	.013	−.420**	−.037***	44.45***	68
	(−.553)	(−1.097)	(.098)	(−.007)	(.012)	(−.224)	(−.010)		
Contract type	−1.219***	.079	−.047	−.003	.013	−.317*	−.754***	50.29***	71
	(.497)	(1.051)	(.099)	(−.007)	(.012)	(.229)	(.167)		
Predicted s.d.	.561	−.048	−.003	−.001	.010	−.476***	−29.269***	48.97***	69
	(.641)	(.001)	(.010)	(.001)	(.013)	(.229)	(6.968)		

* $p \leq .10$; ** $p \leq .05$; *** $p \leq .01$; t-tests are one-tailed for hypothesized effects, two-tailed for control variables.
* The estimated model also includes an unreported block of thirteen industry dummy variables.

incentive compensation from stock options and change in equity value) derived from noncash sources (i.e., changes in the value of stock options and equity ownership). Table 4 reveals that firm risk is negatively related to the proportion of total managerial compensation that is derived from incentive compensation, consistent with hypothesis 3.

Table 4

Regression Models of the Relation between the Proportion of Executive Compensation from Noncash Incentives and Measures of Firm Risk*

$$\text{NONCASH COMP}_i = a + b_1\text{SALES}_i(\times10^{-3}) + b_2\text{EQUITY VALUE}_i(\times10^{-3}) + b_3\text{FIRM AGE}_i + b_4\text{MGT. AGE}_i + b_5\text{RISK}_i + e_i$$

Risk measure	Estimated coefficients						χ^2	Adj. R^2
	a	b_1	b_2	b_3	b_4	b_5		
(Un)profitability	.809***	−1.418***	.028***	.000	−.000	−.092***	5210.09***	.10
	(.105)	(.170)	(.005)	(.001)	(.003)	(.027)		
No. of risks	.796***	−1.422***	.029***	.001	.000	−.003**	5185.94***	.09
	(.117)	(.174)	(.005)	(.001)	(.003)	(.002)		
Contract type	.718***	−1.371***	.028***	.001	.000	−.049*	5059.84***	.09
	(.109)	(.167)	(.005)	(.001)	(.003)	(.033)		
Predicted s.d.	.920***	−1.454***	.030***	.000	−.000	−3.598***	5201.88***	.10
	(.114)	(.177)	(.005)	(.001)	(.003)	(1.322)		

* $p \leq .10$; ** $p \leq .05$; *** $p \leq .01$; t-tests are one-tailed for hypothesized effects, two-tailed for control variables.
* The estimated model also includes an unreported block of thirteen industry dummy variables.

Hypothesis 2, which stated that managerial risk-bearing concerns would result in riskier firms having top managers hold lower levels of equity in their firms, is tested in the models shown in Table 5. The results are consistent with hypothesis 2, indicating that the higher the level of firm risk, the lower the level of managerial stock ownership. This result holds for each of the four risk measures. Finally, hypothesis 4 stated that the level of equity ownership held by the top management group is inversely related to the likelihood that stock options are used to compensate top management. The results in Table 3 are consistent with this hypothesis and the risk-bearing explanation.

Managerial Incentives

Table 5

Regression Models of the Relationship between Management Equity Holdings and Measures of Firm Risk*

MGT. OWN$_i$ = a + b_1SALES$_i$($\times 10^{-3}$) + b_2EQUITY VALUE$_i$($\times 10^{-3}$)
$\qquad$ + b_3FIRM AGE$_i$ + b_4MGT. AGE$_i$ + b_5RISK$_i$ + e_i

Risk measure	Estimated coefficients						χ^2	Adj. R^2
	a	b_1	b_2	b_3	b_4	b_5		
(Un)profitability	.970***	−.067	.001	−.000	−.008***	−.145***	1766.87***	.08
	(.097)	(.043)	(.001)	(.001)	(.002)	(.031)		
No. of risks	.860***	−.060	.001	.002	−.007***	−.002	1670.51***	.04
	(.112)	(.043)	(.001)	(.002)	(.003)	(.002)		
Contract type	.810***	−.053	.001	.003	−.006**	−.048*	1663.79***	.04
	(.097)	(.041)	(.011)	(.002)	(.003)	(.032)		
Predicted s.d.	.958***	−.633	.010	.002	−.008***	−2.438**	1681.14***	.04
	(.126)	(.434)	(.012)	(.002)	(.003)	(1.451)		

• $p \le .10$; •• $p \le .05$; ••• $p \le .01$; t-tests are one-tailed for hypothesized effects, two-tailed for control variables.
* The estimated model also includes an unreported block of thirteen industry dummy variables.

Tables 3, 4, and 5 thus provide evidence that IPO firms with higher risk exhibit significantly lower levels of incentives in executive compensation contracts and managerial ownership. In addition, Table 3 shows that firms whose managers face higher levels of manager-specific risk, based on the level of their equity holdings in the firm, are significantly less likely to have risky incentive compensation contracts. We also examined whether the results were sensitive to the focus on the IPO top management team, rather than the individual CEO. Reestimating the models in Tables 3–5 using CEO data only, we found similar results to those reported in Tables 3–5.

The consistent pattern of statistically significant results in Tables 3–5 suggests a trade-off between risk bearing and incentives, in which firms whose top management groups face substantial risk, due to either the firm's riskiness or their managers' level of equity holdings in the firm, receive diminishing benefits from imposing further risk bearing on managers through compensation contracts. The results thus suggest that firm-specific and manager-specific factors affect managers' willingness to accept contingent compensation and that this results in differential incentive compensation contracts across firms.

Monitoring and Incentives

The second set of results addresses the hypothesized trade-off between the use of incentives and monitoring, i.e., whether firms seek to address the differences in incentive compensation contracts discussed above by increasing the level of monitoring for those firms in which top managers do not bear substantial incentive compensation risk. The tests of hypotheses 5a–5e and 6a–6e, all of which address this trade-off, are shown in Tables 6 and 7, respectively. The results are quite robust in supporting the hypotheses. Table 6 shows that firms facing a weak alignment of owner and manager interests, i.e., firms whose top managers hold smaller equity positions in the firm, are more likely to have (1) a larger percentage of outside directors on their boards (consistent with hypothesis 5a), (2) a larger percentage of outside owner-directors on their boards (consistent with hypothesis 5b), (3) a major non-board-member blockholder (consistent with hypothesis 5c), (4) venture capital backing (consistent with hypothesis 5d), and (5) a separate CEO/board chairman position (consistent with hypothesis 5e). In each case, the greater the magnitude of the agency incentive problem, as defined by lower levels of managerial stock holdings, the greater the level of monitoring provided.

A possible alternative explanation for several of these findings might be that higher equity holdings by top managers could entitle them to a board seat and thus influence the balance between insiders and outsiders. Empirically, we were able to address this issue directly; specifically, the CEO, independent of his or her equity holdings, is virtually always on the board, and the entitlement argument could not apply in this case. We therefore reestimated the models in Table 6, this time using the equity holdings of the CEO only, rather than the top management group, and found that the results were essentially no different from those reported in Table 6. When we reestimated all five monitoring models using CEO equity only, we found that in each case the results were basically unchanged—the level of CEO equity holdings was significantly inversely related to each of the five monitoring variables.

Table 6

Regression and Probit Models of the Relation between Monitoring Structures and Management Equity Holdings*

$MONITOR_i = a + b_1SALES_i(\times 10^{-3}) + b_2EQUITY\ VALUE_i(\times 10^{-3}) + b_3FIRM\ AGE_i + b_4MGT.\ AGE_i + b_5MGT.\ OWN_i + e_i$

Monitoring measure	Estimated coefficients						χ^2	Adj. R^2 (% correct)
	a	b_1	b_2	b_3	b_4	b_5		
% outside directors	−.123** (.060)	.002** (.001)	−.005 (.003)	−.001 (.001)	.016*** (.001)	−.206*** (.029)	2324.65***	.38
Proportion of outside owner-directors	.038 (.058)	−.052*** (.013)	.001*** (.000)	−.002*** (.001)	.006*** (.001)	−.181*** (.029)	464.13***	.15
CEO/chairman split	2.250*** (.499)	1.183 (1.652)	−.845 (2.539)	−.010 (.007)	−.023** (.012)	−1.375*** (.237)	56.00***	(67%)
Blockholder (>5%)	.771* (.465)	1.801 (1.202)	−.110 (.170)	−.015** (.007)	.002 (.012)	−1.688*** (.236)	73.16***	(68%)
Venture capital	−2.418*** (.813)	1.427 (1.324)	−.066 (.116)	−.002 (.010)	−.022 (.020)	−.857*** (.355)	38.13***	(91%)

* $p \le .10$; ** $p \le .05$; *** $p \le .01$; t-tests are one-tailed for hypothesized effects, two-tailed for control variables.
* The estimated model also includes an unreported block of thirteen industry dummy variables.

When extending the definition of the magnitude of the agency incentive problem to encompass the total executive income from stock options and equity ownership, the hypothesized inverse relationship between the levels of incentives and monitoring was also found for three of the five types of monitoring. Results in Table 7 show that firms with managers having a lower proportion of their total managerial compensation derived from noncash incentives are more likely to have (1) a larger percentage of outside directors on their boards (consistent with hypothesis 6a), (2) a major non-board-member blockholder (consistent with hypothesis 6c), and (3) a separate CEO/board chairman position (consistent with hypothesis 6e).

Managerial Incentives

Table 7

Regression and Probit Models of the Relation between Monitoring Structures and the Proportion of Executive Compensation from Noncash Incentives*

$MONITOR_i = a + b_1SALES_i(\times10^{-3}) + b_2EQUITY\ VALUE_i(\times10^{-3})$
$+ b_3FIRM\ AGE_i + b_4MGT.\ AGE_i + b_5NONCASH_i + e_i$

Monitoring measure	Estimated coefficients						χ²	Adj. R^2 (% correct)
	a	b_1	b_2	b_3	b_4	b_5		
% outside directors	−.236***	.022	−.004	−.001	.017***	−.078***	2128.10***	.31
	(.059)	(.014)	(.004)	(.001)	(.001)	(.032)		
Proportion of outside owner-directors	−.111**	−.041***	.009***	−.002**	.008***	.004	415.81***	.08
	(.055)	(.009)	(.002)	(.001)	(.001)	(.026)		
CEO/chairman split	1.695***	.417	−.102	−.011	−.013	−.801***	33.96***	(64%)
	(.492)	(1.547)	(2.175)	(.007)	(.012)	(.263)		
Blockholder (>5%)	.040	.177	−.010	.019***	.013	−.771***	36.80***	(64%)
	(.456)	(.135)	(.015)	(.007)	(.011)	(.236)		
Venture capital	−2.888***	.147	−.064	−.004	.028	−.245	35.28***	(91%)
	(.815)	(.133)	(.122)	(.012)	(.020)	(.334)		

• $p \le .10$; •• $p \le .05$; ••• $p \le .01$; t-tests are one-tailed for hypothesized effects, two-tailed for control variables.
* The estimated model also includes an unreported block of thirteen industry dummy variables.

Taken together, the findings reported in Tables 6 and 7 suggest that firms facing a more severe managerial incentive problem, due to top managers having lower incentives from their compensation contracts and equity holdings, are generally more likely to have governance structures that provide a higher level of monitoring of managerial behavior.

DISCUSSION

Overall, the empirical results provide strong statistical support for the study's hypotheses. The results of tests of the first set of hypotheses relating to the trade-off between incentives and risk bearing consistently show an inverse relationship between levels of firm risk and the degree to which incentive compensation for top managers is used. As an example of the practical significance of the results, a one-standard-deviation increase in the number of risks an IPO firm faces leads to a 63-percent reduction in the probability that a firm offers stock options. This highlights how organizational contingencies, such as firm risk, by tipping the balance between incentives and risk bearing, can influence the nature of incentives used by firms.

Moreover, the relationship between managerial equity holdings and the use of stock options also suggests that manager-specific contingencies can also influence the trade-off between incentives and risk bearing. Taken together, both sets of results support the interpretation that managers' willingness to accept risky compensation varies across firms and that the firm-specific and manager-specific factors examined here contribute to this variance.

An implication of this finding is that future research, particularly the empirical compensation literature, might be well served by devoting more attention to agents' preferences when examining incentive contracts. While Levinthal (1988), in his review of agency models of organizations, noted that such models must take into account the goals of both the individual and the organization, much of the recent literature on compensation neglects the goals of the individual, other than assuming a disutility for effort and a preference for more money rather than less. Lambert, Larcker, and Verrecchia's (1991) theoretical study is distinctive in indirectly raising this issue by examining how stock options may be valuated differently by the firm and the CEO. Similarly, Zajac (1990) noted that differences in managerial preferences imply that identical compensation contracts could have differential incentive effects on the CEO and hence differing implications for firm performance.

In terms of the trade-off between monitoring and incentives, the results are again quite consistent with the hypotheses, showing that the levels of monitoring observed are inversely related to the levels of managerial incentives used. These robust results are obtained with multiple measures of monitoring and considering managerial incentives both in terms of compensation and stock ownership. As an example of the practical significance of these results, a one-standard-deviation increase in the level of managerial stock ownership leads to a virtual 100-percent reduction in the probability that a firm will split the CEO and board chairman positions. More generally, the observed trade-off supports the notion that there are costs to monitoring top management, that the level of monitoring will therefore differ across firms, and that considering firm-specific contingencies such as the use of incentives can contribute to explaining the source of this variance.

Taken together, the findings support our basic contingency arguments: that firms' use of executive compensation contracts to address managerial incentive problems is hampered by risk-bearing concerns stemming from the risk-aversion of top managers and that firms seek to address this problem, which is greatest for the riskiest firms, by structuring their boards of directors to ensure sufficient monitoring of managerial behavior. More specifically, the study shows that the implications of top executive compensation contracts and equity holdings on the magnitude of the agency (incentive) problem cannot be assessed without also taking into account the relative uncertainty of a firm's performance (risk bearing) and the specific composition of a firm's board of directors (monitoring). These arguments and results have implications for three long-standing debates among corporate governance researchers.

First, for researchers interested in the classic problem of the separation of ownership and control (Berle and Means, 1932; Jensen and Meckling, 1976), the study's results suggest that to focus on stock ownership (e.g., Morck, Shleifer, and Vishny, 1988) incompletely defines the problem, since incentive compensation contracts for top executives might be used to address the problem of the separation of ownership and control. In addition, the risk-bearing trade-offs identified in this study, which imply the desirability of some separation of ownership and management, must also be considered in defining the problem. Future organizational research could begin to address these issues jointly.

Second, for organizational and legal researchers interested in establishing guidelines for structuring boards of directors to

Managerial Incentives

ensure maximum monitoring capability (cf. Lorsch and
MacIver, 1989), the study's findings suggest that such
attention to board structure may be misplaced, given that
firms' effective use of managerial incentives can
substantially lessen the need for costly monitoring. Future
research that seeks to assess more explicitly the costs of
monitoring and how those costs may differ across firms
would be particularly valuable, as would examining the
interaction of monitoring and incentives, such as the role of
monitoring in enhancing the specific estimators chosen for
incentive contracts (cf. Stiglitz, 1975).

Third, the results also have implications for the descriptive
pay-for-performance debates in the agency and
organizational literatures (e.g., Kerr and Bettis, 1987; Jensen
and Murphy, 1990). The findings suggest that the current
debate about the effectiveness of incentive compensation
contracts cannot be judged fully without also first
considering (1) the willingness of top executives to bear the
risk of contingent compensation and (2) the potential for
using additional monitoring as a substitute for incentive
compensation. Efforts to observe "optimal" incentive
compensation contracts for top executives empirically should
thus recognize certain inherent conflicts, trade-offs, and
substitution possibilities. This study also suggests that
firm-specific factors such as firm risk, by influencing
managers' willingness to accept contingent compensation,
will also influence the trade-offs made in designing actual
compensation arrangements.

Thus an important issue raised by this study is how much
risk a CEO should be expected to bear in his or her
compensation agreement. While formal theoretical models
of agency recognize the trade-off between incentives and
risk bearing, most empirical compensation studies have
treated compensation arrangements as exogenous (Lambert
and Larcker, 1987). Additional empirical, organizationally
based research is needed to establish the firm-specific and
CEO-specific contextual factors that can shape CEOs'
willingness to accept contingent compensation. This
knowledge about the expected variety in actual
compensation contracts can then be used to address the
CEO pay-for-performance question more clearly. Such an
expected variety of compensation contracts across firms
might explain, in part, the puzzling inability of prior empirical
compensation research to detect a uniform pay-for-
performance relationship for CEOs.

In terms of the organizational literature's potential
contribution to agency research, the results of this study
suggest that future compensation research that considers
both apolitical determinants (e.g., risk aversion) and political
determinants (e.g., CEO power versus board power) of
compensation decisions may be best able to unravel the
ambiguity surrounding pay-for-performance research (see
also Westphal and Zajac, 1994). While Jensen and Murphy's
(1990: 246) inability to find evidence of a pay-for-
performance relationship for CEOs in large corporations led
them to conclude that normative models of incentive
contracts are largely "irrelevant to most compensation

contracts," greater attention to organizational issues could possibly help reconcile normative and positive agency research and thereby enhance its usefulness for organizational research.

Another avenue for future research would involve assessing how and why compensation contracts and corporate governance mechanisms change over time. An interesting descriptive finding of this study is that some compensation and governance features of the firms in this sample, which are generally smaller and younger than the firms often used in this area of research, differ from those found in large *Fortune* 500 firms. The majority of firms in this sample have different individuals in the CEO and chairman roles and also do not offer stock options. In older, larger firms, it is much more common for the CEO also to serve as board chairman and for stock options to be used (Lorsch and MacIver, 1989). Large-scale longitudinal studies, as well as individual case histories, could provide insights into the evolution of firms' corporate governance structures and the role played by institutional and technical factors in influencing that evolution (Westphal and Zajac, 1994).

Finally, while our discussion of firm risk, executive compensation, and governance structure has been oriented toward addressing internal agency issues between owners and managers within their firms, we recognize an alternative perspective that is more externally oriented. Specifically, firms may seek to address executive compensation and governance questions with the intention of signalling information to prospective investors in the IPO market. Leland and Pyle (1977) have argued, for example, that in IPOs, firms attempt to signal inside information about their value. To the extent that signalling is a major issue for IPO firms, it suggests a perspective that may compete with our agency-based contingency perspective. For example, hypothesis 1 stated that, given managerial risk aversion, riskier firms would be less likely to offer stock options to top managers. From a signalling perspective, however, having top managers accept stock options, even when inefficient from a risk-bearing perspective, could be a signal that reduces uncertainty for potential investors in the capital markets: Investors can observe whether top managers are willing to stake their own compensation on the future value of the firm. This suggests a competing hypothesis 1: that firms with higher total risk are more likely to include stock options in their executive compensation contracts. While the competing hypothesis is not supported in this study, this is not to say that signalling is not an issue for firms in our sample but, rather, that the risk-bearing issues raised in this study seem to dominate any signalling concerns. Also, not all of our hypotheses are necessarily at odds with signalling. The directionality of the monitoring hypotheses, for example, could be viewed as consistent with a signalling argument, although the underlying logic for the hypotheses would differ.

Signalling can also be considered in the broader context of a resource dependence perspective (Pfeffer and Salancik, 1978), in which governance decisions such as board

Managerial Incentives

composition are viewed more in terms of their impact on managing external resource needs, as is the case with the role of interlocking directorates (Zajac, 1988). From this perspective, outside directors are seen more as providers of money, expertise, or external contacts, rather than as monitors of managerial behavior. Clearly, boards of directors in large and small firms can engage in both internal monitoring and external resource acquisition activities, such as when an investor gains a board seat to monitor his or her investment more closely. Future empirical research could examine more explicitly the relationship between internal and external board activities, as well as possible changes over time in societal expectations regarding the relative importance of those activities.

While there appears to be a growing consensus for increasing the use of incentive compensation and board monitoring in corporations, this study highlights the need to consider not only the potential benefits of such practices but also the potential costs. The study has shown that there are costs associated with the heavy use of incentive compensation, the costs and benefits of incentives and monitoring vary predictably across organizations, and such differences can explain, in part, the variation in the levels of incentive compensation, ownership, and board monitoring in organizations. More generally, the study suggests that the further development of an agency-based contingency perspective that recognizes explicitly the conflicts, trade-offs, and substitution possibilities among incentives, monitoring, and risk bearing in organizations may have the greatest potential to advance our understanding of top executive compensation, ownership, and corporate governance.

REFERENCES

Aldrich, John H., and Forrest D. Nelson
1984 Linear Probability, Logit, and Probit Models. Beverly Hills, CA: Sage.

Altman, Edward I.
1968 "Financial ratios, discriminant analysis and prediction of corporate bankruptcy." Journal of Finance, 23: 589–610.

Baker, George P., Michael C. Jensen, and Kevin J. Murphy
1988 "Compensation and incentives: Practice vs. theory." Journal of Finance, 43: 593–617.

Beaver, William H.
1966 "Financial ratios as predictors of failure." Journal of Accounting Research, 4: 71–102.

Berle, Adolph, and Gardiner C. Means
1932 The Modern Corporation and Private Property. New York: Macmillan.

Berry, Christopher, Christopher Muscarella, and Michael Vetsuypens
1991 "Underwriter warrants, underwriter compensation, and the costs of going public." Journal of Financial Economics, 29: 113–136.

Black, Fischer, and Myron Scholes
1973 "The pricing of options and corporate liabilities." Journal of Political Economy, 81: 637–659.

Davis, Gerald F.
1991 "Agents without principles? The spread of the poison pill through the intercorporate network." Administrative Science Quarterly, 36: 583–613.

Demsetz, Harold, and Kenneth Lehn
1985 "The structure of corporate ownership: Causes and consequences." Journal of Political Economy, 93: 1155–1177.

Eisenhardt, Kathleen M.
1989 "Agency theory: An assessment and review." Academy of Management Review, 14: 57–74.

Fama, Eugene F.
1980 "Agency problems and the theory of the firm." Journal of Political Economy, 88: 288–307.
1992 "Time, salary, and incentive payoffs in labor contracts." Working Paper, University of Chicago.

Fama, Eugene F., and Michael C. Jensen
1983 "Separation of ownership and control." Journal of Law and Economics, 26: 301–325.

Feltham, Gerald, John Hughes, and Dan A. Simunic
1991 "Empirical assessment of the impact of auditor quality on the valuation of new issues." Journal of Accounting and Economics, 14: 1–25.

Finnerty, John D.
1986 Corporate Financial Analysis. New York: McGraw-Hill.

Holmstrom, Bengt
1979 "Moral hazard and observability." Bell Journal of Economics, 14: 74–91.
1987 "Incentive compensation: Practical design from a theory point of view." In Haig R. Nalbantian (ed.), Incentives, Cooperation, and Risk Sharing: Economic and Psychological Perspectives on Employment Contracts: 176–185. Totowa, NJ: Rowman and Littlefield.

Huddart, Steven
1993 "The effect of a large shareholder on corporate value." Management Science, 39: 1407–1421.

Ibbotson, Roger G., Jody L. Sindelar, and Jay R. Ritter
1988 "Initial public offerings." Journal of Applied Corporate Finance, 1: 37–45.

Jensen, Michael C.
1983 "Organization theory and methodology." Accounting Review, 58: 319–339.

Jensen, Michael C., and William H. Meckling
1976 "Theory of the firm: Managerial behavior, agency costs, and ownership structure." Journal of Financial Economics, 3: 305–350.

Jensen, Michael C., and Kevin J. Murphy
1990 "Performance pay and top-management incentives." Journal of Political Economy, 98: 225–264.

Journal of Applied Corporate Finance
1992 "Stern Stewart roundtable on management incentive compensation and shareholder value." Vol. 5: 110–130.

Kerr, Jeffrey, and Richard A. Bettis
1987 "Boards of directors, top management compensation, and shareholder returns." Academy of Management Journal, 30: 645–664.

Lambert, Richard A., and David F. Larcker
1987 "An analysis of the use of accounting and market measures of performance in executive compensation contracts." Journal of Accounting Research, 25 (Supplement): 85–125.

Lambert, Richard A., David F. Larcker, and Robert Verrecchia
1991 "Portfolio considerations in valuing executive compensation." Journal of Accounting Research, 29: 129–149.

Lawler, Edward E.
1971 Pay and Organizational Effectiveness: A Psychological View. New York: McGraw-Hill.

Leland, H., and D. Pyle
1977 "Informational asymmetries, financial structure, and financial intermediation." Journal of Finance, 32: 371–387.

Levinthal, Daniel
1988 "A survey of agency models of organizations." Journal of Economic Behavior and Organization, 9: 153–185.

Lewellen, Wilber, Claudio Loderer, and K. Martin
1987 "Executive compensation and executive incentive problems: An empirical analysis." Journal of Accounting and Economics, 9: 287–310.

Lorsch, Jay W., and Elizabeth MacIver
1989 Pawns or Potentates: The Reality of America's Corporate Boards. Boston: Harvard Business School Press.

Mace, Myles L.
1971 Directors: Myth and Reality. Boston: Harvard Business School Press.

Mahoney, Thomas A. (ed.)
1979 Compensation and Reward Practices. Homewood, IL: Irwin.

Morck, Robert, Andrei Shleifer, and Robert W. Vishny
1988 "Management ownership and market evaluation." Journal of Financial Economics, 20: 293–315.

Morck, Robert, Andrei Shleifer, and Robert W. Vishny
1989 "Alternative mechanisms for corporate control." American Economic Review, 79: 842–852.

Perez, Robert C.
1984 Inside Investment Banking. New York: Praeger.

Pfeffer, Jeffrey, and Gerald R. Salancik
1978 The External Control of Organizations. New York: Harper and Row.

Ritter, Jay R.
1987 "The costs of going public." Journal of Financial Economics, 19: 269–281.
1991 "The long-run performance of initial public offerings." Journal of Finance, 46: 3–28.

Ross, Steven
1973 "The economic theory of agency: The principal's problem." American Economic Review, 63: 134–139.

Schultz, Paul
1993 "Unit initial public offerings." Journal of Financial Economics, 25: 199–229.

Shavell, Stephen
1979 "Risk sharing and incentives in the principal and agent relationship." Bell Journal of Economics, 10: 55–73.

Stiglitz, Joseph E.
1975 "Incentives, risk and information: Notes towards a theory of hierarchy." Bell Journal of Economics, 6: 552–579.
1987 "The design of labor contracts." In Haig R. Nalbantian (ed.), Incentives, Cooperation, and Risk Sharing: Economic and Psychological Perspectives on Employment Contracts: 47–68. Totowa, NJ: Rowman and Littlefield.

Tosi, Henry L., and Luis Gomez-Mejia
1989 "The decoupling of CEO pay and performance." Administrative Science Quarterly, 34: 169–189.

Wade, James B., Charles A. O'Reilly, and Ike Chandratat
1990 "Golden parachutes: CEOs and the exercise of social influence." Administrative Science Quarterly, 35: 587–603.

Weisbach, Michael S.
1988 "Outside directors and CEO turnover." Journal of Financial Economics, 20: 431–460.

Westphal, James D., and Edward J. Zajac
1994 "Substance and symbolism in CEOs' long-term incentive plans." Administrative Science Quarterly, vol. 39 (in press).

White, H.
1980 "A heteroskedasticity-consistent covariance matrix estimator and a direct test for heteroskedasticity." Econometrica, 48: 817–838.

Managerial Incentives

Zajac, Edward J.
1988 "Interlocking directorates as an interorganizational strategy: A test of critical assumptions." Academy of Management Journal, 31: 428–438.

1990 "CEO selection, succession, compensation and firm performance: A theoretical integration and empirical analysis." Strategic Management Journal, 11: 313–330.

Zmijewski, Michael E.
1984 "Methodological issues related to the estimation of financial distress prediction models." Journal of Accounting Research, 22: 59–82.

[19]

© *Academy of Management Journal*
1996, Vol. 39, No. 2, 441–463.

IMPACT OF CORPORATE INSIDER, BLOCKHOLDER, AND INSTITUTIONAL EQUITY OWNERSHIP ON FIRM RISK TAKING

PETER WRIGHT
University of Memphis
STEPHEN P. FERRIS
University of Missouri at Columbia
ATULYA SARIN
VIDYA AWASTHI
Santa Clara University

The nature of a firm's risk-taking behavior can significantly affect corporate performance. In an agency context, we examined the influence of equity ownership structure upon corporate risk taking. Results support our premise that the wealth portfolios of corporate insiders may influence firm risk taking. They also support our analysis of entrenchment theory and our presumption that financial and nonfinancial benefits or costs may, at high levels of stock ownership, induce executive decisions inconsistent with growth-oriented risk taking. Institutional owners exerted a significant, positive influence on risk taking, but the role of blockholders was negligible. Finally, ownership structure affected corporate risk taking in the presence of growth opportunities, represented by Tobin's q.

Both the finance and strategic management literatures have documented the existence of a variety of agency conflicts within modern corporations. These conflicts arise from the establishment of the agency relationship characteristic of publicly held firms. Inherent in the agency relationship is the separation between the management of a firm by corporate insiders and its ownership (Berle & Means, 1932). In the presence of such separation, "There will be some divergence between the agent's decisions and those decisions which would maximize the welfare of the principal" (Jensen & Meckling, 1976: 482). Agency conflict results from the effects of this divergence between owners and insiders on decision making.

The nature and extent of agency conflict have been examined in the context of a variety of strategic decisions. Included among these decisions are those concerning divestment strategy (Wright & Ferris, 1997), diversification

---

We express our appreciation to Robert Renn, Mark Kroll, Kevin Barksdale, Augustine Lado, and Jeffrey Krug for their constructive recommendations. We also thank this journal's two anonymous reviewers for their significant contributions.

strategy (Agrawal & Mandelker, 1987; Amihud & Lev, 1981; Hill & Snell, 1988; Kroll, Wright, Toombs, & Leavell, 1996), dividend policy (Easterbrook, 1984; Lang & Litzenberger, 1989), takeover resistance (Stulz, 1988), and firm restructuring (Bethel & Liebeskind, 1993; Johnson, Hoskisson, & Hitt, 1993).

One critical agency issue, however, remains largely unexamined—the impact of equity ownership by corporate insiders on firm risk taking. The influence of insiders on corporate risk taking is an important topic for study since their decisions can affect a firm's ability to compete and thus, ultimately, its survival. Also important but underexplored is the role of large but external shareholders, such as blockholders and institutional investors, who exercise significant voting power and can shape the nature of corporate risk-taking activity. Indeed, as active participants in a corporation's governance, both blockholders and institutions can provide monitoring of a firm's strategies to ensure insider responsiveness as well as to enhance corporate performance (Hansen & Hill, 1991; Shleifer & Vishny, 1986).

In this study, we examined the influence of equity holding by corporate insiders and large external shareholders on the risk-taking activity of firms. For the purpose of our study, we defined corporate risk taking as the analysis and selection of projects that have varying uncertainties associated with their expected outcomes and corresponding cash flows. The unpredictability in a firm's income stream (Bromiley, 1991; Conroy & Harris, 1987; Imhoff & Lobo, 1988; Wright, Kroll, Pray, & Lado, 1995) is a result of its risk-taking behavior. The nature of risk-taking behavior is vital since it has significant implications for a firm's asset structure. A proclivity toward risk taking will result in a high-variance asset composition; and risk aversion will result in a correspondingly lower-variance asset structure.

Although shareholders will prefer growth-oriented risk taking, in some situations corporate insiders may actually wish to reduce the amount of such risk taking. This reduction can occur even when insiders are provided with equity ownership incentive programs to promote alignment of their interests with those of shareholders. We suggest that equity ownership programs do not unambiguously give corporate insiders incentives to enhance firm performance and shareholder wealth through growth-oriented risk taking. Inherent in this argument is the presumption that a number of factors significantly influence corporate insiders. These include the nature of insiders' total wealth portfolios, pecuniary and nonpecuniary benefits and costs that insiders derive from their positions, and the potential for entrenchment.

Since we assumed that equity ownership may represent a significant proportion of a corporate insider's total wealth, the result of such ownership may be an increasingly undiversified personal wealth portfolio. Because of this potential for an undiversified portfolio, corporate insiders may make decisions based solely upon an evaluation of personal gains and losses generated by a particular firm strategy. This practice may result in the selection of a set of non–value-maximizing projects for a firm.

Moreover, as Jensen and Meckling (1976), Jensen and Murphy (1990), and Wright and Ferris (1997) argued, the calculation of personal gains and losses from a business decision incorporates both pecuniary and nonpecuniary attributes. Although the capitalization of growth opportunities may be beneficial for shareholders, the uncertainties associated with new ventures and technologies may inhibit insider commitment to corporate risk taking. In particular, when corporate insiders lack appropriate incentives, they may reduce corporate risk taking in order to lower the personal costs of such decisions. Included among these costs would be the potential loss of employment, the extra effort required to master new technologies or manage new ventures, and the anxieties inherent in higher-risk corporate undertakings.

With an appropriate incentive structure, however, corporate insiders may find it personally beneficial to enhance corporate risk taking while developing growth opportunities (Jensen & Meckling, 1976; Jensen & Murphy, 1990; Kroll et al., 1996). Indeed, in order to more closely merge the interests of corporate insiders and shareholders, and thus reduce the potential for agency conflict, insiders have often been provided with an equity interest in firms. This is typically accomplished through discounted stock purchase programs or the granting of stock options. The presumption underlying these programs has been that there is a positive relationship between insider equity ownership and corporate risk taking.

As noted previously, however, insiders may not increase corporate risk taking as they obtain higher levels of equity ownership because of the potential for wealth "undiversification." That is, if a substantial component of an insider's wealth is concentrated in a single investment—as, for example, is the case with owner-managers holding high equity stakes—the insider may not find it prudent to increase risk taking with respect to that investment.

Corporate insiders also face various benefits and costs associated with their employment. The existence of these benefits or costs can create incentives for them that are inconsistent with growth-oriented risk taking (Jensen & Meckling, 1976; Jensen & Murphy, 1990; Wright & Ferris, 1997). Yet, if such benefits or costs influence the insiders to adopt value-destroying strategies, why are those individuals not subsequently discharged?

The possibility of discharge may be a credible threat for insiders with low equity stakes but not necessarily be so for those with high equity claims. According to the entrenchment hypothesis, insiders with greater equity may possess sufficient influence to guarantee their employment (Demsetz, 1983; Fama & Jensen, 1983; Gibbs, 1993). These corporate insiders, then, may abuse their office. Alternatively, since the insiders who own less equity are unlikely to be entrenched, they are less prone to consume perquisites at the expense of shareholders because of the fear of discharge (James & Soref, 1981; Kroll, Wright, & Theerathorn, 1993).

In our study, we assumed that with high levels of stock ownership, the potential for undiversified personal wealth portfolios, the presence of significant pecuniary and nonpecuniary factors, and the potential for entrenchment may elicit insider decisions inconsistent with growth-oriented risk taking. Our analysis provides a different perspective on the subject of corporate risk taking by corporate insiders. As such, it emphasizes a potential shift in the nature of corporate risk taking. The existing literature implies that there is a uniformly positive relation between firm risk taking and equity ownership, with increased insider equity ownership continuously converging the interests of shareholders and insiders. We assert, however, that the relationship between insider ownership and corporate risk taking may become negative at high levels of insider equity ownership. If such an assertion is valid, it will have important implications for the design of incentive contracts and consequent firm performance.

Additionally, we explored the possibility that large external shareholders like blockholders and institutional investors may also exert an influence upon corporate risk taking. Such an influence remains largely unexamined in the literature.

The studies that have examined the impact of shareholder concentration on corporate contingencies have primarily focused on divestment strategy, diversification strategy, corporate restructuring, organizational performance, and firm value (Barclay & Holderness, 1990; Gibbs, 1993; Kroll et al., 1996; McConnell & Servaes, 1990; Morck, Shleifer, & Vishny, 1988, 1990; Wright & Ferris, 1997). Some works in strategic management have contended that significant external stockholders tend to support beneficial corporate strategies but oppose counterproductive strategies (Bethel & Liebeskind, 1993; Hill & Snell, 1988). Scholars in finance have also concluded that equity blockholders and institutional investors tend to promote shareholder-driven corporate strategies (Holderness & Sheehan, 1985; Mikkelson & Ruback, 1991). Since large external shareholders can bring significant pressure that enhances firm performance, an analysis of their influence may provide additional insight on the nature of firm risk taking.

Another contribution of our theoretical and empirical analyses is that we provide further insight into how corporate risk taking is contingent on the presence or absence of growth opportunities. Some firms may have growth opportunities because of valuable internal resources or locations in attractive industries (Barney, 1991; Lado, Boyd, & Wright, 1992; Wright, Ferris, Hiller, & Kroll, 1995; Wright, Kroll, & Parnell, 1996: Chapters 3–5). We can thus examine under what circumstances corporate insiders or large external shareholders may promote risk taking in order to capitalize on the growth opportunities. Other firms may lack growth opportunities because profitable alternatives are absent from their external environments, or they are located in declining industries, or their internal resources are not valuable (Barney, 1991; Lado et al., 1992; Wright et al., 1995; Wright et al., 1996: Chapters 3–5). Increasing corporate risk taking in the absence of growth opportunities may not be economically rational. Consequently, we assert that the structure of ownership may affect corporate risk taking in the presence of growth opportunities but may not be significantly associated with risk taking in the absence of growth opportunities.

We have organized our study into several sections. In the following section, we review the related literature and develop our empirical hypotheses. Subsequently, we describe our research methodology. We then present our results and provide a discussion of their interpretation followed by concluding remarks. Included in these remarks is our view that there is a need for further study of the impact of the equity ownership structure on firm performance. Finally, we discuss the limitations of our work and comment on future research directions.

LITERATURE REVIEW AND HYPOTHESES

A number of scholars in finance have argued that the personal interests of corporate insiders are served when they enhance shareholder wealth. Specifically, insiders may be driven by pressures from managerial labor markets (Fama, 1980), the influence of capital market signals (Easterbrook, 1984; Rozeff, 1982), or the threat of hostile takeovers (Martin & McConnell, 1991) to enhance firm value. From a sociological perspective, James and Soref (1981) as well as Kroll, Wright, and Theerathorn (1993) contended that corporate positions have structural imperatives associated with them that require responsiveness, thereby aligning insider and shareholder interests. That is, "Persons who come to occupy managerial positions tend to be motivated to enhance firm profitability . . . if they wish to remain in their positions of authority" (James & Soref, 1981: 3). Otherwise, they will be discharged.

Other works in finance and strategic management, however, have concluded that personal motivation or political (rather than economic) forces may in some situations drive corporate insider strategies (Bethel & Liebeskind, 1993; Gibbs, 1993; Jensen & Murphy, 1990; Johnson, Hoskisson, & Hitt, 1993; Pound, 1992; Wright & Ferris, 1997). Consequently, insiders may pursue non–value-maximizing strategies unless they have proper incentives (or face appropriate pressures from the mechanisms of corporate governance).

Jensen and Meckling (1976), who examined the relationship between firm value and insider equity ownership in an agency theory context, contended that agency costs decline as insider ownership rises since the financial interests of corporate insiders and shareholders increasingly converge. Consequently, with greater insider equity ownership, the value of a firm should increase. The implication of their model is that the relation between insider equity ownership and firm value is positive.

Hill and Snell (1988) empirically examined insider equity ownership and shareholder concentration and found that both were limiting influences on firm diversification efforts. They suggested that corporate insiders would undertake additional corporate diversification when their incentives were incongruent with the interests of stockholders. Johnson, Hoskisson, and Hitt (1993) analyzed senior executive equity ownership and found that equity stakes were negatively related to board involvement in value-maximizing strategies, particularly with respect to restructuring. The results of these studies indicate a direct relationship between insider share ownership and corporate strategies that enhance firm value.

Alternatively, some researchers have proposed that when insiders possess only minor interests in their firms, such ownership is positively associated with firm value. When insiders own substantial stakes, however, they become entrenched because they possess sufficient influence to guarantee their employment (Demsetz, 1983; Fama & Jensen, 1983; Gibbs, 1993). The implication of such an argument is that the impact of insider equity ownership upon corporate value is negative, but only at high levels of insider ownership.

A number of studies have theoretically and empirically suggested divergent relationships between ownership structure and firm value. Stulz (1988) suggested that the market value of a corporation initially increases and then subsequently decreases with rising insider ownership. McConnell and Servaes (1990) also concluded that the structure of equity ownership had a nonmonotonic impact on firm value. That is, firm value increased as the level of insider ownership rose and then declined as insiders became entrenched. Morck, Shleifer, and Vishny (1988) likewise reported divergence between firm value and insider ownership.

Although insider ownership may be related to corporate wealth creation, institutional investors and blockholders might also affect firm value, through their influence on managerial decisions. Bethel and Liebeskind (1993) found that blockholders' ownership is directly associated with firm value through their lobbying of senior executives for corporate restructuring. In empirical studies, Mikkelson and Ruback (1985, 1991), Holderness and Sheehan (1985), and Barclay and Holderness (1990) have concluded that both institutional investors and large equity blockholders can positively affect firm value. These findings suggest that there is a positive relationship between firm value and large, identifiable external shareholders.

In this study, rather than exploring the impact of a firm's equity ownership structure on its value, we investigated the influence of the ownership structure on corporate risk taking. The existing literature implies that the relationship between equity ownership and firm risk taking is positive. Amihud and Lev (1981), for instance, concluded that the motive behind conglomerate mergers is risk reduction when insiders own small stakes. That is, to the extent that insiders' employment income is linked to changes in corporate value, an increase in the variance of firm returns increases the risk of their employment income. Corporate insiders would consider this outcome undesirable. Amihud and Lev further argued, however, that when insiders possess large equity claims, they are less motivated by considerations of risk aversion in evaluating merger opportunities. That is because with greater ownership, the interests of corporate insiders and shareholders become more aligned, lessening insiders' predisposition for risk reduction.

Agrawal and Mandelker (1987) provided further support for the conclusions of Amihud and Lev (1981). In their study of acquisitions and divestments, the former reported that insiders with large stockholdings are less likely to reduce corporate risk than those with lower equity stakes. These researchers concluded that large equity positions induce insiders to base decisions to acquire or divest upon an asset-variance-increasing criterion.

Other studies have also implied that insider stock ownership is directly related to firm risk taking. Hill and Snell (1988) concluded that as insider ownership increased, corporate diversification was reduced, thus increasing firms' overall level of risk. Johnson and colleagues (1993) reported that corporate restructuring (reverse diversification) was internally induced with greater levels of managerial equity ownership (but board involvement in restructuring was evident with lower managerial ownership stakes).

Contrarily, we propose that the relationship between insider equity ownership and corporate risk taking may not be monotonically positive. In fact, we hypothesize that corporate risk taking initially increases and then subsequently decreases as insiders expand their equity holdings. Inherent in our conjecture is the presumption that at various levels of equity ownership, the nature of insider wealth portfolios, the pecuniary and nonpecuniary benefits and costs derived from their positions of authority, and the potential for entrenchment will differently influence insiders' attitudes toward corporate risk taking.

The components of insiders' wealth portfolios consist of the income produced from their employment with a firm, their ownership of shares and options in the enterprise, and their remaining assets unrelated to the firm. We assume that as insiders increase their holdings of the firm's equity, their personal wealth portfolios become correspondingly less diversified. Shareholders can diversify their personal portfolios by purchasing other investments; corporate insiders are less able to do so if they own substantial equity stakes in the firms they manage. Thus, if a significant portion of an investor's wealth is concentrated in a single investment (as is the case with insiders holding substantial equity), the investor may not find it desirable to increase risk taking with respect to that investment.

Moreover, because of both pecuniary and nonpecuniary reasons, insiders may be reluctant to increase corporate risk taking as they obtain substantial equity investments. Although financial benefits (or costs), such as employment income and stock ownership (or the threatened loss of such rewards), may entice insiders with low equity stakes to enhance corporate risk taking, such may not be the case with respect to those who are entrenched (Demsetz, 1983; Fama & Jensen, 1983; Gibbs, 1993). Similarly, because of nonfinancial benefits or costs, entrenched insiders may be reluctant to increase corporate risk taking. The nonfinancial rewards (or costs) are subject to consumption only by insiders, with shareholder consumption not possible. These nonfinancial benefits may include "the physical appointments of the office, the attractiveness of the secretarial staff, the level of employee discipline, the kind and amount of charitable contributions, . . . etc." (Jensen & Meckling, 1976: 486). The nonfinancial costs relevant to corporate insiders may be the additional effort required to master new technology or manage new ventures or the anxieties inherent in higher-risk corporate undertakings.

Thus, both monetary and nonmonetary benefits or costs may create incentives for the entrenched corporate insiders that are inconsistent with growth-oriented risk taking. As is evident, those insiders with a high degree of equity ownership may adopt non–value-maximizing strategies. Alternatively, insiders with lower levels of equity ownership may be less likely to adopt such strategies for fear of being discharged (James & Soref, 1981; Kroll et al., 1993).

It must be noted, however, that corporate risk taking is most relevant for firms with growth opportunities. If a firm has growth opportunities, it is interesting to examine under what circumstances its insiders may promote (or inhibit) corporate risk taking in order to capitalize on those opportunities. As noted, a corporation may possess growth opportunities because of possibilities in its external environment, such as its location in attractive industries, or because of its internal resources, such as talented human resources, a valuable culture, or proprietary technology (Barney, 1991; Lado et al., 1992; Wright et al., 1995; Wright et al., 1996: Chapters 3–5).

Alternatively, increasing corporate risk taking in the absence of genuine growth opportunities would be economically irrational. Like Jensen (1986), we presumed that the insiders of firms lacking growth opportunities may be primarily motivated by a desire to increase their level of personal consumption. They may selfishly overinvest, adopting projects with negative net present values. Jensen and Murphy (1990) claimed that even an insider with significant equity ownership may adopt a pet project yielding nonfinancial benefits for the insider but generating financial losses for the shareholders.

Firms may lack growth opportunities because of limitations in their external environments, such as their location in declining industries. Enterprises may also lack growth opportunities because their internal resources are not valuable, rare, imperfectly imitable, or without equivalent substitutes, rendering them inefficient and technologically stagnant (Barney, 1991; Lado et al., 1992; Wright et al., 1995; Wright et al., 1996: Chapters 3–5).

Lang and Litzenberger (1989) and Lindenberg and Ross (1981) proposed that Tobin's q, defined as the market value of a firm standardized by the replacement cost of its assets, can represent the existence of growth opportunities. Firms with q's in excess of unity are underinvested, their value largely driven by the existence of growth opportunities. Lindenberg and Ross explained that these growth opportunities are due to firm-specific factors such as operational efficiency, technological superiority, and locational advantages as well as industry characteristics. Firms with q's of unity or less can be judged as overinvested, lacking a set of profitable new investment projects.

We summarize our theoretical discussion as follows. The degree of insiders' equity ownership may exert divergent influences upon corporate risk taking. At low levels of insider equity ownership, the contemporaneous relationship between ownership and corporate risk taking may be positive. At high levels, that relationship may become negative. Growth opportunities will, however, moderate the relationship between insider stock ownership and corporate risk taking. We hypothesized a significant relation between insider stock ownership and corporate risk taking for growth firms, but did not anticipate such a relationship for firms lacking growth opportunities.

Consequently, we do not offer a hypothesis with respect to firms lacking growth potential but submit the following hypothesis for enterprises possessing growth potential.

> *Hypothesis 1: For firms with growth opportunities, the contemporaneous relationship between the level of equity ownership and corporate risk taking will be positive when insiders hold low equity stakes but negative when insiders hold high equity.*

Although equity ownership may exert a contemporaneous effect on corporate risk taking, the potential exists that ownership in one year may also affect firm risk taking in subsequent years (Bromiley, 1991). That is, corporate insiders may analyze and select from projects today, but the impact of their decisions may be felt in the future, in increased (decreased) uncertainties associated with the expected cash flows (Hassell & Jennings, 1986; Wright et al., 1995). Thus, we hypothesize the following lagged relationship between insider share ownership and corporate risk taking for growth firms.

> *Hypothesis 2: For firms with growth opportunities, the lagged relationship between the level of equity ownership and corporate risk taking will be positive when insiders hold low equity stakes but negative when insiders possess high equity.*

The behavior of other large stockholders may also affect shareholder wealth through their influence on corporate risk-taking decisions. Pound (1988), in his efficient-monitoring hypothesis, proposed that large shareholders tend to support managerial decisions enhancing corporate value but oppose strategies detrimental to owners' interests. Jensen and Meckling (1976) and Kroll, Wright, Toombs, and Leavell (1996) argued that, theoretically, stockholder concentration should enhance firm performance. Mikkelson and Ruback (1991) found empirical support for the thesis that large shareholders positively affect stockholder interests.

As previously noted, Hill and Snell (1988) implied that shareholder concentration may limit the adoption of risk-reducing strategies (e.g., diversification strategies) by managers. Bethel and Liebeskind (1993) also suggested that blockholders may inhibit managerial predispositions to invest in risk-reducing corporate strategies that thereby reduce potential shareholder gains. Shleifer and Vishny (1986) proposed that large equity blockholders can theoretically force value maximization through the promotion of firm risk taking. Consequently, we hypothesized that large equity blockholders encourage greater firm risk taking.

We emphasize, however, that corporate risk taking is mainly relevant for firms enjoying growth opportunities. If a firm has growth opportunities, we can examine whether blockholders promote corporate risk taking in order to capitalize on these opportunities. Alternatively, promoting corporate risk taking to take advantage of growth potential, when such potential does not exist, would be irrational. Thus, we only anticipated a direct, contemporaneous relation between the level of equity ownership by blockholders and corporate risk taking for corporations with growth opportunities. For firms lacking growth opportunities, we did not expect a significant relation between blockholders' stock ownership and corporate risk taking. Consequently, we do not offer a hypothesis on firms lacking growth potential but provide the following hypothesis for corporations confronted with growth opportunities.

> *Hypothesis 3: For firms with growth opportunities, the contemporaneous relationship between the level of equity ownership by blockholders and corporate risk taking will be positive.*

The above hypothesis is based on the premise that blockholder stakes have a contemporaneous impact on corporate risk taking. It is feasible, however, that blockholder ownership in a given year may affect firm risk taking in a subsequent year (Bromiley, 1991). It is also possible that although blockholders may influence the process of project selection today, the effect of their influence will be felt later via change in the uncertainties associated with a firm's income stream (Conroy & Harris, 1987; Imhoff & Lobo, 1988). Hence, we hypothesize a lagged relationship between blockholder share ownership and firm risk taking for enterprises confronted with growth opportunities:

> *Hypothesis 4: For firms with growth opportunities, the lagged relationship between the level of equity ownership by blockholders and corporate risk taking will be positive.*

Institutional investors may also affect corporate risk taking. The premise that institutional investors enhance the interests of shareholders is intuitively appealing. Institutions own substantial equity; consequently, it is in their best interests to encourage firm strategies that capitalize on growth opportunities.

Although Chaganti and Damanpour (1991) and Lowenstein (1991) argued that institutional owners may not always play significant monitoring roles, Brickley, Lease, and Smith (1988) found that institutions tended to oppose managerial decisions that were harmful to shareholders. Similarly, McConnell and Servaes (1990) concluded that there was a positive relation between firm value and ownership by institutional investors. Barclay and Holderness (1990) and Mikkelson and Ruback (1985, 1991) also concluded that institutions can force value maximization.

More relevant to this study, Hill and Snell (1988) suggested that institutional investors discourage corporate strategies that reduce firm risk, such as diversification strategies. Also, Hansen and Hill (1991) argued that institutional ownership may be positively associated with R&D expenditures, a proxy for corporate risk taking. In this context, we expected institutional investors to contemporaneously promote corporate risk taking, but only in the presence of growth opportunities. Thus, we specify the following hypothesis:

> *Hypothesis 5: For firms with growth opportunities, the contemporaneous relationship between the level of equity*

*ownership by institutional investors and corporate risk
taking will be positive.*

Institutional ownership in one time period may also affect future firm
risk taking (Bromiley, 1991), through impacts on future income uncertainty
(Conroy & Harris, 1987; Hassell & Jennings, 1986; Imhoff & Lobo, 1988;
O'Brien, 1988; Wright et al., 1995). Consequently, we hypothesized a lagged
association between institutional investors and corporate risk taking for enterprises with growth potential.

> *Hypothesis 6: For firms with growth opportunities, the
> lagged relationship between the level of equity ownership
> by institutional investors and corporate risk taking will
> be positive.*

SAMPLE CONSTRUCTION AND METHODOLOGY

Firms were selected from publicly traded companies satisfying various
data requirements. Our first requirement was availability of ownership data.
We obtained data regarding equity ownership by corporate insiders, external
institutional investors, and blockholders from the *Value Line Investment
Survey.* According to this survey, corporate insiders include firms' senior
executives and the members of their boards of directors. To test the intertemporal stability of these hypothesized relationships, we initially focused our
analysis on the years 1986 and 1992. Later, we incorporated additional data
as we tested for possible noncontemporaneous relationships between equity
ownership structure and corporate risk taking.

Our second requirement was that financial analysts' forecast data about
firms had to be available on the *Institutional Brokers Estimate System.* We
used the standard deviation of analysts' forecasts of earnings per share as
our measure of risk, doing so because uncertainty in analysts' forecasts should
be highly correlated with the unpredictability in cash flows generated by a
firm's assets, which are a result of corporate risk-taking behavior (Hassell &
Jennings, 1986; O'Brien, 1988). Also, evidence suggests that the forecasts of
senior management and analysts are highly correlated (Hassell & Jennings,
1986; McNichols, 1989).

Miller and Bromiley (1990) argued that the advantage of using the standard deviation of analysts' forecasts of earnings per share is that it is an ex
ante proxy for income uncertainty. This is an important characteristic since it
is future income that will be affected by the risk-taking decisions of managers.
Bromiley (1991), Conroy and Harris (1987), and Imhoff and Lobo (1988) also
used this measure as a proxy for corporate risk taking in time series methods.

The third requirement we imposed was that financial data had to be
available in COMPUSTAT files so that Tobin's q's could be calculated. Lastly,
we required that firms have January-December fiscal years so that statistical
estimation would not be biased by varying year-end anomalies. The final
sample satisfying our data requirements consisted of 358 firms for 1986 and
514 firms for 1992.

Our empirical methodology employed a moderated cross-sectional regression analysis in which risk taking was regressed against various measures of equity ownership. It is recognized that when a moderator variable Z, upon which the form of association between X and Y is hypothesized to be contingent, assumes only two values, regression equations should be estimated separately for the two groups (Arnold, 1982; Staw & Oldham, 1978; Stone & Hollenbeck, 1989; Stone-Romero & Anderson, 1994). In our study, the moderator variable is dichotomous—firms with q's in excess of unity represent a group with growth opportunities, and the remaining firms comprise a second group, those lacking profitable investment projects. Thus, using separate sets of regressions, we analyzed the impact of insider, blockholder, and institutional equity ownership upon the firms' risk-taking behavior in the presence or absence of growth opportunities.

We began our examination with a contemporaneous analysis for the years 1986 and 1992, assuming that ownership structure did in fact exert a contemporaneous effect on corporate risk taking. Because ownership structure in a given year may influence later corporate risk taking (Bromiley, 1991), we introduced variables lagged by two years into our regression analyses. More specifically, we estimated the effect of ownership structure in 1986 on corporate risk taking in 1988 and the influence of ownership in 1992 on risk taking in 1994.

Because the goal of this study was to test for nonlinearity in the relationship between insider equity ownership and corporate risk taking, we employed a piecewise linear regression method in our empirical analysis. This approach allowed the estimated coefficient on the insider equity ownership variable to change, if warranted by the underlying data. We anticipated that the association of insider ownership with firm risk taking would be nonlinear because of the following expectations: On the one hand, we expected the impact of insider ownership on corporate risk taking to be positive when insiders possessed low equity stakes—as their ownership rose from 0 to 7.5 percent. On the other hand, we expected this impact to be negative when insider ownership was higher, or beyond 7.5 percent.

Previous researchers using this method have observed a significantly differential impact of equity ownership on firm behavior. Morck and colleagues (1988) reported evidence of insider entrenchment emerging at an equity ownership level of approximately 5 percent. At lower levels, they concluded that the incentive effects of equity ownership dominated and aligned the interests of insiders and stockholders. Similarly, McConnell and Servaes (1990) observed that the ability of equity to mitigate agency conflicts was attenuated at high levels of insider stock ownership. Weston (1979) and Stulz (1988) examined the influence of the takeover market as a disciplining device for corporate insiders and determined that at high levels of insider equity ownership, hostile takeovers were impossible. Thus, equity ownership structure may constrain the effectiveness of the corporate control market to discipline non–value-maximizing corporate insiders.

In our empirical analysis, we examined the possibility of a change in the impact of insider equity ownership on corporate risk taking at a concentration level of 7.5 percent. That is, we partitioned insider equity ownership into low-end (<7.5%) and high-end segments (≥7.5%). Such a partitioning is consistent with that used in earlier studies (e.g., McConnell & Servaes, 1990; Morck et al., 1988) as well as with the previously developed theoretical discussion regarding the emergence of entrenchment effects at higher levels of insider equity ownership. Moreover, alternative partitioning percentages we examined failed to reveal a significant differential impact, suggesting that the entrenchment effects of equity ownership were not adequately separated at other values.

We also controlled for size and industry effects in our analysis. Firm size was captured by total assets, a widely used proxy in the financial economics literature. The effect of industry differences was examined by adding a series of two-digit Standard Industrial Classification (SIC) code dummy variables. This specification controls for possible unique industry effects.

RESULTS AND DISCUSSION

Table 1 presents summary statistics for our measures of the independent variables for the years 1986 and 1992. Also reported are summary statistics for the dependent variable, corporate risk taking.

Table 2 contains the results of the regression models estimating the effects of equity ownership structure on contemporaneous risk taking for 1986 and 1992 and testing Hypotheses 1, 3, and 5. This table presents the results for the full sample and for firms with growth opportunities and those lacking such opportunities. For firms with growth opportunities, the coefficient on low insider equity ownership is significantly positive, and that for insider equity ownership is significantly negative.

These results indicate that when insiders possess a low degree of equity ownership, their ownership positively influences corporate risk taking. As insiders increase their investment in a firm, however, they tend to reduce corporate risk taking. For firms without growth prospects, the impact of insider equity ownership is statistically insignificant. This finding is consistent with our conjecture that increasing corporate risk taking to take advantage of growth potential in the absence of such potential is economically irrational.

The estimated coefficient for blockholder equity ownership is statistically insignificant, indicating that, on the average, blockholders exert no measurable influence on corporate risk taking. This is true for both focal years, 1986 and 1992. The lack of statistical significance for this variable is consistent with the findings of other studies (Holderness & Sheehan, 1988; McConnell & Servaes, 1990). McConnell and Servaes, for instance, contended that many blockholders are passive investors, providing little in the way of monitoring. If passive blockholders dominate, then their monitoring role may indeed be small.

TABLE 1
Summary Statistics for Measures of Independent and Dependent Variables

Variable	Mean	Median	Minimum	25th Percentile	75th Percentile	Maximum
1986 sample						
Managerial ownership[a]	12.60	5.50	0.01	1.00	20.00	78.00
Blockholder ownership[a]	24.14	19.10	1.00	10.00	32.00	79.40
Institutional ownership[a]	42.71	44.23	0.01	31.50	55.86	83.60
Firm size[b]	10,797	1,987	68.0	646.3	8,991.9	208,998
Risk taking, 1986[c]	2.6	1.64	0.05	0.8	3.24	26.03
Risk taking, 1988[c]	2.2	1.35	0.02	0.8	2.4	31.15
1992 sample						
Managerial ownership[a]	12.7	5.3	0.3	2	17	80
Blockholder ownership[a]	17.3	14.3	4.0	9.6	22.1	76
Institutional ownership[a]	51.9	53.4	4.6	40.3	65.6	96.9
Firm size[b]	11,434	2,066	72.0	684.3	9,204.3	213,701
Risk taking, 1992[c]	2.16	1.25	0.01	0.70	2.4	29.05
Risk taking, 1994[c]	2.18	1.27	0.01	0.68	2.5	30.01

[a] Values shown are percentages.
[b] Total assets, in millions of dollars.
[c] This value is the standard deviation of analysts' forecasts.

The results for institutional equity ownership indicate a significant and positive relationship between the level of equity ownership by institutions and corporate risk taking for firms with growth opportunities. Our results are consistent with the arguments of Barclay and Holderness (1990), Brickley, Lease, and Smith (1988), McConnell and Servaes (1990), and Mikkelson and Ruback (1985, 1991). Specifically, these results suggest that institutional investors enhance corporate value through their positive influence on growth-oriented risk taking. The insignificant relationship between institutional ownership and corporate risk taking for firms without growth prospects supports our conjecture that increased risk taking by organizations lacking growth prospects may be without economic justification.

The findings shown in Table 2 support Hypotheses 1 and 5 but not Hypothesis 3. For enterprises possessing growth potential, the contemporaneous association between insider ownership and corporate risk taking is positive when insiders hold low equity stakes but negative when they hold high equity claims. The contemporaneous relationship between institutional investors and corporate risk taking is positive. The contemporaneous relationship between blockholder share ownership and corporate risk taking, however, is not significant.

TABLE 2
Results of Regression Analysis: Contemporaneous Corporate Risk Taking Against Equity Ownership Structure[a]

	1986			1992		
Variable	Full Sample	Firms Lacking Growth Opportunities	Firms with Growth Opportunities	Full Sample	Firms Lacking Growth Opportunities	Firms with Growth Opportunities
Intercept	3.27**	5.86**	-8.90	3.01**	4.62**	-0.80
	(5.69)	(3.21)	(-1.54)	(5.66)	(4.81)	(-0.94)
Low managerial ownership	0.06	0.05	0.21**	0.22**	0.09	0.37**
	(0.87)	(0.53)	(2.27)	(2.10)	(0.33)	(2.23)
High managerial ownership	-0.07*	-0.04	-0.09*	-0.07**	-0.02	-0.09**
	(-1.85)	(-0.74)	(-1.91)	(-2.14)	(-1.19)	(-2.44)
Institutional ownership	-0.15	-0.53	1.89**	0.14	0.03	0.01**
	(-0.56)	(-1.68)	(2.33)	(0.97)	(1.04)	(2.82)
Blockholder ownership	-0.09	-0.18	0.11	0.10	0.27	-0.11
	(-0.86)	(-0.14)	(0.88)	(0.34)	(1.41)	(-1.18)
Firm size[b]	0.44**	0.45**	0.32**	0.39**	0.42**	0.44**
	(2.21)	(2.76)	(2.54)	(2.12)	(2.98)	(3.27)
Adjusted R^2	0.03	0.01	0.17	0.09	0.12	0.21
F	2.08*	1.04	4.48**	5.14**	6.23**	8.50**

[a] For the 1986 samples, $n = 358$, full; 213, no growth; and 145, growth. For the 1992 samples, $n = 514$ full; 308, no growth; and 206, growth.
Standard deviations are in parentheses.
[b] Logarithm of total assets.
* $p < .05$
** $p < .01$

Table 3 presents the results of the regression models estimating the impact of ownership structure on risk taking two years later, testing Hypotheses 2, 4, and 6. As is evident, these results are also consistent with our premise that the relationship between insider equity ownership and risk taking is not uniformly positive. At low levels of equity ownership, insiders enhance corporate risk taking, but at high levels, corporate risk taking declines. There is no significant relationship between insider equity ownership

TABLE 3
Results of Regression Analysis: Lagged Corporate Risk Taking Against Equity Ownership Structure[a]

Variable	Full Sample	Firms Lacking Growth Opportunities	Firms with Growth Opportunities
Risk taking in 1988 explained by 1986 ownership structure			
Intercept	3.31**	5.60**	−8.74
	(5.08)	(2.98)	(−1.17)
Low managerial	0.11	0.06	0.20*
ownership	(1.43)	(1.14)	(2.41)
High managerial	−0.10*	−0.03	−0.14**
ownership	(−2.11)	(−0.54)	(−2.84)
Institutional	−0.12	−0.73	2.05*
ownership	(−0.32)	(−1.31)	(2.37)
Blockholder	−0.06	−0.21	0.29
ownership	(−1.01)	(−0.92)	(1.25)
Firm size[b]	0.51**	0.50**	0.44*
	(4.81)	(3.86)	(3.66)
Adjusted R^2	0.05	0.01	0.18
F	2.14*	1.02	4.89**
Risk taking in 1994 explained by 1992 ownership structure			
Intercept	2.81**	4.09**	−0.77
	(5.17)	(4.71)	(−0.80)
Low managerial	0.22**	0.09	0.40**
ownership	(2.21)	(0.91)	(2.43)
High managerial	−0.07**	−0.02	−0.09**
ownership	(−2.22)	(−1.16)	(−2.39)
Institutional	0.14	0.02	0.01**
ownership	(0.81)	(1.13)	(2.79)
Blockholder	0.12	0.23	−0.14
ownership	(0.58)	(1.29)	(−1.16)
Firm size[b]	0.42**	0.37**	0.48**
	(3.99)	(4.21)	(3.87)
Adjusted R^2	0.09	0.13	0.21
F	5.16**	6.42**	8.88**

[a] See Table 2 for values of 1986 and 1992 n's. Standard deviations are in parentheses.
[b] Logarithm of total assets.
  * $p < .05$
 ** $p < .01$

and corporate risk taking for firms lacking growth prospects, supporting our hypothesis that risk taking is not relevant for such enterprises.

The evidence regarding the impact of blockholder equity ownership on corporate risk taking is insignificant, suggesting that blockholder ownership in a given year does not influence subsequent corporate risk taking. Given the lack of a significant relation between blockholder ownership and corporate risk taking, we conclude that blockholders may not always have a positive influence on firm performance.

The results of the influence of institutional investors on firm risk taking two years later indicate that the association between institutional equity ownership in a given year and future risk taking is positive for firms with growth opportunities but insignificant for firms without such opportunities. This finding is consistent with the argument that institutional owners promote corporate risk taking (Hansen & Hill, 1991; Hill & Snell, 1988; McConnell & Servaes, 1990; Mikkelson & Ruback, 1991), but only for corporations with growth prospects.

Tables 2 and 3 also report results for the control variables. The impact of firm size is significantly positive, regardless of underlying growth opportunities, suggesting that larger firms with greater asset bases are more inclined toward risk taking, irrespective of market valuations of their investment opportunities. The positive association between firm size and corporate risk taking is consistent with Schumpeter's arguments on innovations in his later work (1950) but not with his earlier (1934) contentions (in our context, innovations may be a proxy for corporate risk taking). That is, although in his earlier work Schumpeter proposed that innovations are the domain of entrepreneurial enterprises, later he contrarily argued that large firms are better suited for innovations because many innovations require access to substantial resources (Schumpeter, 1950; Winter, 1984).

The industry dummy variables are consistently insignificant. Because our use of two-digit SIC industry dummies resulted in an extensive number of independent variables, these estimates are not separately reported. Their insignificance, however, indicates that industry-unique factors are absent from an explanation of equity ownership influence on corporate risk taking.

The results in Table 3 are consistently compatible with Hypotheses 2 and 6, which predict distinct lagged relationships between corporate risk taking and the equity ownership of both insiders and institutional investors. We do not find evidence that blockholders significantly influence corporate risk taking. Hence, Hypothesis 4 is not supported empirically.

CONCLUDING REMARKS

Corporate risk-taking behavior is critical to firm performance. The nature of this risk taking, however, may be significantly influenced by insider ownership of a firm's equity. Yet whether such equity ownership consistently inspires corporate insiders to adopt the appropriate level of risk taking remains underexplored in the literature. The influence of blockholders and institutional investors on corporate risk taking likewise remains largely unexamined.

The results of this study emphasize the importance of further study regarding the influence of equity ownership on corporate risk taking. Since the existing literature implies that high insider equity ownership positively affects growth-oriented corporate risk taking, the prescriptive tendency may be to promote increasing levels of insider ownership. This approach, however, may only provide a useful incentive when insider ownership remains low overall.

If our conjecture that the relationship between firm risk taking and insider equity ownership is not monotonically positive is valid, then the practice of increasing insider ownership may require modification. Indeed, if incentive stipulations in contracts permit a substantial accumulation of equity ownership by insiders, their risk-taking behavior may emphasize personal wealth and utility management rather than corporate risk taking and firm performance. We believe that the effective structuring of contracts may be subject to specificities at the firm level of analysis. Thus, broad generalizations concerning the formulation of effective incentives, particularly with respect to insider equity ownership, may be counterproductive.

There is also a need to further examine blockholder and institutional equity ownership and their relationship with corporate risk taking. Theoretically, as vital agents of corporate governance, both blockholders and institutional investors will monitor firm strategies in order to ensure insider responsiveness and promote firm performance (Hansen & Hill, 1991; Hill & Snell, 1988; Kroll et al., 1996; Shleifer & Vishny, 1986). In previous theoretical and empirical studies (e.g., Bethel & Liebeskind, 1993; Shleifer & Vishny, 1986), it has been argued that blockholders enhance corporate performance. Alternatively, our findings are consistent with those of Holderness and Sheehan (1988) and of McConnell and Servaes (1990). In general, the presence of large equity blockholders does not significantly affect firm performance. If passive blockholders dominate, then as a class (McConnell & Servaes, 1990) they are not effective monitors of corporate risk taking and performance. In such an environment, it becomes even more crucial for institutional investors to monitor corporate decision making and performance.

We did find evidence in this study that institutional investors positively influence corporate risk taking. Our results are consistent with the efficient-monitoring hypothesis of Pound (1988) and the empirical findings of Barclay and Holderness (1990), Hansen and Hill (1991), Hill and Snell (1988), McConnell and Servaes (1990), and Mikkelson and Ruback (1985, 1991). It should be noted, however, that institutions may not always be effective monitors of firm performance (Chaganti & Damanpour, 1991; Lowenstein, 1991). Moreover, the impact of institutions on corporate performance may not always be positive, as contended by Pound (1988).

Contrary to the efficient-monitoring hypothesis, Pound (1988) found that institutional investors in some situations may negatively affect corporate performance. Because of financially lucrative relationships with a firm, institutions may be forced to vote with management on issues that are harmful to shareholders. He referred to this contingency as the conflict-of-interest hypothesis. Pound also proposed his strategic alignment hypothesis, claiming that senior executives and institutional investors may in other situations find it mutually beneficial to cooperate to the deteriment of shareholders.

As is evident, the influence of the equity ownership structure on corporate risk taking and firm performance is ambiguous. Consequently, given what we know from the results of the current and related studies, we cannot yet draw clear implications for theory or practice. We conclude that not only the influence of insiders but also the impact of blockholders and institutions on corporate risk taking and performance may be subject to specificities at the firm level of analysis.

Finally, we should emphasize that although corporate risk taking may ordinarily create value, this is not always true. For instance, RJR-Nabisco's smokeless cigarette was the result of a commitment to high-risk product research and development. However, the smokeless cigarette never won consumer acceptance and was withdrawn at a substantial cost. Nevertheless, corporate risk taking may be a prerequisite to value creation.

LIMITATIONS AND DIRECTIONS FOR FUTURE RESEARCH

A number of limitations are inherent in this study. First, because the personal wealth portfolios of corporate insiders are difficult to measure, we assumed in our study that high levels of insiders' equity ownership represented a greater portion of their total financial worth, resulting in increasingly undiversified personal wealth portfolios (as well as entrenchment). Thus, a caveat should be noted since we made this assumption rather than actually examining entrenchment or insider wealth portfolios to determine their diversity. Additionally, although personal benefits or costs may be important determinants of insider decisions, these factors are not readily quantifiable. In particular, nonfinancial factors and their potential influence on decisions are difficult to measure explicitly, especially for a large sample (Jensen & Murphy, 1990). Consequently, another caveat should be stated, since we assume that these factors exist and matter.

We also made no attempt to distinguish between types of large equity blockholders. Explaining the limitations of their study, McConnell and Servaes stated the following: "Some blockholders may be entirely passive investors, whereas others are more active and do perform an important monitoring service. A finer classification scheme might reveal a more important role for active block investors" (1990: 611). Consequently, although our results suggest that blockholders do not influence corporate risk taking, blockholders are not necessarily unable to monitor firm performance. Thus, our results may not be generalizable. Similarly, we have not distinguished between the institutional investors and the consequent applicability of the conflict-of-interest and strategic-alignment hypotheses (Pound, 1988). Hence, our finding that institutional investors positively influence corporate risk taking may not be valid in all cases.

Future research might address some of these limitations. An interesting approach would involve measuring insider equity ownership as an actual percentage of personal wealth portfolios. Such data may be obtainable through a questionnaire. Although responses to such a questionnaire would be limited, they may provide further insight into this issue. Another possible approach would be to examine entrenchment or the impact of personal benefits or costs on risk taking through case study.

Relating blockholders to corporate risk taking may provide interesting insights if they can be classified as either active or passive investors. For instance, blockholders who are descendants of a corporation's founder may be primarily passive investors (McConnell & Servaes, 1990; Shleifer & Vishny, 1986), and blockholders whose profession is the management of investments may provide very active monitoring (Woodruff & Grover, 1994).

Exploring the association between institutional investors and corporate risk taking may alternatively provide interesting results, provided institutions can be categorized in terms of the nature of their relationships with the firms in which they have equity stakes (Pound, 1988, 1992). We suspect that such results would be different from those reported here if, for instance, the sample studied consisted largely of supplier firms (Pound, 1988).

REFERENCES

Agrawal, A., & Mandelker, G. 1987. Managerial incentives and corporate investment and financing decisions. *Journal of Finance,* 42: 823–837.

Amihud, Y., & Lev, B. 1981. Risk reduction as a managerial motive for conglomerate mergers. *Bell Journal of Economics,* 12: 605–617.

Arnold, H. J. 1982. Moderator variables: A clarification of conceptual, analytic, and psychometric issues. *Organizational Behavior and Human Performance,* 29: 143–174.

Barclay, M., & Holderness, C. G. 1990. *Negotiated block trades and corporate control.* Working paper, University of Rochester, Rochester, NY.

Barney, J. 1991. Firm resources and sustained competitive advantage. *Journal of Management,* 17: 99–120.

Berle, A. A., Jr., & Means, G. C. 1932. *The modern corporation and private property.* New York: Macmillan.

Bethel, J. E., & Liebeskind, J. 1993. The effects of ownership structure on corporate restructuring. *Strategic Management Journal,* 14: 15–31.

Brickley, J., Lease, R. C., & Smith, W. 1988. Ownership structure and voting on antitakeover amendments. *Journal of Financial Economics,* 20: 267–291.

Bromiley, P. 1991. Testing a causal model of corporate risk taking and performance. *Academy of Management Journal,* 34: 37–59.

Chaganti, R., & Damanpour, F. 1991. Institutional ownership, capital structure and firm performance. *Strategic Management Journal,* 12: 479–491.

Conroy, B., & Harris, R. 1987. Consensus forecasts of corporate earnings: Analysts' forecasts and time series methods. *Management Science,* 33: 725–738.

Demsetz, H. 1983. The structure of ownership and the theory of the firm. *Journal of Law and Economics,* 26: 375–390.

Easterbrook, F. H. 1984. Two agency-cost explanations of dividends. *American Economic Review,* 74: 650–659.

Fama, E. F. 1980. Agency problems and the theory of the firm. *Journal of Political Economy,* 88: 288–307.

Fama, E. F., & Jensen, M. 1983. Separation of ownership and control. *Journal of Law and Economics,* 26: 301–325.

Gibbs, P. A. 1993. Determinants of corporate restructuring: The relative importance of corporate governance, takeover threat, and free cash flow. *Strategic Management Journal,* 14: 51–68.

Hansen, G., & Hill, C. 1991. Are institutional investors myopic? A time-series study of four technology-driven industries. *Strategic Management Journal,* 12: 1–16.

Hassell, J. M., & Jennings, R. H. 1986. Relative forecast accuracy and the timing of earnings forecast announcements. *Accounting Review,* 61: 58–75.

Hill, C., & Snell, S. 1988. External control, corporate strategy, and firm performance in research-intensive industries. *Strategic Management Journal,* 9: 577–590.

Holderness, C. G., & Sheehan, D. 1985. Raiders or saviors? The evidence on six controversial investors. *Journal of Financial Economics,* 14: 555–579.

Holderness, C. G., & Sheehan, D. 1988. The role of majority shareholders in publicly held corporations. *Journal of Financial Economics,* 20: 317–346.

Imhoff, E. A., & Lobo, G. 1988. *The relations between ex-ante uncertainty, unexpected annual earnings, and unexpected stock returns.* Working paper, Graduate School of Business, University of Michigan, Ann Arbor.

James, R. R., & Soref, M. 1981. Profit constraints on managerial autonomy: Managerial theory and the unmaking of the corporation president. *American Sociological Review,* 46: 1–18.

Jensen, M. 1986. Agency costs of free cash flow, corporate finance, and takeovers. *American Economic Review,* 76: 323–329.

Jensen, M., & Meckling, W. 1976. Theory of the firm: Managerial behavior, agency costs and ownership structure. *Journal of Financial Economics,* 3: 305–360.

Jensen, M., & Murphy, K. 1990. Performance pay and top management incentives. *Journal of Political Economy,* 98: 225–264.

Johnson, R. A., Hoskisson, R. E., & Hitt, M. A. 1993. Board of director involvement in restructuring: The effect of board versus managerial control and characteristics. *Strategic Management Journal,* 14: 33–50.

Kroll, M., Wright, P., & Theerathorn, P. 1993. Whose interests do hired top managers pursue? An examination of select mutual and stock life insurers. *Journal of Business Research,* 26: 133–148.

Kroll, M., Wright, P., Toombs, L., & Leavell, H. 1996. Form of control—A critical determinant of aquisition performance and CEO rewards. *Strategic Management Journal:* In press.

Lado, A., Boyd, N., & Wright, P. 1992. A competency-based model of sustainable competitive advantage: Toward a conceptual integration. *Journal of Managment,* 18: 77–91.

Lang, L. H., & Litzenberger, R. H. 1989. Dividend announcements: Cash flow signaling versus free cash flow hypothesis? *Journal of Financial Economics,* 24: 181–191.

Lindenberg, E., & Ross, S. 1981. Tobin's Q ratio and industrial organization. *Journal of Business,* 54: 1–32.

Lowenstein, L. 1991. Why managers should (and should not) have respect for their shareholders. *Journal of Corporation Law,* 17: 1–27.

Martin, K., & McConnell, J. J. 1991. Corporate performance, corporate takeovers and management turnover. *Journal of Finance,* 46: 671–687.

McConnell, J. J., & Servaes, H. 1990. Additional evidence on equity ownership and corporate value. *Journal of Financial Economics,* 27: 595–612.

McNichols, M. 1989. Evidence of information asymmetries from management earnings forecasts and stock returns. *Accounting Review,* 64: 1–27.

Mikkelson, W., & Ruback, R. 1985. An empirical analysis of the interfirm equity investment process. *Journal of Financial Economics*, 14: 523–553.

Mikkelson, W., & Ruback, R. 1991. Targeted repurchases and common stock returns. *Rand Journal of Economics*, 22: 544–556.

Miller, K. D., & Bromiley, P. 1990. Strategic risk and corporate performance: An analysis of alternative risk measures. *Academy of Management Journal*, 4: 756–779.

Morck, R. A., Shleifer, A., & Vishny, R. 1988. Management ownership and market valuation. An empirical analysis. *Journal of Financial Economics*, 20: 293–315.

Morck, R. A., Shleifer, A., & Vishny, R. 1990. Do managerial objectives drive bad acquisitions? *Journal of Finance*, 25: 31–48.

O'Brien, P. C. 1988. Analysts' forecasts as earnings expectations. *Journal of Accounting and Economics*, 10: 53–83.

Pound, J. 1988. Proxy contests and the efficiency of shareholder oversight. *Journal of Financial Economics*, 20: 237–265.

Pound, J. 1992. Beyond takeovers: Politics comes to corporate control. *Harvard Business Review*, 70(2): 83–93.

Rozeff, M. 1982. Growth, beta and agency costs as determinants of dividend payout ratios. *Journal of Financial Research*, 5: 249–259.

Schumpeter, J. A. 1934. *The theory of economic development.* New York: Oxford University Press.

Schumpeter, J. A. 1950. *Capitalism, socialism, and democracy.* New York: Harper and Row Publishers.

Shleifer, A., & Vishny, R. 1986. Large shareholders and corporate control. *Journal of Political Economy*, 94: 461–488.

Staw, B. M., & Oldham, G. R. 1978. Reconsidering our dependent variables—A critique and empirical study. *Academy of Management Journal*, 21: 539–559.

Stone, E. F., & Hollenbeck, J. R. 1989. Clarifying some controversial issues surrounding statistical procedures for detecting moderator variables: Empirical evidence and related matters. *Journal of Applied Psychology*, 74: 3–10.

Stone-Romero, E. F., & Anderson, L. E. 1994. Relative power of moderated multiple regression and the comparison of subgroup correlation coefficients for detecting moderating effects. *Journal of Applied Psychology*, 79: 354–359.

Stulz, R. M. 1988. On takeover resistance, managerial discretion, and shareholder wealth. *Journal of Financial Economics*, 20: 25–54.

Weston, J. F. 1979. The tender takeover. *Mergers and Acquisitions*, 15: 74–82.

Winter, S. 1984. Schumpeterian competition in alternative technological regimes. *Journal of Economic Behavior and Organization*, 5: 287–320.

Woodruff, P., & Grover, R. 1994. Kerkorian to Chrysler: It's payback time. *Business Week*, November 28: 54.

Wright, P., & Ferris, S. P. 1997. Agency conflict and corporate strategy: The effect of divestment on corporate value. *Strategic Management Journal:* In Press.

Wright, P., Ferris, S. P., Hiller, J. S., & Kroll, M. 1995. Competitiveness through management of diversity: Effects on stock price valuation. *Academy of Management Journal*, 38: 272–287.

Wright, P., Kroll, M., & Parnell, J. 1996. *Strategic management: Concepts and cases.* Englewood Cliffs, NJ: Prentice-Hall.

Wright, P., Kroll, M., Pray, B., & Lado, A. 1995. Strategic orientations, competitive advantage, and business performance. *Journal of Business Research*, 33: 143–151.

Peter Wright is a professor of management and the holder of the University of Memphis endowed chair in free enterprise management. He received his Ph.D. degree from Louisiana State University. His research interests include agency theory, resource-based theory, corporate control, and the valuation of strategic investments.

Stephen P. Ferris is chairman and professor of finance at the College of Business and Public Administration, University of Missouri-Columbia. He received his Ph.D. degree from the Katz Graduate School of Business at the University of Pittsburgh. His research interests include an economic and legal analysis of corporate governance structures, international capital markets, and corporate bankruptcy/financial distress.

Atulya Sarin is an assistant professor of finance at the Leavy School of Business, Santa Clara University. He received his Ph.D. degree from Virginia Polytechnic Institute and State University. His research interests are in the areas of ownership structure and corporate governance.

Vidya Awasthi is an assistant professor of accounting at the Leavy School of Business, Santa Clara University. He received his Ph.D. degree from the University of Washington. His research interests are in the areas of managerial information systems and corporate control.

[20]

ELSEVIER Journal of Corporate Finance 7 (2001) 257–284

Journal of
CORPORATE
FINANCE

www.elsevier.com/locate/econbase

Investment policy, internal financing and ownership concentration in the UK

Marc Goergen [a,1], Luc Renneboog [b,*]

[a] *School of Management, University of Manchester Institute of Science and Technology (UMIST),*
PO Box 88, Manchester M60 1QD, UK
[b] *Department of Finance and CenTER, Tilburg University, Warandelaan 2,*
5000 LE Tilburg, Netherlands

Accepted 22 June 2001

Abstract

This paper investigates whether investment spending of firms is sensitive to the availability of internal funds. Imperfect capital markets create a hierarchy for the different sources of funds such that investment and financial decisions are not independent. The relation between corporate investment and free cash flow is investigated using the Bond and Meghir [Review of Economic Studies, 61 (1994a) 197] Euler-equation model for a panel of 240 companies listed on the London Stock Exchange over a 6-year period. This method allows for a direct test of the first-order condition of an intertemporal maximisation problem. It does not require the use of Tobin's q, which is subject to mismeasurement problems. Apart from past investment levels and generated cash flow, the model also includes a leverage factor which captures potential bankruptcy costs and the tax advantages of debt. More importantly, we investigate whether ownership concentration by class of shareholder creates or mitigates liquidity constraints. When industrial companies control large shareholdings, there is evidence of increased overinvestment. This relation is strong when the relative voting power (measured by the Shapley values) of the combined equity stakes of families and industrial companies and the Herfindahl index of industrial ownership are high. This suggests that a small coalition of industrial companies is able to influence investment spending. In contrast, large institutional holdings reduce the positive link between investment spending and cash flow relation and, hence, suboptimal investing.

* Corresponding author. Tel.: +31-13-466-8210; fax: +31-13-466-2875.
E-mail addresses: Marc.Goergen@UMIST.ac.uk (M. Goergen), Luc.Renneboog@kub.nl (L. Renneboog).
[1] Tel.: +44-161-200-3456; fax: +44-161-200-3505.

258   *M. Goergen, L. Renneboog / Journal of Corporate Finance 7 (2001) 257–284*

Whereas there is no evidence of over- or underinvesting at low levels of insider shareholding, a high concentration of control in the hands of executive directors reduces the underinvestment problem.

JEL classification: G32; G34
Keywords: Investment; Liquidity constraints; Ownership; Control; Corporate governance

1. Introduction

In perfect capital markets, investment decisions are independent of financing decisions and, hence, investment policy only depends upon the availability of investment opportunities with a positive net present value (NPV) (Modigliani and Miller, 1958). In the standard neo-classical model of investment, firms have unlimited access to sources of finance and invest as long as the marginal dollar of the capital expenditure generates at least one dollar of a present value of cash flows (Tobin, 1969). Consequently, firms with profitable investment opportunities exceeding available cash flow are not expected to invest any less than firms with similar opportunities but larger internal cash flows.

However, the empirical literature supports the model about the hierarchy of financing which predicts that the investment expenditure of some firms may be constrained by a lack of internally generated funds. For many firms, the cost of external capital does indeed seem to exceed the cost of internal funds. As profits are highly cyclical, the existence of liquidity constraints makes investment spending more sensitive to fluctuations in economic activity. Differing views on the riskiness of investment projects between shareholders and management and, hence, on the relevant discount rate may result in good investment projects being rejected.

Underinvestment due to asymmetric information (Greenwald et al., 1984) results from the fact that the market requires—even for high quality firms/projects—a premium equal to the one required for investing in the average firm. Consequently, due to adverse selection, it may be the (relatively) lower quality projects which may seek external financing and some positive NPV projects are not undertaken at all.[2] Myers and Majluf (1984) have labelled the hierarchy of financing—driven by asymmetric information and/or the real direct and indirect costs of different sources of financing—the pecking order theory. Firms finance positive NPV projects in the first instance with internal financing, subsequently with debt (as the least risky form of external financing) followed by all kinds of hybrid debt with equity components and finally with external equity as a last resort.

---

[2] This adverse selection process is similar to Akerlof's 'lemons market'.

M. Goergen, L. Renneboog / Journal of Corporate Finance 7 (2001) 257–284   259

Consequently, a positive relation between investment and liquidity may result from asymmetric information because the lack of internal capital and the 'high cost' of external capital create an *underinvestment* problem. However, this positive relation may also be the consequence of an abundance of retained earnings which makes internal funds too inexpensive (from the management's point of view). In firms with insufficient monitoring mechanisms—e.g. in firms without performance-related managerial remuneration schemes, with diffuse ownership, with anti-takeover devices or with CEO dominated boards of directors—high managerial discretion may lead to considerable agency costs. In such cases, managers' interests are not perfectly aligned with those of the shareholders (Jensen, 1986; Bernanke and Gertler, 1989): managerial decision-making may be motivated by 'empire building' and lead to *overinvestment*. In this setting, managers may place a discount on internal funds and overspend by undertaking even negative NPV projects as long as there is excessive liquidity[3] in the firm because managers may derive more private benefits by increasing their firm's size (Hart and Moore, 1995).

The question whether or not the level of investment depends on corporate liquidity has drawn substantial attention over the last decade since the seminal paper by Fazzari et al. (1988) has rekindled the interest in the determinants of investments. However, relatively few papers test the investment–liquidity relation within a specific corporate governance framework. Notable recent exceptions are, e.g. Kathuria and Mueller (1995), Kaplan and Zingales (1997), Hadlock (1998), Gugler et al. (1999), Vogt (1994) and Cho (1998) for the US, Degryse and De Jong (2000) for the Netherlands, Haid and Weigand (1998) for Germany, and Gugler (1999) for Austria.

This paper focuses on the impact of relative voting power and liquidity on investment spending in UK firms. The empirical version of the Bond and Meghir (1994a) Euler-equation model is extended by including variables capturing ownership concentration and shareholder coalition to answer the following questions. Are UK firms liquidity constrained? Does the presence of specific classes of shareholders influence the relation between investment spending and internally generated funds? Do shareholder coalitions influence the investment–cash flow relation in firms with dispersed ownership? Are companies with high leverage more liquidity constrained?

The remainder of the paper is structured as follows. Section 2 presents the hypotheses and embeds them in the literature. Section 3 describes the data and explains the methodology. Section 4 discusses the results and Section 5 concludes.

---

[3] Excessive liquidity is defined as the total cash stock of a firm minus the cash component of working capital, minus cash necessary for all compulsory payments (debt, payables, taxes) and minus cash invested in positive NPV investments.

260   M. Goergen, L. Renneboog / Journal of Corporate Finance 7 (2001) 257–284

2. Models on liquidity constraints and hypotheses

2.1. Types of investment models

In the literature, empirically testable models of company investment can be categorised into four broad classes. The four classes are the neoclassical model, the sales accelerator model, the Tobin's q model and the Euler-equation model.[4] In the neoclassical model, the relative cost of capital is the main determinant of corporate investment (see e.g. Jorgenson, 1963 for an overview). The model is defined as:

$$\left(\frac{I}{K}\right)_{it} = \alpha_i + \alpha_1 \left(\frac{C_K}{K}\right)_{it} + \alpha_2 \left(\frac{C_K}{K}\right)_{i,t-1} + \alpha_3 \left(\frac{CF}{K}\right)_{it} + \varepsilon_{it} \tag{1}$$

where I stands for the investment level, K for the capital stock, C_K for the cost of capital and CF for cash flow. The coefficient α_3 gives cash flow sensitivities for firm i and ε_{it} is the error term. Although today's investment generates tomorrow's output, the model does not include any forward-looking variables.

Similarly, the sales accelerator model (Abel and Blanchard, 1986) does not include expectations about the company's growth potential[5] and assumes that investment grows along with total sales:

$$\left(\frac{I}{K}\right)_{it} = \alpha_i + \alpha_1 \left(\frac{S}{K}\right)_{it} + \alpha_2 \left(\frac{S}{K}\right)_{i,t-1} + \alpha_3 \left(\frac{CF}{K}\right)_{it} + \varepsilon_{it} \tag{2}$$

where S stands for total sales.

A more fundamental criticism of these two types of model is that a positive relation between investment and cash flow is assumed to be evidence of liquidity constraints. However, a positive cash flow coefficient may not reflect the importance of internally generated funds for investment purposes, but could instead indicate higher future profitability.

Investment is likely to depend not only on the current level of optimal capital stock but also on its future, optimal level (Bond and Meghir, 1994b). As data on expectations are not available, the relation between investment decisions, expected future levels of output and the hurdle rate (the minimum required rate of return to accept investment projects) cannot be estimated. The inclusion of current and lagged levels of output and hurdle rate into investment models is not a proper solution because no distinction is made between factors influencing the optimal

---

[4] All the models reviewed in this section include a cash-flow variable, although the original version of some of the models may not have included such a variable.

[5] Fazzari et al. (1988) test alternative versions of the sales accelerator model by adding Tobin's q to Eq. (2). They show that the inclusion of Tobin's q diminishes the effect of the cash flow variable, although the latter remains still significant.

capital stock (the level of capital for which the marginal product of capital equals the hurdle rate) and factors which forecast the future value of the capital stock. Therefore, the cash flow variable of the above investment equations could reflect either financial constraints or the formation of expectations.

Models incorporating Tobin's q (defined as the ratio of market values of equity and debt over the replacement value of the firm's capital stock) have attempted to solve this problem as the expectation of future profitability is captured by the forward-looking stock market valuation (see, e.g. Abel, 1990):

$$\left(\frac{I}{K}\right)_{it} = \gamma_i + \gamma_1 Q_{it} + \gamma_2 \left(\frac{CF}{K}\right)_{it} + \varepsilon_{it} \tag{3}$$

where Q_{it} stands for Tobin's q and γ_1 is the sensitivity of investment to profitability opportunities, which are reflected in Q. If firms are not financially constrained γ_2 is expected to be equal to zero; otherwise, γ_2 will typically be different from zero.

However, estimating q-models is not without problems for various reasons. First, Tobin's q is difficult to measure: the replacement value of assets is not reported in most European countries. Proxying the denominator of Tobin's q by book value of assets also suffers from estimation problems such as the measurement of intangibles. Second, Tobin's q will only include future expectations if the firm is a price taker in perfectly competitive industries, if there are constant returns to scale and if the stock market value correctly measures the fundamental expected present value of the firm's future net cash flows (Hayashi, 1982). In practice, these conditions may not be fulfilled, e.g. if the stock market displays excessive volatility relative to the fundamental value of the companies. Thus, if cash flow (or profitability) variables are included in an investment model along with Tobin's q, these cash flow variables may still be made up of expectations not captured by Tobin's q. It may then be difficult to disentangle the effect of expectations from the one of liquidity constraints in the parameter estimate of the cash flow variable. Chirinko and Schaller (1995) show that average Tobin's q is flawed as it reflects the average return on a company's total capital whereas it is the marginal return on capital that is relevant. Gugler et al. (1999) develop a technique to measure marginal Tobin's q and test the degree of cash flow sensitivity to investment in different Tobin's q scenarios to distinguish between cases with asymmetric information and agency conflicts.

The Euler-equation model of Bond and Meghir (1994a,b) (hereafter called B & M) is based on the first-order conditions of a maximisation process. The model deals with the shortcomings of the neoclassical and average Tobin's q-models. The level of investment relative to the capital stock is a function of discounted expected future investment adjusted for the impact of the expected changes in the input prices and net marginal output. The Euler specification has the advantage that it controls for the influence of expected future profitability on investment spending whilst no explicit measure of expected demand or expected

262   M. Goergen, L. Renneboog / Journal of Corporate Finance 7 (2001) 257–284

costs is required as future unobservable values are approximated by instrumental values. The theoretical model translates into the following empirical specification and tests the wedge between retained earnings and outside financing:

$$\left(\frac{I}{K}\right)_{it} = \alpha_1 \left(\frac{I}{K}\right)_{i,t-1} + \alpha_2 \left(\frac{I}{K}\right)^2_{i,t-1} + \alpha_3 \left(\frac{CF}{K}\right)_{i,t-1} + \alpha_4 \left(\frac{S}{K}\right)_{i,t-1}$$

$$+ \alpha_5 \left(\frac{D}{K}\right)_{i,t-1} + \psi_t + \varphi_i + \varepsilon_{it} \qquad (4)$$

where D stands for the debt of the firm, ψ_t and φ_i stand for time specific effects and fixed effects, respectively, and all the other symbols are as previously defined.

As the time series for I/K is relatively short (1988–1993), it may be influenced by the economic slow-down of the UK economy in this period. As I/S (Investment standardised by Sales) is more stable over time, we test the following variant of the B&M model.[6]

$$\left(\frac{I}{S}\right)_{it} = \alpha_1 \left(\frac{I}{S}\right)_{i,t-1} + \alpha_2 \left(\frac{I}{S}\right)^2_{i,t-1} + \alpha_3 \left(\frac{CF}{S}\right)_{i,t-1} + \alpha_4 \left(\frac{D}{K}\right)_{i,t-1}$$

$$+ \psi_t + \varphi_i + \varepsilon_{it} \qquad (5)$$

2.2. Hypotheses

Empirical attempts to answer our first question—whether or not investment activity is influenced by movements in generated profits (or cash flow)—have a long history and date back to the business cycle research of Tinbergen (1939) and Meyer and Kuhn (1957). Both studies found evidence that financial profitability influences investment decision in the short run. Although these and many other studies have interpreted such findings as evidence of the hierarchy of financing theory, the results could as well imply that liquidity variables are a proxy for omitted variables. We try to control for the latter possibility by using the Generalized Method of Moments in Systems (GMM_{sys})[7] rather than OLS. Within this econometric setting, we hypothesise that:

Hypothesis 1. *There is no relation between a firm's investment decision and its cash flow stock.*

Over the past decade—since Fazzari et al. (1988) have triggered renewed interest in financing constraints and investment activity by testing the neo-classi-

---

[6] We are grateful to Steve Bond for this suggestion.

[7] This estimation technique controls for the potential omitted variables problem by using lagged variables as instruments.

cal, sales accelerator and Tobin's q models—the above null hypothesis has been frequently rejected. The standard approach in the literature has been to test the above models on subsamples of firms which are supposed to be liquidity constrained, e.g. firms with low dividend pay-out ratios and new equity issues. Fazzari et al. (1988) find that the sensitivity of capital expenditure with respect to cash flow fluctuations is highest for fast growing and/or low-dividend firms. However, strong criticism about this study and related articles was formulated by Kaplan and Zingales (1995). They collected additional quantitative and qualitative information on financing constraints for the Fazzari et al. sample. The analysis of subsamples with varying degrees of financing constraints yields results contrary to those of Fazzari et al.: the higher the likelihood that the companies face financial constraints the lower their investment–cash flow sensitivity.[8]

Several papers have since then extended investment models by incorporating different sources of funds such as working capital (Fazzari and Petersen, 1993). They find that the investment–cash flow sensitivity is significantly positive but the coefficient on working capital changes is significantly negative, reflecting that working capital seems to compete for funds with fixed investment. Carpenter (1995) further extends this model by adding changes in debt level and finds evidence of significant financing constraints in firms with low growth opportunities (low Tobin's q) and with low dividend pay-out ratios.

Furthermore, the investment–cash flow relation may be influenced by the concentration and nature of ownership. Managerial discretion may be curbed if shareholders assume an active monitoring role, which reduces overinvestment and is reflected in no or a smaller investment–cash flow relation. Likewise, the positive investment–cash flow relation may be reduced in the presence of large corporate blockholders. For example, Hoshi et al. (1991) distinguish between two samples of Japanese firms, the ones that belong to a keiretsu group and those that are independent. Hoshi et al. investigate whether or not keiretsu membership has an impact on the access to external capital. Keiretsu firms are expected to face fewer or no liquidity constraints because the keiretsu usually comprises financial institutions which can provide soft loans for investments. The results suggest that firms belonging to a keiretsu are less susceptible to financing constraints.

This raises the question whether or not shareholders play an active governance role. There is some, albeit limited, empirical evidence of large shareholder monitoring for the UK. Industrial and commercial companies as well as individuals and families (not related to a top manager) who own share blocks or build up large shareholdings discipline incumbent management in the wake of a performance decline and in the absence of managerial entrenchment (Franks et al., in

---

[8] Fazzari et al. (1996) respond by pointing out a number of inconsistencies in the Kaplan and Zingales methodology and reasoning and mention the arbitrariness of the criteria used for forming subsamples with different degrees of financing constraints.

264   *M. Goergen, L. Renneboog / Journal of Corporate Finance 7 (2001) 257–284*

press; Lai and Sudarsanam, 1997; Lasfer, 1995). Monitoring will only be cost effective if a single shareholder or a coalition of shareholders becomes large enough to internalise the costs of corporate control. A small shareholder pays all the costs related to his control efforts but benefits only in proportion to his shareholding (Grossman and Hart, 1980; Demsetz, 1983). Using power indices to measure relative control, Leech (2000) shows that, given the dispersed ownership structure of UK firms, the equity stake needed to incite a shareholder to actively participate in monitoring is not that large. Three to four percent of ownership in the average company may suffice.

The positive relation between internally generated funds and investment may not be present or may be less strong in the presence of a large outside shareholder for two reasons. First, the problem of overinvestment may be reduced by enhanced monitoring which decreases the squandering of free cash flows by management. Second, asymmetric information between management and large shareholders may decrease if it pays for the large shareholder to spend time and effort to collect more accurate information on the management's quality and its investment projects. Hence, we will test whether:

Hypothesis 2. *In the presence of a large outside share block held by an industrial or commercial company, or an individual or family not related to a director, a (positive) relation between investments and cash flow is absent.*

Institutional investors are the largest owners of firms listed on the London Stock Exchange. However, institutions have been reproached by the Cadbury (1992), Hampel (1998) and Newbold (2001) corporate governance committees to be passive investors. Stapledon (1996), Goergen and Renneboog (in press), and Faccio and Lasfer (2000a) confirm that institutions do not normally intervene in a company's business for two reasons. First, they may lack the monitoring expertise. Second, they may want to ensure investment liquidity as insider-trading regulation may immobilise portfolio rebalancing. In contrast, recent anecdotal evidence seems to suggest that, even if institutional shareholders do not publicly intervene, they act behind the scenes. Moreover, surveys on the actual voting behaviour of investment funds reveal that vote casting by institutions has been growing rapidly (Mallin, 1996). Some institutions have even established voting policies which compel them to cast their votes on, e.g. managerial investment decisions in firms where they hold an equity stake of 3% or more (for examples, see Mallin, 1999). Hence, we formulate our null hypothesis as follows:

Hypothesis 3. *For companies in which institutional shareholders own large ownership stakes, there is no relation between investment and internally generated funds.*

Managerial ownership can be used as a proxy for the alignment of interests between managers and shareholders. However, the relationship between insider

M. Goergen, L. Renneboog / Journal of Corporate Finance 7 (2001) 257–284   265

holdings and the alignment of shareholder and managerial interests may be non-monotonic as suggested by Morck et al. (1988) and McConnell and Servaes (1990). At low levels of insider ownership, increases in managerial ownership may lead to a convergence of interest whereas high levels of insider ownership may result in managerial unaccountability due to entrenchment (Franks et al., in press; Faccio and Lasfer, 2000b). Consequently, increases in managerial shareholdings when managerial shareholdings are low may lead to diminished investment–cash flow sensitivities because of less overinvesting. Conversely, an increased sensitivity is expected when managerial ownership increases and is already large, which may lead to overinvesting. This reasoning hinges on Jensen's (1986) free cash flow argument resulting from the existence of agency costs.

The predictions about the investment–cash flow sensitivity in the context of managerial ownership are different under asymmetric information. Inferior knowledge about the quality of the management and its investment decisions by the capital markets may be the reason why a premium on external capital is required and why an underinvestment problem arises. When insider ownership grows and managerial interests become more and more aligned with those of the other shareholders, managers internalise more of the mispricing of external funds (Hadlock, 1998). Consequently, the underinvestment problem becomes worse as managers are increasingly reluctant to reward external capital with an excessive premium. Investment will rely even more on the availability of internal funds and hence—at low levels of insider ownership—the investment–cash flow sensitivity rises with increasing levels of insider ownership.

In summary:

Hypothesis 4. *Insider ownership does not influence the investment–cash flow relation (null hypothesis). Alternatively (in an agency context), at low levels of insider holdings, high free cash flow will entail fewer investments when insider ownership increases because of increasing alignment of interest of managers and other shareholders. At high levels of insider holdings (leading to managerial entrenchment), free cash flow leads to more investments. In an asymmetric information setting, the investment–cash flow sensitivity increases with insider ownership.*

2.3. Measurement of control concentration

A priori, one would in general expect little shareholder monitoring in the UK as most listed industrial companies (85%) are widely held, i.e. lacking a controlling share block in excess of 25%. Bebchuk and Roe (1999) argue that diffuse ownership persists—in spite of its inherent drawbacks in terms of agency costs—as a result of historic regulatory evolution (structure- and regulation-driven path dependence). For example, for investors who are not interested in acquiring a complete company, the mandatory takeover threshold of 30% is an upper boundary (Goergen and Renneboog, in press).

However, agency costs between management and shareholders may be lower than expected if shareholders can increase control power by forming voting coalitions. Such coalitions are formed on an ad hoc basis because if a coalition were to be formed for longer periods of time, regulatory authorities would consider the coalition as an investor group.[9] Consequently, voting coalitions are usually temporary and are customarily forged with a specific aim (e.g. the removal of incumbent management). They are also commonly kept confidential, although explicit voting contracts may be drawn up (Van Hulle, 1998).

We adjust the B & M investment model described above, using five alternative definitions of ownership and control: (i) the total proportion of shares held by each category of owner,[10] (ii) the largest stake of all ownership stakes, (iii) the Herfindahl index of the largest three stakes held by each category of owner, (iv) the Shapley values of the largest shareholder and (v) the Shapley values for each category of owner.

High and low levels of ownership or control are subjective notions as the levels depend upon the distribution of ownership in the company. The Herfindahl index succeeds in capturing the dispersion of ownership across shareholders and the relative power of a group of shareholders but does not reflect the relative voting power of individual shareholders. For example, if three shareholders own 40%, 40% and 20%, respectively, of a company's equity, the Herfindahl of the three largest shareholdings is 0.36. Shapley values (SVs) can be used to measure the relative importance of a shareholder in forming winning voting coalitions (Rydqvist, 1998). In our example, each shareholder's SV is 0.33 because each is pivotal in coalitions yielding more than 50% of the control rights.

Including SVs instead of ownership percentages or Herfindahl indices allows us to test a dual hypothesis. Not only do we test for the impact of the presence of large shareholders on the investment–cash flow relation, but we also test whether this relation is influenced by coalitions of shareholders rather than individual large shareholders. A stronger statistical relation between SVs and investment than

---

[9] In that case, a coalition owning more than 15% of the shares is required to disclose its 'strategic intention' or, if it controls 30% or more of the votes, the Mergers and Monopolies commission may require the coalition to comply to the mandatory takeover rule (Stapledon, 1996).

[10] In the UK, the percentage of equity held by a shareholder usually equals his or her percentage of votes (one-share–one-vote) since the London Stock Exchange has discouraged the use of multiple voting shares (Goergen and Renneboog, in press) and since ownership cascades are, in contrast to most Continental European countries, rare.

M. Goergen, L. Renneboog / Journal of Corporate Finance 7 (2001) 257–284   267

between percentages of ownership and investment may be interpreted as indirect evidence of shareholder-coalition formation.[11] Within a framework of co-operative games—with transferable utility—in characteristic functional form, Shapley (1953) developed 'Shapley value assignment' ϕ defined as follows (Felsenthal and Machover, 1998):

$$\phi_a(w) = \text{def}\frac{1}{n!}\sum_{X \subseteq N}(|X| - 1)!(n - |X|)!(wX - w(X - \{a\}))$$

where game w is a real-valued function whose domain is the power set (the set of subsets) of N (a non-empty finite set) such that $w\phi = 0$. Any member of N (the grand coalition of w), a, is a player of w. If X is a coalition, the real number wX is called the worth of X in w.

In the UK, the disclosure threshold for shareholders other than directors is 3%. In the average quoted company, 56% of the equity capital is formed by stakes below the disclosure threshold. We assume that these stakes are owned by—de facto small—shareholders who free ride on corporate monitoring as their share-holdings are too small to internalise the cost of corporate control. Therefore, the free float is assumed not to be involved in monitoring the management and not to form voting coalitions. In practice, it is difficult to organise minuscule share stakes into voting blocks (Chung and Kim, 1999).[12] Consequently, rescaling the sum of the disclosed share blocks to 100% is a fair assumption. The resulting SVs reflect the relative voting power whereby a winning coalition is expected to reach absolute control (50% + 1 vote of the rescaled vote).[13]

All potential pacts are simulated by company and by year and the SVs measure the extent to which shareholders are pivotal in (potential) voting pacts. This assumes that every blockholder has an equal propensity to take part in a voting pact and to monitor the firm. However, it is possible that the relative power is better described as the result of a voting game consisting of two stages. It may be

---

[11] Interesting studies relating voting power (measured by power indices) and performance are those by Leech and Leahy (1991) who use probabilistic indices for the UK and by Zwiebel (1995) for the US.

[12] During protracted hostile takeover battles, coalitions of large shareholders may solicit votes of atomistic shareholders to buttress the coalition, but management removal seems to be more the competence of large shareholders due to free-riding behaviour of small shareholders.

[13] There are a few cases where a shareholder who owns only a small share stake is given a disproportionately large relative voting power. For example, when the sole large shareholder holds 3% of the shares, he receives a SV of 1. In order to avoid this problem, companies with only one shareholder owning an equity stake of less than 5% and companies with two shareholders each owning less then 5% are excluded, where 5% is an arbitrary threshold. This results in removing 3% of the observations.

268   *M. Goergen, L. Renneboog / Journal of Corporate Finance 7 (2001) 257–284*

easier for specific classes of shareholders to form ex ante coalitions during the first stage before entering in a voting game as a block during the second stage.

For example, given that executive directors as a group have similar private benefits of control, they may combine their shareholdings to form one block and try to obstruct actions by other shareholders (e.g. attempts to remove executive directors). Evidence of managerial entrenchment in the UK is given by Lai and Sudarsanam (1997) and Franks et al. (in press). In this 'two staged' case, equity stakes of the executive directors are first added and, subsequently, the relative voting power of this aggregate block is calculated. As there is some evidence that non-executive directors support incumbent management (Franks et al., in press; Berger et al., 1999), it is possible that the executive and non-executive directors forge a joint coalition such that the SV of all their combined stakes should be computed.

Examples of private benefits of control which can be reaped by (coalitions of) industrial companies owning large shareholdings by means of influencing the transfer pricing policy or expropriation of corporate opportunities[14] are discussed in Johnson et al. (2000). Some surveys (e.g. PIRC, 1999 and Mallin, 1996) provide some justification for the calculation of SVs for aggregate blocks held by coalitions of institutions. As different types of institutional investors meet regularly through associations such as the National Association of Pension Funds, coalition formation among (types of) institutions may be facilitated.

The rationale of forming coalitions among shareholders from specific ownership classes may justify the calculation of SVs (relative voting power) for each class of owners (after having aggregated all shareholdings by investor class). Further evidence of similar private benefits of control within shareholder classes is presented for the US by Barclay and Holderness (1989, 1991). These studies revealed that blocks were priced, on average, at substantial premiums of 20% and that these premiums differed according to the acquirer's ownership class. The fact that different classes of owner have different abilities to extract control rents is also empirically supported for the US by Holderness and Sheehan (1988).[15]

---

[14] An example of expropriation of opportunities: the French holding company Suez/Lyonnaise des Eaux which is active in utilities (e.g. energy, water, waste recycling, etc) owns a substantial share stake in Tractebel, a Belgian electricity which has pursued an aggressive worldwide growth strategy with operations in Latin-America, the former Soviet Union, etc. As Suez/Lyonnaise des Eaux has electricity subsidiaries which may also attempt to expand internationally, it seems that Tractebel's radius of action has been curtailed.

[15] Banerjee et al. (1997) for France and Renneboog (2000) for Belgium show that the private benefits and reasons for control accumulation by holding companies—which are the largest shareholders in France and Belgium—are manifold: capturing tax reductions by facilitating intercompany transfers, reducing transaction costs by offering economies of scale or by supplying internal sources of funds.

M. Goergen, L. Renneboog / Journal of Corporate Finance 7 (2001) 257–284   269

3. Data description and methodology

3.1. Sample selection

A sample of 250 companies was randomly selected from all the companies quoted on the London Stock Exchange in 1988. Financial institutions, estate companies and insurance companies were excluded. A data panel was constructed for the period 1988–1993. The reason for the relatively short time series is that ownership data had to be collected by hand from company reports. The recession period of 1988 to 1993 was chosen during which corporate liquidity constraints may be more severe. Seven of the 250 companies were dropped because accounting data were not available from Datastream. Only those companies with a minimal panel of 4 years were retained in order to allow for a dynamic analysis. As a result, companies delisted through takeovers or insolvencies between 1988 and 1991 were therefore excluded, but those that were delisted after 1991 were included in the analysis. Subsequent to 1991, 29 of the sample companies were acquired and five were liquidated or entered a formal bankruptcy process. The pattern of ownership is not significantly affected by recent IPOs (where insider ownership is particularly high) because 71% of the sample firms had been listed for at least 8 years.[16]

3.2. Data sources, variable definitions and data description

As the B&M model is the model underlying the investment and liquidity relation, data for the model were collected using the same variable definitions and the same Datastream codes as the ones used by Bond and Meghir (1994a). In Eq. (5), Gross Investments (I) is defined as purchases of fixed assets and fixed assets acquired through takeovers. Cash flow (CF) is the sum of the provision for depreciation of fixed assets and operating profit before tax, interest and preference dividends. Sales (S) are total sales and Debt (L) is total loan capital consisting of all loans repayable in more than 1 year. Dividends (D) are ordinary dividends net of Advance Corporation Tax. Capital stock (K) is the sum of the gross book values of plant and machinery, and land and buildings. New Share Issues are collected from the London Share Price Database. Table 1 shows the evolution of investment and cash flow standardised by sales. The data reflect the start of a recession with investment (on sales) reduced from 15.9% to 6% and cash flow (on sales) decreasing from 14.7% to 11.6%.

---

[16] See Goergen (1998) and Goergen and Renneboog (2001a) for a discussion about the evolution of ownership in IPOs.

270   *M. Goergen, L. Renneboog / Journal of Corporate Finance 7 (2001) 257–284*

Table 1
Descriptive statistics for the financing variables

	I/S	CF/S	D/S
1988	0.159	0.147	0.100
1989	0.129	0.173	0.122
1990	0.084	0.117	0.111
1991	0.057	0.104	0.110
1992	0.051	0.097	0.119
1993	0.059	0.116	0.137
Average	0.091	0.126	0.071
Standard deviation	0.275	0.232	0.417
Observations	1004		

Source: own calculations. Data from Datastream.

Ownership data on the size of shareholdings both for existing and new shareholders for each year in the period 1988–1993 were collected from annual reports. All directors' holdings greater than 0.1% are included as well as other shareholders' stakes of 5% and more (until 1989) and of 3% and above (from 1990 when the statutory disclosure threshold was reduced to 3%). The status of the directors (executive/non-executive) and the dates of joining and leaving the board were also obtained from the annual reports. Non-beneficial share stakes held by the directors on behalf of their families or charitable trusts were added to the directors' beneficial holdings. Although directors do not obtain cash flow benefits from these non-beneficial stakes, they usually exercise the voting rights.

Shareholdings were classed into the following categories: (i) institutions, consisting of funds managed by banks, by insurance companies, by estate firms, by government agencies and consisting of investment/pension funds; (ii) industrial and commercial companies; (iii) families and individuals (not directly related to any director); (iv) executive directors; and (v) non-executive directors. Directors and their families, categories (iv) and (v), are referred to as 'insiders' whereas categories (ii) and (iii) are labelled as 'outside' shareholders. The identity of the owner of substantial shareholdings labelled as 'nominees' was collected from the company secretaries who were contacted by fax. In 96% of these cases, the shareholder behind the nominee company is an institutional investor. We attempted to collect data on shareholder attendance and vote casting for a subsample of companies. The attempt failed as some companies only allowed these data to be consulted on their premises or were not able to disclose historical data on voting.

Table 2 describes ownership concentration over the period 1988–1993. The mean across time for the largest shareholding amounts to 16.6%. The sum of all

Table 2
Descriptive statistics of ownership and control

Panel A: Evolution of ownership percentages and control distribution across shareholders

Year		1988	1989	1990	1991	1992	1993	Mean
Largest shareholder	% Ownership	18.9%	18.2%	17.3%	16.1%	15.3%	13.9%	16.6%
Largest shareholder	Shapley value	0.68	0.68	0.55	0.50	0.50	0.56	0.58
All shareholders	% Ownership	37.6%	36.4%	42.4%	43.6%	41.1%	33.7%	39.1%
All shareholders	Herfindahl	0.46	0.45	0.32	0.29	0.29	0.34	0.36
Average number of shareholders per co.		3.77	3.92	6.08	6.62	6.44	5.45	
Total number of investors in all companies		840	879	1429	1549	1327	839	
Number of sample companies		223	224	235	234	206	154	

Panel B: Ownership, Shapley values and Herfindahl indices by category of owner

1992	Shareholder	Number of companies[a]	%Ownership[a]	%Ownership[b]	Shapley value[a]	Shapley value[b]	Herfindahl[a]	Herfindahl[b]
Total institutions	Largest	187	9.2%	8.4%	0.32	0.29		
Total institutions	Sum	187	24.4%	22.4%	0.68	0.62	0.18	0.16
Industrial companies	Largest	86	12.8%	5.4%	0.34	0.14		
Industrial companies	Sum	86	14.3%	6.0%	0.36	0.15	0.13	0.06
Families and individuals	Largest	31	10.7%	1.6%	0.19	0.03		
Families and individuals	Sum	31	16.4%	2.5%	0.27	0.04	0.07	0.01
Executive directors	Largest	103	8.1%	4.1%	0.16	0.08		
Executive directors	Sum	103	11.6%	5.9%	0.21	0.11	0.07	0.04
Non-executive directors	Largest	58	10.3%	2.9%	0.21	0.06		
Non-executive directors	Sum	58	14.5%	4.1%	0.26	0.07	0.08	0.02
Total directors	Largest	118	10.1%	5.8%	0.21	0.12		
Total directors	Sum	118	17.3%	10.0%	0.31	0.18	0.10	0.06

Panel C: Evolution of financing needs and relative voting power over time

Year	1988	1989	1990	1991	1992	1993	1988–1993
Financing needs[c] % of sample companies	4.68%	8.47%	15.47%	15.22%	11.66%	28.91%	13.45%

[a] Averages are calculated over the number of companies with shareholdings of that specific shareholder category.

[b] Averages are taken over the total number of sample companies (including those companies lacking a shareholder of a specific shareholder category). The averages are calculated for the total number of sample companies (204).

[c] Panel C gives the percentage of the sample companies with financing needs. A company is considered to be in 'financing need' when it issues new equity, reduces dividend payments, omits dividends, has an interest coverage of less than 2 or is financially distressed (files for bankruptcy).

disclosed shareholdings is 39.1%.[17] The Herfindahl index of all shareholders amounts to 0.36 and thus reflects the wide distribution of shareholdings across large shareholders (of which there are about six in the average company). Panel A also shows the relative voting power of the largest shareholder with a Shapley value of 0.58. The increase in the number of shareholders from four in 1989 to six in 1990 results from the decrease in the ownership disclosure threshold from 5% to 3%. Panel B shows the average stake by category of owner. Institutions own the largest cumulative equity stakes (24.4%), but they also have the highest frequency in the average firm. Industrial companies, directors and individuals or families own relatively individual larger shareholdings. Panel B also reports the Shapley values of the largest shareholder as well as the Shapley value of the aggregate stake of each category. If all institutions were to collude to cast their votes as a block, they would be the most powerful investor group with a SV of 0.68 compared to the board which has a SV of only 0.31. Panel C shows the percentage of companies which may have financing needs: they are financially distressed, have an interest coverage below two, reduce or omit dividends or issue rights.

There are two main approaches to test the investment–cash flow relation. The sample can be partitioned by a variable expected to reflect financing constraints (e.g. a low dividend pay-out ratio) and the models are subsequently run for each sub-sample (e.g. Kadapakkam et al., 1998). Alternatively, the model is estimated for the entire sample with the inclusion of interactive terms, each consisting of a dummy variable set to one if the firm's ownership or financial situation satisfies a certain criterion (e.g. Gugler, 1999). The advantage of the latter method is that the ownership concentration and financial status of the sample firms are not restricted into one single subsample over the whole period, but are allowed to vary over time and, hence, move from one category or subsample to another. Cleary (1999) discusses the advantages of such a time-varying approach.

The time-varying variables used to interact with the variables in Eq. (5) are defined as follows:

L_{category^i}	= 1 if the largest share stake is held by a shareholder of category ^{i};
T_{category^i}	= 1 if the sum of all shareholdings owned by shareholders of category ^{i} is higher than the total percentage of equity held by each other category of shareholders;
H_{category^i}	= the Herfindahl index of the three largest stakes held by shareholders of category ^{i}.

---

[17] The reduction in the largest equity stake and the sum of shareholdings is due to the fact that the number of firms in the last few years of the sample period is smaller as a result of bankruptcies and takeovers.

M. Goergen, L. Renneboog / Journal of Corporate Finance 7 (2001) 257–284   273

SV$_{category}$^{i} = the Shapley value of the sum of all shareholdings of category ^{i}, reflecting whether this category of shareholders is pivotal in potential coalitions with other classes of shareholders.

Financing needs   = 1 if more than one (the median value for the sample was
one) of the following five conditions (each of which might
indicate liquidity constraints) are fulfilled: the firm files for
bankruptcy, new equity is issued in the form of a rights
issue,[18] the firm omits dividend payments, the firm decreases
dividend payments, or the firm has an interest coverage of less
than 2.

where i = executive directors; all the directors (inside shareholders);[19] outside
shareholders (defined as industrial company or an individual or family); industrial
or commercial companies; institutional investors (bank managed funds, investment
and pension funds, funds managed by insurance companies).

3.3. Methodology

A panel over a 6-year period (1988–1993) was collected to capture dynamic
adjustment processes and to control better for the effect of omitted variables
(Hsiao, 1986). If there are unobserved fixed effects, dynamic OLS models provide
biased and inconsistent estimates because the error term will be correlated with the
explanatory variables. In this case, the coefficient on the lagged dependent
variable suffers from an upward bias. One of the characteristics of our sample is
that, although the firms are randomly selected, they are selected from a non-random population, i.e. the companies listed on the London Stock Exchange. This can
be controlled for by allowing for fixed effects.[20] In addition, Meghir (1988) shows
that using a fixed effects estimation takes care of the attrition bias resulting from
non-random exit from the sample.

The Within Groups-OLS (WGOLS) allows for the elimination of the fixed
effects (φ_i) in the error term by taking the deviations from the time mean. This
method focuses on time series variation and omits cross-sectional variation.

---

[18] Goergen and Renneboog (in press) report that if a UK company issues new equity for more than
3% of the market value of equity, it has to use a rights issue in order to preserve the rights of the
existing shareholders.

[19] Franks et al. (1998) and Faccio and Lasfer (2000b) cast doubt on the independence of non-executive directors, as advocated by the Cadbury Commission in 1992 and subsequent UK corporate
governance commissions. They find that non-executive directors support the incumbent management
even in the wake of poor performance.

[20] Another example of fixed effects bias is that firms in the South of England may, on average, invest
more than firms in the North of England even when controlling for industry.

274   M. Goergen, L. Renneboog / Journal of Corporate Finance 7 (2001) 257–284

However, in Eq. (5), unless the number of time periods is high, $(I/S)_{i,t-1}$ will be strongly correlated with $\varepsilon_{i,t-1}$ in the time mean of ε_i as:

$$\left(\frac{I}{S}\right)_{i,t-1} = \alpha_1 \left(\frac{I}{S}\right)_{i,t-2} + \alpha_2 \left(\frac{I}{S}\right)_{i,t-2}^2 + \alpha_3 \left(\frac{CF}{S}\right)_{i,t-2} + \alpha_4 \left(\frac{D}{S}\right)_{i,t-2}$$
$$+ \phi_{t-1} + \varphi_i + \varepsilon_{i,t-1} \tag{5'}$$

As a result, the estimate of the coefficient on the lagged dependent variable will be heavily downward biased.

For a short and unbalanced panel, a more efficient method was developed by Arellano and Bond (1991). Their procedure consists in taking the first differences of the model and then applying the Generalised Method of Moments (GMM_{diff}), using the lagged levels of the dependent variable and the independent variables as instrumental variables. By taking the first differences, the fixed error term φ_i is eliminated. Given that the shocks $\varepsilon_{i,t}$ are not serially correlated, the lagged levels dated $t-2$ and earlier of the dependent variable and the independent variables can be used as instruments to obtain a consistent estimator. The advantage of the Arellano–Bond technique over other methods—such as the widely used Anderson and Hsiao (1982) procedure—lies in its efficient use of available instrumental variables.

However, Blundell and Bond (1998) have shown that when the period of study is relatively short the GMM_{diff} estimation procedure performs poorly in two situations. The first situation is where the coefficient on the lagged dependent variable (α_1) is close to unity and the second situation is where the relative variance of the fixed effects (φ_i) is large. In these situations, the lagged levels of the variables are weak instruments and GMM_{diff} provides a downward-biased estimate of α_1, the coefficient on the lagged dependent variable. Using Monte Carlo simulations, Blundell and Bond (1998) show that in these situations the Generalised Method of Moments in system (GMM_{sys}) provides better estimators than GMM_{diff}. The system consists of two types of equations, each of which has its own instruments. The first type of equations is in levels and their instruments are the lagged differences in the dependent variable and the independent variables. The second type consists of equations in the first differences with the levels of the dependent variable and the independent variables as instruments. All the models were estimated using the 1997/1998 version of the Arellano and Bond (1988) Dynamic Panel Data (DPD)-programme written in GAUSS.

For each estimation, we report (i) the p-values for the tests on first-order correlation (m_1) and second-order correlation (m_2) in the residuals, (ii) the p-value for the Sargan test and (iii) the p-values for the parameter estimates, based on standard-errors asymptotically robust to heteroskedasticity. If m_1 is significant, then the instruments dated $t-2$ are not valid, but later instruments such as $t-3$ and $t-4$ may still be valid. Likewise, if m_2 is significant, then the instruments dated $t-3$ are not valid, but later instruments such as $t-4$ and $t-5$ may be.

M. Goergen, L. Renneboog / Journal of Corporate Finance 7 (2001) 257–284   275

The Sargan (1958) test is used to determine the valid instruments for each model and detect over-identifying restrictions. Under the null hypothesis of valid instruments, it is asymptotically distributed as a $\chi^2(n)$ with n degrees of freedom.

4. Results

The basic B&M model was estimated using the three different estimation techniques: OLS, GMM$_{diff}$ and GMM$_{sys}$. Table 3 shows that only for the model estimated with GMM$_{sys}$ (column iii) the dynamics of the structural adjustment costs of B&M model are not rejected and the size, sign and significance of the explanatory variables are in line with the theoretical predictions and the empirical results of the B&M model. As expected, the coefficient of the lagged dependent variable is close to 1 while the coefficient of the squared lagged dependent variable is negative and close to 1 (Bond and Meghir, 1994a). Both OLS and GMM$_{diff}$ provide biased estimates.

Theoretically, an insignificant cash flow coefficient is expected because a company should be able to pursue its investment policy regardless of the amount of internally generated funds and should be able to attract as much external capital

Table 3
Basic Euler-equation model estimated using (i) OLS, (ii) GMM$_{diff}$ and (iii) GMM$_{sys}$

Variable	(i) OLS	(ii) GMM$_{diff}$	(iii) GMM$_{sys}$
Constant	0.095*** (0.000)	−0.039 (0.835)	0.106 (0.135)
I/S_{t-1}	0.486*** (0.000)	0.608* (0.055)	0.821** (0.014)
$(I/S_{t-1})^2$	−0.067*** (0.000)	−0.101 (0.667)	−0.998* (0.075)
CF/S_{t-1}	−0.120* (0.095)	−0.215 (0.454)	−0.232** (0.030)
$(D/S_{t-1})^2$	0.029 (0.431)	−0.212 (0.132)	0.031** (0.036)
p-value of m_1	0.022	0.035	0.169
p-value of m_2	0.009	0.699	0.972
p-value Sargan test	–	0.790	0.172
Observations	814	633	790

(a) $(I/S)_{i,t}$ is the dependent variable in each model. (b) Each model contains time dummies and industry dummies. (c) m_1 and m_2 are tests for the absence of first-order and second-order correlation in the residuals, respectively. These test statistics are asymptotically distributed as $N(0,1)$ under the null of no serial correlation. (d) The Sargan test statistic is a test of the over-identifying restrictions, asymptotically distributed as $\chi^2(k)$ under the null of valid instruments, with k degrees of freedom. (e) Model (i) is OLS in levels. Model (ii) is the model in the first differences with levels dated $t-3$ and $t-4$ of the dependent and independent variables as instruments. Model (iii) is a linear system of the first-differenced and levels equations. The instruments are levels of $(I/S)_{t-1}$, $(I/S)_{t-1}^2$, $(CF/S)_{t-1}$, $(D/S)_{t-1}^2$, IA$*(I/S)_{t-1}$, IA$*(I/S)_{t-1}^2$, IA$*(CF/S)_{t-1}$, and IA$*(D/S)_{t-1}^2$ dated $t-4$ for the differenced equations and first differences dated $t-3$ for the levels equations. (f) p-values, based on standard-errors asymptotically robust to heteroskedasticity, are reported in parentheses. ***, ** and * stand, respectively, for statistical significance within the 1%, 5% and 10% confidence levels.

as needed to finance positive NPV projects. However, the negative cash flow coefficient reflects that for the random sample of companies, there is neither an overinvestment nor an underinvestment problem because companies do not invest more when their generated cash flow is large nor do they invest less when the internally generated funds are low. The negative relation between investment and cash flow may, however, result from the fact that the time window captures a recession in the UK.[21] The results obtained from the OLS estimation in column (i) may also be substantially different from their expected values due to first-order serial correlation. The fact that m_1 is highly significant for the OLS estimation is worrying as the *t*-tests will no longer be valid. If the *t*-tests are still used in the presence of (first-order) serial correlation, this may lead to the wrong conclusions about the significance of the coefficients (Gujarati, 1995, p. 411).

Table 4 investigates the impact of financing needs on investment spending with financing needs being defined as a company issuing new equity, reducing dividend payments, omitting dividends,[22] suffering from financial distress (filing for bankruptcy) or has an interest coverage of less than 2. The interaction term with cash flow shows that the investment spending of companies with financing needs is almost three times as sensitive to the availability of cash flow liquidity constraints as firms without financing needs. This is evidence that companies with financing needs suffer from underinvestment and it leads to the rejection of Hypothesis 1 stating that internal funds do not influence a firm's investment policy. Table 4[23] also reports the impact of the combined voting rights concentration held by institutions on the investment–cash flow relation. Whereas, in the absence of institutional holdings, investment spending is sensitive to the presence of internally generated funds, this sensitivity disappears for companies with high levels of institutional ownership (the coefficient of the cash flow term and the one of the interacting cash flow term cancel out). This suggests that institutional shareholders may somehow reduce suboptimal investment spending. This finding rejects Hypothesis 3.[24] Furthermore, the negative debt coefficient and the positive

---

[21] The models in Tables 3–6 include time dummies, as well as industry dummies interacting with the time dummies The time dummies interacting with the industry dummies control for trends in the (I/S) series, which may be particular to certain industries and are not captured by the simple time dummies.

[22] It may be that a company with positive NPV projects cuts dividends in order to utilise its internally generated funds more. However, as there is ample empirical evidence of the rigidity of a downward adjustment of dividends, we do not consider these marginal cases.

[23] It should be noted that it was not possible to test the hypotheses simultaneously by including them in one model because of the limited time series and the number of lagged instrumental variables used.

[24] However, this finding was not found to be robust as including the relative power of the institutional shareholder category (Shapley value) did not yield statistically significant results. In addition, including the largest institutional shareholder rather than the sum of all institutional share stakes did not yield significant results. Given that a single institution only holds a relatively small share stake, this suggests that institutions only have an impact on investment spending when do they control a large percentage of voting rights.

M. Goergen, L. Renneboog / Journal of Corporate Finance 7 (2001) 257–284   277

Table 4
Investment model with financing needs

Variable	Financing needs	$T_{\text{institutions}}$
Constant	0.200 (0.179)	0.156 (0.137)
I/S_{t-1}	0.933** (0.007)	0.485** (0.044)
$(I/S_{t-1})^2$	−0.401** (0.027)	−0.360*** (0.000)
CF/S_{t-1}	0.296* (0.085)	0.574** (0.020)
$(D/S_{t-1})^2$	−0.138 (0.140)	−0.028*** (0.000)
$IA*(I/S_{t-1})$	−0.676 (0.283)	0.963 (0.115)
$IA*(I/S_{t-1})^2$	0.413 (0.163)	−0.453 (0.153)
$IA*(CF/S_{t-1})$	0.889* (0.100)	−0.512* (0.068)
$IA*(D/S_{t-1})^2$	0.048 (0.505)	−0.034 (0.595)
p-value of m_1	0.366	0.669
p-value of m_2	0.196	0.313
p-value Sargan test	0.422	0.335
Observations	820	820

(a) $(I/S)_{i,t}$ is the dependent variable in each model. IA stands for interaction dummy and is to be replaced by the following dummy variables: (i) Financing needs is a dummy variable, which is set to 1 if a company issues new equity, reduces dividend payments, omits dividends or is financially distressed (files for bankruptcy). (ii) $T_{\text{institutions}}$ is a dummy variable, which is set to 1 if the total proportion of shares held by institutional investors is at least a third of the total proportion of significant share stakes held in the firm. (b) Each model contains time dummies and industry dummies. (c) m_1 and m_2 are tests for the absence of first-order and second-order correlation in the residuals, respectively. These test statistics are asymptotically distributed as $N(0,1)$ under the null of no serial correlation. (d) The Sargan test statistic is a test of the over-identifying restrictions, asymptotically distributed as $\chi^2(k)$ under the null of valid instruments, with k degrees of freedom. (e) The models are a linear system of the first-differenced and levels equations. For all the models the instruments are levels of $(I/S)_{t-1}$, $(I/S)_{t-1}^2$, $(CF/S)_{t-1}$, $(D/S)_{t-1}^2$, $IA*(I/S)_{t-1}$, $IA*(I/S)_{t-1}^2$, $IA*(CF/S)_{t-1}$, and $IA*(D/S)_{t-1}^2$ dated $t-4$ for the differenced equations and first differences dated $t-3$ for the levels equations. (f) *p*-values, based on standard-errors asymptotically robust to heteroskedasticity, are reported in parentheses. ***, ** and * stand, respectively, for statistical significance within the 1%, 5% and 10% confidence levels.

cash flow coefficient point out that a high level of leverage leads to a reduction of investment as the bond market and banks require high premia to compensate for the bankruptcy risk if internally generated funds do not suffice for investment spending.

Table 5 shows the results for the investment–cash flow model with the interaction terms reflecting the ownership and control power of industrial companies.[25] A priori, one would expect more concentrated outside control to lead to a better investment policy for two reasons. First, the management's inclination to

---

[25] Combining the dummy for the financing needs with voting power variables into one model failed due to the irreversibility of the estimation matrix in the GMM method. This is the consequence of fact that the time series is short and that several lags are used as instruments.

Table 5
Investment model with control power of industrial companies

Model	(i)	(ii)	(iii)
Variable	$T_{\text{industrial co's}}$	$H\%_{\text{industrial co's}}$	$SV_{\text{industrial co's}}$
Constant	0.114 (0.170)	0.840** (0.035)	0.204 (0.205)
$(I/S)_{t-1}$	0.400 (0.136)	0.383** (0.019)	0.564** (0.023)
$(I/S)^2_{t-1}$	−0.130 (0.383)	−0.114 (0.186)	−0.223 (0.354)
$(CF/S)_{t-1}$	0.039 (0.741)	0.207** (0.022)	−0.178 (0.542)
$(D/S)^2_{t-1}$	−0.002 (0.819)	−0.044 (0.118)	−0.022 (0.362)
$IA*(I/S)_{t-1}$	−0.831 (0.393)	−0.899 (0.213)	−0.589 (0.241)
$IA*(I/S)^2_{t-1}$	1.067 (0.202)	−1.926 (0.426)	0.050 (0.938)
$IA*(CF/S_{t-1})$	0.860 (0.175)	1.051* (0.092)	1.455* (0.0510
$IA*(D/S)^2_{t-1}$	−0.435*** (0.001)	−0.808 (0.605)	−0.002 (0.983)
p-value of m_1	0.324	0.593	0.371
p-value of m_2	0.174	0.512	0.463
p-value Sargan test	0.413	0.752	0.170
Observations	814	814	814

(a) $(I/S)_{i,t}$ is the dependent variable in each model. IA stands for interaction dummy and is to be replaced by the following: $T_{\text{industrial co's}}$ is a dummy variable equalling 1 if the total proportion of shares owned by industrial companies is higher than the total percentage of equity held by each other category of shareholders. $H\%_{\text{industrial co's}}$ is the Herfindahl index of the three largest stakes held by industrial companies. $SV_{\text{industrial co's}}$ is the Shapley value of the sum of the share stakes held by the industrial companies (combined). (b) Each model contains time dummies and industry dummies. (c) m_1 and m_2 are tests for the absence of first-order and second-order correlation in the residuals, respectively. These test statistics are asymptotically distributed as $N(0,1)$ under the null of no serial correlation. (d) The Sargan test statistic is a test of the over-identifying restrictions, aymptotically distributed as $\chi^2(k)$ under the null of valid instruments, with k degrees of freedom. (e) The models are a linear system of first-differenced and levels equations. The instruments are levels of $(I/S)_{t-1}$, $(I/S)^2_{t-1}$, $(CF/S)_{t-1}$, $(D/S)^2_{t-1}$, $IA*(I/S)_{t-1}$, $IA*(I/S)^2_{t-1}$, $IA*(CF/S)_{t-1}$, and $IA*(D/S)^2_{t-1}$ dated $t-4$ for the differenced equations and first differences dated $t-3$ and $t-4$ for the levels equations (except for the model with $T_{\text{industrial co's}}$ where the instruments for the levels equations are first differences dated $t-4$). (f) p-values, based on standard-errors asymptotically robust to heteroskedasticity, are reported in parentheses. ***, ** and * stand, respectively, for statistical significance within the 1%, 5% and 10% confidence levels.

overinvest would be curbed as a result of closer monitoring. Second, management would underinvest less because asymmetric information may be reduced as a result of the existence of large outside shareholders. Control concentration is captured by four variables: a dummy variable indicating whether or not an industrial company controls the largest equity stake, a dummy variable indicating whether the category of industrial companies holds a larger combined shareholding than any other category, the percentage of the Herfindahl index of the largest three industrial shareholdings and the relative control power (SV) of industrial companies. The models reported in Table 5 show that at low levels of control concentration held by industrial companies, there is no relation—apart from model (ii)—between investment spending and cash flow. When the category of industrial companies has high relative control power (SV in model iii) and when this control power is concentrated in the hands of just a few industrial companies (as measured by the Herfindahl in model ii), a strong positive relation at high levels rejects Hypothesis 2 and suggests that powerful industrial shareholders seem to be able to stimulate investment spending when the company has high (free) cash flow or restrict investments when the internally generated funds are low. The former action may result from the fact that industrial companies can extract private benefits of control from concentrated ownership. Examples of tunnelling are given

Table 6
Investment model with control power of insider shareholders

Model	(i)	(ii)	(iii)	(iv)
Variable	$L_{executives}$	$H\%_{executives}$	$H_{executives}$	$SV_{executives}$
Constant	0.096 (0.129)	0.876 (0.156)	−0.022 (0.866)	0.244 (0.264)
$(I/S)_{t-1}$	0.699*** (0.004)	0.517*** (0.006)	0.690*** (0.004)	0.649** (0.012)
$(I/S)^2_{t-1}$	−0.664** (0.018)	−0.161* (0.053)	0.021*** (0.000)	−0.420** (0.028)
$(CF/S)_{t-1}$	−0.222** (0.018)	0.054 (0.688)	−0.314*** (0.000)	0.491 (0.113)
$(D/S)^2_{t-1}$	0.035** (0.012)	−0.076** (0.028)	0.039*** (0.000)	−0.042*** (0.000)
$IA*(I/S)_{t-1}$	0.577 (0.613)	−0.084 (0.989)	−0.336 (0.140)	1.881** (0.026)
$IA*(I/S)^2_{t-1}$	−1.591 (0.644)	−4.057 (0.606)	−0.148 (0.504)	−2.299 (0.128)
$IA*(CF/S_{t-1})$	0.100 (0.840)	1.670 (0.398)	0.252*** (0.009)	−0.712 (0.151)
$IA*(D/S)^2_{t-1}$	−0.301 (0.735)	0.815* (0.094)	−0.019 (0.580)	−2.971*** (0.007)
p-value of m_1	0.227	0.878	0.614	0.718
p-value of m_2	0.418	0.883	0.258	0.521
p-value Sargan	0.457	0.487	0.633	0.211
Observations	790	814	820	814

(a) $(I/S)_{i,t}$ is the dependent variable in each model. IA stands for interaction dummy and is to be replaced by the following dummy variables: $H\%_{executive}$ is the Herfindahl index of the three largest stakes held by executives. $H_{executive}$ is a dummy variable set to 1 if the ratio of the Herfindahl index of the three largest stakes held by executives over the Herfindahl index of the three largest stakes (whatever their owner) is higher than the median of the ratio for all the firms in that year. $SV_{executive}$ is the Shapley value of the sum of the share stakes held by executive directors (combined). (b) Each model contains time dummies and industry dummies. (c) m_1 and m_2 are tests for the absence of first-order and second-order correlation in the residuals, respectively. These test statistics are asymptotically distributed as $N(0,1)$ under the null of no serial correlation. (d) The Sargan test statistic is a test of the over-identifying restrictions, asymptotically distributed as $\chi^2(k)$ under the null of valid instruments, with k degrees of freedom. (e) The models are a linear system of the first-differenced and levels equations. The instruments are levels of $(I/S)_{t-1}$, $(I/S)^2_{t-1}$, $(CF/S)_{t-1}$, $(D/S)^2_{t-1}$, $IA*(I/S)_{t-1}$, $IA*(I/S)^2_{t-1}$, $IA*(CF/S)_{t-1}$, and $IA*(D/S)^2_{t-1}$ dated $t-4$ for the differenced equations and first differences dated $t-3$ and $t-4$ for the levels equations (except for the model with $L_{executives}$, the instruments for the levels equations are first differences dated $t-4$). (f) p-values, based on standard-errors asymptotically robust to heteroskedasticity, are reported in parentheses. ***, ** and * stand, respectively, for statistical significance within the 1%, 5% and 10% confidence levels.

in Johnson et al. (2000), which show that tunnelling—defined as, e.g. investment in assets subsequently sold or leased to a controlling shareholder, transfer pricing advantageous to the controlling shareholders, loan guarantees granted to the controlling shareholder, expropriation of corporate opportunities—is seldom penalised by courts. The fact that the models capturing that an industrial company controls the largest equity stake and that industrial companies combined own the largest equity stake (model i) do not yield significant results in contrast to models (ii) and (iii) provides some indirect evidence that it is a coalition of industrial companies which influences the investment policy but only if the control power is concentrated in the hands of few industrial companies.

The impact of voting rights concentration in the hands of management (executive directors) is analysed in Table 6. At low levels of managerial ownership, there is no positive relation between investment spending and cash flow availability and, hence, no evidence of consistent over- or underinvestment. High levels of internally generated funds even lead to reduced investments. However, if executive ownership is high and is highly concentrated among a small number of executive directors (measured by the ratio of Herfindahl indices in model iii), there is some evidence that the underinvestment problem is reduced.

5. Conclusion

The empirical literature documents that the level of internally generated funds significantly influences investment spending. The positive cash flow sensitivity of investments can result from excess cash flow which management perceives to be too inexpensive and therefore squanders in negative NPV projects. In contrast to such agency problems, the positive relation may also be the consequence of liquidity constraints which cause the company to pass up valuable investment projects if the premium paid for external financing is perceived to be too high. This paper has investigated this relation for a random sample of companies listed on the London Stock Exchange and has analysed whether the cash flow sensitivities differ for companies with financing needs and for companies with varying degrees of ownership control. To this end, the Bond and Meghir (1994a) model, which overcomes some of the drawbacks of the neo-classical and Tobin's q investment models, was extended. In addition, the model was estimated using the GMM in systems technique which avoids the estimation biases of the usual methods (like weighted least squares, and GMM in differences).

For the whole sample, there was no evidence of a positive relation between the levels of internally generated funds and subsequent investment spending, or no evidence of consistent over- or underinvesting. However, companies with financing constraints seem to underinvest since their investment spending is strongly and positively related to the amount of internally generated funds.

For companies in which institutions own a large amount of the voting rights, the relation between investment spending and cash flow is reduced. Whereas for companies without large share stakes controlled by industrial companies investment is not cash flow dependent, the presence of voting control by industrial companies induces a positive relation between cash flow and investment spending. This may result in either overinvestment—perhaps stimulated by industrial companies desiring to reap private benefits of control by tunnelling—or underinvestment if these large shareholders reduce the company's intention to attract external funding. Given that in the absence of concentrated control by industrial companies, investment spending does not depend on cash flow levels, the first interpretation seems the most plausible one. For the models with industrial ownership, a cash flow sensitivity is only observed for models with the Shapley values or Herfindahl indices. It seems that coalitions of a few industrial shareholders have an impact on investment policy rather than individual shareholders. Finally, there is some evidence that firms with low levels of managerial ownership suffer from underinvestment, a problem which is not present in firms where managers hold relative high stakes.

Acknowledgements

We are grateful to Marco Becht, Steven Bond, Bob Chirinko, Julian Franks, Klaus Gugler, Dennis Leech, Moshe Machover, Colin Mayer, Joe McCahery, Dennis Mueller, Kristian Rydqvist and the participants of the Corporate Investment and Governance Network (chaired by Dennis Mueller) for valuable advice and discussions. This paper was written while Luc Renneboog was a visitor at Oxford University (Trinity Term 2000); he is grateful to the Netherlands Organisation for Scientific Research for financial support. The usual disclaimer applies.

References

Abel, A., 1990. Consumption and investment. In: Friedman, B., Hahn, F. (Eds.), Handbook of Monetary Economics. North-Holland, New York, pp. 725–778.

Abel, A., Blanchard, O. 1986. Investment and Sales: Some Empirical Evidence. NBER Working Paper 2050.

Anderson, T., Hsiao, C., 1982. Formulation and estimation of dynamic models using panel data. Journal of Econometrics 18, 47–82.

Arellano, M., Bond, S. 1988. Dynamic Panel Data Estimation Using DPD—A Guide for Users. Working Paper no. 88/15, Institute for Fiscal Studies.

Arellano, M., Bond, S., 1991. Some tests of specification for panel data: Monte Carlo evidence and an application to employment equations. Review of Economic Studies 58, 277–297.

Banerjee, S., Leleux, B., Vermaelen, T., 1997. Large shareholdings and corporate control: an analysis of stake purchases by French holding companies. European Financial Management 3, 23–43.

282   *M. Goergen, L. Renneboog / Journal of Corporate Finance 7 (2001) 257–284*

Barclay, M., Holderness, C., 1989. Private benefits from control of public corporations. Journal of Financial Economics 25, 371–395.

Barclay, M., Holderness, C., 1991. Negotiated block trades and corporate control. Journal of Finance 46, 861–878.

Bebchuk, L., Roe, M., 1999. A theory of path dependence in corporate governance and ownership. Stanford Law Review 52, 127–170.

Berger, P., Ofek, E., Yermack, D., 1999. Managerial entrenchment and capital structure decisions. Journal of Finance 52, 1411–1438.

Bernanke, B., Gertler, M., 1989. Agency costs, net worth and business fluctuations. American Economic Review 73, 257–276.

Blundell, R., Bond, S., 1998. Initial conditions and moment restrictions in dynamic panel data models. Journal of Econometrics 87, 115–143.

Bond, S., Meghir, C., 1994a. Dynamic investment models and the firm's financial policy. Review of Economic Studies 61, 197–222.

Bond, S., Meghir, C., 1994b. Financial constraints and company investment. Fiscal Studies 15, 1–18.

Cadbury, A., 1992. Report of the Committee on the Financial Aspects of Corporate Governance. Gee & Co, London.

Carpenter, R., 1995. Finance constraints of free cash flow? A new look at the life cycle model of the firm. Empirica 22, 185–209.

Chirinko, R., Schaller, J., 1995. Why does liquidity matter in investment equations? Journal of Money, Credit and Banking 27, 527–548.

Cho, M., 1998. Ownership structure, investment, and the corporate value: an empirical analysis. Journal of Financial Economics 47, 103–121.

Chung, K., Kim, J.-K., 1999. Corporate ownership and the value of a vote in an emerging market. Journal of Corporate Finance 5, 35–54.

Cleary, S., 1999. The relationship between firm investment and financial status. Journal of Finance 54, 673–692.

Degryse, H., De Jong, A., 2000. Investment Spending in the Netherlands: The Impact of Liquidity and Corporate Governance. Working Paper, CentER, Tilburg University.

Demsetz, H., 1983. The structure of ownership and the theory of the firm. Journal of Law and Economics 26, 375–390.

Faccio, M., Lasfer, M., 2000a. Do occupational pension funds monitor companies in which they hold large stakes? Journal of Corporate Finance 6, 71–110.

Faccio, M., Lasfer, M., 2000b. Managerial Ownership, Board Structure and Firm Value: The UK Evidence. Working Paper, City Business School.

Fazzari, S., Petersen, B., 1993. Working capital and fixed investments: new evidence on financing constraints. Rand Journal of Economics 24, 328–341.

Fazzari, S., Hubbard, R., Petersen, B., 1988. Financing constraints and corporate investment. Brookings Papers on Economic Activity 1, 141–195.

Fazzari, S., Hubbard, R., Petersen, B., 1996. Financing Constraints and Corporate Investment: Response to Kaplan and Zingales. NBER Working 5462.

Felsenthal, D., Machover, M., 1998. The Measurement of Voting Power. Edward Elgar Publishing, Cheltenham.

Franks, J., Mayer, C., Renneboog, L., 2001. Who disciplines the management of poorly performing companies? Journal of Financial Intermediation, in press.

Goergen, M., 1998. Corporate Governance and Financial Performance. A Study of German and UK Initial Public Offerings. Edward Elgar Publishing, Cheltenham.

Goergen, M., Renneboog, L., 2001a. Prediction of ownership and control concentration in German and UK initial public offerings. In: McCahery, J., Moerland, P., Raaijmakers, T., Renneboog, L. (Eds.), Convergence and Diversity in Corporate Governance Regimes and Capital Markets. Oxford Univ. Press, Oxford.

Goergen, M., Renneboog, L., 2001b. Strong managers and passive institutional investors in the UK. In: Barca, F., Becht, M. (Eds.), The Control of Corporate Europe. Oxford Univ. Press, Oxford, in press.

Greenwald, B., Stiglitz, J., Weiss, A., 1984. Informational imperfections and macroeconomic fluctuations. American Economic Review Papers and Proceedings 74, 194–199.

Grossman, S., Hart, O., 1980. Takeover bids, the free-rider problem, and the theory of the corporation. Bell Journal of Economics 11, 42–64.

Gugler, K., 1999. Investment Spending in Austria: Asymmetric Information versus Managerial Discretion. Working Paper, University of Vienna.

Gugler, K., Mueller, D., Yurtoglu, B., 1999. Marginal Q, Tobin's q, Cash Flow and Investment. Working Paper, University of Vienna.

Gujarati, D., 1995. Basic Econometrics. 3rd edn. McGraw-Hill, New York.

Hadlock, C., 1998. Ownership, liquidity and investment. Rand Journal of Economics 29, 487–508.

Haid, A., Weigand, J., 1998. R&D investment, financing constraints, and corporate governance. Working Paper, WHU.

Hampel Committee (Committee on Corporate Governance), 1998. Final Report. Gee Publishing, London.

Hart, O., Moore, J., 1995. Debt and seniority: an analysis of the role of hard claims in constraining management. American Economic Review 85, 567–585.

Hayashi, F., 1982. Tobin's marginal q and average q: a neoclassical interpretation. Econometrica 50, 213–224.

Holderness, C., Sheehan, D., 1988. The role of majority shareholders in publicly held corporations: an exploratory analysis. Journal of Financial Economics 20, 317–346.

Hoshi, T., Kashyap, A., Scharfstein, D., 1991. Corporate structure, liquidity and investment: evidence from Japanese industrial groups. Quarterly Journal of Economics 20, 33–60.

Hsiao, C., 1986. Analysis of Panel Data. Cambridge Univ. Press, Cambridge.

Jensen, M., 1986. Agency costs of free cash flow, corporate finance and takeovers. American Economic Review Papers and Proceedings 76, 323–329.

Johnson, S., La Porta, R., Lopez-de-Silanes, F., Shleifer, A., 2000. Tunneling. American Economic Review 90, 22–28.

Jorgenson, D., 1963. Capital theory and investment behavior. American Economic Review 53, 247–259.

Kadapakkam, P., Kumar, P., Riddick, L., 1998. The impact of cash flows and firm size on investment: the international evidence. Journal of Banking and Finance 22, 293–320.

Kaplan, S., Zingales, L., 1995. Do Financing Constraints Explain Why Investment is Correlated with Cash Flow? NBER Working 5267.

Kaplan, S., Zingales, L., 1997. Do investment–cash flow sensitivities provide useful measures of financing constraints? Quarterly Journal of Economics 20, 169–215.

Kathuria, R., Mueller, D., 1995. Investment and cash flow: asymmetric information or managerial discretion. Empirica 22, 211–234.

Lai, J., Sudarsanam, S., 1997. Corporate restructuring in response to performance decline: impact of ownership, governance and lenders. European Finance Review 1, 197–233.

Lasfer, M., 1995. Agency costs, taxes and debt: the UK evidence. European Financial Management 1, 265–285.

Leech, D., 2000. Shareholder Power and Shareholder Incentives: Towards a Theory of Ownership Control. Working Paper, Warwick Business School.

Leech, D., Leahy, J., 1991. Ownership structure, control type classifications and the performance of large British companies. Economic Journal 101, 1418–1437.

Mallin, C., 1996. The voting framework: a comparative study of voting behaviour of institutional investors in the US and the UK. Corporate Governance, An International Review 4.

Mallin, C., 1999. Corporate Governance: Financial Institutions and their Relations with Corporate Boards. Working Paper, Nottingham Business School.

McConnell, J., Servaes, H., 1990. Additional evidence on equity ownership and corporate value. Journal of Financial Economics 27, 595–612.

Meghir, C., 1988. Attrition in Company Panels. Working Paper, University College London.

Meyer, J., Kuhn, E., 1957. The Investment Decision: An Empirical Study. Harvard Univ. Press, Cambridge.

Modigliani, F., Miller, M., 1958. The cost of capital, corporation finance and the theory of investment. American Economic Review 48, 261–297.

Morck, R., Shleifer, A., Vishny, R., 1988. Management ownership and market valuation. An empirical analysis. Journal of Financial Economics 20, 293–315.

Myers, S., Majluf, N., 1984. Corporate financing and investment decisions when firms have information that investors do not have. Journal of Financial Economics 13, 187–221.

Newbold, Y., 2001. Report of the Shareholder Voting Working Group. Fund Managers' Association, London.

PIRC, 1999. Proxy Voting Trends 1999. Pensions & Investment Research Consultants, London.

Renneboog, L., 2000. Ownership, managerial control and the governance of companies listed on the Brussels stock exchange. Journal of Banking and Finance 24, 1959–1995.

Rydqvist, K., 1998. Empirical Investigation of the Voting Premium. Discussion Paper, Norwegian School of Management BI.

Sargan, J., 1958. The estimation of economic relationships using instrumental variables. Econometrica 26, 393–415.

Shapley, L., 1953. A value for N-person games. In: Kuhn, H., Tucker, A. (Eds.), Contributions to the Theory of Games II. Annals of Mathematics Studies, vol. 28, Princeton Univ. Press, Princeton, pp. 307–317.

Stapledon, G., 1996. Institutional Shareholders and Corporate Governance. Clarendon Press, Oxford.

Tinbergen, J., 1939. A method and its application to investment activity. Statistical Testing of Business Cycle Theories, vol. 1. League of Nations, Geneva.

Tobin, J., 1969. A general equilibrium approach to monetary theory. Journal of Money, Credit and Banking 1, 15–29.

Van Hulle, C., 1998. On the nature of European holding groups. International Review of Law and Economics 18, 255–277.

Vogt, S., 1994. The cash flow/investment relationship: evidence from U.S. manufacturing firms. Financial Management 23, 3–20.

Zwiebel, J., 1995. Block investment and partial benefits of corporate control. Review of Economic Studies 62, 161–185.

Name Index